THE EDGE OF GLORY

THE EDGE

A Biography

OF GLORY

of General William S. Rosecrans, U.S.A

WILLIAM M. LAMERS

WITH A NEW INTRODUCTION BY
LARRY J. DANIEL

LOUISIANA STATE UNIVERSITY PRESS, BATON ROUGE

Louisiana Paperback Edition, 1999

08 07 06 05 04 03 02 01 00 99

5 4 3 2 1

Library of Congress Cataloging-in-Publication Data
Lamers, William M. (William Mathias), 1900–
    The edge of glory : a biography of General William S. Rosecrans, U.S.A. / by
William M. Lamers ; with a new introduction by Larry J. Daniel.—Louisiana pbk. ed.
        p.   cm.
    Originally published: New York : Harcourt, Brace & World, 1961.
    Includes bibliographical references and index.
    ISBN 0-8071-2396-X (pbk. : alk. paper)
    1. Rosecrans, William S. (William Starke), 1819–1898.
    2. Generals—United States—Biography.   3. United States.   Army—Biography.
    4. United States.   Army of the Cumberland—Biography.   5. United States—His-
tory—Civil War, 1861–1865—Campaigns.
    I. Title.
    E467.1.R7L3   1999
    973.7´3´092—dc21
    [B]   98-49269
                                                                                              CIP

The author wishes to thank the following publishers for permission to quote from the
books listed. Houghton Mifflin Company: *Letters of Henry Adams,* ed. by Worthington
Ford, 1930, *Memoirs* by Henry Villard, 1904; Liveright Publishing Corporation: *Meet
General Grant* by William E. Woodward ($3.50), Copyright (R) 1956 by Helen Wood-
ward; Robert M. McBride Co.: *Grant and His Generals* by C. E. McCartney, 1953; The
Macmillan Company: *Lincoln Finds a General* by Kenneth Williams, 1949; W. W. Nor-
ton & Company: *Memoirs of a Volunteer* by John Beatty, ed. by H. S. Ford, 1946; G. P.
Putnam's Sons: *New York Commandery Papers* by the Military Order of the Loyal Legion
of the United States, 1901; Charles Scribner's Sons: *The Civil War and the Constitution* by
J. W. Burgess, 1906, *Reminiscences* by J. B. Gordon, 1904; The State Historical Society of
Iowa: *The Civil War Diary of Cyrus Boyd,* ed. by Mildred Throne, 1953.

The paper in this book meets the guidelines for permanence and durability of the
Committee on Production Guidelines for Book Longevity of the Council on Library
Resources. ∞

"Together both, ere the high lawns appear'd
Under the opening eyelids of the Morn,
We drove a-field, and both together heard
What time the gray-fly winds her sultry horn . . ."
—Milton, *Lycidas*

CONTENTS

MAPS

by Arnold Gates

INTRODUCTION

LARRY J. DANIEL

I well remember a pleasant day in October 1988 in Memphis, Tennessee, when I attended a Civil War exhibits show. Hundreds of people were present, the lion's share of whom were gathered around tables displaying flags, buttons, Confederate money, and reenactors brandishing replica muskets and swords. I took a path less traveled and went to the far side of the huge hall, where I spotted a dealer in Civil War books. I had not been browsing long when my eyes focused upon what I considered the crown jewel of the show—an old, used copy of William M. Lamers's *The Edge of Glory*. For years I had vainly searched for a copy. Needless to say, I quickly purchased it, and there could not have been a more thrilled person in attendance that day.

The subject of Lamers's book was William Starke Rosecrans, the commander of the Union Army of the Cumberland. Rosecrans was a general who, at times, could be brilliant, but who could also be infuriating, contentious, and highly opinionated. He represented a study in contrasts—a devout Catholic, but a man who could also erupt into profanity and impatient outbursts. He was as excitable and talkative as General William T. Sherman and as methodical as Don Carlos Buell, both of whom had commanded the Cumberland's predecessor, the Army of the Ohio. It was a single, costly mistake at the Battle of Chickamauga in September 1863 that resulted in a partial rout of Rosecrans's army. For all intents and purposes, his Civil War career was destroyed.

In *The Edge of Glory: A Biography of General Williams S. Rosecrans, U.S.A.*, the commander emerges as a man who was forced to fight a two-front war—one with the Rebels and one with officials in Washington, notably Secretary of War Edwin M. Stanton. This fact, coupled with circumstances beyond his control, kept Rosecrans from being a great general. Yet he came close—he "touched the edge of glory."

Especially penetrating are the chapters on Corinth, Tullahoma, and Chickamauga. Lamers tells not only what happened, but why it happened. Beyond the narrative of events there is an analysis of why Rosecrans so often won, but ultimately failed. Lamers explains the enmity that arose between Rosecrans and General Ulysses S. Grant, revealing a portrait of the latter that is liable to leave readers uncomfortable. In the end, it was a combination of brilliance, fortune, and personality flaws that molded "Old Rosy." Clearly Lamers is correct in concluding that had Confederate general James Longstreet's attack not come at the precise moment that it did, through sheer luck, at the Battle of Chickamauga, the story of Rosecrans might have had a very different ending.

As for the Union responsibility for the Chickamauga defeat, Lamers places the blame largely upon Thomas Wood, who, though strictly following Rosecrans's orders, unnecessarily pulled his division out of line, thus creating a large gap. Lamers points out that Rosecrans was only six hundred yards away and in plain view, yet Wood failed to clarify the order. Yet Lamers fails to state the obvious—if Wood made no attempt to see Rosecrans, the army commander likewise made no attempt at an on-site inspection. "If Wood knew the position of affairs and that the movement was impossible, why did he not tell Rosecrans, instead of moving out of line?" Lamers asks. The answer is that Wood had just been badly reprimanded by Rosecrans for not obeying directives quickly enough. Lamers reports, though underemphasizes, the nasty encounter. Nevertheless, he concludes: "The order was wrong. So was Wood. So was Rosecrans in allowing his testy temper to run off with his tongue, until a subordinate grew irresponsible with anger."

After the war, Rosecrans was in and out of several ventures. He was elected to Congress and served in a diplomatic capacity, but success eluded him as it had during and before the war. He died in 1898 in California. Despite Rosecrans's headstrong tactics and penchant for running his mouth, one cannot come away from Lamers's book without feeling that he somehow deserved a better fate.

Although conceding his subject's character flaws, Lamers is largely sympathetic and at times even defensive, a fact not lost upon the critics. James I. Robertson noted that the author showed "a definite prejudice" toward Rosecrans, while T. Harry Williams declared that Lamers could not resist the temptation to "lay into Rosecrans' many enemies." Historians since have been more evenhanded in evaluating this complex and multifaceted figure. Lamers, nonetheless, succeeded in resurrecting the reputation of this usually maligned general. So thorough was his research (Rosecrans's grandson, William S. Rosecrans III, allowed him first access to the general's papers) that it is probable that *The Edge of Glory* will remain the definitive Rosecrans biography for decades to come. Indeed, only a revisionist work is possible; all of the facts are there.

Reviewers hailed the book as a superb work. In the *New York Times,* T. Harry Williams wrote: "By almost any standards, Lamers' book is a superior piece of historical reporting, one that enlarges our knowledge of the specific subject and at the same time illumines our understanding of the whole war." Robert R. Kirsch, in the *Los Angeles Times,* assessed the book as a "brilliant and carefully researched biography." The renowned Civil War historian Hal Bridges, in the *American Historical Review,* concluded: "William M. Lamers has met the need for an adequate biography of Rosecrans. . . . [He] writes with ease, spirit, and imagination, and he recounts Rosecrans's military career in great detail." John H. Henderson, in the *Nashville Banner,* thought *The Edge of Glory* was "an excellent study of a neglected general," and righted the wrong that had been done to the man.

Lamers's book made its appearance near the beginning of the Civil War Centennial, a period when America's interest in our national trauma peaked. Despite the fact, and the excellent reviews that followed, *The Edge of Glory* was ill-timed for two reasons. First, it was released almost simultaneously with Glenn Tucker's long anticipated *Chickamauga: Bloody Battle of the West.* Ironically, Tucker wrote about the very battle that destroyed Rosecrans's career. The two books became neck-and-neck contenders for the prestigious Fletcher Pratt Award of the New York Civil War Round Table, with Tucker's study edging out its competition. Lamers's received an honorable mention.

Second, despite the renewed fascination with the Civil War, the attention proved largely one-sided, focusing overwhelmingly on the war in Virginia. It would be four more years before Louisiana State University Press would publish Thomas L. Connelly's *Army of the Heartland: The Army of Tennessee, 1861–1862,* followed in 1971 by *Autumn of Glory: The Army of Tennessee, 1862–1865.* Connelly became the father of western revisionism.

What followed was a reexamination of the western theater and its role in ultimate defeat and victory. Authors such as Herman Hattaway, Grady McWhiney, James Lee McDonough, Albert Castel, Richard McMurry, John Marszalek, Nathaniel Hughes, Peter Cozzens, Michael Ballard, Wiley Sword, and Steven Woodworth have successfully reshaped the national dialogue. The issue is no longer North versus South but East versus West. While the Union armies were stymied in Virginia by Robert E.

Lee, the war was pushed to its completion in the west. It is thus appropriate that LSU Press reprint *The Edge of Glory* at this particular time. In the context of the reappraisal of the western theater, one of its major characters, William S. Rosecrans, must also be considered anew.

In 1998, I began a book titled *The Days of Glory: A History of the Army of the Cumberland* for LSU Press. It was during my research that I rediscovered the value of Lamers's book. I consider it to be one of the most thorough and readable Civil War biographies in existence. On many occasions I have stopped to reexamine what Dr. Lamers concluded on a particular issue. While I sometimes see things in a different light, Lamers is always the starting point.

William M. Lamers received his doctorate degree at Marquette University, and he subsequently became the assistant superintendent of Milwaukee Public Schools. Throughout his life he was actively engaged in civic and educational affairs, serving for twenty-one years as the president of the Milwaukee Public Museum and on the board of the Milwaukee Public Library. He authored books on several subjects, but his passion remained Rosecrans. For nearly a decade he labored on *The Edge of Glory,* personally touring the battlefields and all of the places where the general lived. He was sixty-one when the book was published.

On April 5, 1987, at age eighty-six, Bill Lamers died. He was buried at Holy Cross Cemetery in Milwaukee. He surely would be pleased to see a new generation of Civil War historians and enthusiasts revisiting his view of one of the most understudied major figures of the Civil War—William S. Rosecrans.

THE EDGE OF GLORY

Major General William Starke Rosecrans might have become the greatest and most famous commander for the North in the American Civil War. Abler than Joseph Hooker or George G. Meade, he nearly won command of the Army of the Potomac, and might have crushed Robert E. Lee at Chancellorsville or Gettysburg to end the war. He might have led William Tecumseh Sherman's army to Atlanta and the sea. In brilliant campaigns he brought the greater part of that army to Chattanooga. He was in some respects Abraham Lincoln's ablest general, and before Chickamauga, had been his most consistent winner. He and not Ulysses S. Grant might have been, at the war's end, the supreme commander of all the Union land forces. Even as it was, he almost became President instead of Andrew Johnson.

It was December 30, 1864, and Rosecrans brooded in his family home in Yellow Springs, Ohio. His veterans were in at the kill and he had no command. Perhaps James A. Garfield, his former chief of staff, now a leader in Congress, could help. He began a letter to the friend to whom he would turn often in the years ahead.

"Greatly I am puzzled to know how it comes to pass that an officer who minds his own business, labors for the good of the country and the service, aiding merit and honesty to rise, and treating all with kindness and humanity, should be treated as I have been." He had been thrice removed, "without intimation of cause or provision for promotion." He had just restored order to Missouri, unearthed the conspiracy of the Order of American Knights, and repulsed Sterling Price's second Missouri invasion. Yet, "in the midst of congratulations from all Union men, and professions of kindness from all sides, without warning notice, or complaint, or hint of explanation, I am removed, and put in an attitude of disgrace before the nation. Isn't it strange?"

Rosecrans had been at odds with Washington before, but never so seriously. A year ago he had been temporarily sidetracked from command; but now he was shelved. Two years earlier, to the very day, he was leading the second-largest Union army to the great victory of Stone's River. Without that victory, Lincoln insisted, the "nation could scarcely have lived over." And a year before that, in 1862, he commanded the important Department of Western Virginia. His brilliant maneuvering and small victories had elevated General George B. McClellan to command of the Army of the Potomac and then to supreme command, as his victories at Iuka and Corinth later propped district commander Grant's sagging fortunes. Confederate generals and reporters had called Rosecrans the ablest, most dangerous Union general. Now Grant was his arch enemy. Or was it Secretary of War Edwin M. Stanton? or General Henry W. Halleck?

Although he had been on bad terms with Stanton from the spring of 1862, and with Grant from the following autumn, his achievements in the battlefield temporarily put him beyond the power of his enemies. The serious deterioration of his fortunes had not begun until the spring of 1863, when he delayed attacking Braxton Bragg, while Grant cornered John C. Pemberton in Vicksburg. Later that spring he started his forward movement with the Tullahoma or Middle Tennessee campaign that pushed Bragg across the Tennessee River. An almost bloodless achievement, and the greatest victory of pure strategy in the war, it ranked in importance with the simultaneous victories at Vicksburg and Gettysburg. The victor who planned it knew its worth. Then came the brilliant crossing of the Tennessee, the advance into Georgia, and, in mid-September, Chickamauga. The angry War Department peremptorily ordered Rosecrans to advance, but refused to support him from the inactive armies to his right and left. The concentrated Confederates struck hard, and Rosecrans was made the whipping boy for the blunder.

Now, with the war ending, his enemies had seen to it that he would be shut out from the final glory. Grant and Meade sprawled out along the Richmond-Petersburg line watching Lee bleed. Sherman's army kept the death vigil at the sea.

As he sat writing to Garfield of his plight, Rosecrans recalled his forty-five months of service.

"I who began by drilling home guards of Cincinnati, teaching the first Ohio troops how to encamp at Dennison, who fought the first successful battle involving important results in the War; made the first successful campaign against Lee; helped to lay the foundations of the first free State made out of a slave State, receiving for my service a unanimous vote of thanks from the legislature; who invented and had built the first army ambulance now universally used; who first suggested and put into operation the plan of providing photographed information maps of the country for distribution among military commanders now regarded as almost indispensable in all the great military operations in which there are not good topographical maps; whose inspector-general's system has been adopted throughout the army; who built up the cavalry of Mississippi, giving Sheridan the opportunity of winning his first star; who won Iuka and Corinth against great odds; who built up the dispirited mounted force of Buell's Army and brought it to be the victorious cavalry of the Army of the Cumberland; who fought Stone's River; drove Bragg from Shelbyville, Tullahoma and Chattanooga, wresting from a superior force the keys of East Tennessee, Georgia and the centre of the Southern Confederacy; who struck the Ohio and other Copperheads a great blow, virtually killed the OAKS; drove Price from Missouri; and did much to give that State . . . freedom; an officer of sobriety, morality, industry, abstinence from all intrigues military and political, I find myself put into retirement and apparent disgrace, while young men of less age, rank, services, men tainted with pecuniary speculation if not *peculation,* are in command and favor. I want to tax your friendship, in which I confide, to find out and give me an explanation of how and why this is."

He appended a postscript: "You know I consider my present situation an outrage on justice having few parallels in this or any other War. But I am a firm believer in the final downfall of iniquity."

Yet even during his lifetime his history was written by his enemies, and the stereotype which to this day passes for Rosecrans' portrait was created chiefly by Ulysses S. Grant, reporter-Second Assistant Secretary of War Charles A. Dana, and their friends, a portrait frequently copied but seldom examined. It is a popular image distorted with error, an unfriendly caricature.

How and why was it? Rosecrans had asked Garfield. As in the

breakthrough at Chickamauga, an accident in timing, the answer lies partly in historical accidents. It lies partly in a wry piece of bad luck that tossed Rosecrans into a fight to the finish for military place and advancement with persons whose temperaments were incompatible with his. Blame must rest with McClellan, Grant, Halleck, Stanton, and others, even with Lincoln. And although he may have been the last to see it, blame must be assigned to Rosecrans himself.

He possessed virtues and excellencies, some to an heroic degree. He was blessed with a brilliant, resourceful mind, and prodigious energy. No general, North or South, surpassed him in personal leadership, or in his courage in taking necessary risks on the battlefield. His patriotism and personal probity could not be questioned. But in excess his virtues sometimes became faults. He made enemies unwisely and needlessly. A perfectionist, he was critical and impatient of slipshod performance in others, yet he had himself some difficulty in delegating responsibility. He was no compromiser. He could be short of temper and long of tongue. Generally he was kindly and courteous to his inferiors, and sometimes brusque with his superiors. He refused wrathfully "to crook the pregnant hinges of the knee where thrift would follow fawning." He had the dubious good fortune to be both articulate and talkative. His righteousness occasionally led to self-righteousness, and his bristling independence to impolitic speech and action. A man of simple outlook, he could not understand the devious workings of other men's minds. When he was wronged, he spoke out, forgave, bore no grudges—and was at a loss when those who felt the sting of his own tongue were not equally magnanimous. The dislike which his bitterest enemies had for him generally followed some failure of theirs in which he shared, but for which he was not responsible; so that in its genesis, at least, it was partly based on fear of him. Yet something in him would not let that fear subside. Perhaps it was his talkativeness. Perhaps it was his stern, uncompromising moral sense, rooted in firm religious convictions. He would not sacrifice men or armies to advance his personal fortunes. Whatever it was, he was seldom out of trouble, until the question of his survival in high command became a race between his military competence and luck, and the determination of the War Department to be rid of him. But all this oversimplifies.

What manner of man was this who won the unqualified, lifelong esteem and love of the admirable and forthright George H. Thomas, and the violent dislike of the generally moderate and reserved Ulysses S. Grant? Who was worshiped, as few generals are worshiped, by the men whom he commanded, and hated by the Secretary of War?

His life story gropes toward an answer. And it begins by noting that he was a true son of the lusty pioneer breed that begat him. He was a Rosecrans, a "mover."

One

"THE BRILLIANT ROSY ROSECRANS"

In 1807, a group of solid farmers in the Wyoming Valley in north-eastern Pennsylvania decided to migrate to Ohio, and sent ahead two commissioners. One of these was a thirty-five-year-old physician, Dr. Daniel Rosecrans. Son of Captain Daniel Rosecrans, a Revolutionary soldier, Dr. Daniel was of the fifth generation in America, a descendant of Harmon Henrick Rosenkrantz, who arrived in New Amsterdam in 1651. The "movers"—they did not call themselves pioneers—had learned of good, fairly priced lands in Delaware County, Ohio.

After the commissioners returned, these people, in the late spring of 1808, set out overland for central Ohio, a journey of over 400 miles. The movers were a sturdy, vigorous, strong-minded, self-reliant, independent folk. One of them said: "It is not the inert, the irresolute, or stupid who strike out in life in great changes of pursuit, or risks in business. It is men of thought, of enterprise, of resolution." Among the movers were Dr. Rosecrans, his wife Thankful, and their six children. Four more would be born to them. Dr. Daniel Rosecrans first purchased land in Kingston Township along Little Walnut Creek, and later a tract farther south, on Taylor Run. Mahala Rosecrans remembered that Uncle Daniel rode everywhere "with his pill bags in his saddle." He was elected justice of the peace, and was called "Squire."

Crandall, the eldest child, born in Wilkes-Barre, Pennsylvania, August 30, 1794, became the father of General Rosecrans. He took a man's part in clearing the wilderness. A boy in the Ohio wilder-

8

ness learned by observing, listening, doing. Before leaving Pennsylvania, he had learned to write legibly and spell correctly, and his later business dealings showed that he mastered arithmetic.

The Rosecrans family converted a militant patriotism into a tradition of soldiering and adventure. Cousin John Rosenkrantz was typical. He had built a fort in New Jersey, along the Delaware, and with his five sons fought under Washington at Monmouth. During the Revolution, although three of Captain Daniel's six children continued to spell the name "Rosenkrans"—descendants of Harmon Henrick Rosenkrantz finally used twenty-three variants in spelling the family name—two changed it to "Rosencrans," and Dr. Daniel emerged as "Rosecrans." He did not wish to be mistaken for a Hessian, even though he kept the old pronunciation.

Religion, too, was important to these people. Crandall's mother, Thankful Rosecrans, was a Methodist of intense convictions, and threw open her door to Methodist circuit riders. Although she disapproved Dr. Daniel's Universalist leanings, she tolerated Universalist meetings in their home. Crandall adopted neither belief, so that General Rosecrans remembered his father as a "man of religious feeling who affiliated with no particular church." But creed or no creed, the family was deeply religious, with religion expressing itself in a stern moral code.

When war broke out in 1812, Crandall enlisted in the Light Horse Battalion and joined General William Henry Harrison in the campaign to relieve Detroit. He returned home two years later, bearing a captain's commission. He had been Harrison's adjutant.

In 1816, Crandall married Jemima Hopkins, whose widowed mother supported herself with the aid of her husband's $96 annual pension. Timothy Hopkins, who had served in the Connecticut line, was a relative of Governor Stephen Hopkins of Rhode Island, signer of the Declaration of Independence.

For his bride, Crandall built a commodious double cabin on the 160 acres he acquired next to his father's farm on Little Taylor Run. Chauncey, the couple's first child, was born in 1817, but died in infancy. Their second child, the future general, baptized William Starke in the rite of the Church of England, was born on September 6, 1819. The "Starke"—with a gratuitous "e"—was a compliment to Revolutionary General John Stark, one of Crandall's heroes.

While William was a baby, the Rosecrans family moved to Homer, a small town in nearby Licking County. Crandall opened a tavern and store, and prospered sufficiently to acquire a farm, a garden, additional houses and lots, and a potash factory, a source of ready cash. From time to time, he contracted for the construction of public works—probably bridges, roads, and canals. He grew "comfortable," and his home was happy. As a young officer, William wrote: "I have a mother who loves me well," and a father "having for his fortune his father's blessing, his own good hands, and my good mother. He has been active and enterprising. He has grown old, popular, and respected in the humble circle of his acquaintance, but he has not grown wealthy."

Home impressions were dominant in shaping William's character. His lifelong ideal was his strong-willed, self-reliant father, and those who knew both agreed that they talked, looked, and were alike. Crandall had stern, unflinching integrity, and was often called upon to arbitrate neighborhood disputes. People spoke of his "iron will and hot temper." The description fits his son William.

From his father, William inherited the family's patriotism, together with a strong interest in history. A copy of the Declaration of Independence hung in the Rosecrans home. When William memorized it, Crandall stood him on a barrel to recite it for the neighbors. Crandall taught his five-year-old son to "hurrah for Jackson." The family treasured a copy of Frederick Butler's three-volume *History of the United States,* and the account of Jackson's victory at New Orleans so impressed the boy that he committed it to memory.

William's gentle, deeply religious mother reinforced the lessons taught by her husband, among them, to speak the truth regardless of cost or pain. William could not have been more than five, when he killed a gander in attempting to shoo it from his mother's garden. Jemima was firm: "You must carry it back to its owner and tell what happened." Even as an old man he recalled the terror of that confession, though the neighbor lady proved kind and solaced him with bread and jam.

His grandmothers, too, made an imprint on William's character. He remembered Grandmother Thankful Wilcox as "quick, small, dark, and peppery." The "peppery" could as well be applied to him. He confessed to an "uppity" side: "No one ever called me 'Willie.' I would not permit it." Grandma Hopkins, he recalled, had large, mild blue eyes peering out of a pale face, and she wore a cap or bonnet, for she was "very bald." Her charity was much like her grandson's. She gave openhandedly. The poor, the troubled, and Indians sought her door.

Three more sons were born to Crandall and Jemima: Charles Wesley—"Wes"—in 1822; Henry Crandall in 1824; and Sylvester Horton in 1827. Neighbors remembered all the boys as "lively and mettlesome." As the eldest, William was a leader in their games. One of their favorite sports was to fight sham battles with corn-stalks. Imitating his father, who commanded the Homer militia, William organized a boys' military company and was elected captain. Although he resorted to fighting only with strong provocation, his motto was to "lick and not get licked." He could not remember ever breaking that motto.

This was the period in which Ohio was being opened to travel and commerce by roads and canals, and William and Sylvester spent long hours discussing the construction of a roadbed for power-driven vehicles. They concluded that wagons with flanged wheels could be hauled over glass rails, and out of this talk grew William's interest in railroads and engineering.

But William and Sylvester were "studious," too. As a small boy William was described as quiet, slender, thoughtful, kindhearted, sensitive, and endowed with a remarkable memory. Crandall taught him addition, and William taught himself the rest of arithmetic. At eight, he attended the winter session of the log school-house at Homer, and at ten, a summer session. Leonard Wood, one of his early teachers, offered to teach him algebra in the evening. "Come to me when you're stalled," he said.

Books took the place of more formal schooling, and William read and studied everything as it came to hand. When at thirteen he was stricken with bilious fever, he read "with avidity" the works of Flavius Josephus and a volume of literary selections, both the gift of a friend. The great book of his childhood was Jane Porter's *Thaddeus of Warsaw;* when he found the last page of his borrowed copy torn out, he saved for months, and bought another copy to read the missing page.

William helped in the family store, and Crandall sent him at fourteen to close up the store of David Messinger, seven miles away. William kept his father's books and collected the bills until he left home in 1833 for nearby Utica to work as a clerk in George Arnold's new store. William's fellow clerk, John D. Martin, remembered him as a "thin, awkward looking, but remarkably thoughtful and industrious boy," who gave such promise that Martin "never doubted for a moment that he would distinguish himself." William became chief clerk, and when, a year or two later, the business moved to Mansfield, he moved with it.

At sixteen, he traveled down the Ohio and the Mississippi to Vicksburg, where he fell ill, and returned to Mansfield. One day T. W. Barkley, a lawyer and later on Ohio Supreme Court justice, hired him to drive him to Columbus. They talked all the way, and Barkley told him at Columbus: "Your conversation has been so intelligent that I strongly urge you to get more education."

The family could not afford college, and so William found a compromise—West Point. To qualified young men, the United States Military Academy offered a four-year curriculum that appealed to William's taste for history, the military, mathematics, and engineering. A congressional appointment would open the door to entrance examinations, and William went after one "whole hog," trudging fifty miles to interview Congressman Alexander Harper. Harper was reserving the appointment for his own son, but the interview convinced him to nominate William instead.

William immediately sent the required evidences of academic, personal, and physical fitness to Harper, and then waited without reply for three and a half months. Finally he applied directly to Secretary of War Joel R. Poinsett, describing the steps he had taken, and adding references and his father's consent. Another candidate had made a strong bid for Harper's appointment, but with Harper's first recommendation and William's direct application at hand, Poinsett appointed William. He had less than three months—he had had only four quarters of schooling—before the entrance examinations, and to brush up his scholarship he enrolled at Kenyon College.

In June of 1838 young Rosecrans travelled by coach to Cleveland, boat to Buffalo, stage to Batavia, the Erie Canal to Schenectady, train to Albany, and boat again to West Point. He was one of 112 admitted to the class of 1842.

West Point in those years was a small, intimate school. In 1838–39, the corps numbered 231; in 1841–42, 196. In the class of 1842 were a number of such future celebrities as James Longstreet, Don Carlos Buell, Earl Van Dorn, and John Pope. Plebe Christopher Matthew Perry was the son of Oliver Hazard Perry, and Schuyler Hamilton the grandson of General Philip Schuyler and Alexander Hamilton. Among Rosecrans' friends were Abner Doubleday, who invented baseball, and Gustavus Vasa Smith. In classes ahead, among others who would be important in the Civil War were George H. Thomas, to whom he gave the nickname "George Washington," Josiah Gorgas, who became Chief of Ordnance for the Confederacy, and William T. Sherman. He greatly admired "bright-eyed, red-haired" Sherman, who was "always prepared for a lark of any kind, and usually had a grease spot on his pants, from clandestine midnight feasts," at which Sherman made the hash.

The Academy gave Rosecrans his first nickname: "Rosy," or more often, "Old Rosy." Plebes were unmercifully hazed, but when upperclassmen tried to enroll him in a fake French club, he brandished a chair at them, and was not molested further.

Students were sectioned according to ability, and Rosecrans was placed in the superior group. He proved "brilliant" in mathematics, and found French "tolerably easy." At midterm, he ranked eighth in French and fifth in mathematics, and was among the fifty-two survivors receiving warrants—appointments by the Secretary of War as subordinate officers. In June 1839, with twenty-three demerits—standings were computed on conduct as well as academic achievement—Rosecrans stood fifth among the 231 corps members.

That summer, Ulysses S. Grant, a fellow Ohioan, enrolled at West Point. Since third-classmen served as officers of the day, Rosecrans, one evening after taps, found Grant in the yard. "I'm guarding the pump," the naive newcomer explained. "I've orders to stand here until after the next call." "You go to bed at tattoo, and douse your lights at taps," Rosecrans told him. "But how do I know that you're not playing a trick on me too?" "See my chevrons. I'm officer of the day." The two, whose lives were destined to merge, had had their first encounter.

The June 1840 examinations brought Rosecrans a fifth in mathematics, a sixth in French, a ninth in drawing, and a fourth in English grammar, and he was ranked third in his class, his highest rank at the Academy.

For many years after 1835, Episcopalianism was the official religion of the Academy, and all cadets were required to attend Episcopal chapel, under the penalty of "criminalities." Under the influence of Chaplain Martin Parks, who had moved with the Oxford Movement from "low" to "high" church, so many West Pointers became clergymen that the Academy was dubbed a "seminary." Someone charged later that as a cadet Rosecrans himself had been a "recluse and religious enthusiast," though a classmate termed this statement "a mistake," and evidence of Rosecrans' sociability and high spirits is everywhere to be found throughout his correspondence with Academy friends. He thought duelling stupid, yet risked dismissal by consenting to fight a duel in a fracas over a lady. The challenger apologized when Rosecrans, an excellent marksman, chose pistols at six paces.

By June 1841, Rosecrans ranked fifth in his class, and when battalion promotions were announced, although he did not receive one of the four captaincies, he was second among the eighteen lieutenants, and again quartermaster of the corps. This was high achievement.

That autumn he enrolled in Engineering, under Professor Dennis Hart Mahan, for forty years the Academy's greatest teacher. West Point was in fact an engineering school, but only its outstanding graduates were commissioned for the Engineers, the elite corps of the Army. When June standings were published, Rosecrans was thirty-seventh in conduct in the corps of 196 cadets, and fifth in his own class, "the brilliant class of 1842." The top seven graduates, he among them, qualified for the Engineering Corps. Prior to 1842, when he was commissioned, no Westerner had ever achieved this distinction.

At the graduation Miss Anna Elizabeth Hegeman, of New York City, arrived as a house guest at the house of Professor Jacob W. Bailey, and graduates Gustavus Smith and Rosecrans invited the Misses Susan Bailey and Anna Hegeman to a walk to the Crow's Nest, a local scenic rendezvous. That evening William was in love with "Annie."

On the parade ground the graduates, fifty-one strong, saluted, swords and hands rising as one. Fourteen of them would die early, twenty-nine live to be generals, eighteen under the old flag, and eleven under a new. Cadets speculated who would be most distinguished in later life? Cadet John McCalmont was willing to guess that although all the first five might have been chosen, Rosecrans "surely would have been among the foremost named." Others answered unhesitatingly, "Rosy Rosecrans," saying that he talked "interestingly, daily, fast, his imagination racing," that he was "good at everything, his studies, his military duties, his deportment." By general agreement he was the "brilliant Rosy Rosecrans."

West Point education had its advantages and shortcomings. For its time, no better general engineering training was available in America, and West Point graduates proved as much with forts, levees, railroads, canals, bridges, roads, buildings, dams with which they covered the country in the second half of the century. From the military standpoint, their education was less notable. While West Pointers learned how to march, ride, salute, and shoot, and took courses in infantry tactics and military police, artillery tactics and the science of gunnery, engineering and the science of war, the only practical experience they received, except for the drill ground and sentry box, came during the summer encampment on the Plain. Professor Mahan's admiration for Napoleon led him to found a "Napoleon Club," and the club, which studied Napoleon's campaigns, helped to fill a gap in the curriculum. To class instruction in artillery, infantry, cavalry, and military-engineering rudiments, it added an understanding of grand strategy. It is clear that Mahan fired Rosecrans' interest in strategy and made him a lifelong student of the campaigns not only of Napoleon, but also of Frederick the Great.

The regular Army, in which Second Lieutenant Rosecrans now took service, numbered about 11,000 officers and men before the Mexican War and about 8,000 afterward. Among officers, turnover was small, pay meager, promotion slow. His first assignment, to arrest sea encroachments on Fortress Monroe at Old Point Comfort, Virginia, consumed almost a year, and during that time he sought a West Point professorship. "I could name no one more acceptable to myself," Professor W. H. C. Bartlett wrote. In April, 1843, Rosecrans was commissioned first lieutenant, his only promotion in his eleven years of service before the war, and in the summer he won the professorship. On August 24, at St. Paul's Episcopal Chapel in New York City, he and Anna Elizabeth Hegeman were married.

Rosecrans taught engineering in Mahan's department, served as post commissary and quartermaster, and superintended the construction of new cadet barracks. His services, Mahan said, were "entirely satisfactory." War with Mexico was declared in 1844, and although Henry Rosecrans served under Zachary Taylor, and thirty-eight of the fifty-four graduates of Rosecrans' class saw action, the War Department held Engineers Rosecrans, Barton S. Alexander, John Newton, and John D. Kurtz to tasks at home.

In 1847, Rosecrans began a five-year assignment as engineer supervising the fortifications at Newport, Rhode Island. There he constructed a military wharf, completed the interiors and arrangements of the forts, and designed a general system of permanent barracks. Finding fault with the existing plan of permanent quarters, he suggested alternate schemes; and a board consisting of Colonels Rene E. DeRussey and Richard Delafield and Captain Robert E. Lee so enthusiastically approved his recommendations that for thirty years they remained the basis for the barracks plans of the Quartermaster's Department. At Newport, Rosecrans developed dredging machinery which, in open water thirty feet deep, proved eight times as efficient as the former diving-bell process. He also worked out a rapid way of laying concrete piers under water.

In 1852, Congress authorized a survey to recommend permanent improvements to the Massachusetts harbor of Bedford and the Taunton River. While completing this work, Rosecrans was ordered to detached service under the Navy, as "Civil and Constructing Engineer" of the Washington Navy Yard. In nine months, from April through December 1853, "he constructed a marine railway, built a large sawmill, and remodeled and improved the Dahlgren ordnance buildings. . . . He drew up plans for the construction of an immense group of machine shops, combining anchor, chain, cable, blacksmith, carpenter and block shops." A unique feature of his design was his use of a single engine to drive all machinery, and a single chimney to vent all forges. In future buildings, the Navy Department followed these designs, and Rosecrans remained very proud of them.

Though army pay was lean, Rosecrans and his wife considered their months in Washington the happiest of their married life. The couple had four children by now. Rosecrans served as Superintendent of a Negro Sunday School of 600 children during this time. Mrs. Hegeman, who made her home with them, assisted in helping them to meet expenses, and Father Sylvester Rosecrans, now a Catholic priest, with characteristic Rosecrans bluntness said his brother was "living on his wife."

Rosecrans sought several jobs during these years. To increase his income, he applied for the professorship in military tactics and natural philosophy at the Virginia Military Institute in 1851, but Thomas J. Jackson, later "Stonewall" Jackson, received the appointment. In 1853 he tried for the editorship of the Cincinnati *Telegraph,* a Catholic paper, but his health failed, and he requested a leave from the Army. General Joseph G. Totten refused, saying "he could not be spared," and Rosecrans resigned instead, only to receive a prompt three months' leave from Secretary of War Jefferson Davis. "Before it expires you will probably change your mind," Davis said, but in March 1853, Rosecrans resigned anyway, as Annie described it: "to secure rest and make a choice of a civil career more likely to support his family." His recommendations for such a post were excellent. For six months of convalescence he "engaged privately in business as an engineer and architect," and found steady employment in June 1855 as engineer and superintendent for the Canal River Coal Company, a British-American firm with extensive holdings in the mountainous wilderness of Coal River, Kanawha County, Virginia. Rosecrans examined the apparently exhausted mines and the tract, to estimate the extent and availability of its remaining resources, and as a result, the Virginia legislature set up legal machinery for a canal to get the coal out of the mountains. The state itself would hold three-fifths of the stock, and private interests two-fifths; and Rosecrans was elected president of the New Coal River-Slack Water Navigation Company. On Rosecrans' recommendation, the company entered the coal-oil business and hired a "practical" engineer to build a refinery. Basic patents on a fractional distillation process were held by Abraham Gesner, of Williamsburg, New York, and after his own "practical" engineer produced "extravagant" estimates, Rosecrans resigned from the coal company, and using Gesner's

advice, with two partners built a refinery with a rated capacity of
500 gallons a day on Columbia Street in Cincinnati. It was one of
the first three of its kind west of the Alleghenies.

He enlarged his plant and added partners during the panic of
1857, but the process failed to produce marketable kerosene—
customers demanded clear, colorless illuminating oil that would
not foul the wick. While he was testing an experimental product
to meet the demand, one day a patented "safety" lamp exploded,
burned him severely, and set the refinery on fire. He beat out the
flames, and walked home a mile and a half, but it took him
eighteen months to recover. The distorting, livid scars gave a permanent "smirk" to his face. His two partners could not manage
his process, and the business nearly failed.

In April 1860, Sherman resigned as superintendent of the
Louisiana Military Institute to become London representative of
an American banking firm, and a mutual friend from the army,
Charles P. Stone, wrote to Rosecrans that Major Don Carlos Buell
of the Adjutant General's Department, who controlled the appointment, "would be delighted to offer it to you." The post paid
an annual salary of $4,000, and carried with it the command of the
Louisiana arsenal. A month later, Sherman had changed his
mind, and Rosecrans, returning to the refinery instead, soon became, he said, "the first to obtain a good, odorless oil from petroleum." He also discovered a "cheap and sure process" of manufacturing a soap with chlorine properties, and invented the first
kerosene lamp successfully to burn a round wick, and a short
chimney lamp. He received French and English patents on these
and formed a company to manufacture them. By January 1861,
the business was showing a profit, and Rosecrans believed that he
was on the highway to prosperity.

But during these years the nation was dividing. In November
1860, when Lincoln was elected President, Rosecrans, like Grant
and most regular army officers, had voted for Stephen A. Douglas.
South Carolina seceded on December 20, 1860; the cotton states
followed, and early in February 1861, delegates in Montgomery,
Alabama, organized the Confederacy.

Cincinnati lay across the Ohio River from Kentucky. "No one
knew which way the coon would jump," Lincoln said of that
divided state. Months before April 1861, home guards had been

forming in every Cincinnati ward, and men with military training drilled them. Rosecrans selected the "Marion Rifles," the Fourteenth Ward Company, as his charge from the many offered.

Early April 12, men prowled in the dark in Charleston Harbor. Around four o'clock that morning, just before the dawn, a gun spoke and a shell exploded near the Fort Sumter flagstaff.

War was over the land.

Two

"A BRIGADIER'S SWORD AND SASH"

Passionate anger swept over the North at the attack on Sumter, and on April 14 Lincoln called on the governors to raise 75,000 militia to assist in the repossession of the federal forts, places and property. With this call for troops, Cincinnati was filled with martial music, tramping men, bunting, and parades. Recruiting offices sprang up for four new regiments.

"Impelled," as he said, "by a strong sense of duty," Rosecrans withdrew from the active management of the refinery, leaving his two partners to conduct the business. He unpacked his worn lieutenant's uniform, and by Friday, April 19, he was in Columbus, Ohio, to offer his services to Governor William Dennison. On that day the 6th Massachusetts, en route to Washington, was forced to fight its way through Baltimore.

The onset of war had found the small regular Army scattered and poorly equipped, and loyal governors were faced with the task of putting together a militia army. Under existing laws, troops entering federal service were to be fully organized and officered by their states. Because Congress was not in session, it was necessary for the states to supply equipment and transportation. When Governor Beriah Magoffin of Kentucky growled, "Kentucky will not furnish troops for the wicked purpose of making war upon her sister states," Dennison snapped back: "If Kentucky won't, then Ohio will furnish the men for her."

Dennison knew little of military matters, and when he learned that he had the power to appoint major generals for Ohio troops, he thought first of Irvin McDowell. Influential Cincinnatians, however, pressed the candidacy of a young railroad man, Captain George B. McClellan. After hesitating, Dennison appointed him. Then he asked Rosecrans if he would, "as a civilian aide, help McClellan select a camp site for the Ohio militia?" Rosecrans agreed.

West Pointers were already linking McClellan with Rosecrans. When he was asked, who of the Federal officers are to be most feared? Confederate General Daniel H. Hill answered: "Sherman, Rosecrans and McClellan. Sherman has genius and daring, and is full of resources. Rosecrans has fine practical sense, and is of a tough, tenacious fiber. McClellan is a man of talents, and his delight has always been in the study of military history and the art and science of war."

The Little Miami and Ohio Railroad provided a special train for a party of inspection, including Generals McClellan and Jacob D. Cox, a state senator holding a nominal commission as major general in the Ohio militia, and Captain—a courtesy title— Rosecrans. The party picked their site, a place thirteen miles north of Cincinnati, where the Little Miami, in a sweeping bend, enclosed broad fields sheltered to the west by low hills. The tract was named "Camp Dennison" after the Governor, and Rosecrans was assigned to lay out the camp. On April 30, he arrived, brisk, lively, impatient, and voluble. He soon staked out a camp for the two regiments that followed, and by nightfall the men were housed.

In the midst of a windy day, a squall of personalities blew up when Rosecrans discovered that some men were installing floors and bunks in the huts. He ordered these luxuries ripped out. Cox asked Rosecrans: "Has McClellan forbidden floors?" "No, sir, but my position as Chief Engineer gives me sufficient control of the subject." Cox submitted the controversy to McClellan, insisting that huts, unlike tents, were permanent and should therefore have bunks and floors. McClellan sustained him. "Rosecrans seemed to like me better," Cox commented, "on finding I was not carried away by the assumption of indefinite powers by a staff officer."

After three weeks spent in encamping new regiments, Rosecrans was sent by Dennison to Philadelphia to buy muskets, and to Washington to secure uniforms and make arrangements for paying the Ohio troops. Because there was no central purchasing, states bid against one another for arms and equipment, and, until Congress reconvened, paid troops from state funds.

Rosecrans discovered much war fever in Philadelphia, but not enough rifled muskets in the Justus arms factory. He found Washington being converted into an armed camp. With Yankee practicality, he applied to the War Department for a commission as brigadier general of volunteers. Generals Winfield Scott, McClellan, Joseph G. Totten, Joseph Mansfield, and others endorsed his application. McClellan wrote to Simon Cameron, Secretary of War, that "the good of the service would be advanced by giving him the appointment. I do not make this recommendation from any personal feelings, but simply because I am sure he will make a far better general officer than those likely to be urged." Ten days after McClellan's letter, Rosecrans himself "respectfully" requested Cameron to ask Lincoln "to appoint me one of the three-year volunteers lately called into the service of the United States."

A week later, he wrote to Annie: "On Saturday I visited Generals Totten and Mansfield who added their names with most flattering testimonials." They advised him to "take a Brigadier's commission in the three-year troops and trust to the future for the rest." After a long interview with Rosecrans, General Scott endorsed on McClellan's letter: "From my knowledge I cordially concur in this recommendation.—Winfield Scott." Rosecrans spent the morning waiting in the anterooms of the Secretary of War, and finally succeeded in presenting his letter of application to him.

In the meantime, unknown to him, the office of chief engineer of the state of Ohio had been created. Before the bill passed, Governor Dennison and the Senate Committee of Military Affairs agreed that the post should be Rosecrans'. The position, which conferred the rank of colonel, and the pay and emoluments of a colonel in the United States regulars, awaited his return from Washington. A brigadier's commission had not as yet arrived.

Dennison sent Rosecrans the commission, together with an explanation of the circumstances surrounding its origin. Rosecrans' answer was impolitic.

It would be very gratifying to me to stay at home with my family, be at the State Capitol with you and enjoy the many opportunities for having a finger in "fat contracts" which would offer. But our people must go to the front with or without leaders and fight and die for the country. I cannot stay at home and see this; duty demands that I should offer my military acquirements to aid in diminishing the loss of life. I must go with our people to the front.

While disavowing interest in the offer, which was less high than the appointment he sought as brigadier general, Rosecrans felt that because the office had been created for him, he should take the commission to prevent others from seeking it; and he accepted it.

McClellan, meanwhile, had been looking to Ohio's defenses. Mobilization of the Ohio militia, recruitment of three-month volunteers, and the establishment of Camp Dennison, made Ohio's frontiers secure. To aid Unionists in Virginia and Kentucky proved more difficult. Kentucky still maintained its policy of armed neutrality, refusing to allow either Federal or Confederate troops on its soil, and Lincoln wisely refrained from forcing the issue. Kentucky's neutrality closed to possible Confederate counterthrust more than half the front between the Mississippi and the Atlantic. Governor Dennison differed with Lincoln: "We can let no theory prevent the defense of Ohio. I will defend Ohio where it costs least and accomplishes most. Above all, I will defend Ohio beyond rather than on her border."

This determination pointed to Virginia. The crest of the Appalachians divided Virginia into the slaveholding Tidewater, where great plantations lay along waterways emptying into the Atlantic, and the mountainous western portion, in the Mississippi basin, to which the plantation system was unsuited. Pro-Union Western Virginia, embracing a third of the state and one-fifth to one-fourth of its white population, had beeen restive for years, quarreling about the manner in which all her interests and rights were subordinated to the "slave power." Western Virginia in 1860 had a free population of 349,642, with only 12,771 slaves, concentrated mostly in its three southern counties. For long stretches, Western Virginia was wild and primitive. In the north and west, a thin population had sifted over from Pennsylvania and Ohio and settled in the fertile bottoms of the Kanawha River, or along the Baltimore and Ohio Railroad. These simple people wanted no part of secession.

Geography made Western Virginia important to both South and North. The panhandle at its northwestern extremity projects sixty-five miles northward between Ohio and Pennsylvania, to within a hundred miles of Lake Erie. For the South, the Ohio River provided a channel into the Middle West, and for the North, a back door leading to Richmond, Charleston, and Savannah. Whoever held Western Virginia controlled important roads, railroads, telegraph lines, and rivers between the North Central and Middle Atlantic states.

A convention, elected with a clear understanding that an act of secession required popular endorsement, was sitting in Richmond when Sumter fell. Although the delegates had rejected the proposition by a two to one majority less than a fortnight before, on the 17th of April, by a secret vote, they passed an ordinance of secession, to be submitted for ratification to a general election to be held five weeks later, on May 23. By that time Confederate troops had swarmed into eastern Virginia, and the popular endorsement had small significance. When Western Virginians found themselves liable for Confederate military service, they organized meetings to demand separation from the rest of Virginia, and selected delegates from thirty-five counties. These met at Wheeling on May 13, disavowed secession, and asked that Western Virginia be admitted to the Union as an independent state.

Governor Dennison urged Lincoln to protect these neighbors across the Ohio. For the time being, however, Lincoln himself could do little. Critical weeks passed before the War Department established a strong, unified command, and meanwhile loyal governors took effective action with state troops to police and defend their own and to aid neighboring states. Said McClellan: "The Union was saved in the West by the action of state governments." Loyal citizens in border states like Kentucky and Tennessee, and military and political leaders and opinion makers, North and South, watched Unionist Western Virginia. "If the people of the free states could have consented to surrender their brethren of West Virginia to their common foes," Horace Greeley reasoned in his book *The American Conflict,* "they could not have relinquished their territory without consenting to their own ultimate disruption and ruin. West Virginia was thus the keystone of the Union arch."

On April 25 the Virginia militia had been placed at the disposal of Jefferson Davis, now Confederate President, and on May 6 the state had been admitted to the Confederacy. It then looked to its borders, and Colonel Robert Selden Garnett was put in command of the Confederate forces in Western Virginia, while reinforcements from Georgia, South Carolina, Alabama, and elsewhere arrived daily. Governor John Letcher, apprehensive of growing Unionist sentiment in Western Virginia, ordered militia under Colonel G. A. Porterfield to Beverly. From Beverly the militia advanced to Grafton, important because there the Baltimore and Ohio Railroad divided, the main line turning northwest to Wheeling, and the southern continuing west to Parkersburg.

On May 7 Dennison asked that McClellan's department be extended to include Western Virginia. Next day the extension was made. Dennison urged McClellan to cross the Ohio and occupy Parkersburg. McClellan's reply was significant: "I advise *delay* for the present. I fear nothing from Western Virginia. . . . I do not like the idea of detaching raw troops to the frontier. My view is to strike effectively when we move. . . . Let us organize these men and make them effective—in Heaven's name don't precipitate matters. . . . Don't let these frontier men hurry you on."

From the reception of this letter, Dennison dated the beginnings of his doubts as to McClellan's being a man of action. When Senator John S. Carlile telegraphed Dennison on May 20 that Confederate troops were marching toward Wheeling to break up the Unionist convention, the time seemed ripe to rescue Western Virginia. Anxious to take advantage of the opportunity, Dennison telegraphed these facts to both McClellan and Scott. Four days passed without action, but on the 24th Scott ordered McClellan to cross the Ohio promptly. McClellan ordered his men to occupy both Wheeling and Parkersburg, and to push forward to Grafton, repairing the railroad ahead of them. With their advance, Porterfield retreated south fifteen miles to Philippi, where he issued a proclamation: "Rally! Rally at once in defense of your mother!"

The day after he was appointed colonel of the Ohio Volunteers, Rosecrans received a commission as brigadier general in the United States regulars, to date from May 16, 1861. Attached was a brief note to "Dear Rosecrans" from Julius P. Garesché, a West Point friend, now Assistant Adjutant General: "With sincere pleasure I enclose your appointment as Brigadier General in the *regular* army. That affair at Big Bethel, Virginia, has disgusted the people with *Militia* Generals, especially B.—*Republican* ones—and has therefore served your cause. We have just made out others for Pope, J'n. Reynolds, Hurlbut of Illinois as Brig. Gen's. Volunteers." The "B" referred to General Benjamin Butler, who, in a confused scrape, had suffered heavier losses than the Confederates.

"I am appointed a Brig. General in the regular army," Rosecrans wrote to his wife. "So, my dear, your old ambition must now feel gratified." On May 20, he received a telegram directing him to "come down to Cincinnati by the next train, ready for detached service," and the next day he was given command of a provisional brigade of four regiments of three-month men. The four regiments, the 23rd, 24th, 25th, and 26th Ohio, were quartered in Camp Jackson, which Rosecrans renamed "Camp Chase," in honor of Salmon P. Chase. The 23rd Ohio, Rosecrans' personal regiment, contained names destined for greatness. Lieutenant Colonel Stanley Matthews was to become an associate justice of the United States Supreme Court, and Major Rutherford B. Hayes, and Lieutenant William McKinley, Presidents of the United States.

After midnight on the 26th, Rosecrans, with his staff, left Parkersburg to inspect Elk Camp. By 6:00 A.M., they found the crowded wooded site, ten miles below the town, on a bend of the Elk, where recruits were roaming around. When Rosecrans had the long roll call beaten, troops poured from the woods, fields, and ravines. Those not answering were arrested. The lesson taught, Rosecrans dismissed the men and rode ahead to hunt for a better camp site.

The concluding paragraph of a June 29 dispatch to McClellan suggests that Rosecrans may have ruffled McClellan's self-esteem: "No one among your general friends has more disinterested and earnest wishes for the success of your efforts. None under your command are more loyally, cheerfully ready to conform to the duties of a subordinate position. . . . Review, if you please, that letter which you have put on record, and say whether, after you receive this, both private feelings and public interest are likely to be the better for it." What McClellan charged cannot be discovered, since the letter in question is missing.

By June 1, McClellan had gathered between 7,000 and 8,000

men at Parkersburg, and the next night he ordered them to capture Porterfield, sending columns down two separate roads in simultaneous attacks. It was the first taste of war for the eager, uncertain recruits on both sides.

Although the plans were good, in the stormy darkness they miscarried, and Porterfield escaped south, first to Beverly and then to Huttonsville, where he lay for several weeks, reinforced daily with troops and supplies. With 30,000 men, McClellan now faced a scant 10,000 Confederates and he determined to advance. On Laurel Hill, a few miles north of Beverly, lay the main Confederate force, commanded by Garnett, now a general, Porterfield's successor. His headquarters were at Beverly, thirty-five miles south of Philippi, at the eastern base of Laurel and Rich mountains. A smaller Confederate force under Colonel John Pegram guarded the turnpike from Beverly westward to Buckhannon, where, crossing the road and running up the mountain on either side, a mile of entrenchments commanded the important pass.

In rough country, Beverly had strategic importance. Here, facing the mountains, the Staunton and Parkersburg turnpike forked. The Wheeling branch followed the river north to Philippi, while the Parkersburg branch climbed Rich Moutain on its way through the gaps in the southwest Alleghenies to Staunton.

McClellan considered the great Kanawha Valley the logical entrance into enemy territory, but when news came that Garnett was entrenching himself at Beverly with elaborate works, he postponed his Kanawha plan and decided to march on that place. Moving forward with three brigades, Rosecrans' among them, McClellan encamped at Roaring Creek, two miles from the base of Rich Mountain and in sight of Pegram's position.

The mountains of West Virginia lie in long, ancient, parallel ridges that look as though they had been plowed, with occasional wind or water gaps crossing them. Roads wound through these, some of them, says Douglas Southall Freeman, "almost as old as the colony of Virginia. Their badness was a joke when they were at their best, and a calamity when they were at their worst." This was the country which Rosecrans, several years before, had surveyed. Hills were a tapestry of oak and evergreens, brightened in spring with redbud and the pink and white of laurel and dogwood. In this land of tumbled water, mountain creeks and cataracts, of rivers brawling between cliffs, an Ohio private, Ambrose Bierce, breathed deeply of spruce and pine and wandered over mountain sides, to discover "a veritable realm of enchantment," later calling the Alleghenies the "Delectable Mountains" and remembering "their dim blue billows, ridge after ridge, interminable, beyond purple valleys full of sleep in which it seemed always afternoon."

"I expect to find the enemy in position on Rich Mountain, just this side of Beverly," McClellan wrote to Scott on July 5. "I shall if possible turn the position to the south, and thus occupy the Beverly road in his rear. . . . No prospect of a brilliant victory shall induce me to depart from my intention of gaining success by maneuvering rather than by fighting. I will not throw these raw men of mine into the teeth of artillery and entrenchments if it is possible to avoid it. I am trying . . . not to move until I know that everything is ready, and then to move with the utmost energy and rapidity."

When McClellan's scouts reported the enemy divided, he laid plans to beat them in detail, by striking first Pegram, then Garnett. But reconnaissance showed that Pegram's works were strong, and so Rosecrans hatched a better scheme.

At Roaring Creek he was told that David Hart, whose father farmed the top of Rich Mountain, was in camp. The Harts were Unionists, and David had escaped down an obscure trail. Rosecrans took him to McClellan's tent and there plans of attack were agreed upon. The Union force would divide. Rosecrans would detour around the mountain with his brigade and attack the enemy from the rear. At their front, McClellan, on hearing Rosecrans' guns, would attack and between them they would crush Pegram. The plan was Rosecrans'. "About 10:00 P.M.," Rosecrans says in his *Official Report,* "I came to the headquarters with a plan for turning the enemy's position. . . . The General was pleased to direct me to carry it out."

Rosecrans' column would start at dawn on July 11. Secrecy was important, yet in spite of all precautions, at midnight a nervous bugler sounded the call for assembly, and Rosecrans himself discovered several lights in the tents—"they were promptly extinguished."

Garnett had warned Pegram that McClellan might attempt to flank him by a little-used road to his right. He considered his left

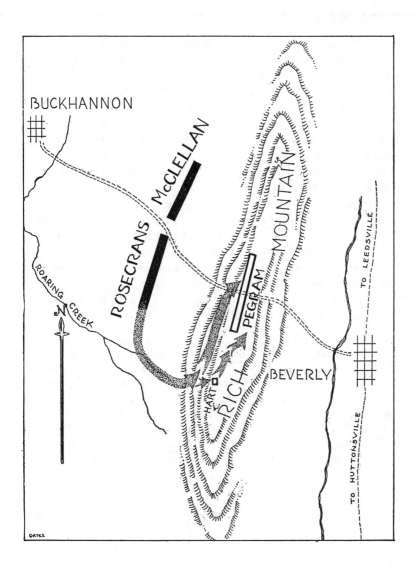

BUCKHANNON

McCLELLAN

ROSECRANS

ROARING CREEK

N

RICH

PEGRAM

MOUNTAIN

HART

BEVERLY

TO LEEDSVILLE

TO HUTTONSVILLE

GATES

BATTLE OF RICH MOUNTAIN

July 11–13, 1861

secure. Pegram, uneasy, aroused Captain Julius A. de Lagnel and sent him with one gun and 350 men to guard the road at the Harts' farm, highest point in the gap. After drinking coffee and chewing their beef and bread, at three o'clock Rosecrans and his men set off in darkness and pelting rain, carrying canteens of water and a day's rations. Because of the unfortunate midnight bugle call, the column of infantry and cavalry, altogether 1,917 men, made a wider detour than first planned. Rosecrans took no artillery with him, for he understood the impossibility of dragging guns up the narrow, tangled paths ahead. The men had orders to parade in silence, but a horse set up a frightening din, "snorting, neighing, and making all the noises possible." Enraged, Rosecrans shouted, "Cut off his head, Adjutant, cut his head off! Damn these stallions, I always did hate 'em anyway." "That was the first time I had ever been addressed by a general officer," said Charles H. Ross. "How Old Rosy did scare me that morning!"

David Hart, who led the way accompanied by Colonel Frederick W. Lander, McClellan's volunteer aide, later wrote:

We started about daybreak . . . through a pathless route in the woods. We pushed along through the bushes, laurels and rocks, followed by the whole division in perfect silence. The bushes wetted us thoroughly, and it was very cold. Our circuit was about five miles. About noon we reached the top of the mountain, near my father's farm . . . A dragoon with dispatches from General McClellan, who was sent after us, fell into the hands of the enemy and thus they found out our movements. They immediately dispatched two thousand five hundred men to the top of the mountain with three cannon. [Actually, it was 300 to 350 men with one cannon.]

They entrenched themselves with earth-works on my father's farm, just where we were to come into the road. We did not know they were there until we came on their pickets and their cannon opened fire upon us. We were then about a quarter of a mile from the house, and skirmishing began. I left the advance and went into the main body of the army. I had no arms of any kind.

In his *Report*, Rosecrans described Hart's departure from the head of the column. At twelve noon, he wrote, "the flanking force halted in the rear of the crest of Rich Mountain and the men lay down to rest" while he and Lander examined the country. "It was found that the guide was too much scared to be with us longer, and we had another valley to cross, another hill to climb, another descent beyond that to make, before we could reach the Beverly road at the top of the mountain."

Hart continued:

The bushes were so thick we could not see out, nor could the enemy see us. The enemy's musket balls could not reach us. Our boys, keeping up a fire, got down within sight and then pretended to run, but they only fell down in the bushes and behind the rocks. This drew the enemy from their entrenchments, when our boys let into them with their Enfield and Minie rifles, and I never heard such screaming in my life. The Nineteenth, in the meantime, advanced to a fence in a line with the breastworks, and fired one round. The whole earth seemed to shake. They then gave the Indiana boys a tremendous cheer, and the enemy broke from their entrenchments in every way they could. The Indiana boys had previously been ordered to fix bayonets. We could hear the rattle of the iron very plainly as the order was obeyed. Charge bayonets was then ordered, and away went our boys after the enemy. One man alone stood his ground and fired his cannon until shot by a revolver.

Throughout this melee, Charles Ross, on his unruly stallion, saw Rosecrans "riding around bareheaded, and as he stops to speak to this or that officer, excitedly opening and shutting a small spyglass."

Captain de Lagnel, the Confederate commander, fell wounded, and the horses hitched to his gun panicked and tore off down the mountain road, smashing into another gun coming up as reinforcement. The two pieces tangled, twisting down the slick mud, while the frightened horses broke loose and ran off through the woods.

A general race [Hart wrote] for about three hundred yards followed through the bush, when our men were recalled and reformed in line of battle, to receive the enemy from the entrenchments at the foot of the mountains, as we supposed they would certainly attack us from that point; but it seemed that as soon as they no longer heard the firing of the cannon they gave up all for lost. They then deserted their works and took off whatever way they could. A reinforcement which was coming from Beverly to the aid of the two thousand five hundred, retreated for the same reason.

In his *Official Report,* Rosecrans says he "rode around to the 13th and drove them into charge up across the road. . . . The whole line at the same time advanced; and by five o'clock the battle was over, and the Union forces occupied the position, with the enemy's entrenched camp three miles to the west, and a column of Virginia rebel infantry a mile or two to the east on the road to Beverly." Written in the margin of his *Sketch of the Life of Gen'l. William Starke Rosecrans,* a manuscript designed as "supplementary to the published records," is a significant insertion: "A prime part of the plan was that General McClellan's attack on the enemy's position should be begun as soon as the guns of Rosecrans' column should be heard attacking the enemy's position at Hart's tavern on top of the mountain three miles in rear of his main entrenchments."

Colonel John Beatty, who served with McClellan, wrote in his diary:

Between two and three o'clock we heard shots in the rear of the fortifications; then volleys of musketry, and the roar of artillery. Every man sprang to his feet, assured that the moment for making the attack had arrived. General McClellan and staff came galloping up, and a thousand faces turned to hear the order to advance; but no order was given. The general halted a few paces from our line and sat on his horse listening to the guns, apparently in doubt as to what to do; and as he sat there with indecision stamped on every line of his countenance, the battle grew fiercer in the enemy's rear. Every volley could be heard distinctly. . . . If the enemy is too strong for us to attack, what must be the fate of Rosecrans' four regiments, cut off from us and struggling against such odds? Hours passed; and as the last straggling shots and final silence told us the battle had ended, gloom settled down on every soldier's heart, and the belief grew strong that Rosecrans had been defeated and his brigade cut to pieces or captured. This belief grew to certain conviction soon after, when we heard shout after shout go up from the fortifications in our front.

"The noise of the engagement had been heard in McClellan's camp," said General Cox, "and he formed his troops for attack, but the long continuance of the cannonade and some signs of exultation in Pegram's camp seem to have made him think Rosecrans had been repulsed. The failure to attack in accordance with the plan has never been explained. Rosecrans' messengers failed to reach McClellan during the 11th, but the sound of the battle was sufficient notice that he had gained the summit and was engaged; and he was, in fact, left to win his own battle or to get out of his embarrassment as he would."

In his own report, McClellan says that during Rosecrans' march to attack Pegram, he was

. . . to communicate with me every hour—the remainder of the force under my command to be held in readiness to assault in front as soon as Rosecrans' musketry should indicate that he was immediately in their rear.

The order to General Rosecrans to advance to attack the rear of the lower entrenchments was not carried out, but his brigade remained at Hart's farm during the remainder of the day and the night, and I received no communications from him after about eleven o'clock A.M. when he was still distant about a mile and a half from Hart's farm.

About the time I expected the general to reach the rear of their entrenchments I moved up all my available force to the front, and remained in person just in rear of the advance pickets, ready to assault when the indicated moment should arrive. . . .

Late in the afternoon . . . I finally determined to return to camp. . . . Orders were then given to move up the guns with the entire available infantry at daybreak the following morning. Some delay occurred in moving from camp, and just as the guns were starting, intelligence was received that the enemy had evacuated their works and fled over the mountains. Then for the first time since eleven o'clock the previous day I received a communication from General Rosecrans.

Of McClellan's failure to support him, Rosecrans says bluntly in his *Personal Report,* a terse summary, dated June 15, 1865, of his military record: "My brigade after a march of ten hours over pathless mountains, gained the gap two miles and a half in rear of the rebel entrenched camp, where he met and fought us with all the infantry and artillery he could spare from his camp, which General McClellan contrary to agreement and military prudence did not attack." Rosecrans heard no firing from McClellan's direction, and disposed his troops in the best defensive position on top of Rich Mountain, and as a dark and rainy night closed down they bivouacked in line of battle on their arms.

Picket firing continued throughout the night, and at 3:00 A.M. a prisoner brought in by Union pickets told Rosecrans that the disorganized enemy were probably dispersing. At five o'clock, an advance disclosed that Pegram and most of his command had fled. The 170 Confederates who remained behind, many of them wounded, surrendered with artillery, camp equipage, and quartermasters' stores. Thirteen Indiana boys were buried among the boulders of Rich Mountain.

"We were rejoiced this morning," Colonel John Beatty wrote in his diary, "to hear of Rosecrans' success, and, at the same time, not well pleased at the escape of the enemy under cover of night. We were ordered to move, and got under way at eight o'clock. On the road we met General Rosecrans and staff. He was jubilant, as well he might be, and as he rode by received the congratulations of the officers and cheers of the men."

With the enemy on the run, McClellan finally advanced and entered Beverly, thus flanking Garnett's position on Laurel Hill with a superior force. To extricate himself, Garnett abandoned his position, crossed the Laurel Mountains eastward, and fled toward the north on a single wretched road up the Cheat River Valley, pursued by a Union detachment. At Carrick's Ford, turning to face it, he was killed.

That evening, McClellan amplified his report of victory. From Beverly, at 8:00 P.M., he sent a dispatch to Scott: "I have the honor to inform you that the army under my command has gained a decisive victory which seems to have accomplished the objects of my march. I turned the very strong entrenchments on Rich Mountain yesterday with General Rosecrans' brigade of four regiments and one company of cavalry." The next day he added: "Success of today is all that I could desire." In his delight, Scott mistook McClellan's account of the occupation of the Confederate camp for a second "success." "The General-in-Chief, and what is more, the Cabinet, including the President," he wrote, "are charmed with your activity, valor and consequent successes of Rich Mountain on the 11th, and of Beverly this morning. We do not doubt that you will in due time sweep the rebels from Western Virginia, but we do not mean to precipitate you, as you are fast enough."

In his *Official Report* of July 14, McClellan referred to "great difficulty and almost superhuman effort of Rosecrans and his men," and added:

I cannot let the present occasion pass without making mention of the services of Brigadier General Rosecrans in conducting his command up the very precipitous sides of the mountain and overcoming the formidable obstacles which impeded his progress; also for the very handsome manner in which he planned and directed his attack upon the rebels at Hart's farm, carrying them after a stout and determined resistance.

Simultaneous with McClellan's advance on Beverly, another column under General Cox pushed forward from Guyandot, at the junction of the Guyandot River with the Ohio, and moved eastward steadily into the Kanawha Valley, reaching Charleston on July 25.

From Beverly on June 16, McClellan proclaimed: "Soldiers of the Army of the West! I am more than satisfied with you.

"You have annihilated two armies, commanded by educated and experienced soldiers, intrenched in mountain fastnesses fortified by their leisure. You have taken five guns, twelve colors, fifteen hundred stand of arms, one thousand prisoners, including more than forty officers. All this has been accomplished with the loss of twenty brave men killed and sixty wounded on your part."

Before July ended, Western Virginia was safely in Union hands, and there it remained throughout the war. While the engagement at Rich Mountain and the later one at Carnifax Ferry, a crossing of the Gauley, were small compared to the great battles of the next three years, "their importance," wrote McCalmont later, "could not be overestimated. Their immediate effect was to give encouragement and spirit to the Union forces, and incidentally to promote McClellan to command of the Army of the Potomac, and to advance the command and influence of Rosecrans."

Rosecrans' private opinion of Rich Mountain is noteworthy. "I called it nothing but an 'affair,' " he wrote to Annie. "The results and its conception were both fortunate. I was as collected under the enemy's fire and as little sensible of danger as at any time in any ordinary business. But while trying to get my troops in proper position I could not help thinking if the enemy had disciplined troops and any enterprise how they would have stirred us up."

He later developed this viewpoint for the Committee on the Conduct of the War:

The first action I was in had 1700 men. I told the Colonel to put three companies upon different points of a ridge, and hold the rest of his regiment in column in the road. . . . He got on the ridge with every man, and it took him forty minutes to get them down. . . . I thought to myself, if I had 500 men on the other side I would make a hole in those fellows they would never get over. . . . There was not a captain there who knew how to manage his men. . . . I saw a captain going around with a cane over his shoulder. No sword at all—haw-bucking his soldiers about with his finger.

With Rich Mountain, McClellan's healthy self-esteem expanded, and by July 19 he considered himself indispensable. When Cox was checked on the Kanawha McClellan complained: "Cox has fought something between a victory and a defeat. . . . In heaven's name give me some general officers who understand their profession. I give orders and find some who cannot execute them unless I stand by them. Unless I command every picket and lead every column I cannot be sure of success."

At Rich Mountain, Cox points out in his "McClellan in West Virginia," McClellan "showed the same characteristics which became well known later. There was the same overestimate of the enemy, the same tendency to interpret unfavorably the sights and sounds in front, the same hesitation to throw in his whole force when he knew that his subordinate was engaged."

In November 1862, J. T. Trowbridge, a popular writer, wrote to Rosecrans:

Do you remember, once when I proposed to join my fortunes in this war to yours, your answer? I venture you don't. It was this: "I shall connect my fortunes with McClellan's." I replied you had better join Mac's to yours. You answered: "No, no. Mac is a lucky dog." And so you joined him, went into Western Virginia with him, and fought Rich Moutain for him and made him commander-in-chief. If, when you were outflanking Pegram, he had whipped you, whose defeat would it have been? Rosecrans'. But as you whipped him it was McClellan's victory.

These minor successes in Western Virginia brought a surge of elation to a victory-starved North. Subordinate Rosecrans was responsible for them, but commander McClellan wrote the Napoleonic reports and became the national hero.

Shortly after, on the Potomac, "On to Richmond" pressures produced disaster for the North. On July 21, Scott telegraphed McClellan at Beverly that "[Joseph E.] Johnston has amused Patterson and re-enforced [P. G. T.] Beauregard. McDowell is this forenoon forcing the passage of Bull Run. In two hours he will turn the Manassas Junction and storm it today with superior force."

That evening, at 8:00 P.M., the first news of the Bull Run disaster reached McClellan from Scott: "McDowell has been checked. Come down to the Shenandoah Valley with such troops as can be spared from Western Virginia, and make head against the enemy in that quarter. Banks and Dix will remain in Baltimore, which is liable to revolt." The next message from Scott explained: "After fairly beating the enemy, and taking three of his batteries, a panic seized McDowell's army and it is in full retreat on the Potomac. A most unaccountable transformation into a mob of a finely appointed and admirably led army . . . Remain in your present command instead of going into the valley of Shenandoah." That night Scott telegraphed to McClellan: "Circumstances make your presence here necessary. Charge Rosecrans, or some other general with your department and come hither without delay." And later: "Bring no troops with you. The successor in the Ohio Department may need them all in Western Virginia." McClellan answered on the 23rd from Beverly: "I leave in the morning. . . . Rosecrans is left in command and will go at once to Kanawha."

After Bull Run, Rosecrans wrote to his wife:

McDowell's army has suffered a defeat. Our army is now in full retreat on the Potomac. . . . Think of such a dispatch to us on an extended frontier with the idea of a victorious enemy banging at our forces while paralyzed with fear they thought not of the blows they were receiving, but of their flight and the obstacles to it. Moreover a paralysis of our forces would increase the enemy's activity and enterprise in our direction. For almost at the same moment with this appalling news came the order relieving General McClellan and devolving on me the care and command of this great department. Day before yesterday General McClellan and I rode from Beverly to this place [Grafton]—forty miles, the General on his way to Washington and I here to prepare for the Kanawha expedition. The day was most beautiful. Both our staffs and staff wagon and baggage were along. Our escort was a company of dragoons. At ten o'clock we reached the great fortified position of the rebels at Laurel Hill. It was the opinion of both of us that it would have been a far easier task to have taken Laurel Hill than to have taken Camp Garnett on Rich Mountain. There can be no doubt that with proper vigor and energy the enemy might have been dislodged before we attacked him on Rich Mountain.

During this campaign and the small battle which climaxed it, Rosecrans displayed both the characteristic excellencies that during the war carried him almost to the top as a commander and the habitual faults that, combined with some poor luck, ultimately caused his removal. His personal courage and his capacity for leadership were as marked as his apparently intuitive sense of strategy, even in a crisis. His military intelligence was high and his nervous energy and industry were prodigious. He never spared himself, and in this can be discerned an element of weakness. In times of stress, he neglected to take proper rest. He attempted to do too much himself, instead of entrusting more to his subordinates. Correspondent Whitelaw Reid commented later that at Rich Mountain Rosecrans' conduct

merited the praise which it instantly and everywhere received. The plan, as has been seen, was entirely his own; and though it was his first action, as well as the first for the troops he commanded, his conduct showed a thorough comprehension of the true method of handling raw volunteers, not less than that disposition to "go wherever he asked his soldiers to go," which always made him a favorite with the men in the ranks. But he already exhibited symptoms of the personal imprudence which was to form so signal a feature of his character, by casual hints as to his dissatisfaction with the conduct of his superior officer—a dissatisfaction which he afterwards expressed officially. . . .

Reid knew. He was there, and well acquainted with both Rosecrans and McClellan. Reid's secondhand account of Shiloh should not obscure much keen observation and accurate reporting. Ohioan Reid knew and understood his fellow Ohioans, and much of the time wrote from firsthand information.

And so they parted; McClellan for Washington, and within a few months to the supreme command of all the land forces of the United States, and Rosecrans to lead fresh recruits, as green as the last, against John B. Floyd, Henry A. Wise, and Robert E. Lee. The echoes of McClellan's departing train sounded through the mountains, and as they died away, a new cry arose: "Lee is coming!"

Three

"LEE IS COMING"

On July 23, 1861, Rosecrans took command of the Department of the Ohio, embracing Western Virgina, Ohio, Indiana, Michigan, and Illinois, with headquarters at Clarksburg, Virginia.

Bull Run had just proved a crushing defeat. It suggested that the idea widely held in the North that the war would last no more than three months was a delusion, and so frightened Washington that tens of thousands of troops who might have upset the balance on the battlefield were immobilized in its defense. It gave impetus to the abandonment by both the South and North of Kentucky's armed neutrality, and put Union arms in Western Virginia on the defensive. "Officers and men are low-spirited tonight," wrote Colonel Beatty. "Our army has been beaten at Manassas with terrible loss."

Through August, Rosecrans fortified Red House, Cheat Mountain, and the Elkwater passes, and prepared to resist Lee, who now undertook to regain possession of Western Virginia. There, as in the east, both armies faced each other in a period of inaction. The Confederates, chased by Cox up the Great Kanawha, retreated until they crossed the Gauley. "In the race up the Kanawha Valley," sneered Greeley, "Wise succeeded, to the last, in keeping ahead, which was the only military success he ever achieved."

Wise's retreat ended at Lewisburg, capital of Greenbrier County, one of the few Confederate strongholds west of the main Allegheny ridge. There he was heavily reinforced, while the Union armies in Western Virginia were depleted by the mustering out of three-month volunteers. To regain Western Virginia, Davis sent General Floyd with reinforcements into the Kanawha Valley, and placed Lee in command of the fragments of Garnett's defeated troops at Valley Mountain. Lee was to direct the campaign. Wise felt that an expedition up the Kanawha Valley might enable him to make a deep foray into Ohio.

With his main force, Rosecrans lay at Clarksburg, on the spur of the Baltimore and Ohio into Parkersburg. General Joseph J. Reynolds and one brigade watched the passes of the Cheat and Greenbrier mountains. Cox remained in the Kanawha Valley near Gauley Bridge. Rosecrans grew anxious when from July 26 to 30 he heard nothing from Cox. Good generalship would oppose fragments with masses.

"Lee intends attacking Cheat Mountain Pass," Scott telegraphed, and McClellan next day warned: "Lee and Johnston are actually on their march to crush you." They would probably attack either Huttonsville or Gauley. Rosecrans should draw heavy guns from the Allegheny arsenal, fortify vulnerable places, and establish headquarters at Buckhannon.

Threat of Lee's invasion set Western Virginia nerves aquiver. Senator Carlile telegraphed Cameron: "For God's sake send us more troops and a general to command, or else we are whipped in less than ten days." Some of the alarms Rosecrans labeled "exaggerations," others "absurd." "I find it most difficult," he later told Senator Benjamin F. Wade, of Ohio, "to get our officers to weigh testimony." A prime example of false rumor was that Lee had met and defeated Rosecrans and taken almost the whole of his command prisoner.

Both commanders held prisoners previously taken, and when Lee proposed exchange, Rosecrans refused. "You ask me for men captured here, hardy mountaineers, who would reinforce your army operating against me. You propose to give me men captured at Bull Run, who know nothing of service here." It was their first contact since Newport.

Correspondent Whitelaw Reid heard Rosecrans say: "Lee will make a splendid plan . . . but I'll fight the campaign before he gets through planning it." Lee proposed to capture and hold the lightly defended passes into the middle section of Western Virginia, proceed southward, join his 10,000 men with the 10,000 of Floyd and

Wise, and, with greatly superior forces, overwhelm Rosecrans. Rosecrans was given almost a month to prepare. Reid's prophecy proved accurate. "General Lee's plan," wrote Confederate historian E. A. Pollard, "was said to have been one of the best laid plans that ever illustrated the consummation of the rules of strategy, or ever went awry on account of practical failures in its execution."

Opposing commanders were fairly matched as to bad roads, the inexperience of their troops, and incompetent officers. During August, Rosecrans had more trouble with his own army than with Lee's. Three-month enlistments expired and he waited for reinforcements from Lincoln's new 300,000 levy. Service in Western Virginia was hard and obscure. No paymaster met returning heroes, no mustering-out officer discharged them, and the dissatisfied men scattered over Ohio.

By August 4, Rosecrans planned to complete defensive works in critical places, clean out guerrillas, organize supplies, and when the new Ohio regiments arrived, carry out McClellan's scheme to seize eastern Tennessee. Lee's advance blocked the last of these plans.

On some days, great cumulus clouds drifted overhead, striping the peaks in alternate sunshine and shadow. From Clarksburg, Rosecrans wrote to his wife on August 13: "It has rained a great deal here this summer. All the vast masses of warm air charged with vapors from the Mississippi valley which come rolling up this way deposit much of their moisture this side of the mountains. . . . My dearest, what a terrible scourge of Almighty God is war! How shameful to complain of the little crosses of daily life when war compels men to sleep on the cold ground, stand in rain, and go out with life in hand, not knowing when they will return. Ah, my own sweet wife, let us humble ourselves."

Recruits proved as undisciplined as children, and as unprepared for the grim business of war. Their average age was seventeen, and they rambled, climbed, and picked raspberries, blackberries, huckleberries, and fox grape. In the easy frontier democracy, privates slapped officers on the back, called them by their first names, and failed to salute. Rosecrans had a professional soldier's standards, and after taps occasionally inspected the camp in person. Seeing lights or hearing talk and laughter, he whacked a tent with his sword, telling the occupants to put out lights and be quiet. The men responded with "rough camp talk and drolleries," and pretended astonishment: "We didn't hear taps and thought it was our regimental wagonmaster playing a trick on us." Cox agreed that "if Rosecrans' method was not an ideal one, it was at least vigorous, and every week showed that the little army was improving in discipline and in knowledge of duty."

Rosecrans demonstrated the common touch, too. One hot day, Company A of the 7th Ohio was detailed to unload supplies freighted up the Kanawha. Captain William R. Creighton permitted his men to take off their coats. As they sprawled out to rest, Rosecrans rode up. Creighton leaped to his feet. "Don't you know, sir, that it is against orders to allow men on duty to remove their equipment?" he was asked. "The man that issued that order never did a day's work, and I'll see him in hell before I let my men swelter with their accouterments on," said Creighton. Rosecrans silently rode to the boat. "Know who that is?" a soldier asked Creighton. "No, and I don't care." "That's General Rosecrans." When Rosecrans returned, the company, in full equipment, gave him a "present." After Creighton had "put his men through the manual," Rosecrans raised his hat and said: "A company that can handle muskets that well should be allowed to unload a steamer without anything on if they want to."

He soon learned that "All want of discipline, loss, and waste of money comes from want of officers. An officer who knows his business, attends to the instruction of his men. Volunteers expect instruction, and if their officers are uninstructed, do not get it." He wrote to the War Department: "Every day's experience convinces me of the absolute necessity of having some officers of military education among them. . . . The detail of a second lieutenant from the Military Academy to act as Major even would in six weeks increase the military power of a regiment at least one-third." The idea possessed him: "Could not the Academy be opened, say, in November, and cadets detailed, one for each regiment as instructors or drill masters?"

"At Beverly," Charles H. Ross remembered, "Rosecrans used to dine with us quite often. Our cook would put an extra basket of crackers on the table, for the General would always give us a lesson in outpost or picket duty, using the crackers to illustrate it."

"Our General is an incessant worker," wrote another close observer. "He is in his saddle almost constantly. He has not had a full night's sleep since he has been in Virginia, and he takes his meals as often on horseback as at his table. . . . His soldiers recognize him as a competent commander."

It was to be expected that, in Unionist Western Virginia, civil war would spawn trouble. To end ambushings, maraudings, brigandage, pillage, lootings, murder, and other such offenses, Rosecrans, on August 20, 1861, addressed the "Loyal Citizens of West Virginia": "You are the vast majority of the people. . . . The old constitution and laws of Virginia are only in force in Western Virginia. These laws you must maintain. . . . Let each town and district choose five reliable and energetic citizens as a committee of public safety, . . . and be responsible for the preservation of peace and good order."

So satisfactory were the results of Rosecrans' civilian policy that the new state government was promptly organized, and guerrilla war almost unknown in Western Virginia. In August, 1861, a convention provided for a new state, to be called "Kanawha," later changed to "West Virginia," though statehood was not conferred until June 20, 1863. For his services, the West Virginia legislature passed a unanimous vote of thanks to Rosecrans. The legislature of Ohio did likewise in the winter of 1861–62.

During the late summer of 1861, rain fell on both armies impartially, and by August 10, after twenty days of downpour, the roads seemed bottomless. Ice formed on puddles the night of August 14, and the Confederates, as uncomfortable as if they were in a Tennessee hog pen, huddled around great fires. Fog shrouded the mountaintops, and on the 19th logs, brush, green trees, and all manner of drift swept down the flooding Elk River. Huddled in his heavy overcoat, Lee wrote: "It is raining now, has been all day, last night, day before, and day before that." He had not yet achieved his great reputation. Although Western Virginia trembled, Richmond papers called him "Granny." In addition to other handicaps, Lee had Floyd and Wise, two former governors of Virginia with political differences. Lee squirmed at their punctilious battle of dispatches, and finally decided that Floyd ranked Wise.

On August 16, as the Confederates massed to retake Western Virginia, McClellan ordered Rosecrans to "Disregard, for the present the interior of Western Virginia, or else hold it with your worst troops. . . . Concentrate the remainder of your available force in the vicinity of Huttonsville. . . . Make a strong reconnaissance . . . towards Huntersville, and if possible drive them out before their works are completed." Further orders said that, having protected vulnerable places, Rosecrans should "attack the enemy on Cranberry or wherever he debouches . . . in succession with overwhelming forces. Never wait for him to attack your main column, but crush the enemy nearest to you, and then go after the next. . . . March with the utmost rapidity."

Floyd opened the campaign by pushing out from Lewisburg against Cox, who was compelled by superior numbers to fall back upon the New River. Leaving a sufficient force under Wise to checkmate Cox, Floyd marched northwestward toward Carnifax Ferry, the crossing of the Gauley, to intercept reinforcements which Rosecrans might send Cox from Clarksburg. Floyd kept to the right of the New River, which joins the Gauley to form the Great Kanawha.

Across the Gauley, five miles below Summersville, the 7th Ohio, one of Cox's outposts, guarded the Gauley road at Cross Lanes. Floyd fell upon the dispersed Union regiment. Because Floyd had now crossed Cox's northern line of communication, Rosecrans knew that the assault was to be made on Cox and that he must be quickly rescued. He assured the War Department that the sixty-five companies of infantry at Clarksburg would be at Bulltown in three days. Anticipating this move, Floyd busied himself with fortifying Carnifax Ferry.

Lee now took the field and turned his attention to seizing the critical passes into middle Western Virginia. He saw that at Valley Mountain he was too far north of Floyd and Wise on the Kanawha to conduct joint offensive operations, or maintain communications with them. He therefore moved southward, taking position before the defiles of Cheat Mountain, in the upper valley of the Greenbrier, which flows southwest into the Kanawha. Advancing on the Huntersville Pike, he threatened Reynolds' single brigade, which held Cheat Mountain, and from September 12 to 15, with an overwhelming force of 9,000 or 10,000 men and eight to twelve pieces of artillery, he maneuvered against Reynolds, and accomplished only his own exhaustion.

Rosecrans set out from Clarksburg with three brigades—4,500 men, under Generals Henry W. Benham and Eliakim P. Scammon, and Colonel Robert L. McCook. West Pointers Scammon and Rosecrans were personal friends—at Yellow Springs, Ohio, their wives and children shared a large house for the duration of the war—but Rosecrans called Benham "selfish, fussy and conceited." Colonel McCook still rode at the head of his "thousand Dutchmen," many of whom had had European military training. Lacking such training, McCook developed a good working arrangement. His men took care of themselves in military matters, and he served as bookkeeper, interpreter, good provider, and defender. Orders were signed by Assistant Adjutant General George L. Hartsuff, a durable young West Point graduate whom Rosecrans greatly admired.

Now the column traversed the rolling country south of Clarksburg, where young Thomas Jackson had played on the river in a canoe hollowed from a tree trunk. When he was dying, he remembered, and said: "Let us cross over the river and rest under the shade of the trees."

After reaching Sutton on September 6, Rosecrans confided to Annie: "The troops are monstrously green." He added: "I would like for you to order me a brigadier's sword and sash."

At Sutton, hills were splashed with the yellow, russet, and red of autumn trees. The Federals crossed the Elk, toiled to the summit of a high ridge, descended, and followed Twolick Run, which was churning white foam as it tumbled over rocks and fallen timber. Next, they crossed Birch Mountain. By now, Confederate skirmishers lurked on neighboring heights, and the country became dangerous to penetrate. It was "seamed with by-roads, blind paths and mountain passes," and infested with bushwhackers. In order to stop up all avenues by which the enemy might strike his lines in rear and center, Rosecrans found it necessary to make minute reconnaissance. "He mapped all Western Virginia, highways, byways, mountain passes, ravines, blind paths, bridle paths, cow paths and negro routes," wrote the New York *Times* correspondent. "If he saw a horse track, he sent an aide to follow it: 'Be sure to observe whether the horseshoes were put on wrong side before or not.'"

About noon on the 9th, when the perspiring recruits dragged

their guns to the summit of Powell Mountain, a deserted camp on the highest ridge showed that a considerable force had been there. All afternoon the column wound down through low wooded hills, to the widening bottoms of Muddlety Creek. Moving cautiously toward the Bottoms, the advance flushed and scattered several hundred Confederates. That night, the main column slept in the meadows, and next morning marched before 4:15. At 8:00, as they entered Summersville, Confederate cavalry whisked out of the other end of town. A burned bridge delayed Rosecrans' entrance.

Until then, Rosecrans had supposed that Floyd lay fortified below Kesler's Cross Lanes. But at noon two cavalry prisoners were brought in. One of them had been in Floyd's camp and reported that Floyd waited on the cliffs overlooking Carnifax Ferry. A mile up the road, another fork, the Salmon and McKee's Creek road, leading through the hills to Kesler's Cross Lanes, gave access to his position. From then on Rosecrans scrutinized every bridle path, ravine, and neighboring cliff.

Moving cautiously, the column traversed a narrow, deeply shadowed section of Peter's Creek Valley. Rosecrans reached Kesler's Cross Lanes about 2:00, and while he halted for the train to close up, picket firing began to his front. In flushing out Confederate pickets, Union skirmishers had encountered a good-sized force encamped on a hill. The news provoked cheers. William H. Lytle's 10th Ohio made first contact. Colonel W. S. Smith and the 13th Ohio were close behind. Rosecrans ordered Benham "to move forward cautiously into the woods for the purpose of reconnoitering." The New York *Times* correspondent heard soldiers agree that the "old general"—Rosecrans—"would not stumble upon a masked battery."

When Benham reached the camp and found abandoned equipment, he concluded that Floyd was retreating. Rosecrans disagreed and repeated: "Feel the enemy closely, but do not engage him unless you see an evident opening."

Whitelaw Reid wrote of Benham:

. . . In the scarcity of experienced officers, this brigade had been entrusted to a . . . brigadier recommended not only by the warm endorsement of General McClellan, but by that lion's skin, so often used . . . to cover the ass's shoulders—'service in Mexico.' . . . The Brigadier had the misfortune of always staying out of reach of the enemy when he was sober, and of being too drunk to understand his surroundings whenever he was likely to have a fight. The Rebel outpost having retreated, this obfuscated officer conceived the idea that he had won a great victory, and plunged ahead pell-mell with his brigade through the woods, contrary to his explicit orders, and without even a line of skirmishers deployed to the front. . . .

Twenty-five minutes after Benham's brigade left the deserted Confederate camp, the remainder of Rosecrans' column was still moving tensely forward. The *Times* correspondent wrote that as "teamsters shouted, whips cracked, and artillery horses strained up the hill . . . suddenly all heads turned at sharp, quick firing in the woods just ahead." It was Benham in serious trouble. After advancing through heavy underbrush, he suddenly found himself before a formidable earthwork, and exposed to fire from seven or eight pieces of artillery and the musketry of Floyd's whole command, which lay concealed some fifty yards to Benham's front.

Rosecrans had two alternatives—order up reinforcements to attack a fortified position of unknown strength or withdraw at the risk of a stampede. Deciding to support Benham and continue the attack, he spurred to the top of a hill and trained his spyglass on the woods. He saw nothing, not even smoke, but the sound of firing described the enemy's right, and he ordered Colonel John W. Lowe's 12th Ohio forward. As the men reached the crest, they cheered Rosecrans and plunged into the woods.

When Benham sought reinforcements, Rosecrans sent in a battery and two rifled cannon, and ordered McCook's and Scammon's brigades to advance. Then he rode forward to examine Benham's position and to reconnoiter more closely the Confederate works. At the front, he learned how the fight began. Hearing but not seeing Benham, the Confederates had fired a volley, and Benham's men had replied.

When the blast from the woods indicated Floyd's position, Rosecrans ordered the 10th up the hill to the right. At its head rode diminutive Colonel Lytle, poet, gentleman, and white-gloved aristocrat from Cincinnati's Laurence Avenue. The batteries had not come up, and the 12th was still advancing. The 10th and the 13th made their way to an enemy abatis. On the rough ground and amid felled trees and tangled brush, the line of the 10th was broken, and the right separated from the center. Not knowing what had happened, Lytle ordered a charge.

"Follow Tenth!" he cried, dashing toward the enemy battery, which at a hundred yards opened a terrible fire upon him and his four cheering companies. A bullet passed through his left leg, wounding his horse also. The animal threw him, dashed over the entrenchments, and was killed. That day the "Bloody Tenth" earned its name.

The 12th struggled up a rough path to the left of the road, straight to the battle line. "In front of one of Floyd's batteries," said Captain James D. Wallace, "we crossed the fence of a cornfield, entered the field, and were ordered by Colonel Lowe to deploy to the right and advance." Colonel Lowe, on foot, was killed by a shot in his forehead.

By this time, from the edge of the cornfield, Rosecrans could see part of Floyd's works. The fusillade which his troops kept up against Floyd's fortifications made the enemy lie close, but did not prevent their rapid return fire.

Rosecrans next sent a party through the woods still farther to the enemy's left, to seek a weak point in Floyd's position, and then, dismounting, he made his way along his front. He later described the confusion: "I saw a regiment that had retired behind a hill under fire and there was but one company formed. . . . I asked: 'Where is your captain?' 'I don't know.' 'Where is your lieutenant?' 'I don't know.' 'Where is your orderly sergeant?' " Telling the orderly sergeant to form the company, Rosecrans went to the next company. " 'Where is your captain?' 'I don't know.' 'Have you a captain?' 'Yes, sir.' 'Is he here?' 'He was here.' 'Where is he now?' 'I don't know.' I found out of the ten companies, but one captain at his post."

Reports revealed that Floyd's entrenchments stretched across a bend in the Gauley, with flanks protected by steep, rocky cliffs, rising to perpendicular heights of from 400 to 500 feet. At their rear was Carnifax Ferry, the only point of crossing in twenty-five miles.

It might be possible to reach and turn the enemy's right, Rosecrans learned, so he ordered an assault. The 13th was to attack the extreme right, while the 10th with part of the 12th was to advance to the right of the cornfield and attack the center and left.

September twilight fell early in the woods, and it was dusk when McCook received orders to assault. As he waved his slouch hat, he roared: "Forward, my bully Dutch! We'll go over their damned entrenchments if every man dies on the other side." The Germans cheered wildly. Captain Hartsuff led the column into position. But in spite of all their shouting, the brigade saw no action. When darkness fell, they were withdrawn.

The 13th climbed a steep, slippery cliff, through blackberry thorns and laurel thicket, attempting to turn the enemy's right. The weary men had been marching since 3:00 A.M.—"more exhausted troops I never saw," Rosecrans said, and decided to withdraw through the ravine and await daybreak. In the darkness, the column doubled on itself, and a stray shot provoked the tense volunteers to fire on one another, killing two and wounding thirty. The mistake was discovered immediately, and the column extricated.

Rosecrans reported:

By dusk I deemed it prudent to withdraw our forces from the woods to the open fields in rear of our entrenched camp. To cover this withdrawal, the batteries . . . were ordered into position, and directed in a tone of voice to be heard by the enemy, to give him "Hail Columbia," and with the same intention the Ninth was called for and ordered to ambush them well. The regimental commanders were then ordered to lead their men quietly out by the flank, while the Ninth and Third brigade . . . were to disperse themselves to cover the movement. Captain Hartsuff directed the columns as they withdrew. . . . I arranged the troops in order of battle on ground still farther to the rear . . . and at 2:00 o'clock retired to an oat loft to sleep.

The men dropped down to sleep without cooking their suppers. Through the night heavy rumbling was heard, as if artillery were being shifted. At 4:00 A.M., as Rosecrans awoke, a sentry brought in a runaway Negro, who reported that the enemy had abandoned their camp, crossed the Gauley, and then destroyed their boats.

Floyd indeed was gone. Between 10:00 P.M. and 4:00 A.M., he had crept down the cliff on a steep, single track road. Discouraged, slightly wounded, overestimating Rosecrans' numbers, and blaming Wise for not reinforcing him, he fell back about fifteen miles on the main Charleston road, and prepared to entrench himself in the mountain passes.

Rosecrans estimated that his forces took 8,000 feet of entrench-ments. The elaborate works protecting the Confederate camp em-braced almost a square mile of ground and lay within a mountain basin, protected from all missiles but shells. The river flowed deep in the rear. In front was a ravine, thickly grown, which so con-cealed the position that it could hardly be seen until it was reached. On the right were strong works which stretched to the very edge of the precipice. The left was the only portion of the works tolerably accessible. When Rosecrans inspected the site he found that:

> The ferry was gone, foot-bridge destroyed, and the enemy's column out of sight. . . . The descent to the ferry from this side is by a narrow wagon track, winding around a rocky hill-side. The ascent from the other side is by a road passing up the Meadow River, which is in a deep rocky gorge, the sides ascending precipitously to the height of nearly 300 feet. . . . Finding we had no means of crossing the ferry, which is here 370 feet wide, pursuit was impossible. . . . The rebels, aware of this, left a body of skirmishers to occupy the cliffs along the Meadow River down the ferry to prevent small parties from crossing.

Rosecrans ordered McCook to drive the Confederates from the other side of the river and take possession of the heights, and Ben-ham to repair the roads and ferry. Cox was to advance cautiously with all his available force on the Lewisburg road.

Rosecrans' report continued:

> Papers found in camp showed that Floyd's force consisted of at least five regiments, two batteries, and a battalion of cavalry. . . . Wise's force, not having been put at less than 2000, I feared they might fall on and crush Cox before we could cross. I was speedily relieved from these fears by a report from him . . . saying that the rebels were in full re-treat, and he had been within two hours of their rear guard. By this time one of the small ferryboats had been got up, and Colonel McCook's brigade was passed over to reinforce Cox.

Gloom in the South followed the news of Floyd's defeat. The Richmond correspondent of the Charleston (South Carolina) *Courier* wrote:

> Advices from West Virginia today are not encouraging. The causes for this failure are twofold: 1st, the inadequacy of our military strength in that section, 2ndly, the superior generalship of Rosencrantz [sic]. Lee,

Floyd and Wise have at the present time less than 15,000 men. The enemy know it. Rosencrantz, Cox and Reynolds have not less than 50,000.

The enemy have in Rosencrantz probably the best general in the Northern armies. What credit McClellan won in West Virginia was due rather to the genius of his subordinate. Our army officers admit that the late maneuvers of Rosencrantz in which he succeeded in surprising Floyd was the most brilliant Federal feat of the war. Leaving his armies in the mountain intact, Rosencrantz proceeded to the Kanawha Valley and raised a fresh force of 15,000 men. [This was incorrect reporting.] With these he suddenly precipitated himself upon Floyd, and though our General gained a technical victory, yet the ultimate result was disastrous to the Confederates.

From Camp Scott, near Carnifax Ferry, Rosecrans wrote on the 11th to Annie: "I have supplied myself with a trunk from the captured property. It contained a beautiful snugglety, an abundance of shirts, drawers and sox." But despite his victory, Rosecrans was disappointed. Floyd had escaped. In his *Official Report*, he complimented his troops, but made no complaint about Benham.

Rosecrans' new orders divided the Department of the Ohio. Ohio, Indiana, and that portion of Kentucky lying within fifteen miles of Cincinnati were to be under General Ormsby M. Mitchel, while that part of Virginia lying west of the Blue Ridge would constitute a separate command, to be called the Department of Western Virginia. As its commander, Rosecrans would continue to requisition reinforcements from the Governor of Ohio, or from the commander in that state.

The sprawling Department of the Ohio, which McClellan and then Rosecrans commanded, had been an efficient military district only so long as it faced a single active front in Western Virginia. But with the Union defeat at Bull Run, and the election in August of a strong Unionist legislature, Kentucky's official neutrality had ended, and, on September 3, General Leonidas Polk led Confederate troops across the Kentucky line from East Tennessee, and on the 4th took possession of Columbus. Learning of this, General Ulysses S. Grant, at Cairo, Illinois, sent detachments across the Ohio to Paducah and Smithfield. "With these movements," wrote historian John W. Burgess, "the farce of Kentucky's neutrality was played to the end."

Rosecrans must have considered the loss of his Cincinnati base a blow, for he sent a dispatch to Scott; it is missing from the *Official Records* and drew a rebuke: "No blow has been struck at you. That phrase objectionable. Draw reinforcements and supplies as before. . . . You are a soldier, a scientific general and confidence is reposed in your judgment and discretion as well as in your zeal and valor."

Shortages of supplies and ammunition remedied, Rosecrans crossed the river with the troops he had brought down from Clarksburg, and, moving to the Lewisburg road, joined forces with Cox. On the 28th, the head of the column, acting as a corps of observation, advanced to the top of Big Sewell Mountain, a long, windswept spur of the Allegheny range thirty-four miles from Gauley Bridge, while two and a half regiments stood at the foot. Reconnaissance showed that on the mountain the Confederates had 12,-000 to 14,000 effectives, compared to Rosecrans' 5,200, and that they had constructed fortifications of from two to four miles in length along the top. To support these main works, Lee developed a secondary line at Meadow Bluff, fifteen miles beyond the first, on the road toward Lewisburg.

Lee in his combined forces mustered 20,000 men to Rosecrans' 8,500, yet he had made no attack other than to send a small detachment on September 25 across the New River at Champanville, where a Union detachment surprised and routed it. Autumn storms had taken their toll in sick Confederates, while the healthy floundered in the mud, short of supplies and equipment. In addition, the quarrel between Floyd and Wise had simmered, until, on September 25, Wise was ordered to "go to Richmond," and departed huffily from the campaign.

From the top of Big Sewell, Rosecrans wrote that "a most terrific rain set in, lasted 31 hours, raised the rivers and streams so as to cut off communications even between regiments separated by tiny rivulets. The telegraphic communications between me and all parts of West Virginia were interrupted and so remain." At Charleston, the Kanawha River, normally forty to fifty feet below the town's plateau, rose some forty-five or fifty-five feet, until water stood four to five feet deep in the houses.

Outnumbered more than two to one, with the enemy behind good defensive works, in a country stripped of forage and subsistence, with roads to his rear turning to jelly, and with men unpaid and supplies in jeopardy, Rosecrans decided to withdraw to Gauley Mountain, to a position nearer his depots. There he planned to remain until the threadbare troops were supplied with food and clothing. Exposure to incessant rain had produced much sickness in both camps, and the "storms at Big Sewell Mountain," Floyd said, "cost more men, sick and dead, than the battle of Manassas."

Withdrawal from Big Sewell Mountain began on the night of October 5. Baggage and the sick were sent ahead. At 10:00 P.M., tents were struck, and at 11:00 wagons moved. The weather cleared briefly, and the rear guard, watching nervously on the crest until 1:30, saw fog and clouds slip away and stars appear. The night grew electric with strain. When a brilliant star rose, someone whispered, "It's a fire balloon!" A picket's gun went off, and anxious watchers felt certain that the Confederates had discovered the withdrawal.

Rosecrans led the struggling column. "Wagons toiled over the steep and slippery hills," Cox wrote. "Here and there a team stalled in the mud. It looked as if daylight would overtake us. Rosecrans now gave his personal supervision to moving the wagons and artillery, wagon-master's work, but work which had to be done if the little army was not to be found in the morning strung out and exposed to the enemy. The result showed that hardly less than the commanding general's own authority and energy could have moved the column forward in the mud and darkness. When day broke we were only three or four miles from our camp of the evening before."

At daybreak, preparing to attack, Lee found Rosecrans gone. The Confederate pickets had mistaken the rumble of Union wagons for a last-minute shifting of artillery. Lee could not make effective pursuit, because his horses were lean and weak. He had been outgeneraled by mud, sickness, and Rosecrans; heckled in the press, he wrote that army movements "cannot keep pace with the expectations of editors."

Rosecrans' new position, a little above the confluence of the Gauley and New rivers, was not quite accessible by river transportation. Supplies could be brought by steamboat from Cincinnati to a point twenty-five miles below Gauley Bridge, but the camp was thirty-five miles beyond, so that a sixty-mile wagon haul was needed. Horses and mules fell dead in the tenacious mire.

Gradually the Union army found camps: Robert C. Schenck's

brigade, ten miles from Gauley Bridge; McCook's, eight; Benham's, six; and Cox at the bridge, with a detachment guarding the steamboat landing below. One regiment was at C. Q. Tompkins' farm, where Rosecrans established headquarters. His men complained that Mrs. Tompkins used a lamp to signal information across the river—her husband, a West Pointer, and Floyd's brother-in-law, was a colonel in Lee's army. When Lieutenant Judson Cross of the 7th Ohio was captured, Tompkins looked him up. "When you see Rosecrans *again*, give him my personal regards and tell him I am a thorough rebel." Cross escaped, and two weeks later, delivered the message in person to Rosecrans.

One morning, headquarters quiet was shattered by a Confederate shell. Rosecrans shouted, waved his arms. Floyd had erected batteries on Cotton Hill, overlooking the Union camp, to blast supply trains struggling in the six miles between Tompkins' farm and the falls of the Kanawha. To silence Floyd, Rosecrans posted a battery of ten Parrot guns at Kanawha Falls. After that, the wagons moved at night, and the noisy shelling did little damage.

Issuance of clothing had begun immediately; and by November 1 all the men except the cavalry were well supplied. Private contributions, including coverlets and woolen socks, had been heavy. Rosecrans was solicitous, too, about the payment of his troops, because slow pay discouraged recruiting and hurt morale. For a family man, the ability to send money home insured some peace of mind. In addition to good clothing, shelter, and pay, Rosecrans wanted proper weapons for his men. Some regiments had four different kinds of muskets, requiring four different kinds of ammunition. He wanted to return his muskets to be rifled, a thousand at once, since smooth-bores could not be used against rifles.

Incidentally an excellent portrait of Rosecrans at the time comes from Cox, who shared a tent with him:

His general appearance was attractive. He was tall but not heavy, with the rather long head and countenance that is sometimes called Norman. His aquiline nose and bright eyes gave him an incisive expression, increased by rapid utterance in his speech, which was apt to grow hurried, almost to stammering, when he was excited. His impulsiveness was plain to all who approached him; his irritation quickly flashed out in words when he was crossed, and his social geniality would show itself in smiles and in almost caressing gestures when he was pleased. In discussing military questions he made free use of his theoretic knowledge, often quoted authorities and cited maxims of war, and compared the problem before him to analogous cases in military history. This did not go far enough to be pedantic and was full of lively intelligence; yet it did not impress me as that highest form of military insight and knowledge which solves the question before it upon its own merits, through a power of judgment and perception ripened and broadened by the mastery of principles which have ruled the great campaigns of the world. He was fond of conviviality, loved to banter good-humoredly with his staff officers and intimates, and was altogether an attractive and companionable man, with intellectual activity enough to make his society stimulating and full of lively discussion. I could easily understand Garfield's saying . . . that he "loved every bone in his body."

Whitelaw Reid described Rosecrans as:

nearly six feet high, compact, with little waste flesh, nervous and active in all his movements, from the dictation of a dispatch to the tearing and chewing of his inseparable companion, the cigar. He is easy of access, utterly destitute of pretence, and thoroughly democratic in his ways. With his staff his manner was familiar and almost paternal; with private soldiers always kindly. In the field he was capable of immense labor; he seemed never to grow weary, and never to need sleep. Few officers have been more popular with their commands, or have inspired more confidence in the rank and file.

By mid-October, the Confederates seemed again to be preparing for action. Virginia militia, which through the summer encamped west of the New River and south of Loop Creek, moved, about October 18, toward Gauley, opposite McCook at Miller's Ferry. Rosecrans ordered McCook to cross the Gauley, capture or disperse the militia, and occupy positions there; or recross, as seemed best to him.

McCook pushed ahead to Fayette, reconnoitered the roads there, and returned to his camp, leaving no force across the river. He found only militia to his front. Although Rosecrans regretted that McCook had not left a company behind at Miller's Ferry, he gave no further orders, and McCook let a week pass without action. When finally he tried to put a small force across, Confederate sharpshooters resisted, and he abandoned the attempt; a movement in strength was required, he informed Rosecrans.

Rosecrans thought it best to delay the crossing. He hoped that the sharpshooters might prove the nucleus of a larger force, which might stand, and be dispersed or captured. On October 27, he heard rumors that Floyd was moving to cut Union communications. From his knowledge of the country, Rosecrans guessed that an attacking force would come in through Fayetteville, which lay across the Kanawha, about ten miles south of Gauley Bridge. On this assumption he based his plan of operations. He would draw them in and capture them. In attempting to surround Rosecrans, Lee would find himself in a trap. Moreover, such defensive action would not impede the clothing and paying of the troops.

Signs of a Confederate advance now magnified. Camps and smoke appeared opposite Miller's Ferry. Although the New River gorge and the crests of hills concealed the enemy, "we learned," said Rosecrans, "that Floyd had about 4000 men," and that orders had been given at Meadow Bluff to W. W. Loring and Tompkins to move secretly. "Lee had said to a person who told me I had intended to occupy Kanawha Valley, very significantly, 'IF HE CAN.' A flag of truce also came from Meadow Bluff, the headquarters of Lee, signed by Col. J. Lucius Davis, showing that Lee was absent."

These clues led Rosecrans to believe that the attackers would descend from both sides of the Gauley, part striking McCook at Miller's Ferry, and part crossing the river beyond Schenck's camp and coming down the west side. On the 29th, Confederates scattered the Union outposts on the Fayette road. On November 1, they brought up a six-pounder rifled gun to Gauley Bridge and another opposite Montgomery's Ferry, and began shelling, so that Rosecrans ordered Cox to operate the ferryboat only at night. As enemy plans clarified, Rosecrans matured his own. McCook would continue to threaten to cross at Miller's Ferry, and be in good position to resist any force Lee might bring down the Lewisburg road. Schenck would move up the west bank of the Gauley and attempt to cross at Bowyer's Ferry, seventeen miles up, and fifteen from Sewell. Although Bowyer's Ferry was equipped only with an old canoe, Schenck must attempt to get on Lee's flank and rear; while Benham, whose camp lay below McCook's, and who could march unseen at night, would move to his right to Gauley, and thence to a point opposite the mouth of Loop Creek. There he would cross, be reinforced, and reconnoiter the roads along the river to gain position on Lee's other flank, and to his rear. These movements would catch the Confederates in a pincers.

To activate this plan, Benham took position, concealing his force of 3,000 at the mouth of Loop Creek, and holding the road beyond for six or seven miles. While Rosecrans had directed Schenck to cross at Bowyer's Ferry, reconnaissance showed two intermediate crossings: Townsend's Ferry, five and one-half miles up, apparently unguarded; and Claypool's Hole, between Townsend's and Miller's Ferry. Schenck and Rosecrans selected Townsend's Ferry as the best, and put men to work improvising boats out of canvas and wagon boxes. In spite of continuous rain, the project was completed by November 9.

The flooding Gauley proved almost impossible to navigate with the crude ferries, bull boats, and skiffs. Still Schenck was reluctant to abandon the scheme of falling on Lee's rear, because it gave promise of complete success, and Rosecrans was willing temporarily to withhold any other movement to avoid interfering with the plan. But when the flood did not abate by the 10th, Rosecrans ordered Schenck to move, telling him that Benham, who was concealed near the mouth of Loop Creek with 3,000 men, was posting himself on all the roadways. If Schenck could cross above, Benham would attack the Confederates in front and left flank, while Schenck would take their rear. If Schenck could not cross, he should come down and attack by front, while Benham would cut off their retreat.

From November 3 to 10, in twenty-three telegrams and one dispatch, Rosecrans attempted to make his plans clear. Benham was to cross Loop Creek, firmly occupy the country as far as Taylor's, see that his men were well supplied with rations, reconnoiter the passes from Loop Creek to the enemy's position, and hold himself ready to act as soon as it was determined whether he could cross New River above Schenck's position.

Benham crossed on the 6th, and from November 5 to 8, Rosecrans labored to instruct him in the necessity of knowing the passes from his position to the enemy's flank and rear, especially the pass by Cassidy's Mill, so that if Schenck crossed to take Lee in the rear, Benham would be ready to attack by that route, by the flank, or by the front and flank. Should the river prevent Schenck's passage, Benham was to co-operate in a combined attack on the front, flank, and rear. "In that case," Rosecrans advised, "Schenck will cross 3000 men, seize Fayette and advance down the road and you will take them by the Laurel Creek route only, or by the Nugent path only, or by both."

On the morning of November 10 Schenck was ready to navigate the Gauley at unguarded Townsend's Ferry, but the river proved too high. McCook remained at Miller's Ferry, with the enemy in force sniping at him, as they had for twenty days. Cox with the bulk of his command was stationed at Gauley Bridge, with one regiment at Tompkins' farm; and Benham lay across the river at Loop Creek.

The movement to encircle Lee and Floyd began on the morning of the 10th when Cox sent Colonel Charles A. DeVelliers with 200 men of the 11th Ohio across the Gauley, on a ferry just above its mouth. Simultaneously, 200 men of the 1st Kentucky crossed at the lower ferry. To block DeVelliers, Confederate skirmishers made a stand. At 6:00 P.M., six companies of the 2nd Kentucky joined De-Velliers and pushed the Confederates from the hills in front of the New River. Next morning, the Union drive resumed until, after a vigorous and brilliant skirmish—the compliment is Rosecrans'—about 700 men of General Cox's brigade drove the rebels from the front of Cotton Hill and their camp at Huddleston's, and held the entire ground for nearly three miles between the Fayette road and New River. During these operations, the remainder of the Union army remained in their positions awaiting developments.

The first of these took place on the morning of the 11th when the enemy broke camp at Laurel Creek and retired to Dickerson's, a fork in the road leading south from Miller's Ferry to Fayette Court House. There they started to fortify themselves. This withdrawal alarmed Rosecrans, because Lee might escape his trap. The entrenching partly reassured him. Lee digging in was still caught. Rosecrans needed only to bring Benham down on his left flank and rear.

Said Rosecrans, "I therefore, on the 11th, . . . directed him to occupy Cassidy's Mill with 1000 men, and dispose the rest of his force to move, stating to him that I only awaited the information from him as to the practicability of the Cassidy's Mill route to say whether he was to come in on the north side of Cotton Hill on their front, or take them in flank and rear." At 11:00 P.M., Benham had still not supplied the information. Rosecrans sent another dispatch, telling him that Schenck had not abandoned the plan of crossing the Gauley at Townsend's Ferry, and ordering him to occupy Cotton Hill, the movement to begin early on the 12th.

Not even an *Official Report* can conceal Rosecrans' indignation:

His failure to furnish me with the information so often required, about the roads by Cassidy's and other routes to the enemy's rear, and many signs of unsteadiness, had impaired my confidence in his management. Nevertheless . . . I indulged the hope that he would fully appreciate his position and the decisive results to be expected from a movement by the enemy's left flank to his rear on the Fayetteville road. [Again and again Rosecrans repeated his orders to Benham, until] . . . about 3:00 o'clock P.M. of the 12th, General Benham's main force reached the extremity of Cotton Hill, 8 miles from Loop [Creek] towards Fayette. About the same time his detachment, which did not march as had been ordered on the previous day, swelled by some mistake from 1000 to 1300, reached Cassidy's Mill.

A slight skirmish ensued between a few advanced companies of General Benham's brigade and the rebels. The command of General Benham halted and bivouacked on their arms. General Benham reported to me by a courier, stating his position, and complaining of the weakness of his main force compared with the supposed force of the enemy, and asking reinforcements, that he might attack them. . . . Calling his attention to former dispatches and the Cassidy's Mill route, informing him the enemy was still at Dickerson's, I directed him again to watch the enemy's movements closely, saying if he did not move, our success was certain; if he did, General Benham should intercept him from the rear, and throw his entire force, except 500 men, by the way of Cassidy's Mill, on the Raleigh pike. The enemy's entrenchments were but 2½ to 3 miles from General Benham's position. . . . This mill was but 2½ to 3 miles from the Fayette road.

General Benham had been instructed *ad nauseum* to look to that way of cutting off the enemy's retreat, which began at 9 o'clock on that night. General Benham did not find it out, according to his report, until 4:30 the next afternoon. That is to say, while the last remnant of the rebel force had left Fayette early in the morning of the 13th, according to General Benham's report, his boldest scouts were desperately engaged from daylight until late in the afternoon in finding their way over a distance of 2½ miles that separated his bivouac from the enemy's deserted entrenchments. His force at Cassidy's Mill had a company in Fayetteville at 9 o'clock the next morning fully informed of the retreat of the enemy, and, as the captain of that company states, he dispatched messengers back to Cassidy's Mill and Benham immediately; yet General Benham did not learn of the retreat, though only 2½ miles off until 4:30 P.M. of the 13th, and did not reach Fayette until 12 o'clock at night of the 13th, being twenty-seven hours from the time Floyd commenced his movement. So little attention had he paid to the reiterated instructions, all tending to enforce the one idea that the real blow ought to be struck at the enemy's rear by the Cassidy's Mill route and that a front attack was only desirable in case General Schenck should cross above or in case the enemy stood fight, and that even in this latter event, General Schenck was to attack in front while he was to attack the flank and rear. He ordered the entire force from Cassidy's Mill, instead of striking across to the Raleigh road, to join him by moving down to Laurel Creek and then to Fayette, thus imposing on it a fatiguing march of 7 or 8 miles.

Advised of all this, and knowing the wretched condition of the roads, and taught by experience that orders for carrying three or more days' rations were never obeyed, I looked upon the game as up and the pursuit of Floyd as not promising much; but on the suggestion of Benham that they might have stopped to sleep, dispatched him to use his discretion in the pursuit.

General Benham pursued and overtook some of the enemy's rear guard in the forenoon of the 14th; but Floyd had twenty-seven hours' head start and Benham's troops were about out of provisions. Schenck, who had joined him, now directed Benham to turn back; together they wheeled and faced toward Gauley Bridge and the angry Rosecrans.

The campaign was over. The enemy had been driven not only from the Kanawha Valley, but from all the country west of Meadow Bluff and north of Raleigh, and the country itself was "more nearly pacified and disposed to return to the Union than they have ever been since the commencement of the war." But Rosecrans was disgusted. Twice Floyd might have been annihilated. Once, the scheme failed because rains flooded the Gauley and prevented Schenck's crossing. The second time it failed because Benham again bungled the execution of plans confided to him.

"Benham was the cause of our losing him," Rosecrans wrote to his wife. "I had two strings to the bow, either of which would have been sufficient to catch him. The general is, I fear, neither brave nor true. Terrible when the game flies; but very easily tamed when it bays."

Benham wrote:

> During the night, at about 2:30 A.M. of the 13th, it was reported to me by a scout . . . that wheels of heavy wagons or artillery were heard rumbling in the direction of the [rebel] camp, but as they became no fainter, it was uncertain whether they were retreating or receiving reinforcements. I immediately sent directions to Colonel Smith of the Thirteenth regiment, to send out two other scouts, to ascertain if the movement was a retreat; but most unfortunately . . . he did not understand it as a command, but merely a suggestion, and they were not sent. On learning this at early light, I immediately sent forward a scout of ten men supported by two companies of the Thirteenth Regiment—but the report of these men of the retreat of the rebels did not come in until after 4 P.M.

Rosecrans concluded his own report: "It has been with great regret that I found it necessary to censure a general officer for failure to capture the rebel forces that were justly ours." He ordered Benham's arrest and requested his court-martial, but was not sustained by McClellan.

Concerning Rosecrans' charge, Benham wrote to the Secretary of War: "With the exception of one remark, *not the threat,* to the man whose carelessness caused my horse to fall into the river with all his equipments on, while I was going at night to attack the enemy, I aver that each and every specification is most foully false." Later, as a result of the unsuccessful attack which he led in June 1862 against James Island in the harbor of Charleston, South Carolina, Benham was severely censured, and for a time deprived of his general's rank. However, he was recommissioned, and gradually worked his way back up in command, to end the war as a major-general of volunteers.

Though his successes at Rich Mountain, at Carnifax Ferry, and at Gauley Bridge were less complete than they might have been, Rosecrans had succeeded better than any other Union general in 1861. The best proofs were Confederate tributes. Confederate historian Pollard wrote that Lee's campaign, "after its plain failure, was virtually abandoned by the Government. Rosecrans was esteemed at the South one of the best generals the North had in the field. He was declared by military critics, who could not be accused of partiality, to have clearly outgeneraled Lee, who made it the entire object of his campaign to 'surround the Dutch General,' and had been outwitted, outmaneuvered and outgeneraled." Lee left shortly to command on the Atlantic seaboard, and Floyd beat an unmolested retreat south, more than fifty miles, to Peterstown.

In the northeast corner of the department, General Benjamin Kelley, who was guarding the railroads, advanced on Romney toward the end of October, and cleared the district, and Rosecrans prepared to go into winter quarters. In Yellow Springs, the children had the whooping cough, but as soon as possible Annie would join him at Wheeling. Jemima was dead; in far-off Iowa, snow was beginning to cover her grave. By the middle of November, the chill of shortening days grew more acid, and weary armies came to a halt in the snow.

Four

"THAT DAMNED LITTLE CUSS, McCLELLAN"

A few optimists found false comfort in Rosecrans' defeat of Lee. From London, Henry Adams, secretary to his father, American Minister Charles Francis Adams, commented: "If you wire us a great victory on your side, the thing's finished. Rosecrans seems to be a great deal of a man if I understand his double victory over Floyd and Lee. The Lee business seems to be a first rate thing, as he was one of their great guns." As 1861 closed, however, the outlook was more grim.

Like most West Pointers, Rosecrans believed that the fight would be to the exhaustion or death of one of the contestants, and that valor would accomplish little unless armies were properly equipped, trained, and led. When the campaign ended, as always he looked to the condition of his troops. Although his own front was quiet, enemy movement threatened Virginia to his left, and Kentucky to his right. To McClellan's question, "What are your plans?" he replied: "To hold Kanawha Valley with its outlets towards Raleigh and Sewell; to hold Cheat Mountain Pass on both roads; to hold Romney and the Red Horse Pass; guard the railroads . . . and recruit and discipline regiments . . . thinned by casualties and discharges for disabilities. The first necessity will be to . . . get rid of the lazy, cowardly, slothful and worthless officers who infest our army."

By now, supply, not Lee, was his chief problem. Hay had to be wagoned seventy-two miles from Cincinnati. While men and animals might pull their feet out of mud, or detour, wagon wheels in mountainous country followed ruts almost as inescapably as train wheels cling to rails. When wagons stalled, the column stalled. Rosecrans himself saw a two-horse wagon stall with only two men in it. Confederate wagoners, too, complained that it was "hard for them to haul from Millboro, a distance of sixty miles, any more than it took to feed their teams back and forth."

Hauling tents was the worst problem. In the backwoods, houses and barns were infrequent and marchers could not depend upon finding shelter. A regiment's tents required twenty four-mule wagons. To eliminate this load for winter campaigning, Rosecrans proposed to substitute waterproof boots for shoes, and use either sleeping bags or knapsack tents. Indispensable baggage would be loaded directly on mules.

Late in November, Rosecrans moved his forces into winter quarters: Schenck to Fayetteville and west along the Kanawha and Gauley; Reynolds to Philippi, Elkwater, and Huttonsville; and Kelley to Romney. On the 30th, McClellan ordered four more regiments—making a total of twelve—to Buell, and transferred the general staff officers at Cincinnati from Rosecrans. Rosecrans felt he had been "rewarded by having his Department cut to a mere cipher," and, as a Cincinnati paper reported it, inquired "if the Government needed his services any longer." He "disdained to draw from the public treasury without rendering an equivalent." On strictly military grounds, McClellan's transfer of inactive men to active fronts, where supply and shelter were simpler, was defensible, but Rosecrans chafed, nonetheless, for he wanted to undertake a winter campaign. When the Confederates grew active around the neighboring Big Sandy, he asked that this region be added to his department, and requested permission from McClellan to visit Washington to see him concerning this and "many other details relating to the good of the service." Buell had made dispositions for the Big Sandy Valley, McClellan answered, and Rosecrans would not *need* to come. Nevertheless, Rosecrans went, probably without further correspondence. A Confederate spy alerted Richmond: "Valuable information: Rosecrans is in Washington."

He should have remained in Wheeling. Washington spirits matched the bad weather. Foreign relations were touchy, armies were stalled, generals were quarreling, and the mood of the Radical

Republicans was black. Lincoln asked Quarter-Master General Montgomery Meigs, "What shall I do? The people are impatient; Chase has no money and he tells me he can raise no more; the General of the Army has typhoid fever. The bottom is out of the tub."

To some, their Western Virginia associations seemed to tie together the fortunes of Rosecrans and McClellan. McClellan's army, well drilled, well equipped, numbered 150,000 on October 15, and on November 1 he succeeded Scott as supreme commander. The Radical Republicans, who had hailed his rise, wanted him to attack. But now McClellan was in trouble. His delays convinced his supporters that the military conservatism of Democratic generals—and especially McClellan—was "infernal, unmitigated cowardice"—or, worse, treason. He must be replaced.

On Rosecrans' arrival in Washington, McClellan was still in bed with typhoid, and when ill was even more inaccessible than when well. Rosecrans called repeatedly and waited long in the parlor below McClellan's bedroom. Finally, General Fitz-John Porter, McClellan's favorite, descended to interview his own and Mc-Clellan's former West Point professor.

Rosecrans explained his plan for a winter campaign. He would quietly concentrate at Romney 25,000 men, gathered chiefly from Western Virginia and from Ohio and Indiana. He would move these less than forty miles southeast, seize and fortify Winchester, and outflank the Confederate position at Manassas. Porter returned with McClellan's answer. McClellan was certain that if he placed 20,000 men in Winchester, the Confederates would send 20,000 men to oppose them. And if he added more, the Confederates would add an equal number. And so on and on. In short, Rosecrans' plan would effect only a transfer of the theatre of war.

Rosecrans persisted: "General Lee could not cross the Shenandoah in the face of 20,000 men in an entrenched position without weakening too much his main command and giving McClellan a chance to beat him; nor can he allow this 20,000 men to occupy Winchester in the rear of his left flank, posted in Loudon County up the Potomac. Such occupation would necessitate a change of the *rebel* front so as to place its left flank in the direction of Ashby's Gap to secure its communications with the rear. This change would expose the right to be crushed by the Army of the Potomac."

How much of McClellan's rejection and of his stripping of Rosecrans' command was based on the fact that Rosecrans was out of his favor and how much on military considerations is not clear. Rosecrans certainly injured himself by blurting out in his *Official Report* of Rich Mountain that: "McClellan, contrary to agreement and military prudence, did not attack." The accuracy of this statement only increased its unpalatability, and widespread comments, even among Confederates, that McClellan's victories were "due rather to the genius of his subordinate," were not likely to smooth ruffled plumage. Rosecrans knew where he stood, and snorted disgustedly when he was told that, ignoring him, McClellan invited Colonel Lander east "to do for me what you did at Rich Mountain." At the height of McClellan's power, less worthy candidates were commissioned major generals, while Rosecrans, who had won McClellan's sole victory and commanded one of the four major districts and armies, remained a brigadier.

In Washington, Rosecrans was summoned to appear before the Committee on the Conduct of the War. This joint committee of the Congress, called by T. Harry Williams the "unnatural child of lustful radicalism and a confused conservatism," grew out of Northern differences regarding war aims. Conservatives, Lincoln the foremost, declared themselves for restoration of the Union, even with slavery. The Radicals considered Lincoln's war policy mild; they shuddered to think that Democratic generals might convert battlefield triumphs into election victories; and they seized upon the minor disaster at Ball's Bluff to set up machinery to investigate the whole conduct of the war. Ohio's Senator Ben Wade revealed their mind; if the "war continues thirty years and bankrupts the whole nation I hope to God there will be no peace until we can say that there is not a slave in this land." The radicals considered the Union holy; abolition holier.

When hearings opened on December 20, the Committee's bugbear was McClellan. Why didn't he advance? The Committee summoned his subordinates because he was ill and questioned them concerning McClellan's supposed schemes. Browbeating failed to cow most of McClellan's generals.

January 31, 1861, was almost springlike as Rosecrans walked

from Willard's Hotel to a smoke-filled basement room in the Capitol, where the Committee, with Senator Wade as chairman, was meeting. With a record of action and achievement, Rosecrans had an easy interview. He discussed such problems as green troops, the loyalties of Western Virginia, the difficulties of winter campaigning. He pointed out that if "we have 50,000 soldiers it is not necessary to run them all upon the batteries of the enemy to whip their force." He wished to move in conjunction with McClellan, and would not condemn McClellan's delay; raw troops needed hardening. Rosecrans finished by noon. He had stood by McClellan.

A week later, unable to "find out what the general wanted him to do," or to outfit his troops, he left Washington. The Radicals had meanwhile scored a smashing victory: Edwin M. Stanton replaced Cameron as Secretary of War. McClellan rose from his sickbed to fight off an attempted ouster. Rosecrans could not have guessed what the change of secretaries meant to his fortunes.

Back in Wheeling, he found that during his two weeks' absence McClellan had transferred over 20,000 of his 22,000 troops to Lander, who guarded the Baltimore and Ohio Railroad, leaving him some 1,700 men. Further to checkmate him, winter struck with intense cold. Heavy snowfall blocked the mountain roads, so that local postmaster James Trotter complained: "If you knock the gable end of Hell out and back it up against Cheat Mountain and rain fire and brimstone for 40 days and 40 nights, it won't melt the snow enough to get your damned mail through on time."

Rosecrans busied himself by developing a pack-mule train. When typhoid became epidemic, he transferred the sick from crowded houses to clean hospital tents. As a result, in a single regiment the sick list dropped from nearly 300 to less than thirty. He had observed, too, that the tipping of the light, two-wheeled ambulance cart was no less agonizing than the jolting of springless, heavy wagons. He therefore ordered the construction of a light, four-wheeled ambulance which was almost immediately adopted throughout the Union armies, and even in Europe. Annie joined him in Wheeling, and the distinguished artist G. P. A. Healy painted their portraits.

The end of January brought Lincoln's General War Order #1, designating Washington's birthday as the day when all Northern military forces should advance upon the "insurgent forces." Rosecrans' was one of four armies named. The order provided for no implementing directives, no meeting of top commanders, no working out of objectives, interlocking details, subordinate plans. McClellan made no advance, and Rosecrans looked at his 1,700 men and ignored the order, with nothing said on either side. The only movement occurred at Forts Henry and Donelson, where Commodore Andrew H. Foote and Brigadier General Ulysses S. Grant won important successes. Grant became a popular hero as headlines played upon his initials.

Meanwhile, unknown to Rosecrans, his affairs were becoming entangled with those of Major John C. Fremont, the "Pathfinder" and Republican presidential candidate in 1856, who had entered the war as Western commander. Fremont's record in the post was undistinguished. He had won no victories, but had declared martial law, confiscated property, disregarded Washington, become involved in procurement scandals, allowed his accounts to become muddled, declared emancipated the slaves of Missourians convicted of bearing arms against the United States, and finally had been removed. The Radicals proclaimed him a martyr, and determined to restore him to command. Lincoln yielded to their pressures. Not wishing to remove McClellan, yet needing a post for Fremont, he created the Mountain Department, which included West Virginia, and on March 11 put Fremont in charge.

"Where am I to go?" Rosecrans telegraphed McClellan when he heard the news. He sent plans to Stanton, and sought reinforcements for a movement up the valley of the South Branch. On March 22, Stanton replied that he liked the plans and would have been pleased to entrust their execution to Rosecrans with "great confidence of successful result," but that it would be for Fremont "to execute such operations as may appear most expedient." A week later, Fremont arrived in Wheeling. Rosecrans remained a few days clearing up business and then left to report to the War Department. Rosecrans found Washington in turmoil. As January ended, Lincoln had ordered McClellan to move overland against Richmond. McClellan proposed instead to transport his army by water to Fortress Monroe, and thence to march it northwest on the peninsula between the James and York rivers. Although Lincoln reluctantly consented, by March 17 he objected that

McClellan's plan left Washington uncovered. A majority vote of division commanders overbore Lincoln's alarm, and he ordered McClellan to begin the movement on the 18th, but without consulting him forbade an advance unless an adequate force was left to protect Washington. Until the Confederate batteries along the Potomac were silenced, McClellan was not to move more than half his army to the peninsula.

Behind Lincoln's hesitancy lay complex pressures, obscure and sometimes contradictory forces. T. Harry Williams comments: "Plots and counterplots boiled beneath the troubled surface. Stanton hatched innumerable schemes to destroy his enemies. McClellan twisted and turned as the Radicals struck. And behind all was the implacable Committee." It seems possible that at a meeting between Stanton and the Committee on the Conduct of the War a scheme was worked out to cause McClellan to fail in his campaign. The Radicals apparently wanted a quick victory, but not at the expense of abolition; a great victory, but not one that would make Democrat McClellan a national hero and hurt them personally or the Radical cause. In these matters Civil War historians still divide sharply. One group charges McClellan with virtual treason; the other accuses the Radicals of a conspiracy climaxed by the assassination of Lincoln. At the time, Lincoln's second secretary, John Hay, observed: "McClellan is in danger, not in front but in rear." And over a half-century ago, John W. Burgess, speaking of McClellan's removal after Antietam, wrote: "Whether a crushing victory over the Confederates, ending at once the rebellion, before slavery was destroyed, was wanted by all of those who composed the Washington government may well be suspected. And it is very nearly certain that there were some who would have preferred defeat to such a victory with McClellan in command. It was a dark, mysterious, uncanny thing, which the historian does not need to touch and prefers not to touch."

Under Lincoln's orders, McClellan kept strong garrisons in the Washington fortifications, at Manassas Junction to cover the Capitol's rear, and in the Shenandoah. On March 13, he ordered General Nathaniel P. Banks to move down the Shenandoah to Manassas, leaving a few regiments to cover Winchester. McDowell's corps waited near Fredericksburg for orders to join McClellan. Fremont occupied Western Virginia. McClellan estimated that to succeed he needed 208,000 men, plus the garrison of Fortress Monroe. Now he was ready to gather this great host and strike.

The Radicals struck first. Senators Wade and Zachariah Chandler, crying that McClellan was leaving only a few thousand men to cover Washington, besought Lincoln to transfer Blenker's division of 10,000 men to Fremont. Lincoln assured McClellan that he would not weaken his army. Nevertheless he did make the transfer. "If you could know the full pressure of the case," he told McClellan, "I am sure you would justify it."

The next blow came on April 2 when General James S. Wadsworth, commanding the Washington defenses, complained to Stanton that his troops lacked strength to repel a Confederate attack. Again Lincoln yielded, and ordered that Sumner's or McDowell's corps be detained in Washington. McDowell's 30,000 men stayed on Stanton's orders. The 40,000 men under McDowell and Blenker who had been under McClellan's command comprised approximately a third of the force he had counted on. McClellan was indeed appallingly cautious, but he did need superior numbers to fight offensively against a strongly placed enemy. Instead, when he locked finally with Johnston and Lee, numbers were roughly equal.

To make matters worse, the Confederates had Jackson. As the reduced Union army shifted to the peninsula, Joseph E. Johnston moved to face McClellan, leaving Jackson with a small army of observation, estimated at 8,000 to 13,000 men, to guard the Shenandoah Valley and the northern and western approaches to Richmond.

The division of the Valley forces by the War Department proved an egregious blunder and was probably the largest single cause for McClellan's defeat in the Peninsula Campaign. In attempting to prevent it Rosecrans incurred Stanton's wrath, thus adversely affecting his own military and personal fortunes.

On April 6, Blenker turned back from Warrenton, Virginia, to join Fremont. A German-born, naturalized soldier of fortune, he had helped to cover the Union rout after Bull Run. His division was outstanding in the multigarbed Army of the Potomac for smartness and color, and heads turned when Blenker cantered through the gray fog in his scarlet-lined military cape. He had grumbled at Stanton's order directing him to leave the delightful

Army of the Potomac, where, surrounded by his staff, he had frequently entertained McClellan with champagne and other delicacies.

On the second day of Blenker's march, a freak storm brought four days of heavy, wet snow. Roads grew deep with slush and mud, streams flooded, communications broke down. Blenker pushed doggedly ahead, although his men lacked tents, supplies ran out, and shoes began to fall apart. He did not know the district even in good weather, and with its gaps and turnings obscured by a white swirl, he was lost, although too proud to admit it even to himself.

Four days passed without word from Blenker. On April 11, Fremont telegraphed: "I have immediate need of all the force in the department." Stanton answered: "Blenker's division will be hurried on to Harper's Ferry where they will be subject to your orders." Then he telegraphed Banks, at Woodstock: "Where is Blenker?" Banks knew only that on the 6th Blenker had left Warrenton for Strasbourg to join Fremont. It seemed ridiculous to say that Blenker might be lost. Ten thousand men could not vanish.

Meanwhile, Rosecrans waited in Stanton's antechamber. Stanton, he understood, held enlarged powers and all departmental commanders reported directly to him. Rosecrans may have heard also that Stanton was a physical coward and a moral bully, that white-haired officers wilted under the whip sting of his voice. Knowing tongues whispered that "McClellan holds his position by a single hair." No one felt secure. Friends told Rosecrans that false reports concerning himself had been spread by Lander: "His slanderous tongue is therefore the poisoner of the public mind in Washington," Rosecrans wrote to his wife. "McClellan's flattering him is to me evidence that he is either a hypocrite or a much poorer judge of human nature than I had supposed. . . . But I do hope he [McClellan] may be successful in spite of all doubts as to his honesty."

Stanton received Rosecrans "with profuse expressions of cordiality." While Rosecrans grumbled, Stanton "expressed pleasure with my plan of operations for West Virginia. His regret was that it was not in his power to prevent me from being superseded or absorbed, and he wished he could give me some command, but there was nothing at present except to go with Banks or Halleck. Meanwhile I am ordered to go up and look after Blenker's division, to see and confer with Banks and return to the War Department. Said Mr. Stanton, 'You may rely upon it that anything which I can do for you will be done,' and when I looked at him without reply, he said very emphatically: '*That's so!*' "

That evening, Stanton's carriage "came for me and I went to the War Office. He asked me to smoke." After some conversation about the Blenker-Banks assignment, Rosecrans "remarked that he must excuse me for grumbling this morning. I considered my luck hard hitherto. Said he: 'You may consider this the beginning of your good luck.'" Stanton regretted that circumstances prevented his assigning to Rosecrans the command of "the only live plan of campaign for the season which he had seen." That plan was Rosecrans'. Stanton said he considered sending Rosecrans to McDowell for he would have liked to see them both get to Richmond "before that damned little cuss McClellan."

These were Rosecrans' written orders:

You will proceed forthwith to Strasbourg by the quickest route and thence to Brigadier General Blenker's division, and cause the force to move as speedily as possible by way of Winchester to Harper's Ferry, there to report to Major-General Fremont for orders.

. . . You will also see and confer with Major-General Banks, ascertain the position of his force, and also the state of the force at Winchester. You are authorized to give such orders as may in your judgment be required for the service in respect to Blenker's division, and may exercise whatever discretionary authority may be necessary to place Blenker's division in its proper position and within the orders of General Fremont. You will report to the Department at every telegraph station, and ask for such other and further instructions as may be required.

Puzzling questions emerge from this. Did Stanton propose to use Rosecrans merely as a *guide*? If so, why didn't Blenker hire a guide and extricate himself, or use the same maps Rosecrans used? Or why didn't Stanton send a staff major who knew the country well? Or if Stanton wanted an expediter, why didn't he assign the task to Fremont? And what was Stanton's purpose in sending Rosecrans to confer with Banks? Was it simply to report the condition of the troops at Woodstock and Winchester? Banks, Fremont, and Stanton were connected by telegraph. Or did Stanton want Rosecrans to serve as an official observer or spy, as Charles A. Dana later served with Grant at Vicksburg and Rosecrans at Chattanooga?

The most plausible answer to all these questions seems to be that a twist of politics had dumped Rosecrans in Stanton's lap. Rosecrans could not long be left without assignment because of his conspicuous success. And he could not be assigned immediately because suitable vacancies were lacking. And so Stanton improvised an errand boy's job out of Blenker's difficulty and sent a strong man to perform it. This was asking for trouble.

Rosecrans probably realized that his orders were vague and his position anomalous. Nonetheless, when he took the assignment, he should have performed the simple minimum tasks and returned to report to Stanton. Instead, he involved his good military judgment, his patriotism, and his conscience, and, unasked, made recommendations for the good of the service. That is when trouble began.

Early on the morning after seeing Stanton, Rosecrans left for Winchester, a thirty-mile ride over "execrable" roads. "Blenker's division is reported to be at Salem, between Front Royal and Manassas Junction," Stanton telegraphed Fremont. "General Rosecrans is on the road between Winchester and Harper's Ferry to take temporary command of the division to bring it into position." Rumor said that Blenker had been injured in a fall from his horse. Fremont telegraphed Stanton that he was sending an officer to direct Blenker's march. "It best suits my plans . . . that the division will march to Moorefield." Stanton replied immediately: "I have sent General Rosecrans to take command until the division is brought in position for your command." He then informed Rosecrans that "General Fremont directs that Blenker go to Moorefield. It may be well to go across to Strasbourg. The route however is left to your discretion." That night at 10:30, Rosecrans arrived at Winchester. "Your dispatch received," he wired Stanton, "and shall assume command and direct column accordingly."

On the 13th, Fremont telegraphed Banks to order Rosecrans to get Blenker's division forward as rapidly as possible. He should send ahead at least one brigade to Moorefield to meet a contingency. Rosecrans meanwhile remained at Winchester. With

Stanton's telegram giving Blenker's position before him, he was "studying distances." He thought that the best route might be toward Thornton's Gap, then down to Harrisonburg, doubling back to Moorefield. The difficulty of getting forage from the ravaged country increased as the troops advanced.

On April 14, Rosecrans was in high spirits. The sun shone, and in full view of the snow-covered Blue Ridge, he rode to Strasbourg on "magnificent" roads. He had learned that Blenker was at Paris, Virginia, overlooking Berry's Ford on the flooding Shenandoah. Blenker would need three days to get across and he had gone too far north to be redirected to the easier route through Thornton's Gap. Rosecrans forwarded Stanton's orders. Blenker was to leave Berry's Ford, and cross instead at Snicker's Ferry. Then, before leaving the vicinity of Banks' headquarters, Rosecrans rode to Woodstock "to see and confer with Banks." Rosecrans himself described this conference in a manuscript sketch of his campaigns which he titled *W.S.R.:*

General Banks received him very cordially; under the Secretary's order to confer with Banks it was assumed that the subject of that conference should be about the best way of utilizing the forces now available but not weighing in the contest which the Army of the Potomac was then waging on the James River. Rosecrans said, "General, what force have the rebels on your front?" General Banks replied: "From eight to thirteen thousand under Ewell and Jackson." "You," said General R., "have about 25,000; Fremont can spare 6,000 from New Creek, and 5,000 from Beverly under Milroy; and McDowell's force including Blenker's division will probably reach 40,000, making in all 75,000 men who do not practically weigh a feather in the scale of the present contest." "True," said General Banks. "Well," said Rosecrans. "Blenker should not cross the Shenandoah but go to Sperryville, McDowell should move up to Culpeper—Jackson and Ewell would then retire to Staunton; you would advance to Mount Jackson—Fremont and Milroy would come in on your right—the enemy would cross the Blue Ridge, thus cutting off the supplies and control of the great valley from the rebels at Richmond, and threatening their left and rear, while your own supplies would be insured and your position safe from any sudden enterprise, the enemy would be obliged to detach largely from his force at Richmond to watch and counter your movements, thus exposing himself to defeat by the Army of the Potomac, or to evacuate Richmond and retire into North Carolina." General Banks was struck with this plan, assented to it, and Rosecrans immediately returned to Winchester, telegraphing the plan in cipher from Strasbourg on his way.

The next morning, Banks reported to Stanton: "Had full interview. Opinions concurring."

Unification of the valley commands would automatically make Washington safe, and provide a second menace to Richmond. The plan would pose a dilemma for Johnston, who was heavily outnumbered by the forces ringing him, even though he possessed interior lines. Without heavy reinforcements, Jackson was likely to be crushed, and the door opened down the James to Johnston's rear. In reinforcing Jackson, by so much Johnston weakened his own army on the peninsula. On April 2 when Jackson first asked for reinforcements, he was told that he must first withdraw closer to the Rapidan. While he would be strengthened, the Confederates could take no risk in dealing with McClellan, who was the main adversary.

On April 15, while Rosecrans conferred with Banks, Jackson heard a rumor that heavy Federal columns, under Fremont, marching on Staunton, would sever his rail communications with Richmond. He knew that Banks, moving up to Harrisonburg, could turn to Johnston's rear and threaten Staunton without exposing the Federal rear, forcing him to fall back or be caught between Blenker's column from the north and another from the mountains. He would then be cut off from Johnston. He knew that Banks could cross the Blue Ridge without opposition, and would have no difficulty in reaching Staunton, and that it was altogether possible that Banks could assure the fall of Staunton without placing his army in material danger of attack.

On the 22nd, Jackson halted Ewell east of the Blue Ridge. It was clear that the Confederates were in for serious trouble. Jackson knew that Rosecrans was now in the valley, and the Confederates thought highly of Rosecrans because of the Western Virginia campaign.

Rosecrans' proposal to unite the Valley armies had provoked such a storm in the War Department that his friend Hartsuff, serving as Stanton's assistant while his wound healed, advised him in a private note that "Stanton has taken a dislike to you," elaborating later: "The Sec'y of War took a senseless but strong

prejudice against you in connection with Blenker's Dutchmen."
Rosecrans himself said that, "Unfortunately for the country this
plan [to unite the Valley forces] was not adopted—and for Gen'l.
Rosecrans—who from that time forth appeared to have made an
enemy of Mr. Stanton." Hartsuff's warning note proves that
Stanton's change of heart toward Rosecrans took place on April
15, 1862. The date is significant.

It took several days for Hartsuff's warning to reach him, and
by daylight of the 16th, unaware of Stanton's distrust, Rosecrans
was galloping north to Winchester on the Valley Pike. From Winchester he reported: "Blenker left Hunter's Chapel on March 10.
They have been since that wandering without tents, shelter or
knapsacks. . . . Their clothing is worn, shoes gone, no pay since
December, not much wonder they stole and robbed. Shoes and
clothing should be sent, and Paymaster-General ordered to pay for
January and February immediately, to arrest demoralization."
Blenker's horses were nearly starved.

Rosecrans reported to Stanton sometime later that his messenger
had met Blenker "at Paris and Berry's Ferry and brought reply . . .
grumbling at your order, and failing to report the strength, condition of ammunition, camp equipage, supplies of subsistence, transportation, and forage. I telegraphed immediately . . . that your
orders and his left me and him no discretion; that he was not to
surrender his command, but obey my orders."

Blenker's woes seemed endless. Two days before, when three
regiments had attempted to cross the Shenandoah, the ferryboat
had tipped, and sixty men and two officers drowned. Rosecrans
reported that the crossing had been stopped at Berry's Ferry. "The
remaining troops go to Snicker's Ferry. If you approve my plan
orders ought to come at once. General Fremont will not need more
than one brigade until he gets down below Staunton. The combined movement will make it easy to reinforce him from General
Banks', while the latter can draw from the remainder of the
division near Luray."

On the 16th Stanton replied: "Last night I had a report from
Blenker, delivered by an officer who left them two days ago.
Neither of them said a word about the destitution you speak of.
If they are in that condition, it shows the greater necessity for you

to have followed your instructions and by going to them found out their true condition." Stanton later scolded: "I have received no information of your plans. Blenker's division is assigned to Fremont's command and no part of it ought to be diverted from that object. Your instructions do not authorize any change in its destination. I expected you would have gone forward and superintended its movements until it came within Fremont's command." From this, Rosecrans should have sensed Stanton's irritation and walked carefully.

"All I have done," Rosecrans replied, "is in careful compliance with your instructions and intentions. The plan referred to was one for combined movement of Banks, McDowell, and Fremont, and was discussed and approved by Generals Banks and Shields. In a military point of view I have no doubt of its superior advantages, but I understand that all Blenker's command is to move to Moorefield with the least possible delay, and am taking steps to conduct them accordingly. As I telegraphed the Secretary, they are without any kind of shelter, and now without provisions."

"I never heard of your cipher telegram until today," Stanton continued on the 17th, "and I deeply regret that you did not follow my instructions. I hope you will now see that the division is placed in its proper command, as I directed in the first instance." With all of Blenker's division except its rear guard encamped on the western side of the Shenandoah, Rosecrans replied: "You will find that I have taken the wisest and most expeditious course to effect what you ordered." An examination of dates and places shows that this statement is accurate.

The next morning Stanton asked Fremont whether there had been any conference or understanding between him and Banks regarding combined operations. Fremont answered that he and Banks had agreed to keep each other informed of their movements. Despite Rosecrans' seven telegraphic reports concerning the condition of Blenker's command, Stanton told Fremont that he could not understand the delay of its advance, and Fremont, who had no way of knowing, complained to Stanton that the "delays of the division are extraordinary."

Rosecrans again petitioned Stanton from Winchester to combine the Union forces, and Stanton's answer arrived on April 18.

The President will not sanction the plan you proposed until it is more fully matured, and after full conferences and agreements by all who are to participate in it. The Department has no evidence from Fremont, Banks, or McDowell that they have been consulted or will co-operate. When you have obeyed your instructions by placing Blenker's division under General Fremont's orders you will return immediately to Washington and await orders.

To this Rosecrans replied:

Every step taken by me since I left Washington has been as directly to the prompt delivery of the Blenker division at Moorefield in serviceable condition as if I had thought of nothing else. Knowing the time that must elapse in getting Blenker forward I suggested what occurred to me, not presuming further than to consult Banks and Shields, for whose approval I gave my word. Fremont's movements were to be what the plan required. Banks wished it, and McDowell probably would have done so.

He made no more strategic recommendations. He had not held Blenker back in order to further his scheme, but when he abandoned the scheme, Blenker was not yet ready for a long march. On the 21st, in the midst of a search for shoes for Blenker's barefoot men, Rosecrans wrote to Stanton that for "forty days without shelter they now lie in the rain." Not until May 4 were they clothed and shod. On that day, accompanied by Rosecrans, they left for Moorefield by way of Romney, planning to join Fremont on May 9. Rosecrans spent three days at New Creek Station "using the authority of my rank to push supplies forward."

In his letter to his wife on April 22, Rosecrans had written: "Hartsuff is now Brigadier General and Assistant Adjutant General of the Army. So far as is in his power he will shield me from the stabs of assassins." Eight days later he added: "I find the public tide sets toward me strongly in many places. What will come of it I cannot tell. It will take me one more week to get back to Washington." That same day, an ungraceful horseman riding a sorry-looking chestnut with shambling gait turned north to strike the head of Fremont's command at Fort Republic. With Jackson's advance, the uncertainties of the Confederates in the valley were resolved.

When Rosecrans reached Washington on May 14, Stanton had no smiles for him, no promises of promotion, no cigars, no flattery.

Instead in an unpleasant interview, he shouted at him: "You mind your business and I'll mind mine."

"From that time onwards Stanton's professions were always 'too sweet to be wholesome' and his practice hostile," Rosecrans wrote. "His whole behaviour left the impression that his antagonism originated in the connection I was not so constituted as to *become useful to him,* and that therefore his sentiments toward me were similar to those which Haman felt toward Mordecai who sat in the King's gate."

Undoubtedly the interview was stormy on both sides. Rosecrans stood in no man's awe. He took no man's abuse meekly. "With his inferiors he was uniformly kind and considerate," Whitelaw Reid wrote. "To those above him he was always punctilious, often testy, and at times deplorably indiscreet. . . . This sturdy honesty, which led him to take upon himself the weightiest responsibilities, and incur the gravest displeasure rather than do that which in his conviction, would prove injurious to the Cause, was at once one of the most striking features of his character, and one of the most potent reasons for his constant embarrassments."

"Calumnious," Rosecrans called the rumor that "my difficult and testy temper" caused the hostility of the War Department. "But for a substitute . . . I will suggest one founded on facts, most of which appear in my Official Record and testimony before the Committee on the Conduct of the War." These facts dealt with his "plain and simple plan" for utilizing "88,000 men" who were doing nothing but holding Richard S. Ewell and Stonewall Jackson with "8,000 to 15,000 men" in check. Two days after Rosecrans forwarded this report he received the private warning note from Hartsuff. From that time onward "Stanton's practice was hostile." There never was "any bitter correspondence to provoke this hostility." The *Official Records* support this statement.

"Senseless," was Hartsuff's opinion of Stanton's anger and Hartsuff should have known, because as Rosecrans wrote to Annie on April 22, 1862, Hartsuff was "now Brig. General and Ass't. Adj. General of the Army for the most important and necessary purposes." But senseless or not, Stanton's anger against Rosecrans was violent and long lasting. Why?

If Stanton believed that Rosecrans had delayed in getting Blenker to Fremont, his belief was in error. Blenker's unwillingness to admit to Stanton the true condition of his division had kept part of the facts from him. What Blenker thought of sending a brigadier errand boy to lead him is not hard to imagine.

Or was his hostility due to a determination to run the war his own way—his unquestioned right within certain restrictions—and to his touchiness about interference from generals? Did he resent the fact that his errand boy was making major strategic recommendations and possibly exceeding orders? The Cincinnati *Times* correspondent commented that "Rosecrans made suggestions at the outset of Mr. Stanton's career eminently useful to the interests of the service. Unfortunately they did not meet with the approval of the Secretary of War. Why should the new fledged director of the military affairs of the nation, fresh from his law library, take any council from a professional soldier? The Secretary grew indignant, and in the excess of his wrath, Rosecrans was sent by him into banishment."

There is another explanation, less simple, much mooted among historians. It rests upon the thesis already mentioned that Stanton and the Radicals hatched a plot to destroy McClellan by preventing him from capturing Richmond. Stanton had admitted that he would have liked to see McDowell and Rosecrans get there before that "damned little cuss McClellan." If such a plot existed, or even a strong subconscious wish, then Rosecrans, suggesting the very campaign that would have enabled McClellan instead to succeed, unwittingly offended Stanton.

Whatever the cause of Stanton's anger, Rosecrans had made a new, powerful, and dangerous enemy, and it is likely that, his protest to the contrary notwithstanding, his testy temper and loose tongue had contributed to the trouble. Stanton was a man of different breed from McClellan, who after a lecture, some talk, and a few gestures of annoyance seems to have decided to disregard Rosecrans. Once Stanton gained the scent of an enemy, he was not likely to lose it. He was a persistent and inexorable stalker. And having pounced upon his victims he devoured them.

Subsequent events proved that in the Shenandoah campaign, Jackson was truly Napoleonic, and that Rosecrans' strategy was right. On May 5, Johnston evacuated Williamsburg, and when McClellan followed him to within seven miles of Richmond, the city panicked. But then McClellan's communications were threatened, and he waited hourly for McDowell, who was promised, to join him. To prevent such junction, Johnston ordered Jackson to move along the Shenandoah Valley and threaten Washington. With the threat of a junction of the Federal forces in the valley removed, on May 23 Jackson, reinforced by Ewell, swooped down upon a detachment of Banks's force at Front Royal and routed it. The next day, Banks, who was at Strasbourg with 6,800 men, began a race with Jackson for Winchester. Although Banks and his fugitives won, Jackson achieved his purpose, and McDowell was not sent to McClellan.

Until May 24, the scattering of the Union forces was largely due to Stanton's orders. Next, Lincoln tried his hand in strategy. He ordered Fremont into the Shenandoah to Jackson's rear, and after countermanding the order to join McClellan, directed McDowell instead to send 20,000 men to the Shenandoah to assist Fremont, or to capture Jackson if he could not effect the junction.

More disaster followed when Jackson routed Banks at Winchester on May 25 and drove him in wild flight thirty-five miles across the Potomac. Stanton, believing Washington in imminent danger, telegraphed the Northern governors to send militia for its defense. Lincoln seized the railroads, recalled part of McDowell's corps to Washington, and ordered Fremont, Banks, and McDowell—still separated—to capture Jackson. On June 8, Fremont overtook the retreating Jackson at Cross Keys, but was repulsed; so was Shields who next day struck at Jackson at Port Republic. Colonel Henderson said that Jackson "fell as it were from the skies into the midst of his astonished foes, struck right and left before they could combine, and defeated in detail every detachment that crossed his path." With 17,000 men Jackson in a month won four battles and captured many prisoners. More important, he terrorized Washington and kept 40,000 men from joining McClellan. Margaret Leech observes: "Divine interposition could scarcely have scattered the Federal forces more perfectly than had those two amateurs of war, Mr. Stanton and Mr. Lincoln."

Rosecrans did not witness the panic in Washington when disaster struck in the valley. After his interview with Stanton, he left without waiting for baggage or horses, under orders to join Halleck before Corinth, where a great battle was expected. His wife was to remain at Yellow Springs, sharing a house with the Scammons. This leave-taking was more poignant. Her health was frail, and before winter she would bear her sixth child.

Never again would Rosecrans be part of affairs east of the mountains. The new assignment committed him. Thereafter he was a "Western general."

ꟻive

UNDER GRANT'S COMMAND

After their defeat at Shiloh on April 6 and 7, the Confederates had retreated southwest toward their fortifications at Corinth, some twenty miles away. Corinth was a key to their inner stronghold, and Shiloh had been fought for its possession. There the Memphis and Charleston, best and most direct railroad from the Atlantic to the Mississippi which they could hope to hold, crossed the Mobile and Ohio railroad, an easy route from the rich midlands to the Gulf of Mexico. With Corinth lost, they would be vulnerable on their left, and without a base from which to rally to support their center. Halleck, who had led the Department of the West since November 1861, had taken personal command of the western Union forces in April from Grant, and with Pope's Army of the Mississippi, Grant's Army of Tennessee, and Buell's Army of the Ohio, moved against Beauregard, who now faced him at Corinth behind extensive fortifications.

While the war in the East bogged down, here in the West generals were jostling for position. Sherman had told Halleck, "I attach more importance to the West than to the East. The man who at the end of this war holds the military control of the Valley of the Mississippi will be the man." Would he be Halleck, John Pope, Don Carlos Buell, George H. Thomas, William T. Sherman, John A. McClernand, or Grant? When the war began, Grant had named the five most likely to lead victorious Union armies: McClellan, Buell, Charles P. Stone, Rosecrans and Simon B. Buckner. Now Buckner was a Confederate, McClellan had made powerful enemies, Buell was mistrusted, Stone under arrest, and Rosecrans demoted in assignment. Sherman and Thomas, too, had their handicaps. Thomas was a Virginian, and Sherman had failed in Kentucky and was considered "crazy."

Although both the West Point and the political groups had supplied able military leaders, resentments brewed between West Point "bullet heads" and "Republican Greenhorns." "I hope we may not be cursed with any more political generals," Halleck confided to Rosecrans. Rosecrans had seen "civilian" generals advanced ahead of him, although he was a professional and senior in years and successful command experience. In Halleck's army, civilian generals Lew Wallace, John A. McClernand, Thomas L. Crittenden, and William Nelson outranked him.

Although Grant was nominally second in command, and still highly rated in Washington, few in the West would then have picked him as most likely to succeed. In May 1862, Grant's troubles were as thick as the flies that tormented the horses. After his capture of Fort Donelson, which brought him his commission as major general of volunteers, he had fallen from favor. Halleck credited the victory to General C. F. Smith, and, charging that Grant had failed to report and had visited Nashville without permission, ordered his arrest. On his release, Grant had caught up with his army at Pittsburg Landing.

Then came Shiloh. While Grant's bald announcement of a victory added to his reputation in the East, in the Middle West where casualties were heavy and where newspapers printed detailed accounts of the first day of the battle, a clamor for Grant's removal arose. He was castigated in editorials, cursed by his troops. When several Midwestern governors requested Grant's removal on charges of incapacity and recklessness, Halleck hurried down from St. Louis to take personal control. One of his first acts was to deprive Grant virtually of all command. Although next in rank to Halleck, Grant was, as he described himself, "little more than an observer." While theoretically Grant commanded the Army of the Tennessee, Halleck ignored him and sent orders directly to Thomas, who was second in command. Embarrassed and frustrated, Grant several times asked to be relieved.

Experiences such as these made Grant extremely sensitive to newspaper criticism and to army gossip. It was his misfortune that whenever he erred, popular judgment harked back to his early record and charged his shortcomings to drunkenness. Grant's troubles merit notice here only because they intruded themselves into his relations with Rosecrans, and set off a chain reaction that lasted for the lifetimes of both. Grant outranked Rosecrans. If one had looked fairly at both men as they met before Corinth, the prediction would have been easy to make that if perfectionist Rosecrans—voluble, highly critical, cocksure, competent—were assigned to Grant's command, and Grant's performance did not measure up to his subordinate's standards, trouble would follow.

Although Rosecrans, too, was down on his luck, his difficulties with Stanton were superficial trifles compared with Grant's deep-rooted insecurity. Rosecrans had commanded a department, planned his own campaigns, communicated directly with the President and the Secretary of War. "To be reduced," wrote Whitelaw Reid, "not merely to the position of subordinate, but to a subordinate's subordinate . . . is never a gratifying change, but Rosecrans bore it handsomely." As he joined Halleck's army, then in sight of Corinth, it numbered 173,000, with 108,000 present and fit for duty. Although this was the largest force ever to be gathered in the West, many were sick and low in morale. "The mumps are raging," wrote diarist Cyrus F. Boyd, of the 15th Iowa volunteer infantry, "and every other disease known to human beings."

Beauregard's army was in worse condition. Although its nominal strength was 112,000, of the 75,000 actually present, only 57,000 were effectives—ready for service or action. Halleck outnumbered Beauregard almost two to one. In smaller forces east of the Mississippi, Halleck had another 18,500 men in Buell's department. Offsetting these, the Confederates had 2,000 at Chattanooga, 12,000 at Knoxville, and 8,000 at Vicksburg and Jackson, but west of the river their numerical advantage was offset by the fact that their forces were scattered and poorly armed. The Confederates were discouraged and demoralized by their reverses. The Union troops were "correspondingly elated."

With such superiority, had Halleck been aggressive, he would have moved rapidly. Instead, he substituted a virtual siege operation.

When Rosecrans arrived at Pittsburg Landing on the dismal overcast day of May 23, 1862, he found little to mark the place beyond the clutter of river craft, until the wind that came with the rain carried the stench of rotting flesh from the wooded bluffs. Shiloh was a vast graveyard, cut with gulleys, interspersed with idle farms and swamps. Rain had scoured shallow graves, and skulls and toes protruded through the thin covering of earth; heavy wagons crushed bodies and turned up bones.

On May 24, Rosecrans reported to Halleck, with whom he was to remain on friendly terms until the summer of 1863, and on the 27th, Halleck sent Rosecrans to Pope, commanding the left, and Pope assigned him to command of his right, consisting of E. A. Paine's and David S. Stanley's divisions.

A lull had fallen as Rosecrans joined his command. Stanley's division formed the advance of the salient of Halleck's line. To its front, a wide, shallow valley sloped up to Beauregard's entrenchments. Stanley's men heard the Confederates talking and caught distant glimpses of Corinth, and on the night of the 26th, listened to them nailing up boxes and driving teams away. Now a bugle could be heard sounding retreat, then tattoo, and taps. Stanley was strengthening newly dug trenches, since Pope felt that any advance might bring on a general engagement.

At intervals a shell lofted into Stanley's lines, and his guns replied, but pickets were quiet, and the front maintained an uneasy silence. That evening, unusual activity in Corinth again kept the Union army alerted. Rosecrans heard railroad trains rumbling from north and west and passing south. He slept little. Rosecrans was general field officer of the day for the whole left.

At 1:20 A.M., Pope notified Halleck that Beauregard was being heavily reinforced by railroad. "Cars are running constantly, and the cheering is immense every time they unload. I have no doubt that I shall be attacked in heavy force at daylight." Halleck replied immediately that the Army of the Mississippi should prepare to sustain attack. Rosecrans toured his lines, ordered the men under arms, and personally supervised their dispositions. At 3:30, the right stood in their trenches, heavy-eyed but ready. At 4:00, the dawn wind freshened, and, coffee cups in their hands, men straightened as a solitary cannon boomed. "Signal for attack," they told one another.

Instead, a series of explosions followed, each flash leaving darker the gray of dawn. After the last rumble, a swirling black mushroom arose, with ragged fires fingering the smoke. Suspecting that Beauregard was evacuating, Stanley hurried forward, while Paine advanced two regiments to seize a Confederate battery. After ordering these movements and dispatching the news to Pope, Rosecrans hurried after Paine. At a deserted battery, he hoisted a flag and then sent his men by different routes into Corinth. There he found Colonel Grosbeck, commanding Stanley's second brigade, in possession. Grosbeck had raised the colors of the 10th Illinois on a building at about 7:00 A.M. A few families remained. Beauregard, however, had slipped away. By switching cars, tooting whistles, ordering bands to play and men to cheer, he had given the impression that he was being heavily reinforced and preparing to attack. "I think we have been fooled," said one correspondent. "The works are far from being invulnerable, and the old joke of Quaker guns has been played on us." Another reporter found "stuffed soldiers and old hats on sticks" grinning from the deserted breastworks.

Rosecrans found Corinth a sizable, prosperous town. It had sprung up only ten years before on land wrested from the Chickasaws. The region's red, sandy soil produced bountiful, quick-cash crops, and had made enterprising newcomers prosperous. In the fat years before the war, owners of the residences on Jackson Street imported their furnishings from Philadelphia and New York. Corinth boasted a hotel, the Tishomingo House, a few good business buildings, a brick courthouse, and a college.

Rosecrans and Pope rode through litter and smoke, past burned wagons, spent ammunition dumps, and ruined commissary stores. Pursuit was in the air, and by nine o'clock Rosecrans relayed Pope's order to the right. "Prepare three days' rations; march . . . in pursuit as soon as possible." Beauregard's army, rattling toward Tupelo on the Mobile and Ohio, or snaking down narrow roads, was demoralized. After the evacuation of Corinth, as after Shiloh, vigorous pursuit by the whole Union army should have begun immediately. Halleck either failed to see his opportunity or was reluctant to commit his whole force to it.

At Pope's headquarters, Halleck ordered Rosecrans to lead the pursuit, pushing on toward the Tuscumbia, and in case he found himself too far in the rear to pursue successfully, to select a camp behind that stream. At 5:00 P.M., Rosecrans led Pope's right wing,

12,000 strong, out of Corinth: Paine in the van, Stanley next, and Charles S. Hamilton last.

A pursuing Union cavalry column, taking the same road as Paine and Stanley, caught up with Beauregard's rear guard before sunset, up the Tuscumbia and four miles to the front, and met strong resistance. In the soggy, tangled lowlands, a Union battery floundered under fire of sharpshooters and artillery. A little after dark, when the artillery arrived, the enemy withdrew across the river, burning the bridge, and leaving sufficient force to prevent its reconstruction.

Next morning, riding half a mile above the burned bridge, Rosecrans found that the Tuscumbia backwaters narrowed, so that great trees felled along its banks would span them. While artillery held the enemy at the bridge, infantry crossed three-quarters of a mile above it, thus opening a way to Beauregard's flank and rear. So threatened, he fled during the night. Engineers meanwhile restored the bridge, and at noon artillery crossed. The right wing followed, and at 5:00 reached Rienzi, where the infantry halted. The cavalry, under Granger, pushed on to Boonesville.

Granger found the road strewn with blankets, knapsacks, small arms, carriages, and wagons, broken and abandoned by the enemy. On the evening of June 2, Pope told Halleck that he would not urge the pursuit beyond Baldwyn, the first large depot, thirty-five miles from Corinth; and he ordered Rosecrans not to advance beyond Baldwyn until his flanks and rear were secured. Next day, however, he felt more confident: "Urge the pursuit at least as far as Baldwyn, and farther, if you find it desirable or practicable." Baldwyn straddles the Mobile and Ohio, about ten miles beyond Boonesville. The road ahead to Boonesville stretched dark, obstructed by three swampy bottoms. Granger arrived on the outskirts of Boonesville about 1:30 A.M. on the 3rd. Pope now crowded Beauregard. "The whole rebel army is probably at Baldwyn," Rosecrans told Pope. "It is likely we will be attacked. Advance Thomas to Blackland to support us."

But battle was not to Halleck's taste. "The main object now," he told Pope and Buell, "is to get the enemy far enough south to relieve our railroads from danger of an immediate attack. There is no object in bringing on a battle if this can be obtained without one. I think by showing a bold front for a day or two, the enemy will continue to retreat, which is all I desire."

Halleck followed his pursuing column at a distance, and from Boonesville, Pope, who was sick, sent a dispatch to him: "Rosecrans and Smith are positive that the whole rebel army lies behind Twenty Mile Creek, which crosses the railroad four miles north of Baldwyn." This position was strong. Roads and bridges were wanting to cross the creek and the bordering wild swamp. Poor roads to the rear and more creeks and swamps made troop and supply movements difficult. Unless Halleck was prepared to follow Beauregard to Okolona, forty miles below Baldwyn, Pope "would not advise any movement of troops in this direction at this moment."

Despite this cautious advice, a fight seemed imminent, and, wishing to see it, Pope joined Rosecrans at the front. Next day, Buell arrived, and while Rosecrans, Pope, and Buell watched, the outnumbered army formed into battle line two and one half miles long, waiting to assault when reinforced. That night, when Buell's army took position beyond Pope's right, Pope reported: "If my operations are successful, I shall at an early hour fall upon the enemy with my whole force."

But the battle of Twenty Mile Creek, into which the entire armies of Beauregard and Halleck might have been drawn to dwarf even Chickamauga as the great battle of the West, was never fought. With Buell's arrival, Beauregard retreated, and by the morning of June 9 had passed through Guntown.

Restrained by Halleck's defensive attitude, the pursuit ended. "Delay in making an attack will favor us more than it can the enemy," Halleck said to Pope. Later, he added: "If confident that the enemy is retiring, you are authorized to assume command and make the attack; but, as the remainder of the army is distant and otherwise occupied, I desire that no risk be run. The enemy will retreat in a day or two, which will satisfy us about as well as if he were defeated in battle."

On June 11, after remaining for eight days at Twenty Mile Creek, the army returned to Corinth. Pursuing Beauregard for about thirty-five miles, Rosecrans had brought him to bay. That no substantial gain resulted was Halleck's responsibility. For the second time in two months, the Confederates were permitted to escape. Sick at Danville for a few days, Pope had relayed to Halleck dispatches from his officers at the front. Pope, condensing into one dispatch communications from Rosecrans, Hamilton, and Granger, had reported that the woods, for miles, were full of stragglers who were coming in in squads. Not less than ten thousand men were thus scattered about. He expected them to come in within a day or two. To the War Department, Halleck had then announced a great victory. "General Pope is thirty miles south of Corinth, pushing the enemy hard. He already reports 10,000 prisoners and deserters, and 15,000 stands of arms captured." When the War Department had released this news, bells had pealed across the North. Then it was learned that very few prisoners had come in. Pope was censured for making a statement which he later claimed he neither made nor authorized, and the North responded with ridicule and anger to Pope's "newspaper victory." Some part of the responsibility, though certainly not all, would seem to have been his.

When the pursuit ended, the breakup of Halleck's army into lesser commands began. For any one of these, the Confederates provided a fair match. On their own grounds, with interior lines, they had some chance of victory if they could meet the Union forces in detail. For dispersing his strength, Halleck has been charged with military imbecility, and with adding a year to the war. The case against Halleck is not simple or wholly free from extenuating circumstances.

Halleck might have sent a portion of Buell's army to move quickly and to seize, fortify, and hold Chattanooga. Still outnumbering Beauregard, with the rest he might have pursued the Confederates vigorously, bringing them to battle without fortifications, or else continuing his pursuit to Vicksburg. But his "orders were cautious to the extent of feebleness."

This failure to seize the last stronghold remaining to the Confederates in the Mississippi Valley was a Union catastrophe. Admiral David G. Farragut's fleet waited below the city for land support. A force of 10,000 men would have been enough at any time during May or June 1862 to capture the place. With Vicksburg's fall, the entire Mississippi would have been securely in Union hands. When, on June 28, after running batteries, Farragut told Halleck that land forces were needed to take Vicksburg, Halleck would detach no troops for the task. As a result, the Navy left Vicksburg, the Confederates regained control of 600 miles of the river from Baton Rouge to Helena, and strengthened the Vicksburg defenses, and Grant's 1863 campaign became necessary.

McClernand was the first to leave Halleck. On June 4 he started for Bolivar with two divisions of the Army of the Tennessee. On the 9th, Sherman moved west with two divisions along the Memphis and Charleston to Memphis, and Buell started east along the same tracks toward Chattanooga. Next day, general orders restored Grant, Buell, and Pope to their independent commands; while Thomas, with a division, was assigned to Corinth.

Buell moved slowly. Meanwhile, President Jefferson Davis had replaced Beauregard, whom he disliked, with Braxton Bragg, one of his favorites. Humorless, competent Bragg, an acquaintance of Rosecrans from Newport days, acted brilliantly and quickly, transporting most of his army by railroad from middle Mississippi to Chattanooga. After he secured Chattanooga, he struck north through Tennessee to regain middle Tennessee, to cover eastern Tennessee, and to invade Kentucky. The remainder of his army encamped at Holly Springs, Mississippi, awaiting reinforcements, supplies, and cooler weather before reopening the campaign.

By mid-June "General Summer" commanded at Corinth. Dust settled six inches deep or rose in dense clouds. Daytime temperatures hovered around 100 degrees. "Terrible weather for marching," Sherman wrote, "dust and heat insufferable." Empty stream beds cracked under the fierce sun, and buckets dangled useless in dug wells. Iuka Spring went dry, one of three times in a century. A half-million men and their horses, mules, beef cattle, and other food animals had so polluted the ground that drinking water stank, and was unfit even for stock. Confederate fleas and body lice now made easy transfer to Union underwear. Flies tormented men and animals, and the high whine of mosquitoes promised fever. Stronger than the familiar smell of horses and sweat was the acid, all-pervading stench of "squitters," or "Mississippi quick-step." Diarrhea and dysentery had no respect for rank. Halleck was confined to quarters in the high-ceilinged Curlee mansion with what he called "the evacuation of Corinth." Pope was sick, and Sherman "quite unwell." Surgeons surmised that diet or exposure to cold was at fault and recommended the wearing of a flannel "belly band."

"Keep the body clean," volunteers read in a U.S. Christian Commission leaflet. "You never take cold, no matter how wet, if in motion. Drinking, unless under medical advice, is your greatest curse. . . . Lewdness makes beasts of men—never risk it. . . . Better use uncooked pork than eat victuals half cooked. Don't smoke beans, skim your soup often. Onions are good, they are antiscorbutic. . . . Don't try to execute the law yourselves. It don't pay." And Private John Tallman complained from Camp Hurlbut—probably near Memphis: "Our diet has been principally sow belly and magets, bacon and crackers, some say the crackers have magets in them, but I don't look for them. All I say is if they get between my teeth they will get hurt."

Rosecrans estimated that 35 per cent of his men were sick. Good sanitation, bathing facilities, and clean drinking water were critically needed, and Pope found a level spot about six miles from Corinth on Clear Creek, a wide, running stream of excellent water, with many springs, but no swamps. Here Rosecrans made his camp on June 12. He established a convalescent hospital, and organized a system of antiscorbutic and antifever diets which soon reduced the sick list from 35 to 12 per cent. "There are but few very sick," Colonel Heg observed on July 9; he thought the camp near Corinth "a fine, healthy place, and plenty of good spring water, but the FLIES are so awful thick, if it was not for my mosquito bar they would eat me up."

The army settled down for almost three months of comparative quiet. With the bulk of his force at Camp Clear Creek, a brigade at Rienzi, cavalry battalions at Booneville, Blackland, and Jacinto, Rosecrans covered the approaches to Corinth from the direction of Columbus, Mississippi. When Pope was ordered east on June 15, to command the combined armies of Banks, Fremont, and McDowell, Rosecrans knew his plan for uniting these armies had been turned over to another. But Pope's transfer brought Rosecrans some advantage. He succeeded Pope as commander of the Army of the Mississippi. Though his rank remained unchanged, he now reported to Halleck.

As summer settled down, Grant paced in the large, angular, white frame house across the street from Halleck's headquarters on Jackson Street. "My position at Corinth," he wrote, "with a nominal command and yet no command, became so unbearable that I asked permission . . . to remove my headquarters to Memphis. I had repeatedly asked, between the fall of Donelson and the evacuation of Corinth, to be relieved from duty under Halleck, but all my applications were refused." At this juncture, Sherman found him, his belongings packed and ready to leave. "I am in the way," he told Sherman. He was going to St. Louis. "I begged him to stay," Sherman said, "illustrating his case by my own." After thinking the matter over, Grant stayed on, but shifted his headquarters to Memphis.

Rosecrans was busy early in July reorganizing his command. Paine now led the first division; Stanley, the second; Hamilton, the third; Jefferson C. Davis, the fourth; Alexander Asboth, the fifth; and Gordon Granger, the cavalry. Rosecrans' relations with Hamilton were less easy and happy than with the rest. Hamilton (West Point '43—Grant's class) was "touchy" and pugnacious.

These local assignments were, naturally, of minor importance compared to Lincoln's appointment of Halleck as general-in-chief of the land forces of the United States. Halleck received Stanton's dispatch on July 11 and ordered Grant to return from Memphis. Then he asked Washington, "Shall I relinquish the command to the next in rank, or will the President designate who is to be commander?"

Lincoln had never met Grant. But Grant had turned in victories, and even more important, he was sponsored by politically important Congressman Elihu B. Washburne of Illinois. And so Grant succeeded Halleck, and on July 15 was in Corinth issuing orders. Halleck, miscast in active service and later in administration, was greatly maligned.

As he left Corinth, Halleck confirmed Grant's assignment; he would command the district of West Tennessee, including Cairo, that part of Mississippi occupied by Union troops, that part of Alabama that might be occupied, and the "forces heretofore known as the Army of the Mississippi." However, these orders did not liquidate the Army of the Mississippi. On July 17, Grant assumed command, with headquarters at Corinth. By the next day, Rosecrans, now directly under him, was bringing routine matters to his attention. Reid points out that Halleck's departure for the first time brought General Rosecrans into relations with Grant, "whose subsequent ill-will was to prove so baleful."

Grant's depleted force consisted of two armies. By the end of July, the Army of the Tennessee, which Grant continued to command in person, showed an aggregate, present and absent, of 65,000 men at Corinth, Memphis, Jackson, Cairo, and scattered elsewhere. The Army of the Mississippi, which Rosecrans commanded, had, present and absent, about 40,000 men at Camp Clear Creek, at Cherokee Station, Alabama, and at Jacinto, Mississippi.

Rosecrans bustled through the torrid days with characteristic energy. He scolded the War Department in an effort to get his cavalry well armed, watched the enemy, and wondered why he was rusticated while others, less well qualified, less deserving, were promoted. He was perplexed about official disfavor—Stanton on the radical and McClellan on the conservative side were angry with him—and he wrote in the summer to a fellow Cincinnatian, Secretary Chase. Chase was equally baffled, and, worse for Rosecrans, he was out of Stanton's favor, and critical of Stanton's generalship; he knew and approved of Rosecrans' plans for unifying the valley armies. Chase wrote: "What the cause of discrimination apparently against you may be, I do not know. My influence with the War Department is not strong. Had it been greater, some serious disasters would have been avoided, and movements been made heretofore resembling those prepared by you. Such as it is, however, you shall have the benefit of it, as in times past you had."

Rosecrans worried, too, about other problems: about his wife Annie—he begged Mrs. Scammon and his mother-in-law to reveal the truth about her health, prayed for her safe delivery, and for their "hope," the unborn child; about the delay in soldiers' mail— he inaugurated a system of daily delivery, and speeded up the bushels, barrels, and even wagon loads of forgotten mail addressed to anxious soldiers.

Because good topographical maps were scarce, Rosecrans contrived a rapid map-making system. He ordered his staff engineers to draw a skeleton map on which to mark topographical information. To get copies of this master map quickly, Rosecrans told a roving photographer, "I want photographic copies. I'll pay you well. Or I'll give your privilege of taking soldiers' pictures to someone else." Rosecrans distributed these maps to his brigade and division commanders, requesting them to place additions and corrections on them, and return them, for the production of a copy for general issue. This innovation became standard army practice by the end of the war.

Civil administration provided another problem. Rosecrans himself pointed out that the native population did not understand that they "were not entitled to protection as citizens who had a right to go with their state and resist Federal coercion, instead of being the subjects of a conquered territory, as Confederate theory defined them." To Unionists, he said: "You are children of Uncle Sam. He'll do what he can for you; you do the rest." To others: "If you want the full privileges of citizenship, take an oath of allegiance." He told objectors: "Take an oath of qualified allegiance to the *de facto* government, pledging yourselves to abstain from mischief, or leave the country."

Runaway or captured slaves who flocked into Union camps or followed columns on the march created another problem which some Federal commanders sought to avoid rather than solve.

As late as June 18, Sherman, in orders No. 43, had stressed the duties of officers and men toward slaves: "The policy of the army is to have nothing to do with the negro. 'Exclude them from camp,' is Halleck's order. We cannot have our trains encumbered by them, nor can we afford to feed them." By July 23, this policy was so amended that Grant, in special orders No. 142, allowed the hospital in Jackson to retain "black labor," to perform "such menial service as should not be put upon soldiers." Rosecrans' relations with the Negroes were more enlightened. "Rising superior to prejudice, and in advance of the times, he organized a battalion of colored engineer troops, the first employed in the Army."

"A good many soldiers and people are *bitterly* opposed to having 'niggers' take any hand in this War," wrote Sergeant Cyrus F. Boyd of the Fifteenth Iowa Infantry. "I am not one of those kind of people. If a *culled* man will dig trenches and chop down timber and even fight the enemy he is just the fellow we want and the sooner we recognize this the quicker the war will *end*."

Once or twice a week, Rosecrans rode over to Corinth and dined with Grant. Grant was glum. Correspondent William Shanks observed that Grant seldom joked, and rarely laughed, and "whittled or smoked with a listless, absorbed air." But his friendliness toward Rosecrans is indicated in his August 9 report to Halleck. He wanted more important assignments for this brigadier general. "Having so many Major Generals to provide commands for, this may be difficult. I regret that General Rosecrans has not got rank equal to his merit to make this easy."

Rosecrans' dispatches to Grant were cheerful, relaxed. One facetious report probably made Grant smile: "The Mackerel—I mean Union brigade, attacked the pigs of Danville, deploying skirmishers who opened a sharp fire and brought eight of the hairy rascals to the ground before Colonel Tinkham . . . informed the commander of the brigade that these natives were non-combatants, as loyal as possible, considering their limited information."

Grant was concerned about Corinth's defenses, for Beauregard had built a circle of earthworks on three sides, two and one-half miles from the center of the town. Realizing the impracticality of manning these, Halleck had begun to construct an inner circle on a mile-and-a-half radius, extending it to cover the southern approaches. Because the Confederates would certainly attempt to retake Corinth, throughout the summer Grant's soldiers sweated to strengthen the "Halleck Line." Rosecrans judged these works useless. His conversations with Grant fell into a pattern.

"How are you coming along?" Rosecrans would ask.

"Well, pretty slowly, but they are doing good work."

"The line isn't worth much to us, because it is too long. We cannot occupy it."

"What would you do?"

"I would have made the depots outside of the town north of the Memphis and Charleston road between the town and the brick church, and would have enclosed them by field-works, running tracks in. Now, as the depot houses are at the cross-road, the best thing we can do is to run a line of light works around in the neighborhood of the college up on the knoll."

After Grant looked over the ground with Rosecrans, he gave orders to Colonel Frederick E. Prime to construct a new inner line of breastworks to include the college grounds and five low hills. On these, he began to build five open batteries: Robinett, Williams, Phillips, Tannrath, and Lothrop. When General Earl Van Dorn fell upon Corinth in October, it was this inner ring which Rosecrans had urged that made the Union victory possible.

Meanwhile, on the morning of July 28, Colonel Philip H. Sheridan's cavalry attacked Ripley, and captured thirty letters. These revealed that the enemy was moving in strength against Chatta-nooga. The writers thought that "with Bragg in the east and Price in the center, the Yankees will be made to skedaddle." They boasted that they would "take Corinth when they please."

"Sheridan ought to be made a brigadier," Rosecrans telegraphed Halleck. "He would not be a stampeding general." Brigadiers Rosecrans, Sullivan, Granger, Elliot, and Asboth recommended Sheridan's promotion: "He is worth his weight in gold." Up to then, Sheridan's fighting qualities had been largely undemon-strated. This recommendation helped bring Sheridan his first star. Rosecrans always proudly claimed Sheridan as his discovery.

Other indications of Confederate purposes appeared. Granger reported heavy troop movements eastward by rail. Only Price, with about 20,000 men, was left in Mississippi. A strong attack on Buell or the Army of the Potomac was expected. Grant told Halleck that if necessary he would reinforce Buell, but Bolivar seemed the point most likely to be attacked by Price. Grant planned to clear the enemy from the front of Corinth, leaving the town with a small garrison.

Even Farragut's distant movements shifted the balances in north-eastern Mississippi. When part of the Union fleet before Vicksburg pulled north to Helena, Arkansas, and the remainder steamed south to Baton Rouge, Sherman wrote from Memphis. "This will embolden Van Dorn, and we must soon expect to hear from him."

In the middle of August, when Grant ordered Rosecrans to de-tach the divisions of John M. Palmer and Jefferson C. Davis to join Buell in Kentucky, Rosecrans marched his whole force toward the Tennessee, and while the two divisions crossed at four widely separated places, the remainder of his army waited at Tuscumbia to cover their crossing. Weather continued hot and dry, although nights were cool in the hills near Iuka.

At Iuka Rosecrans established headquarters at the fashionable Southern watering place—"very pretty, with large country resi-dences"—in the comfortable colonial plantation mansion of Colo-nel Laurence Moore. An encircling veranda shaded its wide, floor-length windows, and the glazed doors in the long central hallway overlooked miles of rolling, wooded country to the south. Rose-crans' bedroom, with its fifteen-foot-high ceilings, was simply furnished, but the front parlor was as lavish as any "secesh Palace" in town. Elaborately patterned silk draperies with brass clasps and heavy, tasseled silk cords hung at the windows. The unobtrusive fireplace was faced with slate, and a coal-oil lamp, shaded with amethyst glass, spread a dim, violet glow on fragile sofas and on the lush tulips and roses of the velvet carpeting.

Halleck wanted the line held west of Decatur, Alabama, ninety miles due east of Corinth, and a hundred miles by road, to keep communications open with Buell. Rosecrans posted his forces along the Memphis and Charleston railroad, facing the enemy on an eighty-mile front. To compensate for his inadequate numbers, he sought improved weapons, asking Stanton for 2,500 revolving rifles and 2,000 revolvers. "We are in the presence of the enemy superior in numbers, having a cloud of irregulars to do their hard riding and messenger work. It is cruel and impolitic to leave us in this condition. . . . You can double our force. . . . I hardly need remind the Secretary it is one of the things he could do for me personally." He entreated Halleck, "I beseech you order me 5,000 first-class muskets and some carbines, or revolving arms."

On September 2, Halleck ordered Grant to abandon the railroad east of Corinth, and to detach Granger's division from Rosecrans and send it to Louisville "with all possible dispatch." A brigade should hold Iuka and Eastport. Although Rosecrans hoped to withdraw undetected from the railroad line—"everything on the front must appear exceedingly strong and have an offensive look" —General Napoleon Buford apparently leaked the secret and risked having Confederate ears hear it, so that Rosecrans, who was in Rienzi, complained to Grant at Corinth: "I am told old Buford learned and blabbed our movements to Major Alger. This is so."

From August 27 to September 1 Pope tangled with Lee near Bull Run, and was so worsted that McClellan replaced him. "In the early days of September," Rosecrans wrote, "after the disaster of the 'Second Bull Run,' the friends of the Union watched with almost breathless anxiety the advance of Lee into Maryland, of Bragg into Kentucky, and the hurrying of the Army of the Potomac northward from Washington, to get between Lee and the cities of Washington, Baltimore, and Philadelphia. The suspense lest McClellan should not be in time to head off Lee—lest Buell should not arrive in time to prevent Bragg from taking Louisville or assaulting Cincinnati, was fearful." To add anxiety, the Union forces in western Tennessee and northern Mississippi became aware that Price was moving in their neighborhood.

On August 29, rumor reported that Price's advance guard, 6,000 strong, threatened Bolivar. Union troops hurried through the town, stirring up dust six inches deep, while thermometers hovered at 100 degrees in the shade. Grant at Corinth was perplexed. "With all the vigilance I can bring to bear, I cannot determine the objects of the enemy," he told Halleck, "everything threatens an attack here, but my fear is that it is to cover some other movement as late as September 10." A day later, Rosecrans told Grant: "I must think the movement a demonstration to cover a move on Buell."

Meanwhile, on September 7, Grant informed Halleck that Sherman commanded his right; Ord, his center; and Rosecrans, his left. Rosecrans commanded the garrison at Corinth; Ord, at Jackson. Grant would probably move his headquarters to Jackson.

From Northern newspapers, Van Dorn learned that Grant would go to Jackson, leaving Rosecrans to command Corinth. Van Dorn knew both, and from his "knowledge of the capacity and character of Rosecrans," he was "convinced that Corinth would be strengthened by the change of its commander." Van Dorn said of Rosecrans: "I knew my antagonist—knew he would avail himself of every resource in his power." "Able," he called him, "skillful," and "astute."

As he advanced north from Chattanooga, Bragg grew confident that by himself he could handle Buell, leaving Sherman and Rosecrans to Price. Price could "dispose of them." He learned that two of Rosecrans' divisions were moving east, and warned Price to watch Rosecrans. Buell was in full retreat, and their junction must be prevented.

On the 12th, still at Corinth, Grant wrote to Halleck: "Everything indicates we will be attacked here in the next forty-eight hours, and at present the route is indicated by the southwest. I will be ready at all points. General Rosecrans is not yet in with all his forces, but will be by tomorrow night." Grant had ordered to Corinth all spare forces at Bolivar and Jackson.

From his information, Rosecrans could not deduce where Price's attack would fall. Supposing Price bypassed Grant to head for

Ohio? Rosecrans expressed his concern to Grant: "As Price is an old woodpecker, it would be well to have a watch set to see if he might not take a course down the Tennessee toward Eastport, in hopes to find a landing."

At moonrise on September 13, Price rode toward Iuka. Over steep hills, through the shadow of sweetgums, oaks, and white-limbed birch, flowed his "multi-colored horde." Richmond considered his army a mob; that night it was well ordered and well supplied, with pay in its pockets and salt beef and bread in the wagon trains. A "Member of G.A.R." described how every segment of Western life marched or rode with Price: "old men and young boys, rich planters on blooded horses and Negro laborers on foot; farmers and clerks; grizzled hunters and tough keelboat men; prosperous merchants and plain backwoodsmen. Some had never been out of Mississippi; some had been bronzed in every latitude. Some wore black, full citizen's clothes, with beaver hats and frock coats; some in drab; some in gray, blue and streaked; some in red shirts, pants and high top boots; some in the old-fashioned militia uniform of their forefathers." On they came, glutting narrow roads, overflowing into the forest; undulating, talking in smooth drawls or emitting shrill, terrifying cries—"as strangely assorted and colorful an army as ever human eye rested upon."

That day, Price's cavalry attacked the small Iuka garrison commanded by Colonel Robert Murphy. Although Murphy repulsed them, when they cut both the railroad and telegraph to Corinth and returned in greater force, he thought it "prudent to retire and save his forces," abandoning a large quantity of stores. Rosecrans commented: "Our rear guard withdrew so hastily that no idea of the hostile movement could be drawn from their report." He ordered Murphy's arrest.

Arriving in Iuka in force on the 14th, Price found that Rosecrans had gone westward with about 10,000 men. Reports were confusing. Two days earlier, Bragg had written to Price that it "seems Rosecrans with part of his army" is at Nashville. "I have anxiously expected your advance and trust it will be no longer delayed."

Bedeviled by conflicting information and orders, Price lay daringly exposed at Iuka for five days. He could not advance into Kentucky, leaving Rosecrans at his back. From Richmond, on September 19, Jefferson Davis telegraphed: "If Van Dorn, Price and Breckinridge each act for himself disaster to all must be the probable result." Van Dorn, who outranked Price, wrote from Holly Springs on the 16th proposing a joint attack on Corinth. "I have but thirty-five miles to march, and can reach you with 10,000 men in three days. . . . Rosecrans is a quick and skillful fellow, and we must be rapid also." They would pluck Corinth.

Meanwhile, Rosecrans advanced Colonel Joseph Mower with the 11th Missouri to "feel Price out." And, pushing vigorously to within two miles of Iuka, Mower learned that Price lay in Iuka with strong infantry, cavalry, and artillery forces. Rosecrans reported this information to Grant; with the enemy divided, they hatched a plan. They would capture Price.

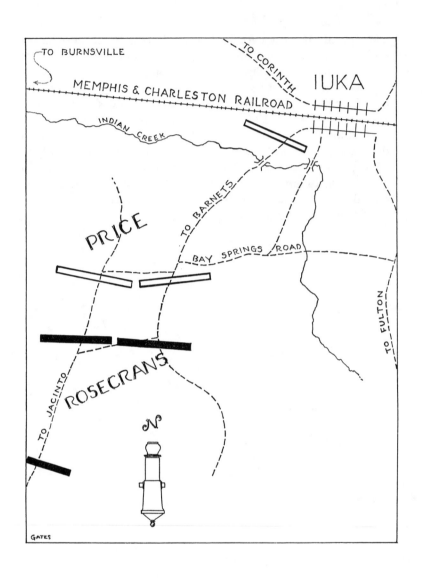

BATTLE OF IUKA

September 19, 1862

Six

IUKA — THE PINCERS DO NOT CLOSE

Grant understood both his danger and his opportunity. Operating jointly, Price might assault Corinth from the east while Van Dorn struck from the south. To catch the pair divided, Grant must move rapidly and crush Price at Iuka before Van Dorn came up. To succeed, Grant needed more troops than he had at hand and he ordered into Corinth 8,000 men from Bolivar and Jackson. Nine thousand additional scattered troops garrisoned the district. Grant acknowledged that he "deferred very much to Rosecrans," who had recently returned from Iuka, for he was more familiar with the ground.

It seemed likely that, if attacked, Price would attempt either to cross the Tennessee and join Bragg or to withdraw southward to join Van Dorn. To checkmate both alternatives, Rosecrans suggested that Grant divide his forces, sending one part north of the railroad to attack Price in front—he lay north of Iuka facing west and north—and interpose between him and Tennessee, and the other part south, to block his escape and prevent his junction with Van Dorn.

Combined military operations are notoriously tricky; this one required close timing and careful leadership for each jaw of the pincers, for Price had sufficient strength to match either Union force. Was Rosecrans too sanguine, too trusting of the capacities of his associates? At Rich Mountain, where McClellan failed to carry out his part in a similar operation, Rosecrans had been left to fight the battle alone. Subsequent events at Iuka proved that

Rosecrans had as much to fear from Grant's failure to co-operate as from Price's army.

Grant approved Rosecrans' plan and gave him command of the right, to block Price from the south. He remained with the left himself, giving Ord nominal command. The left was to open the fight and keep Price busy north of Iuka while Rosecrans covered its southern approaches. Grant expected that Rosecrans would be near enough by the 18th to make it safe for Ord to bring on an engagement on the morning of the 19th.

Danger existed that Van Dorn might learn of this attack and fling his cavalry against Rosecrans' marching column or the weakened Corinth garrison. To screen Corinth's southern approaches, Grant ordered enough troops to Jacinto and Rienzi to resist a cavalry attack. After Ord's troops had detrained at Burnsville, cars would be held ready to carry Ord's column back in an emergency.

Grant first planned to send Rosecrans against Iuka through the woods directly south of the railroad. Rosecrans demurred; for three or four miles east from Burnsville, the tangled swamps of the headwaters of Yellow Creek formed an impassable barrier. Moreover, Hamilton's four brigades, which were assigned to Rosecrans, lay at Jacinto, eighteen miles southwest of Iuka. Rosecrans suggested instead that his command should concentrate, and then move eastward along the Tuscumbia Road to the intersections of the Iuka and Fulton roads, there to divide and march north upon Price's left flank and rear.

Rosecrans would leave a small force at Barnet's, where the Jacinto Road turns northeast, and continue ahead, so that his main force would approach Price on the Fulton Road, which enters Iuka east of the Jacinto Road. Thus Grant hoped to annihilate Price in a four-sided trap. To the north and northeast, seven to twelve miles away, flowed the Tennessee. To the northwest, Ord would lie. Up from the southwest and south, Rosecrans would march. To the east, a few miles from the Fulton Road, ran Bear Creek, its bridges destroyed.

Rosecrans immediately concentrated his sick and disabled, parked them defensively near Corinth, and awaited orders. He advised Grant that because half of his command was fifteen miles away at Jacinto, he needed time to concentrate. He suggested that since Hamilton, at Jacinto, covered the Tuscumbia Road, six or eight miles south of the railroad and parallel to it, he was doing good outpost service.

On the evening of the 17th, Rosecrans reported to Grant: "Stanley's division marches tonight for Davenport's Mill, near Jacinto, where all the regiments meet. Hamilton moves forward tonight. . . . I will then move to Jacinto and connect my headquarters with Burnsville by lines of vedette posts for prompt and rapid communication with your headquarters." Later he reported:

Hamilton has sent out Mizner with a regiment and all our cavalry, toward Barnett's on the Jacinto and Iuka Roads. The only thing that we can do to prevent Price's passing through the defiles of Bear Creek east is to push that division on him and follow it with all Stanley's force while Ross makes a strong demonstration on his front. This is safe for a day or two if we can keep spies from running to Breckinridge and Van [Dorn] and Price and you can hold your hand against [them]. I can pursue with my entire force, which, including Du Bois and Danville, will be about 13,000 men of all arms.

On the morning of September 18, when Grant entrained for Burnsville, Rosecrans had orders to march as rapidly as possible, keeping communications open between his column and Ord's right.

Rosecrans left Camp Clear Creek in an early morning rainstorm. The skies cleared about nine o'clock, leaving the roads slightly muddy but dustless. Before noon, he reported to Grant: "The rain and darkness prevented Stanley from making progress until this morning. We shall all be concentrated at Jacinto by about 2 o'clock and move forward to the vicinity of the Bay Spring Road tonight." Sometime during the day, he added that "if Price's forces are at Iuka the plan I propose is to move up as close as we can tonight and conceal our movements; Ord to advance from Burnsville, *commence the attack,* and draw their attention that way, while I move in on the Jacinto and Fulton Roads, massing heavily on the Fulton Road, and crushing in their left and cutting off their retreat eastward. I propose to leave in ten minutes for Jacinto from whence I will dispatch you by a line of vedettes to Burnsville." (Italics mine.)

When Ord reached Burnsville at noon, Grant was already there.

Ross arrived with his command during the afternoon. At 6:45 P.M., Grant informed Rosecrans of Ross's arrival. McArthur's division was north of the road, two miles to the rear, and Davies, south of the road nearby. Grant had sent two regiments of infantry, with cavalry support, toward Iuka. They had instructions to bivouac for the night about two miles beyond Burnsville.

Ord's column detrained, struck quickly at the Confederate advance, and drove it in. He halted six miles from Iuka to await the command to attack. Grant, at Burnsville, was seven miles from Iuka. His advance lay behind his cavalry and two miles from Iuka. The Burnsville troops, Grant told Rosecrans, would move on Iuka at 4:30 A.M. Rosecrans should advance as rapidly as possible and "let us do tomorrow all we can." Grant guessed that Price's cavalry was cover for his probable retreat.

Meanwhile, by treachery or accident, a guide led Stanley to the rear of Ross, of Ord's command, delaying Rosecrans' movement for four or five hours. When Rosecrans learned that Stanley was still twenty miles from Iuka, he decided to bivouac for the night at Jacinto. At 9:00 P.M., he sent a message to Grant down the vedette line: "Stanley's division arrived after dark. . . . Our cavalry is this side of Barnett's; Hamilton's first brigade 8 miles; second brigade 9 miles this side; Stanley's near Davenport's Mill. We move as early as practicable, say 4:30 A.M. This will give 20 miles march for Stanley to Iuka. Shall not therefore be in before 1 or 2 o'clock, but when we come in we will endeavor to do it strongly."

Referring to this dispatch, Grant later wrote: "I immediately dispatched to General Ord giving him the substance of the above, and directions not to move on the enemy until Rosecrans arrived, or he should hear firing to the south of Iuka. Of this change General Rosecrans was promptly informed by dispatch sent with his return messenger." This dispatch is missing from the *Records*. It may have been written and never sent, or sent and never delivered. If Grant prepared it Rosecrans never received it. In any event, sometime during the 19th, Grant sent a dispatch to Halleck saying that "Rosecrans is south of the enemy moving on him, while Ord *attacks* from the west." (Italics mine.)

Sometime during the late evening or night a dispatch arrived at Grant's headquarters from Cairo telling that McClellan had exterminated Lee at Antietam. Headquarters sent this dispatch down the vedette line to Rosecrans. Rosecrans received this news at 1:30 A.M., in a dispatch which also acknowledged the receipt of his telling Grant that he had been delayed and would come in later than expected. This was the last dispatch, Rosecrans insisted, to reach him from Grant's headquarters before, during and after the battle.

Ord later reported: "In the course of that evening [the 18th] dispatches were received from General Rosecrans, stating that a large portion of his command had been delayed by mistaking the route and following one of my columns and was still about twenty miles from Iuka." Grant's and Ord's reports disagree as to times. Grant says he "immediately" sent a dispatch to Ord. But Ord says: "While making a reconnaissance about ten o'clock that morning [September 19th] I received from you the following dispatch: 'I send you dispatch received from Rosecrans late in the night. You will see he is behind where we expected him. Do not be too rapid with your advance this morning, unless it should be found that the enemy are evacuating.' " This dispatch was signed "Clark B. Lagow, by order of Major General Grant." Colonel Lagow's signature *may* be significant.

It was not "immediately" after midnight, but the following afternoon, fourteen hours later—after 4:00 P.M. on the 19th, Ord contended—that Grant told him to move his "whole force forward to within 4 miles of Iuka and there await sounds of an engagement" before attacking Price.

Rosecrans was unaware that his support had been immobilized at Burnsville and marched at 5:00 A.M. on the 19th; at 6:00 he sent a dispatch to Grant: "Troops are all on the way, in fine spirits by reason of news"—Lee's supposed extermination at Antietam. "Eighteen miles to Iuka, but I think I shall make it by the time mentioned, 2:00 o'clock P.M. If Price is there *he will have become well engaged by the time we come up,* and, if so, twenty regiments and thirty pieces cannon will finish him. Hamilton will go up the Fulton and Iuka road; Stanley up Jacinto road from Barnet's; when we get near, will be governed by circumstances. Cavalry will press in on the right to cover their retreat." (Italics mine.) Grant made no reply.

By 11:40, Rosecrans' cavalry had moved east toward the Fulton Road, and one of Hamilton's brigades had reached Cartersville with orders to turn up into the Jacinto and Iuka Road above widow Moore's. At noon, the column was on schedule. They had covered twelve miles and had reached Barnet's, driving in the enemy's cavalry pickets for the last two or three miles.

Since about 1:30 A.M., some ten and a half hours before, when the false news concerning Antietam had been dispatched to Rosecrans, apparently no messages from Grant had been sent down the vedette line, and no thundering cannon announced that Ord was engaging Price. At Barnet's, Rosecrans faced an unexpected problem. He had planned to send half his command ahead to the Fulton Road intersection, and hence north to Iuka, while the remainder marched north from Barnet's on the Jacinto Road. But as he had reported to Grant at 6:00 A.M.: "When we get near, will be governed by circumstances."

"I telegraphed you," he wrote in his *Report* to Grant, "that the force from Burnsville should attack the rebels from the west and draw them in that direction and then I would move in on their rear by the Jacinto and Fulton Roads and cut off their retreat." The two roads were not parallel. With Iuka as the hub, the Jacinto and Fulton roads are two spokes radiating south, and connecting with a section of rim, which is the road between Jacinto and Tuscumbia on which Rosecrans marched. Between them, northward almost to Iuka, lay a wedge of swampy, brush-covered country.

"I here ascertained," Rosecrans later commented, "that the Fulton Road crossed the Tuscumbia four and a half miles east of this point, and there were no cross-roads between it and that leading hence to Iuka, by which columns advancing on them separately could certainly and safely communicate with each other, and also that the enemy's strength was believed to be between 20,000 and 30,000 strong. I therefore determined that it would be unsafe to move Stanley's division up the Fulton Road, whereby I should divide my command, consisting of only four brigades, into two columns, not within supporting distance of each other."

It is likely that Rosecrans' cavalry reconnaissance, sent by Colonel Mizner early on the 19th to examine the Bay Springs, Fulton, and Iuka roads, correctly assessed and reported the terrain. In any event, Rosecrans' cavalry had been on the Fulton Road. Neither Grant nor Rosecrans had understood this situation in planning their joint attack, but in his *Official Report,* Grant approved Rosecrans' on-the-spot decision: "A partial examination of the country afterward convinced me that troops moving in separate columns by the routes suggested could not support each other until they arrived near Iuka." In keeping with his reappraisal, Rosecrans sent his whole force up the Jacinto Road. Sanborn's brigade of Hamilton's division led. The rest of Hamilton's men followed. Stanley followed Hamilton.

A mile and a half south of Iuka, where the distance between the converging Jacinto and Fulton roads narrows, a diagonal crossroad connected them, and permitted columns advancing on both to give mutual support. This crossroad, the "Bay Springs Road," was long ago abandoned, and today can be traced by a slight depression, and by variations in thicket growth. The relation of the three roads can be visualized in terms of an A. Iuka is the apex. The left leg represents the Jacinto Road; the right, the Fulton. The transverse, placed high and sloping upward from left to right—from west to east—is the Bay Springs Road. Its possession was Rosecrans' goal at noon on the 19th. With Price engaged by Ord, it should have been open, so that Rosecrans could move part of his force across it to the Fulton Road. Rosecrans' awareness of the existence of this road is apparent from his dispatch of the 18th; "We shall . . . move forward to the vicinity of the Bay Springs Road tonight." If, however, Price blocked the Bay Springs Road to Rosecrans, then the Fulton Road lay open to Price, and by not occupying it, Rosecrans would allow Price to escape.

About 12:10, Colonels C. B. Lagow and Theophilus Dickey of Grant's staff pulled rein at Barnet's, where Rosecrans had halted. They brought no messages from Grant. They appeared to have come on their own initiative. "Two of my staff . . . had gone around to where Rosecrans was," Grant said later. He did not say, "I sent them." They bore no orders from Grant, from whom Rosecrans had not heard in more than ten and a half hours.

They asked Rosecrans, "General do you think the enemy is in force at Iuka." "Yes," said Rosecrans. "Are you going to pitch into him?" "Yes, of course, that is the understanding of my movement, and we are only five or six miles from the enemy. We ought to hear Grant's opening guns on the Railroad by this time."

"Maybe he is waiting for you to begin," they said.

"Not so," said Rosecrans, "the main attack should begin on the Railroad to attract the enemy's attention and enable me to surprise his left flank and get the roads in his rear."

At 12:40, when Rosecrans sent another dispatch to Grant from Barnet's, the head of Hamilton's column was a mile beyond town, the head of Stanley's at Barnet's, and Hatch at Peyton's Mill was skirmishing with Price's cavalry.

As Grant's aides rode north with Rosecrans, the noise of Hamilton's advance swelled to a persistent uproar. At 4:30 P.M., Lagow and Dickey left for Burnsville.

Hamilton had encountered immediate resistance on the Jacinto Road, and the last few miles became a steady contest and constant skirmish. At 4:00, his advance climbed a long hill a mile and a half south of Iuka, near the forking of the Bay Springs Road. There it paused briefly to rest the winded battery horses. Thick woods hid the entrance to the Bay Springs Road, below and to the right. They also concealed ten Confederate regiments in battle line.

Grant's failure to engage Price north of Iuka allowed them to be there. Rosecrans had told Grant that he would be in at 2:00 P.M. Only the fact that he was forced to skirmish his way up the Jacinto Road kept him behind schedule at the last. At 2:00, Price was informed that a strong Federal column was moving upon his rear, and, at 3:00, he ordered Little to send Hebert's and Martin's brigades from the inactive Burnsville front down the Jacinto Road to cover the entrance to the Bay Springs Road. Price rode with Hebert.

At 4:00, riding behind his skirmishers, Hamilton saw the Confederates, wheeled, and galloped back to his column, which was strung out along a road no wider than a wagon track. The enemy had dug entrenchments in the light, sandy soil, behind the crest of a densely wooded hill. A deep ravine separated the two armies. Battle opened on a rough and brushy point, falling off abruptly at either side, too tangled with underbrush to allow deployments. Mrs. Woodley, who lived close by, said "they shot so fast it sounded like corn a 'poppin'."

Had Hébert's brigade, which was in position, opened fire immediately, Hamilton would have been routed; but a pause enabled him to throw the 5th Iowa, which led, across the road and to the right. The Confederates meanwhile hurried their nearest battery to the crest of the road. Its high, opening blasts showered twigs and leaves upon Hamilton's regiments as they scurried into positions. No sooner had the Federals crouched in the brush than the whole Confederate force moved down the ravine, up through the woods, and up the road toward the 11th Ohio battery at the brow of the hill. That afternoon, the heaviest assaults fell upon this battery and the regiments flanking it, particularly upon the 5th Iowa, which lost half its men.

Although the charging Confederates advanced to within 150 or 200 yards, the battery waited for orders to fire. Finally, a sergeant screamed: "By God, I guess we're going to let them gobble the whole damned shooting match before we strike a lick." A corporal replied: "I guess we are obeying orders." "Damn the orders," the sergeant retorted. "It was the last straw," Lieutenant Sears said later. "Give them hell as fast as you can! . . . The guns of this battery became the bone of contention"; Sears remembered, "everything else, both flags, Union and Confederacy . . . were forgotten in that all-absorbing handspike-and-ramrod, rough-and-tumble, devil take the hindmost fight for those six guns." Forty-eight out of the fifty-four gunners were killed or wounded.

Price planned not only to strike the center, but to flank Hamilton right and left. As the fight opened, Rosecrans was riding with Stanley a mile to the rear of the head of Hamilton's column. He galloped forward on the clogged road, and on reaching the front found Hamilton's position strong. He ordered a battalion of cavalry to reconnoiter the right and sent an infantry regiment with a section of artillery to take a position a quarter-mile in advance of Hamilton's left. Next he ordered the first of Stanley's brigades to advance on the double quick, pushing three of Stanley's regiments to the right, to plug gaps left by withdrawing troops.

In Price's first assault, his artillery held their fire lest they catch their own advancing lines in their barrage. Front-line Federals, too, waited until the enemy were within a hundred yards, and then fired in volleys. Both sides staggered, wavered, fell back. Reforming, the enemy again advanced, cheering wildly. Again they were repulsed. After this second assault, the three companies of the 5th Iowa, flanking the battery, were so thinned that it seemed that neither battery nor regiment could hold out, and the 26th Missouri, immediately to its rear, advanced four companies to fill gaps. In a third assault, the enemy penetrated the battery, spiked three guns, and in hand-to-hand fighting bayoneted many cannoneers. As twilight deepened, the battle became furious. Major Weber of the 11th Missouri saw Confederates "received on the point of the bayonet, and then shot off, and others were shot by officers, who placed pistols in their very faces."

In the tangled ravines and gulches to the left, the commanding officer of the 17th Iowa was injured, the second in command absent, and the third under arrest. Captain John Young's only instructions were from General Sullivan: he should do his best. Young had rallied his men with difficulty and formed another line when a tremendous Confederate volley was answered by Federal regiments in Young's rear, causing a "dreadful stampede." Young's men commenced firing in all directions, but he rallied them and kept them "in pretty good line" until darkness.

In dusk and smoke, on steep hillsides to the right, a Mississippi regiment came within twenty paces of the 11th Missouri, mistaking them for friends. As the Missourians fired, a Confederate officer ran into their ranks shouting: "For God's sakes don't fire into your own men!" The Missourians answered with a volley. In the twilight the two brigades fought desperately for an hour, the smoke becoming so dense that men five paces away were obscured. Finally the enemy withdrew, and firing dwindled along the whole line. Sunset came at approximately six o'clock, and twilight lasted twenty-five minutes. At nightfall, the troops rested on their arms, with the enemy so close that the Union men could hear Confederates talking. Spasmodic firing bickered until 8:00 P.M. No night wind stirred the unseen branches overhead. Fourteen hundred dead and wounded lay in the brush. Price had never witnessed such fighting. Hamilton agreed: "I never saw a hotter or more destructive engagement."

"Profoundly disappointed at hearing nothing from the forces on the Burnsville Road, and not knowing what to expect," Rosecrans wrote in his *Official Report*, "it became my duty to make dispositions for the battle next morning as if we were alone." He did not dare to divide his force by sending Stanley down the Jacinto Road to Barnet's, and then east and north to block the Fulton Road.

Because Hamilton's division had borne the brunt of the fighting,

Rosecrans withdrew it to the rear, in the next field below, from which place it could be moved to the right and through the woods against the enemy's left. Ammunition was replenished; Stanley's batteries, which had been in reserve, were posted on commanding ground in a field next to the hospital; and a new infantry line developed. When Surgeon Campbell's field hospital was filled, a second was opened. In the calm night, with no breath of air stirring, the candle flames scarcely wavered as Dr. Campbell, in blood-spattered apron, piled up a grisly stack of amputated arms and legs.

At 10:30 P.M., twenty-one hours after Grant's dispatch telling of Antietam reached Rosecrans, Rosecrans sent a report of the battle down the vedettes to Grant: "We met the enemy in force. . . . The engagement lasted several hours. Firing was very heavy. You must attack in the morning and *in force.* The ground is horrid, unknown to us, and no room for development. . . . Push in onto them until we can have time to do something. We will try to get a position on our right which will take Iuka." At the same time, he ordered a reconnoitering party to search for a way across the swampy ground which skirted the field to his east, and to examine the heights beyond with a view to their occupation by his artillery.

The positive tone of this order to his superior might have been regarded as insubordinate and used as a basis for misunderstanding to come. It might also reasonably have been interpreted as good advice from one leader in a joint movement to the other, with whom he was on a friendly basis and who had failed to put in his appearance, on how to get out of a mess.

"Not one wink of sleep visited my eyes," Rosecrans wrote to Annie. Throughout the night he toured the front. In the blackness he heard Confederates "making great noises." They chopped, drove stakes. Someone cried: "Fall in there." Men trudged. Rosecrans surmised that troops were taking new positions. At midnight, teamsters shouted and slapped leather on horses' rumps. "Gee-up!"—and heavy wagons creaked through the darkness. Price is looking to the safety of his train, Rosecrans figured, as the sounds tapered off toward the southeast. He thought, too, that artillery was being posted along the height he hoped to occupy. The Union reconnoitering party had not returned. No news arrived from Grant or Ord. Rosecrans felt "great uneasiness," as he later said.

At 3:30 A.M., ambulance or artillery drivers, evidently anxious and in haste, could be heard moving vehicles. Was Price changing positions or retreating? Rosecrans issued orders to rouse the men, give them breakfast, and make ready to move at daylight. Stanley would lead a pursuit.

Morning's first gray showed the forest ahead empty, and soon after dawn, reports told Rosecrans that Price had withdrawn to a line closer to Iuka. Federal skirmishers probed and, meeting no resistance, pushed forward. Rosecrans ordered a general advance. A civilian bearing a flag of truce met Colonel John M. Fuller, who led Stanley's column. The citizens wished to surrender. The Confederates, he said, were in trenches previously dug by the Union army. As Stanley entered the outskirts of the town, a handful of stragglers from Price's rear guard fired a few shots, and were quickly scattered by musketry and artillery. Rosecrans knew then that Price was not merely changing positions, he was retreating.

Immediately, he ordered all his cavalry, a regiment and a half, to move in on their flank down the Fulton Road. Stanley's division was to follow with all possible dispatch. Hamilton, coming up behind Stanley, was to face about, march back to the forks of the road, and taking the Tuscumbia Road, to fall on the enemy's flank.

At 7:00 A.M., Rosecrans sent a report of the battle down the vedette line to Grant, and at 8:45 and again at 9:45, his courier galloped directly to Burnsville to report that the "rebels left their sick and wounded," at this place and were retreating "with all possible speed." "Stanley follows them directly, and Hamilton endeavors to cut them off from the Bay Springs Road. The men double-quick with great alacrity. . . . Please order hospital stores and attendants for 500 sick and wounded." The dispatch asked bluntly: "Why did you not attack this morning?" Ord endorsed this dispatch afterward: "We didn't hear any sounds of the battle last P.M."

Colonel Fuller, who had joined Rosecrans, saw Ord's forces approaching from the west sometime later "with drums beating and banners flying," and he heard Rosecrans ask Ord: "Why did you not come to me in accordance with our mutual understanding? Why did you leave me in the lurch?" Ord pulled a piece of paper from his pocket and handed it silently to Rosecrans. It was Grant's order to postpone the attack.

Probably no battle of the war showed a higher percentage of casualties to numbers engaged. Rosecrans lost 141 killed, 613 wounded, and 36 missing—790 in all. Of these, nearly 700 were in Hamilton's division. Price reported 86 killed and 408 wounded, but this figure was inaccurate, for Rosecrans' provost marshal certified that he buried 265 Confederates. An additional 120 died in the hospital. Captured were 342 wounded and 361 unwounded. Price retreated with an estimated 350 additional wounded in his wagons. His total losses and casualties without duplication were 1,438.

Even before the battle, Price had planned to evacuate Iuka. On the night of the 18th, as he had awaited Ord's attack, he read Bragg's order to hurry to Nashville. Later, after midnight, Van Dorn's order directed him to rendezvous in Rienzi for an assault on Corinth. Price promptly ordered his troops to load wagons, and to prepare to move toward Baldwyn at daylight of the 20th. Rosecrans' afternoon attack of the 19th interrupted but did not halt these plans, and so, with the Fulton Road open, Price retreated, sending his trains ahead during the night and following with his army shortly before sunrise, marching toward Marietta Springs and Baldwyn, with Hamilton and Stanley pursuing.

Rosecrans waited for Grant in Iuka. Near noon, he "was startled by the sound of music," and, looking up, he beheld the head of General Grant's column entering Iuka. Except for the visit by Lagow and Dickey, this was the first contact he had had with Grant in more than thirty hours. Neither then nor later did Grant discuss the failure of the left wing to co-operate with Rosecrans. Grant said nothing about the fact that he had changed the plan. "No explanation was then or subsequently given," Rosecrans told the Committee on the Conduct of the War, "of the cause which prevented that column from attacking the enemy in front the day before, save that they did not hear our guns."

Grant now assumed command and ordered a brigade to take charge of captured stores and hospitals. In his *Report,* he said: "This was the first I knew of the Fulton Road being left open to the enemy for their escape." He ordered Rosecrans to "pursue the enemy as far as you think pursuit will be likely to result in any benefit to us or injury to them." He and Rosecrans went down the Fulton Road together for several miles, and Grant's examination of the country confirmed Rosecrans' good judgment in not dividing his forces on the roads the day before. When Grant turned back, Rosecrans galloped ahead and overtook Stanley's infantry.

Through daylight of the 20th, Stanley and Hamilton followed Price, his line of retreat marked by castoff clothing, equipment, ammunition, weapons, and supplies. By nightfall, Rosecrans observed, the pursuers were fatigued, out of rations and ammunition—in country which reconnaissance showed was destitute. Hamilton had chased the enemy fifteen miles, until his men were "worn out with labor and fighting and famished for want of food." He discontinued the pursuit "only when the powers of nature were exhausted."

Morning convinced Rosecrans that he had reached the point, mentioned by Grant, where further pursuit would result in no "benefit to us or injury to them," and so, with Grant's approval, he halted the chase. He guessed that Price would push ahead to Bay Springs, and there entrain for Tupelo, where he could unite with Van Dorn and replenish his supplies. He returned to Jacinto on the 22nd.

He reported to Grant the next afternoon that "only two regiments of Price's troops had reached the railroad last evening. Rear guard at least stayed at Bay Springs yesterday. Country all clear and quiet to 4 miles below Blackland and west to the Hatchie. Shall put a brigade of Stanley's division at Rienzi tomorrow. . . . Anxiously await news from you. Oh that Corinth could be left to take care of itself!"

Captain Goddard telegraphed Annie that her husband was alive; and, on his return, Rosecrans himself wrote to her: "The failure of proper co-operation unfortunately lost us the capture of Price and his entire army, which would have been inevitable had the attack from the west side been duly made. We accomplished our task, but the failure of the attack from the west to come up on time brought all the forces in our direction, and prevented us from attaining the point we most desired on the evening of the 19th."

For both Grant and Rosecrans, later events proved that Iuka was more than a brief, sanguinary battle. Questions were asked: Why did Rosecrans leave the Fulton road uncovered? Why did Grant modify the plan? Having done so, why did he fail to inform Rosecrans, or if he notified Rosecrans what happened to his message? Why did Grant stand by during the fight? Charges and countercharges were made by the troops, generals, newspaper correspondents, and the public. The aftermath of Iuka produced a lifetime of bad blood between Grant and Rosecrans.

What had Grant been doing on the left wing? While Ord and Ross took positions before Burnsville, Grant remained there with about 900 of Ord's men. In 1862, as now, the railroad depot was the principal building of Burnsville and Grant made his headquarters there for two days. From evening of the 18th, through the whole of the 19th, and into morning of the 20th, Grant's headquarters seem to have taken small interest or part in the pincer operation. It is likely that they were preoccupied with other business.

Sometime before midnight on the 18th, a Cairo dispatch arrived, telling Grant of a battle near Sharpsburg on the 16th. This was Antietam, in which McClellan stopped Lee. The dispatch erroneously transformed a drawn fight into an overwhelming victory: "Longstreet and his entire division prisoners. General Hill killed. Entire army of Virginia destroyed, Burnside having reoccupied Harper's Ferry and cut off retreat. . . . Latest advices say entire rebel army must be captured or killed, as Potomac is rising and our forces pressing the enemy continually."

Grant directed Ord to have this dispatch read next morning to his troops, and sent a copy of it down the vedette line to Rosecrans. At midnight, with Grant's permission, Ord sent a dispatch to Colonel M. D. Leggett, who commanded this advance, asking him to convey the news to Price: "I think this battle decides the war finally, and that upon being satisfied of its truth General Price or whoever commands here will avoid useless bloodshed and lay down his arms. There is not the slighest doubt of the truth of the dispatch in my mind."

In spite of the fact that Ord signed this dispatch the scheme to get Price to surrender was not his but Grant's. Colonel Arthur Ducat later told Rosecrans as much:

I was Senior officer to Gen. Ord,—a good, brave and competent soldier,—who was in command of Grant's principal column. I know something of the internal workings of matters from Corinth down to Iuka, and the foolish halt at Burnsville, which was none of Ord's fault. Ord told me of Grant's proposition to send in the despatch to Price, informing him of the battle of Antietam and the defeat of the Confederate forces, asking for his surrender. Ord said, "Ducat, what do you think of it?" I remarked, "Why should Price surrender when he can run; and if this despatch goes in, he will get out if he can, because it gives him time. The thing to do is to attack him now."

Under a flag of truce, Leggett contacted the colonel commanding the Confederate troops to his front. He in turn bore Ord's message to Price, who considered the surrender proposal, and finally sent it back by the same time-consuming procedure. The *Records* do not say when this sequence ended. But if it began at midnight, Price's answer probably did not reach Grant's headquarters until at least 10:00 A.M. The distance each way was some eight miles, and the night was without moonlight, so that the Union orderly and Confederate colonel delivering the message to Price picked their way through the dark. The message changed hands at least ten times, and the formalities for two flags of truce had to be arranged. Finally, reporter "Eno"—an obvious pseudonym—of the Cincinnati *Gazette* charged, in his account published immediately after the battle, that Price held up his answer for six hours, immobilizing Grant, while he himself prepared to retreat. "Eno" observed that Price's answer arrived late in the afternoon. Price replied that "if the facts were as stated they would only move him and his soldiers to great exertions in behalf of their country, and that neither he nor they will ever lay down their arms—as humanely suggested by General Ord—until the independence of the Confederate States shall have been acknowledged by the United States." Price called the victories "pretended," and Ord's demand "insolent."

Apparently Grant was not proud of this surrender proposal. He did not mention the episode in his *Official Reports* or in his *Memoirs.*

Even after Price answered, through the remainder of the 19th and the morning of the 20th, Grant apparently was not greatly concerned about Rosecrans. Grant still may have thought, in spite of Price's truculence, that Lee's supposed annihilation would end hostilities. Prior to 9:00 A.M., Ord shared some responsibility with

Grant. But at that time, oddly enough, with the pincer movement in progress, Grant sent Ord on a reconnaissance toward Corinth. Ord reconnoitered until 3:00 P.M., and did not return to Burnsville until 4:00.

Throughout the day, no one at Grant's headquarters appears to have checked weather, wind, or road conditions, or followed Rosecrans' advance on the map. Colonel Ducat, at Burnsville at least part of the time, considered it "most extraordinary" that Grant failed to follow the head of Rosecrans' column, although "it was none of my business." It is obvious from a check on his arrival times that Rosecrans calculated his advance by standard infantry pace.

Later, Grant claimed that an adverse wind prevented his hearing Rosecrans' guns, and Ord supported the statement, saying: "The wind freshly blowing from us in the direction of Iuka during the whole of the 19th, prevented our hearing the guns and cooperating with General Rosecrans."

Yet with the wind toward him, Colonel Dubois, who was guarding the front from Jacinto to Rienzi, heard the guns, fifteen miles on a direct line from Iuka. And with the wind blowing away from them, McArthur's men, watching the railroad, at Ord's extreme left, heard them. Concern may render perception acute and discriminating. Grant's headquarters and most of the right wing apparently were not engrossedly concerned, alert. Ord's statement was obviously sincere and entirely credible, nevertheless it offers a reason only for the failure of the plan as amended.

Other indications of lack of alertness are not wanting. Colonel Lagow signed an order for Grant—an unusual procedure—and at noon, Lagow and Dickey, without orders and on their own initiative, had wandered to the right to see what was happening to Rosecrans. More significant probably was the fact that after the report of the false victory, for some thirty hours between that time and Grant's arrival in Iuka, Grant's headquarters sent no messages down the vedette line to Rosecrans.

At 4:00 P.M., as Hamilton collided with Price, Grant ordered Ord to move to within four miles of Iuka. At sundown, however, Ord was still with Grant at Burnsville. At 11:30 P.M., at the head of his column four miles from Iuka, Ord said: "Ducat, this is too bad." Ducat agreed: "Let us ride in and get permission to go forward at daylight," and the two then returned to Burnsville where they received Grant's permission.

As he marched at dawn, Ord heard the sound of two guns. It was Stanley at Iuka, scattering Price's stragglers with artillery. Now for the first time Ord and Ducat knew that Rosecrans had been engaged. That morning, at least, within four miles, cannon fire was audible. Had Ord been within that distance the afternoon before, prepared either to attack or to support Rosecrans' initial attack, he might have heard the fighting and seen the smoke which Ross described.

Ord now told Ducat to send a dispatch to McArthur to move up and attack. Ducat was to take Grant's bodyguard, the only cavalry with Ord, and feel the enemy. He met no resistance, and finding the Confederate earthworks evacuated, sent a dispatch to Ord to come forward. The whole column entered Iuka.

Several hours later, Grant followed. At 8:35 A.M. on the 20th, when Rosecrans' dispatch of 10:30 P.M. arrived, he first learned of the battle. Grant told Ord: "Get your troops up and attack as soon as possible. Rosecrans had two hours' fighting last night, and now this morning again, and unless you can create a diversion in his favor, he may find his hands full."

By this time, Ord had joined Rosecrans, Price had "skedaddled," and Colonels Lagow and Dickey, who had wandered all night in the woods, had reached Burnsville.

Soon after Grant's dispatch to Ord, Colonel Hillyer reported that Price was in full retreat. Grant later stated that on receiving this news he immediately set out for Iuka.

News of Iuka first appeared in the Cincinnati papers of September 29. The *Commercial* reported:

Great victory against Confederates, and appeared that they were beaten and surrounded. Union forces waited for morning to complete the job, but by that time the enemy had run off in the night.

The question among our troops then arose: how did the enemy get away? Why did not our forces on the Burnside [sic] Road engage them in the rear during the battle, and thus entirely capture them? You may slightly, but not fully, imagine the bitter curses that went up from our subordinate officers and men when they learned that *Hellish Whiskey* was the whole cause. And yet, when we contemplated that "drunkenness in high places" prevented us from capturing General Price with his twenty-three thousand men, which could have been easily done, the enthusiasm of victory was cooled very much indeed.

When Sylvester Rosecrans, now auxiliary Catholic Bishop of Cincinnati, read the story, he wrote to Annie: "The awful charge made against Grant in today's *Commercial* is not so surprising as it is disgusting. I am afraid it is true."

On October 9, the *Commercial* was still critical: "It was a pity that Grant did not attack on time to enable Rosecrans to bag Price. Price would have been splendidly entrapped if someone had not blundered. As it was, it was a wonder he did not crush Rosecrans' whole command."

"Eno" of the Cincinnati *Gazette,* who remained with the Union left from the 17th to the 21st, described Grant's operations during the four days:

Rosecrans marched on Tuesday with most of his division: the left wing marched on Wednesday. A drenching rain fell the greater part of that day, but I never saw troops march with more ease and enthusiasm. There was not a bit of straggling. About two or three o'clock, the Second Division halted for the night a few miles west of Byrnesville [sic]—it was said to allow Rosencrans [sic] time to gain on Price's left. On Thursday it proceeded to Byrnesville, where the entire left wing was encamped. This was seven miles from Iuka. We went into camp at three o'clock and rested. On Friday morning the entire force was in line to march into battle. The wagons were ordered to remain in the rear, and the men to carry thirty rounds of ammunition about their persons. While in line, a dispatch was read announcing McClellan's great victory in Maryland. Upon hearing this, cheer after cheer rent the air. Never were troops in better condition for battle, and yet, although the enemy was in our grasp almost, only a few miles away, we reluctantly heard the order to stack arms, and make detail for picket guard, which we knew meant that we would lie there for some hours at least.

All that clear, bright day we were condemned to be inactive. Gen. Grant sent in a flag of truce to demand a surrender, but that wary old traitor Price detained it six hours, and then sent it back with a refusal. It was now late in the afternoon, and by the time the troops could get in position and in motion it was nearly sundown. All the left wing advanced about two or three miles and encamped, except the Eighty-first Ohio and Second Iowa which remained at Byrnesville [sic] with Gen. Grant.

Meanwhile, "oblivious of the flag of truce business, and solely intent on meeting and fighting the enemy," Rosecrans fought the battle of Iuka.

On Friday evening, while the battle was raging, the advanced portion of the left wing was quietly going into camp, five miles distant, all unconscious of the proximity of a battle. They could not hear the musketry. and the cannonading was either very inconsiderable or none at all, so close were the contending armies. On Saturday morning they formed in line of battle and sent forward skirmishers, who captured some of Price's pickets who had not been called in.

The left wing returned to Burnsville on Saturday evening, and to Corinth on Sunday evening, "a disappointed body of troops," yet, "Eno" continued, "remarkably free from grumbling or criticism. Indeed it is a characteristic of tried troops that they do not grumble. They know their rights, of course, and are not imposed upon with impunity but they do not complain at incapacity or blundering, as the raw troops they were a year ago would have done. Instead they hold in supreme contempt the man who fails to do the best thing with them, be he Corporal or Major-General."

Eno then narrated some "facts" which "in part" explained the inactivity of the left wing. Rosecrans had dispatched Grant that he was twenty-four hours late in starting Friday and asked Grant to detain Price. Grant thereupon sent out the flag of truce, which Price detained

. . . while he could complete his preparations. It is said that Gen. Ord urged that the left wing should take up a position nearer, at any rate, but Gen. Grant overruled him, assuring him that very soon we could advance and completely surround Price.

In the meantime the gallant Rosencrans was using all diligence, and with his eager army had actually marched twenty miles on Friday, before he fought with so much gallantry. As it is, it appears that only a want of proper knowledge of Rosencrans' position, prevented the co-operation which would have insured the capture of Price. . . . It may be that he will catch the rebels; but we have little hope of such a success. But with what he has already done "Old Rosy" has well earned the additional star which is said to have been recently conferred upon him.

Grant wrote two reports of Iuka. The first, dated September 20, 1862, compliments Rosecrans: "I cannot speak too highly of the energy and skill displayed by General Rosecrans in the attack, and of the endurance of the troops under him. General Ord's command showed untiring zeal, but the direction taken by the enemy prevented them taking the active part they desired."

The second was dated October 22, three weeks after Rosecrans' report, and after the Cincinnati newspapers had reached Grant. Now Grant withheld all compliment from Rosecrans: "If it was the object of the enemy to make their way into Kentucky, they were defeated in that; if to hold their position until Van Dorn could come up on the southwest of Corinth and make a simultaneous attack, they were defeated in that. Our only defeat was in not capturing the entire army or destroying it as I had hoped to do. It was a part of General Hamilton's command that did the fighting, directed entirely by that cool and deserving officer." This was a less than accurate statement.

This second report remained "buried" for more than eighteen months, and Rosecrans, without access to it, could not answer. Later in his *Sketch* he referred angrily to it:

That the noise of our battle was heard by Col. Du Bois more than fifteen miles from us in a strait [sic] line over a rolling forest country; that our battle field was not more than five or six miles from our main column on the Rail Road; that our firing was heard by Gen'l McArthur's command on the extreme left of the troops there; are facts well-known to many living witnesses . . . attested by ample documentary evidence —there is not the shadow of reasonable doubt. That they should have been ignored or obscured by Gen'l. Grant under the impulse of instinctive selfishness, and by his sycophant biographer, Badeau, and others who sought to profit by him, or repeated carelessly after these—only shows that there was something more than ordinary to cover up in the conduct of Gen'l. Grant on that occasion. This is further evidenced by the publication in the Chicago *Tribune* and New York *Herald* more than eighteen months after the battle, of Grant's report of the Battle of Iuka, the authenticity of which is attested by the very simplicity of its self-contradictory statements and the almost painful admixture of truth and falsehood unskillfully put together to conceal the truth which it fears to state or deny. . . .

What but a hazy consciousness that there was some "damned spot that would not out" in that Iuka record could have drawn from its resting place this Report eighteen months after its burial and when all its untruthfulness was unthought of by those whom it had wronged and who were absorbed in their perilous duties of fighting the battles of their country?

But the most striking act in this history of falsification is this: When Gen'l. Rosecrans gave his testimony before the Committee on the Conduct of the War in April 1865, he requested Senator Wade to secure and have printed with his (Gen'l. R's) account an authenticated copy of Gen'l. Grant's Report of the Battle of Iuka. In the Committee's printed Reports appears Senator Wade's letter asking for this copy and Mr. Stanton's reply that he transmits the same "herewith," and following these copies of the Report of Gen'ls. Ord, Ross, McKean and other subordinates whose commands participated in the *movements* but *not in the battle*, omitting the entire report of Gen'l. Rosecrans, the *only subordinate who did participate* in it, and omitting *Gen'l. Grant's*, the only one asked for by Senator Wade. Why was such a fraudulent statement made by the Secretary of War? Or if that official supposed that the entire Report was enclosed, who deceived him, or abstracted it? And for what purpose? Can there be any doubt that, by whomsoever done, the design was to prevent the public from knowing what Grant actually did say in his Report of the Battle of Iuka?

The record would have been better served if Rosecrans had written plainly and not in riddles.

Unfortunately for Grant's reputation for accurate and impartial reporting, a comparison of Grant's several reports with each other and with the reports of his subordinates and the correspondence in the *Official Records,* and of all this material with the *Memoirs* provides some basis for Rosecrans' indictment.

The government printed *Official Records* dealing with Iuka and Corinth did not appear until 1887. But in 1885, Grant's *Personal Memoirs* appeared. He declared in them that: "I was disappointed at the result of the battle of Iuka—but I had so high an opinion of General Rosecrans that I found no fault at the time." In the *Memoirs* were many statements that contradicted other testimony:

First: "I remained at Burnsville . . . and communicated with my two wings by courier." Insofar as this statement suggests that Grant communicated with Rosecrans, it is misleading and inaccurate. Unless both the original dispatches and the copies were lost, Grant sent a dispatch down the courier line at 6:45 P.M. on September 18; and around midnight the false report of Lee's destruction. After Grant's 6:45 P.M. dispatch, except for this report, Rosecrans received no more communications from Grant via the courier or any other line for some 30 hours.

Second: "I was very much disappointed at receiving a dispatch from Rosecrans after midnight from Jacinto . . . saying that some of his command had been delayed. . . . However, he would still be at Iuka by two o'clock the next day. I did not believe this possible because of the distance and the condition of the roads, which was bad." Yet Surgeon Campbell had said in his *Official Report:* "On the 19th the roads were in splendid order, hard and entirely free from dust. The men marched with ease and in fine order." Grant added: "Besides, troops after a forced march are not in a good condition to fight," but he knew as he wrote that eighteen or twenty miles in cool weather did not constitute a difficult march.

Third: "I immediately sent Ord a copy of Rosecrans' dispatch." Ord reported "immediately" occurred fourteen hours later.

Fourth: "A couple of hours before dark on the 19th Rosecrans arrived with the head of his column at Barnet's." On September 19, 1862, darkness came at 6:25. At 12:40, Rosecrans reported to Grant from Barnet's that he had "reached here at 12." The *Memoirs,* therefore, subtract between four and four and a half hours from a critical afternoon.

Fifth: "After the engagement Rosecrans sent me a dispatch announcing the result. This was brought by a courier. There was no road between Burnsville and the position then occupied by Rosecrans and the country was impossible for a man on horseback. This made it a late hour of the night before I learned of the battle that had taken place in the afternoon." And speaking of the same lack of direct access, in his report of October 22, 1862: "For this reason his communication was not received until after the engagement. I did not *hear* of the engagement, however, until next day, although the following dispatch [Rosecrans' 10:30 P.M. dispatch of September 19] had been promptly forwarded. *This dispatch was received at 8:35 a.m.* [September 20th]." (Italics mine.) Clearly 8:35 A.M. is not "a late hour of the night." Here Grant subtracts some eight hours.

Sixth: "I at once notified Ord of the fact and ordered him to attack early in the morning." If Grant ordered Ord to attack "at once" after learning of the Rosecrans battle of the 19th, but did not learn of the battle until 8:35 A.M. on the 20th, could he order

Ord to attack at a future hour, but "early in the morning"? Ord reports no such orders, and his account makes it clear that he went into Iuka on his own initiative. Grant did order Ord to attack at 8:35.

Seventh: "Ord also went in according to orders, without hearing a gun from the south of town but supposing the troops coming up from the southwest must be up by that time." Grant wrote this in 1884, although he had read Ord's *Report*—by his own statement he sent it in with his own—in which Ord stated, "The next morning at 8 o'clock, *hearing heavy guns in front of us,* I moved rapidly into Iuka. The guns heard that morning were first heard by us." Perhaps Grant had forgotten by the 1880's that on October 22, 1862, he himself had written: "The statement that the engagement had commenced again in the morning was on the strength of hearing artillery. Ord, hearing the same, however, pushed on *without awaiting orders.*"

Eighth: "Rosecrans, however, had put no troops upon the Fulton Road, and the enemy had taken advantage of this neglect and retreated by that road during the night." Yet in his *Report* of October 22, 1862, Grant approved Rosecrans' decision not to put troops on the Fulton Road: "A partial examination of the country afterward convinced me that troops moving in separate columns by the routes suggested could not support each other until they arrived near Iuka."

Ninth: "Word was soon brought to me that our troops were in Iuka. I immediately rode into town." Burnsville is eight miles from Iuka. Had Grant hurried forward at 8:35 A.M., he could have been in Iuka long before midmorning instead of near noon. The haste exists in the record, not in the events.

Tenth: "[I] found that the enemy was not being pursued even by the cavalry"; and "I ordered pursuit by the whole of Rosecrans' command." The first contradicts Grant's *Report*: "I immediately proceeded to Iuka, found that the enemy had left during the night. *Generals Stanley and Hamilton were in pursuit.*" (Italics mine.) The second, if true, was an empty gesture, because the whole of Rosecrans' command had been in pursuit from four to six hours before Grant arrived. Grant also said that Rosecrans "followed only a few miles after I left him and then went into camp, and the pursuit was continued no farther." Grant's own *Report* asserts that

he had ridden south from Iuka with Rosecrans, leaving him somewhere near the battlefield. At 1:00 A.M. on the 21st—the next
morning—Rosecrans reported to Grant from Jacinto, Mississippi,
twenty-three miles from Iuka by the roads he had taken. During
the day he reported again. The pursuers were fanning out beyond
Jacinto. Grant makes it seem that Rosecrans needlessly, arbitrarily,
and culpably called off the pursuit. Yet Hamilton says explicitly
that the "pursuit was discontinued only when the powers of nature
were exhausted." Hamilton's testimony has unique value—he was
as unfriendly to Rosecrans as he was friendly to Grant.

It is certain that Grant's failure to co-operate at Iuka with Rosecrans did not represent an effort on his part to embarrass Rosecrans. Their relations were friendly through the Iuka episode, and
had the joint plan proved wholly successful, the major credit for a
victory would have gone to Commander-in-Chief Grant. Inasmuch
as the *Commercial* hinted at the charge, Bishop Rosecrans put it
into writing, and local tradition at Iuka today maintains that
Grant lay drunk in the Burnsville depot while Rosecrans fought
Price, the question merits examination. Grant's biographer William Hesseltine writes: "This [Iuka] seems to be the only place
where an issue [concerning Grant's incapacity for active command
because of drink] could arise. . . . Iuka has had little study."

If Grant was drunk, his conduct would not have been excep-
tional in his army, for "hellish rum" was all too popular. The Cincinnati *Gazette* correspondent was "appalled at the ravages of
whiskey among Grant's officers." Reporter Edward Betty wrote
that Hamilton's staff officers were rarely free from the influences
of liquor. "Whiskey, O Whiskey!" sighed Boyd at Memphis three
months later. "Drunk men staggered in all the streets. The men
who had fought their way from Donelson to Corinth now surrendered to Genl. *Intoxication*." And a month earlier the Nashville *Dispatch* had quoted the Cincinnati *Times* correspondent as
saying that the "ravages of whiskey" had been so "terrible" among
the officers of Grant's department that he was "scarcely able to
recognize many men whom he had met a year ago—so awfully had
a free use of the bottle distorted their features. . . . It is a pity that
some means cannot be devised to prevent officers from unfitting
themselves for duty by tippling." There may have been drinking
in the Iuka depot before the surrender proposal was sent to Price.

Perhaps the prospect of the war's speedy ending called for jubilation and the bottle. If so, would Grant indulge? Not if Mrs. Grant or Rawlins had been present; both were dedicated to keeping Grant sober. But Mrs. Grant was not at Burnsville, and Rawlins was in Corinth.

The argument for Grant's incapacity from drink rests on rumors, his demonstrated weakness, the absence of Mrs. Grant and Rawlins, the "foolish halt," the unrealistic surrender scheme, the silence from his headquarters, the relaxation of vigilance, his sending Ord away, Lagow's signing an order—although this did not necessarily mean that Grant hadn't given it—Lagow's and Dickey's wandering off on their own, and on Grant's apparent failure to keep track of weather, wind, road conditions, and Rosecrans' movements.

Direct testimony by a reliable witness is not available. Ord and Ducat, who were intermittently with him, did not report him drunk. Years later, in a personal letter to Rosecrans, Ducat, who disliked Grant intensely, spoke scornfully of his generalship. But he did not charge him with intoxication. Nor at any time did Rosecrans. Bishop Rosecrans may have had news from Corinth before he made his statement. If the newspaper story could reach Cincinnati, so could a telegram or letter. Still the reports could have been based only on Grant's reputation, not on evidence.

The same facts may suggest not so much insobriety as failure to assess a military crisis correctly, a difficulty Grant had demonstrated before at Shiloh and would again demonstrate at Cold Harbor. Unfortunately, so far as Rosecrans' future relations with him are concerned, it makes little difference which interpretation is accepted. Grant was insecure because of his old record and the aftermath of Shiloh. The *Memoirs* amply support the point. Now he was in trouble again. The old charges would be made, or at least hinted at. Newspapers would praise Rosecrans, who fought the battle, and by inference at least, Grant would be given a less flattering role in the accounts. And he did have a talkative subordinate. Such a one is always dangerous.

Naturally Rosecrans was indignant—and reticence was not one of his virtues. At this juncture, said Whitelaw Reid, Rosecrans "could not omit the opportunity to do himself an injury," and not only remarked in his report that he was "profoundly disappointed at hearing nothing from the forces on the Burnsville Road," but "he was even more explicit elsewhere." Such talk threatened Grant, fear begat dislike, and the personal fight was on. Now Stanton had another ally.

As for Grant's slanting his reports to his own and his friends' advantage, and to Rosecrans' disadvantage, such muddying of truth is fairly routine in the *Official Records* and could be shrugged off, were it not that the resultant injury to the personal and military reputation of Rosecrans persists to this day. The inaccuracies of the *Memoirs* are equally understandable. They were written in the eighteen-eighties by a mortally ill man, fighting magnificently, but still smarting from the resounding thwacks of Rosecrans, then Congressman, in a House debate over a "back-pay" bill that was of profound importance to Grant. Unfortunately, for Rosecrans at least, the *Memoirs* are still widely read and highly regarded.

An intriguingly simple and generally accepted account of Iuka holds that Rosecrans did not follow orders, left the Fulton road open (which he did), allowed Price to escape, and thus deprived Grant of the full fruits of a victory.

The truth seems to be that when Rosecrans found that to divide his force was hazardous, to eliminate the risk of being beaten in detail he used good judgment and left the Fulton Road open, knowing that he could occupy it safely over the Bay Springs Road. With Grant attacking, the Bay Springs Road should have been open. But Grant failed to attack, failed to hold Price north of Iuka, and Rosecrans could not cross on the Bay Springs Road. Grant might have destroyed Price. Perryville was to prove that part of Buell's army could match Bragg. In the Mississippi region the weaker Confederate armies had become divided, and for a few days were beyond effective supporting distance of each other. With Price beaten, Van Dorn was no match for Grant, and while Buell held Bragg, the way lay open to seize Chattanooga and Vicksburg, both lightly defended, and to attack Mobile from the rear. As after the siege of Corinth, when by energetic pursuit Halleck, with double his numbers, might have destroyed Beauregard, a great opportunity was lost.

Confederate General Maury, who commanded a division under Price, made a simple assessment of the battle: "Rosecrans struck us a heavy blow. Grant failed to cooperate, fortunately, and we got back to Tupelo considerably worsted."

Whatever the justice of the charges by either man, the failure to trap Price was tragic from a Northern point of view. Union soldiers suffered and died for less than their sacrifices should have bought. Ten days later when Boyd walked to the battlefield, he found about forty men buried in one grave "besides numerous other graves scattered all through the woods. . . . Saw many of the enemies' [sic] dead lying around not more than half covered. The ground in many places was *white* as snow with *creeping worms.* The darkness of the forest and the terrible mortality made it one of the most *horrible* places I was ever in."

Seven

CORINTH

Price's retreat ended fears that he might cross the Tennessee and reinforce Bragg. He was moving to join Van Dorn, and to threaten Corinth. Corinth lay exposed and difficult to hold. The Memphis and Charleston railroad westward, open to frequent cavalry raids, lay abandoned from Chewalla to Memphis. Eastward from Iuka, it lay unguarded and after Granger withdrew to reinforce Buell, Rosecrans lacked force to police it.

Rosecrans posted Stanley and Hamilton, on their return, in a great arc from Rienzi to Jacinto, thus covering the town's southwest approaches. As long as Van Dorn's objective remained obscure, Rosecrans had no choice but to disperse his force. Van Dorn hoped to keep Rosecrans confused and veering, and to overwhelm Corinth before Union outposts at Iuka, Jacinto, and Rienzi could be hurried in.

On September 24 Grant drew his depleted department into a rough triangle and moved headquarters fifty-eight miles north to the greater security of Jackson, Tennessee. General Stephen A. Hurlbut remained at Bolivar and Sherman at Memphis, while Rosecrans held the Corinth salient. Grant wrote to Halleck that things seemed to be quiet so, "I shall go to St. Louis to confer with General Curtis."

As he left Corinth with Grant, Ord recommended to Rosecrans his chief of staff, thirty-year-old Colonel Arthur Ducat. Grant, who needed another engineer, had asked Ducat to become his inspector general, but he agreed to postpone his transfer until after the

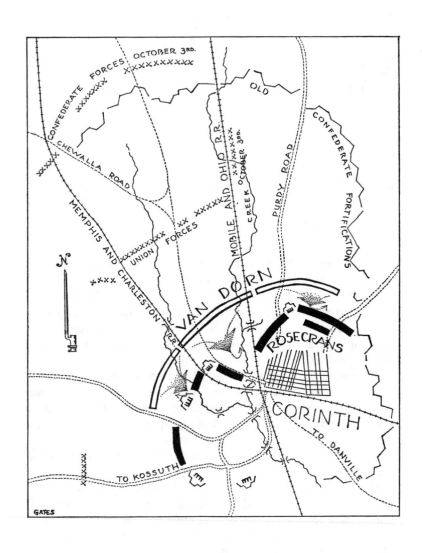

BATTLE OF CORINTH

October 3–4, 1862

Corinth battle when Rosecrans argued that his own need for Ducat was greater—the fortifications were incomplete, and Grant's staff had shipped all maps of Corinth and its environs to Jackson. Ducat professed to know "every rabbit track in that country."

Unlike Rosecrans, the Confederate leader Van Dorn knew the northwest approaches to Corinth well. He had served under Beauregard after Shiloh and had lived in Corinth during April and May. He knew its approaches, its defenses, its topography, and had supervised the construction of one of the roads, which he was to use for his assault of October 3. He had in his possession, moreover, accurate Confederate and Federal maps. His best map, showing the eastern approaches, was one made under Rosecrans' supervision, and had been captured at Iuka. Van Dorn knew little, however, about the new inner fortifications.

The weather turned extremely hot again after Rosecrans left Iuka. Yet work was pushed day and night, and from September 27 through the 30th, breastworks were completed from College Hill to the left. A weak segment, lacking rifle pits and continuity, still remained, extending from the Mobile and Ohio tracks to Battery Powell. Trees were felled for an abatis from Battery Robinett to the Mobile and Ohio tracks. Rosecrans organized contrabands, "shoals of men, women and children," into a colored engineers' corps, with squads of twenty-five and leaders from the line or Quartermaster's Corps.

Price reached Ripley on the 28th. Rosecrans telegraphed Grant at Columbus, Kentucky, for permission to adjust his outposts to the shifting threat by ordering Stanley westward to guard the Hatchie crossings as far north as Pocahontas, Tennessee.

Corinth was garrisoned by 15,000 men, comprising the divisions of McKean and Davies. Stanley and Hamilton, watching twelve to fifteen miles out, had about 6,000. In outposts or on scouting missions, there were another 2,500 cavalry troops. Not all were effectives; the Union force in the battle was estimated at about 18,000 men. Stanley's estimate of Van Dorn's strength as 40,000 was high. According to Maury, Breckinridge's 6,000 had been detached, and Price lost about 4,000, mostly stragglers, on the Iuka expedition. Van Dorn's field returns showed that he brought some 22,000 men into the battle.

Van Dorn marched rapidly from Ripley to Pocahontas, threatening Bolivar and Corinth with his cavalry, and feinting with his infantry toward Bolivar. When Grant returned from St. Louis on September 30, he telegraphed Halleck that he felt threatened at all points. Rosecrans, nevertheless, resolved to act upon the assumption that Corinth was Van Dorn's goal. Accordingly, near midnight on September 30, he ordered the troops at Iuka into Corinth. They arrived two days later, at about 10:00 P.M., and bivouacked two miles west. Simultaneously, Rosecrans drew in Stanley and Hamilton, summoned his outposts from Burnsville, Rienzi, and Danville, and ordered closer the brigade at Chewalla, strengthening it with another battery.

On October 1 Grant told Halleck: "It is now clear that Corinth is to be the point [of Van Dorn's objective], and that from the west or southwest. Price, Van Dorn, Villepigue, and Rust are together." Yet he sent no reinforcements to Rosecrans on the 1st or 2nd, though he knew also that neither Hurlbut nor McPherson could count on the railroads to bring them quickly to Corinth—Van Dorn would certainly cut Corinth's communications with Grant's district before he attacked. On the 2nd, Grant knew from telegraphic correspondence with Hurlbut that Van Dorn held the railroad at Grand Junction, thus severing Corinth from Bolivar; he learned further that he had ripped up the tracks six miles south of Bethel to block or delay reinforcements from that direction. When, at Grant's orders, McPherson finally moved at daylight on the 4th, instead of reaching Corinth at 7:00 A.M., as he easily might have done by rail, he arrived there some nine or ten hours later. He marched on foot the last seventeen miles.

By the 2nd, Van Dorn had almost completed a great half-circle around Corinth. He did not expect to surprise Rosecrans, with whose outposts he had been engaged for thirty-six hours. "I knew my antagonist," said Van Dorn to the Military Court of Inquiry investigating his conduct at Corinth, "—knew that he would avail himself of every resource in his power . . ." Earlier he told the same court that Corinth was the

"key to the whole position. Its strategic importance has been recognized by the enemy as well as by ourselves. I could have taken Memphis, but I could not have held it. . . . No important military result would have attended the capture. . . . The line of fortifications around Bolivar is intersected by the Hatchee River. . . . Besides, an advance upon it would expose both my flanks and rear to an attack from the forces at Corinth and Memphis. While Corinth was the strongest, it was the most salient point, and its capture was a condition precedent to the accomplishment of anything of importance in West Tennessee. The able and astute general who commanded at Corinth well understood the consequences which would have resulted from its fall."

And in his *Official Report* Van Dorn spoke in like vein: "The attack on Corinth was a military necessity, requiring prompt and vigorous action. It was being strengthened daily under that astute soldier General Rosecrans." Van Dorn spoke of the "more than equal activity and determined courage displayed by the enemy, commanded by one of the ablest generals of the United States Army, who threw all possible obstacles in our way that an active mind could suggest."

On October 2 Rosecrans sent a brigade ten miles northwest on the Chewalla road to observe and to take the first shock of attack. If assaulted, the brigade was to resist stiffly, forcing Van Dorn to disclose whether he meant to approach Corinth from the northeast, where the ground was open and the defenses were weakest, or go "north of us, strike the Mobile and Ohio road, and manoeuver us out of our position." Rosecrans himself felt certain that Van Dorn would not be so unwise as to send his army against Union forces behind strong defensive works.

His reasoning coincided with Van Dorn's. Van Dorn told General Bowen that he would not sacrifice his men against fortifications, and Bowen understood that it was Van Dorn's purpose to force Rosecrans to leave his entrenchments, and to fight the Confederates in the open field. Van Dorn himself asserted that he planned his attack carefully, and made it at points with which he was made entirely familiar by reason of his previous service at Corinth. He felt a tremendous need for haste.

With the battle plans completed, at 1:30 A.M. on the 3rd Rosecrans called a meeting of his division commanders. The generals rode through dusty moonlight to the Curlee mansion, received verbal orders, and left immediately for their new positions.

Hamilton was to march his 3,700 men north to a position between the Beauregard fortifications on the Purdy and Hamburg roads. Rosecrans called this a post of honor. He still thought that Van Dorn might circle farther east, so as to strike Corinth's most vulnerable point. Davies, with 3,204 effectives, would march two and a half miles northwest to form the center, with Hamilton on his right and McKean on his left. McKean's 5,315 men were already covering the western approaches, the Chewalla road, and the Memphis and Charleston tracks. The day before, Rosecrans had learned that not one but two good roads led northwest toward Chewalla. Most of Stanley's division was posted in reserve at the extreme left, west of the town, guarding the Kossuth road.

All night at headquarters two patent kerosene lamps blazed. The roads around Corinth's square bustled with shifting troops. Pulleys squealed a constant shrill complaint at the public well, for many private wells were dry. At the western edge of Corinth the intersecting tracks stretched to hairline thinness in the moonlight. Fifty-eight miles north, Grant lay at Jackson.

Through delayed orders, after 3:00 A.M. on the 3rd, Davies' division left Camp Montgomery, south of the town, to seek its new position. The men stumbled past old Confederate campsites as the moon paled, and the east lightened with dawn. Davies found Rosecrans still awake. Two and a half miles northwest, Davies took position near the old Confederate fortifications. The morning grew warm, and the men were hot and tired.

By shifting to new positions north and west of Corinth, Rosecrans hoped to prevent surprise, and to test by adequate resistance any attacking force. If the attack proved formidable, he would receive it behind the new inner line.

Northeast of Corinth, swamps alternated with hills, both heavily wooded. Occasional cleared fields stretched to the left of the tracks. Hamilton's division was posted in rolling land that fell off in front into heavily timbered swamp, so thicketed as to bar passage to infantry in numbers. Davies' right faced the same terrain, while his left lay on hilly ground. Two roads entered Corinth from the north, the Chewalla on the west and the Bolivar on the east. Except for the right center, the northern approaches were without natural defenses.

As the day warmed, a detail went to town and brought breakfast back. The men ate, listening to the firing of artillery northwest of Corinth.

The Confederates, too, had risen before sunrise, and marched along the south side of the Memphis and Charleston tracks from

Chewalla toward Corinth. Lovell's division led, Price followed. As he neared the outer works, Price turned left across the tracks, and formed in battle line opposite Davies and about 400 yards north of Beauregard's old fortifications.

On the 2nd, Van Dorn's advance had struck Oliver's brigade, ten miles out of Corinth on the Chewalla road. When Van Dorn attacked again, early on the 3rd, Oliver's resistance was insufficient to test his intention. Was Van Dorn actually attacking from the northwest, or feinting there, to slide around to the north and northeast? To compel an answer, Rosecrans ordered McArthur of McKean's brigade to reinforce Oliver. McArthur, a pug-nosed, red-faced, heavy-set man, who spoke with a Scotch burr, was a good fighter, drinker, and horseman. He reported from the front that the hill on which Oliver stood could test the advancing force. "Hold it for that purpose," Rosecrans said. By nine o'clock, although outflanked, McArthur was standing up to Van Dorn like a terrier fighting a wolf, instead of feeling him out as ordered. "McArthur's Scotch blood rose," Rosecrans remembered, "and he fought him with the stubborn ferocity of an action on the main line of battle instead of the resistance of a developing force."

Incorrectly assuming that McArthur was obeying orders, Rosecrans ordered Davies to reinforce him with two brigades. "I have already done so," Davies responded. By now Davies was concerned with the length and thinness of his line, which faced a massed army, and he reported to Rosecrans that he could not hold his position with the troops in his command. He was promised reinforcements, and therefore rushed in the last of his reserves.

Even before he reached his assigned position, Davies heard Oliver's artillery, and learning that he was withdrawing from Chewalla, sought Rosecrans' permission to advance a half-mile and occupy the old breastworks on the Chewalla road, thus supporting Oliver. "Do as you think best," Rosecrans replied, but in no event should he cease to touch his left upon McArthur's right. Shortly afterward, Rosecrans cautioned Davies not to let the enemy penetrate beyond the old Confederate breastworks, and to give heed to a bridle path running between the Columbus and Chewalla roads. Davies then formed his first battle line.

By 10:00 Union skirmishers had been driven back into the old breastworks, and the Confederates confronted Davies across an abatis of fallen timber, about four hundred yards wide. When McArthur withdrew, a gap remained between his right and Davies' left. Here Lovell attacked with three brigades. Rosecrans' concern for the bridle path proved proper. The 218 men with two guns covering it were pushed aside, as the Confederates poured over Davies' front and flanked his left. Within twenty minutes, the Union center abandoned the Beauregard line.

When Davies learned that his left had been driven a half mile, he ordered his First and Second brigades to form a battle line 1,000 yards to the rear of the old Confederate entrenchments, hoping to delay Van Dorn's advance until his own left, his Third brigade, could withdraw to the junction of the Chewalla and Columbus roads. Then he ordered his First and Second brigades to withdraw once more, about 800 yards, and join the Third at the road junction.

"Again I sent for reinforcements," Davies reported, "and determined to make my final stand at the white house, 950 yards back of the forks and 725 yards in front of Fort Robinett." Van Dorn had anticipated this withdrawal. By attacking Rosecrans' left and center, he sought to compel him to reinforce from his right. Van Dorn therefore held a portion of his own left in reserve, hidden in the woods north of Corinth, ready to fall on the weakened Union right at the critical moment. Rosecrans, too, kept his reserves well masked.

By noon of the 3rd, encouraged by their success, the Confederates determined to continue to drive against the center. The weather turned hot, about 94 degrees, and the men, who had marched since 2:00 A.M. and fought since 9:00, were so exhausted that many suffered sunstroke. Rosecrans concluded by 1:00 P.M. that Van Dorn would continue to assault the center, "where hopes had been given by our falling back." He dictated orders to bring Hamilton into the fight. He would trap Van Dorn in a great V. McKean was to withdraw until his right met Davies' left. Stanley was to move nearer town and close upon McKean, and Hamilton was to face toward Chewalla and move down his left until it touched Davies' right. Davies was to hold his ground firmly. When Davies had drawn Van Dorn in strongly, Hamilton would swing in on his flank and rear and close the day. Hamilton was "carefully instructed" regarding this movement. Timing was important. If

Davies retreated prematurely, Hamilton would not be in position. If Hamilton showed himself prematurely, his division would be imperiled. At 2:00 P.M., Rosecrans sent a circular to his commanders: "For fear of misunderstanding in relation to my orders, I wish it distinctly understood that the extreme position is not to be taken till driven to it."

By 1:00 P.M., Davies had withdrawn to the high ground to which Rosecrans had assigned him. Before him lay an open field, behind him a stand of timber. Swampy ground covered his right, and Batteries Robinett and Williams his left. From an elevation his artillery could sweep the open field and command the road approaches. While taking position, Davies listened for sounds of heavy fighting by Stanley or Hamilton. Pressure on his front was heavy. No sooner was Davies posted than Price burst from the woods in magnificent style, in columns by divisions. Without firing, the Confederates advanced at double-quick across the open field until within point-blank range of Davies. Then, deploying into line, they opened fire. At a signal, Davies' troops rose from the dry grass and poured in a return fire so deadly that Price reeled, broke, and fled. When the reformed lines attacked again, they were again repulsed with great slaughter, and the attackers fled across the open plain to the shelter of the woods. Price wrote: "Here the fighting was of unparalleled fierceness."

Once more Price reformed and advanced, to be raked by artillery fire and musketry. McKean had closed on Davies' left, and two of Maury's brigades, bayonets fixed, advanced upon him deliberately in three distinct lines, one behind the other. McKean's men had been cautioned not to fire without orders, and even when the attack came so close that the commands of the Confederate officers became distinctly audible, they obeyed. Suddenly the Confederates took aim and with shouting and the familiar yell the whole line blazed. Cyrus Boyd wrote later: "Then somebody commenced firing and we shot away in the smoke. . . . But their first volley laid out many a man. . . . Every one now took to a tree or some place to protect himself."

At about this time, 3:00 P.M., Colonel Mower reported to Davies with one of Stanley's brigades. While these reinforcements were being deployed into the line, a Confederate charge disrupted Davies' front, and some of Mower's men became panic stricken and broke in confusion. In endeavoring to rally them, Generals Oglesby and Hackleman were wounded. So furious was the battle that rifle barrels grew red-hot and cartridges exploded in them prematurely. "Let them burst," cried Colonel Thomas W. Sweeney, "there's no time to cool off now."

For more than an hour and a half, Davies held the enemy at bay. His limbers were twice filled with artillery ammunition from a six-mule team running to Corinth. The afternoon waned and the enemy pressed on. So constant and rapid was Davies' artillery fire that ammunition grew short. Rather than risk the capture of his batteries, Davies resolved to take the "extreme position," and ordered the guns withdrawn in line with Battery Robinett. Davies and McKean trailed the guns. As the artillery filed slowly to the rear, sweat streaked down the faces of the cannoneers, so blackened with gunpowder that they looked like coal heavers, and blood from wounded horses left a glistening red trail in the road. The Confederates greeted the withdrawal with an exultant yell.

Attack subsided at sunset; firing, at dark. That evening every road into Corinth was crowded with Davies' men, all weary, some hatless, spiritless, thirsty, dirty, sunburned, wounded.

Van Dorn concluded that he had caught Rosecrans with the Corinth garrison of 15,000 men. He did not suspect the presence of either Stanley or Hamilton.

After McKean and Davies had fallen back, at 3:30 P.M. Hamilton received an order from Rosecrans: "Davies, it appears, has fallen behind the works, his left being pressed in. If this movement continues until he gets well drawn in, you will make a flank movement, if your front is not attacked, falling to the left of Davies when the enemy gets sufficiently well in so as to have full sweep, holding a couple of regiments looking well to the Purdy road. Examine and reconnoitre the ground for making this movement."

When Hamilton returned this order, endorsing on its back, "I cannot understand it," Rosecrans sent Ducat to explain it.

But Hamilton refused to obey the order or the acting chief of staff. He told Ducat, Rosecrans wrote later, that he wanted a more positive and definite order despite Ducat's explanation of the plan for the immediate movement,—"he was obliged to return to me for an order fitted for the situation. Two orderlies sent on the same errand afterwards were killed on the way." Rosecrans then ordered Ducat himself to return. "I have four children," Ducat pleaded. "You knew that when you entered the service," Rosecrans replied. Ducat went, carrying "further explanations of the most explicit kind; and a little sketch to show what ought to be done." Hamilton finally marched, and by sunset had reached a point opposite Van Dorn's left. Sullivan's brigade, which faced to the left, moved a short distance, crossed the narrow flats bordering the tracks, and entered the thicket. There it engaged Van Dorn's left and fought fiercely. Buford's brigade, circling too far to the west to take position, did not contact Van Dorn. As a result, Hamilton's delayed flanking movement had no effect at all other than to involve a brigade in a sharp fight. It did not trap Van Dorn. "Had the movement been executed promptly after 3 o'clock," Rosecrans complained later, "we should have crushed the enemy's right and rear. Hamilton's excuse that he could not understand the order shows that even in the rush of battle it may be necessary to put orders in writing, or to have subordinate commanders who instinctively know or are anxious to seek the key of the battle and hasten to its roar."

If the sun had only set an hour later, each of the two opposing commanders was convinced, he might have finished the battle that day. Both were confident of victory on the next. Van Dorn said in his *Official Report:* "The army slept on its arms within 600 yards of Corinth, victorious so far. . . . I had been in hopes that one day's operations would end the contest and decide who should be the victors on this bloody field, but a 10 miles' march over a parched country, on dusty roads, without water, getting into line of battle in forests with undergrowth, and the more than equal activity and determined courage displayed by the enemy, commanded by one of the ablest generals of the United States Army, who threw all possible obstacles in our way that an active mind could suggest, prolonged the battle until I saw, with regret, the sun sink behind the horizon. . . . One hour more of daylight and victory would have soothed our grief for the loss of the gallant dead who sleep on that lost but not dishonored field."

"We've got them where we want them," Rosecrans declared, knowing that Van Dorn lay wedged between the converging tracks. At nightfall, his associates reported Rosecrans "in magnificent humor." He quoted Dickens' Barkis: "Things is workin'."

Early that night Rosecrans summoned his division commanders to tell them they were facing the entire army which the Confederates could muster in northern Mississippi, and were outnumbered probably two to one. The time had come to take advantage of the inner defenses. He would form a new, mile-long line close to the northern edge of Corinth. McKean would hold the left, with his division well under the crest of College Hill, Stanley would form an angle which began at McKean's right and had its salient at Battery Robinett. Hamilton would withdraw closer to Corinth, his right extending almost to the old Confederate works, while his left closed up with Davies' division at the Bolivar road. Cavalry would cover both flanks and the rear. Although the other batteries were protected by earthworks, Fort Richardson, hastily constructed that night, was fronted by an apron of hay and cotton bales.

At headquarters Davies informed Rosecrans that he had lost three brigade commanders and many of his officers. Rosecrans must not depend on his command the next day although his men would do all they could. Accordingly, Rosecrans ordered Davies to take position as reserve southeast of Corinth. Davies was en route when Hamilton brought a revised order—he was to take position north of Corinth, facing the Purdy road. Davies' slow movements continued throughout the night.

Twenty years later Hamilton denied that the battle plan had been revised for the second day and cited a 7:00 P.M. order of Rosecrans', signed by Ducat, instructing him to throw out "vedettes, pickets, grand guards, scouts, and a line of skirmishers." Ducat was angry when he heard Hamilton's denial.

"Good heavens! What general with the knowledge of what happened to General Hamilton on the 3rd would not deem this necessary," he wrote in response. "Where is the proof in this of anything, only that it was deemed advisable to look after Hamilton and see that he performed a duty known as necessary to every novice?" The order appears reasonable in view of the vulnerability of the Union right, which Van Dorn planned to assault after demonstrating against the center. Rosecrans appeared to have acted wisely in keeping the enemy's left under close scrutiny.

From mid-afternoon until nightfall, Rosecrans was frustrated by what was either Hamilton's inability to understand or his re-

fusal to obey orders. That night, after he had sent Ducat to check
on the left and left center, Rosecrans himself rode out to his right.
His tour lasted until 3:00 A.M.

Hamilton caught the full blast of his anger, for Rosecrans questioned him "savagely"—so Hamilton said. Hamilton probably
spoke the truth. The conduct he describes is of a pattern with
Rosecrans' occasional behavior both on and off the battlefield. His
way was far more damaging to himself than Grant's, which was to
keep his temper, hold his tongue, and stalk his enemy in silence.
The anger and confusion Rosecrans' berating produced in his
victims must have left them less able and willing to co-operate than
they otherwise might have been. In any event, the effect of the reprimand in the case of Hamilton was marked. Hamilton's resent-
ment burned for years in speech and print. Three months after the
incident, Edward Betty wrote to Rosecrans: "I heard nothing from
Hamilton since you left Corinth but abuses of yourself. I presume
this was done to show me how much I was mistaken in speaking
with reserved praise of your conduct at Corinth." At the time,
however, Hamilton said little, raising only a minor objection. He
wished to use the hill where the batteries stood, against an approach from the west. Rosecrans, against his better judgment,
yielded to Hamilton's wishes.

Between 8:00 and 9:00 P.M., Hamilton later claimed, Ducat
delivered orders from Rosecrans for a night attack: "Place your
batteries on the Purdy Road at 10:00 P.M. and play them for two
hours in a north-west direction . . . where the enemy is massed,
and at midnight attack them with your whole division with the
bayonet." Hamilton criticized these orders. The night was "too
dark to distinguish friend from foe," he said. Hamilton's memory
is inconsistent with the fact that friend and foe found the moonlight brilliant, while at 11:30 Rosecrans, warning Hamilton to
complete his movements before daylight, added: "The moon will
furnish you with sufficient light to distinguish well your ground."
The midnight attack order, whose existence some have questioned,
does not appear in the *Official Records*. Ducat denied carrying it,
and neither Hamilton, Rosecrans, or Colonel John B. Sanborn
mentioned it in his reports.

The Confederates had cut the wires below the telegraph station
at Bethel, Tennessee, twenty-seven miles north of Corinth. Rose-

crans, therefore, sent his dispatches by courier to Bethel to be telegraphed from there to Jackson. Grant found that he and Rosecrans were separated by some seven or eight hours. Rosecrans' first
report of October 3 told that Van Dorn had come in on the
Chewalla road that morning and made a demonstration against
the Union left. However, Rosecrans said, an unusually reliable
scout was satisfied that the Confederates intended to make their
main move on Bolivar. "If we find the force not meant for
Corinth," Rosecrans reported, "or we are in position to do it, shall
move on them steadily and firmly with everything we can spare.
The enemy have since come in on the Chewalla road and have
driven in Davies' left. Our men did not act or fight well. I think
we shall handle them. We are at the outer line of works." The last
sentence establishes the time of writing as approximately 10:00
A.M.

Rosecrans' next dispatch to Grant was sent at 11:30 P.M.: "The
rebels attacked between railroad's northwest. Davies' division—
the right of McKean's—were the only troops really engaged; it was
bushwhacking, our troops knowing nothing of the ground. . . .
Hamilton attempted to swing in from the Purdy road westward,
but it was late in the evening and he was too far advanced to the
north." He discussed his new positions and pointed out that the
Confederates "appear to be still in the angle of the roads. If they
fight us tomorrow I think we shall whip them. If they go to attack
you we shall advance upon them."

With Van Dorn's objective clearly revealed, at 4:30 P.M. Grant
ordered McPherson, with four regiments, to reinforce Rosecrans.
He learned simultaneously that Hurlbut, still in Bolivar, would
not march for Corinth until next morning, and could not be expected to arrive during the battle.

Although Grant knew that Rosecrans was fighting, there was no
operator on duty at the telegraph office at Jackson from the evening
of the 3rd until sometime after 7:00 A.M. on the 4th. At 1:00 A.M.
on the 4th a courier brought in to the Bethel Station a cipher dispatch from Rosecrans, but Bethel could not make contact with
Grant's headquarters. Colonel Isham N. Haynie, who was in charge
of the Bethel Station, told Grant that because he could not reach
the operator at Grant's headquarters he sent the message to the
Henderson, Tennessee, Station, and from there by courier to

Grant. At 7:00 A.M. on the 4th Haynie complained to Grant over the round-about route: "We have not been able to get him. . . . I feel it to be my duty to call this remissness to your attention." As at Iuka, Grant's headquarters seemed asleep. What the reason was is nowhere hinted.

As the day ended, Van Dorn was congratulated by his generals. Even Rust, who had called his assault madness, admitted that, by Friday night, they had come much closer to achieving success than he had hoped for. But because Van Dorn's maps had been prepared before the inner works were constructed, and the fortifications facing Lovell were unfamiliar, he sent a spy into Corinth. At midnight, Lovell bent over a rough and very much defaced sketch of parts of batteries Robinett and Williams. From the spy's drawing, Lovell's generals were led to believe that they faced one or two redoubts with three guns each, information that Van Dorn later labelled as insufficient or unsatisfactory.

At 1:00 A.M. Van Dorn heard a confused rumbling of wheels and surmised that Rosecrans might be retreating. Major Dillon of his staff prowled close enough to distinguish Federal commands, the ring of axes, and hum of voices. Captain Cummins, who listened all night to "a rattling of wagons, shouting of teamsters, and suppressed murmur of hurrying hosts," also guessed a withdrawal was in progress, but General Martin E. Green was skeptical. Retreating soldiers don't fell trees, he said.

But Rosecrans was not falling back at all. During the night, a corps of Negro sappers and miners supplied earthworks for Fort Richardson, the five-gun battery commanding the Bolivar road; and the Yates and Burgess sharpshooters rolled up logs to erect a breastworks before it. The troops in Corinth slept little. Officers looked to their men and positions. Ammunition was distributed. It was 3:00 A.M. before it grew quiet on Hamilton's front. Stanley's men heard the Confederates facing Robinett chopping aisles through the abatis. Rosecrans returned to headquarters, approved Ducat's report, and examined a diagram showing troop dispositions, before he retired for a few minutes at four. General Sullivan described the army's confident mood: "There was no desponding heart in camp that night. Our own general we had tried and Rosecrans had ever been victorious. But two short weeks before we had slept victors on the battle-field of Iuka, and memories of that glorious fight but nerved us to more desperate deeds."

Just before daylight on the 4th, Price placed three batteries upon an advanced ridge only 600 yards from Corinth, and at 4:30 A.M. the guns opened fire. "I had no time for breakfast," said Rosecrans. "The troops got very little. They had not been allowed to build fires during the night and were too tired to entrench."

First high shots missed the front ranks, and crashed into the public square, where they stampeded wagon trains and killed and wounded stragglers and hospital corpsmen. A ricocheting shell struck the Tishomingo Hotel, tearing a wounded man to pieces. Non-combatants were ordered to the rear, and sutlers, shopkeepers, teamsters, and Negroes panicked through the streets.

Stanley warned his shivering men to lie face-down and prepare to receive a charge. As the thirty-pound Parrots of Robinett fired, the earth trembled, bursts of orange and yellow lit the forest, and the hills echoed with thunder. Shells from the five heavy guns of Fort Williams tore up the woods near the Confederate line. One shell penetrated a log house and killed sixteen Confederates. To General Napoleon B. Buford the cannonading seemed like "the chimes of old Rome when all her bells rang out."

When the Union guns replied, the advanced Confederate battery made a frantic effort to withdraw out of range. Gunners lashed the horses or cut dead horses loose, and soldiers tried to withdraw the pieces themselves. At daybreak, a Union squad ran out and hauled back to their lines an abandoned gun and caisson.

Davies watched the flashes of the Confederate guns hidden in the woods, and ordered his ten-pound Parrots to silence them by throwing shells with six-second and then with five-second fuses beyond the tree tops. Soon the Confederate batteries fell silent. About 7:00, both sides held their fire, and the quiet was broken only by the sporadic chattering of musketry. On Stanley's front, Confederate sharpshooters, concentrating upon the gunners in Robinett, climbed trees, the better to view their targets. To clear them out, a howitzer sprayed the woods with canister shot.

During the lull, Rosecrans ordered Stanley to hold part of his division in reserve, to support Hamilton or Davies if attack should come from the north, or McKean, if from the west. Skirmishers should withdraw when an enemy battle line formed. At 8:00, puzzled by Confederate inactivity, Rosecrans ordered Stanley to make reconnaissance to the left with two regiments. Stanley took personal command of one, Colonel Joseph Mower of the other. Some of Mower's men had stampeded the day before, and camp talk reported that "Fightin' Joe" had been "shot in the neck." "Find out what Lovell is doing. Feel them, but don't get into their fingers," Rosecrans ordered. "I'll feel them," Mower promised, and plunged into the woods with a terrifying yell. With him went the 5th Minnesota, most of them Indians. Lovell greeted them with a blast. Mower lost his horse, and was captured. "Mower is killed," Rosecrans was told, but, when Confederate field hospitals were seized, Rosecrans found he had only been wounded.

Rosecrans inspected Battery Robinett while he was awaiting attack, and ordered Chief of Artillery Warren L. Lothrop to guard the reserve guns, many of which were parked in the public square. Riding toward his right, Rosecrans found Davies' men on nearly open ground, unprotected except for an occasional log breastwork. Thomas W. Sweeney's brigade, on Davies' right, lay below a slight crest, but otherwise lacked cover.

Van Dorn had planned a sunrise attack. By shelling Robinett he hoped to divert Rosecrans' attention to that segment of his front, while Louis Hébert began the main Confederate assault on the north. Although the cannonading ceased at dawn, an hour passed without attack, for Hébert was ill, and Van Dorn had to issue new orders. It was eight before his troops, now commanded by General Martin E. Green, were ready.

Masses of Green's men on Van Dorn's left crossed the Mobile and Ohio tracks and moved by the flank for a half-mile, seeking position in the woods behind a spur of the Purdy ridge, a table of land not more than 300 yards in front of the ill-protected center right. There they halted until almost nine. Rosecrans was speaking with Sweeney when the heavy fire of Davies' skirmishers announced Price's advance. Davies immediately ordered in his skirmishers, and commanded his infantry to lie down, so that heavy guns could fire over their heads.

Price charged in two columns. The column west of the railroad crossed the open ground toward the Purdy road; the one east of it, and only 300 yards to Davies' front, marched by divisions up the Bolivar road. As the attackers approached the Union line, they merged to form a "monstrous wedge" which "drove forward impetuously toward the heart of Corinth"—so the correspondent of the Cincinnati *Commercial* wrote. Meanwhile Davies' infantry held their fire, their own shells whining over their heads. The air above the battlefield hung motionless and hot, and sunlight glinted on the bayonets. Regimental colors, state and Confederate flags, were brilliant against the dark woods. Horses and riders loomed above the ridge, leading masses of infantry. Drums thrashed in a continuous snarl. The same observer thought it "terrible and beautiful to see the enemy's column advance, in spite of a perfect storm of grape and cannister, shell and rifle ball. On they marched and fired, though their ranks were thinned at every step." Below the crest where Davies waited, the columns spread out magnificently, "like great wings sweeping over the field." The gray lines were close enough now so that faces could be distinguished, but still the Union center held its fire. One man broke, fired his musket in the air, and ran for the rear. At last came the order, "Fire!" It was a "great slaughter," said General Green. His men closed up, and pressed forward like an army in a nightmare, faces averted like men striving to protect themselves against a driving hail storm.

In a crouching run, the enemy gained the crest of the ridge to the front and right of Battery Powell, shouting, "Butler!" as the armies tangled—a probable reference to the much-hated General Ben Butler, the conqueror of New Orleans. Then the Union line gave way. On Hamilton's extreme left, wounded artillery horses reared and, dragging limbers and caissons behind them, galloped through Davies' artillery, so that his horses, too, became unmanageable. The plunging animals injured twenty-one men, and threw two regiments into disorder. The Confederates swarmed into Battery Powell, and Price soon held the whole of Davies' line and seven of his guns.

The ragged head of Price's columns reached the north side of Corinth, fighting from verandas and doorways, and shooting in and out of windows. At the Curlee house, which was Rosecrans' headquarters, a group of Confederates took cover on the portico, while others hugged the walls and fired from the corners. "Give them grape and canister," Rosecrans ordered Colonel Immel, and the guns of the 12th Wisconsin battery barked, splattering the columns of the classic portico with blood.

"I had the personal mortification," Rosecrans said, "of witnessing this untoward and untimely stampede" of Davies. One of Davies' men, David Henderson, watched Rosecrans as he dashed in front of the Union lines. Bullets carried his hat away. His hair flew in the wind. As he rode along he shouted: "Soldiers! Stand by your country." "He was the only general I ever knew," Henderson said later, "who was closer to the enemy than we were who fought at the front." Henderson, who later was Congressman from Iowa, and speaker of the House of Representatives, recalled then that on the battlefield at Corinth Rosecrans was the "central leading and victorious spirit. . . . By his splendid example in the thickest of the fight, he succeeded in restoring the line before it was completely demoralized; and the men, brave when bravely led, fought again." "It lives in the memory of every soldier who fought that day," wrote Whitelaw Reid, "how his General plunged into the thickest of the conflict, fought like a private soldier, dealt sturdy blows with the flat of his sword on the runaways, and fairly drove them to stand. Then came a quick rally which his magnificent bearing inspired, a storm of grape from the batteries tore its way through the Rebel ranks, reinforcements which Rosecrans sent flying gave impetus to the National advance, and the charging column was speedily swept back outside the entrenchments."

From their reserve position near the depot, Stanley's Indians of the 5th Minnesota sprinted northeast through the town to rescue Davies; and reinforced by Sullivan's brigade of Hamilton's division, Sweeney's brigade retook Battery Powell and turned its guns on the enemy, driving them back 150 yards. A battery on the extreme right of Hamilton's line in its confusion poured its fire into the fort after it had been retaken, and one shell, brushing Davies' adjutant general, tore the legs from two soldiers. The Confederate survivors of the fight in town retreated, exposed to the fire of Stanley's and Hamilton's guns as they crossed the open field. Sullivan and Davies pursued them with banners streaming, and with cheers and volleys. Rosecrans' chagrin turned to elation. Hamilton's artillery ripped awesome holes in the flank of the Confederate column as it advanced and retreated; Batteries Williams and Richardson devastated the column with shell and spherical shot.

Stanley paused near Battery Williams. "Should God spare me to see many battles, I never expect to see a more grand sight," Stanley wrote in his *Official Report*. "The roll of musketry and the flash of artillery was incessant as the enemy tried in vain to form line under fire. As the smoke cleared up . . . I could see every fighting man on the field."

Van Dorn "sat on his horse grimly." "That's Rosecrans' trick," he growled. "He's got Price where he must suffer." The sound of Price's guns was the signal for two of Maury's brigades—his third was with Price—to move against the left. At about eleven, Maury advanced in four columns upon Robinett. His cavalry rode out upon the winding, hilly Chewalla road; one infantry column marched through the woods close to the west of Robinett, and two approached on its eastern flank. The 63rd Ohio, which lay directly before Maury, was so exposed that Colonel Fuller feared it must give way, and he ordered up the 11th Missouri in support. The 43rd Ohio faced west, filling the space of 150 yards between Robinett and Williams. As Maury closed, Fuller brought the 43rd forward, in line with the 63rd.

Officers had warned their men to hold their fire, but as soon as Maury came within range, the heavy guns of Robinett and Williams spoke, delivering, said General Moore, "the severest fire I ever imagined possible to concentrate on one point in front of a fortification." The woods screened the Confederates to within a hundred yards of Robinett. As they emerged, the 63rd and 27th Ohio opened fire, while thirty-pound shells from the Robinett Parrots, and ten-pounders from Battery Williams creased their lines. Yet the Texans and Arkansans did not falter; they closed ranks, and stormed the battery. A Confederate color bearer climbed to the crest, poised there waving a tattered regimental flag, and shouting for the Confederacy, fell forward into the works.

Momentarily the Stars and Bars replaced the Stars and Stripes, to hang limply in the smoke-filled air. After one volley, Stanley's infantry charged and drove the enemy out of the works with heavy loss. In Robinett, clouds of dust and powder smoke obscured the fighting; many collapsed from exaustion and thirst after midday when the temperature rose into the 90's. Men struggled and died in an acrid twilight.

Early that morning, a live eagle, "Old Abe," mascot of the 8th

Wisconsin, had been secured in Robinett by a leather thong. When Maury attacked, Old Abe broke loose, swooping and fluttering, bewildered by smoke and confusion. Incredulous Confederates struck and shot at him as he flapped and screeched above them. He survived, to become a minor legend of the war.

On the first assault, the 63rd Ohio lost nine out of thirteen officers, and half its number were killed or wounded. Colonel Joseph L. Kirby Smith, its well-loved commander, fell during the assault. Stanley heard men in the ranks say: "Kirby Smith is dead," and saw them weep.

Maury's officers called the men together in the woods before Robinett, and made eloquent appeals for volunteers for another assault, reminding them that their first attempt had almost succeeded, and that Corinth held the key to Confederate success in the west. Knowing the desperate odds, they nonetheless stepped forward; and tall, bronzed Colonel Rogers of the Texas Sharpshooters offered to lead them.

The second assaulting force broke from the woods with terrific yells, and with magnificent courage charged over the ridge and up to the ditch surrounding Robinett. At their head rode Rogers. Out of the long hammering of drums leaped the admonition of bugles, the wavering, yipping terror of the rebel yell, mixed with hoarse cries of pain and anger. The guns of Robinett, now reinforced with two twelve-pound howitzers, fired into the face of the attacking column, while Battery Williams poured grape and canister into its left flank. When the Confederates closed, Union gunners fled to their infantry supports. Confederate flag bearers proved conspicuous targets. Three died trying to plant the colors on Robinett. When Rogers saw the banner slip from the dead hand of a fourth, he jumped from his horse, leaped the ditch, scaled the low barrier, and waved the Stars and Bars.

At that moment, a Union drummer boy fired a single pistol shot, and Rogers tumbled backward into the ditch. But as Rogers died, his men swept over the ditch and mound and occupied the works, again raising the Confederate colors. Some wheeled the abandoned guns; others, cheering wildly, raced into Corinth, more than a hundred reaching the public square.

At the rear of Robinett, two of Stanley's regiments rose out of the thin brush to fire upon the attackers' left, while, north of the fort, the 43rd Ohio fired upon their right. The Confederates rushed upon the withdrawing defenders in a brief, furious fight. Bayonets flashed like pitchforks; musket butts rammed into men's bellies or smashed their heads. Thus charging gray remnants were caught, not only in an infantry crossfire, but beneath the guns of Batteries Williams, Phillips, and Richardson. Many surrendered, while others threw down their arms and fled back through the abatis, and toward the woods. Union gunners re-entered Robinett, wheeled and double-charged the guns, and fired on the panicking fugitives as they struggled through the chopped-out aisles or fled down the Chewalla road. Those killed crawling through the abatis hung entangled there. Exhausted and sick of the fight, many fastened handkerchiefs to sticks and waved them, shouting: "Spare us, for God's sake." At 2:00 P.M. fire, which had been heavy up to now, slackened. The evidence for this statement is found in McArthur's *Official Report:* "At 2 P.M., immediately on the firing slacking . . ." At 2:15 P.M. Van Dorn had not as yet ordered a retreat. His dispatch to Price tells as much: "If we are compelled to fall back, take the Oxford road."

From Battery Williams, Cyrus Boyd saw the Stars and Stripes rise over Robinett, and thought "how glorious the old flag looked as it again floated over the works in the smoke and breath of battle." He praised the Confederates. "Such bravery has never been excelled on any field as the useless assaults on Robinett."

One of Maury's captains, Edward Cummins, commented that "Our lines melted under their fire like snow in thaw."

Somewhere, Van Dorn had absorbed a dangerous, compulsive idea: A battlefield is the greatest gaming table. "What does a gambler know of excitement who has millions staked on a card? He loses but millions, he can win but millions. But here, *life* is to lose, glory to win." At Corinth he staked his army and reputation on the chance that he was swifter, stronger, and more astute than Rosecrans; and in the early afternoon the cards were down and he had lost. After the fight at Corinth on October 3 and 4, and on the 5th at the Hatchie Bridge, of the 3,900 Maury had led in from Chewalla, he brought 1,302 back, having lost 245 killed, 926 wounded, and 1,427 missing. Later, when Ducat met Van Dorn under a flag of truce, Van Dorn confessed: "I don't see how the devil Rosecrans held the place, and I don't believe any other man in the service but Rosecrans could have done it." Now, a little after 2:00 P.M., reaching for a dispatch book, he scribbled an order for Price to retreat.

Rosecrans witnessed this last assault: saw the attackers come upon the ridge, and Battery Robinett belching its fire at them. When the attack failed, he watched the 27th Ohio and the 11th Missouri chasing them with bayonets. During the morning, a bullet had struck his left side, cutting the strap of a leather pocket which hung from his sword belt. His gloves were stained with the blood of a staff officer, wounded at his side. Now as he paused, he felt an overwhelming fatigue and faintness, an aching thirst, and the enervating heat of the sun, and he sought the shade of a tree. As he sat there he noticed three white smoke bursts over Van Dorn's lines. "They have blown up some ammunition wagons," he cried. "They are going to retreat. We must push them."

With that he ordered McArthur with a regiment and a half to reconnoiter Van Dorn's right. Then he dictated a dispatch to Grant, describing his lines and the enemy's. Van Dorn had withdrawn some distance to the northwest, massing between the railroads. Water wagons were starting out from Corinth. Satisfied that Van Dorn was retreating, he ordered Sullivan to push the enemy with a heavy skirmish line, and feel them constantly. He then rode his lines, telling the men that he knew they needed rest after marching and fighting for three days and two nights. They should have it, but no longer than was absolutely necessary. He ordered them to return to their camps, provide five days' rations, take rest, and be ready to pursue early next morning.

His tour brought Rosecrans to Robinett. Years later, Colonel Fuller, who commanded Stanley's First Brigade, wrote: "All remember that salutation you gave to my brigade, when you rode over the dead to Battery Robinett, and uncovering your head, said: 'I take off my hat in the presence of men as brave as these.' No man near enough to hear them will ever forget them."

More than 200 of Maury's men lay near Robinett, 56 of them in a tangled heap in the ditch. Cyrus Boyd strolled over to look at them: They had the "most unearthly look upon their dying faces." One of them, preparing to spike the guns, had clutched a hammer tightly in one hand and rattail files in the other. While questioning prisoners along his route, Rosecrans gave a message to Captain Thomas F. Tobin of Maury's artillery: "Tell General Maury . . . I never used to think, when I taught him, a little curly headed boy . . . that he would trouble me as he has today." Dabney Maury had been his student at West Point years before, sitting directly in front of George B. McClellan.

That afternoon, the Confederates were buried in a single trench; Colonel Rogers was placed alone in a smoothly rounded grave, marked with a plain board.

Rosecrans lost his temper when he reached Davies' position. Out of Davies' body of 2,924 officers and men, 114 had been killed, 705 wounded, 25 had suffered sunstroke, and 159 were missing—casualties totaling 1,001, or more than a third of the division. Later Davies wrote to Rosecrans complaining that: "You said upon the battlefield, among the piles of the dead and groans of the wounded, slain by the Second Division . . . that they were a set of cowards; that they never should have any military standing in your army till they had won it on the field of battle; that they had disgraced themselves, and no wonder the rebel army had thrown its whole force upon it during the two days' engagement." Once again Rosecrans had demonstrated by a tactless outburst his unfortunate habit of losing his temper and loosening his tongue.

When Davies later asked Rosecrans to make public retraction, Rosecrans admitted: "They fought nobly the first day, and . . . many of them, especially on the right, did the same the second day, and so much so that I shall overlook the cowardly stampeding of those under my immediate observation on the second day—which gave rise to the public indignation I expressed in your presence and in theirs."

As he rode slowly back toward the town, Rosecrans came upon an Arkansas lieutenant, wounded and leaning against a tree. "General, you licked us good, but we gave you the best we had on the ranch," he said.

"Gen'l Rosecrans, our commanding General came around this evening and was almost taken from his horse by the soldiers," Cyrus Boyd wrote. "The _wildest enthusiasm_ prevailed and every man seems ready to pursue the enemy. We have had but few battles so well managed as old 'Rosa' has managed this one."

Union casualties were 2,520: 355 dead, 1,841 wounded, and 324 missing. The Confederates lost 8,691: 1,423 dead, 5,000 wounded, and 2,268 captured or missing.

That evening, October 4, Van Dorn reported: "Attacked Corinth. Took all the outer works by storm and got within town. Enemy received fresh reinforcements and we could not complete the work; retired." And Lovell wrote: "I received an order . . . to detach my strongest brigade to the support of Price's center, which was being overpowered by large reinforcements of the enemy."

These "reinforcements" formed no part of the columns of Hurlbut and McPherson. They were troops from Rosecrans' outposts which had moved into his new line during the night of the 3rd. Captain Edward Cummins was more accurate: "We scarcely got in when we met and were overwhelmed by the enemy's massive reserves." And Van Dorn later testified how he had hoped to defeat the Corinth garrison, which he estimated at 5,000 men, before Rosecrans could draw in his outposts of 8,000 men, some of which lay twelve to fifteen miles distant. But Rosecrans checkmated him; and Hamilton and Stanley, although comparatively inactive on the 3rd, were in battle line before Van Dorn left Chewalla that morning. On the 4th, with shortened lines, Rosecrans could afford to hold in reserve parts of Hamilton's and Stanley's forces. In a later report Van Dorn referred to the strength Rosecrans gained by his concentration: "The heavy (Union) guns were silenced and all seemed about to be ended, when a heavy fire from fresh troops from Iuka, Burnsville and Rienzi, that had succeeded in reaching Corinth in time, poured into our thinned ranks. . . . Our . . . troops gave way. The day was lost."

By evening, Grant reported the outcome to Halleck. His subordinate had won another victory. He had none of the detail and could not describe the battle. His first three reports were heavy with that phase of the undertaking he best knew—his own part in it. Rosecrans' reports of the 3rd did not convey the magnitude of the operation, and Grant's understatement of the same day is not surprising: "There was some fighting yesterday."

Grant added that "McPherson has gone with a fine brigade . . . to his [Rosecrans'] relief; probably reach Corinth by 7 this morning [October 4]. I have given every aid possible." Yet Grant knew that the Mobile and Ohio tracks had been ripped up south of Bethel, Tennessee, and that McPherson, who was to leave Bolivar at 5:30 A.M., would be forced to march the greater part of 27 miles. McPherson did not reach Corinth until two or three hours after the battle ended.

Grant's report to Halleck on October 3 that "Hurlbut is moving on the enemy's flank from Bolivar," was likewise somewhat less than accurate. Hurlbut actually was out of supporting distance, and did not meet Van Dorn at the Hatchie River crossing until some fifteen hours after the battle. On the 3rd he had telegraphed Grant: "I can't return [to Corinth] before Sunday [October 5] P.M., the distance being 46 miles." After 5:00 P.M. on the 4th, he said in another wire to Grant that he saw no ground "to believe that I can reach Corinth tomorrow [October 5]. A citizen reports Davis' Bridge destroyed; if so the game is up, and I shall return to save my own command." Fifteen hours after Van Dorn blew up his ammunition wagons, Hurlbut still had not engaged the enemy. In his October 4 report to Halleck, Grant did not mention that Hurlbut had started from Bolivar only that morning, and that on the 3rd he had telegraphed: "I can do no more than demonstrate, unless Rosecrans has beaten Price." Grant's statement: "I have given every aid possible," was not quite accurate. He could have sent Sherman from Memphis, but probably decided it was inadvisable to uncover Memphis and his right. But he had acted tardily, nevertheless. In spite of his dispatch to Halleck, up to the moment he ordered McPherson to march he was doubtless uncertain where Van Dorn would strike.

Grant wrote in his *Memoirs* later: "The works built after Halleck's departure enabled Rosecrans to hold his position until the troops of both McPherson and Hurlbut approached towards the rebel front and rear. McPherson got in to the support of Rosecrans just after the repulse. His approach, as well as that of Hurlbut, was well known to the enemy and had a moral effect."

Van Dorn himself refuted this "moral effect" claim. He gave no heed to Hurlbut until after he was repulsed, when "anticipating that the Bolivar force would move out and dispute my passage across the Hatchie Bridge," he hurried to that point. Of McPherson, Ducat wrote: "The enemy did not know of his approach. This I learned from General Van Dorn."

But the popular and sometimes even the scholarly record of these events has tended ever since to rely on Grant's *Memoirs*.

Not all of Rosecrans' army lay in Corinth that evening. At 2:00 P.M., immediately on the firing slacking, Rosecrans himself ordered McArthur, with a regiment and a half, to reconnoiter along Van Dorn's right. McArthur advanced on the Kossuth turnpike and turned north along the line of the abandoned outer works, skirmishing in the woods and taking a few prisoners. When he reached Battery E, on the Smith's Bridge road, he glimpsed the retreating rear guard of Van Dorn's cavalry. McArthur's infantry followed them four miles beyond Corinth, but could not intercept them. McArthur turned north and picketed the line of the Mobile and Ohio, capturing Van Dorn's field hospitals with about 300 unwounded and 550 wounded, among them 50 officers. Without food or rest. McArthur did outpost duty throughout the night. And then, a little before sunset, McPherson arrived with five regiments and bivouacked in the Corinth square.

As twilight settled upon the smoking disorder, thirsty men filled their canteens from lumbering water wagons, or from the few wells that had not gone dry. Scattered soldiers rejoined their commands. Ammunition and rations were brought out of the depots within the inner works. A hospital was set up at Camp Corral, and by night the injured, their wounds dressed, lay on cots, sheltered by tents which the Medical Director, Dr. Archibald B. Campbell, found under the railroad platform.

At day's end, the "air of pursuit filled Corinth." That evening pursuit orders were issued, probably verbally in conferences between Rosecrans and his generals. Written orders, dated October 5, 1862, were distributed after midnight.

Grant was to charge in his *Memoirs* that Rosecrans "failed to follow up the victory, although I had given specific orders in advance of the battle for him to pursue the moment the enemy was repulsed; he did not do so, and I repeated the order after the battle." No orders of this kind appear in the *Official Records*.

Grant's clause, "the moment the enemy was repulsed," demands consideration. Grant pointed out, in his discussion of Iuka, that a forced march of twenty miles does not leave troops "in good condition for fighting the moment they get through." Such a march was about a six-hour stint. The same troops that he would not have expected to fight after a six-hour march [i.e., about twenty miles] on September 18, he expected, two weeks later, after forty-eight hours of marching and fighting, to pursue the enemy the "moment they were repulsed." Yet Rosecrans' troops were exhausted, injured, and out of ammunition, water, and rations. It would have been physically impossible for them to obey such orders. If Rosecrans received them, he may have concluded that he should not transmit them. The precise moment of final repulse of the Confederates, moreover, was not clear until later—if Van Dorn's generals had not objected, he would have made another assault.

Stanley knew firsthand the problems that Rosecrans faced after 2:00 P.M., and when he read that Grant "severely censured" Rosecrans "for not following Van Dorn's retreat of the 4th, and for his tardiness on the 5th," he commented to the New York Commandery of the Loyal Legion: " . . . It is easy to criticize after the fact. The test is, put yourself in his place. Rosecrans' troops had marched for two and three days, had scarcely a supply of even drinking water, the heat was excessive and the men were worn out. They had narrowly escaped a most terrible defeat. . . ." In spite of Rosecrans' orders and Stanley's best efforts, Stanley's division—roughly one-fourth of Rosecrans' force—was not ready, "because of the fatigued condition of my men and having to provide them with ammunition and rations," to pursue until eight o'clock next morning.

Eight

GRANT CALLS ROSECRANS BACK

The Confederates had withdrawn as rapidly as possible after their repulse. "Never was a general more disappointed than Van Dorn," said Dabney Maury, "but no man in our army was so little shaken in his courage as he was. He never looked more gallant than when his broken army, in utter disorder, was streaming through the open woods. Could Van Dorn have gotten his forces together he would have made another attack. Finding that impossible, he brought Lowell's unbroken division to cover the rear, and withdrew to Chewalla, seven miles west of Corinth. During the retreat he encouraged officers and men to reform their broken organizations...."

Rosecrans planned to hold Corinth lightly and to send his army in two columns after Van Dorn. He knew that he could move more rapidly by dividing his force on two roads, but that he risked at the same time being ambushed and beaten in detail. He chose to move.

McArthur, with the rest of McKean's troops following, and Hamilton tailing McKean, would move toward Pocahontas on the road north of the Memphis and Charleston railroad; McPherson's brigade would lead the divisions of Stanley and Davies toward Pocahontas on the road south of the tracks. Cavalry would screen the advance and flanks of each column. Wagon trains were to remain parked in Corinth, and, to provide quick communications, division commanders were supplied with signal rockets. Until the pursuit was well under way, Rosecrans himself would remain in Corinth to co-ordinate his columns and keep in touch with Grant and Hurlbut.

During the night of October 4, the Confederates took little rest, and before dawn Van Dorn moved his cavalry and pioneers on the road to Rienzi. He was determined to march around immediately and attack Corinth from the opposite direction. When his generals objected, he countermanded the orders and retreated at once toward the Hatchie River. For a whole day Hurlbut had been moving toward the same objective from the opposite direction. The previous mid-morning, heavy cannonading had told him of the fight at Corinth. When the firing ceased, he knew that he must meet Van Dorn; whether defeated or victorious, he could not guess. Yet he pressed forward.

Rosecrans' pursuit began slowly. Although McPherson was ready when Captain Joseph Smith with three companies reported to him at 3:00 A.M., he would not march. The night before, after receiving verbal orders to move at 3:00, McPherson received written orders from Rosecrans to "be *prepared* to move. . . ." And so he waited. Shortly after 5:30 A.M.—sunrise came at 5:38—Rosecrans, full of nervous excitement, galloped up. "Why are you not under way?" he demanded. McPherson produced his written orders, Rosecrans gave the command, and McPherson marched. Ducat felt that "Most men breathing the air of pursuit that filled Corinth would have moved at the first streak of dawn on such orders as McPherson already had." The point seems moot.

Although Stanley was to have dogged McPherson's heels, he had not completed the distribution of ammunition and rations, and his tardiness held up Davies, who followed him; the two divisions marched so far behind McPherson's fresh troops that they were out of support most of the day.

The column south of the tracks made an earlier start, but did little better. McArthur, reinforced by two more of McKean's brigades, marched at daybreak. However, McKean was in trouble from the beginning. Contrary to Rosecrans' explicit orders, he took along his divisional wagon trains, and Hamilton, whose only orders were to follow McKean, did not march until 7:00 A.M.

The main pursuit quickly bogged down. The roads leading west from Corinth were poor, narrow, winding, unmarked, interlocking. Even today they are difficult to follow. And on that October morning the good maps lay useless in Grant's headquarters in Jackson.

When Stanley, far behind McPherson, reached the first forks of the Chewalla road, his guide led him down the extreme right fork and across the tracks; and when in less than a mile Stanley ran upon Hamilton, he returned to the forks. Convinced by this time of the guide's ignorance, Stanley determined to follow Van Dorn's beaten trail and to move toward the cannonading heard plainly in the west. And so he took the next fork, only to find that, four miles farther on, this road too crossed south over the tracks. A countryman now pointed out that no road north of the railroad reached Chewalla. At least, thought Stanley, he was following Van Dorn's line of retreat. Wounded Confederates filled outhouses, tents, and barns. Back in Corinth Rosecrans fretted at Stanley's dispatch telling him that Stanley was lost. He told Stanley: "You should have taken the road to the right, this side of Cane Creek, which keeps north of the railroad. If you are not too far advanced it would be better for you to face by the rear and do it now, as you will reach Chewalla sooner."

Before Stanley received this answer, his troubles had multiplied. A mile beyond the tracks his column collided with McKean's crawling division. McKean lumbered along south of the tracks, trailing McArthur; he was lost, and worse, his train clogged the road. McKean now blocked Hamilton who followed him, Stanley who ran up on him, and Davies who followed Stanley. The four generals gathered at the roadside. In this disorder and delay, Hamilton refused to exercise his seniority and untangle the knot. As long as the march was without resistance, he considered himself restrained by instructions from assuming command.

Learning of the delay, Rosecrans scolded McKean: "Halt your train, turn it out, and park it. I am told it is a mile long. You have left our advance guard without a support by your tardy movements. You are in the way of the other divisions." McKean did not obey these orders. At 2:00 P.M. Rosecrans again lectured McKean: "Hamilton says you are waiting for orders. . . . You have your orders to push ahead, follow your advance guard closely, and report frequently." At the same time, Hamilton should take the nearest northern road. Rosecrans was sending another guide. Hamilton should try to overtake McPherson.

Meanwhile McPherson, far beyond the snarl, moved ahead rapidly. Signs of Van Dorn's flight marked his route: abandoned tents, blankets, haversacks, weapons, ammunition, "scarified and broken trees, guns with twisted barrels and shattered stocks, blood stained garments." Fresh mounds of earth marked some of the hurriedly buried dead, while stiffened, unburied corpses began to bloat. Colonel John W. Sprague of the 63rd judged from the litter than Van Dorn was perfectly stampeded.

Before noon, on reaching a point some six miles from Chewalla, McPherson knew that he was dogging Van Dorn. Cannonading from the direction of Davies' bridge suggested that Hurlbut was engaging Van Dorn's advance. McPherson pushed rapidly to Chewalla, and learned that the Confederate rear guard had just left. By now he probably had Rosecrans' dispatch: "If you reach Chewalla ascertain if the enemy passed by Young's Bridge. Halt at that point until Stanley overtakes you. Push an advance guard, but not beyond support, toward Pocahontas."

A few minutes after entering Chewalla, McPherson's cavalry advance brushed with Van Dorn's infantry and artillery. Although the Confederates retreated precipitously, McPherson was forced to halt to remove road obstructions and repair a bridge. When he resumed the chase, he found a large Confederate burial party blocking his path. "Stand aside," McPherson ordered. "There's fighting going on. General Rosecrans is the only one who can suspend *that*." The way was cleared, and McPherson did not halt until he reached Big Hill, on the east bank of the Tuscumbia. There, at nightfall, in dense timber and undergrowth, he found the Confederates strongly posted. His whole force advanced behind a heavy skirmish line and after a short, spirited fight, took the hill.

McArthur, too, made good progress ahead of the snarl, and was near Chewalla—about seven miles from Corinth—when he too was met by a large Confederate burial party. McArthur, unlike McPherson, halted, while his courier galloped to Corinth to ask Rosecrans' orders. During the three-hour interval before his return, three Confederate brigades encamped on the road ahead—Rust's, Bowen's, and Villepigue's—escaped. When McArthur resumed his march, he collided with McPherson, who had crossed from the north road; he fell in behind McPherson and supported him. By nightfall, McPherson's and McArthur's brigades lay on their arms on the east bank of the Tuscumbia facing Van Dorn's rear guard. Meanwhile, the tangle involving the four divisions had been resolved, and the rest of the army lay within supporting distance; Stanley within two miles of the Tuscumbia; Hamilton within four; McKean presumably near Hamilton; and Davies behind Stanley. Hamilton estimated that that day he had marched fourteen miles.

In the meantime, at 9:00 A.M., the Union column out of Bolivar had struck Van Dorn as he tried to cross the Hatchie at Davies' Bridge. Ord had taken command, ranking Hurlbut. In a sharp, four-and-a-half hour fight, faintly audible to the pursuers out of Corinth, Ord was wounded and Hurlbut succeeded him. "No contest of long duration could be made here," Van Dorn insisted, "as it was evident that the army of Corinth would soon make its appearance on our right front and rear." Maury believed that "few commanders have ever been so beset as Van Dorn was in the Forks of the Hatchie." While Ord and Hurlbut held the bridge before him, the pursuers out of Corinth were only a few miles off. The road between was choked with nearly 400 wagons and 11,000 Confederates. To escape, Van Dorn kept to the left bank, veered sharply to the left, on the Boneyard road, and in full moonlight by 10:00 P.M. crossed at Crum's Mill and headed for Ripley. Hurlbut, short of battery horses, provisions, and transportation, did not pursue, but halted to care for his wounded and bury his dead. He listened hopefully for Rosecrans' approach. Prisoners told him of the Union victory at Corinth.

During the day Rosecrans sent six brief reports to Grant. One of them, sent after 11:00 A.M., asked, "Where is Hurlbut? Now is his time to pitch in. If they stand this side of Chewalla we shall fight where there is no water." Another listed Confederate colonels, dead and wounded. A third informed Grant that Rosecrans had provided for the burial of Van Dorn's dead. A fourth reported the enemy three hours ahead of the main pursuit. The Confederates were breaking toward the Tuscumbia for water. A fifth told Grant that "McPherson, Stanley, and Davies were to start at daylight, but through error were delayed. . . . Now is the time for Steele to pitch in, while they are all looking this way." The last dispatch reported that the leading divisions had arrived at Chewalla. "No news from McPherson since 12 A.M. Enemy's rearguard overtaken beyond Chewalla road repairing a bridge to go over. Progress very slow.

McKean in the way. Order us forage at once or our animals will starve."

Having completed his business in Corinth, Rosecrans at 9:00 P.M. sent a dispatch to McKean: "Am coming out to Chewalla with a carload of water. . . . Ord has been heavily engaged with the enemy at Davies' Bridge. . . . Baggage, I understand, has interfered with your progress, which certainly has not been remarkable."

At the Hatchie crossing Hurlbut had constructed a pontoon bridge to replace the structure burned by Van Dorn, and assigned the 8th Wisconsin to guard it. Early on October 6, Captain Albert E. Smith noticed a "prowler" near it. It was Rosecrans, riding to the front. "How are you fixed for breakfast? I'm hungry." While Smith looked for a can for boiling coffee, Rosecrans found bacon and two onions in staff haversacks. He broiled these on a stick and, after breakfast, rode off.

At 3:00 A.M. Rosecrans found McPherson leading the pursuit. "Push the enemy as soon as it is light," he ordered, and then retraced his route to inspect his divisions. When he found McKean still encumbered by his train, he ordered it back to Corinth and sent McKean with it, to command the post of Corinth, said to be threatened by Confederate reinforcements, including 10,000 paroled men. McArthur succeeded McKean.

On the morning of the 6th, with Rosecrans in personal command, the pursuers turned south, following Van Dorn toward Crum's Mill. Now the headlong nature of the flight became more evident. Litter included wagons, six caissons, a battery forge. William H. Warren wrote: "The road was strewed with tents, wagons and clothing knapsacks shugar molasses flower and corn meal besides cooking utensils cannon carriage and ammunition and guns. I did not see enny canon but it was reported that our scouts found ten peaces of canon throed into a gulley one half mile off the road." Boyd wrote: "Artillery caissons had struck trees, and the ammunition exploded tearing everything to pieces around. Many places the canoneers had cut the *traces* and gone leaving their load behind. The hillsides were white with cornmeal and flour and dust on the road fully one foot deep. Thus for several miles it went. We found Genl. Price's buggy with a fine robe in it. But the owner had gone on. All along the roadside under bushes in the hollows and behind logs the panting fugitives were found Glad to surrender. They all agreed in saying that no such terrible calamity had overtaken them in the west as the battle of the 4th." In an understatement, Price described his men at this time as "somewhat disorganized," and General John S. Bowen called them "footsore, weary and starving."

"On Road," on the 6th, Rosecrans asked Grant: "Have you anything further from men or any orders for me? Am at end of telegraph wire, going forward to Woodward's, thence to Hatchie Crossing. Please answer before I leave."

At noon, at Crum's Mill, the bridge and the mill were still burning, and Van Dorn was reported only a half hour ahead. While McPherson's engineers repaired the bridge, some of his men crossed over the mill dam. At 6:30 P.M., Rosecrans reported that his entire force was at Crum's Mill: "McPherson's brigade and McKean's and Stanley's divisions here; Hamilton 4 miles off. Bridge built; part of the troops across; we shall pursue them." Van Dorn's destination was Holly Springs. Hurlbut reported himself too much cut up to pursue. Late that night, Rosecrans ordered rations to Hurlbut, begging him not to return to Bolivar, but to keep his threatening position until Van Dorn was destroyed.

With Van Dorn fleeing, Rosecrans dictated a dispatch to Grant, which it was easy to misinterpret: "McPherson occupied Jonesborough at 9 o'clock last night. Out of rations, having followed the main column of the precipitate retreat of the enemy Hurlbut reports himself out of position and too much crippled to follow the enemy. I have ordered rations sent to Cypress for him and have begged him not to return to Bolivar until I can communicate with Sherman; I want him to appear to threaten the enemy. I think Sherman should go to Holly Springs by all means, and that the road should be opened to take supplies to him. . . . think it could be done without much trouble. I repeat, it is of the utmost importance to give the enemy no rest day or night, but push him to Mobile or Jackson. Beg the authorities North to send us more troops. Ship everything you can; now is our time; we must give the enemy no time to re-enforce or recruit. Every nerve must be strained. Everything will be sent to see that our troops lack nothing of the necessaries to keep them going."

Next day, within about 4 miles of Ripley, Rust, Villepigue, and

Bowen were drawn up in line of battle, only to discover that the position was capable of being turned right and left and was therefore untenable. When Federal troops were reported advancing on three roads, Lovell ordered a further retreat. As the brigades filed out, officers were told to hurry so that the enemy would not cut them off. That day after marching about 18 miles in 19 hours without rations, Bowen's men were considerably worn out and gave evidence of demoralization. General Albert Rust testified that the route may have been more circuitous after getting to Ripley from the fact that the enemy were expected and believed to be threatening the Confederate rear and both flanks. A large portion of the army was supposed to be in a condition not to make a fight.

Hamilton marched twenty-three miles that day in pursuit in excessive heat and dust, finding only one well on the route. In the late afternoon at least 600 men dropped out in eight miles, but rejoined the column after resting. From Goldsborough, Rosecrans again pleaded with Grant. "Do not, I entreat you, call Hurlbut back; let him send away his wounded. I propose to push the enemy, so that we need but the most trifling guards behind us. Our advance is beyond Ruckersville. Hamilton will seize the Hatchie crossing on the Ripley road tonight." A Confederate deserter "says that they wished to go together to railroad near Tupelo, where they will meet 9000 exchanged prisoners, but he says they are much scattered and demoralized. They have much artillery."

In the rain that night, at the foot of a big tree in Jonesboro, Rosecrans held a candle while Ducat wrote at his dictation. "Our advance is now at Ruckersville or near that," he told Hurlbut.

I have been trying to determine whether Price and Van Dorn stick together, and routes of retreat. The question is still unsettled, but a portion of Price's train is camped west of the Hatchie, and a large portion of Van Dorn's train reported to have come west of the Muddy. Looks as if they had not separated. You are a fighting general. You must support us. We have watched railroads and points long enough. Now is the time to make *them* watch. Move heaven and earth to get what you want—your artillery in shape, etc., and let us go into them. We can do it and others must look out for the country we leave in our rear. Sherman must move down on [General Gideon] Pillow and the other people who rally to him. We want you; if we are pressed we must fight and whip. At the very least you must leave your present position now. Your position is a good one. I have ordered 50 wagons of provisions to you. Let us go on. What says Grant?

Within an hour Grant supplied the answer: Rosecrans must abandon the pursuit. The *Official Records* show that this was Grant's *first* and *only* order in the matter.

Rosecrans immediately replied:

I most deeply dissent from your views as to the manner of pursuing. We have defeated, routed, and demoralized the army which holds the lower Mississippi Valley. We have the two railroads leading down toward the Gulf through the most productive parts of the State, into which we can now pursue them with safety. The effect of our return to old position will be to pen them up in the only corn country they have west of Alabama, including the Tuscumbia Valley, and to permit them to recruit their forces, advance and occupy their old ground, reducing us to the occupation of a defensive position, barren and worthless, with a long front, over which they can harass us until bad weather prevents an effectual advance except on the railroads, when time, fortifications, and rolling stock will again render them superior to us. Our force, including what you have with Hurlbut, will garrison Corinth and Jackson and enable us to push them. Our advance will cover even Holly Springs, which would be ours when we want it. All that is needed is to continue pursuing and whip them. We have whipped, and should now push to the wall and capture all the rolling stock of their railroads. Bragg's army alone west of Alabama River and occupying Mobile could repair the damage we have it in our power to do them. If, after considering these matters, you still consider the order for my return to Corinth expedient, I will obey it and abandon the chief fruits of a victory, but I beseech you to bend everything to push them while they are broken and hungry, weary and ill-supplied. Draw everything possible from Memphis to help move on Holly Springs and let us concentrate. Appeal to the Governors of the States to rush down some twenty or thirty new regiments to hold our rear and we can make a triumph of our start.

Faced with this dispatch, Grant turned to Halleck, probably seeking support from a commander whose pursuit of Beauregard after Shiloh is still a classic in extreme caution. He directed Rosecrans to remain at Ripley until Halleck had replied. Halleck answered, surprisingly, "Why order a return of our troops? Why not re-enforce Rosecrans, and pursue the enemy into Mississippi, supporting your army on the country?"

That portion of Grant's dispatch directing him to remain until Halleck could be heard from proved "highly gratifying" to Rosecrans. "Dispositions will be made in conformity, and I will remain here."

The careless language with which Rosecrans listed matters that "should" be done, and told how he had "begged Hurlbut" not to return "until I can communicate with Sherman," stirred Grant to complain that Rosecrans was "communicating with Sherman," and, inferentially, giving orders. "You are misinformed as to my having communicated with Sherman," Rosecrans replied, "as I have never presumed to do so except so far, after having been informed by you of his whereabouts, I sent word to Hurlbut wishing him to tell Sherman where we were and asking cooperation. I should not think of communicating with him in any official way except through you."

But Grant was neither placated nor convinced. That morning he had telegraphed that he had ordered Rosecrans to return. "He showed such reluctance that I consented to allow him to remain until you could be heard from if further re-enforcements could be had. On reflection I deem it idle to pursue farther without more preparation, and have for the third time ordered his return"— but only one order appears in the *Official Records*. Grant described the incident in the *Memoirs:* "I now regarded the time to accomplish anything by pursuit as past and, after Rosecrans reached Jonesboro, I ordered him to return. He kept on to Ripley, however, and was persistent in wanting to go farther. I thereupon ordered him to halt and submitted the matter to the general-in-chief, who allowed me to exercise my judgment in the matter, but inquired, 'Why not pursue?' Upon this I ordered Rosecrans back. Had he gone much farther he would have met a greater force than Van Dorn had at Corinth and behind intrenchments or on chosen ground, and the probabilities are he would have lost his army."

Rosecrans replied: "I shall take the most prompt and efficient measures to carry the orders into execution."

He showed the orders to Ducat. "Ducat, those people have ordered us back. The orders are imperative, and a great part of the fruits of victory will be lost. We must cross the Hatchie tonight, and try to reach Corinth tomorrow."

"But why?" asked Ducat. "Is anything taking place that we

don't know of? It's not possible for any troops in the center to be marching toward Corinth or wedging in anywhere between Chattanooga and Corinth."

"The whole rebel army of the west," said Rosecrans, "and certainly the whole flower of it, is in our front, whipped and demoralized. We could drive them like a flock of sheep. It seems to me that the time has come to win the war in the west, if not the central zone."

Yet he hurried back to Corinth with such dispatch and secrecy that the enemy did not know for a week what his army was doing or where it had gone. Colonel Stevenson said that his brigade marched 46 miles in two days and three hours. North wind scattered cold rain as McPherson led in the last of the pursuers at dusk on the 12th. "Am about pegged out," said an Iowa soldier. So was Rosecrans' whole force. Rosecrans had pursued some forty miles with his main body; some sixty with his cavalry, and with Grant's help had accomplished no more than the legendary king of France who, in the nursery rhyme, marched 20,000 men up the hill and marched them down again.

On the 8th while telling Halleck: "If you say so, it is not too late yet to go on, and I will join the moving column and go to the farthest extent possible," Grant gave Halleck his reasons for recalling Rosecrans: An army could not subsist itself on the country except in forage; Rosecrans started out to follow only for a few days; his men were much worn out; Grant had learned that reserves were on their way to join the Confederates; Van Dorn, at need, could find fortified shelter; the Mobile and Ohio lay open to Van Dorn; Corinth lay exposed by Rosecrans' advance; and while the pursuit might bring temporary and partial success it could only end in disaster. Further: "Rosecrans has been re-enforced with everything at hand, even at the risk of this road against raids." The last statement disregarded the fact that Sherman at Memphis with two divisions, and John A. Logan at Jackson, Tennessee, had not been sent in. Halleck, however, again declined to give orders in the face of Grant's objections.

While Grant was building this case, Hurlbut telegraphed to him from Bolivar: "I have just heard from Holly Springs. There are no forces there; all left on Sunday. There is but one company of cavalry at Davies' bridge. Everything in shape of force above Wolf

River has moved south. I am of the opinion that the rout of Van Dorn's army is complete, and that Pillow's force, late of Holly [Springs] has caught the panic."

Confederate evidence supports Hurlbut's opinion. On the day when Rosecrans reached Corinth, General Ruggles, at Jackson, Mississippi, informed his War Department that "Van Dorn, with about 12,000 men, is at Holly Springs. Price with about 12,000 men, demoralized, is some 10 miles distant. The enemy is concentrating in their front. General Tilghman is about joining Van Dorn with the few remaining exchanged prisoners. I have called on the Governor of Mississippi for the militia. I have called on General Blanchard to prepare to re-enforce Van Dorn. He needs strong reinforcements at once."

Confederate testimony also supports Rosecrans' statement that Vicksburg then was virtually undefended. General M. L. Smith, who commanded there, admitted to Van Dorn: "I am seriously apprehensive that the safety of this important point may be, and actually is, overlooked. My conviction is that this command is today at the mercy of the Army at Helena. . . . Their unaccountable inertness has saved Vicksburg from succumbing, for since the departure of General Breckinridge's division, there has never been a day on which a successful land attack might not have been made by the force at Helena." On October 3, General Ruggles told Van Dorn: "So far as we have received advices of the enemy's strength and intentions we are bound to consider Vicksburg and Port Hudson threatened by land as well as by water."

Corinth was a "disaster which the want of co-intelligence and cooperation suggested," Jefferson Davis said as he replaced Van Dorn with Pemberton. When he learned that he had been supplanted, Van Dorn commented that the War Department had not properly considered the difficulties before him, and that if the forces in Mississippi were not strengthened, the Confederacy would lose the state.

In spite of Rosecrans' failure to catch and destroy Van Dorn, the immediate importance of his victory was well understood at the time by both North and South. Against the perspective of the whole war, it loomed even more important. Greene wrote: "Corinth . . . marks the farthest point reached in the Confederate wave of reaction along the Mississippi. . . . From this time forward, the

Confederates were thrown on the defensive; the Union army resumed the offensive and steadily advanced, slowly at first, but none the less surely."

Sherman agreed: "The . . . effect was very great. It was, indeed, a decisive blow to the Confederate cause in our quarter, and changed the whole aspect of affairs in West Tennessee. From the timid offensive we were at once enabled to assume the bold offensive. In Memphis . . . the citizens openly admitted that their cause had sustained a death-blow."

Death-blow or not—and it should be emphasized that the testimony is from Grant's friend Sherman—Grant had called Rosecrans back, alleging that further pursuit was dangerous. It is true that a long overland march becomes more and more risky as lines of communication are extended. Grant learned that lesson firsthand in the months ahead when Nathan Bedford Forrest checkmated his first movement on Vicksburg by tearing up the railroad and destroying his depot at Holly Springs. But by that time the Confederates had caught their breath, while in the pursuit after Corinth they were demoralized and on the run. Grant pretended not to believe, or did not believe, or perhaps did not want to believe—whatever the evidence might be—that Van Dorn was demoralized. As we have seen, he tried to shove the responsibility on the timid Halleck, but when even Halleck asked, "Why not pursue?" Grant called off the pursuit. Why?

Sherman wrote in his *Memoirs* that because of Iuka, "General Grant was very much offended with General Rosecrans," and while it is not easy to read a man's mind or to put a thermometer to his emotions, could it have been that his rapidly mounting dislike for Rosecrans—based partly on the fact that he was nursing a successful, talkative rival who knew too much, and whose dislike was augmented by army politicians who stood to profit from a quarrel, or enjoyed seeing one—affected his military judgment? From this point on Grant's hostility is spread upon the open record. "Now began to be seen," Whitelaw Reid wrote, "the first developments of a feeling that, growing with age, was to draw after it an expanding train of evil. There is reason to believe that Grant had been nettled by complaints, partly official from Rosecrans himself, far more unofficial from thoughtless staff officers who 'knew all their general knew,' about the failure to support him at Iuka. The order to stop the pursuit renewed this indiscreet chatter, and whispering tongues were soon poisoning truth by reports they made at Grant's headquarters. There was subsequently an effort at explaining away misunderstandings; both Grant and Rosecrans professed themselves satisfied, and they parted promising friendly intercourse in the future; but it is doubtful if the scars were fully erased from the memory of either, till later events came to brand them deeper and broader with both."

Stanley, an eyewitness, gives further support: "This seems to have been the beginning of a breach between Rosecrans and Grant, which I fear was never closed. It seems to me, however, that Rosecrans was not to blame for the estrangement, unless it was by making too much reference to it."

On October 16 the Department of the Tennessee was created with Grant in command.

Disturbing letters meanwhile told Rosecrans that Annie was ill. "Better or worse, I shall expect to hear from you almost every day," he wrote. He wrote to his wife about Corinth: "The victory was complete. The rebs had reported as the result of Friday's flight, the capture of Corinth. But when they came into the ground where I always intended to fight the battle—if there should be a great one—they were utterly routed and fled. . . . Did I tell you I was ordered to report to Major General Wright and the matter is still 'in petto'? I have a letter from General Halleck of a very flattering character."

On October 7 Grant issued General Orders No. 88 congratulating his armies. Whitelaw Reid said of this document: "Passing by the brilliant battle of Corinth with a single clause [Grant] devoted most of the order to extravagant praise of Hurlbut for the brief onslaught he made upon the enemy during their retreat."

In the same orders Grant intimated that a lack of cordial relations existed between the commands of Rosecrans and Ord: "Between them there should be, and I trust is, the warmest bonds of brotherhood." To this insinuation Rosecrans replied: "The part that expresses the hope that good feeling will exist between Ord's command and my own amazes me. So far as I know there was nothing even to suggest the fact that it might be otherwise. Under such circumstances the report is to be regretted, because our troops, knowing that there was no foundation in it for them, will be led to think there is some elsewhere."

Bickham's account of the battle, datelined Corinth, October 9, and published in the Cincinnati *Commercial,* concluded:

And now, to whom is due the honors of the battle of Corinth? The verdict of the whole army is in favor of General Rosecrans. Officers universally assert that it was he who planned the whole series of operations by which the enemy were entrapped under the forts of Corinth. He found the position unprepared for attack, and without orders he made it a powerful place. By skilful manouevering he deceived the enemy. By pretending to be beaten on Friday, he drew them into a place in which he gave them terrible punishment, and almost destroyed their army. It would seem from General Grant's dispatches that he claims the honors. His agency in the victory of Corinth is not apparent. He is perhaps entitled to credit for the affair at the Hatchie, but he did not assist General Rosecrans. After the enemy was defeated he sent General McPherson to Corinth with two thousand men. . . . That is all he did. It is natural that staff-officers should attribute credit to their chief, but armies are not apt to do so without reason. There is no doubt that the public will give the credit to General Rosecrans where it belongs.

Some time before October 21 Grant had a double complaint for Rosecrans: He had incorrectly paroled prisoners, and certain newspaper reporters and members of his staff were "keeping a distinction of feeling and spirit" between Rosecrans' troops and the rest of the army. Rosecrans answered that he had sent away prisoners "in conformity with previous custom, and in supposed accordance" with Grant's views. As for that part of Grant's dispatch

which refers to newspaper reporters and leaky members of my staff showing the existence of any desire or even sentiment at these headquarters of keeping up a distinction of feeling and spirit between the troops of my command or the rest of your troops, as if they were not an integral part thereof, I answer that no such feeling has ever existed at these headquarters. No countenance, either directly or indirectly, has been given to such an idea, nor was I aware that such an idea was abroad until I saw indications of it from members of your staff and your own orders.

I regard it as the offspring of sentiments [rather] than those of a desire for justice or the good of the service, and sincerely hope that you do not participate therein. There are no headquarters in these United States less responsible for what newspaper correspondents and paragraphists say than mine. This I wish to be understood as distinctly applicable to the affairs of Iuka and Corinth. After this declaration I am free to say that if you do not meet me frankly with a declaration that you are satisfied I shall consider my power to be useful in this department ended.

On October 22 Rosecrans told Halleck of Grant's accusation of "getting up a spirit of division," of his own avowal of loyalty, and of his offer to resign if Grant was not satisfied. He explained that, ever since Iuka, "mousing politicians" on Grant's staff had worked to arouse jealousy in Grant's mind; and that as soon as he had completed new defenses for Corinth and his battle report, he hoped for something that should settle the matter.

I am sure these politicians will manage matters with the sole view of preventing Grant from being in the background of military operations. This will make him sour and reticent. I shall become uncommunicative, and that, added to a conviction that he lacks administrative ability, will complete the reasons why I should be relieved of duty here, if I can be assigned to any other suitable duty where such obstacles do not operate. I forbear speaking of points in the operations here. You will see in my report of Iuka that I have observed the same thing. But I must close this personal letter, wishing you were here to command.

Reid's wry conclusion that "He never omitted an opportunity to do himself an injury" has some basis in fact, and his silences sometimes hurt him as much as his speech. Priding himself on what he considered a subordinate's honorable conduct, he said nothing of "operations here," lumping all of Grant's shortcomings in one sweeping judgment: that he lacked ability as an administrator. Concerning his differences with Grant he wrote: "I shall become uncommunicative."

The next day he besought Grant: "Please answer my personal dispatch." Grant never replied. The full-dress showdown that threatened might have cleared the air. But events originating elsewhere prevented it. Because of Rosecrans' victories, Washington could not afford to ignore him.

After Iuka, Rosecrans had written to Annie: "I have been appointed a Major General. I am curious to see the date. I shall accept it, as an act of tardy justice."

When he learned the date, he boiled over in an "unofficial" letter to Halleck:

I have received and accepted the appointment of Major General of Volunteers for "meritorious services in Western Virginia to date from September 17th, 1862." A feeling of shame and indignation came over me as I wrote the acceptance. If fighting successful battles having important results, successfully defending a mountainous country against an active and powerful foe; if pacifying and restoring law and order to a vast region with 300 miles of mountain frontier, and the successful administration of a department deserved anything from the hands of the government, it deserved my promotion from the date of those services crowned with success. But what do I find? Why, I find myself promoted junior to men who have not rendered a tithe of the services nor had a tithe of the success. I find myself separated from the command of an army whose confidence I possess—a separate army in the field—to go and take subordinate position in a new and unformed one, where Buell, Gilbert, Schenck, Lew Wallace, Tom Crittenden, and Bully Nelson are my seniors. Were it not a crisis for the country, I would not trouble you to intercede, but would at once resign. As it is a crisis, I beg you to intercede for me, that some measure of justice may be done me.

If I have deserved anything for my services in Western Virginia, my rank should date from the close of those services, and that is what I ask in the name of justice. I know and the country knows the strength of this demand. I trust that it may seem to the administration, as to me, that no statesman or government ever gains by partiality or injustice.

This slight drew scornful snorts from Rosecrans for years. In 1865, referring to his brigadier's rank, Rosecrans remarked: "I served in this grade long after colonels have been promoted to major generals for camp service."

Kenneth Williams supports the justice of this claim:

It was not Virginia-born Thomas who for awhile had a right to feel that he was discriminated against by the administration, but Ohio-born William S. Rosecrans. He was colonel of an Ohio regiment when made a brigadier general in the regular army, dating from May 16, 1861. It was well known that it was his turning movement that won the Battle of Rich Mountain on July 11th. Yet when good work was being rewarded in March, 1862, Rosecrans was passed over. His name appears at the head of the major generals of that day because he decisively ranked all of them as a brigadier.

Halleck gave Rosecrans a soft answer:

It would have given me the greatest pleasure if your commission could have been dated back, but the War Department has decided that only in the case of reappointments can commissions be dated back of the adjournment of Congress. . . . As soon as I arrived here I tried to get you appointed, but found that there were objections. These I finally succeeded in removing. I know you are ranked by many of less capacity, and by some who have never rendered any service at all, but this cannot now be helped. I hope, however, that we may not be cursed with the appointment of any more *political* generals. . . . You have my entire confidence, and, if it be possible, I will give you a separate command.

Lincoln subsequently back-dated Rosecrans' commission to March 21, 1862.

More disturbing to Rosecrans than his difficulties with Grant or the date of his appointment was a letter from Mrs. Scammon telling that Annie had been dangerously ill, though now recovered. The baby was dead. As if to cheer and distract her, Rosecrans described the meeting of his flag of truce detail with Van Dorn at Holly Springs. Like many husbands, he bragged a little.

They were taken in blindfold from the pickets. The outfit was very stylish. Silver mounted barouche drawn by four white horses, escorts, 40 elegantly clothed dragoons. Van Dorn received them. He was just relieved. John Pemberton of whom I used to write you from West Point in days Lang Syne is his successor. Our officers were received with much courtesy by those belonging to the old Army. They have a wholesome regard for me, praise very highly the style of our troops and the tactics on the field of battle. Part of what they praised—the center giving way— was accidental and I regretted it, but the main feature was my special intention and was so explained to all the division commanders on the battlefield on Friday evening. They are more afraid of me than any other general in the service. Thanks be to God for that.

Rumor was spreading through the Union camp that Price was gathering an army to make another attempt to seize Corinth. Actually such a return was beyond Price's power. When the long-awaited exchanged prisoners reached Holly Springs, they lacked their own transportation, and Price himself did not have half enough for them. As later facts corrected earlier rumors, Sherman told Grant that the whole force at Holly Springs was no larger than Van Dorn's before Corinth.

In spite of these worries, misunderstandings, and threats, Rosecrans was in high spirits. It was clear, Whitelaw Reid wrote later, that "In the War Department, where Grant's hostility, even if existing and exerted, could as yet avail nothing, the star of Rose-crans was now rapidly rising to its zenith." Papers concerning his transfer were in motion on October 23. Halleck's telegram fol-lowed: "You will immediately repair to Cincinnati, where you will receive orders. . . . Go with the least possible delay." On the same day Stanton assured Rosecrans that he could select his own staff.

Yet when Rosecrans—as he should not have done—appealed directly to Lincoln to promote Lieutenant Lyford as his inspector general, Lincoln forwarded the telegram to the War Department, and Stanton, still simmering at what he termed "interference"— Rosecrans had been appointed against his wishes—boiled over. "Your conduct in this matter is very reprehensible, and I am di-rected to say that unless you obey orders you will not receive the command." The signature was Halleck's; the voice Stanton's.

"I was astonished at your dispatch," Rosecrans answered. "I am obeying orders as fast as the ordinary means of travel will carry me. . . . If you desire more, please say what, and it shall be done if possible." He was in trouble again.

When General Grenville Dodge was ordered to Corinth on Oc-tober 30 to succeed Davies, he learned that "there were many pro-tests" regarding Rosecrans' reports, from McPherson, Hurlbut, and other officers. Mrs. Grant, who was at Jackson, told Dodge that these officers appealed to her in the matter, but that Grant was disinclined to rebuke Rosecrans. At this juncture, the telegram transferring Rosecrans came, and Mrs. Grant told Dodge that Grant came out of his tent holding it in his hands. He declared that his greatest trouble "had been solved."

On October 26, Rosecrans took leave of his army. Hamilton succeeded him. Grant represented himself as "delighted" with the promotion of Rosecrans to a separate command: "I still believed that when independent of an immediate superior the qualities which I, at that time, credited him with possessing, would show themselves. As a subordinate I found that I could not make him do as I wished, and had determined to relieve him from duty that very day." And so, with mutual satisfaction, the two parted.

Although they shook hands and pledged co-operation, for Grant at least the gesture indicated no change of heart. Three days later he directed an aide-de-camp to write to Sherman: "Rosecrans has been ordered to Cincinnati to receive further orders. This is greatly to the relief of the General who was very much disappointed in him. This matter the general will explain to you when he sees you."

When Sherman heard of Rosecrans' transfer, he wrote to him, wishing him every success and congratulating him on his "magnificent victory" at Corinth. A few days later, after Colonels Lagow and Dickey had borne Grant's message to him, Sherman confessed to Rawlins: "I note the General's allusions to Rosecrans, and was somewhat surprised but convinced."

The transfer of Rosecrans produced a fresh flurry of newspaper comment, much of it flattering to him, and extravagant and hopeful. This praise nettled Grant, and on November 9, he composed an uneasy letter to Illinois Congressman Elihu B. Washburne, who had become his patron and defender in Washington. Now, ignoring the newspaper charges that it was the generals, and not the men, of the Union left who were found lacking, Grant created and demolished a straw man. He rose to the defense of his troops, as though they had been slighted:

I do not see my report of the battle of Iuka in print. As the papers in General Rosecrans' interest have so much misrepresented the affair, I would like to see it in print. I have no objection to that or any other general being made a hero of the press, but I do not want to see it at the expense of a meritorious portion of the army. I endeavored in that report to give a plain statement of facts, some of which I would never have mentioned had it not become necessary in defense of troops who have been with me in all, or nearly all, the battles where I have had the honor to command. I have never had a single regiment disgrace itself in battle yet, except some new ones at Shiloh. . . .

Grant now looked forward to undertaking his own operations against Vicksburg, and since new levies and other reinforcements continued to reach him, he was prepared by the 2nd of November to take the initiative. His army now numbered some 48,500 men. Grant's campaign against Vicksburg, which did not fall until eight months later, began three weeks after Grant had called Rosecrans back, and one week after Rosecrans left Corinth.

The generally accepted version of the battle of Corinth and the subsequent pursuit of the enemy follows closely the version in Grant's *Memoirs*. As General Dodge puts it: "Van Dorn and Price were completely defeated, and their army retreated completely demoralized, and should have been relentlessly followed, and their trains and artillery captured; and although Grant urged this in dispatch after dispatch,"—a statement wholly unsupported by the *Official Records*—"for some reason there were delays. Grant criticizes Rosecrans severely for his movements in these battles, and censures him for failing to capture Price at Iuka and to follow Van Dorn after Corinth." Typical of the statements of more recent historians is that of Otto Eisenschiml and Ralph Newman, who say in their *American Iliad* that Price and Van Dorn "suffered a bloody repulse, but escaped fatal damage through Rosecrans' dilatory pursuit, for which Grant, who was in command of the district, never forgave him."

In contrast to these is the opinion of Arthur Ducat, Rosecrans' chief of staff:

> If Grant had supported you, and called upon the different garrisons having troops that might have been available to you, to be forwarded from the different depots, using the railroads to Corinth and the steamers to Memphis and below, and put provisions and ammunition on your line . . . the Vicksburg campaign would never have been necessary. . . . More men were lost from sickness and fever and exposure, digging ditches . . . about Vicksburg, than might have achieved its reduction by a few pieces of brilliant tactics on several occasions and before the place fell. . . . I regard the calling back of you at Corinth as an unexplained military crime, and shall so regard it while I live unless your superiors will admit that they were insane or jackasses. But miserable gloryfilchers like to dwell upon it as something attaching to you. It is a burning shame that every honest man who knows about it should not come forward to deny it, and attack such monstrous outrages upon history.

Rosecrans himself expressed much the same judgment in the article which he prepared for *Battles and Leaders*:

> This [the calling off of the pursuit] was early in October. The weather was cool, and the roads in prime order. The country along the Mississippi Central to Grenada, and especially below that place, was a corn country— a rich farming country—and the corn was ripe. If Grant had not stopped us, we could have gone to Vicksburg. My judgment was to go on, and with the help suggested we could have done so. Under the pressure of a victorious force the enemy were experiencing all the weakening effects of a retreating army, whose means of supplies and ammunitions are

always difficult to keep in order. We had Sherman at Memphis with two divisions, and we had Hurlbut at Bolivar with one division, and John A. Logan at Jackson, Tennessee, with six regiments. With these there was nothing to save Vicksburg from our grasp. We were about six day's march from Vicksburg, and Grant could have put his force through to it with my column as the center one of pursuit. Confederate officers told me afterward that they were never so scared in their lives as they were after the defeat before Corinth. . . . Let the judgments of the future be formed upon the words of impartial history.

Had the military career of Rosecrans ended after the pursuit, those judgments would have been most favorable. To his services in Western Virginia, his excellent record in Mississippi would have added much. He had cheerfully made the best of a reduced assignment, led Halleck's pursuit after the siege of Corinth, improved the health and morale of his forces, managed well the civil affairs of the territory which he administered, strengthened the Corinth fortifications, fought two battles. Iuka was a victory, even though Grant's failure to co-operate lost the full fruits; and Corinth was a decisive Confederate defeat, even though Grant called back the pursuit. In both battles the Confederates outnumbered the Federals—a rare circumstance in Union victories. Rosecrans had proved himself skillful and resourceful in planning, and rapid and able in execution; active, energetic, industrious. He had displayed conspicuous personal bravery in battle and until Chickamauga he was the North's most frequent and most consistent winner, an able commander qualifying for a top assignment to give him a chance to test and prove his full abilities.

Nine

"FIGHT, I SAY!"

The Army of the Ohio had been organized by Kentucky Unionists and by Loyalists in neighboring states. Commanded successively by Robert Anderson, the hero of Sumter, William T. Sherman, and Don Carlos Buell, it had fought at the Big Sandy, Mill Springs, Forts Donelson and Henry, Shiloh, and the siege of Corinth. When Halleck sent Buell to seize Chattanooga, General Braxton Bragg with the Confederate Army of Tennessee arrived there first, and advanced through Tennessee into Kentucky. In a race to Louisville, Buell won, and at Perryville he turned back Bragg, who next day retreated toward eastern Tennessee. Great trains moved in Bragg's van, bearing the plunder on which he subsisted during the winter. Buell followed, but Bragg escaped. Buell left a garrison under Negley at Nashville, and then returned to southwestern Kentucky to rest his footsore army. The 1862 fall primaries, in which the Democrats gained, brought a howl from Republicans—"Buell's slows cost us the votes"—and helped Lincoln decide against Democrat Buell. Rosecrans would succeed him.

In Cincinnati, Rosecrans learned that Lincoln had created the Department of the Cumberland out of that part of Tennessee east of the Ohio River and any portions of northern Alabama and Georgia Union troops could seize. Rosecrans would command this department. His troops would constitute a new army corps, the XIV. An enclosure, to be handed to Buell, directed him to report to Indianapolis for orders. In a covering letter, Halleck ordered Rosecrans to drive the enemy from Kentucky and middle Tennessee and to take and hold east Tennessee, cutting the railroad so as to sever Virginia, Georgia, and the Carolinas from the rest of the Confederacy. Cox, moving up the Kanawha, might help; so might Grant. Rosecrans could call on Wright, commanding the Department of the Ohio, for assistance and supplies. If Bragg moved against Grant, Rosecrans could assist Grant. "I need not urge upon you the necessity of giving active employment to your forces. Neither the country nor the government will much longer put up with the inactivity of some of our armies and generals."

"I will leave tomorrow for General Buell's headquarters," Rosecrans reported. To Grant he telegraphed: "We are to cooperate as far as possible to support each other's operations." In transferring command, the War Department usually issued simultaneous orders, thus granting the losing commander the courtesy of a few days to prepare for the change. Buell was denied this courtesy, and Rosecrans said he "felt more like a constable bearing a writ for the ejection of a tenant than like a general on his way to relieve a brother officer."

From the Galt House, famous Louisville hotel, Rosecrans wrote to Buell: "I, like yourself, am neither an intriguer nor newspaper soldier. . . . Propriety will permit me to say that . . . you had my high respect for ability as a soldier, for your firm adherence to truth and justice in the government and discipline of your command."

Buell had known that his removal was imminent. He told Rosecrans: "I have never done anything without reason. I have done my best, if not *the* best."

As Buell bade his army farewell, he expressed concern for Thomas: "Can I do anything for you privately? I can hardly flatter myself that I can do anything officially." Thomas had a seniority problem. His commission and those of McCook and Crittenden antedated Rosecrans'. When Lincoln wanted Rosecrans as Buell's successor he slashed red tape to antedate the commission to March 21, 1862, thus giving Rosecrans recognition for his Western Virginia victories, and seniority over his new subordinates.

Thomas, learning of Rosecrans' appointment, was "deeply mortified and aggrieved," and he wrote to Halleck in protest against the unfairness of jumping a junior ahead of him. Halleck replied that Rosecrans was not Thomas's junior, and that in any event,

Lincoln could pick whom he chose, without reference to seniority. On the eve of the battle of Perryville, Thomas had been offered the command but had refused it because he felt that Buell had earned the right to fight the battle. "I have no objection whatever to serving under General Rosecrans," Thomas answered, "now that I know his commission dates prior to mine." When he learned that Rosecrans' commission had been antedated, Thomas concluded that Halleck had not been frank and he informed Rosecrans that his sense of military propriety was shocked. "There is no one under whom I would more willingly serve than you, but under the circumstances I trust you will cooperate by getting me transferred to Texas."

"My command came to me unsought," Rosecrans replied. "Had the government so willed, I would gladly have served under *you*. Anticipating the question of rank, the War Department antedated my commission. The best interests of the country demand your service with this army." Rosecrans offered Thomas the choice of becoming executive officer and second in command, or of taking independent command. Thomas chose the latter, and was given the center.

The same newspapers that had clamored for Buell's removal now hailed the coming of Rosecrans. The Cleveland *Leader* said in an editorial: "The army is well pleased with the change. The Army in Kentucky will not remain idle long." They wanted a winning general, and had received the North's most consistent winner. A change of commanders, however, did not alter the unique problems of the Department, or the attitude of public or administration. Colonel Beatty assessed Rosecrans' position: "A man from whom the people are each day expecting some extraordinary action, some tremendous battle . . . is likely very soon to become unpopular. . . . It takes two to make a fight. I predict that in twelve months Rosecrans will be as unpopular as Buell."

On November 1, 1862, Rosecrans entrained for Bowling Green, Kentucky, 115 miles south. Brown hills and dry creek beds told of the long drought. "It is reported," he wrote to Sylvester, "that Bragg is making forced marches to get to Louisville before we can. I doubt it. It would be a great thing for us if the rebels would come and fight us near our base. For the only remedy for this evil is *fighting*. We must crush their power. This must be done by battles.

If we can make the enemy wear himself out by marches, and then fight him near our own base and far from his own, he runs the risk of annihilation."

On paper, this second largest Union army showed impressive strength. It consisted of eight infantry divisions, all with cavalry, and some with artillery, engineering, and signal corps. It included an independent cavalry division, many detached units, and Palmer's division from the Army of the Mississippi—an aggregate of 98,795 men, of whom 75,500 were present for duty, and 102 pieces of artillery.

The army, however, was not in fighting condition. When Colonel Hans Heg of the 15th Wisconsin was assigned to it, he commented that "A looser disciplined army could hardly be expected to hold together." And Colonel Frederick Knefler of the 79th Indiana wrote: "Since October we have marched over 700 miles. For 52 days of our march we had not a single tent and had to subsist on half rations of bread, meat, sugar and coffee." Rosecrans found thinned ranks, filled hospitals, empty supply depots, poor discipline, low morale. Nevertheless, he ordered an advance to Nashville on November 4.

He himself took quarters in a private home at Bowling Green, using the front rooms, while his unwilling hostess kept to the rear. The stream of heavy-booted visitors provoked her to action. At night she ripped the carpeting from the floor and carried it off. In the morning Rosecrans ordered it replaced. Next she flavored the barrel of drinking water with a bucket of soft soap. Rosecrans was ill for one night, but quickly recovered. With each party scoring a victory the contest ended in a truce.

During the first week, Rosecrans appointed his staff, but not his commanders. He brought Ducat with him as chief of staff. If he had special favorites, they were Ducat and Major Frank S. Bond, who had served as secretary-treasurer of several railroads. He and Ducat were the type of bright young men Rosecrans wanted as assistants. Older men could not always keep pace with his driving work habits. "My staff should know everything I know," he said. To distinguish his center and wings from the divisions comprising them, Rosecrans called them informally his "grand divisions." Major-General Thomas L. Crittenden commanded the left wing, and Major-General Alexander McDowell McCook, the right.

Crittenden was a member of a great divided Kentucky family. His father, John Crittenden, had served two Presidents as attorney general, and had been governor of Kentucky, and United States Senator, and was the author of the Crittenden Compromise. Thomas Crittenden himself had studied law, and was Zachary Taylor's aide in the Mexican War. His older brother, George, a West Pointer, was a Confederate major general.

The "fighting McCooks" of Ohio were as distinctive as the proud Crittendens. The clan had produced a dozen generals and heroes. Alexander had taught infantry tactics at West Point for three years; and by service at Shiloh earned his second star. "A juvenile," Sherman called the round-faced 31-year-old; and Colonel Beatty, whose troops suffered under what he termed "McCook's foolish haste," called him "a chucklehead." McCook's military ability was repeatedly questioned, but his courage, nevertheless, was legendary.

Whitelaw Reid criticized Rosecrans for confiding the command of the wings to two soldiers "scarcely equal to the command of divisions, excepting when under the eye of a superior officer who could do their thinking for them." He attributed this mistake to ignorance of human nature, and Don Piatt believed Rosecrans did not know the difference between Thomas and McCook. In Rosecrans' defense it should be pointed out that he inherited his grand division, division, and brigade commanders.

From army comments, Colonel John A. Martin of the 8th Kansas concluded, when later he wrote the history of his regiment, "On the whole, the army rejoiced to learn that Rosecrans had been assigned to command. To those who served under him in Mississippi, his presence was peculiarly gratifying, and the enthusiasm with which they hailed his coming was unbounded." He was always a favorite general, and the "glory of his recent victories gave a fresher and greater charm to his name."

"Letters of congratulations pour in on me," Rosecrans wrote to his wife Annie. But none came from Grant, an indication that hostility at Grant's headquarters had not changed. On November 1, Hamilton complained to Grant that "Rosecrans carried off the maps that were most needed." The language almost repeated Ducat's similar complaint against Grant after the removal of

Grant's headquarters from Corinth to Jackson at the end of September.

Salmon P. Chase wrote to Rosecrans: "It was in my power to secure your official appointment as brigadier"—a not quite accurate statement in view of the fact that Scott, McClellan, and others had had a hand in the matter—"and then give you some opportunity of proving your capacity and courage. . . . You are my debtor for little more than friendship. . . . For months and months the country has witnessed with pain and indignation . . . the mishap of movement which has characterized Buell. It has come to be generally believed that his heart was not in the war. . . . These views I know are not yours. You are for earnest, vigorous and decisive action, and now have an opportunity which other generals apparently have thrown away. . . . Now . . . for East Tennessee—the proud central fortress—the key of the whole position of the rebellion. . . .

"I hope that you endorse heartily—not merely acquiesce in the President's proclamation," Chase continued. (The Emancipation Proclamation had been published less than five weeks before.) "Let everybody understand that slavery is to end. It was Buell's pro-slaveryism that caused more than half his halting. . . . I should like to have you write me frankly as to your political views. You know I am a Democrat. . . ."

"Now for East Tennessee," Chase said. But Rosecrans was no more able to advance in that direction than Buell had been. Historian Henry M. Cist, who served with Rosecrans and knew the country firsthand, wrote that: "Halleck's paper campaign into East Tennessee was based on ignorance of the situation and surroundings." It would send an exhausted army 180 miles over mountainous barrens, with only wagon transportation. As it dropped garrisons to cover communications, its fighting front would weaken, so that when it reached its objective, its striking power would be badly depleted. In the meantime, if more of Bragg's army gathered at Murfreesboro, Negley might be compelled to surrender Nashville. The importance of Nashville as a secondary base of supplies induced Rosecrans to prepare to concentrate his forces there. Railroads were open to within forty miles of it. Although the Cumberland River was now too low for freighting, Halleck suggested that when it had risen, supplies could be shipped by water from St. Louis. The problem that would most vex Rosecrans in the year to come—how to keep communications open and sustain his army in the face of overwhelming Confederate cavalry superiority—immediately confronted him.

"We must have cavalry and cavalry arms, and a capable division commander," Rosecrans pleaded. He feared that when Bragg holed up in winter quarters, his cavalry, better led and in overwhelming strength, would scatter, rove for forage and plunder, and cut Union supply lines. The arrival of Stanley, on transfer from the Army of the Tennessee, strengthened the leadership. On November 3, when Rosecrans ordered his cavalry to screen his advance upon Nashville, and to seek out the enemy cavalry, he found them less than half armed. "My cavalry are the eyes and feet of my army, and will be its providers," he told Halleck, as he requested 2500 breech-loading or revolving arms.

Rosecrans reviewed the army by brigades. The men cheered, heartened by his confident manner, and the crack 36th Illinois infantry put on an exhibition. "Now, beat *that* if you can," Rosecrans told green troops. "Boys, when you *drill, drill like thunder!* Don't try how not to do it!" Spying a soldier with a crooked knapsack, he sent for his captain. "Captain, I'm sorry to see that you don't know how to strap a knapsack on a soldier's back." "But I didn't do it, General." "Oh, you didn't. Well, then, hereafter you had better do it yourself, or see that it is done correctly."

Rosecrans obtained permission from Stanton to muster out officers guilty of pillaging, drunkenness, misbehavior, and other flagrant offenses. He asked men and officers to effect a state of discipline "at least equal to that of the rebels."

The New York *Tribune* commented shrewdly that the country and administration wanted handsome accomplishments and expected impossibilities from Rosecrans because he had been invariably successful. Although they had been taught that Buell's army had no equal, they were apparently unaware that the army which Buell had organized was not the army which he left to Rosecrans. Part consisted of splendid but exhausted veterans; part, of raw levies under inexperienced officers. Although little time remained to season this latter group, Rosecrans undertook the task with characteristic energy.

He was shocked at the absenteeism. Nearly one-fourth of the

army—32,966 men—did not muster for duty. Private Cyrus Boyd observed: "Everyone but the Brigadiers and Major Generals are getting *tired* of the war which now looks like it would end like the Kilkenny cats' fight—nothing left but the tails." Lincoln had described regiments which reported two-thirds of their men absent by desertion or with permission of company officers. Deserters outnumbered recruits. "To fill up the army is like undertaking to shovel fleas." Shoot deserters? "No, we must change the condition of things some other way," Lincoln said.

Rosecrans sought that other way. When a lieutenant deserted to southern Illinois, and wrote telling his men how to desert, Rosecrans ordered him brought back in irons, and a court-martial condemned him to death. Then Rosecrans mitigated the punishment. While the culprit's regiment watched, his sword was removed by a non-commissioned officer, his shoulder straps ripped off, and he was driven "ignominiously" from the lines.

Shirkers straggled and allowed themselves to be captured, trusting that they could be paroled. To end this abuse, Rosecrans ordered a supply of the ugliest and cheapest nightcaps for paroled prisoners to wear home. The effect, he said, was "marvellous." The paroling business ended.

Under Buell, the Army of the Ohio had almost no regular army surgeons in its administrative posts, and no regularly organized ambulance and field hospital system. Rosecrans "proved as interested in the Medical Department as his predecessor had been bored." He looked to the men's spiritual welfare, also. Excellent Protestant chaplains were in good supply. That winter, chaplains numbered 32 Methodists, 6 Baptists, 6 Presbyterians, 3 Catholics, and one Campbellite. Although Catholics, largely German- and Irish-born, were numerous, they lacked their quota of chaplains, so Rosecrans advised his commanders that he would secure a priest for any division or brigade in which Catholic soldiers agreed to supply his reasonable wants. Rumor alleged that Rosecrans favored Catholics, and permitted religion to warp his judgment. These charges were false, wrote Correspondent William D. Bickham of the Cincinnati *Commercial,* who lived at headquarters for a year. "He never interferes with the spiritual affairs of any subordinate." Moreover, Stanley, a recent convert, and Garesché were the only Catholics on his staff.

To re-equip the army and repair the railroad to Nashville, Rosecrans established great military depots at Bowling Green. The army lacked an adequate engineering corps, and therefore he ordered details from every company to serve as pioneers—half laborers, half mechanics.

As fast as troops were equipped, Rosecrans pushed them toward Nashville, where the Federal garrison "lacked almost everything except discipline, courage, and ammunition." As McCook advanced, he was to throw rations into Nashville as quickly as possible. He reached the city on the morning of November 7. Next day, Crittenden encamped along the Cumberland, near Gallatin, Tennessee. Meanwhile, three of Thomas's divisions marched along the railroad, while the fourth occupied Scotsville and Glasgow. Rations followed by rail to Mitchellsville. There they were transferred to wagons for the forty-mile haul to Nashville.

November continued mild in Tennessee, but snow fell as Burnside presented McClellan with an order to turn over his command to him. The order was dated the day after the November elections, which raised the number of Democratic congressmen from 44 to 75, and cost the Republican party five states which they carried in 1860—a loss assumed to be a rebuke to the Lincoln administration.

Rosecrans was in buoyant spirits, yet he remained humble. "I do not feel elated, but rather more dependent on God who for his own glory has set me in my present position."

With the army around Nashville, headquarters announced that it would follow on Sunday, November 9. Rosecrans suspended this order for twenty-four hours—he objected to any but indispensable moves on Sunday. Most generals shared this feeling, and on November 15, Lincoln issued a general order to both services: "The discipline and character of the National forces should not suffer, nor the cause they defend be imperiled, by the profanation of the day or name of the Most High."

Before sunrise on November 10, Rosecrans and his staff boarded a train for Mitchellsville, where horses waited to carry them the last forty miles to Nashville. It would have been tempting to take side roads to avoid the slow procession of wagons that plodded after McCook and Crittenden, but Rosecrans warned the staff to keep with the escort because the "natives were not friendly."

Indian summer in Kentucky was a gentle, lingering time. Morning mist rose from streams and rivers, persimmons hung jewel ripe, and opossums were fat. But after the party crossed the Tennessee border, blight appeared. Fields became weed patches. Fences had been ripped down for campfires, which spread through dry woods to set the country smoldering for miles. An occasional blackened chimney stood in a charred space that had been a home. For hours the horsemen rode through wood smoke in a silent and sullen countryside, without barking dogs or laughing and shouting children. Near Nashville, where the land rumpled into cross ridges and hills, and neat stone fences surrounded rich plantations, slaves' quarters and stock barns stood empty now.

Rosecrans and his staff rode for ten hours. Night fell before the lights of Nashville appeared. The hills surrounding the city glowed with bivouac fires, and tattoo echoed through the valleys. Thousands of men's voices mingled with the high, unmusical complaint of mules. The riders clattered through narrow, rough streets, past tightly shuttered windows, crossed the Cumberland, and drew rein at 13 High Street.

Built close to the street, the spacious brick house of George W. Cunningham, Federal headquarters since Buell occupied Nashville in February 1862, had massive dignity. Rosecrans stepped through an iron gate, intricately wrought. Light streamed through tall front windows and the fanlight topping the tall, double front doors, framed in a simply carved, Victorian Gothic arch. McCook offered the riders immediate hospitality.

Next morning, Nashville looked desolate. War had left buildings dirty and dilapidated, and streets rough and filthy. On an impressive acropolis, the unfinished capitol building had been converted into a fort, a Greek temple with cannon snouts sticking over its parapets. Streets were barricaded with cotton bales or earthworks. St. Cloud Hill was an "armed fort," and other forts lay beyond. In wealthy homes pantries were bare, silver coffee pots empty, and fine china plates held scanty rations. Markets stood abandoned and money was scarce. The Nashville *Dispatch,* on November 1, commented that supplies of dry goods and groceries were "lower than ever in the memory of the oldest inhabitant."

Loyal Unionists welcomed the Federals; collaborators played to the winning side for gain, but the majority of Nashville citizens remained sullen and unco-operative. Some smuggled medicine, weapons, contraband, or escaped prisoners.

In nearby Murfreesboro, the *Rebel Banner* proclaimed the presence of Generals Bragg, Buckner, Cheatham, and others, and intimated that something important was at hand. It boasted: "We will give the Abolitionists battle should they dare to venture so far."

The women of Nashville formed an unorganized but determined resistance. Charging that they lied, spied, and smuggled, William Truesdail, Rosecrans' chief of military police, warned: "Don't trust women." Provost Marshal Miles enjoyed conversing with the women, but denied their applications for passes. Undismayed, they established a petticoat blockade in the hallway and on the staircase of headquarters. "They rarely failed to see Rosecrans," said correspondent Bickham, "but often regretted it." Rosecrans wrote to Annie: "The Nashville ladies are very importunate," and chuckling to himself, he turned the women over to Bickham. "He attends to their insinuative applications for 'little passes.'" Sometimes two hundred women applied in a single day. One woman "sprang from her carriage, and two pairs of heavy cavalry boots fell from their 'delicate hiding place.'" A pocket, "spacious as a market basket," was crammed with quinine. Annoyed indeed was one woman who was "politely denuded"; a number of letters addressed to Confederate officers were found "under her chemise."

Nashville women declared that Captain Truesdail "seemed to possess an evil genius for his slimy type of work." The *Kentucky Daily Democrat* told of a Southern girl who refused to take the oath of allegiance on the grounds that it was wrong to swear. Rosecrans nevertheless insisted that she must swear before she left his presence. "Well, general, if I must swear, I will; but all the sin of the oath must rest on your shoulders. God damn every Yankee to hell!"

To Halleck, Rosecrans reported: "Everything quiet." In ten days he hoped to have the forty-mile rail gap between Mitchellville and Nashville repaired. In the meantime his supplies must come by wagon.

Rosecrans was forced to seize serviceable horses, but he allowed three exceptions—the Insane Asylum; aged Major Lewis, once Andrew Jackson's aide-de-camp; and President Polk's widow, were all permitted to keep their horses. From Polk Place came a note: "Mrs. Polk begs leave to return to Major General Rosecrans her acknowledgements for the favor granted to her, and trusts that 'under the historic name she bears' she may always deserve the consideration awarded her." Rosecrans soon learned that his consideration was misplaced—Mrs. Polk expressed the hope that Washington would soon recognize the Confederacy.

For forty-six days the Army of the Cumberland remained in Nashville, a Union island in a Confederate sea. In thirteen days Thomas judged that by moving slowly through the tunnel trains could come through without danger. The line from Bowling Green to Nashville was subject to constant harassment. Improvised bridges were burned again and again. Tunnels were blocked by a single charge of powder. Rails were torn up, heated, twisted out of shape. Between Franklin, Kentucky, and Nashville, the enemy burned the wood supply and destroyed all water tanks. When the long tunnel south of Mitchellville was cleared, engines found no wood for fuel, no water for boilers. Rosecrans roared: "Morgan has sent over a lot of soldiers in citizens' dress to loaf around and injure the railroad. . . . Whoever cannot give a good account of themselves shoot, or hang on the nearest tree."

Rosecrans watched the Cumberland River. How long before he could use it for freighting supplies? The weather continued clear until the night of November 20, when winds shifted and heavy rains flooded streets. Arising early, Rosecrans looked out upon a mist-shrouded city. The river had risen an inch or two.

Rosecrans condensed his activity at Nashville into a sentence. "I bent every effort to repair the railroad, and get supplies to Nashville, which I made my supply depot for future operations." The advance to Murfreesboro and the victory were made possible by his efforts during these forty-six days. He sought to accumulate enough supplies at Nashville so that the army could advance, or withstand a short siege. Even if he accomplished these aims, he was still checkmated by Bragg's superior cavalry. Bragg had four cavalrymen to his one. Only if Bragg should grow overconfident and send some of his cavalry away, could Rosecrans strike at him with fair prospects of success.

Meanwhile, he ordered his topographical engineers to make maps of the country ahead, and established courier lines. Needing officers, he asked for General Schuyler Hamilton, Halleck's brother-in-law, but Hamilton became ill on arrival and had to be sent home. General J. J. Reynolds, who served in West Virginia, reported. Rosecrans appointed Stanley Chief of Cavalry, and Captain James St. Clair Morton, Chief of Engineers and Pioneers. When Ducat grew ill and returned to Chicago, Colonel Julius P. Garesché replaced him as Chief of Staff.

Garesché, West Point '41, had served twenty-one years in the regular army, eight as assistant adjutant general. After Sumter he refused a commission as major general, saying that he wished to earn his stars on the battlefield. He seemed without earthly ambition, half mystic, half saint; he denied himself reasonable comforts to help the poor. Men loved Garesché, although few understood him. Even the Confederates considered him the "most gallant gentleman in the army."

Garesché came to his desk about 10:00 A.M., and seldom left before midnight. Aides Thoms and Thompson worked at deciphering code at a deal table at the foot of Rosecrans' cot. Aides Goddard and Dickson buried themselves in the paper work of the adjutant-general's department. Rosecrans sometimes called Bond, Thompson, and Thoms together, and dictated three letters simultaneously, while he conversed with a fourth person and puffed his cigar.

All day long, staff officers moved in and out, or waited assignments, lounging in comfortable chairs or upon Rosecrans' cot. Though vague answers drew sharp lectures, which reduced squirming juniors to what some called "speechless idiocy," Rosecrans was generous with compliments too, saying of Ducat, for instance, "I like that man. He's a thorough soldier."

Late in the afternoon military business increased, and, toward evening, commanders came in and remained. With darkness, aides lighted stearin dips. When the last chore was done, a general conversation began. The hesitation and occasional stammering that marked Rosecrans' public speech was wanting in his familiar talk, as he discoursed on literature, science, or religion. He loved to listen to mathematician Thoms, and laughed readily at Garesché's whimsy. The talk sometimes continued beyond the midnight report of Provost Marshal W. M. Miles.

In spite of late November showers, mild dry weather predominated—"beautiful, just cold enough to be pleasant." The Cumberland, which needed two weeks of rain to be navigable, became an absorbing conversation piece. Confederates well knew the advantages the drought had for them. A Shelbyville Unionist was startled to hear a preacher intone: "O Lord, let the rain descend to fructify the earth and to swell the rivers; but O Lord, do not raise the Cumberland sufficient to bring upon us those damned Yankee gunboats!" On Sunday, November 30, lightning flashed, thunder rolled through the hills, and rain lasted until midnight.

Strain had developed in the official relations of Military Governor Andrew Johnson and Rosecrans, though fortunately, their personal relations remained friendly and easy. Their spheres of authority overlapped slightly—Halleck wished Rosecrans to join military and civil government in Nashville by appointing Johnson, whom Lincoln had commissioned a brigadier general, to the command of the post of Nashville. Rosecrans had refused.

Meanwhile, as Rosecrans hoped he would, Bragg returned to Tennessee. After reporting to Davis concerning the Kentucky campaign, he left Richmond, and early in November rejoined his army at Knoxville. He moved by rail to Chattanooga, and from there, on November 12, he wired Beauregard: "My forces are rapidly concentrating in Middle Tennessee, and should the enemy move out of his intrenchments at Nashville, we will soon fight him." By the 15th, Bragg's whole army was across the Tennessee and advancing toward Nashville. On December 3, Bragg was between Tullahoma and Murfreesboro, with three divisions already at Murfreesboro.

By November's end, Rosecrans was filling his shortages. "Five days rations ahead!" he exulted. Although not sufficient for a long campaign, clearly supplies were getting past enemy cavalry in his rear. Artillery ammunition was coming down in quantity from Louisville; cavalry arms arrived more slowly. Although the armies were otherwise fairly matched, cavalry remained the sticking point.

Because he himself lacked cavalry, Rosecrans labored to spread the impression that he had holed in for the winter, so that Bragg might send off some of his, and thus give the Federals an opportunity to move. As early as December 9, the Nashville *Dispatch,* quoting the Louisville *Democrat* of November 7, mentioned "rumors of another Morgan raid into Kentucky." On November

17, Rosecrans told Halleck that he was "trying to lull them" into a belief that he "was not going to move soon." He would accumulate two million rations—sufficient to supply 100,000 men for 20 days—in Nashville and, if the river rose, throw himself on Bragg's right and attempt to crush him. In that case Halleck should send gunboats into the Tennessee, and should provide Rosecrans with an adequate supply of cavalry arms.

Washington was sensitive to the rebuke of the November elections, however, and clamored for an immediate victory. "The President is very impatient at your long stay in Nashville," Halleck wrote. "Twice have I been asked to designate someone else to command your army. If you remain one more week at Nashville, I cannot prevent your removal. . . . The Government demands action."

Despite this threat, Rosecrans refused to advance until the Nashville depots were provisioned for the longest possible break in his supply line. Answering Halleck, he telegraphed a "few but earnest words." He had lost no time. Had he advanced prematurely, he would have had neither supplies nor ammunition to fall back upon if defeated. "Many of our soldiers are to this day barefoot, without blankets, without tents, without good arms, and cavalry without horses. Our true objective now is the enemy's force, for if they come near, we save wear, tear, risk and strength; subject them to what we escape, and gain all the chances to be expected from a rise in the river. . . . I need no other stimulus to make me do my duty than the knowledge of what it is. To threats of removal or the like, I must be permitted to say that I am insensible."

This answer brought a hasty retreat from Halleck. His telegram was a statement of facts, not a threat. Lincoln had told Halleck repeatedly that imperative reasons existed for driving the Confederates across the Tennessee River at the earliest possible moment. Halleck imagined that these reasons were diplomatic, and of a most serious character: "You can hardly conceive his great anxiety about it. I will tell you what it is, although it is only a guess on my part. It has been feared that on the meeting of the British Parliament in January next, the political pressure of the starving operators may force the government to join France in an intervention." Actually, almost a half-million working men were idle because the Union blockade shut off Confederate cotton from English mills. Lincoln was pictured in *Punch* with long horns and a tail.

"If the enemy be left in possession of middle Tennessee, which we held last July," Halleck explained, "it will be said that they have gained on us. . . . Tennessee is the only State which can be used as an argument in favor of intervention by England. . . . Your movements have an importance beyond mere military success." The whole Cabinet inquired almost daily: "Why doesn't he move?" Rosecrans' advance might be the "very turning-point in our foreign relations." Halleck continued: "It was hoped and believed when you took the command that you would recover all lost ground by, at furthest, the middle of December, so that it would be known in London soon after the meeting of Parliament. . . . A victory or the retreat of the enemy before the 10th of this month would have been of more value to us than ten times that success at a later date. . . . General Buell . . . was too slow to be in time. . . . Hence the change."

Rosecrans faced a dilemma. If he advanced he risked defeat. If he stood he risked removal. And while a successful advance depended partly upon his ability to convince Bragg that he was holed up for the winter, the telegraph—available to Bragg through tapping—told him to move.

On December 11, Chase wrote: "I have heard a great deal of conflict about your tarrying at Nashville. Perhaps you should not have gone to Nashville at all, but have pushed directly for East Tennessee. Again, censure is bestowed on the many demands you make for many things."

Before this letter reached Nashville, Lee defeated Burnside at Fredericksburg. Charging repeatedly into impregnable positions, the Union army suffered 12,653 casualties. Burnside pointed to his wounded, trapped in the burning grass on Marye's Hill, and cried: "Oh those men! Those men over there!"

In the west, Van Dorn swooped down upon Grant's advance depot at Holly Springs, destroyed his supplies, cut his communications, and forced him to retreat. The depot was commanded by Colonel Robert C. Murphy, whom Rosecrans had recommended for court-martial after he had abandoned supplies at Iuka to Price in September. Then Grant objected. Now Correspondent Edward

Betty wrote: "Murphy was put in command at Holly Springs to refute your just reprimand of his conduct at Iuka. Just before the Van Dorn raid, Hamilton told me that your remarks in the Murphy affair were 'a gross outrage upon the rights and feelings of every officer in that army,' and requested me to say so in my paper. This I refused to do and the matter rested." Murphy, warned of Van Dorn's approach at Holly Springs, made no preparations to meet him, and Grant dismissed him from the service for cowardly and disgraceful conduct. "When the Holly Springs affair developed the total incapacity of Murphy," Betty gloated, "I saw Hamilton again, and he requested me, in a different tone, to say as little as possible about it."

With Grant retreating from Oxford, the enemy on Rosecrans' right was unemployed, and Chase forwarded a rumor that Pemberton might join Bragg against Rosecrans. Burnside's defeat created a threat for Rosecrans' left, so that John Beatty wrote: "Fredericksburg will enable them to spare troops to reinforce Bragg."

Rosecrans was not without defenders among the powerful Radicals. Captain Francis Darr wrote that Senator Wade of Ohio was a "warm friend of yours, and fully appreciates all the obstacles and impediments which thwart any rapid and extended forward movement." He "strongly contrasts your success in Western Virginia, Iuka and Corinth with the snake-like movements of the Army of the Potomac, and makes it a point to interpose when he hears any murmurs of delay at Nashville."

On November 22, Rosecrans confided to Annie: "The Administration expects much of me. I have a bad country to advance over, but my hopes are all in God. . . . I work about 18 hours a day. . . . I am in the hopes of beginning to move very soon with the intention of moving rapidly and continuously. The next battle in this department is likely to decide the war. There must be no failure. I will not move until I am ready."

Continued drought was accompanied by frequent fires. On the night of November 27, fires burned all around the outskirts of Nashville, and at six-thirty on December 18 a large crowd gathered when the stables in the rear of Rosecrans' headquarters caught fire.

By December 19, twenty to thirty days' rations had been accumulated in Nashville depots, and efforts to reorganize and re-equip the army were showing results. "I do not believe that an army exists anywhere that is better organized . . . and more systematically managed, than are the troops of Gen. Rosecrans' command," Heg wrote.

Two conditions necessary for a Union advance were now accomplished. Bragg lay nearby, and necessary supplies were accumulated in Nashville. Weather was ideal for campaigning. The Federal cavalry, however, was still outnumbered four to one. Bragg must grow overconfident and send part of his cavalry beyond supporting distance.

Luck now turned in Rosecrans' favor. Davis decided once more to attempt to capitalize on discontent behind the Union lines by sending Morgan north to "raise the Copperheads." Bragg lacked enthusiasm for the project: "If Morgan's raid showed that 4000 men could ride through Kentucky, it would show that they could not stay there, while if they struck daily at Rosecrans' lines around Nashville, they might well demoralize him until he could not come out." Nonetheless, Bragg consented to the raid, thus giving Rosecrans the wanted opportunity.

Mid-December found merriment in Murfreesboro. Like an inquisitive neighbor, Rosecrans read the Murfreesboro *Rebel Banner,* which printed the news in full. Wives, sweethearts, and guests of Confederate generals arrived. Country people drove in with turkeys, pork, quail, doves, scuppernong wine, moonshine whisky, and peach brandy. Parlors were festooned. Fiddlers scraped anticipatory notes. President Davis made a ceremonial entrance into the town. Lieutenant General Polk, in full Episcopal robes, with miter and crosier, officiated at the marriage of John Hunt Morgan—that day commissioned major general—and seventeen-year-old Martha Ready, "the belle of Murfreesboro." Generals Bragg, Hardee, Cheatham, and Breckinridge attended the groom. Music and dancing, flirting, boasting, and laughter filled the house.

On December 15, Rosecrans reported to Halleck: "Jeff. Davis attended John H. Morgan's wedding last night, was serenaded and . . . urged them to hold Middle Tennessee at all hazards, until Grant could be whipped." Rosecrans concluded hopefully, "Things will be ripe soon."

On the following day the Nashville *Dispatch* announced that Morgan was "reported moving northward to cut off our railroad communications. Forrest, with 2,500 cavalry and five pieces of artillery, left Waynesboro on Tuesday." "I hardly believe we will have any fight here," wrote Colonel Heg. "Rosecrans is evidently waiting for the enemy to attack him. If we can get them to pitch into us, we can give them a big threshing." Confederate General Kirby Smith was uneasy at Morgan's publicity. "His expedition was in every one's mouth. . . . I saw in a Nashville paper a correct estimate of his force and its destination." He wondered that Bragg should believe that Rosecrans would evacuate Nashville. "Rosecrans is enterprising. His force is, I think, underestimated, and I would look for offensive operations rather than the abandonment of Middle Tennessee, which the evacuation of Nashville necessitates."

It seemed that chill winter rains had by-passed Nashville. The weather grew clear and pleasant—warmer every day. Times were hard for Southern families penned in by Bragg's encircling cavalry. Said the Nashville *Dispatch:* "No candies for the little folks, no egg nogs for the old folks," and "no passes on Christmas day."

Four days before, on December 21, past seven cheering regiments, bridegroom Morgan and his staff rode to the head of his column, prepared for a long sweep into Kentucky. "Morgan has finally started for Kentucky," Garesch
é wrote to Rousseau and Negley at Gallatin. "Have your troops in readiness early tomorrow to move if called upon." "Forrest goes toward Corinth," Rosecrans wrote to Wright at Cincinnati. He warned Grant: "Forrest's cavalry may, and probably will, cross and make a raid on you."

Bragg had finally detached two long cavalry arms, and Rosecrans needed to wait only until they had ridden beyond supporting distance. On December 23, he ordered McCook, Crittenden, and Rousseau to be ready to march next day at daylight. He was at his desk before that time, giving orders for setting up the communications needed in a combined movement. By evening, as news of an advance spread through the ranks, an excited clamor rose; and on the hills, at thousands of campfires, men cooked rations for the march, while quartermasters checked supplies and made final requisitions. Other men squatted in the flickering light, writing letters home. Aides and orderlies thundered up and down regimental streets. Officers, meeting outside divisional and regimental headquarters, talked seriously in undertones. Surgeons checked their instruments; wiped and tested cutting blades, blandly ignorant of germs.

The army stirred in the mild dampness of Christmas Eve. Meanwhile, in Nashville back parlors, many a wife wrote to her absent husband in Bragg's army. "I think the enemy as far committed to stand at Murfreesboro," Rosecrans told Halleck, "to protect the raid into Kentucky, as they will be; and having now the essentials of ammunition and twenty days rations in Nashville, shall move on them tomorrow morning at daylight. If they meet us, we shall fight tomorrow; if they wait for us, next day. If we beat them, I shall try to drive them to the wall. The detachment of Forrest to West Tennessee, and of Morgan, will materially aid us in our movement."

McCook, who was to spearpoint Rosecrans' advance by marching down the turnpike to Nolensville, delayed in starting. His men were in line at daybreak, ready except for striking their tents, but he was not under way at noon; and at 1:20 he notified Rosecrans that it would be dark before he could reach Nolensville. He would prefer to postpone the movement until next morning. Meanwhile Thomas on the Nolensville pike reported so serious a lack of forage that two minutes before midnight, he, too, received orders not to move. Crittenden suggested delay until early the next morning. Daylight of the 26th was then set as zero hour.

Rosecrans called a meeting of his corps commanders for Christmas night—"a consultation," he called it. One by one the generals, smelling of tobacco, leather, horses, and the smoke of burning cedar, climbed to the crowded second-floor room of the Cunningham mansion. Sheridan stared into the grate, watching cedar sticks curl into flame. McCook entered, beaming, talkative, confident. After Shiloh and Perryville, nothing could stop him. With one elbow on the mantel, he boasted of the fighting power of the right. Crittenden drawled: "If the rebels stand at all, there'll be damned hard fighting." He knew Bragg personally as a martinet, severe disciplinarian, a good soldier, and a hard fighter. Fifteen years before, at Buena Vista, he and Thomas had watched him command a battery for Zachary Taylor. "A little more grape, Captain Bragg." "Our uniform experience," Crittenden wrote later, "at Perryville, at Stone's River, at Chickamauga, was that whenever we went to attack Bragg, we were attacked by him, and so our plan had to be extemporized."

Stanley paced the floor, his cavalry saber slapping against his long legs. Johnson stared soberly ahead. Father Treacy slipped in, told the latest rumors, and slipped out again. The telegraph clicked busily. Once Thoms rose to throw more wood on the fire. It blazed up quickly, brightening the room and Sheridan's somber face.

Although Rosecrans did not consult with these men, when Thomas came in and settled himself heavily in the narrow space between the bed and the front window, Rosecrans pulled up a chair facing him. Swiftly and earnestly he unfolded his plan, his animated face almost touching the grave, bearded face of his friend. He talked rapidly, in an undertone, sometimes grasping the seat of the chair, sometimes tapping against it. Thomas nodded now and then, or injected a few words. The younger generals glanced from time to time at the favored confidant; "but no one ever seemed jealous of Thomas."

A beaming servant entered the room with a tray of hot toddy. Rosecrans turned to the group, spoke an eager sentence or two, and sprang to his feet. His face glowed as he slammed his mug of toddy down on Garesché's table: "We move tomorrow, gentlemen! We shall begin to skirmish, probably as soon as we pass the outposts. Press them hard! Drive them out of their nests! Make them fight or run! *Fight them! Fight* them! Fight, I say!"

Thomas looked up with a grim smile, Crittenden straightened, and a grin spread over McCook's smooth, round face. Thomas left first; and the others one by one, so that the last did not leave until midnight. It was expected that Bragg would stand at Stewart's Creek. All departed with Rosecrans' admonition in mind: "Fight them. Spread out your skirmishers far and wide. Keep pushing ahead. Expose their nests. Fight and keep fighting. They will not stand it."

Ten

DESCENT TO MURFREESBORO

Cold rain splashed heavily throughout the night of December 26 as the long drought ended. At dawn, under unbroken gray sky, mist puffed from the valleys and billowed down from limestone outcroppings in the hills. Brooks and streams that had trickled through the parched autumn became foaming yellow torrents overnight. But at reveille tents were struck, and breakfasts eaten. Veterans remarked that soldiers are more cheerful on gloomy days. Whether spirits rose as the barometer fell, or with the excitement of marching, the men were stirred and their officers shared their elation. Sheridan remembered later that the army was "compact and cohesive, undisturbed by discord and unembarrassed by jealousies; under a commander who had the energy and skill necessary to direct us to a success. A national confidence in our invincibility made us all keen for a test of strength."

Cavalry trotted ahead to feel out the foe and cover the flanks. Columns of infantry swept over roads and through leafless December woods toward Murfreesboro, where the enemy waited in mist-shrouded cedar thickets. A breeze rose, whipping rain into their faces. In three wide, irregular ribbons, the Federal army moved out of Nashville.

Rosecrans' thorough intelligence had enabled him to ascertain that Murfreesboro was occupied by two corps—Kirby Smith's and Bishop Polk's, with strong outposts at Stewart's Creek and Lavergne. Hardee's corps was stationed on the Shelbyville and

Nolensville Pike, between Triune and Eaglesville, with an advance guard at Nolensville.

Rosecrans planned to send McCook, with three divisions, down the Nolensville pike to Triune and Thomas, with two, down the Franklin and Wilson pikes on McCook's right. After threatening Hardee's right, Thomas would close on McCook by way of side roads to Nolensville. Crittenden, with three divisions, would march down the Murfreesboro Pike to Lavergne. This strategy was to keep Bragg divided and enable Rosecrans to whip him piecemeal.

"With Thomas' two divisions at Nolensville," Rosecrans said in his *Official Report*, "McCook was to attack Hardee at Triune, and, if the enemy reinforced Hardee, Thomas was to support McCook. If McCook beat Hardee, or Hardee retreated, and the enemy met us at Stewart's Creek, five miles south of Lavergne, Thomas was to come in on his left flank, and McCook, after detaching a division to pursue or observe Hardee, if he found him retreating south, was to move with the remainder of his force on their rear."

The country toward Murfreesboro invited delaying action by small forces. Turnpikes wound across great creases of land, which were in turn intersected by transverse ridges. Along roads, cleared patches alternated with woodland and dense cedar brakes. Steep ledges masked creeks with shelving limestone banks. Thickets of evergreen or brush formed natural nests for skirmishers, who must be flushed out.

Two miles down the Nolensville pike, McCook's advance struck a Confederate skirmish line stiffened with artillery and cavalry. In the ensuing daylong engagement McCook's cavalry charged on the flanks, while his infantry and artillery plodded ahead on the roads. Toward evening, at Knob's Gap, a rugged gash through the crest of a hill, McCook smashed through and gained possession of Nolensville and the hills to its front.

Thomas had moved his 13,395 effectives down the Franklin and Union pikes to Brentwood. He did not contact the enemy, although Negley, on the Franklin pike being nearest to McCook, on hearing McCook's guns pushed toward him across side roads and encamped that night near Nolensville.

Crittenden, with the left, moving directly down the Nashville and Murfreesboro turnpike to Lavergne, struck enemy skirmishers two miles out. All day, with cavalry flankers, he drove them from forest and cane brake. That night Crittenden slept on the southern outskirts of Lavergne. Casualties were light that long, sodden day.

While his advance lumbered forward, Rosecrans remained at headquarters until after 11:00 A.M. Then he mounted and, escorted by his staff, cantered down the Murfreesboro pike. At the outskirts of Nashville they heard the first confused rumble of Mc-Cook's shelling, through the rhythmic splash of hoofbeats. "It's McCook—McCook shelling skirmishers." Rosecrans broke into a gallop. Then a booming rolled back. "Crittenden has met the rebels," Rosecrans called. Overtaking the creeping trains, the riders picked their way through or cut around them. Ahead, infantry filled the turnpike.

Seven or eight miles beyond Nashville, Rosecrans spied a distant wigwag and drew rein. Ahead were men of the Signal Corps, and behind them, connecting with headquarters, stretched a vedette line of corpsmen. "McCook must be near Nolensville now," Garesché said, and Rosecrans agreed: "Yes, he will find the enemy there in some force." As they remounted, someone said: "Perhaps the rebels will take advantage of our divided front to concentrate and strike us on our left." Rosecrans retorted: "Now, that would be profitable. Our unengaged right would flank them, and swing to their rear."

They galloped forward, while the wind freshened, brushing the fog away; the rain stopped, and the sun shone. Eleven miles beyond Nashville Rosecrans set up headquarters in a large gray building and rode out to reconnoiter. He returned through dusk and a moonless night after conferring with McCook at his bivouac on the Nolensville pike.

"Hardee is at Triune, seven miles to my front," McCook reported. "We'll have a fight tomorrow."

"Push the rebels hard. Move at daylight," Rosecrans ordered. That day Rosecrans was in the saddle fourteen hours, riding forty-two miles.

Next morning at dawn, McCook was to spearhead the Union advance and crush Hardee before the Confederates could concentrate. But a rain-filled night brought fog that blotted out everything beyond a hundred and fifty yards. Rosecrans was disappointed: "Not much progress today, I fear." Troops passing head-quarters avoided the turnpike, which now was a muddy river. His staff crowded close as Rosecrans demonstrated the points of junction of his columns: "Clearly Bragg intends to draw us as far as possible from our base. With each mile our effective force is diminished, and our communications grow more open to success-ful attack. The farther south he fights us, the shorter is his own line of communication, and the safer his retreat if we defeat him."

In spite of fog, the right advanced at daybreak, Stanley's cavalry leading. Two miles out, McCook found enemy infantry, cavalry, and artillery blocking his irregular front. Then the fog thickened, and Union skirmishers began to fire into their own cavalry. Mc-Cook ordered a halt until the fog had cleared.

Crittenden formed a salient now, and Rosecrans ordered him to halt until McCook had reached Triune and probed Bragg's intentions there. Which of them should Thomas support? Crittenden must wait until Negley had time to get in the enemy's rear, if possible, and Rousseau could support the left. Crittenden's troops had been in line an hour and a half before daylight. At dawn, the Confederates facing them opened a random shelling. At 9:40 Rosecrans ordered Crittenden to advance slowly to Stewart's Creek, there to cross brigades in two places, hold the bridges, and await Negley and Rousseau. Crittenden marched at 11:00 A.M., with Wood leading. Wood believed that infantry could better traverse uneven country if they were not trailing cavalry, and ordered the cavalry to the rear. Lavergne, a mile off, was Crittenden's first objective. The enemy held the village and the woods behind it. Milo S. Hascall's men loped across fields, and at bayonet point drove the Confederates from the village and fought hand-to-hand in the cedar thickets. Wood watched the enemy withdraw toward Stewart's Creek, which flowed narrow and deep, with steep, rough banks. Unless the Confederates kept running, they would fire the bridge. Spurring their lathered horses, George Haney's Confederates whipped across. Colonel Samuel McKee's 3rd Kentucky infantry sprinted behind them, and saw flames lick from the planks. But the weather fought for Crittenden, and rain slowed the flames until the panting infantry beat them out. The left was now clear to Stewart's Creek.

Miles to the right, McCook remained fog-bound until 1:00 A.M.

and Hardee's heavy battle formation slipped away under the fog. McCook told Rosecrans, "I have yet to pursue them six miles before I can well determine whether they have retreated toward Murfreesboro or Shelbyville. Every prisoner I have taken has contradicting statements as to their destination. I will know tonight."

Hardee's withdrawal to Shelbyville might indicate that Bragg was abandoning Murfreesboro. Or had Bragg withdrawn to Murfreesboro, concentrating there for a general engagement? Rousseau, at Nolensville, must have time to join the center. And so the army halted on Sunday, December 28, while Rousseau's mud-splattered division slogged through rough defiles from Nolensville toward the Murfreesboro pike, reaching its assigned position with Thomas after nightfall.

By mid-morning, a strong west breeze freshened; and, toward noon, wintry sunlight broke through the clouds. When Rosecrans cantered down the Murfreesboro pike toward Crittenden's front, from the north bank of Stewart's Creek he saw a battery supported by cavalry on an elevation of the road, a mile south. Enemy pickets swarmed in the woods ahead. Noisy, ineffectual firing clattered along the road. Would Stewart's Creek be the great battleground? Many Union officers believed that Bragg would resist a crossing, because his defensive position was strong. Accordingly, Rosecrans prepared for a battle here, and headquarters were advanced to Lavergne.

McCook had remained in Triune, but he sent August Willich's brigade to reconnoiter Hardee, and Willich pursued Hardee to Rigg's Cross Roads, captured forty-one of his rear guard, and learned that Hardee had withdrawn to Murfreesboro. Here was news for which Rosecrans was waiting. Bragg would stand this side of Murfreesboro. He would not lead him on as he had led Buell the summer before, exhausting him without a fight to the finish.

Before sunrise on Monday the 29th Rosecrans closed toward Murfreesboro. McCook marched on the Bully Jack road, crossing Stewart's Creek where Bragg had been the day before. Although McCook expected strong resistance, Stanley's cavalry found the road clear, and the column moved to the Wilkinson pike on

Overall's Creek. There, three and one half miles from Murfrees-boro, it halted at nightfall.

To support the van and right of Crittenden's corps, which moved on the Nashville turnpike, Negley's division crossed Stewart's Creek two miles southwest and above the bridge on the Murfreesboro pike. Throughout the day Bragg's rear guard fought stubbornly, opposing the Union center. In the morning, Rosecrans moved headquarters from Lavergne to Stewartsboro, seven miles from Murfreesboro, and there Rousseau encamped. Thomas joined him and remained with him most of the day.

The left wing had in the meantime marched down the Nashville turnpike toward Murfreesboro. Palmer's division led, skirmishing, and shelling the woods. Wood followed, and Van Cleve brought up the rear. At 10:00 A.M. Crittenden crossed Stewart's Creek, and after some resistance the Confederates fell back. The left plodded steadily forward, well in advance of the rest of the army, and about 3:00 P.M. reached Stone River.

In sight of Murfreesboro, Crittenden was told that Bragg was running. Garesché ordered Crittenden to "occupy Murfreesboro if you can with one division. Encamp main body of troops on this side, as before directed." This order traveled slowly and before it arrived, Crittenden found Wood and Palmer halted, while they formed their divisions in line of battle. Instead of retreating, Bragg, in plain view and heavy force, was waiting to dispute the passage of Stone River. Just as Crittenden learned this, Garesché's order reached him, and he immediately issued implementing commands. Wood would occupy Murfreesboro, while Palmer advanced on a parallel front to force passage of the river.

Wood argued that it was hazarding much for little to move on unknown ground in the night instead of waiting for daylight. He urged Crittenden to disregard Garesché's order. Crittenden agreed that the movement was hazardous, and the order based on misinformation that he himself had inadvertently given. Yet he must obey, and Wood therefore advanced. Three regiments splashed into Stone River and were met by musket fire from a Confederate regiment hidden behind a thicket and a fence. Wood's regiments drove the enemy back about 500 yards upon their main body, and trotting after them, found, not one regiment, but Breckinridge's entire division.

Wood and Palmer meanwhile went back to urge Crittenden to disregard Garesché's order. Crittenden agreed to halt further advance until Rosecrans could be consulted, though he would not agree to rescind his own order. At 5:25 P.M. Crittenden sent a dispatch to Garesché. "If you were here, you would not order an advance." He said he would wait—about an hour—until he heard from headquarters and then "if ordered to move I will instantly execute it."

"You did right not to attempt its execution," Garesché answered. "General will soon ride to the front." In a dispatch, and later in person, Rosecrans approved Wood's questioning of an order based on incorrect facts.

The incident produced no serious consequences and Hascall's and Harker's brigades safely recrossed Stone River as soon as it grew dark. Yet Wood had raised a question: "Did Rosecrans expect blind obedience of an order based on wrong facts?" Rosecrans had answered "No." The question would be raised again. At Stone River, Rosecrans gave Wood not only a military maxim, but a working arrangement of it.

That night, for the first time, the two armies lay concentrated close together. Crittenden's three divisions extended 500 yards along the bank of Stone River, with Confederate entrenchments only 700 yards away. Negley's division bivouacked close by. After dark, headquarters advanced to a ramshackle, weather-gray log cabin, lying west of the turnpike, four miles from Murfreesboro. There Rosecrans and Crittenden, with many members of their staffs, slept on the rough floor. Rain pounded during the night on the cedar roof shakes, while in the nearby woods Morton's Pioneers felled trees for two bridges.

Long before daybreak on Tuesday the 30th, the wet and shivering Union soldiers rose. Food was plentiful, but fires for drying clothes or making coffee were not permitted. At 3:30 A.M. McCook arrived and received orders from Rosecrans. He was to rest his right line on Negley's left; advance his right until it was parallel with Stone River; then bring his extreme right to rest on the Franklin Road.

It was time to close gaps and place reserves. Rosecrans ordered Rousseau from Stewart's Creek as reserve for Palmer's right. Negley advanced through the cedar brakes until his right rested on the Wilkinson Pike. Morton's Pioneers slashed alleys through the heavy thicket so that ammunition trains and ambulances could follow Negley. One of Rousseau's brigades was left at Stewart's Creek to guard the crossing; another was sent to Smyrna to cover the Union left and rear.

All day Rosecrans remained with the left and center, examining the ground, and hearing sounds of distant fighting, as McCook, slowly pushing into battle position, advanced from Wilkinson's Cross Roads to Overall's Creek. Rain fell anew before 7:00 A.M., and as Rosecrans stood at the door of headquarters, a Confederate sharpshooter hit one of his staff, just missing Crittenden. The Confederates hauled a cannon forward and opened fire on the log cabin. The first shell ricocheted over the road to explode harmlessly. The next landed near Rosecrans. The third tore off an orderly's head. Rosecrans led his staff up the slope, halting under three large trees, about a hundred yards left of the turnpike, from where they could see much of the second line. To protect dispatches from rain, the staff improvised a crude tent out of fence rails and gutta-percha blankets. To keep gun barrels dry, soldiers fixed bayonets, and stuck them into the ground. Orderlies held horses in readiness. Farther back, the 4th U.S. Cavalry formed a semiring. Officers sat perched on fences, warming themselves at nearby fires. Garesché kept apart, his cold hands partially covered by his greatcoat, reading Thomas a Kempis' *Imitation of Christ*. This was to be his baptism of fire. He remembered that an old woman in Washington had predicted that he would be killed in his first battle. Toward noon, a northwest wind arose, clearing ground fog, and scattering smoke; the men coughed and rubbed their eyes.

The armies' preliminary movements were accompanied by a bicker of musketry and a snarl of artillery. The 4th Cavalry band struck up *The Star-Spangled Banner*, a defiant reminder to the Confederates of their old loyalties.

Soon it become apparent that, even with Forrest and Morgan away, Bragg was bent on stretching his stronger cavalry arm around Rosecrans and disrupting communications to his rear. When artillery fire broke out on the left before noon, Rosecrans' reconnaissance discovered that the Confederate cavalry was clinging to the flanks of a sixty-wagon train as it turned into Lavergne. "The rebel cavalry is out on the Franklin Pike," McCook reported at twelve.

General Joseph Wheeler, with 3,000 of Bragg's cavalry, had attacked Starkweather's brigade at Jefferson at daybreak. Starkweather lost 20 wagons and 122 men. Later that morning, riding toward Lavergne, Wheeler captured a small forage train. At noon, he spied the fat prize—McCook's supply train—near Lavergne under insufficient guard. He charged the train in three columns, looted or destroyed supplies and ammunition, and drove off mules and horses. Paroled and disarmed prisoners trudged back to Nashville with the news. Wheeler then rode to Rock Spring where he destroyed another large train, and advanced on to Nolensville without opposition, capturing large trains, stores and arms, and about 300 prisoners. By 2:00 A.M. on the 31st, Wheeler rejoined Bragg's left near Murfreesboro, having circled Rosecrans' army.

Early next morning, while Hardee was attacking McCook, Colonel Moses B. Walker came upon the wreckage of McCook's train. As far as he could see, the road blazed with plundered wagons. Streets were littered, he reported later, with "empty valises and trunks, knapsacks, broken guns, and all the debris of a captured and rifled army train." Walker recaptured eight hundred men and some horses and supplies.

"Give me more cavalry," Rosecrans had begged repeatedly. Now, in forty-eight hours of hard riding, Wheeler had demonstrated the shortage of Union cavalry more cogently than a thousand telegrams could. Bragg's cavalry was still greatly superior, and his defensive position enabled him to concentrate his remaining cavalry into an effective striking force, while Rosecrans was compelled to disperse his as scouts and mobile support among his advancing units. Rosecrans could therefore neither protect his trains with cavalry guards of sufficient strength nor oppose Wheeler with an effective force. He pointed out that the capture of McCook's trains, seven hundred prisoners and nearly a million dollars worth of property, was the penalty for not heeding his requests. As the first day's battle ended, enough ammunition was left for only one more day's fight, and rations were so short that many lacked food.

Throughout the afternoon of the 30th, as reports of the raid accumulated, Rosecrans was anxious and silent, and only at 4:00 P.M., when McCook reported that he had reached the Wilkinson turnpike and connected with Thomas, making the Union line continuous, did his anxiety subside. On McCook's front lay Hardee's corps, with two of Polk's divisions, the whole force extending down the Salem pike. Union engineers lacked maps of the ground before McCook, and Rosecrans described it as "terra incognita."

"Tell General McCook," Rosecrans said to Captain Horace N. Fischer, McCook's aide, "that if he is ready, he may drive Hardee sharply. Tell him to prepare for battle tomorrow morning. While he holds Hardee, the left under Crittenden will swing around and take Murfreesboro. Let Hardee attack if he wants to. It will suit us exactly." Rosecrans warmed his cold hands at one of the fires and observed, "It is looking better." Later, when Thomas reported that he had repulsed the enemy, and that Sheridan's division was up with Negley, Rosecrans talked lightheartedly for the first time: "Things look bright, gentlemen—brighter than they looked this morning."

A Tennessee farmer captured by McCook's men was sent to Rosecrans. He had been up to the Confederate lines twice the day before, and once that morning, he testified. "The Confederates are posted with the right of Cheatham's division on the Wilkinson pike. Withers is on Cheatham's left, with his left touching the Franklin Road. The right of Hardee's corps rests on that road, but extends entirely beyond it towards the Salem pike."

Late that afternoon, McCook talked to Richard W. Johnson, who commanded McCook's right, and therefore the extreme right of the whole army. McCook told Johnson that he had reliable information "that the center of the rebel line of battle is opposite our extreme right, and that we would probably be attacked by the entire rebel army early on the following morning." McCook had communicated this information to Rosecrans. Johnson looked for some change of program, he said, but receiving no further orders, he called together his three brigade commanders, and explained to them the next day's plans. August Willich and Edward N. Kirk were to form his battle line, Willich to the right; William W. Baldwin would form his reserve—"Every precaution was taken against surprise."

Toward evening, McCook informed Rosecrans that his corps

was facing "strongly toward the east." Rosecrans said that "such a direction to his line did not appear to him a proper one, but that it ought, with the exception of his left, to face much more nearly south, with Johnson's division in reserve." This matter "must be confided to him, who knew the ground over which he had fought."

It was dark before Rosecrans left headquarters. At sunset his marquee had been pitched next to a tumbling log cabin on a knoll near the cemetery. Crittenden's marquee stood a short distance to the north. Thomas and Rousseau shared a cabin farther to the rear; McCook established his headquarters behind the Union center.

The army, 43,000 strong, now lay in final position, awaiting the opening of battle. Its front stretched roughly north and south, in a continuous, irregular line between Stone River on the left and the high, wooded ground south of the Franklin turnpike on the right. Its extreme right formed a hook, a "crochet," to prevent flanking. The entire right wing was posted along the wooded ridge, with open ground before it. Beyond, further separating the right from the enemy, stretched a valley, two or three hundred yards wide, covered with cedar thickets and oak forests.

The center was posted on a rolling slope, somewhat in advance of the right and left, but connecting with them. The three brigades of the left veered away from the Confederate line. The right of these bivouacked in a wood; the middle stretched across a cotton field and into a sparse grove; the left brigade had a partial cover of timber. Open ground fronted the whole left.

Except on the left, the ground to the rear was "undulating and rough." Behind the right wing and the center lay fallow fields divided by fences, cedar thickets, and ridges. Behind the left, which was posted in a cornfield, rose a crest which faced the enemy. On the right of the pike, extending south, was an irregular cotton field. The railroad, on high ground to the left of the pike, and the pike itself, on low ground, crossed near the enemy line in a sharply depressed triangle, the base of which, a half mile to Rosecrans' rear, was about 500 yards wide. On a knoll, about halfway between the two lines, stood the walls of a brick dwelling, "Cowan's burnt house." Stone River was fordable at any place where it could be reached. Bragg lay with his right intersecting it, and the rest of his line paralleling the Union army, with the river behind him. His position was strong. In event of disaster, they could easily ford the shallow river to find good defensive positions on the other side.

Crowded into about a third of their usual number of tents, the staff had begun an uncomfortable, wakeful night. In his *Official Report*, Rosecrans wrote: "A meeting of the corps commanders was called at the headquarters for this evening." He made clear that his original purpose in scheduling this meeting at 9:00 P.M. was to give final instructions, but finding it more convenient to instruct his commanders individually, he did so.

"General Thomas arrived early," Rosecrans wrote, "received his instructions and retired." Actually Rosecrans rode to Thomas's headquarters to inquire about his troops and their disposition. Thomas rode back part way with him, and on the way, Rosecrans explained how next morning McCook would engage and hold Bragg's left, while Crittenden, with Thomas supporting, would attack and crush Bragg's right.

Crittenden had been very much fatigued and had fallen asleep during the evening. When Rosecrans heard this from Crittenden's chief of staff, he excused Crittenden from coming for instructions. Crittenden, who was sleeping a few paces off, knew the plan anyway; Rosecrans had talked freely to him that afternoon.

The meeting summons apparently failed to reach McCook, but at 9:00 P.M., according to Rosecrans—10:00 P.M., according to Stanley—"through a sense of duty" McCook, accompanied by Stanley, visited Rosecrans' headquarters to report his movements, the condition of his line, and all he knew of the enemy. At 6:00 P.M., McCook had received orders from Rosecrans to extend his right with campfires, to make the enemy believe that troops were massing there. McCook had relayed the order to Stanley; a half-hour later he had received battle orders, signed by Garesché: "Take a strong position; if the enemy attacks you, fall back slowly, refusing your right, contesting the ground inch by inch. If the enemy does not attack you, you will attack him, not vigorously, but warmly." The time of McCook's attack was to have been designated by Rosecrans. "I was also informed," McCook wrote in his *Official Report*, "that Crittenden's corps would move simultaneously with my attack into Murfreesboro." This information was probably part of McCook's battle orders.

Now Rosecrans ordered Stanley to collect a cavalry force and march to Lavergne to protect the trains. Then he explained the battle plan in detail to McCook and Stanley. He elaborates in his *Official Report:*

McCook was to occupy the most advantageous position, refusing his right as much as practicable and necessary to secure it, to receive the attack of the enemy; or, if that did not come, to attack himself, sufficient to hold all the force on his front; Thomas and Palmer to open with skirmishing, and engage the enemy's center and left as far as the river; Crittenden to cross Van Cleve's division at the lower ford, covered and supported by the sappers and miners, and to advance on Breckinridge; Wood's division to follow by brigades, crossing at the upper ford and moving on Van Cleve's right, to carry everything before them into Murfreesboro. This would have given us two divisions against one, and, as soon as Breckinridge had been dislodged from his position, the batteries of Wood's division, taking position on the heights east of Stone's River, in advance, would see the enemy's works in reverse, would dislodge them, and enable Palmer's division to press them back, and drive them westward across the river or through the woods, while Thomas, sustaining the movement on the center, would advance on the right of Palmer, crushing their right, the Crittenden's corps, advancing, would take Murfreesboro, and then, moving westward on the Franklin road, get in their flank and rear and drive them into the country toward Salem, with the prospect of cutting off their retreat and probably destroying their army.

Rosecrans insisted, so he reported, "that this combination, insuring us a vast superiority on our left, required for its success that General McCook should be able to hold his position for three hours; that if necessary to recede at all, he should recede as he had advanced on the previous day, slowly and steadily, refusing his right, thereby rendering our success certain."

Rosecrans told McCook, "You know the ground; you have fought over it; you know its difficulties. Can you hold your present position for three hours?"

McCook answered, "Yes, I think I can."

"I don't like the facing so much to the east," Rosecrans told him, "but must confide that to you, who know the ground. If you don't think your present the best position, change it. It is only necessary for you to make things sure."

Actually, McCook's line was not well posted or covered; it lay too close to the enemy, and lacked adequate terminal protection for its own open right. Some regiments and brigades, largely through the fault of their officers, were not prepared to sustain attack. Rosecrans shared with McCook the responsibility for this weakness because he did not personally inspect the line or send a responsible staff officer to do so. Rosecrans later said that he moved with Crittenden and the center because "more planning and experience were requisite on that side. I trusted General McCook's ability as to position, as much as I knew I could his courage and loyalty. It was a mistake."

Whatever McCook's reason—too great confidence in his troops, reluctance to yield without a struggle what he considered a strong position, a reasonable hesitation to risk shifting men at night, or unwillingness to disturb their sleep—he did not readjust his position.

That night, in the Union army, few of the men worried about tomorrow's plans or yesterday's fights, even though their commanding officers were awake. Five days of marching and skirmishing had so tired them that they sprawled under the skies on wet fields, limestone outcroppings, and under dripping cedars. Rousseau's staff slept in a cornfield. At 4:00 A.M., Sheridan's sentries thought they saw enemy movement, and when they challenged and fired, the whole division leaped to its feet, seized guns, and waited. Thereafter they did not sleep.

Somewhere, far north, Morgan bivouacked. Bragg's couriers, galloping out from Murfreesboro, could not find him to urge him back. Confederate sympathizers, sending Morgan's men down obscure by-roads, for once overreached themselves and hid him from friends and enemies alike. Next day, when Morgan's column rested, a faint, faraway rumble rolled up from the south. Morgan identified it, but rode ahead toward the wide, free Ohio to raid, sound and battle both behind him.

Rosecrans sat down to compose an appeal to his army. He felt justly confident. He had reunited his divisions and brought them to face the enemy in good array, with an excellent plan for the morrow's fight. Sheridan described the general impression of the entire army: "The precision that had characterized every maneuver of the past three days, and the exactness with which each corps and division fell into its allotted place on the evening of the 30th, indicated that at the outset of the campaign a well digested plan of operations had been prepared for us." The statement made by Correspondent William Shanks, four years later, that the "official reports tell very elaborately of a grand plan, but that plan was arranged after the battle was finished," flies in the face of such competent testimony.

Long after midnight, Rosecrans and Garesché lay down for a brief sleep. A nipping north wind piped a melancholy monody through the black cedar thickets along Stone River, where a hundred thousand men in blue and gray slept, or worried sleepless, in the rain.

Eleven

STONE RIVER

When Rosecrans rose on December 31, mists shrouded the escort which slept around headquarters. In the dawn chill he hurried cheerfully from tent to tent awakening his staff. Morning cleared slowly, except for lingering vapors over the river. By dawn the army was eating breakfast, and the left started for positions from which it would attack Breckinridge. In a small tent, Rosecrans and Garesché heard Mass. A cluster of officers with bowed heads flanked the entrance. Afterward an orderly brought up Boney, Rosecrans' favorite gray—at Stone River, as later at Chickamauga, he alternately rode Boney or Tobey, a mettlesome dappled gray.

About 6:00 A.M., when Crittenden joined him, Rosecrans was listening to firing from the distant right. Behind them, the headquarters guard stood at rest, Captain Otis commanding. Crittenden and Rosecrans dismounted and walked southeast through open fields to consult Wood, whose division waited to follow Van Cleve's. Rosecrans' loose sky-blue overcoat flapped as he walked, the standing collar fastened under his chin by a single buckle. His soft black felt hat was pushed far back on his head.

They found Wood with a bandaged foot, crutches slung beside him in the saddle. In the distance, Van Cleve's men splashed through the river. "Move Harker in front, then Hascall, then Wagner. Send your command across in brigades in front of this position," Rosecrans instructed Wood. Bragg's right lay in strength east and west behind a long timbered ridge. Wood rode off, saying to Crittenden as he went: "Goodbye, general, we'll meet at the

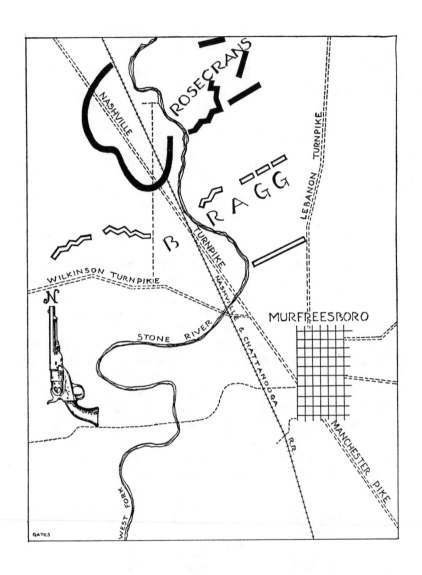

BATTLE OF STONE RIVER

POSITIONS

January 3, 1863

hatter's, as one coon said to another when the dogs were after them."

On their return to headquarters, Rosecrans and Crittenden found their staffs warming themselves at fires in the avenue between the tents. Otis and part of the guard were gone. "A report came in," Garesché explained, "that enemy cavalry had rounded McCook's open flank and gained his rear. I sent Otis out to hunt them." Intermittent firing three miles to the right alarmed no one, for Rosecrans had told McCook the evening before that he expected fighting there, and McCook was confident he could handle it. The skirmishers on Rosecrans' right lay 400 to 600 yards from Bragg's left, but the left had Stone River to cross and from one to two miles to march before it reached Bragg's right. While the left advanced, Thomas rode over, talked to Rosecrans, and returned.

Suddenly, out of the south, a sound rose like the distant, magnified rumble of heavy wagons. Others compared it to the rising of a great wind ushering in a storm. Rosecrans, Crittenden, and Garesché stopped short. Quiet from the left, full roar of battle on the right—Bragg was attacking first. Rosecrans grew concerned, even without knowing the full danger. With all eyes upon him, he paced silently up and down.

Neither semaphore, electric telegraph, nor vedette line connected headquarters with McCook. To take advantage of poor and erratic roads, couriers galloped four miles, some of the distance over limestone outcroppings and through pathless cedar thickets. Rosecrans waited for McCook's report as the rumble swelled to an earth-shaking roll and the booming of artillery emerged from the volleys of musketry. Questions grew urgent. The woods behind Negley came alive with disorganized fugitives. Teamsters, negroes, even soldiers, mules, fugitives, streamed from the cedars and toward the Nashville turnpike. Some plunged on in senseless terror. An officer cocked his pistol. "Tell me what happened." Answers were breathless, hoarse, jumbled. "The right wing is broken!" "Rebel cavalry is in our rear." "General Sill is killed." "Edgarton's and Goodspeed's batteries are captured." No less ominous was the report of Lieutenant Baker who rode hard from Captain Otis. "The right wing is broken, and the enemy is driving it back." On Baker's heels a panting staff officer brought the first official news from McCook. "The right wing is heavily pressed and needs assistance." McCook neglected to report the rout of Willich's and Kirk's brigades, and the withdrawal of Davis's division, and Rosecrans believed his line stronger than it was, to front and flank. With cheerful impatience he reassured his staff: "Never mind, we will rectify it." His next order was based on McCook's statement in his dispatch, that he was "heavily pressed," rather than "broken and driven back," as Baker reported.

"Tell him," Rosecrans ordered McCook's staff officer, "to dispose his troops to best advantage and to hold his ground obstinately." "It is working right," he believed. "If he holds them we will swing into Murfreesboro and cut them off." Crittenden's left still advanced. When Sill's death was confirmed, Rosecrans looked grim. "We cannot help it. Brave men must be killed." At the news of Willich's capture and death, he said, "Never mind, we must win this fight."

Rosecrans and Crittenden now began to appraise the magnitude of McCook's disaster. A second aide galloped up. "The right wing is being driven. It needs reserves." "So soon?" Rosecrans blurted out, and those around him saw his ruddy face blanch. "Tell General McCook I will help him." He assured the staff: "Never mind! We will make it right."

Groundwork for McCook's collapse had been laid the day before, when Bragg decided to strike first, thus choosing the place and terms of the fight. By coincidence, Union and Confederate battle plans were identical—to pivot on the right and attack with the left.

Bragg concentrated heavily on his left. Hardee was to advance at daylight, and Polk, with the center, was to support his attack. The two were then to wheel, thrust the Union right upon its center, seize the Wilkinson and Nashville turnpikes, and thus cut Rosecrans from his trains and block his retreat to Nashville. Both armies moved at daybreak. To attack McCook, Hardee must march in broad formation one-fourth to one-half mile. Crittenden required an hour or more to reach Breckinridge, while Hardee could reach McCook in ten to fifteen minutes.

Had McCook stood firm for three hours, the time differential would not have been disastrous. However, Johnson's line, at McCook's extreme right, lay dangerously close to Hardee. It was not well placed, and lacked a proper terminal hook—"a crochet"—to cover its own open right flank. Furthermore, Johnson was not ready to sustain a heavy assault.

In preparing to attack, Bragg doubled his left, with McCown in front, and Cleburne in support, a few hundred paces to Mc-Cown's rear. Before daybreak Cleburne advanced, and at daybreak McCown moved forward, deflecting to the west and leaving an opening between his own right and the left of Withers' division of Polk's corps. At a double-quick Cleburne came abreast of Mc-Cown, and both assaulted Johnson and Davis. Although the Union skirmish line was not surprised and fired steadily as it withdrew, the assault brushed it aside and quickly enveloped the main line. Bragg's left far overlapped McCook's. In a few minutes, Johnson suffered heavily, Kirk's and Willich's brigades each losing about 500 in killed and wounded.

Colonel Heg, one of Davis's regimental commanders, at daylight "saw solid columns of troops moving through the woods from our right, without making demonstration toward us." Johnson's division lay to Heg's right and rear. "Soon we heard lively musket fire in the direction of his column, which grew heavier and heavier, and fast getting into our rear." Heg knew he was being outflanked, although no one reported the fact to him. "There lay 20,000 of the best soldiers the world has ever seen, destined to be the victims of the imbecility, treachery, and whatever else it may have been, of one of our generals. General Johnson was not with his command when he was attacked. His men had not even been called out of bed. His artillery horses were half a mile off at a creek, watering. And, what was worse, no intimation was given us of the state of affairs, only as we judged from the direction of the firing as it kept getting into our rear. The reports will show how desperately some of our troops fought, only to find out that when they had beaten the enemy in front, heavy bodies of rebel troops would assail them in flank or rear."

As Johnson yielded, part of McCown's charge fell upon Davis, who lay next in line and was already heavily pressed by Cleburne. Two of McCown's brigades and Wheeler's cavalry continued to pursue Johnson's detachments, while McCown's third brigade, McNair's, wheeling to the right, joined Cleburne's attack. Advancing over rough ground, McNair struck Davis at 6:00 A.M. To face him, Davis swung Post's brigade to the right, until it stood nearly at right angles to its former line. To Post's right, Baldwin took position. Connecting with Post, the brigades of Carlin, Woodruff, and Sill held their original places in the main line. Against these seven brigades, numbering 7,000 men and forming a salient which covered the Union right, Hardee hurled seven brigades, numbering 10,000 men. This position lacked natural or artificial defenses.

Despite these odds, for about a half-hour this line held, until Baldwin, at its extreme right, found that the Confederates in pursuit of Kirk and Willich were ranging far beyond his own right. He withdrew to the edge of the woods to his rear and there, attempting to stand, was routed. Meanwhile, three Confederate assaults on the angle of the salient formed by Post's junction with Carlin were repulsed. In the first, General Sill was killed, and in the third, Post withdrew when he found Hardee's left enveloping him. Early in the fight, about half of Johnson's brigade were killed, wounded, or captured.

Reforming his line, Hardee ordered a general advance against the stub of the right which still stood firm—Johnson's remaining brigades and Sheridan's whole division. Sheridan's ammunition was failing, Schaeffer had none, and Robert's supply was low, and so, after Schaeffer had slowed Hardee at bayonet point, and Robert had checked him with his last cartridges, the two brigades withdrew in good order.

Johnson and Sheridan now faced a new crisis. Rampaging behind Rosecrans' lines, Confederate cavalry had destroyed or dispersed ammunition trains that had survived Wheeler's raid. These were now parked to Crittenden's rear on the Murfreesboro pike.

Carlin's brigade was the first to withdraw and reform on the turnpike. Woodruff, who followed, succeeded in bringing off most of his artillery. At 10:30 A.M. Thomas ordered Rousseau with the reserve to take position to the right of Negley. A half-hour later, as Rousseau advanced, he passed Sheridan withdrawing after his five-hour fight. As the last of the right withdrew, Stewart's brigade of Polk's division heavily engaged Negley of the center, while Cleburne and McCown, who had swept in a great arc, were encountering the line that Rosecrans was improvising to check the collapse.

Up to now Bragg's plan had succeeded admirably. He had

routed McCook and held the ground McCook had occupied at daybreak. It remained for Cheatham's and Withers' divisions of Polk's command to drive Thomas back upon Crittenden. Although the stand made by Negley's and Rousseau's four brigades heaped the field before them with Confederate dead and wounded, Negley was forced to fall back slowly, and reform in Palmer's rear when the whole of Cheatham's and part of Withers' division in overwhelming strength fell upon him, front, left flank, and rear, and his ammunition ran out. Rousseau followed. By then it was late morning.

Because McCook reported his collapse tardily, the right was desperately hurt and the whole army jeopardized before Rosecrans had sufficient information to take effective countermeasures. All day he clenched an unlit cigar between his teeth.

Once certain of his facts, Rosecrans scrapped his plan and recalled his left. He surmised that Bragg aimed to cut him off from the Nashville pike, and prepared to form a new line at right angles to the old and across the path of Union fugitives and Confederate pursuers. Into this line he rushed fresh regiments from his left and center, his reserves, stragglers, and commands fighting their way out of the woods in good order. He planned to shelter his trains behind this line. To support it, he massed his remaining artillery. Years later Crittenden alleged that at Stone River "We fought according to Bragg's plan," but the defensive plan which Rosecrans put into operation about 8:00 A.M., and which, by noon, stopped Bragg and saved the day, was uniquely Rosecrans'. Polk's biographer, W. M. Polk, says, "The one that struck first was the one that would probably carry out his plan. On the morning of the 31st both moved about the same time, but as General Bragg had the shorter distance to go, his blow fell first. From that time on General Rosecrans had to conform his plan of action to General Bragg's. He did it so well that ultimately he held the field, and if he had never done anything else, his conduct at Murfreesboro should secure him a high place as a commanding general."

About 8:30 Rosecrans ordered Crittenden to have Van Cleve recross the river. He should cover the ford with one brigade and move the other westward across the railroad to the right of Rousseau. Reserves were needed. Quickly Van Cleve's regiments splashed through the ford, crossed a field, and took position at the right of the turnpike, exposed not only to enemy fire but to the stampeding fugitives from the right. Colonel Frederick Knefler wrote: "May you never see such a spectacle. McClernand's division at Donelson, the field of Shiloh when we arrived, were pleasant sights compared to this. Infantry, cavalry, artillery, came flying in inextricable confusion, horror on their faces. Our line was torn and trampled down. We were compelled to fix bayonets to preserve ourselves. No human voice could have been heard over the tumult. At last the fugitives cleared our front, and as far as we could see the rebels were coming in solid columns, howling and yelling."

Before Wood could move east of the river, Rosecrans ordered him to face about, and send Harker farther down the turnpike to fight on the right of Van Cleve. Hascall would remain in reserve. Morton's brigade was hurried back from the fords to occupy a knoll 400 to 500 yards in the rear of Palmer's center, in support of the Chicago Board of Trade battery.

After he had issued these orders, Rosecrans turned to his staff with a curt, "Mount, gentlemen," and took personal command of the reforming battle lines. Though rash, the action was brave and probably necessary. He had been dogged in less critical situations by the failure of subordinates, and even superiors, to co-operate: McClellan at Rich Mountain, Benham at Carnifax Ferry and again at Gauley, Grant at Iuka, Hamilton at Corinth.

As Rosecrans and Crittenden left headquarters, the swiftly moving Confederate advance caught up with them, and shells from Hardee's batteries fell close by. Orderlies followed him, officers of both staffs, volunteer aides, Major Bond, Father Treacy, and Garesché. At the turnpike, the riders encountered the remnant of McCook's train. This section, stationed to McCook's rear, had barely escaped capture. When Captain Thruston ordered a road cut through the cedars to the turnpike, he saved the wagons but left fighting regiments without reserve ammunition. Frantic mules now strained to drag wagons across the steep railroad embankment. Some balked, while drivers lashed and cursed. Most of the train lurched hastily to shelter behind the tracks.

Rosecrans threaded through to the top of the railroad embankment for a better view. To his right, gunners in their undershirts fired volley after volley. As they paused, bullets flicked through the staff and escort, and an orderly braced himself, half rose, slipped from the saddle, and fell at sword's length from Rosecrans. Smoke rose in blue clouds over the field and billowed among the cedar clumps with a sharp odor and a bitter taste.

Rosecrans descended from the tracks and returned to Wood, to amplify his orders to send Harker across the turnpike to Sam Beatty's right. Riding to Harker, who was next, he told him to form his men in battle line. Then, skirting Harker's left, he met Morton hurrying toward the new concentration. "Front your brigade to the right." There, on a rise of ground from which they had driven a Union battery, Hardee's troops swarmed forward. To check them, Morton called up Stokes' battery, and the heavy field guns strained to the knoll Rosecrans had designated. This advance brought them within enemy range, and a sheet of fire struck them, dropping three horses in a tangle of harness and caissons. Rosecrans rode ahead and urged the artillerymen forward and, when they had cut their guns loose, he led them into the breach.

"Morton, support that battery," he said. As the Pioneer Brigade deployed right and left of the knoll, the Chicago Battery fired canister. Meeting stiff opposition for the first time, the enemy slowed on that segment. Morton asked, "Can't I do something more?" "Take the rise and hold it," Rosecrans said.

As they rode swiftly along the irregular front, Rosecrans and his staff made conspicuous targets. An enemy battery opened on them, and as shells whistled close, all but Rosecrans ducked to the saddle bows. When Garesché begged him not to expose himself, Rosecrans dug his spurs into his horse and replied, "Never mind me. Make the sign of the cross and go in." The only way to be safe, he told them, was to destroy the enemy.

Harker's column tailed the headquarters group, and enemy guns found their range. Men dropped; riderless horses galloped over the field, wild with pain and fright. Pulling rein next to Barnett, his chief of artillery, Rosecrans pointed to the offending guns. "Silence that battery!" When the nearest guns reached a low spot, he shouted: "On the crest! On the crest!" Up went the guns.

Van Cleve's withdrawal exposed the stump of his left to attack by Breckinridge, so Rosecrans sought the ford held by Crittenden's third brigade. "Will you hold this ford?" "I will try, sir," answered Colonel Price. "Will you hold this ford?" Rosecrans asked again. "I will die right here," he said. "Will you *hold* this ford?" "Yes, sir," Price replied. Rosecrans nodded. "That will do." He wheeled and sought the right and Palmer, who was fighting an unequal battle in the Round Forest.

As Rosecrans returned from the fords, the turnpike and fields ahead swarmed with infantry taking positions in the improvised half-mile line beginning to jut at an angle from Sheridan's rear. Rousseau's three reserve brigades were ordered forward, and groped for Sheridan, closing toward his right and rear. Simultaneously Harker's brigade advanced toward Rousseau's right, and Morton's brigade sought position to the right of Harker, later filling the gap between Harker and Van Cleve. Van Cleve with three brigades waited for orders to move into the new position. Rosecrans planned to allow McCook's remnants to filter through, reform, replenish ammunition; and when they had been restored to fighting condition, to post them as needed, or en masse beyond Van Cleve on the extreme right.

Rosecrans galloped along the left in search of the turnpike in range of enemy fire until he reached the vicinity of the burned house, where he drew rein to observe the shifting front. His judgment in repeatedly risking his life when his army depended upon his safety was questioned by his subordinates. He was doing what Cox called "wagonmaster's work"—supervising details that normally should be left to those of lesser rank. Yet some personal supervision was imperative, and his display of courage inspired thousands. During the assault on Hazen, Surgeon Eben Swift saw Rosecrans ride to the front to direct the movements of troops and batteries. Swift saw him draw enemy fire "almost at point-blank range," but he "moved calmly, cheering and inspiring our faltering troops and throughout the day, wherever the battle raged most fiercely, General Rosecrans bore his charmed life."

Years later, an old Cumberlander, J. L. Yaryan, still thrilled to recall for his Indiana comrades how Rosecrans "was at all parts of the field mounted on a large grey horse, his old blue overcoat buttoned to his chin, a stump of cigar caught between his teeth. He left the position usually occupied by the Chief and came to the line of battle, and by his presence and words cheered and encouraged the men of the center and left."

"He is as brave as Julius Caesar," an Indiana veteran confided to General Lew Wallace. And Colonel Heg wrote: "I saw him while riding to and fro at furious rates, the sweat pouring down his face, his clothes splattered over with blood, and I could not help expressing my gratitude to Providence for having given us a man that was equal to the occasion—a general in fact as well as in name." Whitelaw Reid testified, too, "When disaster had enveloped half the army, and from that time to the end, Rosecrans was magnificent. Rising superior to the disaster that in a single moment had annihilated his carefully prepared plans, he grasped in his single hands the fortunes of the day. He stemmed the tide of retreat, hurried brigades and divisions to the point of danger, massed artillery, infused into them his own dauntless spirit, and out of defeat itself, fashioned the weapons of victory. As at Rich Mountain, Iuka and Corinth, it was his personal presence that magnetized his plans into success."

Late in the morning, as Rosecrans paused briefly near the burned house, a shell whined past his head, struck a horse a hundred yards behind him. A hasty observation told him that Negley and Rousseau were fighting desperately, and he rode toward their position. There, in the alternating patches of field and thicket, he met Sheridan leading out his survivors. Sheridan's angry face was smoke blackened; his ammunition was gone, and, forced to retreat, he was swearing savagely. In battle Rosecrans was calm. Not so Sheridan. Ordinarily quiet, in battle he became a bandy-legged fury. Rosecrans cut his tirade short. "Watch your language. Remember, the first bullet may send you to eternity." "I can't help it," Sheridan protested. "Unless I swear like hell the men won't take me seriously." Then he waved to his broken ranks. "This is all that is left, General." Rosecrans pointed toward the tracks. "Crittenden's train is still intact. Replenish your ammunition and get your men back into the fight. Hazen has his hands full at the end of the Round Forest. Support him."

It now became apparent that the junction of the new line with the stub of the left holding its original ground would stabilize into a wedge-shaped salient—a broad, inverted V—open to enemy crossfire. As the weakest, most exposed point, this position would require strong artillery support. To find high ground from which massed guns might cover it, Rosecrans retraced his course, again riding through a storm of minie balls. One of them nicked the muzzle of Garesché's horse, and the animal reared; some of the blood splashed to trickle down Rosecrans' cheek. "Hit, Garesché?" he called back, slackening his pace. Rumor spread that Rosecrans had been wounded.

Rosecrans selected a position for massing his artillery, and paused for a panoramic view. Below, to his right, most of the Union army were finding positions in the new line. Before him a broad clearing formed a long aisle into the stub of the old. Along either side, rusty oaks and bare elms cast diagonal shadows in the winter sunlight. Distant cedar brakes darkened as drifting smoke enveloped them. Fragments of Rousseau's and Negley's divisions, seeking the turnpike, were pursued through the dried cornstalks by solid lines of Confederates, who paused while their front ranks fired. Their goal was in sight now: on reaching the turnpike and railroad, they could cut Rosecrans' supply line. The re-forming line stood or wavered as enemy attack fell on it, or Union reinforcements reached it. Rousseau's withdrawal from the cedars had cleared a path to the Union divisions to his left. After Morton's brigade repulsed one assault, the Confederates swarmed back and threatened to outflank him and capture the battery which supported him.

Van Cleve's division still waited to the right of the turnpike, unable to return enemy fire for fear of hitting Union fugitives from the collapsed right, who sifted through to the rear. Rosecrans heard of Morton's peril and hurried to Van Cleve; he personally led his division into the fight. This may have been the crisis of the battle. Had Morton collapsed, the new Union line might have disintegrated.

Colonel Frederick Knefler of the 79th Indiana described how Van Cleve's division was formed in battle line "under the immediate command of General Rosecrans." The enemy prepared to charge Van Cleve's men as they ran into position before Morton's guns. "Fire over their heads," Morton ordered. The canister, clearing Van Cleve, slowed the Confederates. "I knew the first few minutes would decide the fate of the regiment," said Knefler. "Such a storm broke loose. We were facing each other in an open field, there was no lying down. It rained lead and iron, men were falling in all directions. My horse got frantic and nearly ruined me. My boys stood up like heroes. General Rosecrans cheered them on. Not a man ... flinched. In about ten minutes the rebel ranks began to break. We advanced rapidly, fell upon them like a storm, drove whole ranks behind us as prisoners. . . . We drove them clean back to their fortifications."

Harker's brigade closed on Van Cleve's right flank. Then Harker, Van Cleve, and Morton closed upon Rousseau. With difficulty, the new line became continuous. Hascall's brigade, at right angles to Hazen, anchored its left. Extending in a northwesterly direction from Hazen were Rousseau, Morton, Negley in reserve behind Morton, and Van Cleve and Harker of Wood's division. Curving beyond, in a northwesterly arc across the turnpike, were re-formed remnants of the old right. Cavalry covered this flank, extending several miles on the pike to the vicinity of Overall's Creek. Yelling and firing, Hardee's men plunged out of the cedars to face this unexpected resistance. As he recalled the battle's beginning, Heg wondered that

. . . the entire army was not butchered or captured. Nothing prevented it but the fact that the rebels at first feared that the movement was one of Rosecrans' old tricks to draw them into a trap, and consequently they pressed us slowly and cautiously, giving us time to get out of the way. The whole of the right wing then fell back upon the center, followed by the jubilant and victorious rebel horde—but here they ran against a snag. Column after column came dashing toward the turnpike, like ocean waves against a solid rock. The turnpike and the railroad ran parallel and about 200 yards apart, where old Rosy made his stand, the railroad making a deep cut through the hill. In this cut he massed his infantry and stationed his artillery on the hill which had command of the country around. . . . And as the rebels came pouring on in their drunken revelry, they were slaughtered like sheep in a pen, and our infantry poured out of the railroad cut as if they came out of the gound.

The test of Rosecrans' revised front came with Hardee's full-scale attack. By now, Kniffen believed, the chances of victory were balanced. Although Beatty maintained that "the artillery saved the army," Kniffen felt that much credit was due to the personal courage of the generals, who rode the line. Soldiers took heart when they saw Thomas, whose look struck terror into skulkers; they admired Crittenden sitting easily on "a good hoss"; they noted the genial Rousseau, whom they loved, and the coldly capable Hazen whom they hated but admired. Palmer's solid presence was a rock, and Van Cleve's white beard a banner. Van Cleve rode with an injured heel and Wood fought on with a wounded foot. Rose-crans set a hard pace; blood-splattered, his hat pushed out of shape, he gave orders in a voice that cracked like a teamster's whip. His face was pale, and his eyes, red from battle smoke and loss of sleep, burned with a sullen fire.

Three times the enemy hurled themselves upon Rousseau; three times he withstood them. Then the desperate fourth charge came on. While his men struggled in hand-to-hand fighting, someone yelled: "Reinforcements are coming from the right!" Looking up, Rousseau saw Rosecrans leading the supports. The arrival of troops shifted the advantage, and the Confederates slowly with-drew along Rousseau's front. Again Rosecrans returned to the cemetery knoll. While he paused there, Van Cleve's guns set up a clamor, and he rode toward them. Now Hardee was attacking the line to Rousseau's right.

Hardee struck as Rosecrans reached Van Cleve. An orderly fell at his feet. Staff officers shouted encouragement, waving hats and brandishing swords. "Now, let the whole line charge!" Rosecrans cried. "Shoot low! Be sure of your aim!" A cheer rose. Even scholarly Garesché caught the fever. When bugles blew, he shoved his hat jauntily back on his head, and brandished his sword. By late noon heavy fighting on the re-formed right and center sub-sided; while the Confederates massed before it in strength, they made no further full-scale attack.

Four days later Heg was still furious that the right had been turned and confided to his wife that "we were outflanked and fought to no purpose. The Rebels had it all their own way till about 12 o'clock when Old Rosy met them himself—and routed them terribly."

All morning Rosecrans had been mindful of that remnant of his left which still held its original position. Beginning at 8:30, it had been heavily assaulted. He knew, too, that Breckinridge lay a mile and a half across Stone River with 6,000 fresh troops, without opposition since Van Cleve and Wood had been withdrawn.

When the collapse halted, Palmer's division of Crittenden's corps held the final angle, deep in the original Union left. Bragg considered this salient the key to Rosecrans' position. Both sides called it the "Round Forest." Upon this point, as a pivot, the entire army oscillated all day. At 8:30 Hazen, commanding Palmer's center, moved into a wedge formed by the converging turnpike and the railroad tracks. The first assault on Hazen began at 8:30 and lasted an hour. During a second attack, Hazen's horse was shot between the eyes. The 41st Ohio, short of ammunition, used bayonets. The 110th Illinois, which had no bayonets, used muskets as clubs and held their ground. Although there was no further enemy assault until 2:00 P.M., the Confederates shelled Hazen constantly, so that his men withdrew to the deep cut of the railroad embankment. Rosecrans was assembling fifty pieces of artillery on the high ground covering the salient.

After Polk's first unsuccessful attack upon Hazen, Bragg considered ordering Breckinridge into the fight. Conserve a decisive mass for the critical moment in aggressive battle, is a familiar military maxim. Later, when Hardee's drive against the right slowed, Bragg called upon Breckinridge for troops. Had these reserves been sent into battle before the new Union line consolidated, Bragg might have won. Breckinridge, however, reported that the enemy were crossing Stone River to his front. Minutes later Bragg repeated his request. Now Breckinridge was certain that strong forces were advancing against him. Thus Van Cleve's earlier interrupted advance and a small Union cavalry patrol, scouting far to the left of the river, for more than eight hours pinned down 6,000 Confederates. Bragg subsequently reported that, because of Breckinridge's "unfortunate apprehensions," the reserve was "withheld from active operations . . . until the enemy had succeeded in checking our progress, had reestablished his lines, and had collected many of his broken battalions."

Polk's third attack, at 2:00 P.M., was more easily repulsed because of the fire of the massed Union artillery. Bragg now saw that the battle was becoming deadlocked. An assault upon Rosecrans' left would either carry that point, opening the way to the flank and rear of his new line, or force him to weaken the right, and thus enable Hardee to advance across the turnpike. While Hardee maintained his position, Bragg ordered Breckinridge's four brigades to cross the river for an attack. Polk should throw his entire force against Rosecrans' left.

Rosecrans anticipated this final, desperate charge, and strengthened his line by inserting relatively unhurt regiments where needed. With Hascall, now commanding Wood's brigades at the

Round Forest, he toured his lines, encouraging his troops. Front ranks stood ready to fire; rear ranks lay on the ground. On Rosecrans' right, scattered firing ceased and tension grew with silence. Gauze-like vapors still drifted across the field, thinning in the brilliant winter sunlight. On the right, long blue parallel lines of men intersected the open stretches. Couriers, solitary horsemen, riding out boldly, crossed between regiments.

Then at 4:00 P.M. two Confederate brigades emerged from cover, bayonets glittering. The river had risen during the week's rain, and instead of trotting on a broad front through shallows, Breckinridge's brigades forded in a narrow column. Before his last brigade had crossed, the first two formed a battle line behind a woods and a hill, at right angles to the turnpike. Because daylight was waning, Polk ordered the first two brigades to advance as soon as they formed in line instead of attacking with all four. The mistake was his.

From the crest above the salient, Rosecrans, Thomas, McCook, and Crittenden watched the Confederates, as with banners and thrashing drums, they advanced upon the Union artillery. For a moment pattern marked their attack. Then fifty guns spewed case shot and grape into the compact formations, while below the guns, the divisions of Wood and Palmer fired volleys of musketry. Soldiers plucked cotton to stuff it in their ears against the thundering sound.

McCook called out: "This is a nice mark for shells. Can't you thin out, men?" But Rosecrans ignored this suggestion and remained on the crest, repeatedly sending aides with encouraging messages to the men in the line. It was "about as safe one side as another," Thomas said, but he moved to the right of the turnpike. McCook and his staff pulled up behind him.

Rosecrans saw that Hazen's brigade needed rallying, and, with Garesché at his heels, he plunged down through heavy fire to the right of the tracks. Bond, galloping close behind Rosecrans, saw an unexploded shell whirl past his head and strike Garesché full in the face, leaving only his lower jaw. The headless body rode on for almost twenty paces, until the horse jerked, and it slid off.

Minutes after Garesché's death, an exploding shell killed Sergeant Richman; then two more of the escort fell. All day, "Little Willie" Porter carried Rosecrans' uneaten lunch in a haversack until a shell fragment ripped Willie's trousers and split open the haversack. "Now, all the dinner's gone!" Willie said. The men around him burst into laughter. They roared again when a staff captain whose coat tails were singed by a shell remarked: "It would be damned ridiculous to be killed that way." Bond spurred his horse until it was abreast of Rosecrans, and shouted: "General, do you have a right to expose yourself so much?" But Rosecrans only quickened his pace. As he halted before a regiment, he answered Bond indirectly: "Men, do you know how to be safe? Shoot low. Give them a blizzard at their shins. But to be safest of all, give them a blizzard, and then charge with cold steel. Forward now."

Bond then told Rosecrans of Garesché's death. "I am very sorry," said Rosecrans. "We cannot help it, brave men die in battle. Let us push on, this battle must be won." Minutes later Crittenden saw the fresh blood on Rosecrans' coat. "Are you wounded?" "Oh, no," sighed Rosecrans. "Poor Garesché has just been killed." He commented afterwards: "I had no sensations under fire at Stone's River, I was absorbed in planning how to beat the enemy." But later he cut the buttons from his uniform and saved them in an envelope, marked: "Buttons I wore the day Garesché was killed."

Meanwhile Bragg's assault was being repulsed. As his first two brigades struggled back to the woods, Breckinridge arrived and, judging it fruitless to order them to repeat the attack, sent in his two remaining brigades. They, too, were routed. Bragg concluded bitterly that if all four had attacked simultaneously when summoned at 2:00 P.M., he could have "broken the extreme Union left, driven it back on Rosecrans' panic-stricken right, completed his confusion, and insured an utter rout."

By now the red winter sun silhouetted leafless trees and cedar clumps. Twilight was brief, and the day's fight ended. Beatty gave the Confederates their due. "They fought like devils, and the victory—if victory there was to either army, belonged to them." In ten hours Rosecrans suffered 7,000 casualties. Three of Sheridan's brigadiers were dead; two of Johnson's. Confederate loot included twenty-eight pieces of artillery. Wheeler's raid left the Union army with insufficient rations, though with enough ammunition for another battle. Rosecrans could count these as debits.

As credits he could write in his *Official Report* that the enemy had been "thoroughly handled and badly damaged on all points, having had no success where we had open ground and our troops were properly posted." That night the Union line remained substantially where it stood that afternoon. The extreme left was moved 250 yards to a point above the lower ford. Starkweather's brigade arrived in camp about dusk with many stragglers and about 250 cavalrymen from different regiments and bivouacked to the rear of McCook's left.

Toward sundown, through heavy firing, Hazen, a hard-boiled regular and a spit-and-polish disciplinarian, searched along the tracks for the body of Garesché, his friend. As he found it, the muscles in Garesché's arm contracted and the dead hand reached toward him. He grasped it—warm and lifelike—removed Garresché's West Point ring, picked up his "Bible"—*The Imitation of Christ,* and sent a detail to carry the body to a less exposed place.

"The cold night fell," wrote James K. Hosmer, "the winter heavens dimly lighting up groups shivering by the campfires, and the dreadful field with its burden of mutilation and death." The army was hungry. Heg remembered the day as the "longest I have ever spent in my life. . . . The night came, but we could of course have no fire. . . . As I walked along . . . watching the men sitting on the rocks and cold ground shivering from frost, I could not help but think how little the people at home know of the suffering of the soldier." On high ground at the rear of the Union left, Hazen watched a burial squad dig Garesché's grave. A Confederate deserter wandered over and offered him his blanket, filthy from long use, thick and glazed with blood. Hazen accepted it gratefully.

In Murfreesboro, Bragg ordered all churches and public buildings converted into hospitals, and telegraphed Richmond: "God has granted us a Happy New Year." Union ambulances brought wounded to improvised hospitals. Provost Marshal John Fitch wrote of what he had seen: "Those who witnessed surgical operations at the noted 'Brickhouse Hospital' will never forget many of those scenes. There were the headquarters for cases requiring amputation; and at times three tables were thus in requisition. Human limbs and pieces of flesh cast outside of the house, through the windows, 'would fill a cartload.' The floors 'ran rivers of blood,' and the surgeons and attendants resembled butchers at work in the shambles."

Rosecrans summoned his commanders to headquarters. This was his account of this meeting:

At the close of this day with his right wing refused instead of advanced, his left and center substantially unmoved Gen'l. R. assembled his grand division commanders and cavalry chief, ascertained the condition of their commands and that the last reserves of ammunition would scantily suffice for another day's fighting, ordered their immediate distribution, and then put to them this question: "Shall we fight it out here, or withdraw to an advantageous position covering our depots at Nashville? According to our custom the junior in rank will please answer first." Gen'l. Crittenden said: "On a matter so vital my military experience is so small that I am unable to advise but ready to obey your orders." Gen'l. A. McD. McCook said: "We are the only power capable of opposing the advance of the rebels on Louisville and Cincinnati, and, if broken, it would be an almost irreparable disaster to the country. We have lost but are at present substantially unhurt. We can safely retire on Nashville which is strongly fortified, and with our flanks resting on the river can defy the enemy's efforts to dislodge us; and can cover our lines of supplies to Louisville until reinforcements can be brought down which will enable us to assume a vigorous offensive. I therefore advise that we retire on Nashville and await reinforcements." Gen'l. Thomas said: "The interests at stake are so momentous and the considerations so grave that I would not undertake by my advice to influence the decision of the General Commanding, but I will most cordially support any decision which you may make." Gen'l. Stanley said: "I agree with what Gen'l. McCook has recommended." Gen'l. R. said, "I thank you, gentlemen, for your advice and assurances of thorough willingness to stand by me in any decision I may think best for the country. Please remain here whilst I with Gen'l. Stanley ride out to inspect the ground in our immediate rear over which our first movements in retreat would have to be made." In about two hours he returned from this examination and said: "Well, gentlemen, we shall not retreat, but fight it out here and to the front. Go at once to your posts and hold your commands ready to receive any attack from the enemy. We shall not attempt to attack him until the arrival of our ammunition which I have ordered up from Nashville."

Giving warmest assurances of conformity and support, the friends withdrew to their respective positions while New Year of 1863 was near dawning.

Other accounts indicate that a number of line and staff officers were also there. In a contemporary narrative, Fitch described Rosecrans as "the most conversational and cheerful of all present." He said that "The younger generals were reticent as to whether on January 1st the Union army should hold its ground, advance, or retreat to Nashville"; some were despondent but none advised retreat. Even Thomas, "now calm and placid, waited to hear from his chief, and a stiffness pervaded the assembly" until Rosecrans announced his decision. Even before his tour with Stanley, Rosecrans had declared: "Gentlemen, we have come to fight and win this battle, and we shall do it. Our supplies may run short, but we will have our trains out again tomorrow. We will keep right on, and eat corn for a week, but we will win this battle. *We can and will do it.*"

Colonel Kniffen described Thomas as napping before the fire in the lean-to adjoining the headquarters cabin, while his staff slept in a semicircle around the fireplace, and as saying to Rosecrans that the question of withdrawing was of "such delicacy" that he was willing to leave it to the judgment of the commanding general. Kniffen said: "No thought of retreat had at any time entered the minds of Rosecrans, Thomas, or Crittenden," while McCook, who, after his bloody repulse on the 31st, had advised falling back to Nashville on purely military grounds, accepted the decision of the commanding general "to fight or die right here."

Thirty years after the event, Crittenden wrote that "there was some talk of falling back. I expressed the opinion that my men would be very much discouraged to have to abandon the field"; he quoted Taylor's remark at Buena Vista: "My wounded are behind me and I will never pass them alive."

Twenty years later Don Piatt repeated a story from an undisclosed source, that Rosecrans was "in no condition of mind or body to give the crisis cool consideration," having "outtaxed his strength in his heroic efforts of the day." Rosecrans possessed "some facts not known to the officers present concerning ugly demonstrations on his supply line, and the panic in Nashville, which feared assault." Rosecrans therefore, it was said, considered a retreat to Nashville, while the majority, led by Crittenden, favored "not a retreat but a falling back to better position."

A tour with Stanley toward Overall's Creek—Crittenden

says "McCook," rather than Stanley, an obvious lapse of memory—clarified Rosecrans' purpose. For some two or three miles Overall's Creek runs parallel to Stone River, but west of it. The two streams join north of the railroad and two miles beyond the extreme right of the re-formed line. The inspection was made to ascertain whether the creek and the rise beyond it offered more advantageous ground than that which the army occupied.

As they neared the creek, the generals saw distant riders carrying torches. The torchbearers, kindling piles of combustibles, were wagoners and cavalry covering the extreme right. But as Rosecrans and Stanley did not know their identity, and knew their own orders forbade fires, they concluded that Bragg had moved across their rear and was forming his battle line by torchlight.

Rosecrans came back to the headquarters cabin, and as he entered, Crittenden shouted to him: "My corps is not whipped, and we must not fall back." Rosecrans asked Surgeon Swift if there was transportation to remove the wounded. There was, Swift said, and Rosecrans awakened Thomas. "Will you protect the rear or retreat to Overall's Creek?" he asked. "This army can't retreat," Thomas said and went back to sleep.

"Go to your commands and prepare to fight and die here," Rosecrans said to the group and the effect was "electric." One officer said, "General, I did not know you were so game a man."

Orders went out; all spare ammunition was to be distributed. During the night Rosecrans ordered his empty supply train back to Nashville under guard of a thousand infantry, cavalry, and artillery. Van Cleve and Wood rode with it. Rosecrans knew that the loss of more wagons to Bragg's cavalry would cripple a further advance and render it impossible to bring down supplies from Nashville. As the heavy escort moved up the turnpike, Confederate scouts hurried to Bragg to report that the Union army was retreating. Heavy rain fell and for hours drenched both armies. The old year passed with the midnight hour.

As the New Year of 1863 dawned, Hazen rode to the elevation where the guns stood, to seek signs of impending attack. Crittenden joined him there, and together they watched the drifting ground fog, with its discomforting resemblance to advancing gray-clad troops. On the other side, across Stone River, Bragg beheld an incredible sight—the vapory but certain outlines of Rosecrans' army.

Barron Deaderick, in his *Strategy in the Civil War*, describes Bragg as "surprised and not a little disappointed that the enemy did not beat a hasty retreat to Nashville after the severe pounding received on December 31. Rosecrans was an able commander and he had no intention whatever of withdrawing from the field."

At dawn, Polk pushed forward to occupy the ground where Rosecrans' left had been. Both armies advanced their main lines until they were in plain sight of each other and there they remained knee-deep in mud, as the rain poured down. Heg described their discomfort: "We were now without anything to eat, no coffee, and every man wet to the skin, and the mud getting deeper and deeper." During the morning Colonel Sam Beatty led Van Cleve's division to Polk's rear, crossed the river, and occupied the margin of a wooded slope. Below them the Lebanon road stretched through an open field. To their right, on a similar elevation, a brigade and battery of Breckinridge's division was posted.

The Confederates hauled off the spoils and trophies from the original battlefield, while Bragg's cavalry swept the country to Rosecrans' rear, to scout and to raid supply trains. Throughout the day Rosecrans was busy adjusting his lines and preparing to renew the battle. Captain C. C. Hood, Jr., of the Engineers watched him gallop up and give orders to a brigade of the XIV Corps. He looked "more like a third-rate wagonmaster than a great general, as he is," Hood thought, "as he rode along with a common slouch hat badly battered, a common blue overcoat carelessly put on, pants in his boots—and smoking the end of a small cigar. . . ." Early in the afternoon the Confederates seemed to be massing against the extreme right, but although they appeared in force near Overall's Creek, they did not advance. Just before sundown a noisy exchange of artillery and musket fire broke out, but no engagement followed. Bragg's inactivity throughout the day led Rosecrans to the belief that he had suffered in the earlier fighting.

Raw, blustery night fell, and again the hungry army slept on its arms. As Beatty chewed crackers and raw pork, he wrote, "The night is gloomy enough, but our spirits are rising. We all glory in the obstinacy with which Rosecrans has clung to his position." He read in his pocket Bible: "Thou shalt not be afraid for the terror by night; ... nor for the pestilence that walketh in darkness. ... A thousand shall fall at thy side ... but it shall not come nigh thee," and comforted, he tucked his blanket about him and slept. The night passed undisturbed save for random picket shots. While his staff huddled on the floor of headquarters, "thick as figs in a drum," Rosecrans slept for a few hours in a tent pitched at the building's gable end.

Sunrise brought Confederate artillery fire, and shots rolled up the Murfreesboro pike like balls in a bowling alley. The haze cleared, and sharpshooters, behind fences or in trees, began their hunting. At 8:00 A.M. Morton's engineers hurried over the railroad embankment where they caught the fire of four heavy batteries, and threw themselves to the ground. Their own artillery silenced the enemy while a strong threat to the right was repelled.

The inactivity on New Year's Day had allowed Rosecrans to consolidate his lines. He was gambling on the chance that Colonel Dan McCook would bring ammunition and rations from Nashville, and turned again to his original plan of pushing his left into Murfreesboro, sending more Union infantry and artillery across Stone River to extend Beatty's position on the left bank.

Bragg was aware of this movement and ordered a reconnaissance, learning that "a division had quietly crossed, unopposed, and established themselves on and under cover of an eminence, from which Polk's line was commanded and enfiladed." He ordered Breckinridge to recross and to concentrate his whole command, including twelve guns and 3,000 cavalry, against the Union position. Polk was to cover Breckinridge's advance with an artillery barrage, and skirmishing grew heavier, steadier, and closer as Breckinridge moved forward. Reserve Union regiments moved in echelon to support Beatty, using for barricades whatever material was at hand—fence rails, logs, brush, and stone. Skirmishers watched twelve Confederate guns splash through the ford and strain up the bank to take position against Beatty's left. They counted sixteen gray regiments marching into cover of the woods near Beatty. At the forest's edge, where the trees met open fields, Breckinridge's skirmishers crouched behind fence rails.

Now that Bragg's intention was clear, Rosecrans personally checked the positions at his left. Abruptly, at 3:00 P.M., Confederate skirmishers ripped apart the sheltering fence rails to open paths for the attackers. Beatty ordered a brigade to withdraw from the exposed slope to shelter behind the crest, and as Union men scrambled back, the Confederates emerged from the woods and charged across the field. A double line of skirmishers in gray led heavy columns of infantry, battalion front, with three batteries of artillery. Once beyond the woods, they advanced in three ranks, each six men deep. Another force of equal strength followed in reserve, and behind that, another. Rosecrans was impressed by the Confederates' superb order. Breckinridge hurled the remains of his division—"like three monstrous machines"—against Beatty's three Federal brigades supported by a battery.

At the Confederate charge, both sides opened with volleys followed by irregular, mass firing—"whizzing, whirring, shrieking, tearing sod from the hillside, shattering tree trunks, splintering boughs, knocking the tops from trees." The single, poorly posted Federal battery spoke, as the Union brigades sprang forward to meet the enemy. Beatty's weak line, colliding with Breckinridge's heavy advance, was crushed in front, overwhelmed by the flank, and driven back. The retreating Federals plunged into Stone River, with their pursuers howling triumphantly behind them.

Rosecrans had anticipated this attack, and, to cover the troops across the river, had gathered fifty-eight guns under Crittenden's artillery chief, Captain John Mendenhall. These were so posted on Swain's Hill, a rocky rise west of the river, that they could be shifted easily to sweep the field over which Breckinridge charged. Other guns along the river supported this concentration.

Crittenden and Mendenhall, riding together, heard the assault and, spurring their horses to the hill, saw Beatty retreat. "Can't you do something to relieve Beatty?" Crittenden asked Mendenhall. Mendenhall shifted his batteries to cover the Confederate advance, and withheld fire until Beatty's men were out of range. Then all fifty-eight guns sounded, and the oncoming Confederates, most of them in a brigade of Kentuckians, were ripped with solid shot, grape, and spherical case, until the woods about the knoll seemed "bursting with agony."

Beatty had withdrawn rapidly toward the main body of the Union army, and Breckinridge had suspected a trap, concluding that an assault would be suicidal. Nevertheless Bragg's orders were peremptory. The men advanced in a mass, vulnerable to any attack. Breckinridge cried out: "Oh my poor orphans, my poor orphans!" And so the "Orphan Brigade" was born.

"The firing was terrific and the havoc terrible," Rosecrans reported. Heg wrote that "The rebels were put to flight and old Rosy came galloping down the Pike where we lay, the sweat pouring down his face, and sent for Colonel Carlin. He told Carlin the enemy was routed and ordered him to advance with his brigade and pursue them. His exact words to Carlin were: 'I beg you, for the sake of the Country and for my own sake to go at them with all your might. Go at them with a whoop and a yell.' I had the honor of leading my little regiment in the advance." Although Carlin wondered how much "whoop and yell" his men had left— "out of 2,000, the last three days have left me only 700 effectives"— yet his men cheered and trotted off at double quick. Rosecrans sent in also two of Negley's brigades, followed by Hazen's. Beatty's men joined the chase.

At the fallen fences near the forest's edge the enemy turned. Twilight by now was far advanced, and at nightfall pursuit ended. Darkness brought heavy rain; otherwise Rosecrans might have pushed on into Murfreesboro.

Just as the fighting ceased, Colonel Dan McCook arrived from Nashville with a heavily escorted ammunition and hospital train of ninety-five wagons. Enemy cavalry had ambushed him only seven miles out of Nashville, but he had fought his way through. He told Rosecrans gleefully of a trick he had played on a suspicious-appearing man on horseback. McCook had called out: "I know you're a Union man by your looks, and I want to tell you a secret. Do you see these troops? They're some of old Rosy's Mississippi veterans. There are 25,000 coming, and we're going to give old Bragg hell. Good-by, mind you don't say a word to anyone." "Oh, no," said the civilian. "I reckon he's been at Bragg's headquarters more than three hours by this time," said Colonel McCook.

But perhaps it would be wise to strengthen the impression that he had been reinforced, Rosecrans thought, by encamping an imaginary division on the extension of his right, in full view of Bragg's pickets. Rosecrans had shifted Davis and his division to the left, to strengthen the left and to prepare for an advance into Murfreesboro. The right had been weakened, and Rosecrans feared that Bragg, thwarted at the left, might turn against the right. Accordingly, between 8:00 and 9:00 P.M., a battle front was marked by torches in the cotton fields, and a heavy division of imaginary infantry moved in to the sound of bugles. Three officers, escorted by a troop of orderlies, bawled out commands to imaginary forces. The "light division," as the army called it, halted and bivouacked. A line of campfires, three quarters of a mile long, glowed through the drizzle, attesting to the eyes of enemy pickets the arrival of Rosecrans' "veterans from Mississippi." This ruse may have inspired the passage in Bragg's *Official Report* which began: "The enemy having been largely reinforced. . ."

Rosecrans returned to the night's work. His troops were in good spirits. Not only had they held their ground, they had punished the enemy. Fires were again permitted, and supper was prepared from the limited supplies. All through the night, rain spat into campfires, while troops dug rifle pits and entrenchments along the Union front. At headquarters, with mud halfway to his boot tops, Rosecrans repeated happily: "Things is workin'."

Crittenden came to say he supposed there would be no offensive operations next day because the Old Master would not smile upon any unnecessary violation of his Sunday laws. Rosecrans looked up. "I am just sending a telegram to General Halleck telling him that we shall probably be quiet on Sunday." Crittenden said he considered any advance "extremely imprudent in view of the shortage of supplies." Rosecrans raised an eyebrow. "How many rations do you suppose there are at Nashville?" "Maybe we were seven or eight days ahead," Crittenden said. Rosecrans beamed. "I thought I told you. I know I told Thomas, and probably McCook. I have rations at Nashville to last until the 25th of January, and I can stretch them until the 1st of February." "I wish that all of us had known that," said Crittenden, "we might have worried less."

To move against Murfreesboro while Bragg held the town, the Union army would have to advance on a wide front, ford Stone River, and then cross the fields. By the next morning Stone River had risen so that it no longer could be forded and ten days of recurring downpour had made the open country impassable to artillery. The same weather that stalled Rosecrans' advance shielded Bragg's withdrawal. At noon on Sunday, with his rear protected by a bridgeless stream and fields of knee-deep mud,

Bragg retreated toward Tullahoma, using the railroad and turn-pike, and leaving his severely wounded behind him. At 11:00 P.M. the rest of his army followed, except for cavalry, which departed on Monday. "Sunday morning," Heg wrote, "the sun came out bright, and as we sat by our big fires roasting our pork and cooking our coffee, the reports came that the rebels had left and that old Rosy was pursuing them with fresh troops."

When news reached headquarters that Bragg had fled, Rose-crans had sent out his cavalry to reconnoiter, and then knelt on the rough floor and heard Mass. Father Treacy murmured the familiar prayer: "I will go unto the altar of God." And the soldier acolytes responded: "Unto God who giveth joy to my youth." Wagons lumbered past the cabin, heavy with dead from Ohio, Indiana, Michigan, Iowa, Kentucky, and Illinois. The sun came out brightly as Father Treacy turned from the improvised altar and read the text of his sermon: "In Ramah there was a voice heard in lamentation, and weeping and great mourning—Rachel weeping for her children, and would not be comforted because they were not."

Twelve

On Monday morning, January 5, Rosecrans' army crossed Stone River to the vigorous blare of regimental bands. Stanley's cavalry led, with Thomas, McCook, and Crittenden following. The army took possession of Murfreesboro, and advanced into the empty Confederate camps to cover the roads radiating southward. Cavalry on the Shelbyville and Manchester roads brushed sharply with the Confederate rear guard to clear the last of the enemy from the immediate front. Rosecrans learned that Bragg's main force had reached Shelbyville at noon the day before, and decided that distance, the loss of 557 cavalry horses, and the impracticability of bringing up supplies, made further general pursuit inadvisable.

In Murfreesboro, the finest homes became headquarters for the officers. One group occupied the Ready mansion where, three weeks before, Jefferson Davis had toasted Morgan's bride. Vacant buildings in town and beyond were converted into temporary hospitals. Bragg said he left behind 1,200 seriously ill and wounded Confederates, but Union accounts put the number at 2,600.

In the former drawing room of the luxurious Keeble home, on Monday, Rosecrans sat in a damask-covered armchair. The long mirrors reflected carved doors, the gilt of richly bound books, bric-a-brac, and rosewood furniture. Rosecrans shivered, although a fire burned in the grate, and wretchedly weary, ordered Philip, his steward, to set up a four-poster bed. For the first time in nine days he lay upon smooth, cool sheets. The next day a doctor decided he was more than weary; he was suffering from "lung fever."

As Rosecrans sat propped up in bed he studied his casualty reports: 1,630 killed, 7,397 wounded, and 3,673 captured or missing, an aggregate of 13,249 out of 41,000 to 43,000 effectives. Union casualties were the heaviest of any major battle of the war—223 out of every 1,000 engaged. Each general had overestimated the other's strength. Bragg thought that Rosecrans had 70,000 effectives. Rosecrans reckoned that Bragg had 60,000—it was probably closer to 35,000. With an army twice the size of Rosecrans', McClellan, in a week of fighting before Richmond, had lost only as many men as Rosecrans had had on the battle of the first day. But Rosecrans had taught his fellow commanders an important military lesson: get the whole army into the fight. Spectators don't win battles.

When the news of Stone River reached Washington, Rosecrans rode a crest of popularity. "The unexpected victory," wrote Piatt, "sent a wave of feeling through the North that lifted Rosecrans into high popular favor, and bade fair to make him our foremost military leader."

The victory had pushed the front forty miles farther south. Faith in Union leadership, which had been ebbing since Fredericksburg, now revived. The Stock Exchange steadied, the gold market stabilized, and European governments shied away from recognizing the Confederacy. A long stride had been taken toward Chattanooga, back door to the Confederate heartland. Rosecrans' army exulted, while Bragg's seethed with discouragement. Stone River was, offensively, a draw, but defensively it was a Union victory, for it gave the initiative in the western theater to the North.

Bragg reported 1,236 killed, 7,766 wounded, and 868 captured or missing, an aggregate of 9,870. Never popular, he now was showered by "a deluge of abuse and malignant slanders." A group of his leading generals charged that he lacked the army's confidence to an extent which no longer enabled him to be "useful as its commander." Strangely, Bragg had a complimentary word for Rosecrans. In a talk at Shelbyville the following May with Colonel James Arthur Lyon Fremantle of Her Majesty's Coldstream Guards, who was making a three months' tour of the South, Bragg "allowed that Rosecrans had displayed much firmness, and was the only man in the Yankee Army who was not badly beaten." Bragg acknowledged in his *Official Report* that his lack of success was due to the ability of an enemy who "was enabled to bring fresh troops at every point to resist our progress, and he did so with a skill and judgment which has ever characterized this able commander." The Confederate Secretary of War pencilled on the Report: "Let this be copied . . . leaving out the clause of compliment to Rosecrans."

Congratulatory messages accumulated beside Rosecrans' bed. Among them was one from Lincoln: "God bless you and all with you. Please tender to all, and accept for yourself, the nation's gratitude for your and their skill, endurance, and dauntless courage." Governor Andrew Johnson told Lincoln that the victory had "inspired much confidence with Union men of the ultimate success of the Government, and has greatly discouraged rebels."

Stanton's wire almost purred: "The country is filled with admiration of the gallantry and heroic achievement of yourself and the officers and troops under your command."

When Rosecrans asked that Morton be made a brigadier and the army divided into three corps, Stanton agreed, adding, "There is nothing you can ask within my power to grant to yourself or your heroic command that will not be cheerfully given." Rosecrans proposed to send cavalry back to Kentucky, but Stanton wired: "Retain them with you." When Rosecrans asked to have his commission antedated, Stanton said amiably: "The date of your commission shall be attended to, and arranged to suit you as nearly as possible." But he took no action. Hartsuff, who was still serving in the War Office, wrote to Rosecrans: "I have repeatedly told the Secretary of War that you would belie his opinion if he would give you half a chance. He took a senseless but strong prejudice against you in connection with Blenker's Dutchmen. I think he has yielded it up now. A rare thing for him to do."

After enemy accounts confirmed Rosecrans' report, Halleck telegraphed: "The victory was well earned and one of the most brilliant of the war. You and your brave army have won the gratitude of your country and the admiration of the world. . . . All honor to the Army of the Cumberland—thanks to the living and tears for the lamented dead." The legislatures of Indiana and Ohio passed congratulatory resolutions, and a formal resolution of thanks by Congress followed, one of thirteen passed during the war.

Men who had seen Rosecrans in battle wrote enthusiastically. General John M. Palmer declared later that "Rosecrans, whose courage upon a battlefield was always magnificent, exposed himself at many points to rally his forces, and exhibited the greatest personal bravery. If I was to fight a battle for the dominion of the universe, I would give Rosecrans the command of as many men as he could see and who could see him." From Colonel Heg came "gratitude to Providence for having given us at last a man who was equal to the occasion, a general in fact as well as in name." In a letter to his wife Heg boasted: "Old Rosecrans can and will whip them every time. He will be the great man in this war yet. I think he is the best, bravest, biggest general we have got." From Illinois, Private William Gale: "Our entire brigade must have suffered terribly but stood firm. Rosecrans led it on to a furious charge in person. He is a perfect tiger and certainly bears a charmed life. He has our perfect confidence and so long as he is out of the reach of political warriors will do well." From General Jeremiah J. Boyle at Louisville: "I can feed your army for a year if necessary. What glorious fighting you have done."

Grant, however, sent no congratulations. His first campaign against Vicksburg had failed. Van Dorn had burned Grant's depot at Holly Springs, and Forrest had destroyed the only road by which fresh supplies could be brought up. As a result, Sherman's assault on Vicksburg was repulsed, and, in the shadow of this failure, correspondent Edward Betty judged Grant to be a "bitter, ill-natured, ill-mannered, ordinary man." Not knowing of Rosecrans' victory, as late as January 2 Hurlbut telegraphed Grant, complaining angrily: "Rosecrans still stationary; in God's name why does he not move?" Though Grant sent a dispatch to Hamilton when he learned of the victory, "Rosecrans has whipped Bragg badly and forced him to fall back," two years later he told Lincoln's cabinet, "Murfreesboro was no victory."

Rosecrans planned to halt only until his army had regained fighting trim, and then to advance as rapidly as the army's means of traveling and subsistence would permit. The army understood this purpose. On January 8 Heg wrote: "The army is being put in order again, and in a short time you will hear of old Rosy heading off toward Chattanooga and give them a good threshing."

The victory, however, did not alter the fact that Rosecrans lay deep in enemy territory. By direct line the distance from Murfreesboro to the secure primary base at Louisville was 170 miles; by railroad, 212; and by turnpike, 250.

While the railroad offered the best route, it lay wholly in hostile country, and during and immediately after the battle suffered its worst damage. During the year ending July 1, 1863, trains ran their full distance for a total of only seven months and twelve days; every bridge was destroyed and rebuilt, sometimes three and four times each. The longest tunnel was plugged at one time with rubbish for a distance of 800 feet; rolling stock and stations were burned. Trains were constantly harassed by bitter partisans.

As Sheridan described the problem:

> The feeding of our army from the base at Louisville was attended with many difficulties, as the enemy's cavalry was constantly breaking the railroad and intercepting our communications on the Cumberland River at different points that were easily accessible to his then superior force of troopers. The accumulation of reserve stores was therefore not an easy task, and to get forage ahead a few days was well nigh impossible, unless that brought from the north was supplemented by what we could gather from the country.

With the railroad broken, 18,000 mules and horses, in spans of six each, hauled all supplies for the department's 100,000 men and 50,000 animals. At the standard interval of 100 wagons to a mile, the departmental train stretched thirty miles. The winter rains which had begun on December 26 continued through January, making hog wallows of roads, so that rations were cut and clothing replacements short. Sheridan alone sent 150 wagons weekly to bring in corn reported by his scouts, but the little forage available in Confederate corn cribs could not begin to meet needs. Fruitful foraging was prevented by Confederate superiority in cavalry and by the scoured condition of the farms. "The whole country from here to Nashville is completely ruined," Heg wrote. And when heavy infantry guards were diverted to protect wagon trains, the striking power of the army was reduced.

On January 11, Rosecrans summarized his problem for Stanton:

"Our lines of communication and our depots absorb much force, and that increases as we advance.... The country is full of natural passes and fortifications, and demands superior force to advance with any success." The need for halting until the Union army had restored itself has been unquestioned, then and since. Sheridan described his division as needing "recuperation, reinforcement, and reorganization." By the time this task was well under way, a severe winter made successful campaigning in Middle Tennessee impossible.

Bragg faced no comparable problems. He lay along the Duck River, with camps at Shelbyville, thirty miles south of Murfreesboro, and at Tullahoma, eighteen miles farther south. Tullahoma, his stronghold, was about fifty-five miles from Chattanooga, his principal depot. His supply line was about a third the length of Rosecrans'. He was surrounded by a friendly population, and behind him the barren, mountainous plateau, difficult of access, made a strong defense of his communications.

Bragg's cavalry was also superior to Rosecrans' in all respects. It outnumbered Rosecrans' two to one, even with Forrest and Morgan away, and when they returned, the preponderance became four to one. Bragg's cavalry generals—Forrest, Morgan, Wheeler, Jackson among them—were reckoned among the best; Forrest is recognized today as a military genius, and Van Dorn, who took command, was judged to excel in hardihood, daring, and skill. The best of Rosecrans' cavalry leaders were not equal to the best of Bragg's. So superior were Bragg's cavalry and position that not once in six months was a road blocked or the railroad smashed to his rear.

Meanwhile a difference of opinion, embittered on both sides with personality conflicts, developed between Rosecrans and the War Department. At first it dealt chiefly with reinforcing and equipping the army; later with its advance.

Rosecrans believed that public opinion would compel the Confederates to concentrate to hold middle Tennessee. To advance against such concentration, he needed reinforcements. Concentrating his own army, he ordered Steedman's division to move southwest thirty miles from Gallatin, Tennessee, to near Nashville, and Reynolds' from Nashville to Murfreesboro. Both had been covering the rear and, except for a few regiments, saw no action at Stone River.

When rumor reported on January 13 that Longstreet was coming to Bragg from Virginia, Halleck suggested that Wright should concentrate troops of the Department of the Ohio in one or two places and send the rest to Rosecrans. Accordingly, Wright transferred 14,000 effectives, comprising twenty infantry regiments, four cavalry, and four batteries. This force, with Gordon Granger in command, was transported down the Ohio River and up the Cumberland River to Nashville. The "Army of Kentucky" became Rosecrans' reserve corps. Granger immediately pushed part of it close to Murfreesboro.

Momentarily Rosecrans needed only to ask to receive. Stanton agreed to allocate to him all the revolving rifles manufactured in the United States. Rosecrans was to requisition as many revolving pistols and as much horse equipment as he needed. Forts Donelson and Henry controlled the rivers that supplied his army, and after assigning them to Grant, Halleck transferred them to Rosecrans. Tugs, transports, and barges were needed to keep navigation open on the Cumberland. Stanton sent them to Rosecrans as fast as they could be procured.

On Rosecrans' recommendation, Stanley, Negley, Sheridan, Davis, Palmer, Wood, and Van Cleve were commissioned major generals. Although Rosecrans asked for Buell, Stanton apparently objected. Halleck told Rosecrans that he would not transfer the best officers from other armies: "You already have your full share."

On January 24 a man who would be most important to Rosecrans' whole future galloped into Murfreesboro. He was Brigadier General James A. Garfield, "tall, deep-chested, sinewy, with large regular features, bluish grey eyes, a prominent expansive forehead," a strong, positive, boisterous man, eager of speech, ready to laugh. He had been a minister, professor, president of Hiram College, and member of the Ohio State Senate. He came from Washington, where he had served on the Fitz-John Porter court-martial. Though he was only thirty-one, Garfield knew important people, including Secretary Chase.

Rosecrans received him cordially, and the two talked until midnight. Next morning Garfield wrote:

I am greatly pleased with some features of General Rosecrans' character. He has that fine quality of having his mind made up on all questions which concern his work, thinks rapidly and strikes forward into action with the utmost confidence in his own judgment. The officers have most unbounded confidence in Rosy and are enthusiastic in his praise. He is the most Spanish looking man I know, and though he swears fiercely, yet he is a Jesuit of the highest style of Roman piety. He carries a cross attached to his watch seal.

Later he added:

I find him a man of very decided and muscular thoughts and with a rare Frederick-like quality of having his mind made up on every important question. For sharp clear sense, ready decisive judgment, and bold, self-reliant action he is certainly a very admirable and hence an effective general.

On February 13 Garfield became Rosecrans' chief of staff.

At the end of January, weather had restricted activity to cavalry raids and skirmishes. Rosecrans had hoped that if supplies arrived by mid-February he would have sufficient cavalry and mounted infantry to drive Bragg's cavalry from the field. February, however, proved unseasonably cold, and the deeply rutted roads froze and continued impassable for weeks. Railroad service was re-established to Nashville and beyond by February 12, and with all available methods of transportation, Rosecrans managed to accumulate a fifteen-day supply of materiel in the Murfreesboro depot.

In Washington Lincoln was seeking a successor to Burnside, who had lost the confidence of his army and the administration. Rosecrans' name was put forward strongly by some of his advisers, for he had defeated Bragg and was repeatedly successful. Stanton and Halleck agreed. The military career of Rosecrans was now at its zenith. He was the most successful general in the public eye. But a majority of the Cabinet considered it inadvisable to place a "western" general over the "eastern-dominated" army. And so, on January 28, Lincoln appointed General Joseph Hooker instead. Crowed the radical *Spirit of the Times:* "With Rosecrans in the West and Hooker in the East, there is not treason enough in the North, rebellion in the South, or imbecility or cross purposes sufficient in the

Cabinet, to prevent the War from being brought to an early and satisfactory conclusion."

Rosecrans, still in Murfreesboro, had other more immediate difficulties. Absenteeism was rampant—on its February rolls, his army carried 40,000 non-effectives. "If every Northern soldier able to do duty would do it," Beatty wrote, "Rosecrans could sweep to Mobile in ninety days; but with this skeleton of an army we rest in doubt and idleness." Privates deserted, but so did "officers of white liver, feeble constitutions and Butternut connections." Beatty believed that death might be less painful than the public humiliations which Rosecrans authorized to combat the problem: "Shaving the head and drumming out of camp is a fearful punishment. I could not help pity the poor fellow, as with carpet sack in one hand and hat in the other he marched crest-fallen through the camps to the 'Rogue's March.'" The *Cleveland Leader* told how an Indiana private was branded on the cheek with the letter D.

An important cause of the absenteeism was slow payment of troops. On February 13, when Rosecrans sought to get back pay for his army to December 31, Halleck answered that this would leave other armies unpaid to the beginning of September or October.

By mid-February the sick and the wounded began to return, and stockpiles mounted slowly. Cavalry was still scarce, with not enough to control the country, and too many to feed.

The War Department sent an irritable response to Rosecrans' demands for aid: "Everything has been done and is now being done for you that is possible. . . . Your complaints are without reason. You cannot expect to have all the best arms. Your cavalry is as well armed as that of Grant or Curtis." Rosecrans answered to Stanton that Halleck "treated a request as if he thought it a complaint. . . . I have never asked, and never will ask, anything to increase my personal command. Had this been understood when I went with Blenker's division, this nation might have been spared millions of blood and treasure."

Of all his indiscretions, this statement was perhaps the most damaging. That Stanton's blunder in the Blenker episode had prolonged the war, cost thousands of lives and millions of dollars, made the allusion all the more painful. His new tolerance of Rosecrans vanished abruptly. From here on Stanton was his implacable enemy. Rosecrans could blame only his own loose tongue.

Rosecrans may have been more than ordinarily indiscreet because of his own popularity—he had the solid backing of Chase and Wade and of Governors Andrew Johnson, Oliver Morton, and Richard Yates, who wrote to him: "I entertain a lofty admiration of you and your course which I do not fail to express on all occasions." Rosecrans' army idolized him. But General Stanley said later of that time that in spite of his power Rosecrans' head was marked, and only the slightest excuse was needed to bring his doom.

Rosecrans entered upon an ambitious program better to use what cavalry he had. He transformed Murfreesboro into a citadel. He built blockhouses and stockades to protect the railroad. He covered his front with a string of blockhouses to keep Bragg's cavalry from swarming across. He reduced the use of horses in noncombat services, and centralized control to prevent having his cavalry beaten in detail. His efforts to make one animal do the work of two only aggravated his problem, for he exhausted his animals. He limited the goods, military and personal, eligible for freighting; the adoption of pup tents was in part inspired by his attempt to lighten loads. The Pioneer Brigade loudly complained of the "dog pens" or "dog tents," and on inspection Rosecrans saw signs written in charcoal: "Pups for Sale," "Dog Hole #1," "Rat Terriers," "Purps," "Bull Pups Here," "Sons of Bitches Within." A soldier peered out of one tent and barked: "Bow-Wow!" as he passed. Quickly the door of every tent was filled with pranksters on their knees barking, howling, and baying. Rosecrans roared with laughter.

A mounted honor guard, recruited from soldiers cited for heroism, would have ten times the strength of an equal number of ordinary cavalry, Rosecrans believed, but Halleck objected—the plan would cut across regimental and state authorities, and therefore violate federal law. Rosecrans also saw that horses could be employed to give mobility in a special way—facing the enemy, the riders would dismount, and fight as infantry. Halleck warned Rosecrans that he would weaken his force by much expanding this hybrid arm because mounted infantry were neither "good infantry nor good cavalry," but he consented to the test. To increase his cavalry's effectiveness, Rosecrans sought improved fire power: "If you cannot add to my numerical strength, please . . . to send me

5,000 revolving rifles. Each rifle will add two men for each gun." At the end of April, Rosecrans wrote: "Had I 10,000 more mounted force, I could have all the stock and forage the rebels have taken under our noses; with 20,000 I could have cut off the enemy's subsistence from Middle Tennessee and commanded it myself."

Under harassment by both disputants, Quartermaster Meigs lectured his friend Rosecrans. When Rosecrans demanded 12,000 horses at once, inspectors sent nags. In four months Rosecrans received 33,057 animals, returned 9,000 as unserviceable, and reported the remaining worn out, proof that they were "overworked, underfed, neglected, or abused," Meigs said. "A herd of buffalo resting for four months on a prairie in one place would starve. They must travel to feed, and so with the rebel cavalry. . . . We have over one hundred and twenty-six regiments of cavalry, and they have killed ten times as many horses for us as for the rebels." Rosecrans thanked Meigs for "taking pains to write so fully." The lecture did not solve the horse problem.

A month of wrangling came to a head on March 1, when Halleck, responding to the complaint that the armies were inactive, sought to hasten matters by dangling a prize. He sent identical telegrams to Rosecrans, Grant, and other generals. "There is a vacant major generalcy in the Regular Army and I am authorized to say that it will be given to the general in the field who first wins an important and decisive victory." The "authorization" was Stanton's.

Grant made no verbal reply. He won the appointment four months later after the fall of Vicksburg. Rosecrans would have done well to imitate his silence. Instead he raged. Never before had Bond seen him so angry. He shouted, "Does he seek to bribe me to do my duty? Does he suppose I will sacrifice the lives of my men to serve my ambition? The army is now to be administered on a plan of 'gift enterprise'." The letter "was an insult" to his "open, impulsive nature," John Fiske later said. "The mistake made by Halleck," said Cist, "was that of thinking that what would prove a tempting offer to a man like himself would be so to Rosecrans."

On the 5th, Rosecrans wrote Halleck: "As an officer and a citizen I feel degraded to see such an auctioneering of honor. Have we a general who would fight for his own personal benefit, when he

would not for honor and the country? He would come by his commission basely in that case, and deserve to be despised by men of
honor. But are all the brave and honorable generals on an equality
as to chances? If not, it is unjust to those who probably deserve
most."

Stanley, who knew Rosecrans intimately, considered him "a
most amiable man" who, when he thought himself unjustly assailed, "answered very offensively in writing, and thus made him
enemies, men in high power, who retaliated on him upon his first
misfortune." Rosecrans "may not have been wise," Stanley admitted. "He certainly was not prudent. But he had reason to think
that the offer of Halleck was personal, and savored of a sarcastic
allusion to his delay. Halleck, and the cabinet had got to the point
in which past services were forgotten in anxieties for future successes."

Halleck's answer to Rosecrans was moderate but firm. When the
names of Rosecrans and some others had been presented for major-
generalcies in the Regulars, Stanton had decided to "fill the va-
cancy only when some general could claim it as a reward for a
decisive victory. To this, you return an indignant answer, charac-
terizing the announcement as an 'auctioneering of honors.' . . .
Before receiving your letter, I had not supposed that a Government
which offered and bestowed its highest offices for military success
either depreciated patriotism, encouraged baseness, or bartered
away honor. When last summer, at your request, I urged the Government to promote you for success in the field, and, again at your
request, urged that your commission be dated back to your services
in Western Virginia, I thought I was doing right in advocating
your claim to honors for services rendered."

Garfield later maintained that during this period he attempted
to soften the tone of Rosecrans' dispatches, and even suppressed a
few. Explaining why Rosecrans was not reinforced after Chickamauga, Garfield wrote that Rosecrans' "imperious and curt dispatches" had displeased Stanton and Halleck so that they did not
give that heed to his requests that they "really deserved." Without
minimizing or defending Stanton's truculence, irritability, or habit
of carrying grudges, it is difficult nevertheless to justify Rosecrans'
tactlessness.

Beginning March 4, the Union army pushed south in a series of complicated movements to test Bragg's strength, a general reconnaissance that demonstrated Bragg's positions, but not his numbers.

Among Confederate countermoves was a scheme by Polk to kidnap Rosecrans. Lieutenant Colonel James C. Malone, Jr., of Wharton's cavalry, and Lieutenant W. B. Richmond, Polk's aide-de-camp, were to cross the lines, seize Rosecrans and his adjutant-general's papers, and bring both to Shelbyville. Malone promised that unless Rosecrans started shooting, he would not "harm a hair of his head," and Polk insisted, "From the work of assassination we would recoil with just abhorrence." The adventure came to naught. Malone and Richmond set off. What they accomplished seems nowhere set down.

Through winter and spring the overlapping authorities of Johnson and Rosecrans had produced a few more flurries, but without disturbing their fundamentally friendly relationship. The operations of William Truesdail, Rosecrans' Chief of Police, proved their most trying common problem. Police operations at Nashville quickly assumed vast proportions. All the vices of war named and nameless became "openly and shamelessly rampant," said Lieutenant John Fitch: "Stolen horses, mules, and arms were pilfered and sold for a trifle. Boots, shoes, uniforms, camp equipage, ammunition, and supplies of every kind," were daily spirited beyond the Union lines.

To halt this illicit traffic, Truesdail expanded the military police; in January, Johnson had complained that the police administration was wholly incompetent, if not corrupt. "So far as I am aware," Rosecrans said, "the complaints have generally come from unscrupulous persons." The statement did not include Johnson. When the complaints finally reached Lincoln, Rosecrans wrote to him: ". . . if there be anything wrong, I want to know it. If the fox is unearthed, I will promise to skin him or pay for his hide." Johnson confided to Rosecrans his feeling that "some designing person" was trying to disturb their mutual and well known good feeling. Rosecrans appointed Captain Temple Clark, Johnson's own chief of staff, to examine into the operations of the army police. Clark's report not only cleared Truesdail personally but showed that he had accomplished much in checking crime and smuggling.

On March 13 Annie arrived in Murfreesboro, and the weeks that followed were happier for Rosecrans, who had been with his family only forty-eight hours in the ten preceding months. At that, generals enjoyed privileges denied to privates.

The third week of March saw Tennessee fields turning green. Murfreesboro was fortified, and rations sufficient for an advance were on hand. Cavalry remained the sticking point, and the wrangle over horses continued. Should Rosecrans have moved, horses or no horses? Some have surmised that after Stone River Rosecrans, like many another general, dreaded, perhaps unconsciously, the decision of another battle. It may be that such a consideration influenced him, though he doubtless felt that real military considerations counseled delay. That Rosecrans overemphasized these considerations seems apparent now.

On March 25, Burnside replaced Wright in the Department of the Ohio. His orders from Halleck read: "The Armies of Generals Grant and Rosecrans have in their fronts nearly all the troops that are available in the Southwest. . . . The movement of your troops will depend in no small degree upon those of the army under General Rosecrans. . . . His first object is to occupy and injure as much as possible the army to his front, and secondly, to rescue the loyal inhabitants of East Tennessee. . . . It is, therefore, of vital importance that the line of the railroad is well protected." With May 1 in his mind as the date when fair weather and dry roads would permit campaigning, Rosecrans sent Ducat, who had returned from sick leave, to work out joint plans with Burnside. The partnership seemed to promise well.

Before the armies moved, other matters intruded. The Streight expedition, for one, had ended badly. In retaliation for raids by Morgan, Wheeler, and Forrest, Colonel Abel D. Streight of the 51st Indiana had suggested the formation of a provisional mounted brigade to raid far to Bragg's rear. When Bragg's communications were severed, the Union army would strike. Streight's objectives lay in a distant, wild country, possessed of little forage and poor roads; his chance of returning was small. The project became a favorite of Garfield's and Rosecrans allowed him to organize it, although he denied his request to command it.

Streight received marching orders from Rosecrans on April 7, and left Nashville for Fort Henry. Only half his men were mounted; he planned to seize enough mules on the raid to mount the balance. From Nashville Streight shipped to Eastport on the Tennessee River, where a column from Grant's army, under Colonel Grenville M. Dodge, joined him. The two commands set off together, and Forrest's cavalry took up the pursuit. Dodge was a decoy, and Streight hoped that when he rode off to rejoin Grant, Forrest would follow him. But the ruse failed, and Streight could not shake off Forrest. Streight did penetrate deep into enemy territory, destroying an iron works, a commissary depot, and other important installations. But in May, cornered, exhausted, and far beyond Rosecrans' succor, he surrendered 1,446 officers and men. Had Rosecrans been able to mount Streight's force immediately and well, it might have eluded Forrest and completed its long tour of destruction successfully and quickly. Stanley called the expedition a "fool's errand," in which Garfield sacrificed three excellent regiments.

That spring, the war dragged miserably. At Fredericksburg, Lee's 60,000 men observed Hooker's 130,000, and vice versa. The Army of the Potomac had not moved since the January "mud march." At Murfreesboro, Rosecrans was clamoring for horses. Only Grant kept busy, laboring to gain a position from which he could reduce Vicksburg. The people detested the draft; Lincoln was dubbed the "Widow Maker"; soldiers' pay was slow; and secret societies clamored for peace.

As anti-war sentiment spread, generals were forced to declare themselves against "incipient treason." A meeting of Ohio officers in Rosecrans' army adopted resolutions: "If some miserable demagogues amongst you must vomit forth their treason, let them keep it at home. We know for what we engaged in an abolition war." Rosecrans issued an open letter. "This is war for the maintenance of the Constitution and the laws. I am amazed that anyone could think of peace on any terms. He who entertains the sentiment is fit only to be a slave; he who utters it at this time is a traitor to his country."

Lincoln was grateful for Rosecrans' declaration, but the Copperheads were not. On April 10, the Cleveland *Leader* reported that "Rosecrans' letter on patriotism and home traitors had been refused printing," by the Ohio legislature, with 22 Democrats voting no. "No man in the Union army has more the confidence of the soldiers and the people than General Rosecrans. Of the contemptible acts of the Copperhead party we know not one as low and meanly partisan as this." The letter gave "mortal offense" to Stanton, who flew into a passion, declaring that "that man, Rosecrans, should drop letter writing." He felt that Rosecrans was trying to become a two-fisted military hero of the Radicals and he had reasons to be suspicious, even though Rosecrans was not at fault. For a half year at least a strong movement was under way, headed by Republican Horace Greeley, editor of the New York *Tribune,* to put in another President. Greeley had lost confidence in Lincoln, whom he had helped nominate and elect. And he had less confidence in Stanton. Greeley's first plan had been to force Lincoln to resign—which step Lincoln himself had at least twice suggested—to put Vice-President Hamlin in his place and to compel Hamlin to give Rosecrans command of the army as Secretary of War. Seward he had planned to replace with Unionist Robert J. Walker of Mississippi. But now Greeley's dissatisfaction with Lincoln had grown so that he asked himself if putting Rosecrans and Walker in the cabinet was enough. He feared that Lincoln's administration could not save the Union, that Lincoln had pitted such soldiers as McClellan, Burnside, and Hooker against the ablest Confederates, giving the South magnificent armies to slaughter; while he had sent Grant and Sherman with 33,000 men to take Vicksburg—the figures were Greeley's—leaving Rosecrans, the only Union general who had proved himself a match for Lee, immobilized in Tennessee for want of a few horses.

The Union defeat at Fredericksburg in mid-December deepened Greeley's concern: If the country survived until then, Lincoln's re-election would complete its ruin. Greeley's first choice to succeed Lincoln was Walker. His next, as "best and most available candidate," was Rosecrans, a "uniformly successful, a coming man," whose religion would prove, on the whole, advantageous, for he would receive the solid Irish vote. Greeley's only question was, was he "sound on the goose"—would he consent to a compromise peace: Union *with* slavery? James A. Gilmore, a rich merchant and writer, who served as Greeley's intermediary with Lincoln, was to investigate.

Gilmore consented. He would not, however, take sides against Lincoln, who had failed from the incapacity of his commanders —"All except Rosecrans," Greeley interrupted; in spite of inferior forces, Rosecrans always won. Promising letters that would carry Gilmore "through a stone wall," Greeley revealed his associates: Thaddeus Stevens, Wade, Henry W. Davis, Field, and Andrew—all the important Republicans except Roscoe Conkling, Sumner, and Wilson. While their positions did not allow Chase and Seward to commit themselves, Greeley felt confident of their sympathy, too. After Lee defeated Hooker at Chancellorsville at the beginning of May, Greeley was to tell Gilmore: "If you find Rosecrans the right man I will go personally to Lincoln and force him to resign. Then Hamlin will give Rosecrans command of the armies and there'll be a chance of saving the country."

It is unlikely that so ambitious a scheme involving Stanton's intimates could have escaped his notice. The plot put Stanton's own job and future in jeopardy, and Gilmore's visit must have further kindled Stanton's wrath against Rosecrans.

How much of this plot Rosecrans himself suspected when he greeted Gilmore is hard to guess. Gilmore felt the instant warmth of Rosecrans at his best—his graciousness, wit, charm. He was "magnetized with a sense of Rosecrans' genius." Grant, he added, did not so affect strangers. And so he took residence at headquarters for two weeks, ostensibly to gather material for articles.

When work was done late at night, Rosecrans talked to Gilmore. "The Negro," he believed, "should be given a Bible, a spelling book, freedom, and a chance for something more than six feet of earth." Then he should be left alone. Gilmore was getting his answer. On April 27, Rosecrans congratulated the editor of the Cincinnati *Catholic Telegraph* "on the splendid stand you take against slavery. Slavery is dead." Greeley promptly reprinted this letter in the *Tribune*. Clearly, Rosecrans seemed "sound on the goose." But for the time being Gilmore withheld the big question.

About the same time, the New York *Herald* sent correspondent Henry Villard, an immigrant German, to Murfreesboro. Rosecrans offered him the same courtesies that he extended to all reporters, but Villard misjudged the gesture and rejected the hospitality, explaining later that he considered it a bribe. He judged that Rosecrans "tried to work the press systematically for his personal benefit." Rosecrans, he said, was a "great talker, voluble, earnest, and persuasive—one of the great elements of his strength." Yet Villard was as reluctant to believe what he heard as he was to accept a place at Rosecrans' table. He concluded that Stone River had been a "relative reverse" which took much "starch" out of Rosecrans and diminished his confidence in his army. He informed his editor that Rosecrans had "flaws in his moral and intellectual composition and professional capacity, which the future will surely develop into shortcomings." Among these flaws were the facts that Rosecrans' hair was thin and his legs were short and rather bowed.

Rosecrans' favorite correspondent, W. D. Bickham of the Cincinnati *Commercial,* who had left the army, could not be dismissed with Villard's sneer that Rosecrans bought his friendly pen with small favors. Bickham and Rosecrans had admiration for each other. At Stone River Rosecrans appointed Bickham to his staff as an aide, and Bickham rode at Rosecrans' side throughout the battle. Bickham's accounts were friendly, but a comparison of them with the *Official Records* and other sources indicates that he was a competent and honest reporter with a feeling for color and life in news.

It is probable, though, that Bickham never saw Rosecrans at his worst, or he might have revised this opinion at least: "Men who knew Rosecrans socially had inferred some proneness to hasty judgement, deficiency in executive skill, and lack of coolness and deliberation. It is plain that the original estimate of his character was incorrect." A negative illustration in point came from Brigadier General John Beatty, who hurried to headquarters one day on learning that unwittingly he had disobeyed an order. Rosecrans interrupted Beatty's explanation by shouting, "Why in hell did you not come to headquarters and inquire what it meant?" Beatty saw Rosecrans' face "inflamed with anger, his rage uncontrollable, his language most ungentlemanly, abusive and insulting, and utterly inexcusable." Beatty was tempted to strike Rosecrans, but instead, five days later, he wrote a note asking for an apology. Rosecrans provided no full apology, but he made such amends that Beatty wrote: "His magnanimity made me feel like a new man. I left feeling a thousand times more attached to him; and more respect for him than I had ever felt before."

Meanwhile, as Grant worked doggedly at his own projects, time did not lessen his dislike for Rosecrans. Correspondent Shanks commented about the Western generals that "Jealousy did more actual damage to the cause during the war than incompetency."

And Correspondent Albert D. Richardson of the New York *Tribune* who "messed at Grant's headquarters, with his chief of staff; and around the evening camp fires . . . saw much of the general," made much the same observation: "Military men seem to cherish more jealousies than members of any other profession, except physicians and *artistes*. At almost every general headquarters, one heard denunciations of rival commanders. Grant was above this 'mischievous foul sin of chiding.' I never heard him speak unkindly of a brother officer. Still, the soldiers' taint had slightly poisoned him. He regarded Rosecrans with peculiar antipathy. . . ."

Grant's "taint" of jealousy against Rosecrans was evident to others also. On April 1, Murat Halstead, Cincinnati *Gazette* correspondent attached to Grant's army, wrote to "Governor" Chase —Chase had been governor of Ohio:

> You do, once in a while, don't you, say a word to the President, or Stanton, or Halleck about the conduct of the war? Well now, for God's sake say that Gen'l. Grant, entrusted with our greatest army, is a jackass in the original package. He is a poor drunken imbecile. He is a poor stick sober, and he is most of the time more than half drunk, and much of the time idiotically drunk. . . . Now, are our western heroes to be sacrificed by the ten thousand by this poor devil?
>
> Grant will fail miserably, hopelessly, eternally. . . . Grant is shamefully jealous of Rosecrans, just as such an imbecile would naturally be of his superior, and he and his staff would chuckle to see Rosecrans cut to pieces. Anybody would be an improvement on Grant. If nothing else can be done, now while the Cumberland River is up, send all Grant's army at once, except a division or two, to join Rosecrans and he can instantly penetrate to Georgia.
>
> Or let me suggest a plan. Have Grant's army withdrawn from below Memphis, and suddenly, without warning, send the force amounting to at least 50,000 men up the Tennessee River as far as it is navigable. This would throw them in the rear of Bragg. Anything to get the army of the Mississippi out of the control of that horrible fool, Grant!
>
> There is another plan of operations. Here is Burnside's corps in Kentucky. The rebel invasion of Kentucky is "played out." Now then, order Burnside to secure with *his* troops just arrived all the places in Kentucky, and the Louisville and Nashville R.R. and order a division of Grant's wasting and useless army instantly up the Cumberland to garrison Nashville. Then Rosecrans can have concentrated in a mass all the old

troops of his and Wright's command now in Kentucky, and at Gallatin, Tennessee, and Nashville. He will thus have 120,000 men . . . and he will with absolute certainty break the enemy's center. He will destroy Bragg's army utterly, this side of the Tennessee River.

Rosecrans is the man to strike the blow. For Christ's sake and the country's sake, put the weapon in his hands.

With any sort of handling of the troops we have in the West under Grant, Rosecrans and Burnside, and our enormous steamboat transportation, not ten men of Bragg's army of 65,000 should escape beyond the Tennessee River. All that is wanted is concerted action—that can only be had through an impulse from headquarters, which shall subordinate the proceedings of Grant and Burnside to those of Rosecrans who is in the center, at the post of danger; is *the* fighting man, and has the absolute and enthusiastic confidence of his troops.

Can you not do something to put the spear in his hands?

Chase sent Halstead's letter to Lincoln on April 4 and on the 10th wrote to Rosecrans: "I see but two generals who have as yet given such proof of capacity and devotion to the country as to inspire very confident hopes. These two are yourself and Hooker. . . . The country is longing for . . . some victory with results. . . . I contemplate little of importance achieved since your success at Murfreesboro and McClellan's at Antietam, the last lost as soon as won. . . . I must hope that all our lost possessions will be regained by the opening campaign." In spite of this friendly urging, Rosecrans did not move.

Rosecrans' feud with the War Department dragged on. When Halleck, as a "personal friend," complained about his "enormous" telegraph bills, alleging that they were as great or greater than the combined bills of all other generals, and that his telegrams reported only his successes, Rosecrans replied that he telegraphed frequently only because he wanted to leave nothing important undone. He considered the accusation that he failed to report his losses "grievous, cruel and ungenerous."

At the beginning of May, Rosecrans' friend, Hartsuff, now second in command to Burnside, paid a two-day visit to further the joint plans of the two armies. It was agreed that Burnside would move against General Simon Buckner in East Tennessee while at the same time Rosecrans attacked Bragg. Rosecrans' main advance, following the railroad line, would thrust east to surprise and maneuver Bragg out of his intrenched camps, threaten his communications, and punish him as he withdrew, thus driving him across the Tennessee. Rosecrans would follow, maneuver Bragg out of Chattanooga, get between him and the town, and fight him on grounds of Rosecrans' choosing. Burnside's simultaneous advance would cover Rosecrans' left flank. Since Grant's forces would be endangered by Johnston, Bragg should not be driven beyond the Tennessee until it was too late for him to reinforce Johnston. Rosecrans told Stanton, "What we want is to deal with their armies piece for piece, which is good when we have the odds."

The conferees agreed that, in holding Rosecrans in check, Bragg performed so important a service that large detachments would not be ordered from him. Rosecrans put it vividly: "Bragg is holding us by his nose which he has inserted between our teeth for that purpose. We shall keep our teeth closed on his nose by our attitude until we are assured that Vicksburg is within three weeks of its fall." Burnside agreed to the proposals.

While this conference was being held, Lee beat Hooker at Chancellorsville. Grant, too, was moving, even though he skillfully concealed his purpose. On April 6, Johnston suggested to Richmond that Grant might transfer a large force to Rosecrans. He thought it unlikely that Grant's troops could be "intended for any other field than this." The problem posed would be difficult: If any large part of Grant's army were involved, Bragg "must be expelled from Middle Tennessee. . . . Should we be compelled to abandon Middle Tennessee, it would be difficult to feed this army; the cavalry, amounting to nearly 15,000 could not be kept together in East Tennessee or Georgia. . . . If we had the means of crossing large rivers, I would, in the event of its being compelled to move, send the whole army into West Tennessee to cooperate with that of Mississippi." Again, On April 11 and 13, Johnston told Richmond that Rosecrans was being strongly reinforced by Grant. As late as the 14th, Johnston thought that the Union movement would be against Bragg and looked to the abandonment of Union attempts against Vicksburg. Only when Grant marched down the west bank of the Mississippi and was ferried across below the town were his objectives disclosed: Pemberton's army and Vicksburg itself.

Instead of moving on Bragg, Rosecrans on May 21 wired Halleck: "If I had 6,000 cavalry, in addition to the mounting of the

2,000 now waiting horses, I would attack Bragg in three days. As it is, all my corps commanders and chief of cavalry are opposed to an advance, which, they think, hazards more than the probable gains. Could not all the cavalry possibly disposable be sent down quietly and promptly from all points?" Halleck's response was patient: "I have only to repeat . . . that there is no more cavalry to send you." At the same time Rosecrans dispatched Burnside: "If you would come down soon, I think we could strike a blow that would tell." It had been agreed that Burnside, with the longer distance to march, would start first. "Troops of the main column start tomorrow," he answered. But he did not start.

Through this period Gilmore had some opportunity of learning the views of Rosecrans' generals regarding an advance. Garfield had, on his arrival, told him that Stanton was badgering Rosecrans to advance, and a day or so afterward that he had ordered him to do so. Later, with Gilmore present, Rosecrans asked his corps commanders to comment on a peremptory order to advance at once. "Absolute madness," declared Crittenden. "You should not move a mile with less than 100,000 infantry and 6,000 to 10,000 cavalry." Thomas agreed, holding that if Rosecrans advanced, the Confederates would reinforce Bragg. He should not move, therefore, unless he had assurance that Meade would keep Lee occupied.

Rosecrans, Gilmore narrated, announced that he would waste no more words on Stanton—who was not, as McCook claimed, a "natural born fool," but who needed victories. Rosecrans would deal with Lincoln, with Gilmore as intermediary. Here was another failure of judgment on Rosecrans' part.

Rosecrans had other messages for Lincoln's ears. He had got wind of a scheme: Throughout the South on the night of August 1, in concert with Northern armies, certain of whose officers were at the root of the scheme, Negroes would rebel, arm themselves, and destroy the railroads. "It would end the rebellion," said Rosecrans, "but the South would run with blood." Gilmore agreed to warn Lincoln to keep the military from entering the scheme.

Burnside sent Colonel Loring to Rosecrans for further consultation. Burnside was magnanimous ". . . Down below the Kentucky line, you are in command, and the conventionalities of rank, etc., must not be regarded. You having the largest command, must command. There is no man in the Union army under whom I would

sooner serve than you." On May 18, Halleck informed both Rosecrans and Burnside that Johnston had left Tennessee with a considerable force to reinforce Vicksburg. The enemy would probably try to cover this movement by raids and a threat of advance
against Rosecrans. Rosecrans and Burnside should counteract this
movement by concentrating and threatening East Tennessee.

Again Rosecrans demurred. His spies reported no such news.
Quite the contrary, rumor had the Confederates reinforcing Bragg.
General Andrews, Chief of Staff of the 19th Corps, reported to
Washington that the "rebels are massing their western forces
against Rosecrans." Andrews felt that Grant should reinforce
Rosecrans to the utmost, leaving only enough men before Vicks-
burg to watch the Confederate garrison.

Johnston understood Bragg's problem. Bragg might join Pemberton against Grant only by withdrawing to that strong place
Chattanooga. In so doing, however, he would virtually abandon
East Tennessee, since he then could communicate only by its
flanks. False rumors also confused the Confederates. A report
reached General Boggs that Johnston had "utterly annihilated
Rosecrans."

The confusion continued. On May 1, while Grant was defeating
Pemberton's advance at Port Gibson, Farragut wrote to him: "The
enemy have sent every man they can spare to Johnston in anticipa-
tion of the coming battle between him and Rosecrans." Rosecrans
sought reinforcements, while Grant, hearing that Johnston was
coming to Pemberton's aid, pushed ahead to Jackson, Mississippi,
thus preventing the junction between Johnston and Rosecrans.
"Should not Rosecrans at least make a gesture of advancing?"
Grant inquired of Halleck. On the 9th Johnston was ordered to
assume active command of the Confederate forces in the Mississippi theater. He was to take from Bragg's army 3,000 good troops
to be replaced by a large number of pioneers recently released
from the Arkansas Post.

This further effort to help Pemberton failed. Grant had the bit
in his teeth, and on May 14, after defeating Pemberton at Jackson
while Johnston hovered helplessly nearby, Grant drove him from
successive positions back into his Vicksburg defenses.

Burnside in the meantime had issued order No. 38, which forbade not only treason, but giving aid or even spoken sympathy to

the enemy. Having spread an unwise net, Burnside caught a vocal bird, ex-congressman Clement L. Vallandigham, champion of the Copperheads. A sentence of confinement for the war's duration had made Vallandigham a popular martyr. To end the disapproving clamor, Lincoln ordered Burnside to hand him to Rosecrans for expulsion beyond the lines.

Reporter R. S. Furay watched as Democrats Rosecrans and Vallandigham eyed each other at Murfreesboro. "Why, sir!" cried Rosecrans, "do you know that unless I protect you with a guard my soldiers will tear you to pieces?" "That, sir, is because they are just as ignorant of my character as yourself. But draw your soldiers up in a hollow square tomorrow morning, and announce to them that Vallandigham desires to vindicate himself, and I will guarantee that when they hear me through they will be more willing to tear Lincoln and yourself to pieces." Rosecrans shook his finger angrily. "Vallandigham, don't you ever come back here. If you do, I'll be God damned—and may God forgive me for the expression—I'll be God damned if I don't hang you." Early next morning Vallandigham was thrust beyond the picket lines.

Gilmore's visit had come to an end and now he confided its true purpose to Garfield. "If the country were canvassed, so fit a man could not be found," Garfield said, and at his suggestion, Gilmore went immediately to Rosecrans. Rosecrans listened with "evident surprise and gratification," but declined unhesitatingly to become a candidate. "My place is here. The country gave me my education, and so has the right to my military services. This and not the presidency is my post of duty, and I cannot, without violating my conscience, leave it." Gilmore should tell his friends that Lincoln was in the right place. When Greeley heard of this, he understood Rosecrans correctly as refusing, and turned to Chase as his next choice.

Gilmore delivered Rosecrans' messages of confidence to Lincoln, who asked what he thought of Rosecrans.

Gilmore answered: "He is one of the most all-accomplished men I ever met, with remarkable executive ability, quick unerring judgment. Quincy Gillmore told me that he was the most tenacious fighter and the ablest strategist in our army; and this is the opinion of every one of his general officers. Moreover, he is a thorough Christian gentleman." "But, on occasions somewhat irascible," said Lincoln. Gilmore spoke bluntly. "Rosecrans is all right and Stanton is all wrong. If I had been in Rosecrans' boots, I would have resigned at once." In his opinion, Rosecrans was the right man in the wrong place. Halleck should be returned to field command, Stanton given a clerical position, and Rosecrans made commander-in-chief.

Lincoln then asked: "What's your opinion on the forward movement to Chattanooga?"

Gilmore believed that a premature advance would cause the defeat, perhaps the "total destruction of our army." Lincoln flicked through Gilmore's reports of Rosecrans' generals, and observed, "They all think alike; they must be right. Tell Rosecrans the order will be countermanded." Lincoln said that Stanton desired victories "so badly he would stop at little to get them." Gilmore should make this clear to Rosecrans and recommend patience.

Gilmore learned the sequel from Chase. "When Lincoln told the Cabinet about the Gilmore interview and his countermanding of the order, Stanton snarled that he thought it about time to stop the practice of taking advice of civilians in military movements." Lincoln objected, Gilmore had given no advice. "He merely read to me the opinions of sixteen of Rosecrans' general officers as he took them down. He did say after I had told him that I might write or telegraph Rosecrans, that I should recall the order. And so I did, and consequently, if any one sinned in this matter it has been your humble servant."

On May 23, when Grant's assault on Vicksburg failed, he determined to besiege it instead. By the 26th, his investment was complete, and he was concerned lest Bragg should reinforce Pemberton or unite with Johnston, who hovered futilely to Vicksburg's rear. "I learned that Davis had promised, if the garrison can hold out 15 days, he will send 100,000 men, if he has to evacuate Tennessee to do it," Grant reported to Halleck, Hurlbut, and Rosecrans.

On the 29th, Dana observed that nothing but heavy reinforcements could save Vicksburg. These must come from Bragg. Dana reported, less than a week later, that three divisions had been detached from Bragg, although they had not arrived at Vicksburg. "Nothing can save Vicksburg except a heavy force attacking Grant in the rear." Hurlbut reported to Rosecrans, "Our batteries are playing all day and night."

With Grant's telegram before him, Rosecrans ordered Thomas to hold his command in "readiness to march at a moment's warning." He asked Burnside, "How soon will your troops reach their destination? The time appears ripe for a movement here, and much depends on the position of your forces."

Lincoln's concern grew, and he telegraphed to Rosecrans, "I am very anxious that you do your utmost, short of rashness, to keep Bragg from getting off to help Johnston against Grant." "I will attend to it," Rosecrans replied. When Forrest disappeared from Granger's front, Rosecrans and Stanton were both concerned lest disaster had befallen Grant. Still Burnside hesitated, and did not answer dispatches. Rosecrans grew emphatic. "While waiting your answer to my last dispatch, I deem it proper to say that I wish to make a forward movement within the next four days. It is of the utmost importance that your force be as far to the front as possible, so as to protect my left flank and be prepared to support me by an advance on McMinnville, if necessary. I inquired about your transportation and supplies because we may be able to unite our forces and move straight on Chattanooga." After a week of futile waiting, Rosecrans finally started alone, trusting that Burnside would follow.

On June 2, as Rosecrans repeated, "Our movement has begun, and we want you to come up as near and as quickly as possible," Halleck ordered Burnside to "hurry reinforcements to Grant." "Rosecrans is now relying upon my advance into Tennessee and I am all ready," Burnside objected. Halleck's order: "You will immediately dispatch 8,000 men to General Grant, at Vicksburg," brought a wail from Burnside: "My plans are all deranged." Halleck stood firm. "Johnston is being heavily reinforced from Bragg's army. If you cannot hurt the enemy now, he will soon hurt you."

Thus, ironically enough, Rosecrans' plans were disarrayed by the War Department itself. Rosecrans now felt the need to reassess his position; he halted for another three weeks.

On June 8, Rosecrans circulated a confidential note to his three corps and thirteen division commanders, and his cavalry chief, asking them to answer three questions immediately and independently: "1. From the fullest information in your possession do you think that the enemy in front of us has been so materially weakened by detachments to Johnston or elsewhere that this army could advance on him at this time with strong reasonable chances of fighting a great and successful battle? 2. Do you think an advance of our army at present likely to prevent additional re-enforcements being sent against General Grant by the enemy in our front? 3. Do you think an immediate or early advance of our army advisable?"

The corps commanders opposed the advance. While the judgment of McCook and Crittenden may be questioned, the opinion of so able and levelheaded a general as Thomas cannot be lightly dismissed. Thomas denied that Bragg had been weakened. An advance would provoke a great battle with heavy casualties and no gain. An immediate advance, he said, would give Bragg a decided advantage, and either bring on battle, or cause Bragg to fall back, draw Rosecrans from his base, and destroy his communications. Bragg then could reinforce Johnston. But if the Union army stood, threatening Bragg's flanks, Bragg would not dare to reinforce Johnston. If a reinforced Bragg attacked Rosecrans, he would weaken himself as he advanced. Thomas hoped for such an attack. Rosecrans needed 6,000 more cavalry to change matters.

Thirteen of the seventeen generals did not believe that Bragg had been substantially weakened, while two, Stanley and Brannan, disagreed. Turchin thought that Bragg lost some strength, but not enough to make him vulnerable. Sheridan skirted the question. Two of the generals held that a Union advance would not prevent Bragg from reinforcing Pemberton; one was less certain, and fourteen did not so believe. All answered "no" to the question, "Do you think an immediate or early advance of our army advisable?"

Garfield's opinion was not sought because he was a line officer, nonetheless at the conclusion of a long written argument he listed nine considerations in support of an immediate advance:

1st. Bragg's army is now weaker than it has been since the battle [of Stone's River] . . . while our army has reached its maximum strength. . . . 2nd. Whatever may be the results at Vicksburg, the determination of its fate will give large reinforcements to Bragg. . . . 3rd. If Grant fails, the same result will inevitably follow, so far as Bragg's army is concerned. . . . 4th. A retreat could greatly increase both the desire and the opportunity for desertion [among the Confederates]. . . . 5th. But the chances are more than even that a sudden and rapid movement would compel a general engagement, and the defeat of Bragg would be in the highest degree disastrous to the rebellion. 6th. The turbulent aspects of politics in the loyal states renders a decisive blow against the enemy at this time of the highest importance . . . at the polls, and in the enforcement of the conscription act. 7th. The Government and the War Department believe that this army ought to move upon the enemy. . . . 8th. Our true objective point is the rebel army. . . . 9th. . . . Your mobile force can now be concentrated in twenty-four hours, and your cavalry, if not equal in numerical strength . . . is greatly superior in efficiency and *morale*.

The line officers resented Garfield's trespass, and Stanley spoke of "a little cheap glory" claimed by his friends for "at least one person for his bold advice, but, as he had no command, and no right to vote, I cannot see the propriety of the claim."

If conditions can be presumed to have been essentially the same on June 23 as on June 8, the Tullahoma campaign proved that although one of Garfield's premises was wrong—he estimated Bragg's effectives at 41,680 instead of the actual 50,777—his conclusion was right. A successful advance was possible.

Did Rosecrans' generals know the answer he wanted, and answer to please rather than to inform him? There is no firsthand testimony to support this. Granger, Reynolds, Sheridan, and Thomas in particular were not likely to serve as puppets.

If Rosecrans sought to use the questionnaire as a device for building support for his opinion rather than for getting a critical judgment, he was wrong. If he sought to employ it as a means of shifting the responsibility for command to a committee of subordinates, he was wrong. If he wished to use it as a sword against his superiors or a shield against their criticism—and in this point at least he seems vulnerable—he was wrong. It is impossible to say.

Meanwhile, more troops were drawn into Grant's semicircle of besiegers, so that at Memphis Hurlbut found his flank and rear open. He had abandoned Jackson and the upper line to reinforce Grant. "It is of the most serious importance that Rosecrans move at once," he telegraphed Halleck. Hurlbut's abandonment of Jackson in turn alarmed Asboth, commanding at Columbus,

Kentucky. Asboth, too, had stripped his command to reinforce Grant. He wanted Rosecrans to cover him.

On June 11, Rosecrans communicated his officers' opinions to Halleck, recommending, "Better wait a little to get all we can ready to insure the best results." He added that by waiting it would be possible "to observe a great military maxim not to risk two great and decisive battles at the same time."

Halleck answered that while the maxim applied to a single army, it did not apply to two armies acting independently of each other. It was to the interest of Johnston and Bragg to fight at different times. They were acting on interior lines between Rosecrans and Grant.

Halleck scored on that answer. He scored again when he pointed out: "There is another military maxim, that 'councils of war never fight.' "

Still Rosecrans waited. Nor did he take seriously the rumors that Bragg was reinforcing Johnston. Intercepted enemy letters, and his commanders' reports, convinced him otherwise, in spite of Halleck's belief that Bragg's army had been greatly depleted. Actually, Bragg had lost by detachment. On May 18, he reported that a brigade of cavalry had left Northern Alabama for Mississippi several days before and that another was leaving; and on May 22 he told Davis that Breckinridge with most of his division had also left. Another division, however, would be organized immediately to replace Breckinridge. By the 26th, all of McCown's division of Van Dorn's corps had departed for Mississippi. Rumor told the Confederates that 30,000 of Rosecrans' troops were reinforcing Grant.

Finally, on June 17, Burnside telegraphed that he had sent out "those two expeditions and am very much inclined to follow them with all my available force into East Tennessee, say to the extent of 5,000 or 6,000 men. Will it be of service to you if the move is made?" "It will help me very much," Rosecrans replied.

There were no excuses for halting now. Burnside was moving. The fall of Vicksburg was inescapable and imminent. On June 22, Rosecrans exclaimed, "Thank God, Vicksburg is now in our grasp and the Army of the Cumberland can move." At midnight he ordered Granger to "move tomorrow morning with your whole force to Salem. . . . This is a permanent movement, and not a mere expedition." Next day, marching orders went to Crittenden, Mc-Cook, Stanley, Thomas, and Van Cleve.

The statement has been made and often repeated that Rosecrans moved at last in response to what in effect constituted "peremptory orders" of June 16 from Washington. The *Official Records* show no orders of that date. On June 12, Halleck answered Rosecrans' telegram of June 11 reporting the polling of the officers: "If you say that you are not prepared to fight Bragg I shall not order you to do so, for the responsibility of fighting or refusing to fight at a particular time and place must rest upon the general in immediate command."

The long halt had lasted 169 days, from Monday, January 5, to Wednesday, June 23. Opinions still are divided concerning Rosecrans' military judgment in this matter. His critics outnumber his defenders.

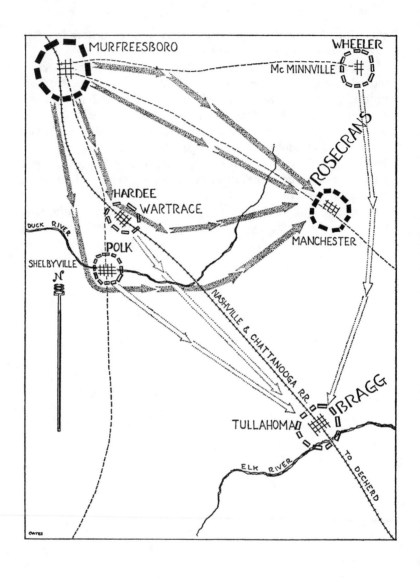

TULLAHOMA CAMPAIGN

MOVEMENTS

June 26–30, 1863

Thirteen

TULLAHOMA—"OUTSTANDING OPERATION OF THE WAR"

On the eve of Rosecrans' advance, the striking forces of the two armies were approximately equal. Bragg's effective strength was 46,665: 30,449 infantry, 13,962 cavalry, and 2,254 artillery; Rosecrans' was 50,017: 40,146 infantry, 6,806 cavalry, and 3,065 artillery. Behind Rosecrans' force stood a reserve corps of 12,575, and garrisons at Nashville and elsewhere. As the aggressor, Rosecrans had to move and fight in the open, while Bragg defended fortifications. To reach him, Rosecrans was forced to extend lines of communication already much longer than Bragg's, in the presence of Confederate cavalry outnumbering him two to one. Bragg's supply base lay nearby. His cavalry superiority enabled him to command all forage in the Duck valley, an area extending almost to Murfreesboro.

Again, as at Stone River, Morgan's departure was a signal for Rosecrans' advance. On June 23 Rosecrans notified Burnside that Morgan with 2,300 cavalry had crossed the Caney, heading for East Tennessee. This second raid led Morgan through Kentucky, Indiana, and Ohio, and into the Columbus, Ohio, penitentiary as a prisoner of war.

Bragg's main depot lay at Tullahoma, a straggling town at the intersection of the main line of the Nashville and Chattanooga railroad and a branch line, the Wartrace-Manchester railroad, jutting northeast through Manchester to McMinnville. Tullahoma lay astride the route to Chattanooga, objective point of all campaigns of the armies of the Ohio and the Cumberland.

East of the railroad's main line and about eleven miles south of Murfreesboro, a range of rough, rocky hills in a lean country corrugated with ridges and crossed infrequently by poor, winding roads extended nearly east and west, dividing the deep and narrow waters of the Duck River from the headwaters of Stone River. Only a few bridges and fords crossed the Duck. A few widely separated gaps led upward toward the south through extended canyons. The terrain compelled an army to keep to the roads.

Bragg's main force waited along the top of the hills which concealed them. The bulk of his infantry was posted parallel to the Wartrace-Manchester railroad. Polk's corps lay behind formidable works fronted by an abatis—a defense of felled trees with sharpened branches turned outward toward an enemy—beginning at Shelbyville and extending from the Duck River on the west to Horse Mountain on the east. Rosecrans judged Polk had 18,000 infantry and artillery. Hardee's corps, 12,000 strong, with headquarters at Wartrace, held the Shelbyville fortifications and Hoover's, Liberty, and Bellbuckle Gaps. In this line Bragg mustered some 8,000 cavalry, spread out in an immense arc, from McMinnville on his right to Columbia and Spring Hill on his far left. Forrest menaced Franklin and Nashville from Spring Hill. Bragg had constructed a large entrenched camp with formidable breastworks—to cover his Tullahoma depot—"nearly as extensive and much stronger than those of Corinth," Rosecrans described them. They were screened by an abatis of felled trees, 600 yards wide.

The unusual strength of this whole position arose from the fact that Bragg's communications were covered not only by his army but by natural barriers; and the approaches to it were easily defended, difficult of access, and few in number. The principal routes southward would bring an attacker into a half-dozen Thermopylaes, all held by Bragg.

One route led almost directly east before turning southwest by a 75-mile detour through McMinnville. Distance and wretched roads between Manchester and Tullahoma made this route an unlikely choice, particularly as easier routes were available. The Manchester turnpike entered the hills on Bragg's front through Hoover's Gap and ascended the Barrens through Matt's Hollow, a long, difficult canyon. To the right of this pike, the Wartrace road made the ascent through Liberty Gap, and for a considerable distance ran parallel with it but east of the railroad. The Shelby-ville turnpike led almost due south from Murfreesboro to Shelby-ville through Guy's Gap. Two other routes, which avoided difficult passes and numerous defiles, were available—the Middleton dirt road and the road leading by way of Versailles into the Shelbyville and Triune roads.

Rosecrans had full and accurate descriptions of Bragg's defenses and forces. He knew that a frontal assault on this citadel would be excessively costly and hazardous, and that even if defeated, Bragg could safely retreat along narrow, winding roads into the Barrens, fighting an easy withdrawing action, constantly shortening com-munications, and punishing the Union army without much en-dangering his own line of withdrawal to Chattanooga. Rough country and cavalry superiority would enable Bragg to keep the railroad open.

Rosecrans determined therefore not to assault Bragg frontally but to turn his right and seize the railroad bridge over the Elk River, south of Tullahoma. He would threaten Bragg's line of retreat and force him to emerge from his fortifications and either do battle on open ground less advantageous to him or retreat along a more vulnerable route.

To effect this stratagem, Rosecrans used the arts of the presti-digitator who diverts attention to meaningless motions of one hand while performing tricks with the other. In complex move-ments designed to confuse and fool Bragg, Rosecrans feinted in one direction and thrust elsewhere.

Military common sense would lead Bragg to assume that Rose-crans would take advantage of the level country and good roads west of the railroad to send his attack down the Shelbyville route against the Confederate left. In outline, Rosecrans' strategy aimed at diverting Bragg by a massive feint against his left. Rosecrans thus hoped to hold Hardee in his Shelbyville defenses so that he could not reinforce Polk. While Bragg was preoccupied with his left, Rosecrans planned to send the corps of Thomas and McCook down the Manchester route to threaten Polk and the Confederate center and right. Again, while Bragg was engrossed with this new threat and holding Polk to meet it, Crittenden would be marching far to the east, down obscure, difficult roads through the Barrens, to gain Bragg's right and rear. When Crittenden had gained position to threaten Bragg's communications, the Union army would concentrate to face the Confederates as they emerged. Further to confuse Bragg, Rosecrans supported feints with feints. Actually the movements of McCook and Thomas and the Reserve Corps constituted a giant feint to cover Crittenden's advance. The campaign contemplated two phases: the first to force Bragg out of his defenses; the second—never reached—to compel him to fight at a disadvantage. The first was directed against Bragg's communications rather than against his army.

Manchester was the key to the center of Bragg's Tullahoma line, and the destination set for McCook and Thomas. It was difficult to reach it with a large body of troops without disclosing the stratagem. The Manchester turnpike, the only practicable road connecting the towns, led for part of the way through Hoover's Gap, a three-mile defile between high hills, and then through Matt's Hollow, a two-mile gorge so narrow that wagons could scarcely pass. Enemy detachments holding these were within easy supporting distance of their main bodies.

To feint for the movement of McCook and Thomas, Rosecrans would send Granger to Triune, almost due west from Murfreesboro. Granger's change of position was designed to make Bragg believe that the attack would come upon Shelbyville by the Shelbyville and Triune pikes.

In plain view, Union supply trains moved out on the Shelbyville pike, and Stanley's cavalry rode to Eagleville, twenty miles west and a little south of Murfreesboro. Stanley was to advance boldly against Shelbyville on the night of June 24 and, after bivouacking, to fill the country to his rear, from Hardee's left and beyond, with immense campfires to suggest that heavy infantry columns followed him. Rosecrans supported the feint on Bragg's left with a feint on Bragg's right. To this end he ordered a cavalry and infantry advance to Woodbury, almost due east of Murfreesboro. The ruse accomplished its purpose. It held Hardee at Shelbyville while the movement against his right took position.

Granger's feint began when he ordered Mitchell's cavalry down the Shelbyville Pike to attack Bragg's cavalry and drive his infantry outposts back into the Shelbyville-Wartrace main line. Simultaneously, three divisions of Granger's Reserve Corps, and Brannan's division of the XIV, moved to Salem, almost on a direct line from Murfreesboro to Shelbyville. While this masking movement developed, Palmer's division with a brigade of cavalry was ordered to the vicinity of Bradyville, where his advance was to seize the head of the defile which led by an obscure road to Manchester. The rest of the army prepared to move.

That evening Rosecrans issued orders to his corps commanders. McCook would advance on the Shelbyville road, and with two divisions seize and hold Liberty Gap. His third division would cover Granger's crossing from the Middleton road and then rejoin the others. Granger would advance on the Middleton road, threatening Middleton, and having covered Brannan's crossing, take position to McCook's rear. Thomas would advance on the Manchester pike, seize Hoover's Gap, and bivouac within supporting distance of McCook.

Crittenden would leave Van Cleve's division at Murfreesboro, concentrate the remaining two at Bradyville, east of Murfreesboro, and there await orders. Turchin's brigade of cavalry would accompany Crittenden toward McMinnville. Stanley with the remaining cavalry would unite with Mitchell, returning from his engagement at Versailles, and attack the enemy cavalry at Middleton.

At daylight on the 25th the Union army moved. Headquarters followed McCook. All morning, unopposed, McCook's three divisions filed south toward Shelbyville, arriving at noon at Millersburg.

That afternoon, when Johnson reconnoitered Liberty Gap, he found two enemy regiments, and drove them out. Strong reinforcements joined the retreating Confederates at the south extremity, but the gap itself was in Union hands before nightfall.

At 4:00 A.M., led by Wilder's brigade of mounted infantry, Thomas marched. Reynolds followed Wilder; at 7:00, Rousseau followed Reynolds; and at 10:00, Negley followed Rousseau.

As the campaign opened, continuous, heavy, unseasonable rains began, making the dirt roads almost impassable. They lasted seventeen consecutive days, and proved particularly disastrous in a region in which, as Rosecrans put it, it is a singular characteristic of the soil that it "becomes so soft and spongy that wagons cut into it as if it were a swamp, and even horses cannot pass over it without similar results."

At nightfall, nonetheless, Rosecrans held the defiles and southern exits of two of the gaps leading to Bragg's stronghold. Crittenden still halted at Bradyville, awaiting developments; he had not contacted the enemy.

To checkmate Rosecrans' advancing columns, Bragg could have chosen one of two alternatives. He might have emerged from the strong positions at his left to block McCook, or he might have concentrated on his right and attacked the flank of Thomas at Fairfield. Union orders for the 25th provided for several contingencies. Swinging to the left, Crittenden would advance to Lumley's Stand, six miles east of Beech Grove, and open communications with Thomas, who would pass there. Thomas was to attack the enemy on the flank of his position in advance of Hoover's Gap, and drive him toward Fairfield. At Liberty Gap, McCook would advance in force toward the Wartrace road, the middle one of three roads leading from the gap. Stanley, with the greater part of the cavalry, would keep the Confederates occupied at Fosterville. Behind him, at Christiana on the Shelbyville turnpike, Granger and the Reserve Corps waited in support.

If Thomas succeeded in driving the enemy on his right down the Wartrace pike, he was to cover that road with one division and march rapidly toward Manchester with his two remaining divisions. McCook, if his feint toward Wartrace succeeded, was also to leave a division to cover Liberty Gap and hurry after Thomas to Manchester. The purpose of this stratagem was to force Bragg to concentrate on his left, while the bulk of the Union army skirted his right to strike at his rear.

Wilder's mounted infantry surprised the Confederate vedettes at Hoover's Gap, broke up their frequent attempts to stand, pushed them back on their supports, and then drove the whole force through the three-mile chasm and beyond McBride's Creek. When Wilder was attacked by Bushrod Johnson's brigade, he took advantage of the superior fire power of his Spencer repeaters, to hold off Johnson until Reynolds, marching six miles to his rear, came up and seized the bridge. That day Thomas advanced seventeen miles.

Continuous rain fell through the 25th, slowing all movements. Brannan was late in joining Thomas, and as a result Reynolds on the right of the 14th Corps was tardy in moving toward Fairfield.

When stiff enemy resistance developed on the heights, Reynolds halted. On McCook's front during the day, Bragg attempted to regain possession of Liberty Gap but was repulsed. Crittenden meanwhile slowly floundered forward through the mud.

Movements that started but slowed on the 25th were completed on the 26th under a soaking rain. On the Fairfield road Thomas's three divisions dispersed the Confederate pickets, and Union pickets advanced toward Fairfield. Early that afternoon Wilder's mounted infantry seized Matt's Hollow, thus gaining access to Manchester, and during the night Reynolds and the train entered the town. Rosecrans and his staff splashed in behind them on the 27th.

Rosecrans' legerdemain was succeeding. Bragg had waited for the main attack to come down the Shelbyville route. Now with Rosecrans' army concentrating at Manchester, uncovering both the railroad and the rear of the Shelbyville-Wartrace line, Bragg was compelled to order Hardee out of his elaborate Shelbyville defenses to the support of Polk's threatened left. During the night the remainder of Thomas's corps reached Manchester, and with two-thirds of his army concentrated, Rosecrans saw that the time had come to close columns for possible battle. He determined to break the railroad to Bragg's rear, and sent Wilder to burn the Elk River bridge, about six miles south of Tullahoma, and to rip up six miles of track between Decherd, which lay about six miles south of the Elk River bridge, and Cowan.

On Rosecrans' left, through the 24th, 25th, and 26th, Crittenden's corps dragged itself through the mud on roads worse than any Crittenden had ever seen. When horses and mules mired— some floundered up to their noses and smothered—they were unhitched, and men strained at ropes themselves, and pulled, pushed, and lifted the guns and wagons.

Crittenden halted two miles from the top of the long ascent, on the 25th, at the only well capable of supplying his corps. There a messenger reached him with Rosecrans' orders to march directly to Manchester. Officers and men set themselves to drag the trains of Palmer and Turchin over the hill; though they worked around the clock, fifty men to a wagon, the road was not cleared until Saturday the 27th. Again, as in West Virginia, Rosecrans did wagon master's work. Thirty-five years later the Reverend David

H. Moore wrote that he watched a group of officers ride up to a gun mired in a cornfield, and wade in to assist, cursing the weather, mud, horses, and particularly Rosecrans, who had got them into the mess. When the gun was extricated and the officers rode away, the only soldier who had not joined the cursing blurted out, "Don't you know, you damned fools, that that was Rosecrans pushing the wheel with me?" As soon as the trains moved, Wood followed. He marched with minimum baggage, as ordered, and crossed his train in eleven hours. Rosecrans sent a dispatch to Crittenden that he would not hold him to schedule, but Crittenden fumed: "If this army fails it will be mainly due to the fact that our wagons have been loaded down with unauthorized baggage."

Stanley wrote of the trials of the men:

> The narrow valleys became sloughs, and the narrow roads winding around the hill were so cut up that hours were taken in moving wagons and artillery a few miles, but it remained for the oak barrens to illustrate how impassable a road may be, under such circumstances as this continuous rain gave. The pale clay of the barrens turned to veritable mortar, and it needed only the molding and the burning to furnish the whole world with brick. Foot soldiers moving over the pale clay deployed like slow moving skirmishers; horsemen sought their own course, and as for artillery and supply wagons, they sank in the mud to their axles and stayed there. The mules were unhitched and led off by their drivers, seeking a place where they could stand without swamping. Details of foot men waded through mortar to the wagons, and carried from them upon their backs such packages of hard bread, bacon, corn, or other stores as would serve to keep men and animals alive.

To reach campsites lying clear of sheeted water, men marched up to their knees far into the night and sometimes into gray morning. The 8th Kansas did not find a campground until 2:00 A.M. Their commander, Colonel John A. Martin, wrote that he had experienced nothing so "disagreeable and exhausting" as this march. That night, for several miles, the route "ran up a narrow, muddy ravine, then into a deep forest, where the road led through holes knee deep, with slushy, dirty water, and crossed every mile or so, a running stream, which generally had to be forded. In the dense darkness we blindly groped our way, stumbling over fallen trees, rocks, and stumps, wading through creeks and crossing tumbledown bridges until we reached camp."

On the morning of the 28th, the last of Crittenden's corps mounted the crest of the plateau and crawled toward Manchester. Crittenden found Rosecrans there, and received permission to halt Wood's exhausted men and animals on the first suitable ground. In four days Crittenden had marched only 21 miles, and for two days Thomas and McCook had lain before Tullahoma, awaiting him. Colonel Gilbert C. Kniffen who was with Crittenden wrote later: "But for the heavy rains, Crittenden would have joined McCook and Thomas two days earlier, and the campaign might have had a different ending."

Stanley's cavalry, supported by Granger's infantry, made a direct attack on Guy's Gap on the far Union right, and the Confederate cavalry fled toward Shelbyville with Stanley pursuing. At the fortifications four miles north of the town a considerable cavalry force under Wheeler, part of Hardee's rear guard, attempted to stand, only to flee again, when Colonel Robert H. G. Minty, in Stanley's van, galloped through the abatis. When the Confederates turned once more, Union cavalry scattered them again in the town. Five hundred ninety-one Confederates were captured, and 200 killed, wounded, or drowned in the Duck. Much equipment was lost. General Wheeler and General Martin swam to freedom.

The bulk of Hardee's corps was hurrying by this time to support Polk, although the mud that slowed Rosecrans proved equally trying for Bragg. At midnight Stanley learned that Forrest was still four miles south after a day's floundering in the mud in a desperate effort to escape to Tullahoma. It became evident to Rosecrans that Bragg was evacuating the elaborate Shelbyville-Wartrace fortifications, which had taken months to build, and that he was concentrating behind his Tullahoma stronghold.

"Find out if we can move in force in line of battle to gain the rear of the Confederate works at Tullahoma," he ordered. When Chief Engineer Morton found the movement practicable, Rosecrans ordered Crittenden to form on the left of Thomas, about six miles from Manchester, with one division in reserve.

Union infantry reconnaissances felt out the Confederates on four separate roads, and confirmed the reports of scouts that Bragg lay in force across all highways except the road to Estill Springs; it was generally believed Bragg would fight a defensive battle behind his Tullahoma works. Now, finally, the three Federal corps were assembled in battle line as though prepared to assault Bragg's works.

It was another ruse, for Rosecrans had no intention of attacking. He knew that the ground between the armies was treacherous, filled with quicksand, and impassable—Kniffen later commented that to plunge into this morass, "through a dense abatis of tangled tree-tops, in the face of a storm of grapeshot and minnie-balls, would have been to doom one-half the army to destruction." Bragg had hoped that Rosecrans would underestimate the difficulties and make a frontal assault, and he awaited it. The ruse worked and Rosecrans kept Bragg immobilized while his smaller movements forced Bragg to evacuate his citadel.

Wilder rode back from his railroad-smashing expedition to report partial success: A detachment of his pioneers had destroyed the trestle work on the McMinnville branch, four miles from Tullahoma, but when his entire brigade attempted to cross near Pelham, they found the Elk River so swollen and turbulent that horses could neither swim nor ford it, and were swept away. Another detachment, sent ahead to destroy the main-line bridge at Estill Springs, had crossed six miles up at Pelham only to find an infantry division guarding the bridge. The outnumbered detachment fell back without loss or accomplishment.

The main body of the brigade, bent on damaging the railroad, crossed the Elk on the Pelham bridge, swam its horses through smaller streams, rafted the mountain howitzers, and struck the railroad at Decherd. After a stiff fight with the Confederate guard, Wilder destroyed tracks and water tanks on the main line and the trestle work on the Manchester spur. He burned the depot, and wrecked the telegraph, before he was driven off.

Bragg realized now that the center of the Tullahoma defenses lay vulnerable to the mass of Rosecrans' army. On the 26th Bragg had wished Polk to move his corps by night to Guy's Gap and attack Rosecrans' flank and rear, while Hardee pressed his right. Polk told Bragg to his face that the position he was asked to take was "nothing short of a man trap." By 5:00 P.M. that day, as Union forces were turning both of Stewart's flanks, Bragg and Polk agreed that the McMinnville-Wartrace line could not be held, and that a retreat to Tullahoma was unavoidable. Polk struggled through the rain-soaked roads to reach Tullahoma, and at 7:00 A.M. on the 29th he posted his corps in battle line and reported to Bragg for orders.

Bragg had then announced that he was determined to stand at Tullahoma although Rosecrans had destroyed the railroad at Decherd and cut the Confederate communications. "An injudicious determination," Polk protested. At a conference that day Polk insisted that it had been Bragg's first duty to re-establish communications with his base. "They have been re-established since this morning's interview," Bragg answered. "How do you propose to maintain them?" Polk asked. "By posting cavalry along the line." "But you do not have cavalry enough at your disposal to cover other points and that line also," Polk reminded him. "The enemy will possess our line of communications by driving off our cavalry in thirty-six hours with a force sufficient to hold the communications. In that event you will be as effectually besieged as Pemberton in Vicksburg, his sources of supply cut off. The enemy will not strike you a blow, but reduce you by starvation either to surrender on the spot, or to retreat along the line by way of Fayetteville, Huntsville, and across the Tennessee in the vicinity of Decatur. In this event animals and men, being exhausted for want of food, would be unfitted for resistence, and your whole wagon train, including ordnance and your artillery, would fall a prey to the enemy. It is doubtful also in such a case if you could get the army itself across the river. But suppose you succeeded in this last, you would find yourself in the hills of North Alabama without food, and your army would be forced to disperse to avoid starvation. In the meantime the enemy would pass over the mountain, take possession of Chattanooga, and march without interruption into Georgia and the Carolinas, taking possession of the heart of the Confederacy. To avoid all these results you should fall back in the direction of your base, so as to keep the line connecting you with it all the time covered."

"Then you propose that we shall retreat?" Bragg asked. Polk's answer was blunt. "I do, and that is my counsel." When Bragg asked Hardee's opinion, Hardee replied that while Polk's view carried great weight with him he was not prepared to "advise a retreat." Instead, he thought, infantry should be sent along the line, to support the cavalry, and to wait for further developments. But Polk finally prevailed, and during the night of the 30th Bragg evacuated the great Tullahoma citadel, the second line of defense made untenable by Rosecrans' strategy.

In the early hours of July 1, a citizen brought the news to Thomas. Thomas advanced cautiously, and at noon Steedman entered the works without resistance. Bragg's infantry had marched off in the dark, and at daylight his cavalry followed.

With Tullahoma in his hands, Thomas ordered the divisions of Negley and Rousseau to pursue east of the railroad along the route of Spring Creek. Late that afternoon their advance overtook Bragg's rear guard at Bethpage Bridge, two miles above the intersection with the Elk. The enemy crossed after a sharp skirmish, took position on the heights south of the river, covering the bridge with artillery, which was screened by rough earthworks, and then burned the bridge.

When Turchin with a brigade of Union cavalry advanced from Hillsborough on the Decherd road, he found Confederate cavalry blocking the fords of the Elk near Morris Ferry. Turchin engaged them until Mitchell came up, and forced the passage. During the rainy night the Union advance halted at the crossings of the Elk.

Lack of ammunition held up McCook through Wednesday, July 1, giving the 20th Corps a badly needed respite. Colonel Martin recalled that Heg's brigade, soaked and chilled in the rain, had "suffered terribly." At every step they sank "almost half knee deep in the soft and glutinous soil, so that a march of twelve miles caused greater fatigue than an ordinary march of twenty."

An officer of the 8th Kansas produced a muster roll in the rain, and ruefully appended:

I make this roll lying flat on my belly on the ground with a rubber blanket for a desk. If I was in Washington in a comfortable room with a hundred dollar desk, a gold pen, black, blue, red and purple inks, the latest and best patent rulers and plenty of "red tape," I could make a more artistic copy. But I have been constantly soaked with rain for seven days and nights, there isn't a bone in my body that doesn't ache, my fingers are as numb as though they were frozen, and my clothes are as stiff with Tennessee mud as my fingers are with chill. Under the circumstances this is the best I can do. If any first class clerk in the department thinks he can do better, let him duck himself in the Potomac every five minutes, and wade through mud knee deep for six days, and then try it on.

Confederates found the mud equally frustrating. "What does 'Tullahoma' mean?" one officer asked another. " 'Tulla' is Greek for 'mud'," was the answer, "and 'Homa' means 'more mud'!"

When McCook's train struggled in on Thursday, he sent two divisions after Bragg down roads west of the tracks. At 3:00 A.M. Sheridan started down the Manchester road. He found the Elk River, three and a half miles from Manchester, impassable, and marching parallel to it reached Red Creek, only to find that flooded also. But near the raging junction of the two he discovered a rough but usable ford, guarded by a Confederate cavalry regiment.

A detachment crossed and drove off the defenders of the ford, and the rest of Sheridan followed, to hold the south bank. A cable was carried across the stream for the weariest soldiers to cling to. After them, the cheering main body of infantry, forming a human chain, breasted the waters without losing a man. To the east of Sheridan, Thomas halted throughout the day beside the raging Elk and the smoldering Bethpage Bridge.

The next afternoon, July 2, Rosecrans reported to Halleck that Tullahoma had fallen, and that the pursuers had struck Bragg's rear guard near the Elk, too late to save the bridges. The stream was falling rapidly, however, and he hoped to overtake Bragg, who had already been forced from the easier Pelham route across the mountains to the longer interior route through Decherd.

At 4:00 A.M. the following day, Sheridan advanced toward Winchester, and in an eleven-hour march pushed on toward Cowan, at the foot of the Cumberland plateau. There he learned that Bragg's infantry and artillery had climbed the mountain and were bivouacked near University, seven miles beyond, with Wharton's cavalry screening them. Thomas, too, crossed the Elk that day, and one of his divisions advanced toward University.

The next morning, on July 4, Sheridan sent two cavalry regiments to penetrate Bragg's cavalry screen to determine if the Confederate army lay behind it. Bragg was gone.

Rosecrans' headquarters had been shifting with the advance. On Wednesday and Thursday it was at Big Spring Branch; on Friday at Beech Grove; for four days, beginning Saturday, it remained at Manchester; and on July 1, it had transferred to Tullahoma, where it remained most of the month. On the 3rd Rosecrans pushed ahead in person to Estill Springs; and on July 4 he rode over to Winchester, where McCook got up an Independence Day dinner party, while two brass bands entertained the men.

There was reason to be festive, for McCook's advance discovered at Cowan that Bragg had entrained the last of his regiments for Chattanooga. Demolition squads had wrecked the railroad to block a further Union advance. Bragg was south of the Tennessee.

That morning another uncertainty was resolved. Rosecrans' headquarters had known from Washington dispatches that Lee was striking north through Maryland and into Pennsylvania, and that Meade had replaced Hooker as commander of the Army of the Potomac. They could not have known that from Charleston, South Carolina, Beauregard was complaining to Joseph E. Johnston: "Of what earthly use is that 'raid' of Lee's army in Maryland? Is it going to end the struggle, take Washington, or save the Mississippi Valley? Why not have kept on the defensive in Virginia, sent Longstreet's 20,000 men to reinforce Bragg, who, with the 10,000 men I sent you, could have crushed Rosecrans, and then sent about 50,000 men to Memphis and Fort Pillow and then to your assistance?"

From June 30 until the morning of July 4 anxious questions were asked in Middle Tennessee concerning the fate of the Army of the Potomac. Then Stanton's dispatch announcing the victory at Gettysburg reached Rosecrans.

Rosecrans' answer told Stanton how he had driven Bragg from his entrenched positions at Shelbyville and Tullahoma, "either of them stronger than Corinth." He was now making an effort to hold Bragg. "I pray God that every available soldier may be sent to me."

The day before, Bragg had reported to Johnston that when Rosecrans advanced in heavy force

. . . we offered him battle, but he declined, and while holding a strong position, which we could not successfully attack, threw a force to our right and rear by which he successfully assailed our communications. No adequate force could be placed at these several points along the line without too much reducing our main body. I accordingly withdrew to Tullahoma, and reached there just in time to prevent an attack upon its feeble garrison.

The enemy established himself again in strong position on the defensive, and moved another heavy column against our bridges over Elk River, now swollen by heavy rains. By making a rapid march and using the railroad successfully, we saved all our supplies, and crossed the Elk just before a heavy column appeared at the upper bridge. We were now back against the mountains, in a country affording us nothing, with a long line of railroad to protect, and a half dozen passes on the right and left by which our rear could be gained. In this position it was perfectly practicable for the enemy to destroy our means of crossing the Tennessee, and thus secure our ultimate destruction without a battle. Having failed to bring him to that issue, so much desired by myself and troops, I reluctantly yielded to the necessity imposed by my position and inferior strength, and put my army in motion for the Tennessee River. . . . The Tennessee will be taken as our line.

And so the Tullahoma campaign ended, with the Confederate army crossing the Tennessee and posting guards along the south bank. It occupied Chattanooga and Tyner's Station, and began to fortify Chattanooga and all crossings as far up as Blythe's Ferry.

Union losses in this, the least bloody major victory of the war, totalled 83 killed, 473 wounded, and 13 captured or missing. Confederate losses were much higher. The Union army captured 1,634 Confederates, 59 of them commissioned officers. Of this Provost-Marshal-General William M. Miles reported, "616 claimed to have delivered themselves to our forces voluntarily, being conscripts or tired of the war." Ninety-six of these enlisted in the Union army. Bragg made no casualty report; his losses, he said, were "trifling."

Rosecrans' advance into Middle Tennessee apparently attracted small attention even among Union generals. Thirteen days after it had begun, Sherman, who did not know of its successful conclusion, wrote to his wife: "I read of Washington, Baltimore and Philadelphia being threatened and Rosecrans sitting idly by, writing for personal fame in the newspapers."

That the campaign had not ended even more gloriously could be blamed only on the weather. Garfield said: "We could have got in ahead of Bragg as our plan was, but for the extraordinary rains which rendered the roads almost impassable. If we had reached Tullahoma before Bragg we should have destroyed his army." Rosecrans made substantially the same statement to Burnside: "Nothing but excessive rains and the impassable condition of the roads prevented us from overtaking and destroying the entire army." And Henry Villard, reporter and severe Rosecrans critic, said in his *Memoirs:* "Had the full execution of Rosecrans' strategic programme not been prevented by the extraordinary inclemency of the unseasonable weather, he would probably have succeeded in inflicting a complete defeat."

Even today this most brilliant campaign remains little known, little appreciated, perhaps because in its own day, by perverse chance, it competed for attention with more dramatic news. Villard pointed out that:

> The most creditable achievement of the Army of the Cumberland in maneuvering Bragg into a retreat was not appreciated in the North as it should have been. The reason was that the news of it reached the loyal public while it was trembling over the issue of the mighty struggle at Gettysburg, and was in feverish expectation of the final outcome of the siege of Vicksburg. The authorities at Washington, in their elation over the defeat of Lee and the fall of the Mississippi stronghold, and in their angry remembrance of Rosecrans' conduct, also failed to award the meed of praise the latter had expected.

Piatt substantially agreed with Villard: "This masterly campaign was neither appreciated at Washington nor known to the people. So accustomed were we to big battles and frightful slaughter that a great victory like this obtained without the useless loss of a man, seemed tame and insignificant."

Yet some appreciative voices spoke out. Seward sensed the importance of the campaign and notified the European powers that Tennessee again was in Union hands. In his *Official Report* Halleck called the campaign "admirable." Lincoln added his praise: "The flanking of Bragg at Shelbyville, Tullahoma and Chattanooga is the most splendid piece of strategy I know of." And soldier Stanley said: "If any student of the military art desires to make a study of a model campaign, let him take his maps and General Rosecrans' orders for the daily movements of this campaign. No better example of successful strategy was carried out during the war than in the Tullahoma Campaign."

Official news of the fall of Vicksburg traveled more slowly to Middle Tennessee than the news of Gettysburg had done. But by July 7, Grant's victory was clear. "We have just received official information that Vicksburg surrendered to General Grant on the 4th of July," Stanton telegraphed Rosecrans. "Lee's army overthrown; Grant victorious. You and your noble army now have a chance to give the finishing blow to the rebellion. Will you neglect the chance?" Grant now received the major generalship in the regulars which had been dangled in March, and Meade was commissioned Brigadier General in the regulars.

But Rosecrans was cut as much by Stanton's neglect to mention the remarkable achievement of the Tullahoma campaign as by the sharp edge of his telegram. Temper flared in his answer: "Just received your cheering telegram announcing the fall of Vicksburg and confirming the defeat of Lee. You do not appear to observe the fact that this noble army has driven the rebels from Middle Tennessee. . . . I beg in behalf of this army that the War Department may not overlook so great an event because it is not written in letters of blood." Nevertheless, Rosecrans ordered a hundred guns set amid the beeches of Tennessee to thunder the tidings of victories in Pennsylvania and Mississippi.

Rosecrans' army could not pursue Bragg because of a problem in logistics. Bragg's biographer Seitz says that although the nine-day campaign "had resulted in a great strategic gain for Rosecrans, Bragg had preserved his army," due to the impassable roads Rosecrans faced, and a railroad in "private hands which served him none too well and as it pleased." Rosecrans, Seitz said, "knew his business too certainly to come to grips with Bragg, unless the better prepared."

Fourteen

"A WALL FULL OF RATHOLES"

With Middle Tennessee cleared, Washington could be expected to demand a further advance. Bragg's army constituted one major objective for Rosecrans. The other was Chattanooga itself. Once, Richmond, Corinth, Chattanooga, and Vicksburg had been the four bastions in the Confederacy's frontier. Now, with Corinth and Vicksburg taken, Richmond and Chattanooga were the two most important points held. And while as a symbol Richmond enjoyed greater importance, from a strategic standpoint Chattanooga was its equal. From it railroad lines radiated to the Ohio, the Mississippi, the Gulf, and the Atlantic. Chattanooga commanded the approach to the east Tennessee coalfields, best Southern suppliers. It guarded the only avenue by which Virginia could be reached from the southeast. Its possession by the Union would practically isolate Virginia and North Carolina, and detach Alabama and Mississippi. It gave access to interior Georgia. When this region was penetrated, the war of movement would be pushed from the middle into the Atlantic zone. Chattanooga was the gateway which enabled the enemy to shift troops between Virginia and the West. It enabled them to dominate the Southern Alleghenies, a territory extending into North Carolina, Tennessee, Georgia, and Alabama, and even South Carolina. Chattanooga had political as well as military importance. Many inhabitants, who had no slaves, were pro-Union. Thomas observed: "Holding Chattanooga enabled us to strike at its belly where it lived."

Chattanooga was more difficult to take than Tullahoma. From

Winchester, where Rosecrans lay, Chattanooga was about sixty-nine miles by railroad, and much farther by roads. Fronting the army soared the Cumberland plateau, 2,200 feet high; and beyond it stretches the Sequatchie Valley, three or four miles wide and sixty long. East of the Valley, Walden's Ridge rose, 1,300 feet high. East of this ridge flowed the Tennessee, 400 to 600 yards wide above Chattanooga, 400 to 900 below it. Unlike the Mississippi, which was navigable for war vessels from the Gulf to the North, the Tennessee was blocked to military traffic 200 miles below Chattanooga by Muscle Shoals. The navy could not aid Rosecrans as it aided Grant.

Chattanooga itself was a stronghold. To its back extended rich, friendly Georgia and a railroad network connecting it with points west and south and with the coast. South of the Tennessee lay Sand Mountain and Raccoon Mountain, rising from the river valley to heights of 600 or 700 feet, with broad, flat, wooded tops. Then, beyond the narrow valley of Lookout Creek, reared Lookout Mountain, a massive ridge 85 miles long, terminating in a perpendicular crag a little south and west of Chattanooga. A road leading south from Chattanooga skirted the point of Lookout Mountain. The nearest crossing of Lookout was 26 miles southwest, the next nearest, Valley Head, 40 miles southwest. Adding to this natural strength, fortifications covered Chattanooga's southern approaches.

Even without these obstacles, Rosecrans faced serious problems in attempting to seize Chattanooga. Each mile south brought him farther from his primary base at Louisville, and his depots at Nashville and Murfreesboro. His cavalry was still inferior, and the hostile country behind him was scoured of forage. The railroad was smashed to the Tennessee, and every bridge damaged or destroyed. Worse, creeks and rivers were still flooding. Roads across the Cumberland plateau were bad. Even when they were dry, their steepness made wagoning difficult. Surfaces were rough, sometimes rocky, and curves numerous and sharp. As far north as Murfreesboro, the roads forming the secondary supply route—the only route available when the railroad failed—were poor. Granger found them impassable and the country a perfect quagmire in which it was almost impossible to move man or beast except upon the pike. That summer, the Cumberland fell so low that navigation became problematical—hence the critical importance of the railroad; at least one-quarter of the army was required to guard it. "Push the repair of the railroad night and day," Rosecrans ordered. "Speed is the only consideration." Repairs had to be extended ahead on the main line to Stevenson, Alabama, and Bridgeport, ten miles northeast of Stevenson on the Tennessee River, and on the branch line to Tracy City, towns which could serve as secondary depots after the army had crossed the Cumberland Plateau.

Rosecrans faced a sevenfold task: (1) to convince a "wary and experienced" Bragg that he would cross above Chattanooga; (2) without attracting attention, to repair the railroad to Bridgeport; (3) secretly to accumulate twenty days' rations; (4) to construct pontoon trains, train pontooners, bring the trains forward, and conceal them; (5) to cross the river and the mountains beyond with twenty days' rations and ammunition for two battles; (6) to wait until the new corn ripened for fodder; (7) so to threaten Bragg's rail communications as to cause him to retreat and permit a concentration between him and Chattanooga.

Ten days' forage was needed to cross the Cumberland Plateau. By July 7, lack of forage remained the biggest obstacle to an immediate advance. The district Thomas occupied was scoured so clear that he found it difficult to stay. Rosecrans pointed out to Halleck that the army was now as far south as supplies permitted. The railroad reached the Elk, where engineers were building a bridge, and entered McMinnville and Pelham. A cavalry division sent up the Central Alabama railroad would open connections with Hurlbut at Tuscumbia. Would Burnside advance and hold the left? Halleck answered wryly that Burnside had been told repeatedly to do so, but he did not know what Burnside was doing. He seemed to be "tied to Cincinnati."

When the rumor that Bragg was burning the sawmill and railroad bridge at Bridgeport proved correct, the guard at Stevenson, Alabama, intervened and saved part of the sawmill but not the long bridge.

The main line was opened to the Elk River Bridge by July 13, and to Bridgeport by the 25th. Repairs to the Tracy City branch line proved more difficult. Constructed to bring coal down the mountain, it required a special engine and cars for the steep grades and sharp curves. The only available locomotive was smashed.

Without it, no supplies could be freighted to Tracy City, and until the depot there was established, a general advance was impossible. For seventeen days the army was held up by a broken piece of machinery, and Thomas, on the 26th, did not have a half day's subsistence ahead for man or beast.

Once rain stopped, the weather turned delightful, with days warm and nights cool. The Cumberland highlands stood forth thinly veiled with dawn mist that clung to them through the morning. However, cool weather failed to cool Rosecrans' tongue. When the Ohio Democratic State Central Committee asked him if his Provost Marshal was destroying newspapers and other political material, he roared that he felt bound to prevent the circulation of "lying, traitorous, libelous stuff."

During July, Rosecrans sent Rousseau and Colonel J. P. Sanderson of the 15th U.S. Infantry to Washington with a plan to re-enlist 10,000 two-year veterans. Several governors had offered to organize seven regiments apiece of men willing to re-enlist if they could fight as mounted infantry in Rosecrans' army.

When he reached Washington, Rousseau handed Stanton Rosecrans' letter. It emphasized the need for reinforcements to cover his communications. Sanderson heard Stanton comment rudely: "I would rather you would come to ask the command of the army of the Cumberland. He shall not have another damned man." Rousseau concluded that Rosecrans' official destruction was but a question of time and opportunity.

Some days later, after Sanderson and Rousseau had been courteously received by Lincoln, Sanderson observed in his daily diary letter to his wife: "Halleck is violent against granting our wishes, and Stanton but little better. But the President is decidedly favorable. The prospects are that he will take the matter in his hands, and act accordingly, giving us a triumph over the bullheaded general-in-chief and the bearish and unmannerly Secretary of War." Next day, Lincoln told Rousseau Stanton wished to see him again. Stanton proved affable, announced that Rousseau's division should be mounted on horses at once—"if the Quartermaster General and Chief of Ordnance approved, he would equip it with the best repeating rifles." A few days later, Stanton's affability disappeared. Rousseau's division was now to be mounted on mules, and repeating rifles would not be delivered until

January. Rousseau and Sanderson then left Washington for other points east, before returning to Chattanooga.

On July 24, the celebrated series of double letters from Halleck to Rosecrans began. In official letters Halleck lectured Rosecrans impersonally; in "private and confidential" letters he spoke more kindly and personally and at greater length. "You must not wait for Johnston to join Bragg, but must move forward immediately against the latter," Halleck ordered officially. "There is great disappointment felt here at the slowness of your advance. Unless you can move more rapidly, your whole campaign will prove a failure, and you will have both Bragg and Johnston against you."

A private letter followed: "The tone of some of your replies lately would indicate that you thought I was unnecessarily urging you forward. . . . The patience of the authorities here has been completely exhausted, and if I had not repeatedly promised to urge you forward, and begged for delay, you would have been removed from the command. . . . I deem it my duty, as a friend, to represent it to you truly and fairly . . . because it was at my earliest solicitation you were given the command." At the same time Halleck prodded Burnside to move into eastern Tennessee.

The next day Halleck urged Rosecrans: "The great object you will have in view is to drive Bragg from East Tennessee before he can be reinforced by Johnston. . . . The pressure for this movement at this time is so strong that neither you nor I can resist it. Unless it is made while Grant's army occupies Johnston, there probably will not be another opportunity this year."

Rosecrans answered moderately. "Your views accord with my own. . . . To move our troops beyond our means of supply would break down and disable both men and horses without result. . . . I confess I should like to avoid such remarks and letters as I am receiving lately from Washington, if I could do so without injury to the public service. . . . What movements of General Grant will affect us?"

Halleck's private response was firm. Rosecrans must perceive that he had acted from motives of friendship: "Having now explained to you frankly that you can have no possible grounds for your tone of displeasure toward me, I shall not again refer to this matter." That evening Rosecrans asked Halleck to assure Lincoln that "we shall work to save and hold" eastern Tennessee: "But these must go together, or the last state of those loyal men will be worse than their present condition."

On August 1 Rosecrans thanked Halleck for his notes, and for his support and confidence. "But as my ambition is something like your own—to discharge my duty to God and our country—I say to you frankly that whenever the Government can replace me by a commander in whom they have more confidence, they ought to do so, and take the responsibility of the result."

Rosecrans stated his immediate problems, but Halleck did not take them seriously and confided to Quincy Gillmore that Burnside and Rosecrans were hesitating to advance until they could be reinforced, and he had no reinforcements to give them.

On August 1, an unnamed general, returning from Washington, reported that Lincoln would not consider improper an unofficial letter from Rosecrans. Rosecrans wrote a lengthy explanation of his delays. Lincoln's answer was kindly:

> Since Grant has been entirely relieved by the fall of Vicksburg, by which Johnston is also relieved, it has seemed to me that your chance for a stroke has been considerably diminished . . . but I can see and appreciate the difficulties you mention. The question occurs . . . does preparation advance at all? Do you not consume supplies as fast as you get them forward? . . .
>
> I am not casting blame upon you . . . I rather think that by great exertion you can get to East Tennessee; but a very important question is, Can you stay there? I make no order in the case; that I leave to General Halleck and yourself.
>
> And now be assured once more that I think of you with all kindness and confidence, and that I am not watching you with an evil eye.

Rosecrans responded to this very understanding letter with an argument. "Permit me to assure you that I am not and have not been touched with any of that official pride which desires to have its own way. . . . You think Johnston was freed by the fall of Vicksburg. Was not Bragg set free by the evacuation of Middle Tennessee? You think we ought to have prevented Bragg from reinforcing Johnston. Why cannot Grant keep Johnston from reinforcing Bragg? Has he not a nearer base of supplies and a more favorable country; a better railroad and more rolling-stock than we have here?"—and much more in the same strain. "Thanking you for your kindness, may I ask you, when impulsive men suppose me querulous, to believe I am only straightforward and in earnest...."

Lincoln declined to rejoin, and on August 31 sent this gracious reply:

When I wrote you before, I did [not] intend, nor do I now, to engage in an argument with you on military questions. You had informed me you were impressed through General Halleck that I was dissatisfied with you; and I could not bluntly deny that I was, without implicating him. I therefore concluded to tell you the plain truth, being satisfied the matter would thus appear much smaller than it would if seen by mere glimpses. I repeat that my appreciation of you has not abated. I can never forget whilst I remember anything, that about the end of last year and the beginning of this, you gave us a hard-earned victory, which had there been a defeat instead, the nation could scarcely have lived over. Neither can I forget the check you so opportunely gave to a dangerous sentiment which was spreading in the North.

Pressures were great on Lincoln and the administration on the day he wrote this letter. Chase told Stanton that the amount of suspended requisitions, including army pay for July and August, would be short $35,000,000, and that he could raise only $5,000,000, and unless the war were prosecuted more vigorously and ended sooner, the government would be financially embarrassed. Stanton cited Rosecrans' delay as the principal difficulty.

Meanwhile, at noon, August 4, Halleck telegraphed to Rosecrans: "Your forces must move forward without further delay. You will daily report the movement of each corps till you cross the Tennessee River." Rosecrans inquired if the order was intended to take away his discretion regarding the time and manner of moving his troops. "The orders for the advance of your army, and that its movements be reported daily, are peremptory," Halleck replied. At the same time he telegraphed Burnside to move immediately on East Tennessee with Knoxville as his objective. The Ninth Corps would serve as reserve. When Burnside reached East Tennessee, he was to connect with Rosecrans' forces.

Rosecrans said, "We were ordered forward alone, regardless alike of the counsels of the commanders, the clamors of the press, the principles of military art and science, and the interests of the country."

From the long wrangle over horses and an advance, and from

other signs, Rosecrans knew that Washington would not listen favorably to him. It was clear that at best Halleck was a sort of well-intentioned office boy and that Stanton was running affairs and was after Rosecrans' head. Yet it would be beyond credibility that the Secretary should so hate his commander as consciously to jeopardize an army and the cause for which it fought. Stanton in his way was as much of a patriot as Rosecrans. But patriotism can be blind, and had Rosecrans understood his position with the War Department, he certainly would have resigned instead of plunging into the Confederate trap. At that, he narrowly escaped to confound his enemies, and the trap was triggered only by an accident. But the hazards of fighting Bragg to the front and Stanton to the rear were frightful. Certainly Rosecrans had not made full inventory of his obstacles and enemies when he took a soldier's way out and obeyed.

In his first daily report, Rosecrans informed Halleck that he would move the following Monday. He was uncertain whether to cross the Tennessee above or below Chattanooga. Preliminary movements would be much different in each case: "If, therefore, the movement which I propose cannot be regarded as obedience to your order, I respectfully request a modification of it, or to be relieved from the command."

Halleck disregarded Rosecrans' offer to resign. The means and the roads he left to Rosecrans' discretion—"In such matters I do not interfere."

Halleck's double letters should have ended with Rosecrans' promise: "This army shall move with all the dispatch compatible with the successful execution of our work." But Halleck was loquacious, and on August 7 remarked: "If you suppose the Secretary of War has any personal hostility to you, or would not rejoice at your success as much as that of any other general, I think you are mistaken. . . . You seem to be laboring under the impression that the authorities here were making war on you. There was never a greater mistake. . . . Nevertheless, many of your dispatches have been exceedingly annoying to the War Department. . . . It is said that you do not draw straight in the traces, but are continually kicking out or getting one leg over."

Rosecrans considered the horse metaphor "very unjust." As for his delays: "I assure you I have given these matters my careful attention, and had the counsels of my best officers. The contempt of the War Department toward these officers' opinions, and the contemptuous silence with which our success was treated, has produced a feeling that the Secretary is unjust. As for myself, I am quite sure you, even you, wholly misunderstand me. You take my remonstrances and importunities for complaints. I know that from your dispatches last Autumn."

"The War Department did not think it prudent to relieve me," Rosecrans said later, "and therefore gave consent in terms sufficient to convict it of reckless ignorance or worse."

By August 13, the repaired locomotive was hauling freight to Tracy City. Sheridan's division followed the rebuilt line forward, two brigades advancing to Bridgeport and one to Stevenson to guard the rapidly accumulating stores. Only a want of forage held up a general advance. A cavalry division was posted on the north bank of the Tennessee while Negley opened a road across the Cumberland plateau, mechanics repaired the Stevenson sawmill, and soldiers felled trees for lumber for rebuilding the Bridgeport bridge, which had been burned by Bragg. The fodder supply continued on a day-to-day basis. Rosecrans bought 50 railroad cars to ease the shortage. His mules and horses needed 28 carloads a day to subsist.

Marching orders were issued on the 15th, and next morning all three corps were crossing the plateau. Although Burnside's simultaneous advance covered Rosecrans' left, Stanton refused similar protection from Grant's army for his right, and so Rosecrans sent Mitchell's cavalry from Fayetteville, Tennessee, to Huntsville, Alabama, and thence along the Memphis and Charleston railroad, to protect the line of the Tennessee river from Bridgeport to Vicksburg. "The rebels expect us above Chattanooga," Rosecrans told Halleck. Such expectation was good military sense. The junction there of the armies of the Cumberland and Ohio would have permitted Rosecrans to beat Buckner and Bragg in detail. Rosecrans would seem to threaten Knoxville, when actually he would be concentrating near Bridgeport and Stevenson. Rosecrans confided to Halleck on August 16:

All three corps are crossing the mountains. It will take till Wednesday night to reach their respective positions. I think we shall deceive the enemy as to our point of crossing. It is a stupendous undertaking. The Alps, with a broad river at the foot, and not fertile plains, but 70 miles of difficult and most sterile mountains beyond, before reaching a point of secondary importance to the enemy, in reference to his vital one, Atlanta.

On August 16, 1863, the campaign to take Chattanooga, which had brought the army to Nashville, through Murfreesboro, and beyond Tullahoma, entered its fourth phase. This phase consisted of three movements in sequence: one, to the Tennessee; two, across the river; and three, against Bragg's communications south of Chattanooga. The strategy was identical with that of the Tullahoma campaign: to feign a direct thrust while reaching behind the enemy, though in this campaign it could be a greatly reinforced enemy. Rosecrans had moved against Bragg in middle Tennessee, while Johnston and Pemberton were busy with Grant at Vicksburg, and Lee was marching to meet Meade at Gettysburg. Now with Meade and Grant idle, Rosecrans risked facing a Confederate concentration. Unless the War Department reinforced him from all quarters, or kept Union armies busy, thus tying down the Confederates, Rosecrans was in danger of ambush by superior forces.

Routes to the river depended on points of crossing. Three alternatives faced Rosecrans. He might cross above Chattanooga, or to its front, or below. To cross at Chattanooga was difficult. The Tennessee gorge is narrow there and commanded from heights on both sides. Confederate John B. Gordon wrote that "Rosecrans was too able a soldier and wise a strategist to assail Bragg in his stronghold when the country was open to him on either flank. His policy therefore was to cross the Tennessee rim not in front of Chattanooga, where Bragg was ready to meet him, but at a distance either above or below it. Both were practicable, and he set his army in motion toward points above and below the city, thus leaving Bragg in doubt as to his real purpose."

That purpose was to cross his main body below Chattanooga while feinting directly at and above it. The railroad to Bridgeport turned east at Stevenson. These depots were south and west of Chattanooga. While an advance below the town covered both, it was necessary for Rosecrans to mask his intent so that Bragg would withdraw his heavy guards at the downstream crossings; and then to prevent him from moving his forces back to block the crossing or to fall upon the divided forces during it. Fortunately the Confederates did not concentrate then against Rosecrans as they did a few weeks later. A spy from Bragg's camp reported that common soldiers felt they were not able to contend with Rosecrans' army, and officers and men believed "Bragg will retreat as soon as an advance is made." They expected and feared a Union movement toward Rome, Georgia.

To open the campaign, the left under Crittenden, which was to feint directly at Chattanooga and upstream, crossed the Cumberland Plateau and occupied the Sequatchie Valley between Jasper and Pikesville. All three divisions built extensive campfires and moved openly, to suggest to Confederate watchers that the whole army was present. Minty's cavalry, riding far to the left, drove Debrill's Confederate cavalry across the Tennessee. This show by a column of all arms convinced Debrill that Rosecrans' whole army was moving by that route.

The XXI Corps hurried to cross Walden's Ridge. On the extreme left, Minty demonstrated along the Tennessee, thirty miles upstream from Blythe's Ferry. Hazen reached the river near Dallas, and posted two brigades on the eastern brow of the Ridge, so that they were visible to Confederate watchers at Blythe's Ferry. At night, their bivouacs were greatly extended by the campfires of a ghost army scattered among the empty hills. In the daytime Hazen marched the same troops, repeatedly and always in the same direction, past the same openings, returning them behind cover. Drummers moved from place to place, beating calls to phantom divisions, and bugles sounded from widely separated, empty mountain spots. Artillery fired across the river, was moved inconspicuously, and fired again. Minty's cavalry swept down the Tennessee bottoms to near Chattanooga, while Wilder moved upstream, scattered the Confederate crossing guards, and occupied all fords for seventy-five miles, from Williams Island to Kingston. At Blythe's Ferry, axes, saws, and hammers noisily worked as though pontoons were being built for the whole Union army.

On August 21, when Wilder reached the opposing heights, he shelled Chattanooga for seven hours, choosing two steamboats and a pontoon bridge for targets, but killing a little girl, a woman, and a ferryman. The Confederates were astonished: their scouts and pickets had given no warning of Rosecrans' approach. But their batteries replied; rolling stock and depot supplies were hurried out of range; Forrest was ordered to Kingston to block a Union crossing there; Hill's corps and other forces were moved upstream in support; heavy guards posted downstream were withdawn; and Buckner was ordered from east Tennessee to Blythe's Ferry, there to join with Bragg.

In the five days before Rosecrans' army had crossed the plateau to face the Tennessee, extensive reconnaissances were made, pontoon bridges were brought forward by railroad and concealed behind woods and hills back of Stevenson. To provide for more permanent river communications, Rosecrans contracted for the rebuilding of the Bridgeport and Running Water bridges. He also ordered the immediate construction of five flat-bottomed, sternwheel steamers, for service between Bridgeport and Chattanooga.

Rosecrans suffered a serious loss when Chief Engineer Morton resigned; he pleaded poor health, but Hazen saw another reason. When McCook complained that Morton's Pioneers blocked his way, Rosecrans had abused Morton with "coarse and unjust language" in a scene Hazen considered "humiliating." The War Department informed Rosecrans that only two engineers were available to replace him—"Baldy" Smith, known to him from West Point, or Benham, who had failed him in Western Virginia. Smith received the assignment on September 5 but did not arrive for a month, and Morton served through the Chickamauga campaign.

While the left feinted, sixty to eighty miles southwest of Chattanooga the crossing of the center and right proceeded quietly. Again, Rosecrans covered his feint with a feint, by sending a cavalry force west to Decatur. Thomas's advance brought Reynolds, followed by Brannan, to the mouth of Battle Creek, Negley to Crow Creek, and Baird to Anderson, Tennessee. McCook simultaneously advanced Johnson to Bellefonte, and Davis to Mound Top and Crow Creek. Sheridan already lay at Bridgeport, openly building a trestle through the shoals to shorten his pontoon bridge, but demonstrating so little strength that General Patton Anderson's brigade, the only infantry force opposing a downstream crossing, withdrew to Chattanooga. As the center and right neared the Tennessee, they halted under the forest's concealment. Rosecrans' headquarters had paused at Winchester on the 15th, Decherd on the 17th, and Stevenson on the 18th. By the 18th, Burnside advanced into east Tennessee.

Lofty cliffs provided Confederate lookout posts so that it was difficult to screen the crossing points, even though Bragg's heavy guards had been withdrawn after the shelling of Chattanooga, and on the 24th, Confederate pickets who had an informal understanding with Union pickets not to fire across the river ended their truce. John Beatty heard it told that they said the "Yanks were becoming too damned thick."

The evening of August 28, before McCook crossed at Caperton's Ferry, ten miles below Bridgeport, Heg's brigades reached the Tennessee, and labored through the night. Enemy pickets stood in full view and bandied talk. At daylight, 4:00 A.M., Heg's brigade rowed across in fifty pontoons, each containing fifty men. After dispersing the enemy, Heg's men laid the 1,254-foot-long pontoon bridge in four and a half hours; and artillery and infantry hurried across it and moved up Sand Mountain. There, in the afternoon, they were visited by Rosecrans and McCook.

At Bridgeport heavy traffic crossed over Sheridan's bridge, but its pontoons separated on August 29, necessitating a five-day repair. At Shellmound, Reynolds floated his command across on captured boats, and at Battle Creek Brannan's men navigated log rafts, launching from behind bushes. Others had constructed enormous dugouts from poplar trunks. As these improvised vessels set forth, strong swimmers, growing impatient, piled clothing and arms on rail platforms, and leaping into the river, swam across. Cavalry spurred their mounts into the water at Caperton and Island Creek. With nothing above the surface except the upper portions of the men's bodies and horses' nostrils and tails, cavalry seemed to Confederate observers a "mass of moving centaurs rather than an army of mounted soldiers." Leaving Minty, Wilder, Hazen, and Wagner behind to observe and annoy the enemy, Crittenden's corps descended the Sequatchie Valley and followed Thomas, using Sheridan's bridge at Bridgeport, boats at Shellmound, and rafts at Battle Creek.

Hill found Bragg's lack of information concerning Rosecrans' movements in "striking contrast with the minute knowledge Lee always had of enemy operation," and concluded that "it was to be a haphazard campaign on our part."

While Rosecrans crossed, a rumor spread that Bragg was planning a countermove in which he would cross above Chattanooga to strike at the railroad behind Rosecrans. Bragg had moved his pontoon bridge to Chattanooga. On September 2, Union troops guarding upstream fords watched Buckner's corps moving down the south bank to join Bragg and halting several times as if preparing to cross. Had Bragg crossed, Rosecrans would have sought battle north of the river. When feints and rumors proved false, he resumed his own crossing.

Hazen was given command of the 7,000 troops north of the Tennessee. With these he demonstrated, threatening to cross, so that even after he knew the heads of columns had reached the south bank, Bragg believed that this real movement was a feint to cover a threat from above. Although his passage of the river was completed by September 4 Rosecrans still took measures to sustain Bragg's illusion that his real attack would be made upstream, and well earned General John C. Gordon's praise: "The apparent movement above Chattanooga and the real preparation for crossing far below, were admirably planned and consummately executed by Rosecrans and showed a strategic ability perhaps not surpassed by any officer during the war." On the same day, without resistance, Burnside occupied Knoxville, Kingston, and other important points. A detachment of Rosecrans' cavalry sent to Kingston entered with Burnside's advance and reported that Buckner and Forrest were heading for a concentration to the rear of Chattanooga.

Beyond the river, the army faced Sand Mountain, and its ascent proved difficult and slow. Negley's men found the road as steep as the roof of an ordinary house, and several wagons skirted too close to the brink and toppled over the precipice. At night, under a brilliant moon, the campfires of the immense army twinkled in the valley and along the mountainsides.

Once the army had crossed, its movements were screened by the towering bulk of Lookout Mountain. Headquarters followed, and on September 4 advanced nine miles by way of Bridgeport to Cave Spring. There it remained on the 5th, and on the 6th moved to Trenton, between Raccoon and Lookout mountains.

From Trenton Rosecrans telegraphed his wife in New York that they were in Alabama, and would be in Georgia the next day: "A great battle will probably ensue. Request the most Reverend Archbishop to offer the Divine Sacrifice for our success." Dana reported to Stanton: "Rosecrans has telegraphed to the clergy all over the country that he expected to fight a great battle today and desired their prayers." Robert Colby, a New York attorney and a Baptist, applauded in a letter he subsequently wrote to Rosecrans: "What other general has asked his church to do the same—hold up the arm of Moses while the fight went on?"

By the 6th, all three corps lay on the western slope of Lookout, from Rawlinsville on the south to within six miles of Chattanooga, and Rosecrans faced a more difficult problem: to cut loose from his base with twenty-five days' rations and ammunition enough for two battles in his wagons, cross two mountain ranges at widely separated points in enemy territory, then enter the valley at the rear of Bragg's stronghold, through defended passes, there to reconcentrate to fight or take such other action as events dictated. But only by advancing over Lookout could he flank Bragg and force him from Chattanooga.

On the 7th, Rosecrans ordered Thomas to cross his corps by Frick's or Cooper's and Stevens' gaps through Lookout Mountain. The gaps lay about twenty-six miles from Chattanooga. Through them ran the only practicable roads into McLemore's Cove, a broad valley lying at the eastern base of Lookout and stretching northeasterly to the rear of Chattanooga. McCook moved to Valley Head, far down Lookout Valley, and seized Winston's Gap, which crosses Lookout forty-six miles south of Chattanooga. Crittenden sent a brigade north to Wauhatchie in Lookout Valley, to feel Bragg's strength over the front of Lookout and across the river road. The cavalry concentrated at Rawlinsville and reconnoitered boldly toward Rome and Alpine. Reconnaissance showed that strong infantry and artillery forces held the river-level approaches to Chattanooga between the Tennessee and Lookout. It was reported simultaneously that Buckner was still withdrawing before Burnside to join Bragg.

Now began the great wheeling movement to bring Rosecrans upon the roads and railroad to Bragg's rear. Crittenden's two brigades before Chattanooga formed the axle, the cavalry under Stanley many miles to the right, the rim. On September 8 and 9, Union cavalry near Alpine, supported by a division of McCook's infantry, swung eastward to Summerville in Broomtown Valley. Alpine lay about twenty miles southerly of LaFayette; Summerville about fifteen miles due south. Both places gave access to the rear of LaFayette, and on roads leading from Broomtown Valley to the railroad in Bragg's rear, and to Rome. From here Rosecrans could threaten the railroad between Resaca Bridge and Dalton. At the same time Thomas crossed Lookout Mountain and reached the middle of McLemore's Cove. He lay within easy striking distance of LaFayette, and formed the inner of the concentric circles seeking to flank Bragg.

Crittenden remained near Chattanooga; part of his corps was still across the Tennessee making noisy diversion and part in Lookout Valley, prepared to reconnoiter, or to support reconnaissance with strength if need be to keep Bragg from twisting southwest down Lookout or Chattanooga Valley, or even to seize Chattanooga if Bragg evacuated it or held it lightly. While reconnoitering the front of the mountain, the men of one of Crittenden's brigades scrambled like goats up the precipitous Nickajack Trace leading to Summertown on the brow of Lookout. From here, Chattanooga, the coiling Tennessee, the Cumberlands, and even the distant Smokies could be seen in panoramic splendor.

Fatigue produced irritability, and Wood balked when Rosecrans ordered Crittenden to send Wood's division to reconnoiter Lookout Valley. Such movement, he alleged, was extremely hazardous: Wood could not believe Rosecrans desired such "blind obedience to the mere letter of his order." When Wood attempted to justify this insubordination in more than fifty pages of foolscap, Rosecrans merely repeated the order.

On the 9th Rosecrans became convinced that Bragg had been abandoning Chattanooga for three days and he ordered Crittenden to advance and push past Lookout. He was to seize the town, bring his remaining forces across the river, drop a brigade as garrison, and pursue vigorously, following Bragg's line of retreat along the railroad. Thomas was to cross McLemore's Cove and Pigeon Mountain and strike at Bragg's flank and rear. McCook was to move on Alpine and Summerville, and, falling behind Thomas, support him.

As at Tullahoma, Union encirclement put Bragg in a quandary. He could easily have resisted assault at Chattanooga. But if he allowed Rosecrans to cut his communications, he might find himself in a predicament similar to Pemberton's at Vicksburg. He might be starved out of his citadel. If, conversely, he divided his army, garrisoning Chattanooga with part of it and attempting with the rest to break Rosecrans' hold on his communications, he risked being beaten in detail. "As a prudent commander," Rosecrans observed, "Bragg could not afford to leave us quietly concentrated south of his position between him and Atlanta."

Bragg therefore withdrew thirty miles south, halting most of his army near LaFayette, behind Pigeon Mountain, another ridge running parallel to Lookout Mountain and Missionary Ridge and terminating eight miles south of Chattanooga. From here he planned to pounce upon the divided Union army as it debouched through the passes. At the same time he took measures that deserters, spies, former slaves, and civilians should spread rumors that he was falling back in disorder through Ringgold and Dalton to Atlanta. Other reports told that he might stand at Rome, or if pushed, might retreat to Atlanta. He had followed the railroad in withdrawing from Murfreesboro and Tullahoma. He might do so again.

Up to this point Rosecrans' strategy again had been masterly. General Emerson Opdycke who served with Rosecrans considered it "brilliant and faultless." Historian James Ford Rhodes spoke of the "campaign of brilliant strategy" which accomplished the occupation of Chattanooga, "a momentous gain for Union arms." And General Montgomery Meigs described it as "not only the greatest operation in our war, but a great thing when compared to any war."

Opinions are divided, however, concerning Rosecrans' next move.

He faced two alternatives. He could push Crittenden southward and advance McCook and Thomas across Lookout to concentrate with Crittenden in an effort to force Bragg to stand and fight. Or he could withdraw McCook and Thomas into Lookout Valley, send them around the mountain's extremity, and with his reconcentrated forces hold Chattanooga strongly while preparing for a further advance. Opdycke believed that this should have been Rosecrans' choice: The moment he entered Chattanooga he "should have concentrated his army there long enough to accumulate supplies, ascertain the position and intentions of his adversary, and whether or not Burnside would reinforce him. He was now 337 miles from the Ohio River, 150 from Nashville, and his prudence, not his impetuosity, should have increased." John Fiske wrote: "The seeds of calamity were sown by the enormous extension of the Federal lines."

Theirs was the wisdom of hindsight. The question was, what would any other competent commander have done in Rosecrans' place? Rosecrans had defeated Bragg at Stone River, flanked him out of Tullahoma. His army already was scattered by the crossing of the Tennessee. Bragg was retreating. Washington pooh-poohed talk of Lee's reinforcing Bragg and encouraged Rosecrans' advance. Rosecrans had reason to believe that Burnside would cover his left, and that McCook would, if ordered, directly and expeditiously close on Thomas so that the two corps might close on Crittenden. He did not foresee McCook's five-day meandering on Lookout.

Moreover, had Rosecrans occupied Chattanooga without first dealing with Bragg, he would have found himself in a worse predicament than Bragg's when Bragg evacuated the town. Bragg evacuated Chattanooga because he did not want to be trapped there. And neither did Rosecrans. Bragg's numbers exceeded Rosecrans'. The Tennessee River to Bragg's front was a strong defense; to Rosecrans' back it was an additional hazard. Chattanooga and its environs were friendly territory for Bragg, unfriendly for Rosecrans. Rosecrans' long communications were as strong as thread, Bragg's short communications as rope. Bragg's cavalry superiority continued overwhelming, and it was as simple for him to reach behind Rosecrans with cavalry as it was difficult for Rosecrans to reach behind Bragg with infantry. As events proved, reinforcing Bragg was easy, while reinforcing Rosecrans was the most difficult single problem of its kind during the war.

The destruction of Bragg's army, the campaign's second and more important objective, appeared to Rosecrans to be well within his power. With a brilliant plan, promising hope of the highest military success, Rosecrans took the calculated risks that any competent general would take. In war, the battle is not always to the strong, but sometimes to the audacious. That accidents and misadventures interfered and denied Rosecrans full success is another matter.

At 1:00 P.M., September 10, 1863, the XI Corps took peaceable possession of Chattanooga. That night Crittenden bivouacked at Rossville, five miles south, where the LaFayette road crosses Missionary Ridge. "Chattanooga is ours without a struggle and East Tennessee is free," Rosecrans telegraphed Halleck. He added: "Messengers go to Burnside tonight, urging him to push his cavalry down. No news from him or his cavalry."

On the 10th, Union headquarters was moved from Trenton to Chattanooga, and doubt regarding Bragg's intentions appeared. Perhaps he had not withdrawn down the railroad. By evening Rosecrans knew that Bragg had retreated down the LaFayette road, how far was not clear; and he ordered the 4th U.S. Cavalry down the Dry Valley road, to see if Bragg was moving on Critten-den's right, and to open communications with Thomas. Thomas was descending Lookout through Cooper's and Stevens' gaps, and preparing to cross Pigeon Mountain through Dug Gap, to strike at LaFayette. Negley, leading Thomas in, found Dug Gap obstructed and a talkative prisoner suggested that he'd better not advance or he'd get licked. The obstruction concealed a strong Confederate force.

For two days there were rumors that although Bragg had evacuated Chattanooga, he would return to attack Rosecrans between Chattanooga and LaFayette. On the 10th Garfield thought such reports "hardly worthy of a moment's consideration." "I am in hopes to be able to report to you tomorrow the capture of LaFay-ette," Thomas informed Rosecrans in a dispatch on the 11th. Had Wilder's brigade been present, he was certain that he could have prevented the enemy from blocking the road. Halleck was equally sanguine. On the 11th he telegraphed Rosecrans that Burnside held all East Tennessee above Loudon. Burnside had advised Lincoln on the 10th that since the "rebellion now seems pretty well checked," he would like to "retire to private life."

"A cavalry force is moving toward Athens to connect with you," Halleck informed Rosecrans on the 11th. "After holding the mountain passes on the West and Dalton . . . to prevent the return of Bragg's army, it shall be decided whether your army shall move farther south into Georgia and Alabama. It is reported here by deserters that a part of Bragg's army is re-enforcing Lee. It is important that the truth of this should be ascertained as early as possible." Halleck announced even more ambitious plans to Burnside: "General Rosecrans will occupy Dalton or some point on the railroad to close all access from Atlanta, and also the mountain passes on the West. This being done, it will be determined whether the movable forces shall advance into Georgia and Alabama or into the Valley of Virginia and North Carolina." On the same day, with Rosecrans' approval, Crittenden telegraphed Burnside that Bragg was retreating and asked only that Burnside send his cavalry south, lending support to Burnside's apparent unwillingness to send anything south.

Independent reports on the 11th suggested that Bragg might not be retreating along the railroad. Crittenden found no enemy at Ringgold. And Wilder, advancing toward Tunnel Hill, skirmished heavily. It seemed that Bragg's rear guard had halted near Lee and Gordon's Mill, six miles north of LaFayette on the LaFayette Road. For three days Crittenden had carried on vigorous movements there, with some lively, minor fights along the Creek, north of the Mills, but south of Rossville. His surmise that Bragg's rear guard lay nearby ended his exploratory movements for he refused to be beaten in detail. Yet even this surmise—Crittenden himself was not greatly alarmed—did not constitute sufficient evidence to justify Rosecrans in calling back the pursuit, when the level-headed Thomas thought that if Bragg was running, he could capture LaFayette.

As Rosecrans grew increasingly uncertain about Bragg's whereabouts, and his own dispersal, a guest appeared at headquarters, Charles A. Dana, acting second Assistant Secretary of War, with a letter of introduction from Stanton. He had come, said Stanton's letter, to confer upon any subject which Rosecrans might desire to have brought to the notice of the department, and possessed the "entire confidence of the Department." Dana had been to Vicksburg and thought highly of Grant.

Dana later wrote that after he read Stanton's letter, Rosecrans "burst out in angry abuse of the Government," complaining that it failed to sustain him, ignored his requests, and thwarted his plans. Stanton and Halleck, he said, had "done all they could to prevent his success." Again he had demonstrated a fruitless show of temper and careless, immoderate language.

"I have no authority to listen to complaints against the government," Dana rejoined. "I was sent here for the purpose of finding out what the government could do to aid you, and have no right to confer with you on other matters."

Thus began a peculiar relationship. Dana ate, slept, poked around with the staff, and gossiped. Each evening he reported to Stanton. The army received him as if he were "a bird of evil-omen." There were whispers among the staff that he was a spy seeking justification for removing Rosecrans, and when he rode behind Rosecrans, men shouted: "Hey, sutler, when are you going to open up?" Apparently mistaking Dana for a sutler because of his civilian clothes was a cutting insult. Sutlers were civilians who followed the army and sold provisions, liquor, and knicknacks to the troops. Fighting men generally held them in low esteem, charging them with greed, dishonesty, and cowardice. Someone withheld from publication with the *Official Records* or destroyed Stanton's instructions to Dana during this visit, for it is unlikely that they were lost, and they are missing from the *Official Records*. In their absence, questions concerning Dana's assignment remain unanswered.

On the morning of September 11, Bragg sprung his trap prematurely. In the wooded gaps of Pigeon Mountain seven Confederate divisions attacked Negley near Dug Gap. Just as it seemed that Negley might be destroyed, Baird arrived, and Negley skillfully extricated both Union divisions and brought them into strong position before Stevens' Gap. That night Brannan and Reynolds crossed Lookout and joined Baird and Negley, and Thomas's force was reassembled. Thomas advised Rosecrans that he was safe and covering the entrances to Stevens' and Cooper's Gaps, but that he was unable to move without danger, except as the whole army moved. Behind Pigeon Mountain, billowing dust clouds indicated marching Confederates. For both Rosecrans and Thomas it was an anxious day.

At Alpine, eighteen miles below Thomas, McCook stared at the dust clouds far north of him. Were they stirred by Bragg, or by Thomas? To find out, he ordered Crook's cavalry to penetrate Bragg's picket screen. Was Bragg marching toward Resaca? If investigation proved otherwise, McCook would join Thomas over the top of Lookout, a distance of seventeen to twenty miles by a fair road. "I am not desirous of fighting Bragg's whole army," he wrote to Thomas, "and in case he is concentrated at LaFayette I am in a false position, for I could not reach you. Where is Crittenden's corps? I will keep my wagon train on top of Lookout Mountain and my troops in the valley. LaFayette is the strategic position for Bragg; he then has his road open to Dalton, or to points farther south on the railroad. His object will be to oppose his whole force to our fractions as they debouch from the Mountain. All citizens here, both Union and Secession, say that he will fight, and . . . I think so also." When a prisoner told McCook that Bragg and not Thomas was at LaFayette, he recalled how retreating Confederate cavalry had headed there. Yet his mind remained divided.

Bragg's strategy was becoming clearer, and Rosecrans as a "matter of life and death," he wrote in his *Official Report,* took measures to reconcentrate his army. McCook was in the tightest spot, still advancing toward Summerville, his wagons far behind him. Stanley must close upon him. McCook was to move his trains, escorted by one division, to the crest of Lookout, and thence as needed into Lookout Valley toward Stevens' Gap or LaFayette. He was then to march his two remaining divisions to the immediate support of Thomas. If Thomas found Bragg at LaFayette, he would order McCook to close. McCook's trains were a drag.

Crittenden was to concentrate his corps and take a strong position north of Chickamauga Creek, near Lee and Gordon's Mills. If attacked and defeated, he would fall back on Chattanooga; if Thomas were attacked, Crittenden would support Thomas. "There is far more probability of his attacking you than his running," Rosecrans insisted to Crittenden.

While Crittenden marched to the right, Wilder again screened his movement, and at Leet's Tan-yard became heavily engaged. Crittenden was still not greatly alarmed, for Bragg always made strong defenses while retreating. As yet Crittenden was not convinced that a large force of Confederates lay at LaFayette.

Meanwhile, on the 11th, Dana wavered, thinking that perhaps the attack on Negley indicated that Bragg had abandoned his retreat on Rome and was bent on destroying Rosecrans in detail. Later that morning, however, he was certain that Bragg was standing only to check pursuit.

With mounting concern, Rosecrans left Chattanooga at 1:00 P.M., September 13, and accompanied by his staff and Dana rode down the Ridge road on Lookout, to join Thomas before Stevens' Gap. He expected to be away at least three days, and to direct in person the reassembling of his army. Departmental headquarters remained behind. Before leaving, he wrote to Crittenden that the "evidence accumulates that the whole of Bragg's army is not only in the Valley, but even over in McLemore's Cove, near the foot of Lookout. Hence the necessity of great caution."

That concentration was effected was remarkable. Hill places the responsibility on Bragg, maintaining that his military intelligence was inadequate, and that he did not personally supervise the execution of orders.

But Rosecrans' very dispersion bewildered Bragg. "It is said to be easy to defend a mountainous country," Bragg said. "But mountains hide your foe from you, while they are full of gaps through which he can pounce upon you at any time. A mountain is like the wall of a house full of rat-holes. The rat lies hidden at his hole, ready to pop out when no one is watching. Who can tell what lies hidden behind that wall?" For several days Rosecrans, with equal perplexity, asked identical questions about Pigeon Mountain.

Captain J. C. Duzer, Chattanooga telegraph chief, read the signs correctly and telegraphed to Colonel Anson Stager, his chief, in Washington: "The enemy are between Thomas and McCook on the south and Crittenden and Granger on the north and the day before yesterday gave Negley a thrashing. . . . Rosecrans went down this P.M. . . . We are in a ticklish place here, but hope to come out with whole skin." And Garfield wrote to Rhodes: "A battle is imminent. The enemy has a large force and the advantage of position. Unless we can outmanoeuver him, we shall be in a perilous situation. Our strategic success has been most brilliant thus far."

The race now was to reassemble, defeat or at least hold off Bragg, and take firm possession of Chattanooga. Once Rosecrans was certain that Bragg was concentrated at LaFayette, and not running, the orders he gave for the concentration of his own army were immediate, urgent, and explicit and sent the XIV and XX Corps on the shortest route by which they could reach Chattanooga while he could watch Bragg.

Dana's enthusiasm was exceeding his usual common sense,

and he continued to supply misinformation to Stanton. Even before reaching Rosecrans, he had telegraphed: "Judicious men here think there will be no battle, and that Bragg has only the shadow of a force at Chattanooga to delay Rosecrans' advance." Though Rosecrans was gravely concerned, Dana on the 14th reported to Stanton from Stevens' Gap: "Everything progresses favorably; concentration of the three corps already substantially effected." And later that day: "This army has gained a position from which it can effectually advance upon Rome and Atlanta, and deliver there the finishing blow of the war."

Rosecrans' corps moved with immense distances between them, from Lee and Gordon's Mills on the left to Alpine on the right, an air distance of 40 miles, but 57 by McCook's meanderings. Facing Bragg's concentration, his army had to concentrate rapidly in a hostile country, with inadequate maps and over mountain roads. Out of sight themselves, Confederates from the crests could watch blue columns toiling in the valleys. Rosecrans held no depots, no railroads. He had to live and fight off the country, or out of his wagon trains. And he had to meet an adversary who overmatched him in strength—Confederate aid was speeding from all points; it was certain now that assistance would arrive from Lee. Signs of Confederate concentration were public and plentiful. As August ended, Sherman had told Grant that Breckinridge's and Walker's divisions had been sent to Bragg. Colonel Jacques, returning from Richmond to report Longstreet's movement after trying vainly for ten days to interview Stanton or Halleck, finally left Washington and reached Chattanooga in time for Chickamauga. Lee himself later criticized Southern newspapers for reporting Longstreet's detachment, when the Confederate Army tried to keep it secret.

Grant had anticipated this problem immediately after Vicksburg and wanted to act to prevent such concentration against Rosecrans. "I knew," Grant wrote in his *Memoirs*, "the peril the Army of the Cumberland was in, being depleted continually, not only by ordinary casualties, but also by having to detach troops to hold its constantly extending line over which to draw supplies, while the enemy in its front was as constantly being strengthened. Mobile was important to the enemy, and in the absence of a threatening force was guarded by little else than artillery. If threatened by land and from the water at the same time the prize would fall easily or troops would have to be sent for its defense. Those troops would necessarily come from Bragg. My judgment was overruled, and the troops under my command were dissipated over other parts of the country where it was thought they could render the most service." Stanton's wrath against Rosecrans apparently caused him to disregard a military maxim obvious even to amateur strategists: Successful war pits masses against fractions.

When Rosecrans' statement that "All reports concur that Johnston and Breckinridge are with Bragg, Buckner is closing down," finally penetrated Halleck's complacency, he cautioned Rosecrans on September 6: "You and Burnside unite as quickly as possible so that the enemy may not attack you separately." But Rosecrans wanted no misunderstanding, and next day he warned Halleck: "Your apprehensions are just, and the legitimate consequences of your orders. The best that can now be done is for Burnside to close his cavalry down on our left, supporting it with his infantry, and, refusing his left, threaten the enemy, without getting into his grasp, while we get him [Bragg] in our grip and strangle him, or perish in the attempt."

Stanton's concern seemed fixed elsewhere. On September 5, Halleck sent a dispatch to Meade: "Rosecrans and Burnside must so occupy the enemy as to remove any danger of an attack on you."

As late as September 6, Washington remained complacent. Although Halleck had before him a dispatch from General Peck in North Carolina, telling that Longstreet's corps was passing south by railroad, Halleck told Meade that Rosecrans seemed apprehensive that reinforcements had been sent from Lee's army to East Tennessee via Lynchburg. If Meade found facts as alleged, Halleck would reinforce Burnside. Meade's scouts and Confederate deserters, however, reported no such movement, although some days before, McLaw's division had marched ten miles, to be nearer supplies or to cover a withdrawal. Shrewdly Rosecrans inquired of Halleck: "Is it not possible that these movements cover the temporary detaching of troops to Bragg?"

"The failure to give Rosecrans effective flanking support was inexcusable," General Henry V. N. Boynton maintained. "No friends of Stanton's or Halleck's have even yet attempted to explain, much less defend it. These and other high officers arraigned Rosecrans as solely responsible for what they chose to designate as the disaster and defeat of Chickamauga. It was the shortest way for some of them to divert attention from the terrible neglect and responsibility which rested on their heads." Opdycke was convinced that Gettysburg and Vicksburg should have led Halleck to concentrate and end the war in 1863. Rosecrans, reinforced by Grant, could have marched "irresistibly," Opdycke wrote later, through east Tennessee to aid Meade against Lee, whose army "could not have existed a single day against such a concentration."

But the Confederates reinforced Bragg from all sides while the War Department decided Rosecrans must go it alone. Toward the end of August Rosecrans had asked Halleck "whether Grant is to do anything to occupy Johnston's attention?" and Halleck had answered that "Grant's movements at present have no connection with yours." On September 5, Rosecrans advised Burnside: "Indications are the rebels will concentrate and fight us at Chattanooga."

Despite this information, for nine days, from September 6 to 15, the War Department took no effective measures to cover Rosecrans' flanks or to reinforce him. Signs multiplied that Bragg was being reinforced and on the 12th, Mobile papers predicted a "great and terrific battle" between Rosecrans and Bragg. Yet the next day Halleck still doubted whether Lee was reinforcing Bragg, although he advised Grant or Sherman "—whichever was at Vicksburg—" that it is quite possible that "Bragg and Johnston will move through Northern Alabama to the Tennessee, to turn Rosecrans' right and cut off his communication. All of Grant's available forces should be sent to Memphis, thence to Corinth and Tuscumbia, to cooperate with Rosecrans, should the rebels attempt that movement." Halleck relied on Burnside to cover Rosecrans' left; as for his right: "Hurlbut will aid you all he can, but most of Grant's available force is west of the Mississippi."

At daylight on the 13th, McCook began to close on Thomas by marching toward Daugherty's Gap, which opens into the head of McLemore's Cove, nine and a half miles south of Dug Gap. He had expected to be with or near Thomas by nightfall, but by noon his optimism lessened. Marching proved slower than anticipated, although the need for haste increased. A Confederate prisoner volunteered that he had never seen so large an army as Bragg's at LaFayette. Among others, he had recognized Johnston, Bragg,

Polk, D. H. Hill, Forrest, Wharton, Harrison, Pegram, Scott, Breckinridge, Preston, Hodge, and Wheeler. Reinforcements from Virginia, he reported, were coming by way of Atlanta. Natives told McCook falsely that no good road lay in the direction of Daugherty's Gap. Judging that Confederates held the Cove, he concluded he would have to join Thomas by way of Stevens' Gap, either marching along the plateau, or crossing the mountain into Lookout Valley and marching up the valley and through the gap. Again natives misinformed him, and considering it imprudent to grope along an unfamiliar road, he chose the second route, thus retracing his advance. With his train ahead of him, he crossed Lookout and followed the Valley until he came to Johnson's Creek and Stevens' Gap. Through these he recrossed Lookout, and through Cooper's Gap he crossed Missionary Ridge, to debouch into McLemore's Cove. For five days he struggled through mountainous country, each needless moment delaying the concentration of the whole army and increasing its jeopardy. Until McCook closed on Thomas, Thomas could not close on Crittenden.

As early as noon on the 14th, on learning of McCook's meandering, Rosecrans ordered him to turn back immediately toward the head of McLemore's Cove. Maps showed a practicable road. Reading this order at 5:30 P.M., McCook fumed. His troops would think he was "trifling with them," he said; his road was longer but more rapid; he was now under Thomas' command. Meanwhile his train clogged the road and delayed the whole column in its ascent of the mountain. With his road full of wagons, he received fresh orders from Rosecrans—to join Thomas with two divisions and cover his trains with a third.

Bragg's army was in McLemore's Cove, Rosecrans realized, and to cover Union communications he had ordered Crittenden to advance Wood to Lee and Gordon's Mills. If attacked there by a superior force he was to resist stoutly, and fall back upon Rossville. If he could not hold Rossville, he was to cover the roads to Chattanooga over the foot of Lookout. Granger meanwhile hurried a division from Bridgeport with orders to proceed immediately to Rossville, and to guard the roads to Ringgold and LaFayette, and along Chattanooga Creek.

By forced marches from Bridgeport, Granger reached Rossville at midnight on the 14th with the Reserve Corps. Crittenden meanwhile had laboriously marched to the top of Missionary Ridge at Henson's. He knew of no enemy force to his front, and none between Lee and Gordon's Mills and Chattanooga. He was sanguine. If attacked, he thought he could whip "all of them" and turn their position. Bragg would not dare by-pass him. If he tried, Crittenden would close on Thomas, and the Union Army would concentrate at LaFayette.

Rosecrans was less optimistic, and ordered Crittenden to leave the Mills and take position with his right on the southern slope of Missionary Ridge. Crittenden remained thus for three days, until McCook closed on Thomas. Then he returned to the Mills.

The flag-of-truce boat at Hampton Roads, a favorite listening post, had brought news from Richmond that, on the 14th, trains carried troops night and day either to Knoxville or Chattanooga. On the 15th, a civilian, Abram Wakeman, telegraphed Stanton from New York that a reliable person who had left Atlanta nine days before, on his way to Richmond, passed "three of Lee's divisions enroute to reinforce Bragg at Dalton, Georgia, and that the general report was that the rebel forces were concentrating at or near there to overthrow Rosecrans." Meade, too, grew convinced that Longstreet had gone south through Richmond.

From Trenton early on the 15th, Rosecrans ordered departmental headquarters to follow him at midmorning from Chattanooga up Chattanooga Valley, and at 8:00 A.M. on the 16th, they reached Crawfish Springs and were established in the F. M. Lee house. There Rosecrans learned from McCook that Sheridan was finally descending the mountain. Three miles behind, Johnson followed; nine miles behind Johnson, Davis. McCook's train was still on Lookout, and he considered ordering it to its destination along the mountain road, because the descent used by the infantry was bad. When in midafternoon Rosecrans learned that Thomas was still waiting at Stevens' Gap for McCook to close, before moving northeasterly along West Chickamauga Creek to close on Crittenden, he told Thomas that he feared the movement might be too late. At 9:00 P.M. Thomas agreed to begin his concentration at daylight between Gower's Mill and Bird's Mill on West Chickamauga Creek. It was none too soon. Wilder's reconnaissance showed the enemy thick along the line of the Creek, but some distance back from it. Minty had observed much the same the day before. Bragg was massing against Rosecrans' left, to block his retreat on the LaFayette road. With this much clear, Rosecrans pleaded with Burnside to cover his left. Rosecrans' army, moving up the Chickamauga valley fifteen to twenty miles south of Chattanooga, could not prevent Forrest from crossing the Tennessee to its left and striking its communications. Bragg seemed to be planning such a move. Worse, General George D. Wagner reported that Jackson's old corps, some 30,000 strong, was coming to reinforce Bragg.

By late afternoon of the 15th Halleck had admitted the probability that three of Lee's divisions were reinforcing Bragg. "I fear that Rosecrans will be hard pushed," he telegraphed Meade; and he advised Rosecrans that "all troops of the departments of the Ohio and Cumberland should be brought to the front to meet the enemy." Sherman and Hurlbut would bring reinforcements to the Tennessee as rapidly as possible. Simultaneous telegrams flashed to Schofield in St. Louis, Burnside at Knoxville, the Department of the Ohio at Cincinnati, Pope in Milwaukee, Hurlbut at Memphis —all should reinforce Rosecrans immediately.

Finally, on the 17th, Halleck ordered Grant to send all available troops on the Mississippi to Tuscumbia or farther up the Tennessee to cover Rosecrans' right and secure his communications. "It was early apparent that while you and General Banks were operating west of the Mississippi, the enemy would concentrate his available forces on General Meade or General Rosecrans. It was believed from all the information we could obtain that Lee's Army was to be greatly reinforced. It now appears that all of Johnston's forces and at least three large divisions of Lee's Army have joined Bragg. . . . Rosecrans is now the main object of their attack, and he must be strengthened by all the means in our power. Burnside is joining him with all the available troops in Kentucky, and I wish you to afford him all possible aid. Vicksburg and other places on the river cannot require large garrisons under present circumstances. . . . It is also understood that they intend to put in the ranks against Rosecrans, without exchange, all the prisoners parolled by you and General Banks." Grant alone had parolled 16,000 prisoners at Vicksburg.

Rosecrans later wrote that when the Union army was in the mountains, and the orders were too late for useful results, "aroused by fear of consequences" Halleck began to telegraph orders for reinforcements. The telegrams, he said, "constituted a confession that support ought to have been ordered at the proper time, and might serve for ulterior operations after our fate was decided." Next day, the 18th, Rosecrans reported to Halleck that he had reason to believe Lee's reinforcements had arrived in Atlanta.

By evening of the 17th, for the first time in ten days, Rosecrans' three corps had finally marched within mutual supporting distance. All day, rumor reported that Bragg was emerging to attack. All day, the armies moved in lines roughly parallel, with the head of Bragg's column north of Rosecrans', and the foot of Rosecrans' below Bragg's, so that each might have flanked the other, Bragg at the risk of getting the creek to his back and losing his trains, and Rosecrans at the hazard of sacrificing a safe line of retreat and of losing Chattanooga. Twelve hours before Bragg's battle orders were issued, Rosecrans predicted them: Bragg would try to seize the Dry Valley and LaFayette roads north of him.

To prevent being cut off, Rosecrans determined to fight defensively and ordered his whole force to move at once northeastwardly down the Chickamauga to cover the LaFayette road toward Chattanooga and to face the most practicable route to the enemy's front. He sought a position to command the roads in which his artillery would have full use and his flanks would be covered. The movement was extremely difficult, along narrow roads in the face of a strong and moving enemy, who constantly threatened and occasionally struck in sharp attacks.

Rosecrans was not ready on the 18th to stand and fight. Great gaps separated his columns. Throughout the day Thomas marched far behind Crittenden. When roads narrowed, the pace slowed, and commands ran up on one another. Conflicting orders sometimes assigned two commands to the same temporary position and confusion resulted. Disputes between officers added to the turmoil. Both Minty's cavalry at Reed's Bridge and Wilder's mounted infantry at Alexander's Bridge encountered Confederate infantry and toward evening were driven into the LaFayette road, a certain indication that Bragg moved in strength within five miles of Rossville and had crossed Chickamauga Creek. Near Lee and Gordon's Mills, Union observers saw heavy enemy forces three or four miles beyond the creek. Most ominous, a thick wall of dust, indicating strong forces marching on dusty roads, appeared at the extremity of Pigeon Mountain and crawled slowly northward.

Confederate orders called for battle on the morning of the 18th. Bragg's army then lay between LaFayette and Lee and Gordon's Mills, with its right extending beyond Crittenden and the Union left. Crossing some distance below the Mills, Bragg's attack was planned to push Crittenden back on Thomas and McCook, separate Rosecrans from Chattanooga, retake Chattanooga, and drive Rosecrans into the mountains, where escape would be difficult. But Bragg's movements, too, were slowed by narrow roads, dense woods, difficult fords, and small bridges; he would barely be ready to attack a day later.

Autumn was chill in the uplands and skies were clouded before the morning. Although by midday of the 18th the weather grew comfortable, by evening everyone wore a coat, and fires blazed before the few tents. During these frantic hours Rosecrans made a final, supreme effort to gain a strong defensive position. In the face of the enemy and at the last minute, he needed to exchange the order of two of his corps, so that his center became his left. He had to move his entire army north to the vicinity of Rossville to cover roads leading to Chattanooga, and thus deny Bragg the advantage of fighting with Chattanooga at his back.

For the moment Crittenden held the extreme left and front, his lines masking and defending the movement "by which the entire army was to pass in his rear leaving him on the right." When a scout reported Bragg's concentration, Crittenden galloped to headquarters. Rosecrans listened, and then "several times" asked the question, "Can you hold your position?" Crittenden firmly declared that he could and promptly rejoined his corps.

At 4:00 P.M. on the 18th, Thomas set out from Pond Springs to move to the left, along West Chickamauga Creek to Crawfish Springs. At Crawfish Springs he was to turn, march to Crittenden's rear up the Dry Valley road, and pass the Widow Glen's house. When he reached the LaFayette road, he was to take position there, with his left extending obliquely across the road near the Kelly farm house, five miles north of Crawfish Springs. In addition to screening Thomas's movement, Crittenden was to extend his line toward the position which Thomas was to take. McCook was to close behind the moving Thomas, occupy Crawfish Springs, and cover Crittenden's right. The main body of Union cavalry, operating under McCook's orders, was to move upon him and guard the upper crossings of the Chickamauga.

As Thomas marched through the twilight and night into the morning of the 19th, it seemed to Bragg that the Union center was closing on Crittenden. At Crawfish Springs, Negley, commanding Thomas's leading division, turned to the right and occupied the Chickamauga fords and the roads intersecting there, to prevent Bragg from cutting the moving column in a night attack. The three divisions that followed, Baird's, Brannan's, Reynolds's, advanced on the Crawfish Springs road, far to the rear of Crittenden's position, their trains on the turnpike and their infantry strung out in the fields on both sides. Thus the column was shortened, the trains covered, and the movement speeded. To the right, well toward the creek, heavy flanking forces paralleled the main column. Progress was slow and constantly interrupted. As the men halted, they made fires of logs and fences to warm themselves. Within an hour a line of fires stretched along the LaFayette Road, "illuminating the clouds above," wrote the reporter of the Cincinnati *Gazette*, "and showing the silent columns of Thomas gliding by like an army of spectres." By midnight the wagons rode through two ribbons of embers and flame.

"Thank God we have wind and dust in our favor," McCook said during the afternoon, as he waited for Thomas to clear from the roads ahead. At 8:30 P.M. he said he hoped that "orders will be given so that Thomas' wagons will not impede my march. I have no baggage with me, nor do I intend to have, save ammunition and rations. Let us in." Orders to move came at 12:15 A.M. of the 19th.

The night was anxious and wakeful. Rosecrans slept briefly, if at all. To their great annoyance, Rosecrans and Thomas were called upon to settle a bitter dispute between Hazen and Negley. Negley had received orders from Thomas to take a position before Hazen received Crittenden's order to yield it. Yet, despite dust and quarrels, the columns struggled ahead.

Eastern skies were graying as Baird reached the Kelly farm, and daylight broke as his division veered diagonally across the LaFayette road. By dawn, McCook's three divisions swung out on the road to Crawfish Springs. McCook rode ahead and reported to Rosecrans; he was told to mass his troops nearby and await orders.

Although the Confederates had been roused in the dark and moved at dawn, Rosecrans' extreme left now lay two miles north of Bragg's right. The night march put Thomas on the left and Crittenden on the right.

By morning of September 19, 1863, the unsupported Army of the Cumberland stood between Chattanooga, its insecurely held prize, and the enemy returning to reclaim it. The fight no longer could be avoided or deferred.

Fifteen

CHICKAMAUGA—"THE GREAT BATTLE OF THE WEST"

As the footweary Union army sought a favorable position about 4:30 A.M., the sky began to lighten and tired men saw that the unseasonably cold night had whitened the grass with a heavy frost. Even after a brilliant sunrise at 5:25, the crests of the long, autumn-striped mountains remained half shrouded in mist.

According to his custom in the field, Rosecrans rose early, and at 6:30 he sent Sanderson to tell Thomas that the center was quiet and to get a report on the left. Later the Signal Corps strung telegraph wires between Crawfish Springs, Chattanooga, Rossville, and the Kelly Farm. At this early hour, however, communication was still by courier. As Sanderson rode past dense oak woods filled with heavy undergrowth, the Union army was cooking breakfast. Tramping feet had filled the air with choking dust clouds that hung for hours, and smoldering stubble and brush and breakfast fires added billows of acrid smoke. Sanderson found Thomas breakfasting under a great oak. His front was quiet.

Sanderson returned to report to Rosecrans and his staff who were seated on the ground, while orderlies held their horses. Rosecrans was awaiting Bragg's attack. Meanwhile, two orderlies brought in a prisoner, one of Bragg's orderlies, who volunteered: "Bragg is being reinforced." Rosecrans' questions were interrupted by artillery fire at the left. The rumble swelled to a battle roar, as Rosecrans mounted and, followed by his staff and escort, galloped toward the left, to observe operations there.

Bragg's battle order was based on the erroneous assumption that

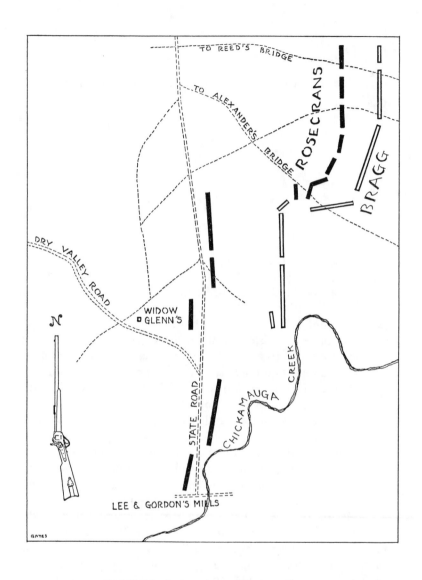

BATTLE OF CHICKAMAUGA

September 19, 1863

FIRST DAY

Crittenden at Lee and Gordon's Mills would continue to form Rosecrans' left. While a detachment posted across the Chickamauga held Crittenden there, Bragg's main force was to cross below him and, wheeling to the left, to fall on him in overwhelming force, thrusting him back on Rosecrans' center and right. Above Lee and Gordon's, the stream was widened by the mill dam; below, it was spanned by bridges and many easy fords.

To execute Bragg's plan, late on the 18th, Bushrod Johnson crossed at Reed's Bridge and pushed upstream. Nightfall found him a mile and a half north of the Mills and a mile west of the LaFayette road. Simultaneously, Walker's corps waded the creek at Lambert's Ford near Alexander's Bridge and halted. The progress of these columns was strongly contested by McCook's cavalry and Wilder's mounted infantry.

While Thomas crossed to Crittenden's rear, to become the new left, the rest of the army guarded the Chickamauga fords and bridges or traversed the narrow roads to find positions in Rosecrans' battle line. After bivouacking, the Confederate army moved at dawn, crossing the Chickamauga on a broad front from Thedford's Ford to Reed's Bridge, a direct distance of about a mile and a half, but of almost six miles along the winding banks. After crossing, Bragg deployed toward Crittenden. He expected the battle to open at the Mills.

He was astonished, therefore, at about 9:00 A.M. to hear heavy firing toward Rossville, where Thomas had inadvertently precipitated the fight four miles north of the Mills.

The chain of events which led Thomas to open the battle began the previous afternoon, when Colonel Dan McCook, commanding Granger's cavalry, led five regiments and a battery to join Minty, on guard at Reed's bridge. By dark, Dan McCook had arrived within a mile of the bridge and when he struck McNair, he halted and passed the night there. Meanwhile another regiment joined Mitchell. Since the bridges might provide access to Rosecrans' flank and the LaFayette road, next morning before daylight McCook ordered the 69th Ohio to burn Reed's Bridge. Charging across, the regiment drove off the enemy and fired the bridge. Then, at 7:00, Dan McCook was ordered to retire—and "not a moment too soon"—to Rossville. Although he believed that he had driven away the only division of Longstreet's to cross during the night, actually three had crossed. One lay three-quarters of a mile to Dan McCook's rear, and another to his front. The driven division had halted in good order beyond the bridge.

By now, two-thirds of Bragg's army had crossed and, covered by the forest, groped upstream. The battle noise toward Rossville puzzled Bragg, who judged it time for his center to close on Crittenden. Bragg first thought that Confederate reconnaissance was meeting stiff cavalry opposition. But when the firing continued, he surmised that during the night Rosecrans' left had moved far downstream; and fearing that his own right might be turned, he modified his plans, shifting his weight to his extreme right by sending a portion of the troops still east of the Chickamauga across Reed's Bridge. This movement proved slow and difficult. It was six dusty miles by winding roads to Thomas's front, and as morning advanced, the weather turned warm.

Thomas was at Baird's headquarters when Colonel McCook reported that only one enemy brigade had crossed Reed's Bridge the day before. McCook thought he could isolate it, because he had burned the bridge. Thomas found the bait tempting and ordered Brannan to cover Alexander's Bridge and to advance his two remaining brigades on the road toward Reed's Bridge, to flush out and capture the enemy brigade. By 9:00 Brannan had taken this position. Next, Thomas ordered Baird to advance his right in line with Brannan. As Baird moved, he met strong opposition. These troop movements precipitated the battle, which began west of Reed's Bridge at about 9:00, when Croxton, who commanded Brannan's right, collided with Forrest, who with two divisions formed Bragg's extreme right. When the fight opened, neither Rosecrans nor Bragg knew that the other had heavy forces in these woods.

Lieutenant Ambrose Bierce later described Chickamauga as a throbbing of guns, a turbulent rain of musketry mixed with plunging shells, long rows of dead under sheets of low-lying blue smoke, a hidden battle roaring and stammering in the darksome forest behind a smoking gray front. The noise, Beatty said, was as the "thunder of a thousand anvils." Co-ordinated troop movements were difficult. The wooded ground was unfamiliar to Rosecrans and his generals. Dense timber concealed the enemy and made signaling difficult. From High Point and Summertown on Lookout,

Signal Corps men tried vainly to penetrate the foliage, dust, and smoke below. Commanders were ordered to maintain communication, and Rosecrans assigned his escort and a cavalry battalion to courier service, but communications were poor. Much responsibility was left to the field commanders.

"Unfortunately for the Confederates," wrote General Hill, "there was no general advance. . . . It was desultory fighting from right to left, without concert, and at inopportune times. . . . From daylight on the 19th until after midday, there was a gap of two miles between Crittenden and Thomas, into which the Confederates could have poured, turning to right or left, and attacking in flank whichever commander was least prepared for the assault." Throughout the morning, Rosecrans made a supreme effort to close up his line, aided accidentally by Thomas's order sending Brannan to burn the bridges. This took the initiative from Bragg. Once Thomas attacked, the battle seesawed, with Bragg constantly compelled to reinforce his right as Rosecrans reinforced his left. Thus Bragg was diverted from his opportunity of beating the Union army in detail.

Croxton, who was heavily engaged, reported that he had driven Forrest nearly a half-mile, but he was roughly pressed and was short on ammunition. He faced many brigades with a dry sense of humor: "General, I would have brought in *one* if I had known which you wanted."

Thomas sent in Baird's whole division on his return from Croxton, and Baird repulsed Forrest. Soon Forrest was clamoring for reinforcements from Polk, and Wilson's brigade of Walker's division was rushed into the fight near Alexander's Bridge. Relieved by Walker, Forrest now turned on Brannan, and Croxton's skirmish turned into a full-scale battle. While Thomas rode slowly behind his six engaged divisions, the enemy attacked Baird and Brannan and threatened to overwhelm them.

By 11:00 Bragg was convinced that Rosecrans was forcing battle far north of the point where he had planned to open it himself, and he rushed heavy reinforcements from all parts of his line, automatically terminating his movement on Crittenden. First Walker's division, then Cheatham's, strongest in his army, was hurried to the right. On its heels Bragg sent Stewart's brigade of Buckner's corps, which waited to move against Crittenden.

The Union army, too, was sucked into the widening fight. As the battle opened, Crittenden experienced a momentary qualm. The night before, Rosecrans had asked him repeatedly, "Can you hold your position?" Now Crittenden was doubtful. Perhaps he would weaken his own line by reinforcing Thomas. Yet at 9:00 he ordered Colonel Grose, with a brigade of Palmer's, to reconnoiter the LaFayette Road to see if communication with Thomas was open. Grose reported the enemy near—should he engage them? No, Crittenden answered. Two hours later, however, with his own front quiet, Crittenden ordered Palmer to reinforce Thomas, and report the transfer to Rosecrans. At 12:20 Rosecrans approved Crittenden's "great good sense." Now Thomas could probably advance with his left to threaten Bragg's right.

As soon as Rosecrans was certain of Bragg's intention to drive against the Union left, he established his headquarters near the right of the center, where the fighting, which had moved down the line, was the heaviest, at the Widow Glenn's house, a log hut on a high hill at the point where the Dry Valley road branches from the Crawfish Springs road. Woods blocked the view to the sides and the rear of the hut, but most of the battlefield lay in a semicircle fronting the yard, even though much of the battle was concealed by woods. This limited view was the most extensive that could be gained. The staff found the Widow Glenn inside, with eight or ten of her children—mostly girls—clinging to her dress. She had already packed their bedding into an ox-drawn wagon, and she left hurriedly. The telegraph moved with the headquarters, and in an hour was operating again. That day Dana sent Stanton eleven brief reports.

Three hours after it began, the fight still seesawed as reinforcements shifted the weight of numbers back and forth. Johnson, with McCook's second division, had left Catlett's Gap at dawn; at Crawfish Springs he received McCook's orders to reinforce Thomas and marched toward the sound of the guns. He plunged directly into battle, just as the reinforced Confederates scattered Baird's troops. Johnson entered to Baird's right and in turn drove the Confederates back a half mile, but Johnson was overlapped and yielded. Palmer arrived to support Johnson with Rosecrans' order to advance *en echelon* by brigades—that is, with units marching in parallel lines, but each somewhat to the left or right of the one to rear, in formation somewhat resembling a series of steps—keeping his right back and out of alignment and closed up on Thomas. Palmer fought forward to the right of Johnson and checked the Confederate advance. Then he too was overlapped and in trouble.

Directly behind Palmer came Reynolds who had left Pond Springs at 4:00 P.M., marched all night, halting an hour for breakfast, before moving into the line northeast of the Widow Glenn's house, only to be rushed to Palmer's right and rear. Reynolds, too, quickly became engaged.

As fast as the Union left was extended north and south, it was assaulted by the Confederates, who now swarmed west of the Chickamauga. East of it, about a mile and a half below the Mills and at Bragg's extreme left, Cleburne's division waited all morning unengaged. These were ably led, battle-proved troops. At 1:00 P.M., Bragg ordered Cleburne against Thomas, but before he had reached his assigned position Davis brought up two of McCook's brigades. Davis had received orders to support Thomas the night before, and he had marched about a mile before hearing the distant thunder of battle. New orders told him to report either to Thomas or Rosecrans, and it was turning afternoon before he halted at the Widow Glenn's. "Place a cannon there"—Rosecrans said, designating a position in front of headquarters. "Then move forward with your command toward the heaviest firing, and attack with a view to turning the enemy's left." The fight by now had moved into the center, so that Davis entered the line almost directly east. Sanderson reported that "About 2:30 P.M. a terrific scene" commenced, which continued without interruption until 4:00 P.M., and at one time the fight drew so near to headquarters that Rosecrans ordered the staff to mount, to be prepared to fall back to a less dangerous place. At that moment the battle died down.

Although Davis's arrival gave Rosecrans a temporary advantage, Bragg slowly regained his superiority as he brought up divisions from his left. Davis too began to yield. Meanwhile, at 3:00 P.M., Rosecrans ordered Wood up from Lee and Gordon's, where he guarded the crossing. Bragg still held forces at the Mills, and by midafternoon he had transferred so much of his strength to Thomas's front that, when Rosecrans sent two of Sheridan's brigades to follow Wood, Sheridan's third, commanded by Lytle, seemed ample force to watch the crossing. Lytle now held Rose-crans' extreme right.

Wood took position to the right of Davis, pushed the enemy hard, and was attacked. Sheridan's arrival took some pressure off Wood, and rescued him. As the battle moved deeper into the center and right, spent musket balls pattered around Rosecrans' headquarters, and shells burst about it. Nevertheless, Rosecrans seemed everywhere present, everywhere alert.

Bragg ordered one division after another to attack: Cheatham's, Stewart's, Liddel's, Johnson's, and, at 4:00 P.M., Hood and three brigades of Texans, the first of Longstreet's corps to reach the battlefield. Rosecrans ordered Negley, who still held the line of the Chickamauga at Crawfish Springs, to become reserve for the center and to march to the Widow Glenn's house. At 6:30 A.M., Rosecrans had directed Negley to report immediately to Thomas, to be posted on the extreme left. McCook would take his place. "Move with dispatch, gathering up all stragglers," Rosecrans urged. But Negley was ill, and ten hours passed before he reported, to be rushed to the support of the hard-pressed center. Once there, he reversed the tide of battle, and pushed the enemy until darkness. Pressure on the Union right eased when Sheridan's two brigades repulsed the attack of Preston's division.

Success at his extreme left meanwhile permitted Rosecrans to shift Brannan to the support of the center, so that at nightfall he lay to Reynolds' right. The gap between Thomas and the rest of the army was now fairly well closed. But Rosecrans was fighting with all his troops except for two brigades and the Reserve Corps.

As the afternoon ended, the wounded began to move painfully to the rear. Water was scarce at the center and right, and in the central portion of the battlefield canteens could be filled only at the sinkhole near the Widow Glenn's house. Once, when Wilder fought his way to the "Bloody Pond," he found men and horses lying in it, that had died of their wounds while drinking. Bragg, holding both banks of Chickamauga Creek, had no such problem.

An hour of silence, beginning about 5:00 P.M., was broken after sunset when Cleburne and Walker burst from the woods and fell upon Baird and Johnson on Rosecrans' extreme left. To gain position, Walker's men crossed fields over which they had fought that morning and looked upon their own unburied dead. Then they assaulted magnificently. Cleburne charged over a front a mile wide. When dusk melted butternut and blue into shadow, both sides used gun flashes as targets. The attack ended without Confederate gain.

Night turned cold, but fires were forbidden because they might reveal Union positions and illuminate targets for sharpshooters. Canteens were empty, and without fire and water, the men could not make coffee. Many had marched through the preceding night and fought all day on empty stomachs. Now they sat down in the feeble moonlight to munch a dry meal of hardtack and bully beef out of their haversacks. The headquarters staff suffered too. At 8:00 P.M. Sanderson wrote: "Here we are without a morsel to eat during the day or a drop of water to drink." Nearest accessible water was at Crawfish Springs, some three miles away. And yet there was "everything to cheer us."

The Union army had reassembled so that it could not be beaten in detail and had survived a day's hard fighting. It had gained secure command of the LaFayette and Dry Valley roads, and a safe line of retreat. Its spare trains were parked in Chattanooga Valley west of Missionary Ridge, covered now by Union cavalry. The heaviest fighting on the left had been defensive and behind breastworks, and consequently, Confederate losses were heavier. However, Rosecrans had thrown his whole force, except for two brigades, on the field into the fight—Granger with the Reserve Corps covered his rear and left. Bragg, whose forces outnumbered Rosecrans', possessed masses of unengaged troops. Rosecrans knew that the next day's battle might determine the survival of his army and the possession of Chattanooga; he determined to renew the fight himself at daybreak if Bragg did not retreat.

Dana's telegrams to Stanton reflected the shifting tides of battle. At 2:30 P.M. he reported: "Decisive victory seems assured to us"; at 4:00: "Everything is prosperous:"; at 4:30: "I do not yet dare to say our victory is complete, but it seems certain. . . . Longstreet is here"; at 5:30: "Enemy holds his ground in many places. Now appears to be undecided contest." After the Confederate repulse at dusk, he spoke with guarded optimism: "Negley . . . drove him back half a mile. . . . This gives us decidedly the advantage in respect of ground."

That night tired armies lay down on earth that by morning was again covered with frost. At Crawfish Springs, the XX Corps converted for hospital use a large brick building with outhouses, and set up extra tents. The wounded of the XX Corps and most of those of the XIV were brought in and by 8:00 P.M. buildings and tents were filled, and the rest lay on open ground in the biting air. Attendants built immense fires, brought extra bedding, and served beef soup and coffee. The correspondent of the Cincinnati *Commercial* tried to sleep near a field hospital where hundreds of desperately wounded men lay with their feet toward the fire. Their soft moans, he said, "sounded like the plaintive cries of a flock of doves."

On Rosecrans' orders, corps and division commanders gathered at headquarters. Of the nineteen holding such rank, Dana estimated that ten or twelve were present, including the corps commanders. All agreed that Bragg outnumbered them, and that the morrow's fight would be bloodier and more decisive. Rosecrans asked McCook, Crittenden, and Thomas to describe their positions and to recommend improvements. The entire group then discussed each suggestion. Thomas drowsed intermittently. Throughout the previous night he had not slept. Rosecrans spoke to him, and he straightened up, said, "I would strengthen the left," and slept again. To all suggestions that the left be reinforced, Rosecrans responded, "Where are we going to take the troops from?"

Rosecrans lectured Hazen for his delay in yielding position to Negley the night before. "You greatly detained the movements of two corps and greatly imperiled the safety of another." Hazen was to charge later that Rosecrans would not "heed my plain statement of the facts," and that he made the accusations "in a tone and a spirit I never before listened to and did so only from the fact that we were upon the eve of an important engagement."

Although Rosecrans' line had to be shortened if seven brigades were to be put in reserve, Rosecrans observed that tired troops should be disturbed as little as possible. He then issued orders for the next day. Thomas was to hold his position unchanged and to the last but, if beaten, he was ordered to retire to Rossville and Chattanooga, and send his trains to Chattanooga immediately. The whole army, except for ten brigades, was now fighting under Thomas.

McCook was to close on Thomas and cover the position at the

Widow Glenn's house; Crittenden, to shift his two remaining divisions near the junction of Thomas and McCook so he could reinforce either. Orders were written, read to the group, and explained carefully. Business lasted until almost midnight, when coffee was brought in and the generals drank as McCook sang the ballad "The Hebrew Maiden."

Night had become extremely cold, and Dana lay down on the plank floor of the headquarters cabin. Sleep was difficult. Cold sliced through the cracks of the puncheon floor, and the sleepers turned to each other for warmth.

Bragg, meanwhile, was preparing his own plans for the morrow. Shortly after dark he had called a campfire conference and reorganized his army into two wings commanded by his senior lieutenant generals. Polk would lead the right, consisting of the corps of Hill and Walker, Cheatham's division, and Forrest's cavalry; and Longstreet, who had not yet reported, the left, composed of the corps of Buckner and Hood, Hindman's division, and Wheeler's cavalry. At daybreak, at the extreme right, Hill would open the attack, which would be taken up successively by Bragg's divisions, until the army revolved like a wheel, with the extreme left as pivot.

Not all soldiers slept that night. At 11:00 Longstreet reported. For seven hours after detraining at Ringgold he wandered lost with McLaw's division and the remainder of Hood's. In the Union camp, McCook left the meeting and undertook an immediate change of position. The night was far spent before he returned to snatch some rest. Thomas reached his headquarters about midnight and slept under the trees. He was awakened at 2:00 A.M. by Baird, who found that his line could not be extended to Reed's Bridge Road without thinning dangerously. At 2:00 and 6:00 Thomas's messenger reported the difficulty to Rosecrans, who replied both times that Negley would be sent immediately to take post on the left. At 2:10, Rosecrans directed Mitchell to report at the Widow Glenn's. At 3:00 A.M., Lieutenant Moody visited Negley's picket line to learn that between 1:00 and 2:00 pickets had heard chopping and other sounds, suggesting the movement of men and guns to Bragg's right. Negley sent Moody to Rosecrans, and Garfield sent him to Thomas. "No firing took place during the night," Rosecrans reported.

Rosecrans slept little if at all and was up before dawn to hear Mass, although he needed sleep so badly that his exhaustion imperilled the army. During the reassembling of his corps, he had lived through ten tense days—the last four burdened with much worry. "Rosecrans habitually used himself badly in time of excitement," said General Stanley. "He never slept, he overworked himself, he smoked incessantly. At Iuka and Stone River, the stress of excitement did not exceed a week. His strong constitution could stand that, but at Chickamauga this strain lasted a month, and Rosecrans' health was badly broken." General McCalmont thought that perhaps "the lateness of the hours Rosecrans kept possibly interfered with his tactical combinations in the field in the early part of the first day at Chickamauga." It is reasonable to assume that his exhaustion was even greater on the second. That morning the correspondent of the Cincinnati *Commercial* saw him emerge from headquarters.

He was enveloped in a blue army overcoat, his pantaloons stuffed in his boots, and a light brown felt hat, of uncertain shape, was drawn over his head. A cigar, unlit, was held between his teeth, and his mouth was tightly compressed as if he were sharply biting it. He stalked to a heap of embers where I was standing, and stood a moment silently by my side. An orderly brought a rawboned, muscular, dappled grey horse to him, and mounting without a word, he rode down the lane towards the road, his staff clattering after him, and understanding his mood, perhaps as silent as himself.

I knew, for I had seen Rosecrans often under widely differing circumstances, that he was filled with apprehensions for the issue of that day's fight. I recognized a change instantly, although I could hardly say in what it consisted. Rosecrans is usually brisk, nervous, powerful of presence, and to see him silent or absorbed in what looked like gloomy contemplation, filled me with indefinable dread. Remember this was just for an instant, and when the leader thought he was entirely unobserved. Rosecrans is too good a soldier to let his face reflect to his men, either his hopes or his forebodings.

At daybreak, leading his staff, Rosecrans rode to the highest nearby hill. From here he could overlook the entire valley and trace, by the dust clouds hanging above it, the position of each army. Again the Confederate cloud moved toward his left. Bragg was still trying to seize the roads to Chattanooga. Rosecrans made a thorough inspection from right to left. Toward morning the cold, clear night had turned foggy. The mists rose at 8:00, some said, at 10:00, others observed. The air seemed "smoky"; and men later spoke of the "bloody dawn" of Chickamauga. Rosecrans himself wrote: "The sky was red and sultry and the atmosphere and all the woods enveloped in fog and smoke."

That morning Rosecrans' lines were extended to cover the LaFayette and Dry Valley roads. Beginning on a crest 400 yards east of the LaFayette road and lying from 50 to 100 yards within the woods which skirt the Kelly farm, the divisions of Baird, Johnson, Palmer, and Reynolds awaited the attack in positions slightly withdrawn from those of the previous day. Breastworks of logs and rails, rough but substantial, covered these divisions. As the veering Union line recrossed the LaFayette road, to the right of Reynolds lay two more of Thomas's divisions: Negley's and, to Negley's right, Brannan's. To Brannan's right were posted two of McCook's divisions, Sheridan's and Davis's. Behind these, two of Crittenden's divisions, Wood's and Van Cleve's, lay in reserve. Minty's cavalry at Missionary Mills covered the left, and Wilder's mounted infantry brigade the right.

Battle lines were about half as long as those of the first day. Rosecrans estimated his line on the 19th at about 3,400 yards to Bragg's 6,880; and on the 20th, as 1,750 yards to Bragg's, 3,310. His shorter line and defensive position gave him an advantage that might have been more significant had numbers been more nearly equal. Reinforcements, however, had swelled the Confederates to near 72,000, minus the first day's casualties. Against these Rosecrans could barely muster 57,000, minus his casualties. Moreover Bragg had a psychological advantage. Prisoners from many regiments had given Rosecrans the impression that the enemy numbered in excess of 90,000. He did not know that many Confederate regiments were badly depleted. Yet, as Hill points out, even ghost regiments have psychological value if an opponent credits them at full strength.

Rosecrans' tour began with McCook. At midnight, McCook had orders to form the right, taking position around headquarters. Before daylight he had moved Sheridan's three brigades to the right and rear of the Widow Glenn's. To the left and rear of Sheridan, as reserve, he posted two small brigades, Carlin's and Heg's, of Davis's division. Davis's third brigade, Post's, was guarding a supply train and missed the battle. At 6:00, Wilder reported to McCook with his brigade of mounted infantry. The fire power of his Spencer repeaters, and his mobility made him a valuable addition to the attenuated right. Inspecting these dispositions, Rosecrans found Sheridan too far up the crest, and Davis too far to the right. McCook must move them at once.

Next, Rosecrans checked on Crittenden. That morning Crittenden was reduced to two brigades of Wood's and three of Van Cleve's. He had posted these five brigades on the eastern slope of Missionary Ridge, as reserves for Thomas, McCook, or both. Rosecrans ordered Crittenden to take a position farther to the left.

At the extreme left Rosecrans found Thomas and approved his dispositions, commenting only that Palmer's line lacked compactness. Thomas's readiness put Rosecrans in good humor. From the left, Rosecrans again ordered Negley to join Thomas, and McCook to relieve Negley.

Inspection completed, Rosecrans retraced his tour to check performances—"probably with Murfreesboro in mind," wrote Dana, who rode with him. Tired men looked at their even more tired commander. Two Illinois soldiers later wrote: "By and by Rosecrans came around. He was in bad plight, but his voice was ringing and cheery. 'Boys,' he said, 'I never fight Sundays, but if they begin it, we will end it.' "

But by the time he reached his extreme right, his good nature had vanished. Instead of moving immediately, Negley was preparing slowly to move. He argued that no one had relieved him, that he was ill, and that the enemy was reported on his front. Rosecrans instructed him to hold his position until relieved, but to hurry his reserve brigade, John Beatty's, to Thomas. By this time Thomas needed reinforcements so badly that, when Negley failed to arrive, he sent Captain Willard to find him and lead him to his assigned position.

It seemed simpler to Rosecrans to provide replacement for Negley by drawing on Crittenden, who was near by, than from McCook; and so, about 8:00, he ordered Crittenden to bring Wood and Van Cleve out of reserve. Two of Wood's brigades and one of Van Cleve's would replace Negley, while Van Cleve's two remaining brigades would be posted to the rear and in support of Wood.

Rosecrans personally reported these dispositions to McCook. While they were talking between 8:00 and 9:00 A.M., Lieutenant Moody brought a request from Negley for reinforcements. "Go tell General Crittenden," Rosecrans ordered, "to make General Negley's line strong and good." Then: "Has General Wood reported to General Negley?" Moody knew nothing of Wood's whereabouts.

Meanwhile, Bragg had found unexpected trouble. He had risen before daylight, and waited impatiently for dawn, when Polk's guns would signal the opening of battle. Instead he heard intermittent musketry. Early that morning, there was sporadic crack of rifle and musket fire, reminding Sanderson of a giant hunt. Bragg learned from reconnaissance that he still could seize the LaFayette road. Several hours passed and yet Polk's guns remained silent. Then a search began for Polk, and riding to the right, Bragg found his army unready. Hill was to have attacked first, but orders went astray, and while the generals argued, Bragg's army took their positions tardily, and Rosecrans improved his line. It was between 9:00 and 10:00 A.M. before the Confederate right struck.

The battle opened with the abrupt first crash of Confederate artillery, as Breckinridge, swinging around with three divisions in an overlapping single line, endeavored to take Baird in front and to outflank his left. Breckinridge was gaining Baird's rear, when Willard rode up, followed by John Beatty. Although Beatty took position to Baird's left, extending it, Confederate pressure forced Beatty back, until Breckinridge again was in Baird's rear.

Fighting spread slowly toward the Union center and right, but the fact that it had begun again on the left set a pattern which saved the army. Again constant support flowed to Thomas; since the previous noon Johnson's and Davis's divisions of McCook's corps and Wood's of Crittenden's had fought under him.

To restore the left, part of Palmer's reserve was sent in, and with their assistance, Beatty and Baird repulsed Breckinridge after much fighting. Nevertheless, the attack on Baird continued to be heavy and moved down the line with unabating fierceness, falling successively on Johnson, Palmer, and Reynolds, until all were simultaneously embroiled. Waves of Confederates rushed upon the barricades; many were injured or killed.

When this assault had spent itself, Bragg's divisions re-formed, attacked, and again were beaten off. Only at Bragg's extreme right

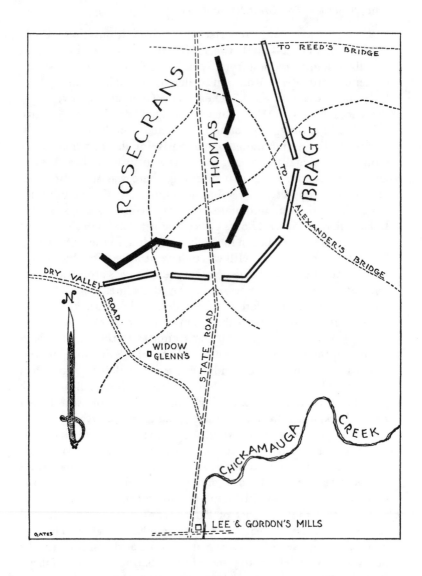

ROSECRANS
THOMAS
BRAGG
TO REED'S BRIDGE
TO
ALEXANDER'S BRIDGE
DRY VALLEY ROAD
STATE ROAD
N
WIDOW GLENN'S
CHICKAMAUGA CREEK
LEE & GORDON'S MILLS
GATES

BATTLE OF CHICKAMAUGA

September 20, 1863
SECOND DAY

did a temporary promise of success appear. There Breckinridge extended his lines so that he overlapped Beatty by two brigades. These formed at right angles to the road and burst from the woods in a direction parallel to it. Less than a half-mile ahead, across open fields, stood the Kelly farmhouse, and directly behind it Reynolds's rear lay exposed. Thomas was outflanked. As the Confederates gained Baird's rear, attack blazed out against the entire left. Walker and Cleburne struck Baird, while Stewart assaulted Reynolds and Brannan to Baird's right. It seemed that the left, enveloped front, flank, and rear, must be crushed.

Thomas watched this movement develop as he rode his line, and, when disaster threatened, he asked Rosecrans to shift Brannan, who was then unengaged, to support Baird. Rosecrans agreed, but when the order reached Brannan, he too was threatened. Brannan consulted Reynolds and remained in line reporting his changed situation to Rosecrans. He did partially comply, however, and sent Van Derveer, then commanding his reserve brigade, to Baird's support. Van Derveer repulsed an attack on the way.

Beatty's brigade, still a thin extension from Baird's left, began to yield ground, and the Confederates gained a foothold on the Union line. Then Palmer sent Grose's brigade to drive them out, and Thomas placed Barnes of Van Cleve's division on Beatty's left. Near noon the attack on Thomas subsided with the exhaustion of the attackers. For the moment, he was secure. Not until 5:00 P.M. would Bragg renew the fight against the divisions that lay behind breastworks on the Kelly farm.

Through the morning hours, disaster had been building up for the Union right. Shortly after the battle opened, Rosecrans inspected his left a second time. Next day Sanderson wrote: "The General approached so close I trembled for his safety. The balls came flying thickly around us, and one solid shot came whizzing not more than perhaps six feet over his head, and struck the ground about a hundred yards behind him, quite near."

Rosecrans took position on a hilltop and paused to give orders. Heavy fighting had broken out on the left when Rosecrans met Wood moving slowly to Negley's rear. Negley had orders to join Thomas, and Wood to replace Negley, but to Rosecrans' alarm, Wood argued that his orders were to *support* Negley, not *relieve* him. For a third time since Lookout Valley, Wood was having trouble with orders; Rosecrans gave him peremptory orders, meanwhile dressing him down. In no mood to co-operate, Wood did what he should have done a half hour earlier, but his delay "subsequently proved of serious consequence," Rosecrans said. It was 9:30 when he relieved Negley.

By now the fight had reached the center, and Thomas sent two aides to request reinforcements. They reached Rosecrans a few minutes apart. Rosecrans told the first that Negley should be nearing Thomas; the second, that Van Cleve would be ordered to Thomas immediately. Still the battle moved toward the right. Negley began to withdraw, and Wood to enter the gap. That morning, Rosecrans suffered apprehensions: it seemed to him that the distance from the Widow Glenn's to Brannan's right was greater than he had supposed, and that the line there was thin and weak. In an effort to strengthen it, he rode to Crittenden, in a peach orchard about 300 yards to his right, and ordered Oldershaw, Crittenden's aide, to hurry to Van Cleve, and tell him to march quickly to the front, in the direction of a certain tree. Next he summoned McCook and lectured him roundly on his line's faulty placement. McCook should move Davis up from the rear of the hill earlier occupied by Negley's reserve, to fill a gap on Wood's right. Then Rosecrans returned to the Widow Glenn's.

There Captain Kellogg, Thomas' aide-de-camp, found him. "Thomas is heavily pressed," Kellogg cried breathlessly. Could he have Brannan? Brannan was out of line and Reynolds's right was exposed. Thomas could have Brannan, Rosecrans said, but must hold his position. "We will reinforce you, if need be, with the whole right."

Sometime that morning Rosecrans telegraphed Granger, "Is Missionary Ridge available, supposing we should fall back?" And at 10:35 he asked Thomas to refuse his left—that is, to bend it back out of regular alignment so that its open end could be covered. He should then use his reserves to extend his line. Rosecrans preferred to have McCook and Crittenden rather than Thomas's reserves cover the Union right. But the enemy was pushing Thomas. He could not shift his troops while he was under attack. Besides, to move that portion that lay behind breastworks would be to send them from their defenses into the open.

To strengthen the left and center, and to close gaps as portions of the right were withdrawn, Rosecrans issued a series of orders. One told Davis to close on Wood. Another went to Wood himself. Garfield, who signed most of the field dispatches of the 19th and 20th, was busy. Rosecrans turned to Major Bond, saying, "If Brannan goes out, Wood must fill his place. Write him that the commanding general directs him to close to the left of Reynolds and support him." And Bond wrote, "the general commanding directs that you close up on Reynolds as fast as possible, and support him." Dating the order 10:45, he marked it "gallop." Clearly this dispatch, signed by Bond, embraced more than Rosecrans intended. Minutes afterward, Brannan's dispatch arrived, and Rosecrans approved his good judgment in not withdrawing while facing attack. Unfortunately, Kellogg's observation that "Brannan is out of line and Reynolds's right is exposed," had been hastily made on the gallop and was inaccurate. Brannan lay to Reynolds's right, slightly to his rear, and because he was not engaged, his men were lying down or sitting in the underbrush. Reynolds's right was not exposed. However, having told Kellogg that Thomas might move Brannan out, Rosecrans now had a double reason to believe that a dangerous gap in the line existed to Reynolds's right—that is, in the military term, his right was "in the air." Rosecrans therefore dictated two orders to Garfield. The first told McCook that Thomas was heavily pressed and directed him to make immediate dispositions to withdraw the right so as to reinforce him as much as possible: "The left must be held at all hazards even if the right is withdrawn wholly back to the present left. Select a good position back this way and be ready to start reinforcements to Thomas at a moment's warning." The second order instructed McCook to hurry two of Sheridan's brigades to Thomas, and to send a third brigade, as soon as he had shortened his lines. After these orders were issued, McCook was to report to headquarters. On second thought, Rosecrans felt that the wording of the latter order was "too precipitate," and he supplemented it by another, directing McCook to report in person. He presumed that McCook, who was close by, would ride over before Sheridan moved, to seek more specific directions. Rosecrans departed to examine the ground to the rear of his left center.

Perhaps this series of orders was too complicated. Crittenden had observed of Rosecrans at Stone River, "I regard Rosecrans as of the first order of military mind. He was both brave and generous, impulsively so; in fact, in his impulsiveness lay a military defect, which was to issue too many orders while his men were fighting." This same defect may have hurt him at Chickamauga.

These orders involved a number of organizations in simultaneous movements in the presence of the enemy and momentarily weakened the right. But, had Rosecrans' luck held, and had the Confederate charge upon the right developed a little sooner or a little later, with reinforcement from the unengaged left the right would have sustained itself, and Chickamauga might have been a Union victory. "Thirty minutes earlier Longstreet would have met well-organized resistance," said Colonel Thruston. "Thirty minutes later our marching divisions could have formed beyond his column of attack."

Even with the attack falling when it did, it might have met substantial resistance if the angry Wood had not opened a division-wide gap in the Union lines. At about 11:00 A.M., while Rosecrans' orderly watched, Wood read the dispatch. He was "glad the order was in writing, as it was a good thing to have for future reference," and carefully tucked it into his notebook—so the aide reported.

When the order arrived, Wood told McCook, who was near by, he would execute it immediately; he suggested that McCook should close his command to the left to fill the gap. As McCook rode away, Wood dispatched staff officers to his brigade commanders. Because Brannan lay between him and Reynolds, it was impossible for him to close up on Reynolds and support him, and in his anger he did not evoke the principle enunciated for him by Rosecrans at Murfreesboro, that an order clearly based on misinformation need not be literally and immediately obeyed.

Nine months later it was bruited that Wood had said: "Gentlemen, I hold the fatal order of the day in my hand and would not part with it for five thousand dollars." And the question was still: If Wood knew the position of affairs and that the movement was impossible, why did he not tell Rosecrans, instead of moving out of the line?

The order's obvious purpose was to maintain a strong and continuous line. Wood neither asked whether it was correct, nor waited for the conditions which would permit its literal execution. He disobeyed both its intent and its letter, even though he asked

Reynolds where and how he should bring his command into action. He did not use Brannan's good sense; nor did he unbend to consult Rosecrans, who was in plain view less than six hundred yards away. Wood began to evacuate, disregarding the fact that the attack on Reynolds was reaching him, and that his skirmishers were being driven back. If he could not support Reynolds, by entering the line and closing upon him, he would support him by getting behind him. Wood emerged with precipitation, "at double quick," Rosecrans testified later, "thus giving General McCook no time to close his troops properly and fill the vacant space." McCook added: "There was not only no time to fill the space, but I had no troops to fill it with, unless a small brigade could cover a division interval."

Wood admitted that no gap existed when he said later that "Reynolds' division was posted to the left of Brannan's division, which, in turn, was on the left of the position I was just quitting," and when he reported that he withdrew hastily when he was "well satisfied the enemy was in considerable force in my immediate front."

Searching for Reynolds, Wood found Thomas and learned that while Reynolds did not require support, Baird did. Wood showed Thomas the order, asked if he would accept the responsibility of changing it, and told Thomas he would obey cheerfully. Thomas agreed, and Wood hurried off. "Intent on maintaining his dignity," Cist observes, "he refused to ride a short distance to ask Rosecrans what the order meant. To this extent he is responsible for the great disaster which swept the right wing from the field of battle on the 20th." Wood disobeyed the order completely, using Thomas as a shield. The order was wrong. So was Wood. So was Rosecrans in allowing his testy temper to run off with his tongue, until a subordinate grew irresponsible with anger.

Some of Rosecrans' friends believed that his exhausted condition "accounts for his debatable order to Wood," Stanley reported later. "But it matters not, whether Rosecrans who dictated it, Bond who wrote it, or Wood who construed the order, committed the grand mistake; we now know that if Wood's division had remained in line and had met Longstreet's attack, Bragg's left, under Longstreet, would have been beaten as badly as was his right under

Polk, and Chickamauga would have been a victory for the Union army."

By another unfortunate coincidence, Rosecrans' second order reached McCook at 10:55. An orderly checked its arrival against his watch. By that time Wood had withdrawn to support Reynolds, and Sheridan was trying to spread into the division-wide opening which Wood had left.

To the right of Wood's emptied position, McCook and Sheridan found some hastily constructed barricades. McCook had directed Sheridan to bring up a brigade to close the gap toward Wilder, when, turning to go, he met a column advancing within a hundred yards of the vacated space. It was Davis with two brigades, marching under orders from Rosecrans to fill this gap. McCook realized the importance of keeping the line continuous, and immediately ordered one brigade of Davis's into the barricades, and the other into reserve. When Sheridan's brigade came up, it was posted as support to the right and rear of Davis. McCook later complained that he knew nothing about Wood's withdrawal from the line until he accidentally met Wood as the movement began: "There was not only no time to fill the space, but I had no troops to fill it with, unless a small brigade could cover a division interval."

Nevertheless, McCook sent in Laiboldt, Sheridan's reserve—and so "the reserve is gone, and my own weak reserves, my only reliance for a second line, have to be put on the first. An interval of two brigades separates Wilder from Laiboldt, and a division interval separates Davis from the nearest troops on his left." The cavalry which had been placed under McCook's direction had not reported to him.

Earlier, McCook had been "calm and confident," but now he became anxious. Dust rose in the woods before him, and he told his staff that he believed Rosecrans had made a mistake, and that a heavy attack was about to fall upon him. If it came, he could not sustain it.

When Davis was ordered to move to the left and close on Crittenden's right, he thought that Wood occupied that position. Instead, he found that the troops to his left, moving out slowly because of the rough terrain, were Van Cleve's. He adjusted his line to them, and sent an aide to Rosecrans or McCook to ask if he had taken the right position, and if not, where he should go. Davis should move to the front and connect with Wood, Rosecrans answered. Davis met Colonel George P. Buell of the 51st Indiana. Buell was moving to the left and feared an attack was imminent. As Davis adjusted his line the attack came.

Rosecrans, who was inspecting the line with Crittenden, had stopped earlier at a battery posted on a narrow strip of woods and suggested that the artillerymen improve their time by cutting aisles through the underbrush to allow the guns to be moved forward easily. Just then Van Cleve came up. "I'm posting them now," he said. Rosecrans thought nonetheless that they were 150 or 200 yards back of where they ought to be, and that it would be difficult for them to support the main line. Crittenden said to Rosecrans, "General, as this is the last of my command, I presume I had better go with it." "Certainly," Rosecrans replied. "And take them where you see that smoke and heavy firing, and do what you can there."

Crittenden followed Van Cleve and at the forest he found that Van Cleve had run up on Wood and halted. Crittenden ordered Van Cleve to move to the left, to cross the Union lines at the first gap, and to seek the enemy. A few minutes later another messenger arrived, calling for support from Thomas. Crittenden did not halt Van Cleve, who was proceeding by the left flank anyway, but sent the messenger to Rosecrans, who was nearby. Rosecrans' order returned. Van Cleve was to hurry to Thomas.

Then came a message from Wood: it was useless to bring artillery into the forest. And so Crittenden ordered Mendenhall to post his guns back on the ridge to cover any retreat across the open field in front of them. As he watched the placing of the guns, Crittenden was amazed, as he described it afterward, "to see them suddenly and unaccountably thrown into great confusion. There was but little firing at this moment near the troops, and I was unable for some time afterward to account for this confusion. In a moment, however, the enemy had driven all before them, and I was cut off from my command, though not 100 yards in the rear, and in full view." The Confederates had attacked and simultaneously run over the extreme right.

This was the breakthrough at Chickamauga. The Confederate attack on the right, although it had been forming all morning, by strange and disastrous coincidence, was not ready until 11 o'clock,

precisely at the time when the forces to its front were least prepared to meet it.

In the deep woods, scarcely a stone's throw from the Union right,
the Confederates had quietly massed and advanced. Here were
Stewart's, Johnson's, Hindman's, Hood's, and Preston's divisions,
each with two brigades in front and one or two in support. Hood's
division, which constituted the main column, was strengthened by
Kershaw's and Humphreys' brigades. Longstreet informed Bragg
by messenger that he was ready: "I had better make my attack."
His messenger had not had time to return when he learned that
Bragg had issued orders directly to certain of his division commanders, and that some were already advancing. Earlier Confederate plans to pivot on the left and attack with the right had been
predicated upon the successful issue of Polk's battle. With Polk
checkmated, Longstreet amended the plan.

He ordered a general attack. The bugles blew, and the Confederates rose with a prolonged yell. Bierce felt his soul tingle when
the screaming rebel yell shrilled above the rattle of rifle fire. The
assaulting troops, flags flying, rushed across the narrow space, yelling, shooting, with the spearhead probing the thin line. Davis
hurled his troops into the gap, but his 1,200 men were unprotected
on both flanks. Coolly his veterans fired several rounds and then
used clubbed muskets on the enemy, who poured over and around
them, the Confederate front line being everywhere repulsed or
shot down by Carlin's brigade. Yet the Gray overlapped Carlin's
right and brushed him aside. Major James E. Calloway's regiment
opened a terrible fire until but three men of the enemy's first line
and about half his second line were standing. The rest fell, he said,
"in windrows." Then, to his horror and surprise he too was
crushed. Colonel John A. Martin of the 8th Kansas saw that the
Confederates were terribly punished, but to no avail. McCook
called Longstreet's attack a "most furious and impetuous assault
in overwhelming numbers"—the enemy's line of battle extended
from beyond Brannan's right to a point far to the right of the
Widow Glenn's house, and in front of the strong positions just
abandoned by General Sheridan's two brigades.

As the blow fell, Davis galloped back to Laiboldt, posted in an
open field several hundred yards to his rear and right: "If you're
going to support me, do it immediately." Laiboldt quickly de-

ployed his troops to form a line on Davis's right, but before they could take position, the enemy, who had skirted the right unopposed, struck and routed the line.

Davis's division, resisting and in good order, fell back several hundred yards, until its withdrawal brought it clear of the shelter of the woods and into an open field. There the Confederate fire took full effect, and the division was routed.

At a rocky ridge extending across the field, officers made valiant efforts to rally their commands, but the tidal attack poured through the break and smashed both sides of the line beyond the breach. First to break through were Bushrod Johnson's three brigades of Longstreet's center, and on their heels came the five brigades under Hindman and Kershaw. Johnson, a competent soldier, turned the head of the attacking column to the right, and the rest followed, shouting, yelling, running over batteries, taking prisoners, seizing Rosecrans' headquarters at the Widow Glenn's, until they found themselves facing the new Federal line on Snodgrass Hill. By the time Hindman cleared the gap, panic was spreading through the Union right.

Buell's was the last of Wood's brigades to leave the line. Buell had been apprehensive about withdrawing while the enemy threatened not more than 200 yards away; he had scarcely begun to march when the attack struck his right flank like an avalanche. Remnants of Buell's command stopped to resist at every hilly crest. As Wood rode back toward Buell, he found the valley south of him swarming with the enemy. With Buell gone, Brannan's right was exposed and flung back, although his left held.

The brigades of Lytle and Walworth from Sheridan's extreme right, which were marching double quick to support Thomas, were deflected and were in the path of the breakthrough. For a moment they stemmed the gray torrent, broke a wave or two, but when it swirled through far to their left, they, too, collapsed.

Other commands were caught up in the disaster. As Van Cleve's division hurried to the left, a routed brigade with a panicked Union battery at its heels cut diagonally across it. The terrorized horses trampled Van Cleve's men, running some down and scattering others, until the ranks broke, and the division was flung shattered on the ridge to the rear. When infantry supports gave way, gunners in the artillery reserve of the center were helpless, and as horses were slaughtered, men could not drag guns away through the heavy undergrowth. In three-quarters of an hour the right was driven about a mile.

In the midst of this collapse the Confederates struck a single, final, sharp bit of Union resistance. When McCook ordered Sheridan to the left, he sent Gates Thruston, his aide, toward Crawfish Springs to order up cavalry to fill the gaps left by his infantry. Thruston delivered the orders to Wilder, who was still posted on Sheridan's flank. Galloping back, with Wilder's cavalry pounding the road behind him, Thruston met Colonel Thomas J. Harrison, who commanded the only mounted regiment in McCook's corps. The regiment was armed with repeating rifles and guarded an ammunition train.

At the crest of a hill Wilder and Harrison suddenly faced the left of Longstreet's charging column. Less than fifty yards away, bayonets fixed and hats pulled down, six lines of yelling Confederates rushed before them. "Fire at will," Wilder shouted. Four times the Confederates charged; four times they were repulsed. They did not return for a fifth charge, and Wilder escorted the train to safety. This attack led Longstreet to believe that another Union corps had emerged unexpectedly at Rosecrans' right, and this error helped to check effective Confederate pursuit. Further attack was directed against Rosecrans' left.

Although Brannan's right was scattered, his left held firm and changed position to face the attack. Other unrouted commands did likewise, until men who for two days had looked east for the enemy now stared south. The abbreviated line commanded the Dry Valley road and down it drifted the fugitives from the right. Casualties had been heavy. In the breakthrough the five small brigades of the XX Corps lost more than forty per cent of their number. Hill said he had never seen so many Federal dead, save before the sunken wall at Fredericksburg.

When opposition on his front and left died down, Hindman wheeled to the right and there joined Stewart, Hood, and Bushrod Johnson before the shortened circle of the Federal army waiting on Snodgrass Hill. It was 2:30. The mopping up had taken over three hours.

Rosecrans and his staff witnessed the breakthrough from a point directly behind the Union center. Rosecrans had watched Crittenden's two brigades, until only their rear was visible between him and the trees. Then a staff member cried, "General, our men are giving way yonder." "Impossible," Rosecrans declared. "Van Cleve is there with two brigades. So is Brannan. Thomas countermanded the order to shift him to the left." But his confidence vanished quickly as the battle exploded in front of him and the rear of Van Cleve's column fell to pieces.

Two sleepless nights and noon warmth had made Dana drowsy, and he slept on the ground, to awaken to the "most infernal" noise he had ever heard. He sat up, and the first thing he saw was General Rosecrans crossing himself. "Hello!" he said to himself, "if the general is crossing himself, we are in a desperate situation."

As he leaped into the saddle, Dana saw "lines break and melt away like leaves before the wind." Then headquarters disappeared. Sanderson watched as "the gray backs came through with a rush, and soon the musket ball and cannon shot began to reach the place where we stood. The whole right of the army apparently had been routed."

Negley's men scurried, and shot and shell began to fly thickly over and around the headquarters group; Morton, who stood near Rosecrans, was wounded. Rosecrans rode off, followed by the headquarters cavalcade, and still showered by shot and shell, he ascended a hill, to the rear of Davis's right, and reached the crest, out of enemy range. There, while he ordered the troops to rally behind the ridge west of the Dry Valley road, Davis's division collapsed. Just as Rosecrans prepared to order McCook to "throw Sheridan on the rebels' flank," he realized that the opportunity to counterattack in detail had passed. He watched Davis and Sheridan attempt to rally their men, and saw Longstreet's long line sweep up from the southwest, outreaching the Union right by at least a half-mile. Effective Union resistance would have to be offered on more advantageous ground, so he ordered Davis and Sheridan to withdraw northward, and to stand at the first strong defensive point on the Dry Valley road.

The hill now swarmed with stragglers, and with his staff Rosecrans recklessly tried to halt, rally, and send fugitives back to the battle. Whenever Captains Porter and Drouillard attempted to stem the tide, a handful would form into a makeshift company, only to take to their heels when cannon shot tore through trees. A fugitive charged him with a bayonet, but Porter stood his ground and was not run through. Correspondent William Sumner Dodge reported later that "here General Rosecrans threw himself into the very thickest of the fight."

Dana was wide awake by now, and he mounted and galloped off, headed toward the enemy, until he met Wilder, who was organizing his line on the crest of Missionary Ridge so as to command the Dry Valley road. "It's a worse rout than Bull Run," Dana said. "General Rosecrans was probably killed or captured." Wilder turned Dana around, and pointed him toward Chattanooga.

Confederate cavalry charged through the widening gap, and cut off access to whatever resistance still stood on the right. They reached the rear of the hill, and began to take prisoners. The Cincinnati *Gazette* reported that even the "personal exertions of Rosecrans himself, who with drawn sword at the head of his devoted staff, endeavored to check the rout," was ineffectual. He saw that he could do no more, and ordered his staff and escort to mount and ride back a hundred yards to the base of the ridge toward the rear of the center. Calls for reinforcements continued to reach him, the last from Negley.

Negley had posted sixteen fully equipped and six partially equipped guns on a ridge at the left, and at their foot, a brigade had thrown up rail breastworks. Before this position flowed the confused debris of battle. When massive gray columns, enveloped in dust, marched forward, Negley guessed that the right had collapsed. And so by different routes he sent two messengers to Rosecrans seeking reinforcements. One of them, Lieutenant William H. Moody, made a circuit to the rear of the ridges and about a half mile beyond Negley's position found Rosecrans upon the top of the ridge. He was endeavoring to halt stragglers. "I saw General Rosecrans, as near as I can judge, at noon on Sunday immediately in front about 500 yards, alone. The yell of the enemy could be heard to the right and front and very close," Moody said. He reported Negley's need to Rosecrans and rode with him a short distance to the rear. "It is too late," Rosecrans said. "I cannot help him."

Immediately after the collapse, Rosecrans stopped with McCook for less than a minute, but did not speak. In the confusion he became separated from part of his staff. As Sanderson rode toward the ridge, he saw Rosecrans turning left in the ravine, and passing to the point where McCook had been posted that morning. Garfield, Bond, and a few others were with him. He was attempting to join Thomas by way of the Dry Valley road.

For three hundred yards the party galloped through a shower of grape, canister and musketry. At the rear of his shattered right, Rosecrans observed the magnitude of the collapse, and when he heard heavy musketry fire and cheers and noted how the Confederates veered across the road, forming a barrier between himself and Thomas, he began to doubt whether even the left had held its ground. The party headed up the Dry Valley road for Rossville, in an attempt to reach Thomas through the Rossville gap. They forced their way through masses of fugitives. Although men on foot, officers on horseback, wagons, caissons, ambulances, clogged the road, the first wild panic had subsided. Rosecrans urged Van Cleve's fugitives to look for Sheridan. Garfield later told Cox that Rosecrans "rode silently along, abstracted, as if he neither saw nor heard." The correspondent of the Cincinnati *Commercial* wrote: "A rumor came back to several of Rosecrans' staff that he had last been seen leading a charge. He was either missing or dead. I heard it, and thought involuntarily of Libby Prison."

At Rossville the group drew rein. Around them milled fragments of the right, stragglers, and wagons. "What happened?" men asked. Some answered: "The whole army is licked. Rosecrans and Thomas are killed, and McCook and Crittenden captured."

A small detachment of Negley's men rode up. "Where is General Negley?" Rosecrans asked. The answer was disheartening. One of Rosecrans' last orders had sent Negley to Thomas' extreme left. Now his men reported Negley beyond the gap, but short of the battlefield. His division had been "knocked to pieces," and he was trying to rally stragglers. Rosecrans knew that such information, if true, meant that the center and left had also collapsed. He could not know that Negley, instead of joining Thomas immediately, had disappeared from the line, and drifted from the field to Rossville, and while two of his brigades reached the left, they arrived so tardily as to be of small help to Thomas.

Because heavy firing from the Kelly farm might indicate that Thomas still fought, Rosecrans and Garfield knelt and placed their ears to the ground. The sounds were difficult to identify. Were they irregular musketry or regular volleys?

What now took place became vague and confused in the remembering, and telling, and retelling. Historian Cist, of Rosecrans' staff, says that the sound of scattered musketry without artillery convinced Rosecrans that his army was "entirely broken." Garfield thereupon argued that it was his duty as commander-in-chief to go to Chattanooga, there to make such reorganization of the broken army, as it straggled in, as would prevent its complete destruction.

Cox maintains that Garfield told him that he and Rosecrans both heard regular volleys and knew that the left still made organized resistance. To Garfield's offer to return to investigate, Rosecrans assented "listlessly and mechanically," ordering him to tell Thomas that he could withdraw at his discretion.

Rosecrans himself insisted:

In view of all the interests at stake I decided what must be done. I said to General Garfield and Major Bond: "By the sound of the battle over to the southeast, we hold our ground. Our greatest danger is that Longstreet will follow us up the Dry Valley Road. Post, with all of our commissary stores, is over the ridge, not more than two or three miles from the Dry Valley Road. If Longstreet advances and finds that out, he may capture them. This would be fatal to us. If he comes this way, he will turn the rear of our left, seize the gap at Rossville, and disperse us. To provide against what may happen: *First,* Sheridan and Davis must have renewed orders to resist the enemy's advance on the Dry Valley Road. *Second,* Post must be ordered to push all our trains into Chattanooga and securely park them there. *Third,* orders must go to Mitchell to extend his cavalry line obliquely across that ridge, connect with the right of Sheridan's position on this valley, and cover Post's train from the enemy until they are out of danger. *Fourth,* orders must go to Spear's brigade, now arrived near there, to take possession of the Rolling-Mill bridge across Chattanooga Creek, put it in good order, hold it until Post arrives with his trains, then turn the bridge over to him and march out on the Rossville Road and await orders. *Fifth,* Wagner in Chattanooga must have orders to park our reserve artillery defensively, guard our pontoon bridge across the Tennessee, north of the town, and have his men under arms ready to move as may be required. *Sixth,* General Thomas must be seen as to the condition of the battle and be informed of these dispositions.

General Garfield, can you not give these orders?" I asked. Garfield answered:

"General, there are so many of them I fear I may make some mistakes, but I can go to General Thomas for you, see how things are, tell him what you will do, and report to you."

"Very well, I will take Major Bond and give the orders myself. I will be in Chattanooga as soon as possible. The telegraph line reaches Rossville, and we have an office there. Go by Sheridan and Davis and tell them what I wish, then go to Thomas, and telegraph me the situation."

Rosecrans himself said in his *Report* that the safety of his trains was uppermost in his mind: "It was to provide for the security of these trains . . . and that they should be moved into Chattanooga after our right was driven back . . . that I directed special attention."

In any event, whether he did or did not know that Thomas still held the field, it was a catastrophe that Rosecrans did not himself ride to Thomas, and send Garfield to Chattanooga. Had he gone to the front in person and shown himself to his men, as at Stone River, he might by his personal presence have plucked victory from disaster, although it is doubtful whether he could have done more than Thomas did. Rosecrans, however, rode to Chattanooga instead. Says Cist: "That was the turning point and his hour had arrived." Five years after Chickamauga, Swinton wrote that "if Rosecrans had been correct in his theory as to the fortune of the day, he did the best thing that could possibly be done in returning to Chattanooga. He was not right in his theory, and his action in accordance with that theory was a great error." For while Rosecrans went to Chattanooga, Thomas and two-thirds of the Union army were making a desperate yet magnificent stand that has become a proud part of the military epic of America. Thomas, Rosecrans' firm friend and loyal lieutenant, would thereafter justly be known as the Rock of Chickamauga.

Unaware of the disaster that had crushed the right, the four divisions that that day constituted the left—Baird's, Johnson's, Palmer's and Reynolds's—continued to face the exhausted Confederate right under Polk. To the right of these four divisions, but for hours separated from them, the withdrawing divisions of Wood and Brannan fell into line. These were joined by fragments of other scattered divisions, until finally Thomas held a more or less continuous line, stretching in a great semicircle from the LaFayette road across the Kelly farm and on to Snodgrass Hill. Against the right of this line Longstreet and the Confederate left made heavy and costly assault. When it seemed that it too must be crushed, Granger and Steedman with the Reserve Corps, marching without orders to the sound of fighting, arrived and turned the tide. Thomas miraculously held this position until nightfall, and then, on Rosecrans' orders, successfully withdrew, first to Rossville to cover the gaps through which the roads to Chattanooga run, and later to Chattanooga itself.

If Rosecrans could not correctly assess his defeat, neither could Bragg his victory. Thomas had so punished Polk that Bragg refused Longstreet's request at 2:30 for reinforcements so that, while part of his command held its gains, the rest might pursue the remnants of Rosecrans' right down the Dry Valley Road. He said that only Longstreet's troops had any fight in them. Longstreet believed that at 3:00 P.M. Bragg thought the battle lost, "though he did not say so positively."

It is probable that as Rosecrans rode into Chattanooga and drew rein at General Wagner's headquarters sometime between 3:30 and 4:00 P.M., he did not know that Thomas was saving the day and the army. The uncertainty must have added to his exhaustion, which by now so consumed him that he had to be helped from his horse into the house. Crittenden and McCook, whose destinies were tied to his, came after him into Chattanooga after heroic efforts to rally resistance.

Crittenden arrived first—sometime between 3:00 and 4:00 P.M. —and reported to departmental headquarters. McCook wandered miles out of his way and, arriving sometime between 4:30 and 5:00, reported to Rosecrans at General Wagner's headquarters. He was ready to take the field, he said, and asked for orders. "Wait a short time until I hear General Garfield's report from the extreme front," Rosecrans advised. "We hold the field. Granger has gone up from Rossville. A portion of yours and Crittenden's corps are reported near Rossville, and the arrival of a further report from General Garfield will enable me to give more definite instructions both to you and General Crittenden." Captain Joseph Hill heard Rosecrans order McCook to "lie down and rest." Rosecrans said:

"I am nearly worn out and I want someone with me to take command, if necessary to assist me."

But his exhaustion had not kept Rosecrans from giving immediate attention to the business he had outlined for Garfield. He dispatched messengers to Mitchell and Post; gave orders in person to General James G. Spears, whose brigade of the Reserve Corps guarded the bridge across Chickamauga Creek near the tannery, to prevent all able-bodied soldiers below the rank of major-general from entering Chattanooga, and to Wagner; and at 4:15 sent an aide to Thomas, ordering him to "assume command of all the forces, and with Crittenden and McCook, take a strong position and assume a threatening attitude at Rossville. Send all the unorganized forces to this place for reorganization. I will examine the ground here and make such dispositions for defence as the case may require and join you. Have sent out ammunition with rations."

After Crittenden's arrival, but before McCook's, Rosecrans ordered Garfield to "see General McCook and other general officers. Ascertain extent of disaster as nearly as you can and report. Tell General Granger to contest the enemy's advance stubbornly, make them advance with caution. Should General Thomas be retiring in order, tell him to resist the enemy's advance, retiring on Rossville tonight."

Ducat's report—it lacks indication of the time of sending and receiving—brought a measure of cheer and security. Ducat was at the McFarland house in the Dry Valley, south of Rossville. There he had made a "strong rally, say of 10,000 men, and some seven or eight batteries, from many commands. . . . The enemy cannot well drive us from this point, as we command the gap. Generals Crittenden and Van Cleve have gone through this line to the rear." Ducat had not seen McCook. Sheridan, Davis, and Negley had just joined him, and he and Sheridan were going to join Thomas through Rossville by the LaFayette Road. "Things are not as bad as they might seem. Where are McCook and Granger? Hurry up Granger."

The first definite news of Thomas's stand apparently was brought by Captain Joseph Hill, who reached Sheridan by way of Rossville, with a message for Rosecrans that Thomas was "all right; had stood his ground, and driven the enemy from the front."

At 5:00 P.M. Rosecrans telegraphed to Halleck: "We have met

with a serious disaster; extent not yet ascertained. Enemy over-whelmed us, drove our right, pierced our center, and scattered troops there. Thomas, who had seven divisions, remained intact at last news. Granger, with two brigades, has gone to support Thomas on the left." And he advised Burnside: "We have met with a severe disaster. . . . If you are near enough to join us, do so at once."

But Washington already knew. At 4:00 P.M., Dana had tele-graphed: "My report today is of deplorable importance. Chicka-mauga is as fatal a name in our history as Bull Run. . . . It was wholesale panic. . . . Enemy not yet arrived before Chattanooga. . . . Preparations making to resist his entrance for a time." Acting as his own cipher clerk, Dana sent the message in the War Depart-ment secret code, which was broken only once, and that at this inopportune moment. The operator at Nashville guessed the content of the telegram and passed the news around, so that the Associated Press representative in Louisville was able to prepare a circular which quoted Dana's statement, "Chickamauga is as fatal a name in our history as Bull Run." The army telegraph later that evening revealed more. A laconic telegram signed "Stevens" reached Major Thomas Eckert at Cincinnati at 7:45: "You may expect bad news from Department of the Cumberland. General Rosecrans is in Chattanooga."

Garfield's dispatch, datelined, "General Thomas' Headquarters, Battlefield, Five Miles South of Rossville—3:45 P.M.," reached Rosecrans about 5:00.

General Thomas has Brannan's, Baird's, Reynolds', Wood's, Palmer's, and Johnson's divisions still intact after terrible fighting. Granger is here, closed up with Thomas and is fighting terribly on the right. Sheridan is in with the bulk of his division, but in ragged shape, though plucky and fighting. . . . I hope General Thomas will be able to hold on here till night, and will not need to fall back farther than Rossville; perhaps not any. . . . I think we may in the main retrieve our morning disaster. I never saw better fighting than our men are now doing. . . . Granger thinks we can defeat them badly tomorrow if all our forces come in. I think you had better come to Rossville tonight and bring ammunition.

To this good news Rosecrans responded: "Your dispatch of 3:45 received. What you propose is correct."

News continued to improve. Wilder reported at 6:00 P.M. that he had driven the enemy from their position at Widow Glenn's and nearly to the LaFayette road, when they came in at his rear and threatened to cut him off. He then fell back to Chattanooga Valley. His five regiments were in good condition. Rosecrans ordered Wilder to push forward on Missionary Ridge, and there open communications with Mitchell, who had been holding the Chickamauga fords all day. At 7:15 P.M. Rosecrans warned Mitchell to watch Wheeler, "lest he go over the mountains and seize our bridges."

As the picture clarified it improved. At 7:00 P.M. Negley reported from Rossville that he and Davis, on a tour of observation up the Crawfish Spring road, had reached a point within a mile and a half of the Widow Glenn's without finding any Confederates, and at 7:05 Captain A. S. Burt sent another dispatch from Rossville: "We have succeeded in getting the troops organized at this place with some six or seven batteries intact." From Ringgold Road, Minty reported that he had finally gathered enough of his scattered details together to drive Scott—not Forrest—across the creek.

Now the broad outlines grew clear. Thomas blocked the direct road to Chattanooga, while cavalry covered both flanks of the army. At Rossville, behind Thomas, were thousands of disorganized but serviceable troops. While much artillery had been lost, most of the trains were safe. By 8:00 P.M. Dana telegraphed:

I am happy to report that my dispatch of 4:00 P.M. today proves to have given too dark a view of our disaster. Having been myself swept off the battlefield . . . my own impressions were naturally colored by the aspect of that part of the field. . . . Thomas, with the remainder of the army still holds his part of the field. . . . Some gentlemen of Rosecrans' staff say Chickamauga is not very much worse than was Murfreesboro. I can testify to the conspicuous and steady gallantry of Rosecrans on the field. He made all possible efforts to rally the broken columns; nor do I say that there was any fault in the disposition of his forces. The disaster might perhaps have been averted but for the blunder of McCook in marching back from his previous advanced position. That blunder cost us four days of precious time.

On Rosecrans' orders, at about dusk Crittenden had left for his own headquarters to rest, in order to be ready to return to the front. At 9:00 P.M., Crittenden sent Starling to Rosecrans' headquarters to see if news of importance had arrived. Starling remained there until 10:30 and returned to find Crittenden asleep; he did not wake him since no report of importance had come in. Crittenden's orders were to report at midnight and proceed with McCook to the front. At the appointed time Crittenden was present.

Granger brought in Garfield's long dispatch at 8:40 P.M., although he failed to mention the incident in his *Official Report*.

> General Thomas has fought a most terrific battle and has damaged the enemy badly. General Granger's troops moved up just in time and fought magnificently. From the time I reached the battlefield (3:45 P.M.) till sunset the fighting was by far the fiercest I have ever seen. Our men not only held their ground, but at many points drove the enemy splendidly. . . . The disaster on the right . . . must be considerable in men and material, especially the latter. The rebels have, however, done their best today, and I believe we can whip them tomorrow. . . . Granger regards them as thoroughly whipped tonight, and thinks they would not renew the fight were we to remain on the field. . . . The troops are now moving back, and will be here in good shape and strong position before morning. I hope you will not budge an inch from this place, but come up early in the morning and if the rebs try it on, accommodate them. . . . I am half dead with fatigue. Answer if I can do anything here.

As Rosecrans finished reading, he burst out with "Thank God"; read it aloud, and waved it over his head. "This is good enough. The day isn't lost yet!" "Gentlemen," he cried—one version says "to McCook and Crittenden," an obvious error since Crittenden was at his own headquarters—"this is no place for you. Go at once to your commands at the front." Then he ordered Wagner to go to the outskirts of Chattanooga and stop all stragglers from the front. Rations and ammunition were to be sent out to meet the troops at Rossville.

When he began to prepare detailed orders for Thomas, Granger interrupted. "That's all nonsense, General. Send Thomas an order to retire. He knows what he's about as well as you do." And so Rosecrans sent a simple order. Finally, he sent a dispatch to Garfield: "You may stay all night. If the enemy are drifting toward our left . . . have men ordered up. I like your suggestions."

Rosecrans' account of the same incident tells how he read Garfield's dispatch to McCook, and at 9:30 directed him to proceed to Rossville and there assume command of his corps. He told Mc-

Cook that the Union army would occupy a position near Rossville, which Thomas had been ordered to select. By 9:45, full communications between headquarters and the army in the field were apparently re-established, because at that time Garfield expressed the "pleasure of the general commanding" to Wilder for his report of 6:00 P.M.

Crittenden returned to Rosecrans' headquarters at 11:00 P.M. Three hours later, Rosecrans ordered him to proceed to Rossville, gather his two divisions, and report to Thomas. Rousseau, McCook, and Crittenden then set out together on the LaFayette road.

In the early hours a telegraph operator brought in Lincoln's message, dated 12:35 A.M., September 21, 1863:

> Be of good cheer. We have unabated confidence in you and in your soldiers and officers. In the main you must be the judge of what is to be done. If I was to suggest, I would say save your army by taking strong positions until Burnside joins you, when I hope you can turn the tide. I think you had better send a courier to Burnside to hurry him up. We cannot reach him by telegraph. We suppose some force is going to you from Corinth but for want of communications we do not know how they are getting along. We shall do our utmost to assist you. Send us your present posting.

Sixteen

THE EYES OF THE FERRET

John Fiske has pointed out that "Chickamauga was the greatest battle fought by our western armies, and one of the greatest of modern times. In our Civil War it was exceeded only by Gettysburg and the Wilderness; in European history we may compare it with Waterloo."

Livermore estimated that in troops engaged, Bragg had an advantage of some 8,000 or about 14 per cent more than Rosecrans. He puts Bragg's total at 66,326; Rosecrans' at 58,222. Underwood and Buell give Bragg an even greater advantage: 71,551 to Rosecrans' 59,965. Livermore estimates Union losses at 1,657 killed, 9,765 wounded, and 4,757 missing, for a total of 16,179. Bragg lost 2,316 killed, 1,320 wounded, 1,468 missing, for a total of 16,986. The collapse of Rosecrans' right and his retreat spared Bragg heavy loss from capture. Nevertheless, the percentage of Confederate losses was the war's heaviest.

Union General O. O. Howard maintained that "Chickamauga resulted, notwithstanding our heavy losses and partial defeats, in a substantial success, for Rosecrans had gained Chattanooga, and thus firmly seized the left bank of the Tennessee."

Bragg's immediate claims were modest: "We have driven the enemy from several positions, and now hold the field, but he still confronts us. The losses are heavy on both sides." Whereupon Lincoln telegraphed to Rosecrans: "You see he does not claim so many prisoners or captured guns as you were inclined to concede."

While calling the battle "decidedly victorious," the Richmond

Sentinel expressed its fear that "as Rosecrans is an obstinate fighter, and his army was yet unbroken, the finale might be like Shiloh, Corinth and Murfreesboro."

"We suppress exultation," said the Richmond *Whig*, "at the thought of what yet remains to be done. The victory that does not disperse or capture his whole army is a lost opportunity. If he is permitted to hold Chattanooga, then our victory will be without profit. If he holds it, he holds a point from which he may at any moment strike at the vitals of the Confederacy." Confederate historian Pollard wrote: "Chickamauga had conferred a brilliant glory on our arms, but little else. Rosecrans still held the prize of Chattanooga, and with it the possession of East Tennessee," with easy access to Virginia, North Carolina, Georgia, and Alabama.

Stanton concluded, after reading the Richmond papers, that the Confederates felt that their army had barely escaped a fatal defeat. And Lincoln wrote to his wife: "We are worsted, if at all, only in the fact that we, after the main fighting was over, yielded ground."

The importance of Chickamauga is indisputable. "Except Petersburg," said Archibald Gracie, "where the final issue was settled, there was no more important battle of the Confederate war than Chickamauga." And years later the temperate judgment of a competent Confederate authority, General Daniel H. Hill, who fought under Bragg, appeared. In spite of Chickamauga, Hill pointed out, Rosecrans held Chattanooga, "the objective point of the campaign. . . There was no more splendid fighting in '61, than was displayed in those bloody days of September, '63. But it seems to me that the *elan* of the Southern soldier was never seen after Chickamauga. . . . He was too intelligent not to know that the cutting in two of Georgia meant death to all his hopes. . . . He fought stoutly to the last, but, after Chickamauga, with the sullenness of despair and without the enthusiasm of hope. That 'barren victory' sealed the fate of the Confederacy." Hill's opinion agrees with Rosecrans' statement to Halleck: "Enemy confronts us, but we have taken the starch out of him."

A week after Chickamauga, Quartermaster-General Montgomery Meigs reported to Stanton from Chattanooga: "It is difficult for the leaders to abstain from claiming a complete victory. . . . Chattanooga is fast becoming a fortress and depot which will serve as a base of future operations. . . . It appears to me that the great effort of the rebels, by which concentrating in Georgia, they hoped to crush this army and recover possession of Tennessee and Kentucky, has failed. If so, the fruits of victory are with General Rosecrans"—though he admitted the trophies were Bragg's.

Stanton certainly knew that some blame for the disaster would be put on him. His dislike of Rosecrans was public knowledge, and after Chickamauga, Sanderson heard "denunciation, fierce and strong, from all quarters against the Secretary of War for not reinforcing this army. If the demands of General Rosecrans . . . had been granted, instead of being here we should now be upon the Atlantic seaboard." If Sanderson heard such talk, Dana heard it, and if Dana, then Stanton also heard it. From West Virginia, Governor Pierpont wrote to Rosecrans: "For two days I have been blue with anxiety . . . for the safety of your brave army. I have known for many days, as I suppose the Department in Washington has known, that a strong force had been taken from Lee's army to reinforce Bragg. I trembled for the consequences."

When news of the battle reached Henry Adams in London he was "painfully impressed with the conviction that our government has again proved incompetent, and has neglected to take those measures of security which it ought to have done." Adams, the son and secretary of the minister to England, was far from affairs at Chattanooga; yet it is interesting to note that he and others were beginning to hold Washington—rather than the field commanders —responsible for Union reverses.

From midnight until near noon on September 21, the day after Chickamauga, Bragg possibly might have retaken Chattanooga. When the defensive weakness of the Rossville position became apparent, Rosecrans ordered Thomas to maintain his line until night and then withdraw. Beatty considered the Union army "simply a mob. . . . Were a division of the enemy to pounce upon us between this and morning, I fear the army would be blotted out." In the morning, Garfield notified Rosecrans that he was not sure the Rossville line was suitable, or that much reliance could be placed on the stampeded troops. "On the whole, I do not feel sure but that you ought to remain in Chattanooga till we see the developments and organize the rear."

Forrest rose early on the 21st and surveyed the Union army from a treetop on Missionary Ridge. He concluded that it was routed. Below him masses of men struggled to the rear, while others felled trees to prevent pursuit. Artillery and wagons were terribly tangled. "Every hour is worth a thousand men," he informed Bragg. However, knowing his losses, Bragg ordered no general advance.

Gracie believed that "the halt to Confederate pursuit was the most stupendous blunder of the war," and Confederate Daniel Hill maintained that "the great blunder of all was that of not pursuing the enemy on the 21st." Hill felt that Bragg did not know that he had won a victory until the morning of the 21st.

The Confederates spent the day burying dead and gathering loot, and Bragg's opportunity vanished, and with it the major profit of his victory. Slowly the Union chaos subsided. At Rossville, Beatty saw the confusion end as "officers found their regiments, regiments their brigades, and brigades their divisions." Except for outposts and parties of observation, the whole army was in Chattanooga by midnight, and "in wonderful spirits considering their excessive fatigue and heavy losses," Dana reported to Stanton. Although 2,200 of Rousseau's division had been killed or wounded, he rode out that night to meet them on his return from Washington, to find the survivors in fine spirits and ready to fight: "As I write, cheers are going up."

No immediate shortages existed in Chattanooga except forage. Rosecrans' urgent task was to hold the town. Outnumbered and in a rugged and hostile country, his army had lost offensive power. It was vulnerable on both flanks; it required rest, reorganization, and cover for its communications and, to resume the offensive, it needed reinforcement, but despite his declared good intentions, Lincoln was not very helpful in providing it. He preferred to suggest rather than to issue orders to his generals. The phrases, "This is more social than official," or "This is not an order," characterize his letters. Such expressions failed to move Burnside.

Orders had specified that Rosecrans' campaign would be a joint operation by the Armies of the Cumberland and the Ohio. Burnside, however, failed to co-operate. He considered Buckner's withdrawal a defeat, and, instead of uniting with Rosecrans to prevent Buckner's junction with Bragg, marched sixty miles from Knoxville to Cumberland Gap and there won an inconsequential victory. While there he received Crittenden's dispatch telling that

Rosecrans had occupied Chattanooga while Bragg was retreating to Rome. Crittenden's last sentence was clear: Rosecrans "requests that you move down your cavalry and occupy the country recently covered by Colonel Minty . . . who has been ordered to cross the river." Burnside concluded that Rosecrans needed no help.

The three-way correspondence between Rosecrans, Burnside, and Washington constitutes not only a portrait of Burnside but an indictment of the Washington administration. Halleck's repeated theme was: "The enemy will concentrate to give Rosecrans battle. You must be there to help him." And Burnside's response was no less unvaried: "Am now sending every man that can be spared to aid Rosecrans." Yet he sent no one. When news of Chickamauga reached him, Burnside assured Halleck that although he was hurrying troops toward Rosecrans, he had undertaken to capture Jonesboro. Finally at 11:00 A.M. on September 21, Lincoln stepped in. "If you are to do any good to Rosecrans, it will not do to waste time with Jonesboro. It is already too late to do the most good that might have been done, but I hope it will do some good. Please do not lose a moment." Lincoln's telegram only confused Burnside. Did he want him to evacuate east Tennessee? He denied delaying; besides, he needed more information regarding Rosecrans' position.

Lincoln answered patiently: "My order to you meant simply that you should save Rosecrans from being crushed out, believing if he lost his position you could not hold East Tennessee in any event; and that if he held his position, East Tennessee was substantially safe in any event." He concluded: "This dispatch is in no sense an order." And Halleck said: "These orders are very plain, and you cannot mistake their purport. It only remains for you to execute them." "I am ready to do it immediately if ordered," was a typical Burnside response, and so was Halleck's: "I can only repeat former instructions. I cannot make them plainer."

Beatty wrote in his diary that at Chickamauga, officers "shouted Burnside at the boys until we became hoarse. But, alas, by nightfall Burnside had played out. . . . [He] is now regarded as a myth, a fictitious warrior, who is said to be coming to the relief of men sorely pressed, but who never comes." Greeley sneered: "The military reading of General-in-Chief having been very extensive, he can probably cite numerous instances wherein the leader of a small army has made haste to unite that army with a large one, which would necessarily absorb it, without having been placed under the orders of its commander; but, in the recollection of this writer, such instances are rare. At all events, Burnside did not add another." Halleck's summary is deadly: "As Burnside could not be persuaded to go to Rosecrans' assistance (I telegraphed him fifteen times to do so, and the President three or four times), it became necessary to send him two corps from the Army of the Potomac, thus destroying all our plans here."

Although War Department orders were issued on September 15, Grant's relieving column under Sherman did not reach Chattanooga for two months, and as far as Rosecrans was concerned gave no more aid than Burnside's, which failed to arrive. When Grant was made supreme Western Commander, he cut red tape, and Sherman arrived. The Vicksburg correspondent of the Cincinnati *Commercial* was to write a month later: "I have heard the very pertinent question asked whether it was the design to succor Rosecrans in this war or the next."

Effective rescue was to come from the Army of the Potomac, and through Stanton's energetic action. Stanton had ordered the Army of the Cumberland across the Tennessee into Georgia. Then came Dana's dismaying telegrams: "The Confederacy seems concentrated here"; and, if "Ewell be really here, Rosecrans will have to retreat beyond the Tennessee"; and, a few hours later, "There is no time to wait for reinforcements, and Rosecrans is determined not to abandon Chattanooga and Bridgeport without another effort. Battle here will probably be fought tomorrow or next day."

Dana's "disaster" telegram moved Stanton to action. He sent for Lincoln, aroused Halleck and the Cabinet, and told them that he thought he could send 20,000 veterans from Meade's army, the force to reach Chattanooga in five days. Lincoln was skeptical. "I bet you can't get them even to Washington in ten days," he said. But if 20,000 bales of cotton could make the trip in five days, 20,000 soldiers could. Halleck estimated that forty days would be needed. Stanton then asked General D. C. McCallum how long the job would take him. "Seven days," said McCallum. Stanton turned to Halleck: "Forty days!—when the life of a nation is at stake." He immediately ordered the XI Corps, under Howard, and the XII, under Slocum, to Chattanooga, with Hooker commanding the movement.

The rail operation that followed has been called the most dramatic of the war. Marching orders were issued on Tuesday, September 22. On Sunday, September 26, troops, artillery, and horses were crowded into cars, and the train, six miles long, pulled out in sections at half-hour intervals. On Friday, October 2, five days after starting the 1,200-mile journey, the advance reached Bridgeport, where Howard established headquarters. Hooker set up headquarters at Stevenson, eight miles east.

Stanton's determination to remove Rosecrans strengthened. "If Hooker's command got safely through, all the Army of the Cumberland can need will be a competent commander."

The army at Chattanooga began digging itself in. Entrenchments were weak and guns were unmounted. On Tuesday, the 22nd, fires were kept to a minimum. At 3:00 A.M. every man stood on the line. All day soldiers improvised rifle pits. The defensive position, laid out by Morton, extended about three miles across the peninsula, some two miles from its extremity. McCook held the right, Thomas the center, the line's weakest part, and Crittenden the left. Throughout the morning Bragg menaced in three columns but made no assault.

The Union army still mustered 35,000 effectives and had ten days' rations, which could, if necessary, be stretched to twenty, and enough ammunition for a two days' fight in the field, and a longer fight behind rifle pits. Although Rosecrans first believed that, unless ample reinforcements were assured within ten days, retreating would be safer than remaining, by 9:30 on the 22nd he had decided to hold Chattanooga at all hazards. The headquarters staff, however, still kept baggage packed. Rosecrans toured each regiment and battalion. Sanderson wrote that he was everywhere "vociferously" applauded. Throughout the day regimental bands played patriotic airs.

Lincoln telegraphed on the 24th: "With Burnside, Sherman, and from elsewhere we shall get to you from 40,000 to 60,000 additional men." And Halleck promised: "In addition to the expected assistance to you from Burnside, Hurlbut and Sherman, 14,000 or 15,000 men from here will be in Nashville in about seven days. The government deems it very important that Chattanooga be held till reinforcements arrive."

On the 23rd, the regiment at the head of Lookout Mountain

was threatened with being cut off, and on Rosecrans' orders withdrew, destroying the wagon road behind it. Rosecrans believed that if he were reinforced, he could retake the position. Dana wrote that Rosecrans was "obstinate and inaccessible to reason" about the matter.

Rosecrans ordered ammunition brought up to Chattanooga, fifty wagons at a time, along the north bank of the Tennessee. He sent Mitchell to scour the country for eight or ten days' forage. He made provisions to arm convalescents in the Bridgeport hospital, so they could defend the Tennessee river line. He dispatched Minty on a reconnaissance in front. Until rifle pits were ready, he stationed Thomas along a narrow path covered by the railway embankment. He directed Crittenden to cut all available timber on Palmer's front for an abatis. He ordered Crook to cover the ford four miles above Island Ferry, and to employ his spare time in constructing an inner line, to be masked with bushes. Officers apologized as tired men complained, but orders kept the soldiers digging in relays around the clock, and shovels were handed from squad to squad.

Dana telegraphed Stanton on the 24th: "This place . . . will hold out. . . . It can be taken only by regular siege. The labors of this army for the last forty-eight hours have been herculean. As soon as Hooker arrives and Sherman and Hurlbut make their appearance in Tuscumbia Valley, it will be able to resume the offensive irresistibly." And Quartermaster General Meigs, who had hurried to Chattanooga, agreed: "I have seen the men, vigorous, hearty, cheerful and confident. The position is very strong already, and rapidly approaching a perfect security against assault. Nothing but a regular siege could, I think, reduce it."

Union lines extended across the widest portion of the peninsula. To the rear of rifle pits, breastworks of solid earth were constructed, and behind these rose an interior chain of redoubts connected by another line of breastworks. Cameron Hill, a steep elevation on the western side, was crowned with a citadel in which heavy guns were mounted in a bombproof shelter. The opposing Confederate lines, concealed in timber, stretched facing the town for a distance of about eight miles, from near the abutment of Missionary Ridge, along the brow of the ridge, across Chattanooga Creek, and up the slopes of Lookout Mountain.

Work on restoring the railroad was pushed with vigor. Dana passed through Bridgeport on the 27th and saw the railroad bridge there nearing completion, and the Running Water bridge almost ready to be put up. One of Rosecrans' major inventions was born at this time out of the need to move his wounded to hospitals farther north. Upon Rosecrans' orders—although credit is sometimes given to Medical Director Cooper—railroad coaches were prepared for transporting the wounded in some degree of comfort. "An arrangement of slats converted ordinary day-coach seats into 'lower berths.' Litters hanging from braces attached to the side walls formed 'uppers'." In this arrangement lay the basic scheme of the Pullman car.

"All the eastern troops must concentrate at Bridgeport," Rosecrans telegraphed to Colonel Thomas A. Scott at Louisville on September 29; and he ordered Colonel William P. Innes, military superintendent of the Nashville and Chattanooga Railroad, to "strain every nerve to send through Hooker's corps."

Again the question of supply became all absorbing. Railroad trains were running from Murfreesboro to Bridgeport. The Bridgeport depot was not empty, but how to haul freight from Bridgeport to Chattanooga was a difficult problem.

Five routes, four short and one long, joined the towns. The first was the railroad, temporarily useless because the trestle bridges across the Tennessee and at Running Water had been burned. The second, the wagon road, ran along the south bottoms, parallel to the tracks. The third was the river, unnavigable after six weeks of drought. The fourth was the road along the north bank. Although wagon trains at first traveled this route, the Union withdrawal from Lookout brought it within easy range of Confederate sharpshooters. These did most damage along the Narrows, where the road lay fifty yards from the bank, and the river was about 300 yards wide. Soon trains abandoned this road for the fifth route, the long road, a difficult, hazardous trail leading over the pontoon bridge at Chattanooga, across the bottoms, over Walden's Ridge, through the Sequatchie Valley, over the Cumberland plateau, and westerly across the barrens, to Bridgeport. It crossed country stripped of forage, and without drinking water during drought. After rains it became a greasy, washed-out hell. No one at first realized how bad it was, and Dana telegraphed Stanton:

"It will be difficult for the enemy to interfere with our hauling from Bridgeport via Jasper." Dana proved a poor prophet.

Disagreements between Bragg and his generals assisted Rosecrans. Immediately after Chickamauga, Longstreet proposed to flank rather than besiege Chattanooga. The whole Confederate army should cross to the north bank and menace Rosecrans' communications, compelling him to evacuate Chattanooga and retreat to Nashville. If Bragg were handicapped by a lack of transportation, he could move against Burnside, destroy him, and return to Rosecrans, again to menace his communications. Bragg condemned this plan for

. . . its entire lack of military propriety. It abandoned to the enemy our entire line of communication and laid open to him our depots of supplies, while it placed us with a greatly inferior force, beyond a difficult and at times impassable river, in a country affording no subsistence for men or animals. It also left open to the enemy, at a distance of only 10 miles, our battlefield. . . . All this was to be risked and given up for what? To gain the enemy's rear, and cut him off from his depot of supplies by the route over the mountains, when the very movement abandoned to his unmolested use the better and more practicable route, of half the length, on the south side of the river.

Bragg's plan was to hold Rosecrans in Chattanooga, meanwhile striking at his vulnerable supply route with cavalry. If he were so harassed, Bragg believed, Rosecrans' destruction would be "only a matter of time." Bragg arranged his army in a semicircle to the south and west of Chattanooga.

Bragg occupied the point of Lookout on September 24, and Longstreet crossed into Lookout Valley and pushed his pickets along the south bank almost to Bridgeport, simultaneously closing all four short routes to Rosecrans. South and east of the burned Bridgeport bridge, the Confederates controlled the railroad. As Longstreet approached, the Federals disconnected the pontoon bridge from the south bank. The south bank road, over the nose of Lookout, was completely controlled by Bragg, and his artillery on Lookout dominated the river. Only the long route remained available.

Rosecrans' most urgent problem, therefore, was to reopen short supply routes into Chattanooga. Accordingly, he immediately ordered four steamboats to be built there and one at Bridgeport, and the damaged Chattanooga ferryboat to be converted into a transport. He further ordered several sawmills to be repaired, and a dismantled foundry to be turned into a smithy. As September ended, these establishments were producing lumber and metal fittings. Later, when Hooker arrived, Rosecrans directed him to select enough material at Bridgeport for one bridge, and to ship the rest to Chattanooga.

To improve the long route, on the 24th Rosecrans ordered Ducat to ascertain the most practicable wagon road from Chattanooga to Jasper. Ducat thought he could "wiggle a road through that will be 50% better" than part of the long road. His report marked the beginning of a struggle to improve and keep open a road so vital to the army that men charged with its maintenance reported directly to Rosecrans. The efforts availed little. Heavy traffic and rains quickly cut through its surfacing so that, by the middle of October, the road was deeply rutted, and in low spots mules sank belly-deep in the mud; and causeways were needed to get wagons across "innumerable sink holes and beds of quicksand."

To permit direct hauling into Chattanooga, two trestle bridges were begun, with knowledge that a flood would sweep them away. Rosecrans ordered the construction also of two pontoon bridges. On September 27, Meigs reported: "The roads are rocky and mountainous, yet trains get through without much destruction of wagons. When the river rises the bridges will go, but the river will become navigable. One steam-boat and a few flats are ready for service. . . . When the troops understood to be on their way here arrive, General Rosecrans expects to recover command of the river to Bridgeport. Supplies can then be accumulated by water."

Chattanooga soon looked like a place besieged. Earth was parched and cracked, and after two months' drought, the grass was burned and gray. Trees had been cut down for fuel or fortifications. Dust covered everything, so that moving men or animals stirred up choking clouds. Cavalrymen took shortcuts over sidewalks, showering pedestrians with dirt. Teamsters cursed, while loungers listened and laughed.

The army lay quartered in tents on the outskirts, while headquarters personnel occupied town houses. A single room in a small cottage with a leaky roof served Rosecrans as office, conference room, and bedchamber.

Colonel Joseph F. Fullerton wrote later that Missionary Ridge, visible from the porch of the cottage, "summit, side, and base, was furrowed with rifle-pits and studded with batteries. The little valley of the Chattanooga was damned up with earth works; and Lookout Mountain, now a mighty fortress, lifted to the low-hanging clouds its threatening head crowned with seige-guns." With a glass, Rosecrans could watch Bragg's headquarters on Missionary Ridge, while from Lookout Mountain the whole Union camp lay exposed. By daylight, Fullerton said, "our troops could be counted, our reveille heard, our roll-call noted, our scanty meals of half-rations seen. . . . The enemy's signal flag on Lookout talked over our heads, with the signal flag on Missionary Ridge."

Each morning Union pickets stood at arms until the daylight fog rolled back. Picket stations were given signal rockets. Bragg first posted a battery of heavy, rifled guns on the east slope of Lookout and fired them for range, and soon the Confederates were moving much artillery up the mountainside and constructing placements for it. On October 5, regular, heavy shelling began. The army took the bombardment in stride. As Negro boys played marbles nearby, Union troops commented on the accuracy of the shooting and its probable damage. Early in the siege it was agreed unofficially that Chattanooga Creek should divide the two armies. Along its banks, pickets carried on daily conversation and in the evening, Confederate bands played "Dixie," and Union bands "Hail Columbia" and the "Star Spangled Banner." Headquarters forbade excessive fraternizing.

As September ended, the estimated ten-day supply of rations and forage for Rosecrans in Chattanooga was exhausted. However, a large supply and ammunition train, 800 wagons, was expected from Bridgeport. During the night of September 29, shifting winds broke the long dry spell. Next morning steady rains flooded out some regiments, pouring a foot and a half of water into their trenches. Most serious damage was to the long road. Meigs wrote to Stanton: "I never travelled on such roads before."

Rosecrans had been apprehensive that Bragg would strike at the long road and had assigned to General Crook and 2,000 men the impossible task of guarding the Tennessee River line for 50 miles, and to Mitchell the job of obstructing the approaches to all fords. He begged Halleck: "Cover my flanks." Warnings had come on the 24th when a prisoner told Rosecrans that Forrest's men were cooking rations to go to middle Tennessee. "The old general himself" said "he was going to cut off the supplies." Two days later a Louisiana deserter reported that the Confederates planned to cut communications in Rosecrans' rear, and Atlanta newspapers announced that Wheeler would raid even before he crossed the Tennessee. Upstream, for 50 miles, in addition to main fords, lay lesser-known crossings and shallows where fords could be improvised. Infrequent roads led to the water and were not connected along the thickly grown banks.

About noon on October 1, a mud-splashed courier brought the first news that Confederate cavalry were crossing at Cotton Port Ford. Crook was resisting. The next report told that Wheeler had broken across in several other places, with 5,000 or 6,000 cavalry and mounted infantry, and was off to the mountains with five days' rations. Crook could not concentrate quickly enough to prevent the crossings, and Wheeler outnumbered him. Forrest rode with Wheeler, with three badly armed brigades, scarcely five hundred men in each. As they passed before Wheeler the horses were foam-flecked and skinny. They had been driven hard for three days and nights without being unsaddled, and the riders were hollow-eyed and hungry.

Rosecrans ordered Crook to concentrate and give chase, while Dan McCook out of Bridgeport must intercept the raiders at Anderson's Crossroads. By now Wheeler had a half-day's start. Again Rosecrans besought Burnside: "You will have to close with them. We have sent ours."

On the 2nd, Wheeler reached the Sequatchie Valley and there divided his forces. Next morning, at 3:00 A.M., a detachment of 1,500 men, lunging toward Jasper, ten miles down the road, over-took a fleeing train of 32 six-mule-team wagons. Setting fire to the wagons, the Confederates rode on, the glow on their backs and the mules trotting beside them.

This destruction was prelude to a greater disaster. Near Anderson's Crossroads, Wheeler's main column brushed aside infantry and cavalry guards to uncover the great prize. Coiling slowly over the mountain struggled a train of 800 six-mule-team wagons, and an immense number of sutlers' wagons. The procession stretched for ten miles, from the top of Walden's Ridge to Jasper, and was so long only half was visible.

Panic seized the train, and teamsters leaning forward to lash their mules succeeded only in getting their wagons dragged halfway down the other side of the hill. At the summit, an ammunition wagon blew up. Soon the whole train stalled helplessly, and the raiders herded Union soldiers, teamsters, and sutlers into miserable groups. Then gray-clad horsemen dismounted and rummaged through wagons. They shouted gleefully about cases of whisky in sutlers' wagons, and women's clothes in nurses' trunks. Shoeless raiders tried on shoes; others replaced worn butternut pants with new Yankee trousers. Some shucked coats, boots, and shoes from Union officers and even demanded their money and watches. Confederate officers rode along the train selecting wagons and mules to be driven away. The order was given: "Kill the mules and burn the wagons!" The mountain road now became a slaughterhouse on fire. Men ran from wagon to wagon with torches, and at the crack of carbines mules reared and screamed in death agonies, hauling and upsetting blazing wagons. Two or three hundred mules were dispatched with cavalry sabers, and horses whinnied shrilly at the smell of smoke and blood. Some mules tore loose from their traces and crawled away; others rolled and tried to bite their wounds. Flames lapped at the canvas wagon covers, and sutlers turned their faces from the heat and their dreams of profit. Finally, taking with them what they could wear, or carry, or drive before them, including some unburned wagons and some horses and mules, the raiders galloped away from the smoke and the smell of singed animal hair, smoldering canvas, burning wood, and from the fetid fumes of leather, grease, gunpowder, and fresh blood. A light rain began to fall, but they were snug in new clothes, and warm with victory and sutlers' whisky. In eight undisturbed hours Wheeler ravaged the train and sent 400 of Rosecrans' wagons skyward in a great curving mane of smoke and fire which was visible for miles. The remainder were looted, driven off, or scattered. It was the funeral pyre of Rosecrans in top command.

Dan McCook's infantry and cavalry, slowed by heavy rain, had been splashing northward over narrow, slippery roads. When McCook saw the spiral above Anderson's Crossroads, he did not need croaking country people to tell him what had happened. Mc-Cook thundered past the smoldering wagons, caught up with Wheeler at dusk, and clung to his rear until dark. In the running fight, he recaptured about 500 mules and most of the unburned portion of the train and rescued some of Wheeler's prisoners, including a number of "benevolent ladies and gentlemen" who were going to the front as nurses. Captured Confederates were "wholly or partially" clothed in federal uniforms, and almost all were stuffed with plunder.

The ravaged wagons belonged to the divisions of Brannan, Negley, and Rousseau. In addition, an ammunition train and forty sutlers' wagons had been burned. While McCook salvaged what he could and then bivouacked, Wheeler's column pounded through the night, crossed the Cumberland highlands, and, descending the north slope about dawn, joined Wharton's force in moving upon McMinnville. By 10:30 A.M. on October 3, Wheeler faced the fortified town, and by noon Major M. L. Patterson, the Union commander, surrendered a large supply of quartermaster's and commissary stores, and a garrison of 587 men, with arms, accouterments, and horses. Wheeler spent a day and a night in destroying stores, a locomotive and train of cars, and a bridge. Once more, through no fault of his own, Dan McCook arrived too late, and once more evil tidings reached Chattanooga. Checking losses, Meigs fingered Stanton's telegram: "All quiet on the Potomac. . . . All public interest is now concentrated on the Tennessee and at Chattanooga."

On October 4 Burnside dispatched Rosecrans: "Is there any truth in the crossing of the enemy's cavalry at Cotton Port, which you reported?" And Rosecrans next day lashed back: "Having warned you often of the danger for the last ten days, and reported the catastrophe to you on the 1st, and got your promise to send your cavalry to help mine, I am amazed at your dispatch. I now say that your failure to close your troops down to our left has cost 500 wagons loaded with essentials, the post of McMinnville, and Heaven only knows where the mischief will end. . . . If you don't unite with us soon, you will be responsible for another catastrophe, I fear."

Two miles beyond McMinnville, Crook's cavalry had overtaken Wheeler. Twice Wheeler stood and twice fell back. With darkness,

Wheeler rode toward Murfreesboro to destroy the railroad. Guessing his purpose, however, Crook crossed to the Liberty turnpike, posted his force along Murfreesboro's approaches, and thus saved both the immense depot and the railroad to its north. Again Wheeler veered off, and with Crook pounding hard behind him, sacked Shelbyville on October 6, and near Wartrace tore up rails and burned a large trestle bridge. At Shelbyville, when the chase grew hot, Wheeler divided his force, and although many of his men were captured, killed, or wounded, by riding hard he reached Muscle Shoals with the remainder and on the 9th safely recrossed the Tennessee.

The XI Corps, of 5,834 effectives, had arrived at Bridgeport on October 2, while the XII Corps, of 9,245, was still passing through Nashville.

Rosecrans had ordered Hooker to bring his command to Bridgeport, cross the pontoon bridge there, and join him near Chattanooga, but Wheeler's raid modified this plan. Hooker was now to distribute his men along the railroad. "We can hold this point [Chattanooga] if we can keep up communications and supplies," Rosecrans telegraphed Hooker. Hooker himself set up headquarters at Bridgeport.

Had Hooker brought with him from the East, as Grant later maintained he did, a "full supply of land transportation," animals in good condition that had "not been subjected to hard work on bad roads without forage," Hooker might have supplemented Rosecrans' exhausted facilities. But over Hooker's protest, his "choice and efficient trains" were kept in Virginia—additional rail transportation for 6,000 mules and horses plus thousands of wagons obviously was impossible to supply. Hooker's need for animals was met out of the dregs of the Nashville corral—unbroken or broken-down horses and mules, many of which died as they were being driven down—not hauled by railroad—to Bridgeport. This sorry procession did not arrive at Bridgeport until late in October.

As October began, before the impact of the heavy rains and Wheeler's raid, optimism prevailed in Chattanooga. Fortifications grew strong and men worked "cheerfully, and with skill and ingenuity." As late as Sunday, October 4, the featured front-page story of the New York *Times* bore the headlines, "*General Rose-*

crans Army—Its Position Perfectly Secure, and The Prospect Bright." Part of the army's confidence grew from its knowledge of troubles in Bragg's camp. Deserters talked. A Kentuckian said that, given an opportunity, his regiment would desert almost to a man. Georgia troops balked at crossing the state line.

Rumor told that when a Tennessee regiment tried to desert it was repulsed by one of Longstreet's divisions, with 880 casualties, and that Bragg fired his artillery so that the Federals could not hear the fight. When Bragg rejected Longstreet's plan to move the whole Confederate army across the Tennessee and to undertake an active flanking campaign with it instead of laying siege to Chattanooga, Longstreet joined the anti-Bragg faction by writing to his Secretary of War: "I am convinced that nothing but the hand of God can save us or help us as long as we have our present commander."

Rosecrans informed Halleck: "Jeff. Davis was on our front Saturday and Sunday. He told the troops he would give them 30,000 reinforcements; he would sacrifice Richmond and Charleston before he would lose this place, and bid them be of good cheer; they should be in Kentucky by November." While Davis undoubtedly contributed to morale, his chief purpose was to referee his generals' quarrel.

In Chattanooga rain, hunger, and now news of disaster weighed heavily upon spirits formerly high. At first the army welcomed the rain, but it soon became a nuisance and a hazard, and men abandoned their flooding entrenchments. By the morning of the 3rd, increasing currents had lapped the floor of the trestle bridge. Sheet water turned lowlands into lakes, and horses and mules sank belly deep in muddy stretches of road. Even the fire of Confederate siege guns slackened.

On October 2, Rosecrans had ordered the army on two-thirds rations and authorized corps commanders to reduce these to one-half. Further shortage appeared inevitable, and on the 6th, Hooker, lacking forage, ordered all such wagons as he had—the transportations walking down from Nashville had scarcely taken the road—out to hunt for unravaged cornfields, and Rosecrans personally checked to see that his supply officers were functioning efficiently. When beef contractors failed to meet quotas, Hooker reported an arrearage of 3,000 animals and sent Rosecrans a mere

300 head. Priorities were set for the railroad: in order, forage, beef cattle, overcoats and blankets, troops and equipment. Horses began to starve in Chattanooga, although many had been turned loose to shift for themselves on the north bank. Without horses, artillery could not be moved to attack Bragg if he crossed the river in force. Sutlers were ordered to sell their extra horses to the army.

A second raiding column, commanded by General Philip Roddy, crossed the Tennessee, striking toward Winchester and Decherd. At dawn, the Federal cavalry undertook pursuit, and riding all day, overtook Roddy, but only after he had blocked the long railroad tunnel by dumping trash and rubble down the airshaft. When Roddy learned at Salem that Wheeler was falling back toward the Tennessee, he turned his own column south. With Wheeler and Roddy withdrawing, a third raiding column halted before crossing, and returned to its camp.

Although Bragg's massive cavalry raids on Rosecrans' communications ended, guerrillas continued to maraud, telegraph lines and railroad bridges, tracks and tunnels proving attractive targets.

On October 3, Rosecrans wrote to Lincoln with a proposal: "If we maintain the position in such strength that the enemy are obliged to abandon their position, and the elections in the great States go favorably, would it not be well to offer a general amnesty to all officers and soldiers in the rebellion? It would give us moral strength, and weaken them very much." In making this well-intentioned but presumptuous proposal Rosecrans possibly was thinking of Colonel Jacques' belief that once they were assured of amnesty, the war-weary Confederates would surrender. Lincoln had even suggested that Jacques should conduct informal negotiations with Richmond, with Rosecrans as intermediary. Lincoln told Jacques that he would grant amnesty if the Confederates surrendered.

Lincoln's answer to Rosecrans' suggestion of amnesty arrived next day while headquarters was stunned by the McMinnville disaster: "If we can hold Chattanooga and East Tennessee, I think the rebellion must dwindle and die," Lincoln wrote. "I intend doing something like what you suggest whenever the case shall appear ripe enough to have it accepted in the true understanding, rather than as a confession of weakness and fear." Villard, however, later called Rosecrans' letter a "senseless suggestion" and maintained that it "gave great offense and raised suspicions of political aspirations on his part," and caused Lincoln to consider his removal from command.

Almost twenty years later another story showed that the amnesty letter gave offense not so much to Lincoln as to Stanton, who garbled it to convince Governor Morton of Indiana that Rosecrans' removal was necessary. Colonel Holloway remembered that when Morton and Stanton met on October 17 in the Indianapolis railroad depot, Stanton declared that the "cause of Rosecrans' removal was a telegram which the General had sent to President Lincoln after the battle, recommending an armistice with a view of agreeing on terms of peace." This untrue statement filled Morton with "apprehension for the success of the Union cause and with grief at the discovery that Rosecrans should have proved so weak and faltering."

On October 9, Ohio was to choose for governor a pro-war Republican, John Brough, or Clement C. Vallandigham, an anti-war Democrat. The nation eyed this election, for if Vallandigham carried Ohio, he might carry the Union later. To Rosecrans the connection between desertion and Copperheadism was so close that he proclaimed his support of Lincoln's administration publicly and vigorously and encouraged his officers and men to do likewise.

The election results proved Rosecrans' efforts successful. Out of 10,000 Ohio votes cast by the Army of the Cumberland, Brough received some 9,700 and Vallandigham, less than 300. Reporter William Shanks believed that the way was now open, if Lincoln chose to take it, to remove Rosecrans. Rosecrans' popularity with the Ohio electorate was so great that to remove him before the election might have cost the pro-war Republicans the state.

Bickering had arisen among the Union generals after Chickamauga. "After a battle," John Beatty noticed, "there is always more or less bad feeling—regiments, brigades and corps claiming that other regiments, brigades and corps failed to do their whole duty and should therefore be held responsible for this or that misfortune." At the root of some of the bad feeling was Rosecrans' hot temper and careless language. Hazen had responded to Rosecrans' tongue-lashing of the night of September 19 by allying himself with the anti-Rosecrans faction. Wood had had his revenge in the break-through. Earlier, after a dressing-down by Rosecrans, Chief-

Engineer Morton had requested another assignment. The transfer had been delayed until after Chickamauga. On October 5, Halleck sent William Farrar—"Baldy"—Smith to Rosecrans. The replacement did not operate to Rosecrans' advantage or comfort. Morton was easy to get along with. Not so Smith.

Smith was still only a brigadier general and out of favor. He was an able but sour, frustrated West Pointer, who talked well and sometimes too much. Dana wrote bluntly to Smith: "If you had neither been able to speak or write, I have no doubt that you would now have been in command of one of the great armies." At Chattanooga Smith began by attempting to browbeat Captain William C. Margadent, Superintendent of Topographical Engineers. When Margadent refused, as Rosecrans had ordered, to show confidential maps to unidentified civilians sent by Smith, Smith arrested Margadent. Rosecrans released him after eight days, and Smith then ordered him to tour the outer picket line each morning at 3:00 A.M. while keeping his full daytime assignments. For ten days Margadent, who was not easily cowed, woke up Smith by bawling out his pre-dawn reports at Smith's headquarters. On the eleventh day Smith capitulated and rescinded the order.

During this minor comedy Smith wrote his impression of Rosecrans, calling him

. . . a real study. He was able, with a rapid, working mind capable at times of effort requiring determination of character. But while many plans of action came into his head, he was not usually persistent in any, having generally some new plan which he would think better than a previous one. He was optimistic to such a degree that I am convinced he expected his military record would carve a way for him to the White House; and I think the same quality blinded him to the peril his army was in at Chattanooga.

It should be added that Smith was scarcely a detached, competent witness.

Smith claimed that shortly after he arrived at Chattanooga he told Rosecrans he could not supply the army over the mountain roads once the rains started, and that Rosecrans informed him that he was mistaken, because he was then hauling twice as many rations as were needed. Smith dropped the subject but hurried work on the defenses, looking meanwhile for some way to reopen a shorter route.

Carlin and Davis were also quarreling again. Carlin requested Rosecrans to assign his brigade to another division or replace Davis—he had "a total want of confidence in Brig. Gen. Jef. C. Davis." Davis endorsed Carlin's request: "These reflections and insinuations are false representations throughout . . . introduced by motives of malice," and McCook recommended Carlin's transfer.

The next day Palmer sent a note to Garfield. Palmer was so certain that "important changes must be made in the organization of this army before it again takes the field, that as soon as safety of this army is placed beyond doubt, I will either tender my resignation or ask to be relieved from further duty in this department." Palmer's reference was clearly to McCook and Crittenden. It was bruited in the army that Rosecrans had so little confidence in the pair that on the battlefield he gave orders directly to their division commanders, bypassing the corps organization, and fighting their units as independent divisions and regiments under his immediate personal command.

The matter of who had run off, and who remained to fight, might have been settled within the family had Dana not been present.

In his *Truth About Chickamauga* Archibald Gracie took Rosecrans severely to task for submitting to Dana's presence:

I know of no other army, Federal or Confederate, which ever had an official . . . in its camp . . . whose sole duty was . . . that of custodian of all the gossip . . . that could be collected against the general officers, from the commander-in-chief down, to be retailed daily to the authorities in Washington, and thence to percolate through the newspapers to the public, and to be actually used as the basis for the history of this battle, as generally accepted, even to this day.

How any general of a great army, or any man of self-respect could have tolerated, as did Rosecrans, the presence in his camp of such an official, whom he knew to be there to spy on him and to criticize his every action, is incomprehensible. . . . If we read Dana's dispatches, and then mark the effect produced by them in Washington, not only in the disposition of Rosecrans and in the appointment of his successor, but also in connection with the future careers of officers whom he vilified, we must conclude that his authority was supreme and that he was the only full ranking general of them all. The *Records* prove that this doughty warrior accepted the camp gossip for truth, and used it to destroy the future sphere of usefulness in their service of their country, of some general officers who deserved a better fate, including even those whom courts of inquiry—but to no purpose—rightly exonerated from blame; while two generals whom he especially honors in these dispatches escaped without even exposure for conduct deserving of court-martial.

Correspondent Villard had returned to Chattanooga on October 4. While he had no love for Rosecrans, he found serious fault with Dana, saying:

He received and conveyed impressions, like the professional journalist that he was, hastily, flippantly, and recklessly. He thus involved himself in glaring inconsistencies, contradictions and humiliating self-corrections. This criticism certainly holds good of his official correspondence relative to the Chickamauga and Chattanooga campaigns as represented in the *War Records.* . . . His zeal often degenerated into officiousness, and he fell at times into the role of the informer, without perhaps being conscious of it. . . . As my own eyes observed at the time, Dana had intimate intercourse, day and night, with General Rosecrans, and he enjoyed his personal hospitality, sitting at the same table, and sleeping in the same building. His reports also prove that he deliberately drew the general into confidential communications, the substance of which he used against him, and that he held talks with general officers regarding Rosecrans which were nothing less than insubordination on their part.

Nor could General Cox swallow Dana whole: "The gifted journalist had known how to give his communications the most lively effect, and they had great weight with the Secretary. They were not always quite just, for they were written at speed under the spell of first impressions, and necessarily under the influence of army acquaintances in whom he had confidence." Neither could General McCalmont: "Stanton's confidential correspondent kept busy his prolific and unscrupulous pen in sending dispatches, giving free and injurious opinions of the characters and capacities of the generals. Whether he took his cue from the War Department is not known." Since Dana's dispatches were "sent in secrecy, and the instructions and letters he received were not published with them, it would have done no harm if they had remained buried in secret until the end of time," McCalmont said.

A week after Chickamauga, Dana had said in a dispatch to Stanton that "A very serious fermentation reigns in the Twentieth and Twenty-first army corps, and indeed, throughout this whole army. . . . The generals of division and brigade feel deeply this desertion of their commanders," and threaten to resign rather than serve longer "under such superiors." While only "two or three" had actually spoken to Dana, he was informed, "on good evidence," of the opinions of such men as Palmer, Wood, Sheridan, Johnson, and Hazen. He thought Davis agreed with the rest. The dissatisfied generals had not told Rosecrans that they would no longer serve under McCook and Crittenden, but several had private conversations with him concerning the matter.

Part of the problem, so Dana reported, was Rosecrans himself:

The defects of his character complicate the difficulty. He abounds in friendliness and approbativeness, and is greatly lacking in firmness and steadiness of will. He is a temporizing man, dreads so heavy an alternative as is now presented, and hates to break with McCook and Crittenden. Besides, there is a more serious obstacle to his acting decisively in the fact that if McCook and Crittenden fled to Chattanooga . . . he fled also; and it may be said in his excuse that, under the circumstances although it was proper for the commanding general to go to his base of operations, while corps commanders ought to remain with their troops, still he feels that that excuse cannot entirely clear him either in his own eyes or those of the army. . . . While the subordinate commanders will not resign if he is retained in the chief-command . . . their respect for him as a general has received an irreparable blow. And that not from his abandonment of the army alone, but from his faulty management on the field especially in leaving a gap of a whole brigade distance between the divisions of Wood and Davis. . . . If it be decided to change the chief commander also, I would take the liberty of suggesting that some western general of high rank and great prestige, like Grant, for instance, would be preferable as his successor to anyone who has commanded in the East alone.

The effect of Dana's suggestions was immediate. On the next day, September 28, by Lincoln's directive the XX and the XXI army corps were consolidated under the command of Gordon Granger, and a court of inquiry was ordered for McCook and Crittenden.

Dana further told Stanton that the soldiers had lost their affection for Rosecrans and no longer cheered—except on orders—when he passed among them. General officers of "prominence and worth"—Dana specified only Garfield and Wood, and Colonel Emerson Opdycke—had "spontaneously" visited him to tell him the army's mind.

. . . While few people possess more estimable social qualities, I have never seen a public man exhibiting talent with less administrative power, less clearness and steadiness in difficulty, and greater practical incapacity than General Rosecrans. He has inventive fertility and knowledge but he has no strength of will and no concentration of purpose. His mind scatters; there is no system in the use of his busy days and restless nights, no courage against individuals in his composition, and, with great love of command, he is a feeble commander. He is conscientious and honest, just as he is imperious and disputatious; always with a stray vein of caprice and an overweening passion for the approbation of his friends and the public outside.

Under the present circumstances I consider this army very unsafe in his hands; but do know of no man except Thomas who could now be safely put in his place.

The next day, Dana gave some indications of his ability to judge generals when he asked Stanton: "Would it not be possible for General Halleck to come here? What is needed to extricate this army is the highest administrative talent, and that without delay."

Stanton answered: "I wish you to go directly to see General Thomas and say to him that his services, his abilities, his character, his unselfishness, have always been most cordially appreciated by me, and that it is not my fault that he has not long since had command of an independent army."

Dana read Stanton's telegram to Thomas. Thomas admitted that he would like an independent command. However, he said, "I would not like to take command of an army where I should be exposed to the imputation of having intrigued, or of having exercised any effort to supplant my previous commander." Thomas made it clear that he would not consent to become Rosecrans' successor.

Another version of this episode is found in Dana's report of October 8, to Stanton:

"General Rousseau, who seems to be regarded throughout this army as an ass of eminent gifts, having reported to General Thomas that you had inquired how the army would like to have him in the chief command, that officer has sent a confidential friend to me to say that while he would gladly accept any command out of this department to which you might see fit to assign him, he could not consent to become the successor of General Rosecrans, because he would not do anything to give countenance to the suspicion that he intrigued against his commander. Besides he has as perfect confidence in capacity and fidelity of Rosecrans as he had in those of General Buell."

Thomas, who scorned intrigue, reported the matter to Rosecrans: "I asked General Garfield to speak to you about the traitors from Washington now in camp, and I want now to tell you that I should consider your removal from this army a national injury. Should it be done, I will no longer serve with it, but ask to be relieved and sent elsewhere." Touched by "the noble sincerity of Thomas," Rosecrans answered: "Of this be sure. No cloud shall ever come between us."

For six days, from October 4 through 10, Rosecrans worked on his battle report while Dana predicted: "I judge from informations that have reached me that in writing his own report General Rosecrans will elaborately show that the blame of his failure rests on the administration; that is, on the Secretary of War and General-in-Chief, who did not foresee that Bragg would be reinforced, and who compelled him to move forward without cavalry enough, and very inadequately prepared in other respects."

Rosecrans could with propriety have so slanted his report, but in fact he made no mention of Stanton or Halleck, nor did he speak of the army's being compelled to move forward with insufficient cavalry, nor assess blame against the Administration.

The army first learned that it was being reorganized when a Nashville newspaper arrived with the story that the XX and XXI corps were to be consolidated as the IV corps under Granger. Crittenden excitedly announced that he would resign rather than draw pay while not working, and Rosecrans assured him, "Every act of yours in the battle of Chickamauga met my cordial approbation." McCook took the news calmly; so did the soldiers of the two corps, until home letters arrived, showing, Dana reported to Stanton, that their friends regard the consolidation as a token of disgrace and punishment. "It is very desirable to obviate any such feeling, especially as of the six divisions composing the consolidated corps, three fought with heroism and success throughout the battle." Washington, he said, should justify the consolidation on the basis of battle losses and Halleck announced that the consolidation was intended to reduce the number of corps and corps commanders. Palmer was not mollified by this flimsy excuse and tried to resign; such consolidation, he felt, "implied censure" of the men and officers. Rosecrans refused to accept his resignation.

McCook and Crittenden left on the 10th, and Granger took command of the IV corps, with Sheridan leading the troops of the former XX, and Palmer those of the former XXI.

Next to depart was Congressman-elect Garfield. Garfield had been debating regarding the proper course for a soldier elected to political office—to remain in the army or resign? He resolved this uncertainty on October 15 and left for Bridgeport. The party was joined by General Steedman, also going to Washington. Rosecrans' congratulations accompanied Garfield: "His high intelligence, spotless integrity, business capacity, and thorough acquaintance with the wants of the army will render his services, if possible, more valuable to the country in Congress than with us." Garfield was under official orders from Rosecrans, to describe to Stanton and Halleck the problems of the army: "Report to me frequently until your mission has been accomplished . . . when you will have leave of absence to await orders from the War Department."

Thomas told Garfield as they parted: "You know the injustice of all these attacks on Rosecrans. Make it your business to set these matters right." Neither Thomas nor Rosecrans suspected that Garfield had been secretly undermining Rosecrans with Dana. Garfield carried a personal letter to mail; it was from Baldy Smith to his wife, and gossiped that: "We will have a change of commanders, and General Thomas is to be the man."

Reynolds succeeded Garfield as Chief of Staff. Sanderson thought Reynolds a "decided improvement." "Garfield, though smart," Sanderson wrote, "is by no means a strong man, and with less confidence and assurance of his own superiority would be a much safer and more valuable chief advisor. I do not believe, though he was a useful man, his absence will prove any serious loss."

Chattanooga was isolated when the pontoon bridge separated the day after Garfield's departure on October 16. Although it was repaired in a few days, by the 14th Baldy Smith was thinking "with horror of the long, impassable road between here and our supplies. We are really in a very dangerous condition, and this place may have to be given up because we cannot get enough to eat so far from the depot." Dana shared his concern.

Rosecrans was continuing his efforts to find an alternate supply route. The steamboat would be finished in a week, but even though the work was being rushed, Captain William LeDuc, who was in charge, rode out from Bridgeport seeking another land route along the north bank. He discovered a railroad bed without rails, but with a twelve-mile flood-proof connection to Jasper, twenty-one miles shorter than the wagon road. On the 14th, Rosecrans ordered construction to begin at once.

"Nothing can prevent the retreat of the army from this place within a fortnight . . . except the opening of the river," Dana wrote on the 16th. Rosecrans had ordered Hooker to prepare for the movement to open the river, by crossing at Bridgeport and seizing the south bank, but believed this should be delayed until Hooker's wagon trains arrived from Nashville. Although they had left on the 8th, they were being walked down and not transported by railroad, and had not yet arrived at Bridgeport. "In the midst of all these difficulties," Dana continued, "General Rosecrans seems to be insensible to the impending danger, and dawdles with trifles in a manner which can scarcely be imagined. . . . Meanwhile, with plenty of zealous and energetic officers ready to do whatever can be done, all this precious time is lost because our dazed and mazy commander cannot perceive the catastrophe that is close upon us, nor fix his mind upon the means of preventing it. I never saw anything which seemed so lamentable and hopeless."

On the following day, Rosecrans and Dana had a "full" conversation upon the situation. Rosecrans told him, Dana reported, that the possession of the river to the head of William's Island, at least, was a *sine qua non* to the holding of Chattanooga, but that he had to wait at least five days until Hooker's troops were reconcentrated, and his wagon trains had come up. Then Hooker would cross the Tennessee and move on Raccoon and Lookout mountains. Rosecrans believed that Bragg was gathering a great army with which, weather permitting, he would cross on the Union left and probably attack Burnside.

On the 17th Dana complained to Washington that "The general

organization of this army is inefficient and its discipline defective. The former proceeds from the fact that General [Rosecrans] insists on personally directing every department and keeps everyone awaiting and uncertain till he himself can directly supervise every operation. The latter proceeds from his utter lack of firmness, his passion for universal applause, and his incapacity to hurt any man's feelings by just severity. There is thus practically no discipline for superior officers."

Dana's final report, dated October 18, told Stanton that "conditions and prospects grow worse and worse." Starving horses were everywhere. Each day, as fewer wagons arrived, supplies grew scantier, and with every animal that died of hunger and exhaustion, survivors were given heavier burdens; so that, progressively, they collapsed sooner, until half-empty wagons lurched from Bridgeport to Chattanooga through a stinking wall of 10,000 dead horses and mules. As teams grew weaker, steep inclines proved too difficult. By the 17th, over 500 wagons were stalled between Lookout Mountain and the Tennessee, and no forage was at hand. When the animals floundered, teamsters jettisoned part of the load, but even for those who got through, the trip took ten days. As transportation failed, rations were reduced to half or less, and hungry men followed the wagons across the pontoon bridge, to pick up grains of corn and cracker crumbs that were shaken out. At feeding troughs, guards prevented soldiers from poaching on the scanty rations of the artillery horses. "Amid all this, the practical incapacity of Rosecrans is astonishing," Dana wrote, "and it often seems difficult to believe him of sound mind. His imbecility appears to be contagious, and it is difficult for anyone to get anything done."

Such talk raises the question, "What was to be done?" Dana himself supplied the answer: "If the effort which Rosecrans intends to make to open the river should be futile, the immediate retreat of this army will follow. It does not seem possible to hold out here another week without a new avenue of supplies."

In this complaint Dana disregarded Rosecrans' efforts to discover and make ready alternate supply routes. Although theoretically the railroad remained the best of these, it would continue to be unavailable until bridges had been rebuilt and Union troops held the south bank. To repeat, Rosecrans had planned to send

Hooker across the river immediately, to drive out Longstreet, but Hooker brought no wagon trains, and as he arrived, Wheeler was crossing the Tennessee. With no men of his own to spare, Rosecrans sent Hooker to protect the railroad. At the same time he directed Hooker to "push forward preparations for crossing the river as soon as the situation will warrant it." Hooker was to set up a sawmill to produce enough material to eliminate the trestle portion of Sheridan's bridge. It was obvious that Rosecrans could force passage at Bridgeport and support his beachhead from across the river much more rapidly and easily than Bragg could send reinforcements the twenty-four miles from Chattanooga. The ease of Hooker's subsequent operation proved the correctness of Rosecrans' assumptions.

Theoretically the next best supply route was the Tennessee. When October rains made it navigable, one obstacle to water freighting was removed. However, others remained. The first was the lack of steamboats. Although work on these was being rushed, they could not have made the Bridgeport-to-Chattanooga trip even if they had been ready. Confederate guns on Lookout and sharpshooters' rifles at water level on the south bank still commanded the river. How to get by these?

A map provided Rosecrans with the answer.

The Tennessee, as it winds through the mountains, makes six giant loops west of Chattanooga. The first of these, extending southward, is Moccasin Bend. The second and much larger loop extends northward around the upper extremity of Raccoon Mountain. If supplies could be brought upstream to the ferry at the west end of the loop, carried by wagon across the peninsula out of range of Lookout Mountain, and then over the bridge at the east end of the loop, both the most difficult of the narrows—particularly the wild stretch called "The Suck"—and the guns would be avoided, and the freight would be within a few miles of Chattanooga itself. This was the short river route which could reduce the hauling time from Bridgeport by one day, and eliminate the need to use the worst of the road through Jasper. By river the distance around the Moccasin was ten miles; across the neck of the peninsula, it was one mile. In addition to a steamboat, a pontoon bridge was needed to cross a column into Lookout Valley, and as early as September 25 Rosecrans had ordered its construction. By

October 5 the damaged steamer *Paint Rock* had been repaired, although low water still prevented its use, and on the 6th the pontoon bridge at Bridgeport was ready for Hooker's men to cross as soon as they could be withdrawn from guarding the railroad.

Night and day, steamboat building at Bridgeport went on. Finally work was concentrated on a single craft, a little stern-wheeler, the *Chattanooga*, which finally opened the "Cracker Line," a mongrel, the hull a scow of rough planks, its cabin a canvas-covered room. Rosecrans' concern for the boat is indicated in two dispatches to Hooker on the 12th. "Push Edwards to hasten on the steamboat. The preparation of that is of primary importance, both for your movements and mine." And "Edwards says materials are wanted for the steamboat. Let nothing be wanted." When Garfield left for Washington, Rosecrans asked him to investigate the progress of the boat. "The steamboat will be finished next week," Garfield reported.

On the evening of the 18th, all preparations were completed for the opening of the river, and Rosecrans telegraphed Hooker to prepare his command to march at short notice. A week before, he had ordered Hooker to concentrate, telling him that: "The object is to get possession of the line of the river to this place." All that remained to be done was to finish the steamboat, complete the pontoon bridge, settle final details for the seizure of the Brown's Ferry crossing, and assign a commander for this detail of the operation. When Baldy Smith asked permission "to go down the river tomorrow, to see if we cannot hold it as far as William's Island, and use that as a depot," Rosecrans told him: "go by all means and I will go with you."

During the night, mists cleared away, and Monday morning, October 19, was brilliant Indian summer as Rosecrans, Smith, Reynolds, and Bond rode out across the pontoon bridge, leaving Granger in charge of headquarters. On the north Tennessee bank Rosecrans and Bond visited the hospital, and then rode to Brown's Ferry to make a personal inspection of the point on which the pontoon bridge was to be located. Earlier that day Smith had spent an hour at the same spot.

When a telegram arrived from Washington during the day, Granger read it and laid it on Rosecrans' table. Later, General Butterfield, Hooker's chief-of-staff, rode down from Bridgeport to

settle final details of the joint plan, and Granger, pledging Butterfield to silence, showed the wire to him. "Rosecrans is out on a
tour of inspection," he told Butterfield. "He doesn't know this
himself."

It was dusk when Rosecrans returned to headquarters. Granger
halted Reynolds to tell him: "The old man has been relieved.
Thomas is in command."

Rosecrans picked up the dispatch. He was to go to Cincinnati
to await further orders. The dispatch, he said later, contained the
"lying implication that Chattanooga was in extreme peril of surrender and must be held at all hazards."

To Sanderson, the actual order came as a complete surprise. "No
one dreamed it, and none seemed to be able to realize the truth of
it." However, the reports from Sanderson and Rousseau on their
return from Washington had prepared Rosecrans, and "he be-
haved accordingly, took it coolly and composedly, exhibiting
neither surprise nor chagrin, but laughed and talked with those
who came in and had faces as if they were mourning the death of
a near kin."

Rosecrans sent for Thomas immediately and announced to the
few officers present that he would leave the next morning at 5:00
A.M. Thomas came alone, sat down, and Rosecrans handed him the
dispatch in silence. Rosecrans later described the scene. "Slowly
and solemnly," Thomas read the papers, "turning pale and drawing his breath harder as he proceeded." When he finished, Rosecrans continued, he paused a moment and then began: "General,
you remember what I told you some two weeks ago—" Rosecrans
interrupted: "George, but we are in the face of the enemy. No
one but you can safely take my place now; and for our country's
sake, you *must* do it. Don't fear; no cloud of doubt will ever come
into my mind as to your fidelity to friendship and honor." With
this assurance, Rosecrans said, Thomas's agitation began to subside, and "in silence he accepted the situation, his indignation at
injustice yielding to the exigencies of the situation and its consequent duties."

"I can't bear to meet my troops," Rosecrans told Thomas, "I
want to leave before the announcement is made, and I will start
early in the morning." His friends remonstrated, but Rosecrans
refused to change his mind. Thereupon, he and Thomas began a

long, final conference that lasted until after midnight, when he wrote out and signed his order relinquishing command. "Now, General," said Thomas, "I want you to be kind enough to explain the exact plan for the taking of Lookout Valley as you proposed it." Again Rosecrans went over the scheme, carefully describing, he wrote, how and where the jointly operating forces were to cross the Tennessee, and how he intended to occupy Lookout Valley and secure use of the road on the south side of the river.

Rosecrans and Thomas were still talking when a dispatch from Grant arrived for Thomas: "Hold Chattanooga at all hazards. I will be there as soon as possible. Please inform me how long your present supplies will last, and the prospect for keeping them up." Rosecrans asserted that both he and Thomas were indignant at the order, which suggested that they might abandon Chattanooga, regarding it as one that "only ignorance or malice could have inspired." Thomas, nevertheless, sent the information, and added that the town would be held—"until we starve."

After Thomas had left, there remained only final routine to be cleared away. Then, as some of the staff lay down for a few hours of sleep, Sanderson wrote in his diary: "What the effect of this removal will be upon the morale of this army, I know full well. I dread the consequences. It is as yet, even here, known only to a few, and before it will be known to many, the General will have crossed the river and be gone. Of course he hurries off thus early and quickly to avoid the trial of parting with his beloved soldiers. To-morrow when it becomes known, we shall have a gloomy, desolate and sad day."

Under oath, to the Committee on the Conduct of the War, Rosecrans testified: "In General Grant's official report of the battle of Missionary Ridge there is an implication that when he assumed command there was great danger of my abandoning Chattanooga. Nothing could be more mistaken, or more unjust to me than that impression."

Sheridan confirms this statement:

When Rosecrans was relieved, he was busy with preparations for a movement to open the direct route to Bridgeport. . . . With this force [the XI and XII corps] Rosecrans had already strengthened certain important points on the railroad and given orders to Hooker to concentrate at Bridgeport portions of his command, and to hold them in readiness to advance to Chattanooga. General Grant arrived at Chattanooga on October 23rd, and began at once to carry out plans that had been formed for opening the shorter or river route to Bridgeport.

Villard wrote that before Garfield left Chattanooga, Rosecrans talked over the plan with him and with Baldy Smith, Garfield, Dana, and other generals. He was satisfied that Rosecrans "had fully made up his mind to carry it out; had already issued preliminary orders, including one to Hooker to concentrate his command, when his powers as Commander-in-Chief were suddenly cut off."

In fairness to Grant, it should be added that the operations planned by Rosecrans to open the Cracker line proceeded successfully, and that within two months the Army of the Cumberland under Grant's command, reinforced by two corps under Sherman and two under Hooker, so that it outnumbered the dispersing Confederates two to one, won a great victory over Bragg.

It might have been Rosecrans' victory because it was in the making when he was removed. "The enemies whom he made by his sturdy honesty," says Whitelaw Reid of Rosecrans, "dealt him their fatal blow at the unkindest moment. Rosecrans had never been more active, more enterprising, more skillful, than after Chickamauga. His plans for an advance were matured, the preliminary steps were all taken, the troops for which he had so long begged had nearly reached him. In a few days more the glory of Lookout Mountain and Mission Ridge might have been his. But the fields he had sown it was left for others to reap; from the coign of vantage he had won, it was left for others, with larger armies, and the unquestioning support of the government, to swoop down on Georgia and march to the sea."

Seventeen

"THEY SLEW HIM WITH POISON"

Early on the morning of October 20, 1863, a handful of men saw Rosecrans off. Some wept openly, but Rosecrans kept a cheerful face. He had a kind word for everyone, despite his sorrow. Fog hung on Chattanooga as Rosecrans, and his aides, Captain R. S. Thoms and Bond, and Father Patrick Treacy, left headquarters with General Daniel Butterfield, Hooker's chief of staff and Lieutenant Paul Oliver, who were returning to Stevenson, and who at Rosecrans' invitation had joined the group.

Oliver noticed that along the road country people turned round to talk and ride with Rosecrans: "He had the faculty to draw people toward him. No one could be more unassuming or more friendly."

Rosecrans did not complain or speak of his removal, except to express satisfaction at Thomas's appointment. Thomas commanded universal respect but, as Oliver put it, "above all 'Old Rosy' seemed to loom up" in the army's affection. "I do not think," he said, "that any other appointment than that of General Thomas would have at all satisfied it to the loss of the former."

Back in Chattanooga Sanderson wept as he wrote: "He is gone. In him this army has lost its idol and the country the best of its commanders. May he soon again be restored to a command for which he is so eminently fitted."

The day was gloomy. To Sanderson the few officers who visited headquarters seemed more like "mourners at a funeral than rollicking soldiers"; privates "bitterly denounced those who did the deed." Sheridan said that Rosecrans had submitted uncomplainingly, and "modestly left without fuss or demonstration" but that when the men learned of his departure, "deep and almost universal regret was expressed, for he was enthusiastically esteemed and loved by the Army of the Cumberland from the day he assumed command until he left it."

As Thomas assumed command, Rosecrans' farewell message was circulated among the men: "In taking leave of you he congratulates you that your commander comes to you not as he did, a stranger. To his known prudence, dauntless courage, and true patriotism, you may look with confidence that under God he will lead you to victory." Thomas immediately ordered Hooker to "use all possible dispatch in concentrating your command and preparing to move in accordance with the instructions of General Rosecrans," though a change of command could not change the fact that the steamboat at Bridgeport was not quite ready.

The change of commanders of the Army of the Cumberland was part of a bigger shake-up and unification of Western commands. Unification under a single general had been in process even before Chattanooga. Good military sense demanded it, and of the three independent major Western commanders, Grant, Rosecrans, and Burnside, Burnside had disqualified himself by his proved incapacity at Fredericksburg, and Rosecrans was under a cloud after Chickamauga. Vicksburg made Grant the inevitable choice. He got along well with his superiors, despite the trouble he had had with Halleck in 1862, and he was on excellent terms with Washington.

First indication of a new assignment for Grant can be found in Halleck's October 3 telegram instructing him to proceed to Cairo and to report as soon as he was able to take the field. A week later Sherman wrote to him: "I feel sure you will be ordered to Nashville to assume a general command over all the forces operating to the southeast, say, Rosecrans your center, Burnside left wing, and Sherman right." Four days later Sherman added: "Accept the command of the great army of the center; don't hesitate. By your presence at Nashville you will unite all discordant elements and impress the enemy in proportion." And the next day, he was more explicit: "I am very anxious you should go to Nashville. . . . Rosecrans and Burnside and Sherman, with their subordinates would be ashamed of petty quarrels if you were behind and near them, between them and Washington." Several weeks earlier Sherman apparently had queried Grant if he would retain Rosecrans in command and Grant responded that he had "no intentions upon which to base the idea of such a change, except my own feelings. I may be wrong and judge Rosecrans from a prejudiced view, instead of impartially, as I would like to try and do."

On October 11 Halleck promised Grant, who was at "Cairo or Memphis"—Grant was on his way north from New Orleans where he had injured his leg by falling from his horse—that he need not fear being left idle: "The moment you are well enough to take the field you will have abundant occupation." And on the 16th, when Grant reached Cairo, he opened Halleck's order telling him to proceed immediately to the Galt house in Louisville, there to receive further instructions.

The journey took Grant through Indianapolis, and as the train was leaving the station, a messenger halted it. Stanton was arriving. He handed Grant two orders signed by Halleck. Both put Grant in command of the Armies of the Ohio, Cumberland, and Tennessee, but one retained Rosecrans, the other substituted Thomas. Grant chose the order relieving Rosecrans. But even before he joined Grant, Stanton told Governor Morton he was removing Rosecrans because of his "disaster" telegram to Lincoln after Chickamauga.

Grant remained for a day with Stanton at Louisville and on the evening of the 18th, Grant maintained, Dana's telegram arrived, telling Stanton that "unless prevented Rosecrans would retreat." He advised "peremptory orders against his doing so." Stanton held out the dispatch to Grant. "We must prevent this," he said. Grant maintained later that he wrote an immediate order assuming command of the new military division—actually he had written such an order the day before—and sent the wire, dated 11:30 P.M., October 19, to Rosecrans, together with Halleck's order assigning Thomas to command. Thomas "must hold Chattanooga at all hazards," he said; he himself would be at the front as soon as possible. At that time, Grant's order relieving Rosecrans had been in Chattanooga for at least three and a half hours; it had been sent *before* and not *after* Grant said he had seen Dana's telegram saying that "Rosecrans would retreat."

Dana's final Chattanooga dispatch in the *Official Records*—and presumably the telegram to which Grant refers—was dated 11:00 A.M., October 18, and described the possibility of a retreat as contingent: "If the effort which Rosecrans intends to make to open the river should be futile, the immediate retreat of this army will follow. . . . If, on the other hand, we regain control of the river and keep it, subsistence and forage can be got here and we may escape with no worse misfortune than the loss of 12,000 animals." And this telegram reached Stanton on the 18th, not the 19th. Dana himself says that he telegraphed Stanton before leaving Chattanooga on the 19th that, unless ordered otherwise, Rosecrans would retreat immediately. This statement has no basis in the records.

Reporter Villard denies emphatically that Rosecrans was about to retreat:

> I can personally bear witness to the contrary. I saw the General daily, and knew that the opening of the Tennessee and the proposed movement of General Hooker absorbed his attention. Moreover, I recollect clearly that Dana expressed regret to me, an hour before his departure, that he was not to be present when the attempt to seize William's Island and the south bank be made. But his message was effective, in that in consideration of it Stanton and Grant agreed to act at once by removing Rosecrans and appointing Thomas in his place.

On the morning of the 21st (Grant says the 20th), Grant reached Nashville, and on the 22nd he arrived at Stevenson, Alabama, to find Rosecrans already there. "He came into my car," Grant wrote later, "and we held a brief interview, in which he described very clearly the situation at Chattanooga, and made some excellent suggestions as to what should be done. My only wonder was that he had not carried them out." Grant gave Rosecrans the impression that he had played no part in his removal.

At Chattanooga, Dana reported, Rosecrans' removal had been received by all "intelligent" officers "with satisfaction," although, he continued, Rosecrans' friends could not understand the reasons for it, and reported that he was to be made commander of the Army of the Potomac instead. At headquarters, Dana said, order prevailed instead of "universal chaos."

On the 23rd, Grant arrived in Thomas's headquarters to find Thomas staring into the fire; he did not even offer Grant the hospitality he would have given a stranger. Grant understood this deliberate slight—Thomas was again a subordinate, and moreover, Thomas respected Rosecrans. General Wilson of Grant's staff broke the uneasy silence: "General Thomas, General Grant is wet, hungry, and in pain. Can't you find quarters and some dry clothes for him, and direct your officers to provide his party with supper?" Thomas asked Grant if he wished to change his clothes. Grant refused, and lighted a fresh cigar.

Sanderson, who was there, studied Grant. "If he be a truly great man, his looks are very deceptive," he wrote afterward. "Yet withal I have formed a rather favorable opinion of him, not as a great man, but as a clever and affable gentleman. So far as the army is concerned, most of the officers and men feel cool, doubtful and distrusting. They have not the confidence in him they had in Rosecrans."

Most of the general officers called that evening and "pointed out on the map the line, marked with a red or blue pencil," which, Grant understood, "Rosecrans had contemplated falling back upon." No one said that Rosecrans had determined to retreat. That was Grant's interpretation.

Baldy Smith arrived to explain the army's problems so clearly that Grant understood them without a tour. Smith spoke of the sawmill *he* had improvised, *his* lumbering, the boat *he* was completing at Bridgeport, the bridges *he* was building—all to be used in opening the river route. Apparently he did not say that the plan was Rosecrans' and that these preparations had been in the making before his arrival. The next day, Grant, Smith, and Thomas rode to Brown's Ferry, and that night, Grant ordered the opening of the "Cracker Line." Grant says in his *Memoirs* that he "deemed it but just" to put Smith in command of the troops detailed to execute the movement.

Grant then regarded Smith highly, but Smith did not reciprocate. He wrote of Grant: "Ability ordinary; sense of responsibility, utterly wanting, except so far as his personal interests were concerned; professional acquirements absolutely wanting, so far as related to the direction of movements, and conduct of battles. He was malignant in his hatred, but would forgive for a consideration. Utter disregard of truth where his own interests were concerned; the moral qualities drowned in rot-gut whiskey."

Hooker's concentration at Bridgeport, ordered on the 19th by

Rosecrans and confirmed by Thomas, was not completed when Grant arrived. But on the 26th Hooker was ready, and crossing his pontoon bridge, he turned east, to become the right of a pincers movement. At 3:00 next morning, 1400 men under Hazen and Turchin embarked in Chattanooga in 52 pontoons for Brown's Ferry, nine miles below. Meanwhile another column crossed to the north bank at Chattanooga, turned west, and traversing Moccasin Point, waited for the waterborne column near the Ferry.

The river column first rowed and then turned toward the shadowy north bank to drift through "The Suck." At daybreak, reaching Brown's Ferry, they crossed and seized the south bank, to lay a bridge across the ferry. At night Hooker encamped at Whitesides, and next day his men entered Lookout Valley, and by 5:00 P.M. had contacted Smith at Brown's Ferry. The Brown's Ferry route now was safe and on the 29th the *Chattanooga* was plying the river, and the partial siege and starvation were over.

Here was a competently conceived and executed plan in which many persons had part and for which many therefore deserved praise. Grant inferentially claimed the whole responsibility for it by writing in the *Memoirs* that he had "got the Army of the Cumberland in a comfortable position." The public and even some of the soldiers gave him the credit that belonged, in reality, to Rosecrans first, and to Thomas, under whose immediate direction the enterprise was conducted, second, and to Hazen, Hooker, and Smith. A smaller part of the glory was rightfully Grant's.

As the years passed the principal claimant of credit was Smith. By February 5, 1864, Hooker was fuming because Smith claimed authorship of the advance into Lookout Valley. The movement was "pointed out to me," Hooker said, "before I left Washington and afterward communicated to me by Rosecrans long before I ever saw Chattanooga." Smith pressed his claims, as against Grant, Thomas, Hooker, and especially Rosecrans, for more than forty years, until in 1900 Secretary of War Elihu Root appointed a full Military Court of Inquiry. The Court failed to "find any evidence that Smith was the originator of the plan for the relief of Chattanooga by military operations conducted in Lookout Valley. On the contrary, there is abundant evidence in the *Official Records* to show that the plan was devised and prepared by General Rosecrans."

Rosecrans meanwhile was without a command. Garfield waited for him for two days at Cincinnati, and left for Washington, having written some advice: "Allow me to suggest that in the magnificent reception that awaits you here and elsewhere you be careful not to inaugurate a contest with the War Dep't. There are doubtless those who are ready to pick up anything you may say in criticism of the Secretary of War. Your past career is your best vendication."

The news that Rosecrans was on the way to Cincinnati led to the organization of a tremendous civic reception, inspired in part by indignation at the rumors that he had been removed for dishonorable reasons. Rosecrans asked an immense, cheering audience, "to remember that whenever we hear the voice of government it is our duty to yield to it with prompt obedience [cheers], to recognize its right to issue orders, and to presume it has good reason for what it does until we know to the contrary."

For weeks the removal of Rosecrans was headline news and editorial material. On October 20 the special correspondent of the Cincinnati *Times* wrote from Chattanooga: "There is wailing and weeping in the Army of the Cumberland today. They slew him with poison whom they feared to meet with steel. Already the maggots are active on the carcass of the fallen lion." General Palmer noted that the newspapers were filled with the "most false and extravagant" reports of Chickamauga, causing the War Department to "perpetrate the most signal injustice to officers and men." McCalmont said that "Rosecrans' religious as well as political opinions were used exaggeratedly by his enemies to his disadvantage. That they did not succeed in crushing him, or in materially lowering him in the estimation of his army, or the country, is the best proof of his eminent merits." The New York *Times* on October 21 said that many contradictory reasons had been given for Rosecrans' removal: McCook and Crittenden had preferred charges against Rosecrans; he had fled from the battle at Chickamauga; he had considered the battle lost; he had disobeyed orders in advancing beyond Chattanooga; he had mismanaged the battle. The statement that he had an attack of epilepsy during the battle was untrue; but that he was constitutionally and by education "subject to fits of religious depression of the profoundest character" was correct, the *Times* said. It was further charged, the

Times continued, that Rosecrans made "excessive use of opium." It was also understood that his relations with Halleck were "strained," and that his removal had been contemplated for some time. Yet, said the *Times,* the reputation for courage that Rosecrans had won at Stone River was "plea in bar to the imputation of cowardice in his abandonment of his battleground."

Next day a *Times* editorial said of Rosecrans: "No history of the rebellion will ever be written in which his name will not occupy a leading place. We feel confident that he will bear a prominent part in finishing the work in which he has already borne so brilliant a share in beginning. There is but one living military man who has accomplished more, and that is Grant."

The *Times,* on November 2, printed a "private" letter from Rosecrans:

I have only to say that I pray God that the country may be as well or better served by another. As for the infamous lies which are put forth by the press to blast my reputation, such as disabling mental disease, the use of opium, disobedience of orders in not advancing when ordered— if I thought they came from our government I would despair of a nation headed by such a government. Personally I commend myself to the Just and Merciful One, Who knows what is best for me.

Rosecrans "refused to credit" occasional newspaper reports which asserted that he was removed at Grant's request. He held Stanton responsible.

The most vicious attacks on Rosecrans, then as later, came from William F. G. Shanks, a reporter for the New York *Herald.* North and South, the war spawned incompetent generals, among them Lee and Sherman, he wrote later, but the worst of them all was Rosecrans:

Politics nor war ever thrust upon the nation a more incompetent leader than Rosecrans. He was neither a strategist nor a tactician, and all he knew of the art of war were its tricks. He was known throughout the camps of the foe as "that wily Dutchman, Rosecrans." He was eminently fitted by nature and education to be the Provost-Marshal and chief of spies to a great army, but nothing more. Nature unfitted him for the task of directing a great army by making him extremely nervous. He possessed no control over himself, and consequently was not capable of directing others.

In forming his estimates of generals—and his opinions of Lee and Sherman were scarcely higher—Shanks turned to the pseudo-science of phrenology. Others went astray by reading character meanings into Rosecrans' facial expressions. Reid, who knew him well, wrote that Rosecrans' "brow is ample; the eyes are penetrating and restless; the face is masked with well-trimmed beard; but the mouth, with its curious smile, half of pleasure, half of some exquisite nervous feeling, which might be intense pain, is the feature which will linger longest in the mind of a casual visitor." Historian John Fiske wrote: "In later years I used occasionally to meet Rosecrans, and I always thought that I could see the shadow of Chickamauga upon his noble face. The first time that I was introduced to him I was reminded of the strange look that haunted the face of Barnaby Rudge . . . the dim but abiding shadow of a look to which an instant of terrible and overwhelming experience only could have given birth. Afterward I always noticed the look. . . ."

Years later, an unnamed Washingtonian confided the true secret of Rosecrans' "smirk," "curious, nervous smile," and "strange and haunted look" to the editor of the Washington *Post*. The expression had nothing to do with Rosecrans' personality; it was caused by scar tissue that puckered his face as a result of burns he received in the refinery fire. Beneath his beard his smile was one-sided.

The Richmond *Examiner* on October 26 told its Confederate readers gleefully: "Lincoln is helping us. He has removed from command the most dangerous man in his army. Rosecrans thus retired is unquestionably the greatest captain the Yankee nation has yet produced."

From London, Henry Adams wrote to his brother, Charles Francis Adams, Jr.: "I suppose Meade will be removed. Nothing indeed can surprise me since the removal of Rosecrans. In the end Stanton must be turned out, but he has been probably as bad a Secretary of War as circumstances allowed him to be, and if he can deprive us of success, he will."

To bring his case to the public, Rosecrans asked Lincoln's permission to publish his own report of Chickamauga, along with those of Thomas, McCook, Crittenden, and Granger: "It is an act of justice I solicit from one in whose justice I confide." Lincoln answered, "With every disposition not only to do justice but to oblige you, I feel constrained to say that I think the publications had better not be made now."

Many wrote to Rosecrans to express affection and loyalty. General Abner Doubleday said: "I simply write to say that no one who knows you believes for a moment the accusations which are floating about in a certain class of newspapers. . . . Letters from your army speak of you in a most affectionate manner and show that the troops have undiminished confidence in you." And Truesdail, chief of Rosecrans' police, who was now out of assignment, wrote: "O Gen'l, the conspirators long at work have accomplished their end in your case. . . . It was necessary to turn public attention to some cause for such an event. True and just causes could not be found. . . . Some men who stooped low with uncovered heads before your person and smiled in your face were engaged in this unholy work."

Nine months later "Burke"—almost certainly Colonel Joseph W. Burke of the 10th Ohio—reported from Chattanooga that he had been dismayed to hear a rumor that Rosecrans' enemies in the army were increasing in "numbers and malevolence." This he said was false; except for a few "bigots and malcontents," the army was friendly to Rosecrans, and "the impression prevails here that Dana is nothing but a respectable spy" whose operations have caused "the most intense disgust and hatred. Stanton is despised on general principles, and Halleck because it is his desire to dishonor the character of every rising man."

After his release from Libby Prison, Colonel Streight wrote to say: "I cannot express my deep regret and mortification at your removal from the Army of the Cumberland. I consider your military operations around Chattanooga as the masterpiece of your eventful military career."

It was not easy for a man of Rosecrans' temperament to swallow his humiliation in silence, and he did not always succeed. One man wrote to Garfield that "Old Rosy has been about as busy as usual since he arrived—talking—talking—talking. The newspapers bother him terribly. Every little squib must be answered or corrected. In the meantime, Andrew Ward, Secretary of the meeting of the War Democrats at Chicago, has been stuffing the General with the idea that he will be nominated by them for the Presidency against Old Abe and the Peace Democrats' candidate, and the no-tion seems to please him much." Rosecrans was disturbed in particular by a letter from General Wood, published with Stanton's authorization and maintaining that the responsibility for the collapse at Chickamauga was his, not Wood's. He protested to Lincoln against such "violation of military usage and courtesy," and told Adjutant General Lorenzo Thomas that: "as the best of generals are liable to mistakes, I should have been content to leave those of General Wood to the simple historical statement of them, presuming that he regretted them far more deeply than even myself; and so feeling I called attention to his military virtues. . . . But his mean and unsoldierly defense of error shows him wrong both in head and heart."

The weeks went by and Rosecrans wondered when and where he would be returned to active duty. He wrote to Colonel Rutherford B. Hayes: "The views and motives of my removal . . . are not known to any one outside of the War Department. Various stories will be started and lies will be propagated, but in the integrity of my conscience I stand quietly biding the call of Providence and the judgment of my country and of history."

Who had wielded the final knife against Rosecrans—was it Grant, or Stanton, or Lincoln himself? What part did Dana and Garfield play?

It is clear that Lincoln's consent was needed, but why did he give it? Correspondent R. S. Furay thought that: "The clear sighted Lincoln yielded to some sinister influence. It was the one act of measureless injustice, which while not Abraham Lincoln's fault, stains the annals of his otherwise spotless career." Important among influences on Lincoln, as the diary of Navy Secretary Gideon Welles shows, were Dana's dispatches.

After the Chickamauga reports arrived, Welles wrote that "we" —presumably Welles and Lincoln—concluded that Halleck "had frittered away time and dispersed our forces" while the Confederates concentrated against Rosecrans. Welles, who did not like either Stanton or Halleck, complained on September 22: "I do not find that Stanton has much to say or do. No offensive movements here; no assistance rendered Rosecrans. Halleck has done nothing, proposed nothing, and is now beginning to take measures to reinforce Rosecrans." He reported that Stanton had said that same night: "Rosecrans ran away from his fighting men and did not stop for thirteen miles. McCook and Crittenden made pretty good time to Chattanooga, but Rosecrans beat them both." Reasons may have existed for Rosecrans' withdrawal, Welles wrote, but "these defects are always painful."

On September 28, Lincoln read to Welles and Seward a detailed and confidential dispatch, apparently Dana's dispatch charging that Crittenden and McCook had "wilted" on the battlefield, then had run back to Chattanooga, and gone to bed. This dispatch absolved Rosecrans from blame. Seward felt that all three should be removed. Welles wrote that Lincoln had lost all confidence in Rosecrans.

Hooker, too, had some part in shaping Lincoln's opinion of Rosecrans. In a gloomy telegram he described Rosecrans as "swayed entirely by passion." Hooker added: "It seems that he aspired to the command of the Army of the Potomac, and that mortal offense was given in not naming him first."

Fifteen years later General Steedman said that Lincoln had ordered him to Washington some weeks after Chickamauga. "What is your opinion concerning Rosecrans?" Lincoln asked him. "Well," said Steedman, "Rosecrans is a splendid man to command a victorious army." "But a defeated army?" Lincoln persisted. "I think there are two or three other men in the army that would do better." "Who besides yourself, General Steedman, is there in that army who could make a better commander?" Steedman had only one choice: "George H. Thomas." "I am glad to hear you say so," Lincoln replied, and that evening, Steedman said, "The order relieving Rosecrans went out."

Yet Steedman saw Lincoln *after* and not *before* Rosecrans' removal. Steedman left Chattanooga with Garfield, and on the 19th was in Nashville. Rosecrans was removed at least three days before his interview with Lincoln.

In November Sherman told Rosecrans in Cincinnati that he was astonished to see the newspaper reports that Grant was the cause of his removal. "I think Grant had no hand in it, for on the arrival of my corps I said to him, 'Why in the devil did you have Rosecrans relieved and Thomas placed in command of the Army of the Cumberland? Rosecrans is a better soldier than Thomas ever could be.' Grant replied to me, 'I had nothing to do with it and knew nothing of it till the morning after it was done.'"

Next spring Lincoln describes his own motives to James A. Gilmore:

I couldn't do anything but remove him [Lincoln declared]. The army had lost confidence in him. We could not have held Chattanooga three days longer if he had not been removed. His own dispatches after the battle confirmed that. I think Stanton had got a pique against him, but Chickamauga showed that Rosecrans was not equal to the occasion. I think Rosecrans a true man, and a very able man, and when the War Department merged the departments, I fully expected Rosecrans would remain in command. But you wouldn't have me put him in active service against Grant's express request, while Grant is commander-in-chief? I try to do my best. I have tried to do justice by Rosecrans. I did the most I could.

Lincoln repeated this explanation for Senator Doolittle of Wisconsin. He "knew and esteemed" Rosecrans' military talents and patriotism, he said, and removed him at Grant's request.

When Mary Hurlbut, fiancée of Grant's aide Colonel Rawlins, wrote him that there was much dissatisfaction about Rosecrans' removal, Rawlins replied:

While General Grant is no enemy of General Rosecrans, he could not in justice to himself and the cause of his country think again of commanding General Rosecrans, after his experience with him in the summer and fall of 1862. Of this the authorities at Washington were fully advised in General Grant's reports of the battles of Iuka and Corinth, in the former of which, in consequence of his deviation from the entire plan and order of battle the enemy was enabled to escape with much less loss than he should. To this might also be added the general spirit of insubordination toward General Grant, although to his face he professed to him the highest regard both as a man and officer.

Rawlins then described the Brown's Ferry operation.

The necessity of this movement had been canvassed here for weeks prior to General Grant's arrival, but until General Rosecrans was relieved and General Thomas succeeded to the command no steps had been taken to carry it into execution that I am aware of. The army is in fine spirits, and whatever may be their feelings of love and respect for General Rosecrans no regrets at his removal are evinced and all are unanimous in according to General Thomas the glory of saving the honor of our arms at Chickamauga.

Without intending censure of General Rosecrans, of one thing the country may be assured. When General Grant leaves the field of battle under the impression that all is lost there will remain no heroic Thomas to give a different coloring to that impression.

Greeley's man, Gilmore, had another explanation.

John Hay, Lincoln's second secretary, remembered that when he had warned Lincoln that the politically ambitious Chase would make capital out of the Rosecrans business, Lincoln had laughed. "I suppose that like the blue bottle fly he will lay his eggs in every rotten place he can find."

On December 24, 1863, Gilmore dined with Chase, and Chase told him that he learned that Rosecrans had lost his head at Chickamauga. "Up to that battle I had persistently stood by him, often to the strong displeasure of Mr. Stanton," Chase said. When Stanton proposed that Lincoln should remove Rosecrans, Lincoln said Rosecrans was the only Union general who had shown any ability to cope with Lee, and that his flanking of Bragg out of Shelbyville, Tullahoma, and Chattanooga was the "most splendid piece of strategy he knew of."

In the Rosecrans-Stanton feud Chase's sympathies had been with Rosecrans, he said. Finally, after Chickamauga, as Gilmore reported the conversation later, Chase "had received a letter from an officer in high rank under Rosecrans, and in whom he had great confidence, which said that after the breaking of our line, the general was totally unfitted to command. Nothing but the immovable firmness of Thomas saved the army." Chase had carried this letter for several days before showing it to Lincoln. Lincoln expressed "both surprise and incredulity, but said we could not afford to take any chances. We had already ordered Sherman to the support of Rosecrans, but he thought we had better do even more—merge the Departments of the Ohio, Cumberland and Tennessee, each with its present commander, but all three under Grant." Chase approved the plan and Lincoln presented it immediately to the cabinet. When, at Lincoln's request, Chase read the letter to the cabinet, Stanton suggested that Thomas replace Rosecrans. Lincoln objected; he did not believe the charges, nor wish to do Rosecrans an injustice. Finally he compromised with the decision that the "superseding of Rosecrans by Thomas should be left optional with Grant."

Chase had an orator's feeling for climax. "That letter," he said to Gilmore, "was written by Rosecrans' professed friend and admirer, James A. Garfield."

Chase made no further disclosure of the letter, and when he died in 1873, his secretary and biographer, Shuckers, withheld it from publication until 1882 when he gave it to Dana, who published it in the New York *Sun*. Rumors concerning it circulated, however, and Garfield denied to Rosecrans having written it, although it was whispered that he had indeed been disloyal to Rosecrans. Finally the still-buried letter became an issue in the presidential campaign of 1880.

The story of Garfield's secret and contradictory role was important in Rosecrans' career from January 1863 on.

After Garfield joined Rosecrans at Murfreesboro, he had told Chase that if the "country and the government will stand" by Rosecrans, "I feel sure that he will justify their highest expectations." When he wrote the next time, in April, he considered Rosecrans wise in not advancing unless he was prepared to hold the ground he won. "The impression is very general that the Grant expedition is a failure," he said; the Confederates planned to transfer their Vicksburg forces to Rosecrans' front. On May 5 Garfield wrote that he was eager to impress on Rosecrans the truth that Bragg's army, and not any particular position or territory, was the primary objective: "Nothing but hard blows will break their armies. I am, therefore, for striking, striking, and striking again, till we do break them." Four days later Garfield again wrote to Chase: "We are holding everything in suspense here till we have solid ground to go on."

During the next three months a mood of frustration and criticism seized Garfield, and he confessed to Chase that the "continued inaction of the army" was driving him into a depression like that he had endured a year before. On June 14 he wrote to Mrs. Garfield, "I have been so distressed at the long delay of this army to move, that I could hardly write to anyone more than to utter my disgust."

He was vexed, too, by the Tullahoma campaign: "If we had reached Tullahoma before Bragg, we should have destroyed his army." When Rosecrans halted again, Garfield wrote to Chase in a letter marked "Confidential":

I have for a long time wanted to write to you confidentially on the movements of this department, but I have refrained hitherto lest I do injustice to a good man. We have now, however, reached a point upon which I feel it proper to acquaint you with the condition of affairs here.

I have been greatly tried and dissatisfied with the slow progress that we have made since the battle of Stone River. It would be in the highest degree unjust to say that the 162 days which elapsed between the battle of Stone's River and the next advance of this army were spent in idleness or trifling. But for many weeks prior to our late movement I could not but feel that there was not that live and earnest determination to make "the army's" power felt in crushing the rebellion. At that time the strings began to draw sharply upon the rebels, both on the Mississippi and on the East. They began to fear for the safety of Vicksburg, and before the middle of May they began quietly to draw away forces to aid Pemberton. I pleaded for an advance, but not till June began did General Rosecrans begin seriously to meditate an immediate movement. I was the only one who urged upon the General the imperative necessity of striking a blow at once, while Bragg was weaker and we stronger than ever before. After an advance was agreed upon, it was delayed through days which seemed months to me, till the 24th when it was begun. The wisdom of the movement was not only vindicated, but the seventeen dissenting generals were compelled to confess that, if the movement had been made ten days earlier, while the weather was propitious, the army of Bragg would, in all human probability, no longer exist.

On the 18th instant the bridges were rebuilt, and the cars were in full communication from the Cumberland to the Tennessee. I have since then urged with all the earnestness I possess a rapid advance, while Bragg's army was shattered and under cover, and before Johnston and he could effect a junction. Thus far the General has been singularly disinclined to grasp the situation with a strong hand, and make the advantage his own. I write this with more sorrow than I can tell you, for I love every bone in his body, and next to my desire to see the rebellion blasted, is my anxiety to see him blessed. But even the breadth of my love is not sufficient to cover this almost fatal delay. My personal relations with General Rosecrans are all that I could desire. Pleasant as are my relations here, I would rather command a battalion that would follow and follow and strike and strike than to hang back while such golden moments are passing. If this inaction continues long, I shall ask to be relieved and sent somewhere where I can be part of a working army.

After Chickamauga, Garfield sent letters to Chase on September 22 and 23. The second of these told that the Union army had given as much as it had taken, and could remain where it was for ten days if help would come then. "If we hold this point, we shall save this army."

Further evidence of Garfield's duplicity came from Villard:

Garfield took me freely into his confidence. He told me how fully convinced he was that his chief was making a mortal mistake in going to Chattanooga, how he tried to dissuade him from it, and how relieved he himself was to be permitted to join Thomas. While he did not say so directly, it could be inferred that his faith in Rosecrans' military qualifications was shaken, if not lost, and that he was not sorry to part official company with him. His changed opinion naturally made his position very embarrassing to him.

But this was not all. At Louisville on October 21, the day after Rosecrans had been removed, Stanton waited to cross-examine Garfield. He had just interviewed Dana, and it was impossible, therefore, for Garfield "to avoid mention of incidents which bore unfavorably upon Rosecrans." Besides, Garfield told Cox, "Stanton knew well how to question him." Stanton questioned Steedman also. It is easy to visualize the brilliant trial lawyer using the advantage of his secretaryship to bully and wheedle from the squirming and eager-to-please generals the answers he wanted against Rosecrans.

With Stanton's dispatch unavailable—the *Official Records* of the Chickamauga campaign were published in 1890, and those of the Chattanooga campaign still later—Garfield wrote to Rosecrans in 1880: "On my way to Washington I met Stanton in Louisville and when he denounced you in vigorous language I rebuked him and earnestly defended you against his assaults." Yet Stanton's telegram of October 21, 1863, to Assistant Secretary of War Watson said: "Generals Garfield and Steedman are here. Their representations of the incidents of the battle of Chickamauga more than confirm the worst that has reached us as to the conduct of the commanding General and the great credit that is due Thomas."

In 1881 General Anson Stager, former Superintendent of Military Telegraph, told Rosecrans' friend, General Francis Darr, that "at an interview [October 21] in Louisville between Garfield and Stanton, Andy Johnson and I were present, Garfield and I being the only survivors. Garfield in my presence denounced Rosecrans as incompetent, unworthy of his position, as having lost the confidence of his army, and should be removed."

Two days after Garfield left Stanton in Louisville he visited Cox in Cincinnati, and both agreed, as Cox afterwards recorded, that Rosecrans' "perceptions were acute," but that he lacked the "poise and steadiness to handle great affairs successfully." He had a "fatal defect," a tendency to lose control of himself and others at a time of crisis when control was most needed.

Garfield described the break-through at Chickamauga to Cox, and when he said that Rosecrans "listlessly and mechanically" gave him permission to attempt to reach Thomas, Cox reported that Garfield "leaned forward, bringing his excited face to mine, and his hand came heavily down upon my knee as in whispered tones he described the collapse of nerve and of will that had befallen his chief. . . . Unfortunately there was no doubt that the general was defeated, whether his army was or not." Yet later that same day Garfield wrote to Rosecrans: "I have waited for two days and would be exceedingly glad to see you, but I must go tonight or I cannot reach home before Monday. I therefore must go away without seeing you. The action of the War Dep't. fell upon me like the sound of a fire bell. I am sure that it will be the verdict of the people that the War Dep't. has made a great mistake and have done you a great wrong."

Garfield left for Washington and an interview with Lincoln. When Postmaster General Montgomery Blair later criticized to the President Rosecrans' removal on charges of misconduct at Chickamauga, Lincoln told him that he had not acted on rumors; that Garfield had substantiated the charges. It was Blair's impression that Garfield had done so in person. Blair thought that Garfield hoped to gain military advancement, even to succeed Thomas as commander of the Army of the Cumberland. Garfield, Blair said, told Lincoln that:

. . . he had come on to look over the ground with a view of deciding the question of accepting his election to the House of Representatives. He was not inclined to leave the Army; he had become thoroughly identified with the Army of the Cumberland, and believed that as a commander of troops he would be a success. Mr. Lincoln replied that the Administration wanted a soldier from the field, who knew the wants of the armies from practical knowledge, and he hoped that the General would not hesitate about accepting his election; and as to commanding troops, they had more generals around loose than they knew what to do with.

Blair described a large dinner party given after that by his father, Francis P. Blair, and attended by his brother General Francis P. Blair, Jr., Governor Dennison, and Garfield: "Dennison, I recollect, condemned strongly the removal of Rosecrans, and there was a general concurrence in his views and I recollect that Garfield especially was loud and pronounced in condemning the act. I was of course very much astonished at his duplicity."

Garfield's letter of December 16 to Rosecrans told him how he and Senator Ben Wade of Ohio—Wade described himself to Garfield as a "staunch and ardent friend of R."—had had a "full, direct, and very satisfactory talk" with Lincoln about Rosecrans' future. They argued the justice of assigning Rosecrans to active duty and Lincoln said to them, as Garfield's letter reported it: "I am anxious to do it for several reasons and not the least of them is to show Rosecrans that he is my friend." The letter went on:

He said that the service you rendered at Stone's River was, at the time it was rendered, ONE of the most if not THE most important props of support the country has had since the war. If that battle had been lost it is difficult to see where our fortunes would have landed, and to you personally the country was deeply indebted for its salvation. In the next place, he said, your support of the government in the two letters to the Democrats of Indiana, was, if possible, more important than your service at Stone's River. He said that it was the tone of your dispatches from Chickamauga several days after the battle that led him to fear that you did not feel confident that you could hold the place; and hence the consolidation of the three armies to make Chattanooga sure. It was still at that time his intention to keep you at the head of the Army of the Cumberland, as before with Grant the ranking officer in command of the whole, BUT GRANT MADE IT A CONDITION OF ACCEPTING THE COMMAND THAT YOU SHOULD BE REMOVED. The statement (concerning Grant) I would not like to have repeated except in the strictest confidence. In view of the fact that Schofield has been ordered to Washington and is now here and the fact that the President wants to assign you to a command leads me to expect that you will be assigned to the Department of Missouri.

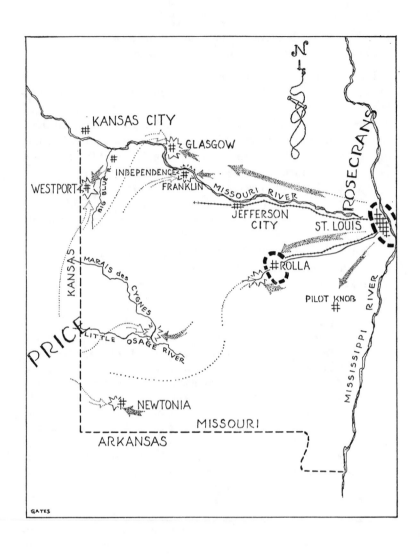

MISSOURI CAMPAIGNS

July–October 1864

Eighteen

MISSOURI

Rosecrans was neither the sort of man to sit idly by without assignment while others won glory in ending the war, nor the sort of general to accept a subordinate assignment. He was not easily silenced, squelched, or discouraged. His self-confidence was enormous, his sense of duty stern, his energy heroic, and his self-righteousness strong. The public receptions after his removal and the letters of powerful friends persuaded him that he was not yesterday's hero.

"There is very little chance of your being assigned by the present head of the War Department to any command, unless it be of Missouri," Bond wrote to him from New York, "and as I am told there now is nothing to do there except to quarrel with politicians." And from Washington, Postmaster General Dennison reported: "The President is your friend and will send you to Missouri."

Except for Halleck, who was saved only by his subordinates' victories elsewhere, every commander in Missouri had emerged with a diminished reputation. Missouri was now scarcely more than a noisome, muddied backwater. But it was still an independent department and command, and in receiving it, Rosecrans was treated better than McDowell, Pope, Buell, McClernand, McClellan and others who had fallen from official favor had been. None of them had been given a real second chance. The assignment might have been worse, and indeed within months Rosecrans would again find himself within the heart of a critical campaign.

John M. Schofield, who had been made commander in Missouri

in May, 1863, had been drawn into the quarrel between the Missouri Radicals and Conservatives. The leaders of both factions reached a single point of common agreement: if Schofield would request his own removal, he would be generously treated. Lincoln found it "scarcely less than indispensable . . . to do something for General Rosecrans . . . Senators Henderson and Brown will agree to him for the Commander of their department." He explained that Grant and Sherman, for reasons he did not understand, disliked Rosecrans but regarded Schofield highly, and that while Missouri Radicals disliked Schofield, they considered Rosecrans acceptable. The change would therefore satisfy all parties, though neither Halleck nor Stanton wanted Rosecrans. Rosecrans' appointment was dated January 28, 1864, and next day he arrived in St. Louis. He brought with him Major Bond as senior aide-de-camp, and Thoms and Drouillard and, after assuming command on January 30, left immediately for Nashville to appear before the courts of inquiry on McCook, Crittenden, and Negley. Rosecrans appeared before all three. The Court found that McCook's leaving the field was an "error in judgment," but that it was reasonable for him to suppose that since Rosecrans had gone to Chattanooga the scattered troops would rally there, and it might be proper for McCook to follow, to confer with Rosecrans. McCook's known gallantry forbade reflections on his courage. The Court did not censure Crittenden for going to Chattanooga. Nor did it censure Negley. Wood had apparently indulged in "coarse and offensive epithets" reflecting on Negley's conduct, but when he failed to support these accusations, the Court condemned his own conduct as leading to "vexatious and unprofitable investigations prejudicial to the service."

Rosecrans returned to his command, and studied the problems posed by his new post. St. Louis, he found, was the principal mid-continent depot for all quartermasters and subsistence stores for the armies on the Mississippi and Red rivers, in Kansas, and in Indian Territory. It was a chief depot for the army in Tennessee. As late as December 1863, the Department of Missouri reported an aggregate of 68,425 troops. Transfers to Arkansas and Kansas left Rosecrans with some 25,000 officers and men, present and absent, but with only 660 officers and 16,323 men present for duty. Some 3,100 of these were in or about St. Louis, and the remainder were scattered over the entire state—an area of some 69,000 square miles. Eleven regiments of militia were being recruited as a second line. For months these had only a paper existence. In the whole state there were forty-two pieces of field artillery. This force must guard St. Louis, protect persons and property, and restore law, order, and industry, especially tillage. Assuming that a dispersal of this force in seven garrisons represented War Department policy, Rosecrans maintained it. Northwest Missouri was guarded by about 2,800 provisionally enrolled militia, sneeringly called "Paw-Paws," and charged often by Union men with disloyalty. Ultra-Unionists, or "Radicals," wanted the Paw-Paws dissolved, and luke-warm Unionists, who called themselves "Conservatives," wanted them kept. Rosecrans told both factions that the Paw-Paws would keep their officers: "We ought to leave those who behave rightfully in peace, notwithstanding their former conduct."

When Rosecrans asked Halleck for out-of-state troops to police Western Missouri Halleck approved the scheme but could send no men. For two years Halleck had himself advocated such a policy but political influences had opposed it. Grant believed, on the other hand, that Missouri had more than enough troops and sent General Hunt to investigate, and Hunt told Rosecrans: "I think the people will behave themselves. I don't think you need even the troops here now."

Echoes of past events followed Rosecrans. When a resolution to thank Thomas for his stand at Chickamauga reached the House, Rosecrans wrote to Garfield that it had his "hearty approval for what it contains," but his "protest for what it does not contain," and Garfield sought to amend the measure by having it thank Rosecrans also, for the campaign culminating in Chickamauga. The House agreed to include Rosecrans, but the Senate never voted on the bill as amended, and Thomas failed to receive the thanks of Congress. In protecting his own reputation, Rosecrans had proved less than generous to his consistently loyal friend.

Rosecrans bustled to put Missouri affairs in order, even though Halleck told Grant that there was no more danger of a disturbance in St. Louis, than in Chicago or Springfield or Cincinnati, and ordered him to send forty-two companies of infantry and cavalry to General E. R. S. Canby in Mississippi and to telegraph their progress daily.

Four regiments marched immediately, though their departure left Rosecrans without sufficient forces to guard his grand depots, railroads and communications, and he asked Lincoln whether Negroes might be enlisted. It was popular nonetheless to joke of "wringing" troops from Rosecrans.

On March 2 Rosecrans, in the first of a series of ill-advised, somewhat pathetic, and futile attempts to regain a key military position, proposed that he accompany the governor of Missouri to Washington to lay plans for policy changes before the Secretary of War. Stanton wisely declined "for the present to give the order asked for." Rosecrans' arrival would have coincided with Grant's. On March 9 Grant received his lieutenant general's commission, and on the 10th became commander-in-chief.

Grant decided to remain with the Army of the Potomac, leaving Meade in nominal charge, and chose Sherman to lead the Western armies. He hoped himself to destroy or capture Lee's army; he hoped Sherman would crush Johnston. Richmond was a collateral objective in the one case, Atlanta in the other. Union activity on other fronts was to be reduced almost to nothing. It was a sensible —the inevitable—strategy.

On the 15th, Rosecrans outlined his own plans to Halleck: to bring troops to Missouri from other states, to muster the Missouri militia into Federal service, and to convert the ten regiments of Missouri state militia into U.S. Volunteers or disband them. State troops had their disadvantages. They owed divided allegiance, and refused to fight outside of the state. Missouri, Kansas, and Arkansas troops should then combine to sweep the country west of the Mississippi to the gulf. The division of the trans-Mississippi region into independent departments put all of them on the defensive and immobilized them.

Rosecrans still had firm friends in Washington and elsewhere. For instance, Garfield wrote to him in March: "I have known but few men so deeply and intimately as yourself, and I feel that ours was not a mere official or even social acquaintance, but a meeting and mingling of spirits. I am glad to tell you that the Missouri men are well satisfied with your administration."

Next, Rosecrans attempted to influence policy by reaching Grant and Sherman via Sherman's brother-in-law and foster brother, and his own friend, Thomas Ewing. At Rosecrans' request

Curtis transferred Ewing from Kansas to him, and Rosecrans wrote to Sherman: "I wanted to have General Ewing see you in reference to a plan for combining all the Kansas, Arkansas, and Missouri troops, with cooperation from Banks, to sweep the country west of the Mississippi clear to the Gulf, including Texas ultimately." Ewing presented Rosecrans' plan to Sherman, and Rosecrans wired Sherman hopefully that he could move south if he received four regiments of infantry and two of cavalry. Even without reinforcements he could still advance with four or five thousand cavalry, fifteen hundred infantry and five batteries. Sherman's answer was prompt: "I start for Cincinnati with Major-General Grant this morning. Have had a full consultation with him. No extended movement west of the Mississippi is under contemplation save the one now in progress up the Red River by Banks."

Rosecrans should have dropped the matter but instead, on March 21, he telegraphed to Lincoln: "I hope all the policy submitted to the War Department in a letter a few days since will be approved." There was no response.

Another snub followed. At Rosecrans' request Colonel John P. Sanderson had been transferred to Missouri. Rosecrans had appointed him Provost Marshal General, and recommended him for a brigadier's commission. The Senate Military Affairs Committee refused to concur in the promotion. "This comes upon me like a thunderbolt from a clear sky," Rosecrans wrote to Halleck. To plead Sanderson's case and to discuss military plans Rosecrans sent Bond to Washington, whereupon the War Department ordered Bond arrested, "on pretense," Rosecrans said, and returned to St. Louis for trial, on charges of violating an army regulation prohibiting an officer on leave of absence from visiting the Capitol. Rosecrans was very angry. It was apparent to Rosecrans, Bond wrote to Garfield, that Bond's arrest was an "attack upon himself." The court-martial appointed by Rosecrans not surprisingly found Bond not guilty. "There is a great feeling of indignation against Halleck and the War Department among members of Congress for the way Major Bond was treated," Garfield wrote to Rosecrans.

Rosecrans sent Garfield the documents in the Bond case, and declared: "History will demand why this nation suffered its interests to remain in the hands of a such a cabinet minister. But I fear the President's kind professions are not to produce any good fruit for me. If they do, I shall consider him more 'cunning' than 'honest Old Abe.' "

On March 26 Grant proposed to Rosecrans that as long as Steele's Arkansas army stood between Missouri and Confederate threat he would cut the forces west of the Mississippi to minimum garrisons. Rosecrans was to guard Missouri with light cavalry against "irresponsible squads of guerrillas and restless but dissatisfied citizens, dispatching 5,000 to 7,000 infantry for service elsewhere."

In the midst of these frustrations, a conspiracy on his doorstep provided Rosecrans with an apparent opportunity to rebuild his diminished reputation. It dogged him from March through November 1864. Of his services in its suppression James A. Gilmore said: "The full discovery he made of this Conspiracy is one of the most important of the many great services he rendered to the country." His connection with it came through Sanderson's activity.

About March 1, Sanderson learned that most of the Paw-Paws belonged to the Order of American Knights or the OAKS. Evidence of the Order's existence appeared throughout the West Central States, and it became clear that Vallandigham was connected with it.

During the middle months of 1864 there were desperate hopes of subversion in the North. Deep in Virginia and Georgia, Grant and Sherman drew reinforcements to themselves, until remote garrisons were reduced below the point of safety. The Knights planned to have Vallandigham attend the Democratic Convention in Chicago, which began July 4. Next they would rise and seize poorly guarded Union prisons. Grant and Sherman could free no troops to quell them. Thus they hoped to terminate the war.

William Forse Scott points out:

Missouri was even more important to the Confederates than to the Federals. If a Southern army could occupy Missouri just before the Presidential election, the vote of the State could not be taken, or if taken, would go to McClellan; the vote of the neighboring states would or might also be turned to McClellan, and Sherman would be compelled to retire from Atlanta to the Ohio. A rosy dream it looks, but such visions were not uncommon in the warm Southern imagination.

The alarm spread to the Middle Western governors. To gain access to Lincoln, Rosecrans wrote to Garfield, and Garfield reported that Lincoln "requested me to write to him freely on the matter. My own opinion is that he is afraid of a clash between you and someone else, probably Gen. Grant, and he would rather have the matter written about at a distance." On June 2, Rosecrans wrote directly to Lincoln: "To convey the facts to you and avoid such an outrage on my messenger as was perpetrated on Major Bond, I respectfully request an order from you to forward the documents by a staff officer."

Lincoln answered: "Send it by express. . . ." Rosecrans, however, considered the information "too grave," although Lincoln could not understand "how a message can be less safe by the express than by the staff officer." Involved, say Nicolay and Hay, was Rosecrans' "ill-concealed desire to have countermanded an order of the Secretary of War. The President had no desire to sustain Rosecrans against Stanton."

To break this impasse, on June 9, Lincoln sent his second secretary, John Hay, to St. Louis: "Please communicate in writing or verbally, anything you would think proper to say to me."

On June 22 Rosecrans sent Sanderson's 1000-page report to Lincoln. Lincoln refused to take the OAKS conspiracy seriously. Hay sustained his judgment, and official silence and inactivity followed Hay's report.

Fortunately, events proved Lincoln right. The OAKS did not possess the strength they boasted, nor did they act promptly. Nor could they act secretly, because the North had been alerted by Rosecrans and General Samuel P. Heintzelman, who commanded in Ohio. Publicizing their plans was in itself a powerful weapon against successful execution.

Late in May, General Edward R. S. Canby was appointed commander of the newly created West Mississippi Division and Missouri was included in his command. Stanton ordered Halleck to inform Rosecrans, who probably desired the assignment himself, that "any orders issued by Major General Canby in his name will be obeyed by you." Rosecrans knew that the authority of commanders of geographical departments could be abridged only by Lincoln, and therefore protested; two weeks later, by presidential decree, Missouri was attached to Canby's division. "Whatever I may think of the course pursued by the War Department," Rosecrans wrote to Canby, "I have no hesitation in assuring you of my cordial cooperation. . . ." But whether Rosecrans would obey Canby's orders, Halleck told Grant, "remains to be seen."

On May 4 Grant crossed the Rapidan River in Virginia to begin his great offensive against Lee, while two days later Sherman marched South against Johnston, with Atlanta as his objective. On May 5 Lee attacked Grant in the Wilderness, and, scorning grand strategy, Grant ordered his army into a slaughter that in three days cost him twenty thousand casualties to Lee's ten thousand, but produced no other definite result. By the 8th Grant was again marching and on the 10th made a second massive assault, losing thirteen thousand more men. Again on the 12th, he attacked with heavy losses, but doggedly kept moving south.

To replace these casualties other commands were stripped. Halleck complained to Grant on the 12th that, despite repeated orders, Rosecrans still retained the 9th Iowa cavalry. "I am powerless to make dispositions without troops," Rosecrans said. Except for city militia St. Louis would soon be unguarded. By the middle of June, Missouri had only three or four Union regiments.

Guerrilla activity intensified in Missouri where there was much divided allegiance, and Rosecrans, finding himself powerless to protect depots, communications, and people, asked Halleck: "What shall I do?" Halleck answered: "Use hundred days men." "If more troops are called for," said Rosecrans, "it may be necessary to abandon the whole southwest portion of Missouri."

On June 3 at Cold Harbor Grant flung his army of 150,000 men against Lee's 75,000 in an effort to destroy Lee before he could withdraw into the Richmond fortifications. The Union attack lasted less than an hour, and was repulsed with a loss to Grant of between seven and eight thousand men. By June 20 Lee had crossed the James River and was safely behind the Richmond intrenchments, and Grant had lost the great chance to take Petersburg and by victory on the eastern front to end the war that summer. The campaign left the Army of the Potomac so worn that its reconstruction and reorganization required most of the following summer, fall, and winter. Meanwhile it besieged Lee on the Richmond-Petersburg line. From May 4 to June 12 Grant's losses in killed, wounded, sick, and captured had been some sixty thousand men, as many as Lee had when the campaign began. Grant needed replacements, and reacted bitterly when Halleck told him that "Rosecrans and Curtis"—Curtis commanded in Kansas—"are continually calling for more troops in their departments. . . . They want 20,000 men to oppose 2,000 guerrillas." "I am satisfied that you would hear the same call if they were stationed in Maine," Grant replied. ". . . Rosecrans should be removed and someone else placed in command. It makes but little difference who you assign, it would be an improvement."

Left with skeleton commands, Rosecrans and Curtis had to deal with a swarm of bushwhackers produced by ten years of disorder. Distant, sparsely settled areas were particularly vulnerable. Inspector General Randolph B. Marcy, on a visit to Missouri, found feeling so bitter that some Union officers and soldiers executed guerrillas, even after surrender. Not even the threat of death by hanging put an end to the activities of the bushwhackers, whose maraudings and pilferings Rosecrans called "hellish." The bushwhackers, he said, were "demons."

To combat them Rosecrans authorized investigations by one Harry Truman—sometimes designated as "H.T." and sometimes as "Captain" Truman. A few weeks after Truman entered Northern Missouri in disguise reports began to filter back that this "cruel scourge . . . did more harm in a week than the Confederates had done during the war . . . was drunk all the time [in a] 'pilgrimage' that had become a personal raid for plunder. He was said to be travelling in a 'state of beastly intoxication with a notorious prostitute.'" Rosecrans ordered Truman jailed, and there the *Records* leave him.

Rosecrans asked Missourians to co-operate with him by setting up county committees of safety. Disloyalty lurked everywhere, and to control it, in one quarter at least, Rosecrans on March 7, 1864, issued Special Order No. 61, requiring that members of larger representative church organizations, such as conventions, synods, and councils, should take an oath of allegiance. Lincoln admonished him mildly: "I somewhat dread the effect. I have found men who have not even been suspected of disloyalty to be averse to taking an oath of any sort as a condition to exercising an ordinary right of citizenship. The point will probably be made that while men may, without an oath, assemble in a noisy political meeting, they must take the oath to assemble in a religious meeting. So far you have got along in the Dept. of Missouri rather better than I dared to hope and I congratulate you and myself upon it."

The glory denied him elsewhere, Rosecrans came near achieving in the presidential race of 1864. Because war aims split the major parties, Republicans proclaimed themselves the National Union Party, and sought a war Democrat to run as vice-president with Lincoln. The National Union convention met in Baltimore on June 7.

Garfield controlled the Ohio delegation, and therefore had a strong voice in the councils of the Republican party, controlling enough votes to name the vice-presidential candidate. While Lincoln was popular, the inner circle of politicians guiding the Convention felt that someone else, preferably a soldier and a war democrat, was needed to balance the ticket and produce a winning vote. Garfield turned to Rosecrans. Rosecrans had won brilliant victories and had a large following in and out of the army. Many people had come to feel that after Chickamauga he had not been dealt with fairly, and the tide of popular sentiment was running so strongly in his favor that well informed Republicans thought that his presence on the national ticket could strengthen it.

Garfield wired Rosecrans from the floor of the convention, "Will you allow your name to be used for vice-president on the ticket with Mr. Lincoln?" Rosecrans consulted friends and replied: "The convention must discharge its high and responsible duties, in view of our national exigencies, according to its judgement and conscience, leaving me to the exercise of mine when I shall know its decision. The nomination of any man acceptable to the loyal people of the Union would satisfy me." A simple "yes" would have been clearer.

Garfield did not receive Rosecrans' answer. No one seems to know what happened to it, but L. W. Mulhane, who corresponded with Rosecrans and whose views were likely those of Rosecrans himself, felt that it had been "pretty well established" that Stanton had intercepted and suppressed it. Active service kept Rosecrans in the public eye and made him important politically. Election to high office, or even nomination for it, would give him a rostrum from which he might inveigh against them. Removal from command would partially silence him, discredit him, cost him followers, an audience, a chance to stir up trouble. The telegraph line to Baltimore cleared through Stanton's office. Such action would have been in conformity with Stanton's established character, personal advantage and prior conduct. This story was freely circulated among both the friends and enemies of Rosecrans and never questioned. The incident could not have escaped the notice of Rosecrans' enemies and certainly must have added to their determination to shelve him. With no reply, Garfield acquiesced in the naming of Andrew Johnson.

From January 1864 until June, Confederate forces west of the Mississippi were chiefly concerned with turning back the threat of the Red River Expedition. This joint land and water undertaking, commanded by General Nathaniel Banks, with Admiral David D. Porter in charge of the large river flotilla, was organized to capture Shreveport, Louisiana, chief strategic point west of the Mississippi. While Banks and Porter advanced up the line of the Red other trans-Mississippi forces acted in concert with them.

Throughout the winter of 1863–64, General Frederick Steele, Commander of the Army of the Arkansas at Little Rock in middle Arkansas, and General James G. Blunt at Forth Smith on the west, had held the line of Arkansas River for the Union while Price occupied southern Arkansas for the Confederacy. March ended as Banks moved up the Red River, where Steele and Blunt converged to unite with him at Shreveport, Louisiana. Steele drove Price back until Price was reinforced by 8,000 infantry, whereupon he forced Steele to retreat to the flood-swollen Saline River. There Steele turned to beat Price so badly that he returned to southern Arkansas, to prepare to invade Missouri instead.

On April 8, after being driven back at Saline Cross Roads, Louisiana, Banks began a retreat down the river, reaching Alexandria by the end of the month. There with great difficulty the fleet was floated through the shallows of the rapidly falling river. The whole expedition was lucky to escape, Banks to New Orleans and Porter into the Mississippi.

With the defeated Union forces cleared from Louisiana Rosecrans by July was satisfied from the "utter feebleness" of his own command that an attack on Missouri was inevitable. He finally received permission to raise such troops as needed to strengthen his forces and set about recruiting eleven regiments of twelve-month volunteer infantry. Intensified guerrilla activity in the northern counties of Missouri was another harbinger of invasion. It was bruited that 23,000 Missouri OAKS waited to greet their Confederate deliverers. Beyond the frontiers of Missouri Price listened for the rumble of revolt, as the season brought good weather and ripe corn.

Price's plan was able. Confederate forces in Indian Territory and western Arkansas were to demonstrate against Forts Smith and Gibson and thus threaten Union communications with Kansas. Simultaneously, other Confederates would menace Little Rock. These demonstrations would prevent the dispatching of aid to Missouri from the small forces in Kansas, Indian Territory, and Arkansas, and Price, with 15,000 mounted veterans and twenty pieces of artillery, would then invade Missouri in three columns. About September 1, while Fort Smith and Little Rock were threatened, Price crossed the Arkansas midway between these two places and marched toward Missouri.

To repel him, Rosecrans had only policing forces, fully occupied in controlling an unruly state. Five of the eleven regiments he had received permission to recruit had been enlisted when the invasion began. By consolidating his force, Rosecrans might have fought a successful defensive campaign against Price, but he would have been compelled to surrender the remainder of Missouri, which would then be unguarded, to Confederate sympathizers and bushwhackers; recruits would then certainly have flocked to Price. Rosecrans did not abandon Missouri. Instead, when he learned that General A. J. Smith, with a division from Banks, was passing Cairo, Illinois, on his way to Sherman, he asked Halleck to halt Smith until Price's intentions were clarified. Halleck's order to "operate against Price and Co.," reached Smith on September 9. Halleck thought that Smith should cross the Mississippi from Cairo to Missouri, permit Price to get north of his point of entry, and then, moving in Price's rear, join his 4,500 veterans with Blunt and Steele out of Arkansas. Smith, however, marched to the vicinity of St. Louis, from which he could proceed by rail and water as the situation demanded. Halleck gave Smith authority to act independently of Rosecrans, but fortunately Smith did not excercise this option of hunting Price's 15,000 cavalry with 4,500 infantry. Rosecrans wrote later: "Too much of a soldier to take literally orders so little suited to the circumstances and so at variance with the usage of the Service, General Smith reported to me for orders."

Sherman meanwhile had occupied Atlanta at the beginning of September, and when late in the month the defeated Hood struck north to make a diversionary thrust through Alabama and Tennessee, to cut Sherman's communications and strike at Nashville, Sherman sent Thomas to beat Hood to Nashville and resist him. Sherman was poorly informed about Rosecrans' dilemma and did not believe that Price could enter Missouri except on minor raids. He grumbled to Grant: "The truth is Rosecrans should be ashamed to take my troops for such a purpose." And Grant wired him that "the only way a soldier can ever be taken from Rosecrans is by sending a staff officer directly to him to execute the order. I do not know that he had any troops to spare, but it would be all the same if he had double the number he has."

On September 23, Price crossed the Arkansas, and entered Missouri along the White River. Three invasion routes were open to Price, but Rosecrans believed that strong military reasons favored a main invasion by the central or Springfield route, with a sortie by way of Pocahontas to isolate southeast Missouri, and he disposed his garrisons accordingly.

As Price swept toward St. Louis, Sherman asked Rosecrans to return Smith's division. Rosecrans answered that Smith confronted an enemy outnumbering him two or three to one; "We are arming every available citizen and militia man in St. Louis to defend the city."

On the morning of the 27th, at Pilot Knob, a natural citadel of great defensive strength eighty-six miles from St. Louis, mounting his artillery in Fort Davidson which frowned down upon a valley, Ewing, with only a thousand men, threw Price back. Union losses were 150 men killed, wounded, and missing; Confederate, 1500 men. That night, having spiked his heavy guns, Ewing began a slow retreat. It was now clear that Price was heading for St. Louis, two days' march to the north. Rosecrans therefore hastily assembled a garrison consisting of Smith's 4,500 infantry, 1,500 volunteer cavalry, skeletons of the eleven regiments of enrolled Missouri militia, and about 4,000 or 5,000 citizen volunteers. Five regiments of Illinois hundred-day volunteers began to arrive on the 30th.

They had come on the understanding that they would not be sent beyond the city limits.

When Halleck learned that Rosecrans at this juncture had ordered to St. Louis two regiments belonging to Sherman, he telegraphed Grant: "I have telegraphed him to forward them on immediately, but I presume he will, as usual, disobey orders. . . . General Canby telegraphs that the forces under Steele and Rosecrans are greatly superior to those of the enemy." Halleck apparently forgot that Steele was at Little Rock, 300 miles in direct line southwest of St. Louis, wholly beyond support. Grant replied: "If Rosecrans does not send forward the regiments belonging to Sherman as ordered, arrest him, by my order, unless the President will authorize his being relieved from command altogether."

Fortunately Rosecrans' makeshift garrison caused Price to veer westerly, and by October 2 he had massed his forces at Union, practically equidistant from Rolla and Jefferson City. He was trailed by the Federal forces, and on the 5th, General Joseph A. Mower arrived at Cape Girardeau, Missouri, from the Red River expedition, and was brought by transports to St. Louis, whence Rosecrans sent him to join Smith at Jefferson City. With only 6,000 U.S. volunteers, augmented by some Missouri militia and a civilian legion, Rosecrans had not dared to attack Price's 15,000 mounted men, but considered it prudent to dog Price, without risking St. Louis, until Mower arrived. On October 6 Price began to cross the Osage river, covered by his artillery and in the face of Union cavalry.

McNeil, Sanborn, Fish, and Brown had united their small commands, thus raising Union forces at Jefferson City to 4,000 cavalry and 2,600 infantry; the generals were agreed that they would make moderate resistance at the Moreau, five miles east. On October 7, when Price struck this "moderate resistance," he withdrew, Jefferson City behind him and St. Louis a hundred miles to his rear. He now proposed to seize Kansas City and Fort Leavenworth, and to invade and desolate Kansas. Curtis learned that Price was coming, and concentrated his regulars in eastern Kansas, south of Kansas City, stationing twenty-four regiments of militia, under Blunt's command, along the eastern Kansas line. Blunt crossed into Missouri to Lexington, some forty miles east on the Missouri River, hoping to delay the Confederates until Rosecrans and Mower could catch up with Price. Although Price remained strong, the direction of his movement gave Rosecrans an opportunity further to concentrate his forces.

By now Rosecrans had taken personal command in the field. He left St. Louis on October 12, reached Jefferson City two days later, and advanced to Warrensburg, Missouri, where he was to remain through November 1.

Price was hugging the south bank of the Missouri, with Sanborn behind him. On October 18, Price hurried westward between Marshall and Waverly. That day Mower's infantry disembarked at Jefferson City and was pushed by rail to join Smith, who was marching three days ahead. At Marshall, Price considered attacking, but pursuing Union cavalry changed his mind, and he fled toward Lexington on the south Missouri bank, forty miles to the west.

Price was now within reach of Curtis, and on the 19th, Curtis telegraphed Rosecrans that the head of Blunt's column had arrived at Lexington, skirmished sharply with Price, and had fallen back toward Independence, which he captured, burning bridges behind it. Price was therefore trapped between Rosecrans on the east, Curtis on the west, and the Missouri River on the north. Curtis and Blunt were resolved to hold Price east of the Big Blue River until Rosecrans arrived, but on the 21st Price gradually forced them back.

During this period, for whatever reason, in a campaign in which Curtis and Rosecrans were operating against a common foe, Curtis reported to Washington and was credited with having won a victory or at least with putting up a fight, while Rosecrans did not report. Some grounds existed, therefore, for Lincoln's question on October 21 to his secretary J. G. Nicolay, who was in St. Louis: "While Curtis is fighting Price have you any idea where the force under Rosecrans is, or what it is doing?" And for Halleck's statement to Grant: "Nothing satisfactory from Missouri. . . . General Curtis seems to be fighting near Independence, but I hear nothing of Rosecrans, A. J. Smith's, or Mower's divisions. No action yet as to change of commanders"—a reference to the efforts of Grant and Stanton to remove Rosecrans.

Rosecrans now considered Price tightly cornered. Approaching Chapel Hill, Missouri, far southeast of Independence, Smith closed southern routes. And yet, in spite of this encirclement, the trap failed to catch the quarry. On the morning of October 22, while Pleasonton's Union cavalry charged and captured Independence, Price's main column drove Curtis back upon Kansas City. Curtis' inability to hold the line of the Big Blue River caused Rosecrans to send Smith to his support and thus opened an escape route to the south for Price. As soon as he had driven Price's rear guard through Independence, Pleasonton sent a message telling Curtis that he was on the field.

On the 23rd, Curtis attacked General Joseph O. Shelby, and Pleasonton moved against Price, who held the Big Blue crossings, routing him in a six-hour fight so that he fled due southward for twenty miles beyond Little Santa Fe, on the Missouri–Kansas border. When Smith reached Independence at five that evening, he set out on a forced night march, but by the time he reached Hickman Hills, both Price and Pleasonton had passed through it. Had he gone there directly from Chapel Hill—the air distance was twenty-five miles, about half the distance from Chapel Hill to Independence and down to Hickman Hills—he would have trapped Price, with 9,000 men, five batteries, and his train.

From here on, Price's flight and the pursuit became headlong. On the 24th, after defeating Price at the Marais des Cygnes River, Pleasonton pursued for ten hours before overtaking him and winning a second victory at the Little Osage River. About midnight, Price blew up his surplus ammunition. Meanwhile, Pleasonton and Curtis rode into Fort Scott, Kansas.

Price now lacked means to strike back. For Rosecrans the battle all but ended the campaign. He was bitterly disappointed at his failure to destroy Price completely and disappointment sharpened his tongue, as Lieutenant George T. Robinson, chief engineer for Curtis, found, when he visited Rosecrans on the 25th. When Rosecrans criticized Curtis, Robinson responded insolently in a conversation that seems to have been to the credit of neither.

Price's rout at the Marais des Cygnes and Little Osage rivers gave Rosecrans a chance to inventory his needs. Pleasonton was exhausted; he had ridden six days and 204 miles and fought four battles, and he recommended that Sanborn and McNeil, who were in better shape, should support Curtis in the pursuit, as long as hope of damaging Price remained. Rosecrans agreed. Convinced that Pleasonton was not needed, Rosecrans ordered him to return to Warrensburg. At Newtonia, Price made his last Missouri stand. There, on the 28th, Blunt overtook him, and was being roughly handled, when Sanborn, who had ridden 102 miles in thirty-six hours, came up in support. Again Price fled.

The pursuers now faced a dilemma. Price's army was entering lean Arkansas country. Would military advantage result from further pursuit? Curtis recognized grounds for an honest difference of opinion. In his *Report* Rosecrans wrote that: "In a country destitute of food for man or beast, five times defeated, pursued 400 or 500 miles, with loss of nearly all their artillery, ammunition, and baggage train, demoralization and destitution and want of supplies would drive the rebels across the Arkansas for supplies at the risk of falling into the hands of Thayer's forces or Steele's cavalry, and if allowed would almost certainly disintegrate and disband them on the way thither." Curtis thought "pushing them was best," Rosecrans added; and in spite of his belief to the contrary, at the urgent insistence of Curtis, and against the better judgment of Sanborn and McNeil, Rosecrans sent three brigades to the Arkansas border. Even then, however, he did not report to Washington, and consequently suffered from the reports of others less well informed than himself.

On October 29, Senator Jim Lane, commanding the Kansas militia, growled to Stanton from Fort Scott, "Curtis and Blunt are pursuing Price with about 4,000 men. Can they not be reinforced?" Curtis likewise complained to Stanton that Rosecrans' orders were taking McNeil to Rolla and Sanborn to Springfield: "Deeming it improper to continue a pursuit in another department suspended by its proper commander, I shall return by slow marches to my own department command." On October 30, Curtis acknowledged the receipt of Grant's dispatch ordering him to pursue Price to the Arkansas River. Curtis forwarded this message to Rosecrans' commanders, who, he reported to Grant, "had abandoned the pursuit" by Rosecrans' orders.

On the next day, Curtis again reported. He had held the pursuit together until the joint force had arrived at Charlot, opposite Fort Scott. Price's men were "actually falling dead of starvation in his rear. They hang together under the impression that we kill all prisoners, a falsehood well calculated to retain his forces intact."

Pleasonton considered further pursuit useless. While Curtis did not know where Rosecrans was, as his "headquarters had been shifting fifty or sixty miles in the rear," he desired "to avoid all reproachful imputations" against Rosecrans and Pleasonton.

Halleck reported this inaccurate statement to Grant, saying that "contrary to repeated orders Rosecrans had recalled his troops." Halleck then, in Grant's name, ordered Curtis to take command of the Missouri troops in his column and continue the pursuit. After this flurry of misinformation, Halleck finally got the facts from Rosecrans. He was withdrawing only Pleasonton. Winslow's brigade had been ordered to Sherman. When Sanborn wrote to Rosecrans on October 30 that Price "will be pursued by General Starvation across the river—a most formidable enemy to him," Rosecrans patiently reminded him: "It was my intention that you and McNeil should follow the retreating column of the enemy, giving it no rest until it was brought within the grasp of Steele's troops at Fort Smith." And so the pursuit continued, even though Sanborn was convinced, as Curtis was not, that if it were abandoned, in the desolate region ahead men would desert in droves; while if Price were pushed nearer to his supplies, none would desert.

On November 6, McNeil reported to Rosecrans from Cassville: "Our movements from here will be regulated by supplies. I greatly fear that the belly impediment will stop our further progress." On the next day he reported that Price was scattering his forces in order to subsist, and that he himself was not much better off. Curtis was heading for Fort Smith. If McNeil attempted to join him there, to forage the horses would be "difficult on the route and impossible when we got there." But he hung on until November 8, when Price crossed the Arkansas, abandoning another gun and his carriage.

Now, with the letter of Grant's order fulfilled, the pursuers turned back. Sanborn was still convinced that Curtis had been wrong: "Had it not been for fear of the pursuing foe, half of Price's army would have deserted north of the Arkansas."

Rosecrans had remained with his army until Price was routed and Curtis had taken command of the Missouri pursuers, and had left Warrensburg, Missouri, on November 2, for St. Louis—he considered his presence advisable at Departmental Headquarters during the presidential elections. The OAKS were threatening turmoil, and in a close contest the loss of Missouri might cost Lincoln the election. Lincoln, believing that he needed the soldiers' vote, had written to Rosecrans on September 26: "I have a report that you incline to deny the soldiers the right of attending the election in Missouri on the assumed ground that they will get drunk and make disturbance. Wherever the law allows soldiers to vote, their officers must also allow it." On October 12, to provide for the "preservation and purity of the election francise," Rosecrans issued General Orders No. 195 in which he set forth particulars to govern voting. Voting was prohibited to those who had borne arms against the United States. The right of eligible persons to vote was declared to be inviolate. The military were to keep order at polling places, and the right to vote must not be denied to Missouri soldiers.

Events proved that Lincoln's concern was needless. On November 8, he beat McClellan by a popular vote of 2,213,665 to 1,802,237, and an electoral vote of 212 to 21. Missouri gave Lincoln 72,991 votes to McClellan's 31,026. The soldier vote for Lincoln was 3 to 1.

The defeat of Price brought Rosecrans no commendations from the War Department. Instead, Halleck complained to Sherman: "Rosecrans has made very bad work of it in Missouri allowing Price with a small force to overrun the State and destroy millions of property." In his *General Report,* Grant observed that when Price "with about 10,000 men" invaded Missouri, the addition of Smith's command made Rosecrans superior to Price and "no doubt was entertained that he would be able to check Price and drive him back, while the forces under General Steele in Arkansas would cut off his retreat. . . . The impunity with which Price was enabled to roam over the State of Missouri for a long time, and the incalculable mischief done by him, shows to how little purpose a superior force may be used. There is no reason why General Rosecrans should not have concentrated his forces and beaten and driven Price before the latter reached Pilot Knob."

In their biography of Lincoln, Nicolay and Hay called this criticism "rather harsh," and assert that the "history of the War had shown that heavy columns of veteran cavalry were not easily prevented from making raids of this character, especially when they were willing to encounter the risk of gradual depletion and dispersion. There seems little doubt that the raid was as much political as military."

It was cavalier for Grant and others to speak lightly about Rosecrans' difficulties and achievements in a campaign in which, as W. Forse Scott of the 4th Iowa cavalry wrote later,

. . . a part of the Union troops and most of the Confederates marched 1500 miles, beginning in torrid heat and ending in snow and zero cold; a campaign beginning in politics and ending with dramatic coincidence on the day on which politics were finally swept out of the war in the defeat of McClellan and re-election of Lincoln; a campaign so disastrous to the enemy that from Iowa to the Gulf peace prevailed during the remaining six months of the war. . . . The value of the campaign hardly needs to be stated. The disastrous defeats of the enemy in the last week of October tell the story; and the ruin of his political scheme was even more hopeless. Price's twenty thousand had melted to nearly nothing. He had no army worth mentioning after that, nor does he again appear in any record of the War in any affair of consequence. No campaign was attempted by the rebels west of the Mississippi after his overthrow.

None of these facts prevented Lieutenant Robinson from charging Rosecrans with treason and with trying to sacrifice Curtis. Robinson's suspicions had grown since he rode off near Little Santa Fe, flinging a huffy impertinence behind him. On December 3, Curtis sent a report from Robinson to Halleck, adding that Rosecrans showed "much eccentric conduct and disrespectful attitude toward a comrade in the field as to preclude our future kind cooperation. . . . Extraordinary delay manifested in bringing forward forces and subsequent hasty and unfortunate orders which withdrew them from my support, may also deserve your notice." Halleck forwarded this report to Grant.

Unaware of these charges Rosecrans turned back to the perennial problem of bushwhacking. The Missouri bushwhackers were a peculiarly cruel and detestable breed. More than four months before, General Brown at Warrensburg had asked Rosecrans to allow him to order shot the first bushwhacker he captured, but to suspend execution until the next time mail, stage coach, or telegraph services were interrupted, when the prisoner would hang. Rosecrans said no, but when bushwhackers treated Union prisoners brutally in October, Rosecrans ordered eye-for-eye reprisals.

Toward the end of October advancing Federals found the bodies of Major Wilson and six soldiers of the 3rd Missouri cavalry. Price's men had captured the seven and turned them over to a well-known bushwhacker. Wilson's body was pierced with many bullets and partially eaten by hogs. Ewing suggested that if Rosecrans lacked a captured Confederate major to shoot, fourteen privates, eight for Wilson and one for each Union private, should be shot. Joseph Darr, now the provost marshal general (Sanderson had died on October 17) had executed six Confederates on October 29. He had no major to sacrifice, and so the Commissary General of Prisoners supplied Major E. O. Wolf, and a ball and chain was riveted to his ankle. Wolf was to be shot to pay for Major Wilson's death. "Suspend execution of Major Wolf until further orders," Lincoln telegraphed on November 10. Wolf was not shot.

After the victory at the Marais des Cygnes and Little Osage rivers on October 24, Rosecrans had ordered Smith to return by the most expeditious route to St. Louis, to embark there and join Thomas at Nashville. The records indicate that Rosecrans left nothing undone to move Smith rapidly, yet Rosecrans' enemies in Washington professed dissatisfaction, and even his accurate reports concerning the steps he was taking to return Smith failed to end the nagging of Grant and Halleck.

Grant had sought to strip Missouri of troops, even while urging Price's destruction. On October 26 he had told Halleck that: "An order, with an order to see it enforced, should go to Missouri" to send to Thomas "all troops not actually after Price or guards for public stores." Sherman was marching to the sea, and Thomas, having beaten Hood to Nashville, faced Hood there. On November 1, Rosecrans informed Halleck: "There are no available troops in St. Louis."

Grant still professed to believe that Rosecrans had concealed 6,000 to 8,000 troops, and on October 29 he sent Rawlins to Rosecrans' headquarters and to "such other points" as Rawlins might "deem necessary" to uncover them. Rawlins was to remain with Rosecrans until his orders "were complied with." He was authorized to issue such orders of his own as would secure the carrying out of his instructions. He was empowered to give orders to Rosecrans or directly to his subordinates.

Rawlins arrived in St. Louis on November 3, the evening Rosecrans returned from his army, and next day Rawlins reported to Grant that the commands embraced in Grant's order were already marching to the Mississippi River—A. J. Smith to St. Charles, Missouri, and Mower, to St. Louis. Rosecrans had transmitted the necessary orders to Sherman's two divisions in the Department of Missouri to "expedite their movements to the points designated by Thomas." Rosecrans had ordered General Winslow's cavalry, which was with Sanborn, to return to the Mississippi the moment it could be safely withdrawn from pursuing Price. In addition, Rosecrans was sending Thomas a regiment of colored infantry. Rawlins could find no fault with Rosecrans, nor did he rescind any of Rosecrans' orders or issue orders of his own. On the contrary: "Rosecrans seems to appreciate fully the conditions of affairs on the Mississippi and Tennessee Rivers, and will use every exertion, I have no doubt, to forward troops there."

Later that day, after talking to Smith, Rawlins reported to Grant that Rosecrans had given Smith "all the necessary orders for the return of the whole of Sherman's troops to Thomas." Rawlins added, "Smith being so anxious to get off and so alive to the importance of doing so at the earliest possible moment, together with Rosecrans' disposition to facilitate his purpose to the fullest extent, I deem it unnecessary for me to remain here longer." Rawlins left St. Louis on November 7, satisfied that Rosecrans had shown "every disposition to hurry troops forward" to Thomas, and "for that purpose to strip his command to the least possible number," and to send more when the pursuit of Price ended. Not even Rawlins' testimony, however, could convince Grant and Halleck, and on December 3, Halleck complained to Grant that "General A. J. Smith's command was 31 days, after General Rosecrans received the order, in reaching Nashville."

Rosecrans' *Personal Report* dated June 15, 1865, summarizes the Smith episode: As soon as Price had been beaten and dispersed

. . . on receipt of Gen'l. Sherman's dispatch that he was about to set out on that march which ended in the capture of Savannah I ordered Gen'l. A. J. Smith with all his command to join Gen'l. Thomas and soon after received an order from Gen'l. Halleck, Chief of Staff, to send them to that destination. I then consulted with Gen'l. Smith as to the most expeditious method of accomplishing this, ordered it to [be] done with all possible dispatch and reported the plan proposed with reasons to Gen'l. Halleck for the information of Gen'l. Grant. It has been reliably reported to me that Gen'l. Grant has said in conversation that it took thirty days to transfer those troops when it could have been done in three days, and because having written him on the subject some three months since, I am yet without reply and have no other mode of putting these facts of history on public record as a contradiction of delay in sending those troops to Gen'l. Thomas which would have been as motiveless as it would have been inconsistent with my judgement and contrary to my feelings.

This statement agrees fully with Rawlins' reports to Grant. Nevertheless Rosecrans was marked for removal. In June 1864 Grant had so twice recommended, and in July he had told Dana that the "most useful way to employ Rosecrans would be to station him at some convenient point on the northern frontier with the duty of detecting and exposing rebel conspiracies in Canada." When Halleck confided to Grant that he would have to remove Ben Butler, who perhaps could be sent to Missouri, he added: "It might not be objectionable to have a free fight between him and Rosecrans. Inveterate as is Rosecrans' habit of continually calling for more troops, Butler differs only in demanding instead of calling."

Although for a few days in October Grant thought it might be inadvisable to remove Rosecrans while Price was in Missouri, by the 11th of that month he had changed his mind: "On reflection I do not know but that a proper regard for the present and future interests of the service demands the removal of Rosecrans. . . . Present movements of Hood's army . . . may make it necessary to have a commander in Missouri who will cooperate." He spoke of Sheridan, Hooker, and Logan as possibilities. On the 20th Grant was asking Halleck, "Has Rosecrans yet come upon Price? If not he should be removed at once." He repeated: "Anybody will be better than Rosecrans." When Canby was injured, Grant suggested that J. J. Reynolds should be given the trans-Mississippi command; he wanted General Dodge to have Missouri. "I think it of very great importance that General Rosecrans should be removed," Grant said. And on December 2, Stanton telegraphed to Grant at City Point: "Where shall Rosecrans be sent by the order placing Dodge in command of the Department of the Missouri?" Grant answered: "Rosecrans will do less harm doing nothing than on duty. I know no department or army commander deserving such punishment as the infliction of Rosecrans on them."

By this time Rosecrans had undoubtedly read the signs aright, because on December 3 he accepted Bond's resignation, probably to spare Bond from the humiliation of being rusticated or shelved for his loyal services to him. Six days later the removal order arrived, and Dodge took over; Rosecrans left for Cincinnati, accompanied by his aide James P. Drouillard. He had commanded the Department of the Missouri eleven months. He had done as well as any man could in a difficult assignment, and better than most, and when he was removed his removal was accomplished by Stanton with the same harshness and lack of courtesy that Stanton had shown in removing Buell.

On April 24, 1865, Rosecrans testified to the Committee on the Conduct of the War that "no reason was ever assigned to me [for his removal at the end of the Missouri episode], nor have I ever, directly or indirectly, heard of any reason for it until within the last six weeks. I have lately heard, from three or four different sources, that I was removed at the personal request of General Grant, who was supposed, by the parties giving me that information, to be extremely hostile to me. As no occasion for any such hostility has ever been given by me so far as I know, I am at a loss to understand it. General Grant's chief of staff, General Rawlins, visited me after the close of the campaign of General Price. He mixed freely with the citizens, and took pains to volunteer the statement, in my office, in the presence of various members of my staff, that he was satisfied that things had been managed wonderfully well during that campaign; that few could have done as well, and probably none better."

Senator Ben Wade, the Chairman, asked Rosecrans, "Has there been any misunderstanding between you and General Grant at any time?" Rosecrans answered, "Never. On one occasion, when some of his staff told my staff that he was under the impression that the newspaper correspondents who, in 1862, attacked him in the Chicago *Tribune* and other papers, had received some countenance at my headquarters, I had a conversation with him upon the subject. He expressly stated that he did not suppose that it came from me; and after conversation with him, in which I answered him that there was not the slightest foundation for such a feeling, he not only expressed himself satisfied, but we parted, promising friendly intercourse wherever duty might throw us."

Looking back later on this second and final removal, Rosecrans said with much right, and a little self-righteousness:

Thus a second time rewarded for fidelity and untiring devotion to the cause of the nation and the interest of my command, unsustained by a single act of insubordination or intrigue or malevolence in all my military career, and thank God without ever having suffered defeat or made a failure in a single great undertaking, I retired to my home where for the country's sake I have submitted to my wrongs without a public complaint.

He wrote privately to Governor Dennison, now Lincoln's Post-master General: "I will take it as a personal favor any information you give as to the cause of this last removal." And he wrote to Garfield, enumerating his military services in Missouri and else-where and adding: "Without warning notice, or complaint, or hint of explanation I am removed and put in an attitude of disgrace before the nation. Isn't it strange?" The letter carried a postscript: "You know I consider my present situation an outrage on justice having few parallels in this or any other war. But I am a firm believer in the final downfall of iniquity."

During the closing months of the war Rosecrans waited in Cincinnati for an assignment, and when the war ended with a Union victory he remained on leave for six months and in December 1865 resigned from the army.

Yet men remembered and respected him and sought him out. His refusal to accept nomination for public office during the sixties and seventies was perhaps his greatest mistake. Although the Republicans continued to hold the White House until 1885, nevertheless it seems certain that had Rosecrans run he would have been elected to high office. In 1866 the Union party of Ohio, in 1868 the Democratic party of California, and in 1869 the Democratic party of Ohio sought him as a candidate for governor, and in 1876 the Democrats of Nevada wanted him to run for Congress. But each time some business venture that promised a degree of success it did not yield caused him to refuse. His unwillingness during this fifteen-year period to accept these public nominations—and dozens of private requests—won him the title "The Great Decliner."

He tried to build a personal fortune but wealth eluded him. His partners had frozen him out of the Cincinnati refinery, and he turned to California and mining, hoping to clear $500,000 in five years. He built a comfortable home in San Rafael, and purchased— probably on borrowed money—14,000 acres of cheap land, the Rancho Sausal Redondo, near Los Angeles.

He had hoped to get his finances in order and then bring charges of conduct unbecoming an officer against Grant, but making a living was too absorbing and he never got around to it.

Rosecrans' diminished fortunes were reflected in his appearance. In 1867 the San Francisco correspondent of the New York *Times* wrote:

Yesterday, sitting opposite to me at the table was a man who stared at me, and I stared at him. That must be Rosecrans, I thought to myself, but how changed. I spoke to him, and after bowing, he said, "Truman isn't it?" To which I replied, "yes." But how changed! When last I saw him he had his martial cloak about him, and was in the zenith of his glory and popularity. No man who ever saw him upon the field of action can forget him, his dash, his excited manner, and his great personal intrepidity. Now he looked sad and careworn, dismal and unfriendly. His clothes were clean, but old and rusty, and his hair and whiskers looked uncombed and shaggy. But his friends, and he has hosts of them, will rejoice to hear that old Rosy has at last been successful, and that his mining operations are O.K.

He became interested in railroads, and in 1865 he was one of the eleven incorporators of the Southern Pacific. For years he served as chief engineer or promoter of one railway or another. The same perverse luck that thwarted his mining ventures and gave him empty holes, or sent a Pacific tidal wave to flood his shafts, now dogged his railroad schemes. His greatest losses were his Southern Pacific holdings. The completion of the Union Pacific made these very valuable, and distrusting certain associates, he hired a judge to scrutinize every newspaper of regular issue during his frequent absences from California. Financiers controlling the company levied a small assessment against Southern Pacific's capital stock, in a campaign to freeze him out, and advertised the levy in an obscure weekly paper with fewer than 200 subscribers. The judge who had been hired as a watchdog failed to see the item, Rosecrans failed to pay the levy, and his stock was secretly auctioned off. To discourage Rosecrans from carrying the case through the courts, squatters were put on his Rancho land. Rosecrans cleared his title but he lost his railroad stock.

In 1868 President Johnson appointed Rosecrans to be Minister to Mexico. Five months later, President Grant terminated the appointment.

His brief diplomatic career convinced him that a prosperous Mexico would need peace, immigration, and railways, and he applied for a concession to build a narrow-gauge railway and telegraph line from Tampico to the Coast. The record of toil and travel, scheming, waiting on rich men and politicians, and of the final collapse of his Mexican dreams, forms a wearying chapter of the frustrating years from 1869 through 1873. Yet he was almost the first, and perhaps the most important, in a long line of Yankee railroad promoters in Mexico.

Rosecrans' military experience led him also to an interest in civil administration, and in collaboration with a former newspaperman, Josiah Riley, he wrote a book, *Popular Government.* The authors advocated such reforms as the honest registration of voters, the clearing of polling places of political pressures, the setting of statutory machinery for initiation and recall—recommendations for practices now commonplace in good government everywhere.

Much of the time Rosecrans had several business ventures afloat simultaneously. He remained active and inventive. Out of his mining experience he developed a patented fuse cutter and became a manufacturer of blasting powder, again running into trouble when a coalition of competitors trimmed their prices to a fourth of his. He and his associates ran out of money and left the business.

In 1867 Rosecrans declined the directorship of the San Francisco mint. Later, when his mining, Mexican, railroad, and manufacturing ventures proved less profitable than he had hoped, he sought that appointment in vain. The election of Rutherford B. Hayes in 1876 brought a friend—even though a Republican—to the White House. Rosecrans hoped that he might return to the Mexican post or at least be appointed to the mint position. Sherman, among others, interceded for him, and Rosecrans journeyed to Fremont, Ohio, from California to meet Hayes at a reunion of the 23rd Ohio. Hayes was friendly to his old commander, but gave him no appointment.

The drive behind these difficult and frustrating labors was not only personal ambition but the desire to provide for Annie and the family. Rosecrans' efforts kept him apart from them frequently and for prolonged periods, yet in spirit the family remained close, and the letters he wrote to Annie and the children, and theirs to him, were rich in affection. At the height of Rosecrans' business troubles, his older son Louis, who had become a Catholic priest, died suddenly in 1876. His father wrote: "Bury him beside his Paulist brethren to await the great Resurrection day, and God bless all those who have been kind to him." Within a year his daughter Mary—Sister St. Charles of the Brown County Ursulines—died of tuberculosis. "The circle beyond is broadening, the circle here narrowing," wrote Bishop Sylvester Rosecrans. Tears were scarcely dried for Mary when Sylvester himself went. He had lived a life of austerity, and left two silver half-dollars and a watch: "Give my watch to my brother. I am ready, Jesus, Mary and Joseph." Next Rosecrans' beloved Annie died, probably of cancer. The letters of William and Annie throughout the years had shown rare, unfailing tenderness and understanding; he did not speak often of her after her death. The hurt was too deep.

Though Rosecrans' attendance at reunions was infrequent, old army comrades remembered him with affectionate respect. In 1869, when the Cumberlanders met, Wood disregarded the bickering over the breakthrough at Chickamauga and called Rosecrans "brilliant in imagination, ardent in temperament, and impetuous in action, with much ability for rapid, comprehensive, and striking generalization." And Thomas responded: "Chickamauga, a battle in which I received great credit at the expense of a better soldier, General Rosecrans." When Thomas died in 1870, Rosecrans was a pallbearer, with Generals Meade, Schofield, Hazen, Hooker, Gordon Granger, Newton, and McKay. Grant attended the funeral. As president of the Society of the Army of the Cumberland, Rosecrans labored for the erection of the statue of Thomas in Washington.

In the midst of Rosecrans' difficulties, Garfield stood staunchly by him, writing friendly, encouraging letters to him, defending him in his absence, using his good offices in Congress to assist Rosecrans' various projects. Rosecrans knew nothing of Garfield's loose talk after Chickamauga—and even in that episode Garfield's criticism was of Rosecrans the general and not the man—and the genuine friendship the two bore each other might have continued to the end had it not been for Dana—that "loathsome pimp," in the phrase of General Gordon Granger.

Dana, who had now become editor and part owner of the New York *Sun,* and who disliked Garfield, in 1877 charged in his column that the cause of Rosecrans' removal from command was a "private letter by Garfield to Chase." "A piece with his false and slanderous life," cried Garfield. "It is a lie." When Dana repeated the charge in 1879, Garfield told Rosecrans that "any charge, whether it comes from Dana, or any other liar to the effect that I was in any sense untrue to you has no particle of truth in it. I met Mr. Stanton in Louisville, and when he denounced you in vigorous language, I rebuked him and earnestly defended you. I fearlessly challenge all the rascals in the world to publish any such letters written by me."

Unfortunately for their friendship, when Garfield ran for the presidency on the Republican ticket in 1880, Rosecrans ran for Congress from the 1st district of California on the Democratic. By that time Garfield's role in Rosecrans' removal was an open secret. More trouble was created when Rosecrans read in Garfield's campaign biographies careless eulogies which magnified Garfield's courage and military exploits at Rosecrans' expense. As a result, when the editors of the *Alta Californian*, a San Francisco Republican newspaper, taunted Rosecrans with inconsistency for listening to attacks on Garfield though he had praised him seventeen years before, Rosecrans retorted angrily: "Seventeen years is a long period, and many a splendid young man, in less time, has descended from honor to infamy, and mortified admiring and devoted friends by being put in the penitentiary."

Both men were elected, and Rosecrans extended the hand of friendship, but Garfield found Rosecrans' "opinion of me, an insuperable barrier to the restoration of the old relation." In this unworthy squabble, Rosecrans had the last word: "No one knows better than you that subserviency to *men in power* is not one of my distinguishing virtues." Garfield should understand, Rosecrans said, that his letter was not "dictated by any such motives. And there I leave it, cordially respecting the saying of a great man: 'I would rather be right than President.'"

The breach was never healed.

Rosecrans proved an effective Congressman, although a Washington correspondent noticed that his "formerly erect carriage showed signs of age, and the elastic step, and quick, nervous movements of twenty years ago had departed."

Garfield died on September 19, 1881, from an assassin's bullet which had struck him down two months before, and in February, both Houses joined to listen to James G. Blaine's eulogy of the dead president. The speech touched off the old trouble, for Blaine described the poor condition of the army before Garfield restored it. "The distinguished gentleman has been wholly misinformed," Rosecrans rejoined, and Ben Butler sneered: "Nothing but good about the dead." But Dana was delighted. The controversy gave him a chance to exploit a windfall, and he published Garfield's "confidential" letter to Chase. Again tongues wagged, some pronounced the letter spurious; and others pointed out that it had been written *before* and not after Chickamauga. Puzzled, Rosecrans asked Dana, did he have a letter written after Chickamauga? He did not. And what was Dana's part in the business?

In view of his dispatches—then safely buried in War Department files—Dana's long answer contains some remarkable statements, among them: "I never went to see him [Thomas] about taking your place, either alone or with anyone else. No doubt there are passages [in these telegrams] which you will regard as having been unjust to you; many concerning which you will tell me, probably with justice, that I was entirely misinformed."

On June 14, Dana published eight letters from Garfield to Chase and revealed his source as John W. Shuckers, Chase's former secretary and his literary executor and biographer. Their authenticity was settled, as was the use which Chase had made of the damaging "confidential" letter. He had shown it to Lincoln only after Chickamauga. Garfield had spoken the truth, but not the whole truth.

In 1882, Rosecrans was re-elected, and became chairman of the House Military Affairs Committee. In this position he conspicuously opposed the Grant retirement bill. Grant was broke, bankrupt. He had drawn his general's salary for eight years; the President's for another eight. In addition, friends provided $250,000, to yield an annuity of $15,000. But Grant wanted to be rich and had become a silent partner in the Wall Street firm of Grant (U.S. Grant, Jr.) and Ward. When the firm closed its doors in 1884, Grant, who was meticulously honest, threw everything into the pot—cash, trust fund, houses, farm, war trophies. His everything was not enough. To aid him, friends proposed that Congress should restore his lieutenant general's rank, and backdate his pay to 1869.

In February, 1885, Rosecrans, who apparently did not know the full extent of Grant's financial troubles, as one of his final acts in Congress spoke against the bill, calling it a "proposition to reward Grant for his distinguished military service," and said he could not vote for it, because "when true history is written," that service would be pared down to very different dimensions. His opposition, Rosecrans maintained, was not due to personal dislike, or to the fact that Grant had made official statements that "were false, and which he knew to be false at the time he made them, and which I have shown in my official reports to be false. I cannot say to the people of this country that a business which has been conducted as to rob poor people of millions, and which, if done on a smaller scale, would have sent its managers to prison, shall be considered as important when the principal manager has allowed a great name to be used as the instrument of the robbery." Despite his objections, the bill passed.

Throughout these years Rosecrans was occasionally mentioned as a possible Democratic candidate for the presidency, and Cleveland's election in 1884 provoked newspaper talk that Rosecrans would be appointed Secretary of War. Instead, in May 1885 he was appointed Registrar of the Treasury.

Grant, meanwhile, was writing his *Memoirs*. Dr. Douglas, his physician, tells how Grant lay awake "worrying about being fair to all concerned." However sincere his intentions and otherwise successful his performance, when the *Memoirs* touch Rosecrans they are unfair and generally inaccurate. Perhaps it was too much to expect a dying man, with Rosecrans' bitter House speech ringing in his ears, to write impartially. In December 1885, the *North American Review* published a brief article by Rosecrans, "The Mistakes of Grant." This answer has been lost in the obscurity of a once influential, though now defunct, periodical; Grant's *Memoirs*, however, still are widely read.

Although Cleveland was not re-elected in 1888, Benjamin Harrison did not remove his old commander from the office of Registrar. Additional honors came to Rosecrans. He was elected a regent of the University of California, and a member of the Board of the Chickamauga Battlefield Commission, and in 1889, Georgetown University, observing its centennial, awarded a single honorary degree, making him a Doctor of Laws.

Rosecrans mellowed with the years. Money came to mean so little to him that his son Carl was sometimes appalled at his father's generosity. Before Rosecrans left San Francisco, an indigent vagabond knocked at his hotel-room door, and his pockets empty, Rosecrans gave him the collection of gold coins he had received from

President Porfirio Diaz. In Washington he customarily walked to his office at the Treasury, and if a veteran asked him for a meal and Rosecrans was short of cash, he brought him to the Willard Hotel and charged the meal to his account.

In 1889 when a bill was introduced in the House to restore Rosecrans' rank and place him on the retired list, Congressmen opposed to it pointed out his opposition to the Grant retirement bill. Support unexpectedly came for Democrat Rosecrans from Republican ranks, David Henderson of Iowa, a veteran of Corinth, remarking that when justice to a soldier was involved he knew no politics. Another congressman commented: "We can afford to forget what General Rosecrans may have said. We cannot afford to forget what he did." The bill itself concluded by saying that it would be a "solace to him in his declining years to be made the recipient of this evidence of his country's gratitude." The bill passed on February 22, 1889.

Frances Thomas, General Thomas's widow, wrote to Anita Rosecrans that she could not help but compliment her and her father: "It is a deserved compliment, though tardily paid. General Thomas' warm affection for General Rosecrans and admiration for his military science I well know. . . ."

Memories of the war died hard. In 1885 with a voice trembling with age Rosecrans told the Society of the Army of the Cumberland the story of his removal, and in 1890 the publication of Volume XXX of the *Official Records* finally laid bare Dana's role. Garfield's biographer puts it well: "For mingled affrontery and mendacity" Dana's effort to put the full blame on Garfield "is unsurpassed by anything even in Dana's record." Rosecrans' friends were furious —as one said, Dana was "satanic."

By 1892 Rosecrans was aging rapidly. At the encampment of the Grand Army in Washington, in the dark when the electric lights failed, former President Hayes introduced him, and Rosecrans began to speak in low tones: "I speak as loud as I can." "We would like to see his face," cried a voice from the darkness. Hayes lighted a match, and held it close to Rosecrans; the flame glowed upon his face with its trim white beard. A sustained roar of applause shook the great tent. It was his soldiers' last public salute to their commander.

Rosecrans became "ill" soon after, and growing no better, he resigned from the Treasury on July 1, 1892, and returned to California, to live at the Redondo Hotel at Redondo Beach. Most of the lands of the nearby Rancho Sausal Redondo, where his son Carl now lived with his family, had been sold in parcels to finance Rosecrans' mining ventures.

After a year, Carl noticed that his father seemed to have lost his sense of time—or perhaps time no longer mattered. He might leave for an hour's ride and be away two days. Carl brought him to the Rancho, added a wing to the sprawling wooden house for him, and engaged a colored man named Charles to attend him.

Life on the Rancho proved happy. Rosecrans loved to stroll through the fields and orchards, and to talk with the neighbors. He read history, and scientific journals. In the evenings, while fragrant eucalyptus logs burned in the grate, he spoke of famous people and events. Old comrades, McCook among them, arrived on the "Cottontail," the narrow-gauge railroad, to visit him; and humble men wept when he recalled their names, regiments, and feats. His former orderly, Mike Patton, wrote to tell him: "Dana is dead. When I wrote to you last I hoped that you would outlive your enemies. You have done it as far as I know of."

The affairs of his grandchildren were of particular interest. When Carl's son William was about four years old, he visited his grandfather at the Redondo Hotel. "Boys don't wear curls," the General said, and William carried his locks home in a paper bag. By the time he was seven, William was an excellent horseman, and when he returned, his grandfather asked, "Whom did you see? What did they say? What were they doing?" He repeated, "Observe." William remembered him as "about the most cheerful person imaginable." His grandfather loved dogs, horses, all animals, and delighted in telling William and his small sister Carmelita about his battle steed, Boney. He talked about oil from the seepage in his water well. He talked much about many places, things, persons. But his grandson is positive: "He never mentioned Grant."

Rancho orchards were white next spring when Bishop Montgomery and a distinguished group of Catholic clergy brought Rosecrans a coveted honor, the Laetare Medal, annually conferred by Notre Dame University on an eminent Catholic layman.

In the summer of 1897, Rosecrans grew seriously ill, but recovered. Thereafter he spent more time in his rooms, even eating his meals there. The following February, he came down with a cold, which turned into pneumonia. His mood was good; he was patient and cheerful and quipped with his nurse. His daughter Lily had married Joseph Porter Toole, and it seemed useless and cruel to tell Rosecrans that Lily's boy, whom he loved dearly, and whose father was first governor of Wyoming, had died suddenly of diphtheria. But the old man heard the news and remained rigid for some time with grief. He rallied, asked for the boy's picture, and failed fast after that; the next day he could not recognize familiar faces. He lay thus for two weeks, and at 7:10 on the morning of March 11, as a sharp north wind whipped over the Rancho, he died. Newspapers across the nation carried the story. The Los Angeles *Times* captioned the story: "Last great general of the Civil War goes to the bivouac with the boys in blue in the silent camping ground. Rosecrans is dead."

He lay in state at the Los Angeles City Hall, while in hourly shifts the National Guard of California stood watch. Draped over the casket was the headquarters flag that had flown at Stone River and Chickamauga. Messages of sympathy poured in, including a touching tribute from President William McKinley. In his sermon at the Requiem Mass Bishop Montgomery recalled that: "He served his country in its perilous need with fidelity, courage and zest. In that duty he served a higher power."

In May 1908, the body of Rosecrans was removed from the receiving vault in Los Angeles to Washington, where in the presence of a distinguished company, including President Theodore Roosevelt, members of the Cabinet and the Congress, Union and Confederate veterans, and friends and relatives, it was reburied in Arlington Cemetery. As the coffin was lowered, the deep-voiced artillery spoke in prescribed sequence and at measured intervals.

In 1895, at the dedication of the Ohio Monument at Chickamauga, Governor—later President—William McKinley had said of Rosecrans in his absence: "He was the first colonel of the regiment to which I belonged, my boyhood ideal of a great soldier, and I gladly pay him tribute." The nation which he served well has been less generous. In June 1864, in a moment of prophetic vision, General Gordon Granger had written to Rosecrans: "The battle is neither to the swift nor to the strong but to him that holds on to the end. If Grant and Sherman squelch out the rebellion they will be heroes and we will be forgotten. So let it be, provided we are once more a happy, united people."

Partly due to circumstances beyond his control, partly to something within himself, it was Rosecrans' lot not to be able to hold on to the end.

But he came close. He touched the edge of glory.

ACKNOWLEDGMENTS

So many kindly, competent persons have made such large and varied contributions to this book that it is difficult after ten years of writing to remember, and much more to acknowledge them all. To them collectively and individually: "Thank you."

In a more particular way I must acknowledge the extensive contributions of Mrs. Lamers to this volume. Knowing it genesis to conclusion, I recall her activity at all stages: in gathering material, writing, editing —and more, in sustaining interest and providing inspiration and encouragement. My gratitude is reflected in the dedication.

While many persons contributed materials, the outstanding contribution was made by Mr. William S. Rosecrans III, of Los Angeles, General Rosecrans' grandson, who allowed us to be the first to have access to the rich stores of documentary and other material gathered throughout his lifetime by General Rosecrans himself. The Rosecrans collection undoubtedly represents one of the greatest collections of Civil War documents. The General's other living descendants, his granddaughter, Mrs. Carmelita Rosecrans Ewing, of Los Angeles, and his grandson Mr. Joseph Porter Toole, of Mexico City, have also been kind to the project. I would like to mention by name the many men and women, collateral relatives of the General among them, who have escorted us around battlefields, well known and obscure, walked us through historic houses, written letters, entrusted us with valuable books and papers, opened doors, and in many other ways served us. Because their contributions are all important, all deeply appreciated, I dare not begin to attempt to list them here lest I offend by inadvertent omissions.

Scholars have been very helpful, as have many of my friends in the Milwaukee Civil War Round Table. The preparation of the book involved much touring of libraries and much help from library staffs, in the form of personal assistance, correspondence, the loan of books and the supply of pictures, photostats, and microfilm.

Involved were the National Archives, Washington D. C.; the Manuscript Division of the Library of Congress; the Huntington Library of San Marino, California; the library and archives of the United States

Military Academy; the Ohio State Reference Library; the state historical libraries of Illinois, Indiana, and Tennessee; the Ohio Archaeological and Historical Library; the Rutherford B. Hayes Memorial Library of Fremont, Ohio; the libraries of Georgetown, Marquette, and Ohio Wesleyan universities, the universities of Notre Dame, Chicago, Michigan, and North Carolina, and Oberlin College; the public libraries of Chicago, Cincinnati, Cleveland, Corinth (Miss.), Iuka (Miss.), Los Angeles, Milwaukee, Murfreesboro, New York, St. Louis, and San Francisco; and the library of the Milwaukee County Historical Society.

BIBLIOGRAPHY

General Sources

A great deal of the material of the War chapters—Two through Seventeen—has been derived from the *Official Records of the War of the Rebellion* (U.S. War Department, Washington, D.C., 1880–1901, 128 vols.). These records are well organized and indexed. Series I, dealing with army operations, is arranged chronologically by military campaigns. Reports and communications are grouped separately and are divided into Union and Confederate.

While there are references to Rosecrans in almost all of the volumes comprising these reports, of particular importance are the following, in each case in Series I:

Volume II: Rosecrans' campaign under McClellan in Western Virginia.

Volume V: Rosecrans' own campaigns in Western Virginia.

Volume X (2 parts): the seige of Corinth, with Rosecrans coming to the west.

Volume XVII (2 parts): Rosecrans' victories at Iuka and Corinth.

Volume XVI (2 parts): The Army of the Cumberland.

Volume XX (2 parts): Rosecrans' victory at the battle of Stone River.

Volume XXIII (2 parts): Rosecrans' Tullahoma campaign.

Volume XXX (2 parts): Rosecrans' Chickamauga campaign, and the seige of Chattanooga.

Volume XXXIV (4 parts): Rosecrans in Missouri.

Volume XLI (4 parts): Rosecrans' defeat of Price in Price's second Missouri invasion, and the removal of Rosecrans.

Volume LI (2 parts): Supplement to above volumes.

Volume LII: Further supplement.

Second only as general sources to the *Official Records* are the four volumes of *Battles and Leaders of the Civil War* (R. W. Johnson and C. C. Buell, eds., New York, 1884, 4 vols.). The reader will find the Rosecrans campaigns as follows:

Volume I: Western Virginia, pp. 126–148.

Volume II: Iuka and Corinth, pp. 734–760.

Volume III: Stone River and Chickamauga, pp. 600–678.

Volume IV: Missouri, pp. 374–377.

Rosecrans appeared twice before the Committee on the Conduct of the War, in December 1861 and in April 1865. His testimony is found in *Reports of the Joint Committee on the Conduct of the War*, Washington,

D.C., 1861, 1863, 1865. Testimony of December 31, 1861, is in the Committee's 1863 *Report*, Part I, pp. 199–209. Testimony of April 22–24, 1865, is in the 1865 *Report*, Part I, pp. 100–119.

Appleton's Annual Cyclopedia and Register of Important Events, 1876–1893

Appleton's Cyclopedia of American Biography, 1888

Biographical Dictionary of the American Congress, 1928

Catholic Encyclopedia, 1907–1922

Cullum, G. W., *Biographical Register of the Officers and Graduates of the United States Military Academy*, 1891

Dictionary of American Biography, 1936

Encyclopedia Americana, 1937

Encyclopaedia Britannica (with American Supplement), 1881

Heitmann, F. B., *Historical Register of the Officers of the Continental Army*, Washington, D. C., 1893

Irwin, B. J., ed., *Official Register of the Officers and Cadets of the United States Military Academy*, New York, 1819–40, 1841–60, 1861–78

Lamb's Biographical Dictionary of the United States, 1900–1903

Military Order of the Loyal Legion of the United States, Commandery Papers:

District of Columbia: *War Papers*, 1887–1897, 25 vols.

Illinois: *Military Essays and Recollections*, 1899, 3 vols.

Indiana: *War Papers*, 1898

Iowa: *War Sketches and Incidents*, 1893–1898, 2 vols.

Maine: *War Papers*, 1898, 3 vols.

Massachusetts: *Civil War Papers*, 1900, 4 vols.

Minnesota: *Glimpses of the Nation's Struggle*, 1887–1903, 5 vols.

Nebraska: *Sketches and Incidents*, 1902, 2 vols.

New York: *Personal Recollections*, 1883–1901, 3 vols.

Ohio: *Sketches of War History*, 1888–1890, 3 vols.

Wisconsin: *War Papers*, 1891–1914, 4 vols.

Powell, W. H., *List of Officers of the Army of the United States, 1879–1900*, New York, 1900; *1900–1903*, New York, 1903

U.S. Army, *Official Registers of the Army of the United States*, Washington, D. C., 1861–1865, 5 vols.

U.S. Military Academy, Association of Graduates, *Annual Reunions*, 1890–1900

U.S. Military Academy, *Regulations*, West Point, N.Y., 1838–1842

——— *Register*, West Point, N.Y., 1838–1842

West Point Alumni Foundation, *Register of Graduates and Former Cadets*, New York, 1942

Manuscripts

The William S. Rosecrans Papers (designated Rosecrans Papers in Notes) were consulted while in the possession of his grandson William S. Rosecrans III, of Los Angeles, California, but they are now in the archives of the University of California at Los Angeles. This extensive collection was made during his lifetime by General Rosecrans himself. It includes his military, business, political, and diplomatic correspondence; letters to him from his mother, brothers, wife, children, and other family letters, and letters or copies of letters from him to them and others; correspondence between members of his family; Rosecrans' letter press books; the original field dispatches of the Battle of Chickamauga; unpublished manuscripts by him of his personal and military history; the scanty beginnings of a biography by his daughter Anita ("Mss. Notes for a Biography of Her Father, General Rosecrans," approximately 20 pp., not continuous or complete); notebooks, account books, letters patent, cards, orders, congratulatory resolutions, diplomas, lectures, articles, awards, photographs, and newspaper clippings. Among manuscripts in Rosecrans' handwriting are: "Chivalry," a lecture, 37 pp.; Document designated "B," describing his removal from the Army of the Cumberland, 4 pp.; *General Rosecrans' Personal Report*, 1865, 28 pp.; "Our Country," a lecture, 42 pp.; *Sketch of the Life of Gen'l William Starke Rosecrans Intended to Give Some Facts, Incidents, and Personal Characteristics of His Civil and Military Services Supplementary to What Is Generally Contained in Popular Official Published Records*, n.d., 56 pp.; *W.S.R., a Sketch of his Campaigns with Analysis of His Qualities as a Commander, and an Estimate of the Importance of His Services to the Success of the Union Arms*, n.d., 86 pp.

Fourteen cases of papers, which had been stored in the Treasury Building, Washington, D.C., from 1892 to 1902, were burned at the direction of his daughter Anita. Included was much of Rosecrans' extensive foreign correspondence with military leaders such as Bismarck.

The William S. Rosecrans collection in the possession of his grandson Joseph Porter Toole, of Mexico City. A small collection of family papers, photographs, and pamphlets.

The William S. Rosecrans appointment papers, valuable particularly for information concerning Rosecrans' West Point appointment, and the William S. Rosecrans Diplomatic Papers, covering the period when he was Minister to Mexico, in the National Archives, Washington, D.C.

The William S. Rosecrans Papers in the archives of the University of

Notre Dame, Notre Dame, Indiana. Letters, chiefly relating to mining and other business, and newspaper clippings.

William S. Rosecrans Paper in the archives of Georgetown University, Washington, D.C. Rosecrans' account of the death of Garesché.

William S. Rosecrans' *Commonplace Book* (414 pp.) on deposit in the Ohio State Library, Columbus, Ohio. Rosecrans' notes on military and other engineering matters and on the refining of petroleum.

In the Memorial Library of the Wisconsin State Historical Society, Madison, Wisconsin: the papers of Hans Heg, Charles S. Hamilton, and Frederick Jackson Turner.

In the Manuscript Division of the Library of Congress, Washington, D.C.: the papers of James A. Garfield, Fitz-John Porter, Abraham Lincoln (Robert Todd Lincoln Collection), U. S. Grant, Samuel P. Heintzelman, Hamilton Fish, Grover Cleveland, James B. McPherson, Andrew Johnson, Edwin M. Stanton, Benjamin Harrison, Rutherford B. Hayes, William F. Trenholm, Benjamin F. Butler, John A. Logan, and C. C. Hood.

In the archives of the University of Notre Dame, Notre Dame, Indiana: the papers of the Reverend Patrick Cooney and of Bishop Sylvester Horton Rosecrans. Bishop Rosecrans' papers include his "Diary."

In the archives of the Ohio State Historical and Archaeological Library, Columbus, Ohio: Sr. M. Felicitas, S.S.N.D., "Notes Concerning Bishop Sylvester Horton Rosecrans," Dayton, Ohio, 18 pp.; the William H. Smith Papers and the John P. Sanderson Papers. Sanderson's papers include his "Letter Diary," July 7, 1863 to April 10, 1864.

In the archives of the Illinois State Historical Society, Springfield, Illinois: the Benjamin Grierson Papers.

In the library of the Chicago Historical Society, Chicago, Illinois: the John A. Rawlins, William Butler, John R. Smith, John Tallman, and William Gale papers.

In the library of the Indiana State Historical Society, Indianapolis, Indiana: the Lew Wallace Papers.

In the archives of the library of the U.S. Military Academy, West Point, New York: various manuscripts relating to Cadet Rosecrans. These include library records, faculty proceedings, orders; *Headquarters— General Orders, Special Orders, Vol. I, Dec. 11, 1839–Aug. 29, 1842,* 431 pp.; *Cadet Circulation Records, 1836–1841;* and *Staff Records, No. 2, 1835 to 1842.*

In the archives of the Hayes Memorial Library, Fremont, Ohio: the Rutherford B. Hayes Papers.

In the library of Oberlin College, Oberlin, Ohio: the Jacob D. Cox Papers.

In the Milwaukee Public Library, Milwaukee, Wisconsin: the Selby V. I. Brown Papers (one Rosecrans letter).

In the National Archives, Washington, D.C.: the Earl Van Dorn Papers.

In the library of the Brown County (Ohio) Ursulines: papers relating to Bishop Sylvester H. Rosecrans and the family of General Rosecrans.

In the Genealogical Division of the New York Public Library: records of the Hegeman family.

Books

Abbott, J. S. C., *History of the Civil War in America,* New York, 1866, 3 vols.

Abbott, W. J., *Story of Our Army,* New York, 1914, 2 vols.

Adams, G. W., *Doctors in Blue,* New York, 1952

Addison, J. T., *The Episcopal Church in the United States,* New York, 1931

Alcott, C. S., *The Life of William McKinley,* Boston, 1916, 2 vols.

Allan, William, *History of the Campaign of Gen. T. J. Jackson in the Shenandoah Valley,* New York, 1880

Armies of the Cumberland, Tennessee, Ohio, Georgia, *The Army Reunion,* Chicago, 1869

Art Work of Nashville, Tenn., Chicago, 1901

Ayers, J. T., *Diary,* Springfield, Ill., 1947

Baldwin, Mrs. A., *When Our Mother Was a Little Girl,* Columbus, Ohio, 1888

Bancroft, H., *History of the Pacific States,* San Francisco, 1884–1890, 19 vols.

Beard, C. A. and M. R., *The Making of American Civilization,* New York, 1937

Beatty, John, *Citizen Soldier,* Cincinnati, 1879

—— *Memoirs of a Volunteer* (ed. by H. S. Ford), New York, 1946

Belknap, C. E., *The War of the Sixties,* New York, 1912

Bemis, S. F., and Griffin, G. G., *Guide to the Diplomatic History of the United States, 1775–1921,* Washington, D.C., 1935

Bennett, L. G., and Haigh, W. M., *History of the 36th Illinois Regiment,* Chicago, 1876

Berard, A. B., *Reminiscences of West Point,* Saginaw, Mich., 1881

Beyer, W. F., and Keydel, O. F., eds., *Deeds of Valor,* Detroit, 1905, 2 vols.

Beymer, W. G., *On Hazardous Service,* New York, 1912

Bickham, W. D., *Rosecrans' Campaign with the XIV Army Corps,* Cincinnati, 1863

Bierce, Ambrose, *Collected Writings,* New York, 1946

Blegen, Theodore C., *Civil War Letters of Hans Christian Heg,* Northfield, Minn., 1936

Bowers, C. G., *The Tragic Era,* New York, 1929

Boyd, Cyrus, *The Civil War Diary of Cyrus Boyd* (ed. by Mildred Throne), Iowa City, Iowa, 1953

Boynton, E. C., *History of West Point,* New York, 1863

Boynton, H. V., *Chattanooga and Chickamauga,* reprint of General Boynton's letters to the *Commercial Gazette,* Washington, D.C., 1888

———— *The National Park—Chickamauga-Chattanooga,* Cincinnati, 1895

Brockett, L. P., and Vaughan, M. C., *Woman's Work in the Civil War,* Philadelphia, 1867

"Brown County Ursuline," *Fifty Years in a Brown County Convent,* Cincinnati, 1895

Browne, J. H., *Four Years in Secessia,* Hartford, Conn., 1865

Buchanan, Lamont, *A Pictorial History of the Confederacy,* New York, 1951

Buck, Irving, *Cleburne,* New York, 1908

Buley, R. C., *Old Northwest,* Indianapolis, 1950, 2 vols.

Bundy, J. M., *Life of J. A. Garfield,* New York, 1880

Burgess, J. W., *The Civil War and the Constitution,* New York, 1906, 2 vols.

Burton, K., *Celestial Homespun,* New York, 1943

Caldwell, R. G., *James A. Garfield,* New York, 1931

Calkins, W. W., *History of the 104th Illinois Regiment,* Chicago, 1895

Callahan, J. M., *American Foreign Policy in Mexican Relations,* New York, 1932

Carrington, H. B., *Ohio Militia,* Indianapolis, 1862

Catton, Bruce, *A Stillness at Appomattox,* New York, 1953

Chesnut, M. B., *A Diary from Dixie,* London, 1905

Church, R. W., *The Oxford Movement,* London, 1922

Cist, Henry M., *The Army of the Cumberland,* New York, 1882

Cleaves, F., *Rock of Chickamauga,* Norman, Okla., 1948

Cleland, R. G., *California in our Time,* New York, 1947

Cockrell, M. F., ed., *The Lost Account of the Battle of Corinth,* Jackson, Tenn., 1955

Coffin, C. C., *Boys of '61,* Boston, 1896

———— *Four Years of Fighting,* Boston, 1866

————*Freedom Triumphant,* New York, 1891

Cole, A., *Irrepressible Conflict,* New York, 1934

Commager, H. S., ed., *The Blue and the Gray,* Indianapolis, 1950, 2 vols.

Condon, W. H., *Life of Major-General James Shield,* Chicago, 1900

Conger, A. L., *The Rise of Grant,* New York, 1931

Congress of the United States, *Reports of the Joint Committee on the Conduct of the War,* Washington, D.C., 1861, 1863, 1865

Corrigan, Raymond, *The Church and the Nineteenth Century,* Milwaukee, 1938

Cortissoz, Royal, *Life of Whitelaw Reid,* New York, 1921, 2 vols.

Cox, J. D., *Atlanta,* New York, 1882

————*Military Reminiscences,* New York, 1900, 2 vols.

Crane, J., and Keeley, J. F., *West Point,* New York, 1947

Dana, C. A., *Recollections of the Civil War,* New York, 1898

Deaderick, Barron, *Strategy in the Civil War,* Memphis, 1945

De Peyster, W., *The Decisive Conflicts of the Civil War,* New York, 1867

Dodd, W. E., *The Cotton Kingdom,* New Haven, Conn., 1921

Dodge, W. S., *Chronicles of the Army of the Cumberland,* Chicago, 1864

Donald, David, *Inside Lincoln's Cabinet,* New York, 1954

Duffield, *Under the Old Flag,* New York, 1912

Dupuy, R. E., *Where They Have Trod,* New York, 1951

Dyer, Frederick H., compiler, *A Compendium of the War of the Rebellion,* Des Moines, 1908

Eckenrode, H. H., and Conrad, B., *George B. McClellan,* Chapel Hill, N. C., 1941

————*James Longstreet,* Chapel Hill, N.C., 1936

Egan, J. B., and Desmond, A. W., eds., *The Civil War, Its Photographic History,* Wellesley Hills, Mass., 1941, 2 vols.

Eisenschiml, Otto, *The Celebrated Case of Fitz John Porter,* Indianapolis, 1950

Eisenschiml, Otto, and Newman, R., *The American Iliad,* Indianapolis, 1947

Elsen, H. W., *The Civil War Through the Camera,* Springfield, Mass., 1912, 16 parts

Emerson, Edwin, Jr., *A History of the 19th Century,* New York, 1901, 3 vols.

Famous Adventures and Prison Escapes of the Civil War, New York, 1885

Farley, J. P., *West Point in the Early Sixties,* Troy, N.Y., 1902

Fatout, P., *Ambrose Bierce,* Norman, Okla., 1951

Ferteg, J. W., *The Secession and Reconstruction of Tennessee,* Chicago, 1898

Fish, C. R., *The American Civil War,* New York, 1937

Fiske, John, *The Mississippi Valley in the Civil War,* Boston, 1900

Fitch, John, *Annals of the Army of the Cumberland,* Philadelphia, 1864

Fitch, M. H., *The Chattanooga Campaign,* Madison, Wis., 1911

Ford, Worthington, ed., *A Cycle of Adams Letters,* Boston, 1920, 2 vols.

────── *Letters of Henry Adams,* Boston, 1930

Forder, S. W., *History of Medicine of Delaware County, Ohio,* privately published, 1910

Forman, S., *History of the United States Military Academy,* New York, 1950

Freeman, D. S., *Lee's Lieutenants,* New York, 1946, 4 vols.

Fremantle, Arthur, *Diary,* Boston, 1954

French, S. G., *Two Wars,* Nashville, 1901

Gabriel, K. H., *Lure of the Frontier,* New Haven, Conn., 1929

Geer, Walter, *Campaigns of the Civil War,* New York, 1926

Gilmore, J. R., *Personal Recollections of Abraham Lincoln and the Civil War,* Boston, 1898

Gordon, J. B., *Reminiscences,* New York, 1904

Gorham, G. C., *The Life and Public Services of Edwin M. Stanton,* Boston, 1899, 2 vols.

Gracie, Archibald, *The Truth about Chickamauga,* Boston, 1911

Grant, U. S., *General Grant's Letters to a Friend* (ed. by J. G. Nelson), New York, 1897

────── *Personal Memoirs,* New York, 1885, 2 vols.

Gray, W., *The Hidden Civil War,* New York, 1942

Greeley, H., *The American Conflict,* Hartford, Conn., 1864–1867, 2 vols.

Green, H., *General Grant's Last Stand,* New York, 1936

Greenbie, M. C., *Lincoln's Daughters of Mercy,* New York, 1944

Greene, F. V., *The Mississippi,* New York, 1882

Hale, H. G., *Horace Greeley,* New York, 1950

Harlow, Ralph, *The Establishment of the Nation,* New York, 1943

Hart, A. B., *Salmon P. Chase,* Boston, 1899

────── *The Welding of the Nation,* New York, 1925

Hazen, W. B., *Narrative of Military Service,* Boston, 1885

Headley, J. T., *The Great Rebellion,* Hartford, Conn., 1862

Hebert, W. H., *Fighting for Hooker,* Indianapolis, 1944

Henderson, C. C., *The Story of Murfreesboro,* Murfreesboro, Tenn., 1929

Henry, R. S., *As They Saw Forrest,* Jackson, Tenn., 1956

"His Comrades" (Emily Van Dorn), *A Soldier's Honor,* New York, 1902

History of Delaware County, Ohio, Chicago, 1880

History of Milwaukee, Chicago, 1881

Hittel, J. H., *History of California,* San Francisco, 1897, 4 vols.

Homes, W. J., *The Loyal Mountaineers of Tennessee,* Knoxville, 1888

Hood, J. B., *Advance and Retreat,* New Orleans, 1880

Hopkins, J., *John Hopkins and Some of His Descendants,* Palo Alto, Cal., 1932

Horn, E. A., *Wisconsin Women in the War,* Madison, Wis., 1911

Hosmer, J. K., *The Appeal to Arms, 1861–1863,* New York, 1907

Howard, O. O., *Autobiography,* New York, 1907, 2 vols.

Howe, Henry, *Historical Collections of Ohio,* Cincinnati, 1848

―――― *Historical Collections of Ohio,* Cincinnati, 1889, 3 vols.

Howe, M. A. D., *Home Letters of General Sherman,* New York, 1909

IRC, *Independent Roystering Club,* privately printed, n.d., West Point Archives

Johnson, Clifton, *Battleground Adventures,* Boston, 1915

Johnson, R. W., *Memoir of Major General George H. Thomas,* Philadelphia, 1881

Jolly, R., *Nuns of the Battlefield,* Providence, 1930

Jones, J. L., *An Artillery Man's Diary,* Madison, Wis., 1914

Ketteil, J. P., *History of the Great Rebellion,* Hartford, Conn., 1865

Kier, M., *The Epic of Industry,* New Haven, Conn., 1926

Lee, R. E., *Recollections of General Robert E. Lee,* New York, 1904

Leech, M., *Reveille in Washington,* New York, 1941

Lewis, L., *Captain Sam Grant,* Boston, 1950

―――― *Sherman, Fighting Prophet,* New York, 1932

Livermore, J. L., *Numbers and Losses in the Civil War,* Boston, 1900

Longstreet, J., *From Manassas to Appomattox,* Philadelphia, 1896

Lossing, B., *A History of the Civil War,* Yonkers, N.Y., 1927

Lytte, J. R., ed., *Twentieth Century History of Delaware County,* Chicago, 1908

Martin, J. A., *Military History of the 8th Kansas Infantry,* Leavenworth, Kan., 1869

Maury, D. H., *Recollections of a Virginian,* New York, 1897

McCalmont, J. S., *28th Annual Reunion of the Association of Graduates of the U.S. Military Academy* (Additional notes by Gen. David S. Stanley), Saginaw, Mich., 1897

McCartney, C. E., *Grant and His Generals,* New York, 1953

―――― *Lincoln and His Cabinet,* New York, 1931

―――― *Lincoln and His Generals,* Philadelphia, 1925

McClellan, G. B., *McClellan's Own Story,* New York, 1887

McElroy, J., *Chickamauga,* Cincinatti, 1896

McRaven, H., *Nashville, Athens of the South,* Chapel Hill, N. C., 1949

McSorley, J., *Father Hecker and His Friends,* St. Louis, Mo., 1952

"Member of the G.A.R.," *The Picket Line and Camp Fire Stories,* New York, n.d.

Monica, Sr. M., O.S.V., *The Cross in the Wilderness,* New York, 1930

Moore, Frank, *Rebellion Record,* New York, 1862–1865, 12 vols.

Mottelay, D. F., and Campbell, C. I., *The Soldier in our Civil War,* New York, 1885, 2 vols.

Nashville City and Business Directory, 1860–1861, Nashville, 1861

Nevins, A., *Fremont,* New York, 1939

———— *Grover Cleveland,* New York, 1932

Nevins, A., ed., *Letters of Grover Cleveland,* Boston, 1933

Newmark, H., *Sixty Years in Southern California,* New York, 1916

Nicolay, J. G., and Hay, J., *Abraham Lincoln,* New York, 1890, 12 vols.

"Non-Vet of Co. H.," *The Eagle Regiment, 8th Wisconsin Volunteers,* Belleville, Wis., 1880

Ohio Writers' Program, *The Ohio Guide,* New York, 1940

Owen, W. M., *In Camp and Battle with the Washington Artillery of New Orleans,* Boston, 1885

Palmer, J. M., *Personal Recollections,* Cincinnati, 1901

Park, Rosewell, *A Sketch of the Topography and History of West Point,* Philadelphia, 1840

Pemberton, J. C., *Pemberton, Defender of Vicksburg,* Chapel Hill, N.C., 1942

Photographic History of the Civil War, New York, 1912, 10 vols.

Piatt, Don, and Boynton, H. V., *General George H. Thomas,* Cincinnati, 1893

Polk, W. M., *Leonidas Polk,* New York, 1893, 2 vols.

Pollard, E. A., *Southern History of the War,* New York, 1865, 3 vols.

Porter, G. H., *Ohio Politics during the Civil War,* New York, 1911

Pulestan, W. D., *Mahan,* New Haven, Conn., 1939

Reid, Whitelaw, *Ohio in the War,* Cincinnati, 1895, 2 vols.

Rhodes, J. F., *History of the Civil War,* New York, 1930

———— *History of the United States,* New York, 1920, 8 vols.

Richardson, A. D., *The Secret Service,* Hartford, Conn., 1865

Riddle, A. G., *Life of Benjamin F. Wade,* Cleveland, 1886

Riley, J., and Rosecrans, W. S., *Popular Government,* San Francisco, 1878

Rosecrans, W. S., *Report of the Battle of Murfreesboro,* 37th Congress, Special Session, Washington, D.C., 1863

———— *Rosecrans' Campaigns* (testimony to the Committee on the Conduct of the War, April 22–24, 1865), Senate Document #142, Washington, D.C., 1865

Rosenkrans, Allen, *The Rosenkrans Family in Europe and America,* privately printed, 1900

Sandburg, C., *Abraham Lincoln: The War Years*, New York, 1940, 4 vols.

Schafer, J., *Carl Schurz*, Madison, Wis., 1930

Schaff, M., *The Spirit of Old West Point*, Boston, 1907

Scharf, J. L., *History of St. Louis*, Philadelphia, 1883, 2 vols.

Schuckers, J. W., *Life and Services of Salmon Portland Chase*, New York, 1874

Schurz, Carl, *Reminiscences*, Garden City, N.Y., 1917, 3 vols.

Scott, W. F., *Philander P. Lane*, privately printed, 1920

——— *The Story of a Cavalry Regiment*, New York, 1893

Seitz, D. C., *Braxton Bragg*, Columbia, S.C., 1924

Shanks, W. F. G., *Personal Recollections of Distinguished Generals*, New York, 1866

Shannon, F. A., *The Civil War Letters of Sergeant Onley Andrus*, Urbana, Ill., 1947

Sheridan, P. H., *Personal Memoirs*, New York, 1888, 2 vols.

Sherman, W. T., *Memoirs of General William T. Sherman*, New York, 1875, 2 vols.

Smith, J. C., *Life and Letters of James Abram Garfield*, New Haven, Conn., 1925, 2 vols.

Smucker, I., *Centennial History of Licking County, Ohio*, Newark, Ohio, 1876

Society of the Army of the Cumberland, *The Burial of Rosecrans*, Cincinnati, 1903

——— *Reports of Reunions and Proceedings*, Cincinnati, 1868–1907, 34 vols.

Society of the Army of the Tennessee, *Reports of Reunions and Proceedings*, Cincinnati, 1866–1914, 43 vols.

Speed, J., *The Union Cause in Kentucky*, New York, 1907

Spooner, Walter W., ed., *Historic Families of America*, New York, 1907

Stevenson, A. F., *Battle of Stone's River*, Boston, 1884

Stewart, N. B., *Dan McCook's Regiment*, Alliance, Ohio, 1900

Stille, S. H., *Ohio Builds a Nation*, Chicago, 1939

Stillwell, Leander, *The Story of a Common Soldier*, Chicago, 1875

Stryker, L. P., *Andrew Johnson*, New York, 1929

Swiggett, H., *Rebel Raider*, Indianapolis, 1934

Swinton, William, *Twelve Decisive Battles*, New York, 1867

Taggart, Joseph, *Biographical Sketches*, Kansas City, Mo., 1927

Taylor, B. F., *In Camp and Field*, Chicago, 1875

Taylor, R., *Destruction and Reconstruction*, New York, 1879

Temple, O. P., *East Tennessee and the Civil War*, Cincinnati, 1899

Tennessee Historical Commission, *Tennessee Old and New: 1796–1946*, Nashville, 1946, 2 vols.

Terrell, W. H. H., *Indiana in the Civil War*, Indianapolis, 1869

Thayer, W. M., *From Log Cabin to White House,* Boston, 1880

Thompson, E. P., *History of the Orphan Brigade,* Louisville, 1898

Tomes, R., *War with the South,* New York, 1862–1865, 3 vols.

Tonn, E., *Foreigners in the Union Army and Navy,* Baton Rouge, La., 1951

Townsend, E. D., *Anecdotes of the Civil War,* New York, 1884

Turchin, J. B., *Chickamauga,* Chicago, 1888

Turner, G. E., *Victory Rode the Rails,* Indianapolis, 1953

Union Soldiers' and Sailors' Monument Ass'n., *Union Regiments of Kentucky,* Louisville, 1897

U.S. Army, *Report of a Board of Army Officers upon the Claim of Maj. Gen. William Farrer Smith that He and Not General Rosecrans Originated the Plan for the Relief of Chattanooga in Oct., 1863,* Washington, D. C., 1901

U.S. Military Academy, *The Centennial of the U.S. Military Academy,* Washington, D. C., 1904, 2 vols.

———— *Regulations,* New York, 1839, 1842, 4 vols.

Utter, W. J., *The Frontier State,* Columbus, Ohio, 1942

Vandiver, F. E., *Ploughshares into Swords,* Austin, Tex., 1952

Van Horne, J. B., *History of the Army of the Cumberland,* Cincinnati, 1875, 3 vols.

Villard, Henry, *Memoirs,* Boston, 1904, 2 vols.

Walker, R. S., *Lookout: The Story of a Mountain,* Kingsport, Tenn., 1941

Weber, Thomas, *Northern Railroads in the Civil War, 1861–1865,* New York, 1952

Weisberger, B. A., *Reporters for the Union,* Boston, 1953

Welles, Gideon, *Diary,* Boston, 1911, 3 vols.

West, R. J., Jr., *Gideon Welles,* Indianapolis, 1943

West Virginia Writers' Program, *West Virginia, A Guide to the Mountain State,* New York, 1941

Whipple, H. P., *Diary of a Private Soldier,* Waterloo, Wis., 1906

Williams, C. P., *Diary and Letters of Rutherford B. Hayes,* Columbus, Ohio, 1926, 5 vols.

Williams, Kenneth, *Lincoln Finds a General,* New York, 1949, 5 vols.

Williams, T. H., *Lincoln and His Generals,* New York, 1952

———— *Lincoln and the Radicals,* Madison, Wis., 1941

Wilson, J. G., *General Grant,* New York, 1897

———— *General Grant's Letters to a Friend, 1861–1880,* New York, 1897

Woodbury, A., *Major General Ambrose E. Burnside,* Providence, 1867

Woodward, William E., *Meet General Grant,* New York, 1928

Pamphlets, Periodical Articles, Articles
in Longer Works, Brief Items

Amended Complaint in the District Court of the 12th Judicial District of the State of California in and for the City of San Francisco, William S. Rosecrans, Plaintiff, The Southern Pacific Railroad Company et al, Defendants, San Francisco, 1873

Army of the Cumberland, "Program, 1870 Meeting," Cleveland

Army of West Virginia, Printed Invitation to Reunion, Sept. 19, 1879, at Marietta, Ohio

Bacon, Charles R., "Life at West Point," *Van Nordine Magazine,* Nov. 1907

Bailey, W. W., "My Boyhood at West Point," *News of the Highlands,* 1941

Basso, H., "St. Louis," *Holiday,* Oct. 1950

Belknap, W. W., "The Obedience of a Common Soldier," Iowa Commandery Papers, Vol. I.

Best, K., and Hellyer, K., "Iuka, Mississippi," *Good Housekeeping,* July 1951

Board of Trustees of the Veterans' Home Association, *Appeal to the People of California,* San Francisco, 1881

Boase, P. H., "Interdenominational Forensics on the Ohio Frontier," *The Gavel,* March 1953

Carnahan, J. R., "Indiana at Chickamauga," Indiana Commandery Papers

Catholic Columbian, "In Memoriam: Rt. Rev. S. H. Rosecrans, D.D.," Columbus, Ohio, 1878

Certificate of Election of Rosecrans as Delegate from the G.A.R., Post #2, Dep't. of California, to Nat'l. Encampment in Baltimore, June 21, 1882

Chickamauga Memorial Association, *Proceedings, Sept. 19–20, 1889,* Chattanooga, Tenn., 1889

Chitton, A. L., "Battle of Corinth," Illinois Commandery Papers, Vol. I

Cist, H. M., "Comments on Gen. Grant's 'Chattanooga,'" *Battles and Leaders,* Vol. III

City of St. Louis, Board of Common Council, *Resolution of Thanks to Officers and Soldiers Engaged in the Late Battle of Murfreesboro,* Jan. 23, 1863

Congregation of St. Paul the Apostle, "Father Deshon, Architect, Engineer, Builder," *Paulist Calendar,* Dec. 1943

Congressional Committee, *To the Voters of the First Congressional District,* San Francisco, 1880

Copeland, W. P., "International Railroad Project between Mexico and the United States," reprint from the New York *Journal of Commerce,* Jan. 1, 1872

Cox, J. D., "McClellan in West Virginia," *Battles and Leaders,* Vol. I

———— "War Preparations in the North," *Battles and Leaders,* Vol. I

Crittenden, J. L., "The Union Left at Stone's River," *Battles and Leaders,* Vol. III

Crosby, C. L., *Rosecrans' Victory March,* Cincinnati, Ohio, 1863

Cross, J. N., "The Campaign in West Virginia," Minnesota Commandery Papers, Vol. II

Curtis, H. B., "Pioneer Days in Central Ohio," *Ohio Archaeological and Historical Publications,* I, June 1887–March 1888

Dodge, G. M., "Personal Recollections of General Grant," New York Commandery Papers, Vol. III

Ehrenclou, V. L., "The Water Well of 1886," *Bulletin of the Union Oil Company of California,* April 1924

Ewing, Thomas, *An Address to the Unpledged Voters of the United States—and the Rosecrans-Lee Correspondence,* Democratic State Executive Committee of Ohio, Columbus, Ohio, 1868

Foraker, J. B., *Remarks in Connection with the Reinterment of Gen. W. S. Rosecrans at Arlington Cemetery, May 17, 1902,* Washington, D.C., 1902

Forman, S., *Cadet Life before the Civil War,* West Point, N.Y., 1945

Frost, W. B., *William Starke Rosecrans, His Life and Public Services,* San Francisco, 1880

Fuller, J. W., "Our Kirby Smith," Ohio Commandery Papers, Vol. I

Fullerton, J. S., "Army of the Cumberland at Chattanooga," *Battles and Leaders,* Vol. III

———— "Reinforcing Thomas at Chickamauga," *Battles and Leaders,* Vol. III

Furay, R. S., "Sketch of W. S. R.," in Howe, Henry, *Historical Collections of Ohio,* 1889, Vol. I

Garfield's Death Warrant (handbill containing the Morey letters), San Francisco, Cal., 1880

G. H. Thomas Post, G.A.R., *Roster of Members,* San Francisco

Gilmore, J. A., "Why Rosecrans Was Removed," Atlanta *Constitution,* Dec. 22, 1895

Grant, U.S., "Chattanooga," *Battles and Leaders,* Vol. I

———— "The Battle of Shiloh," *Battles and Leaders,* Vol, I

Hamilton, C. S., "Hamilton's Division at Corinth," *Battles and Leaders,* Vol. II

Hamilton, C. S., and Ducat, A., *Correspondence in Regard to the Battle of Corinth, Miss.,* Chicago, 1882

Hedden, Warren Rosecrans, Hedden, J. S., Hedden, E. H., Earle, T., Earle, A. W., *Glimpses through Portals of the Past,* New York, 1921

Hemstreit, W., "Little Things about Big Generals," New York Commandery Papers, Vol. III

Henderson, D. B., "Speech at the Dedication of the Chickamauga National Park," 1895

Hill, D. H., "Chickamauga," *Battles and Leaders,* Vol. III

Holden, E. S., "The United States Military Academy at West Point," *Overland Monthly,* July 1891 (reprint)

House of Representatives, 50th Congress, 1st Session, #643, *Chattanooga Battlefield,* Washington, D.C., 1890

House of Representatives, 50th Congress, 2nd Session, *Bill to Place Upon the Retired List Certain Officers with the Rank of Major General,* Washington, D.C., 1888

House of Representatives, 50th Congress, 2nd Session, Report #3675, *William S. Rosecrans,* Washington, D. C., 1889

James, J. B., "Life at West Point One Hundred Years Ago," *Mississippi Valley Historical Review,* June 1944

Kelley, R. M., "Holding Kentucky for the Union," *Battles and Leaders,* Vol. I

Kniffen, G. C., *The Army of the Cumberland and the Battle of Stone's River,* District of Columbia Commandery Papers, Vol. 68

—— "The Battle of Stone's River," *Battles and Leaders,* Vol. III

—— *Major General William Starke Rosecrans,* District of Columbia Commandery Papers, Vol. 74

—— "Manoeuvering Bragg out of Tennessee," *Battles and Leaders,* Vol. III

Le Duc, W., "The Little Steamboat That Opened the Cracker Line," *Battles and Leaders,* Vol. III

Marks, S., "Experiences at the Battle of Stone's River," Wisconsin Commandery Papers, Vol. II

McClay, J. H., "The Defense of Robinette," Iowa Commandery Papers, Vol. I

McCrory, William, "Early Life of Sherman," Minnesota Commandery Papers, Vol. I

Minnesota Commission to Locate Positions on the Battlefields of Chickamauga and Chattanooga, *Report,* Minneapolis, 1895

Mulhane, L., "Major General William Starke Rosecrans," *Proceedings* of the American Catholic Historical Society of Philadelphia, Sept. 1924

Opdycke, E., "Notes on the Chickamauga Campaign," *Battles and Leaders,* Vol. III

"Paulists and Their Work in Our Parish," *Paulist Calendar,* Dec. 1943

Piatt, Donn, "The General Who Heard Mass before Battle," *The Collector,* Jan. 1942

Pletcher, D. M., "General William Rosecrans and the Mexican Transcontinental Railroad," *Mississippi Valley Historical Review,* March 1952

Polk, W. M., "General Polk at Chickamauga," *Battles and Leaders,* Vol. III

"The Removal of General Rosecrans," *U.S. Army and Navy Journal,* Nov. 14, 1863

"The Rosencrans Family," *Old Northwest Genealogical Quarterly,* IX, 313

Rosecrans, W. S., *Actual Estade de Asunte del Ferrocarril Interoceanice,* Mexico City, 1873

——— *Announcement: Headquarters Blue and Gray, Hancock Central Legion,* San Francisco, 1880

——— "The Battle of Corinth," *Battles and Leaders,* Vol. II

——— "Bibliography of Writings," U.S. Military Academy, *Centennial,* Washington, D.C., 1904, Vol. II

——— "The Campaign for Chattanooga," *Century Magazine,* May 1887

——— *Chinese Immigration,* Washington, D.C., 1882

——— *Confidential: The Substance of the Business,* 1871

——— "Edler Brief des General Rosecrans," in *Ein Schmackhaftes Gericht für Loyale Männer,* printed for free distribution, Philadelphia, 1863

——— *El General W. S. Rosecrans: La "Doctrina Monroe," el "Destino Manifesto" y el Ferrocarril de Tuxpan al Pacifico,* Mexico City, 1870

——— *Letter from General Rosecrans to the Ohio Legislature,* Murfreesboro, Tenn., 1863

——— *Letter to the Hon. Horace Greeley,* New York, 1866

——— *Letter to the State Executive Committee of Ohio,* San Francisco, Aug. 8, 1869

——— *Letters to the Voters of Indiana,* Philadelphia, 1863

——— *Major General Rosecrans on Contributions for the Sick and Wounded,* Murfreesboro, Tenn., Feb. 2, 1863

——— *The Memorial of General W. S. Rosecrans,* San Rafael, Cal., 1870

——— "The Mistakes of Grant," *North American Review,* Dec. 1885

——— *Prefatory* (Prospectus of the Southern Pacific R.R. Company), San Rafael, Cal., 1869

—— *The Proposed Monument to General Thomas,* San Rafael, Cal., 1871

—— *Remarks, Feb. 16, 1885 on Bill (S. 2169) to Place Gen. Grant on the Retired List of the Army,* Washington, D.C., 1885

—— *The Veterans' Home Association,* San Francisco, 1881 (2 pamphlets)

—— *W. S. Rosecrans, Nominee for Congress,* San Francisco, 1880 (card)

Rosecrans, W. S., and Lee, R. E., *Reconstruction,* Columbus, Ohio, 1868

—— *Rosecrans' Letter to Lee and Reply of the Latter,* Columbus, Ohio, 1868

Ross, C. H., "Old Memories," Wisconsin Commandery Papers, Vol. I

Safety Powder Company, *The Safety Powder Company,* San Francisco, 1878

Sanborn, J. B., "Reminiscences of the Department of Missouri," Missouri Commandery Papers, Vol. II

Scott, W. F., "The Last Fight for Missouri," New York Commandery Papers, Vol. III

Sherman, W. T., "The Grand Strategy of the War of the Rebellion," *Century Magazine,* Feb. 1888

Smith, A. J., *Acknowledgement of Tribute in Memory of the Late General Rosecrans,* San Francisco, April 6, 1898

Smith, A. S., "Wisconsin Volunteers at Iuka and Corinth," Wisconsin Commandery Papers, Vol. IV

Smith, Francis H., *West Point Fifty Years Ago,* New York, 1879

Smith, W. F., "Comments on General Grant's 'Chattanooga,' " *Battles and Leaders,* Vol. III

—— "Postscript," *Battles and Leaders,* Vol. III

Snead, J. L., "The First Year of War in Missouri," *Battles and Leaders,* Vol. I

Sociedad Mexicana de Historia Natural to William S. Rosecrans, Diploma, Washington, D.C., February 24, 1880

Society of the Army of the Cumberland, Banquet Program, November 25, 1870

—— Invitation, 11th Reunion, 1879

—— Prospectus, 7th Annual Reunion, 1875

Stanley, D. S., "The Battle of Corinth," New York Commandery Papers, Vol. II

—— "Tullahoma Campaign," Ohio Commandery Papers, Vol. III

State of Indiana, *Resolution of the Senate and House of Indiana Congratulating Rosecrans and the Army of the Cumberland on Stone's River*

State of Virginia, *Congratulatory Resolutions Passed Dec. 18, 1861 on Rosecrans' Victories in Western Virginia*

Stone, Charles P., "Washington on the Eve of the War," *Battles and Leaders,* Vol. I

Taylor, Stuart, *A Union Soldier's Views* (Speech at mass meeting to ratify the nomination of Rosecrans), San Francisco, 1880

Thruston, G. P., "The Crisis at Chickamauga," *Battles and Leaders,* Vol. III

Touching Tribute to the Memory of the Late Father Christy, Pittsburgh, September 22, 1879

Urguhart, David, "Bragg's Advance and Retreat," *Battles and Leaders,* Vol. III

U.S. Patent Office, Letters Patent #224, #957, to W. S. Rosecrans, Washington, D. C., Feb. 24, 1880

Waggoner, C., *Honors at Chickamauga,* privately printed, Toledo, Ohio, 1881

Waterman, A. G., "Battle of Chickamauga," Illinois Commandery Papers, Vol. I

Wood, F. M., Sr., *The James A. Garfield Home (Lawnfield),* Mentor, Ohio, 1950

Woodruff, J. M., "Early War Days," Minnesota Commandery Papers, Vol. III

Yaryan, J. L., "Stone River," Indiana Commandery Papers, Vol. I

Newspapers

Atlanta, Ga., *Constitution*
Charleston, S.C., *Courier*
Chattanooga, Tenn., *Daily Times*
Chicago, Ill., *Chronicle; Journal; Tribune*
Cincinnati, Ohio, *Commercial; Gazette; Times*
Cleveland, Ohio, *Catholic Telegraph; Leader*
Columbus, Ohio, *Catholic Columbian*
Indianapolis, Ind., *Times*
Los Angeles, Cal., *Herald; Times*
Milwaukee, Wis., *Sentinel*
Murfreesboro, Tenn., *Rebel Banner*
Nashville, Tenn., *Dispatch*
New York, N.Y., *Herald; Spirit of the Times; Sun; Times; Tribune*
Parkersburg, W. Va., *Catholic Messenger*

Richmond, Va., *Examiner; Whig*
San Francisco, Cal., *Alta Californian; Examiner*
Shakopee, Minn., *Minnesota Courier*
St. Louis, Mo., *Missouri Democrat; Missouri Republican*
Toledo, Ohio, *Journal*
Washington, D.C., *Journal; Post; Tribune*

ABBREVIATIONS: R for Rosecrans
A.E.R. for Annie Rosecrans
W.M.L. for William M. Lamers
M.M.L. for Mrs. William M. Lamers
C.C.W. for *Reports of the Joint
Committee on the Conduct of the War*

Prologue

Lincoln on Stone River: Official Records, Series I, Vol. LII, 442. R to
J. A. Garfield, Jan. 30, 1864, Garfield Papers. The first draft of this
letter, dated Jan. 29, 1864, is in the Rosecrans Papers.

Chapter One: "The Brilliant Rosy Rosecrans"

Family, childhood, and youth: Rosenkrans, Allen, *Rosenkrans Family;*
R, *Sketch,* 1–5; *History of Delaware County,* 564; Frost, *Rosecrans,* 2;
Fitch, J., *Annals,* 1–9; Rosecrans, Anita, "Mss. Notes"; Baldwin, A.,
When Our Mother Was a Little Girl; Hopkins, *John Hopkins,* 187;
Mulhane, "Rosecrans," 243; Howe, *Historical Collections,* 1889, I, 216,
II, 339; *Catholic Columbian, In Memoriam,* 3; Mary E. Reed to W.M.L.,
Oct. 23, 1952; R to L. W. Mulhane, n.d., Notre Dame Archives; W. A.
Rosenkrantz to W. S. Rosecrans III, June 24, 1937. Frontier life: Curtis,
"Pioneer Days," 249; Utter, *Frontier State,* 144–151, 235 ff., 370–372;
Buley, *Old Northwest,* I, 162 ff., II, 419. "Father not wealthy": R to
A.E.R., Aug. 9, 1842. "No Willie": statement, W. S. Rosecrans III to
M.M.L., April 1951. Clerk R: J. A. Martin to R, April 26, 1864. Walked
fifty miles: statement, W. S. Rosecrans III to M.M.L., April 1951. Ap-
pointment: R to J. R. Poinsett, Feb. 4, 17, and March 6, 1838.
A. Harper to R, Feb. 15, 1838, National Archives. West Point: Park,
Sketch, 475 ff.; James, "Life at West Point," 21; U.S. Military Academy,
Regulations, Register; Cullum, *Biographical Register,* I, II; Lewis,

Sherman, 54 ff.; McCrory, "Early Life," 314–316; Lewis, *Captain Sam Grant*, 66, 69, 81; McCalmont, *Reunion*, 66; Pulestan, *Mahan*, 5–10; Society of the Army of the Cumberland, *Burial*, 43. Dating Annie: Susan Bailey to R and G. V. Smith, June 11, 1842. Appointment and marriage: W. C. Bartlett to R, Oct. 21, 1842; Fitch, *Annals*, 10; Frost, *Rosecrans*, 3. Catholicism: Anna E. Hegeman to R, July 28, Oct. 22, 1842; McCalmont, 54; M. Parks to R, March 12, 1844; R to L. W. Mulhane, Nov. 11, 1866, Notre Dame Archives; Rosecrans, S. H., "Diary," Notre Dame Archives; statements, W. S. Rosecrans III to W.M.L., July 1951, W. J. Morton to W.M.L., Aug. 1951. Assignments: A.E.R. to T. A. Scott, April 28, 1871; R. E. Lee to R, Aug. 28, 1848. Life in Washington: Fitch, 11; R to A.E.R., Nov. 17, 1870; S. H. Rosecrans to J. P. Purcell, July 17, 1868, Notre Dame Archives; R resigns: Eckenrode and Conrad, *McClellan*, 11; S. H. Rosecrans to R, Jan. 27, 1852; A.E.R. to T. A. Scott, April 28, 1871; D. H. Mahan to R, Nov. 12, 1853; Kier, *Epic of Industry*, 92–107; R to A.E.R., Nov. 17, 1853, March 8, 1857; R, *Commonplace Book*, 280 ff.; R to J. Fraser, July 14, 1875. R and supporting his family: S. H. Rosecrans to R, Jan. 27, 1852; Gleaner, R. C., in Columbus, Ohio, *Catholic Columbian*, undated newspaper clipping in Rosecrans Papers. Louisiana Military Institute: C. P. Stone to R, April 13, May 9, 1860. Home guards: Fitch, 14.

Chapter Two: "A Brigadier's Sword and Sash"

Wartime Cincinnati: Howe, *Historical Collections*, 1889, II, 42–47. R tenders services: Fitch, *Annals*, 14; Frost, *Rosecrans*; R, *Personal Report*, 1. Ohio enters war: Reid, *Ohio*, I, 32–35; Cox, *Reminiscences*, I, 7–10. Hill on Union leaders: "Chickamauga," 638. R at Camp Dennison: Cox, *Reminiscences*, I, 21–25. R tours East: R, testimony, *C.C.W.*, Dec. 31, 1861. R's commission: G. B. McClellan to S. Cameron, May 18, 1861; R to S. Cameron, May 28, 1861; R to A.E.R., May 25, 1861; R, *Sketch*; Reid, I, 46–51. Divided Virginia: Greeley, *American Conflict*, 477–481; R, testimony, *C.C.W.*, Dec. 31, 1861; Burgess, *Civil War*, I, 206–211. "State governments saved Union": McClellan, *McClellan's Own Story*, 43. B. & O. R.R.: Weber, *Northern Railroads*, 76. McClellan's delay: Reid, I, 47; Greeley, I, 520 ff. R commissioned brigadier: J. P. Garesché to R, June 14, 1861; R to A.E.R., June 18, 1861. Poor roads: Freeman, *Lee's Lieutenants*, I, 684 ff. Western Virginia: Fatout, *Bierce*, 8. R at Rich Mountain: Ross, "Old Memories," 150, 155. Hart's account of Rich Mountain: Tomes, *War with the South*, I, 334 ff. McClellan's inactivity:

Beatty, *Memoirs*, 24 ff. "No explanation": R, testimony, *C.C.W.*, April 22, 1865. R summarizes battle: R, *Personal Report*, 1, 3. McCalmont's comment: McCalmont, *Reunion*, 15. "R jubilant": Beatty, *Memoirs*, 26. "Rich Mountain an affair": R to A.E.R., July 18, 1862. Troops green: R, testimony, *C.C.W.*, Dec. 31, 1861. McClellan's character: Cox, "McClellan," 137. "My fortunes with McClellan's": J. J. Trowbridge to R, Nov. 10, 1862. Bull Run: R to A.E.R., July 25, 1861. Reid describes R: Reid, I, 316. Reports and correspondence: *Official Records*, Series I, Vols. II and III.

Chapter Three: "Lee Is Coming"

Army dispirited: Beatty, *Memoirs*, 35 ff. Floyd's retreat: Greeley, *American Conflict*, I, 523 ff. False rumors, and exchange of prisoners: R, testimony, *C.C.W.*, Dec. 31, 1861, April 22, 1865. Lee's splendid plan: Reid, *Ohio*, I, 55 ff.; Pollard, *Southern History*, I, 171. Service hard: Reid, I, 55. Heavy rain: R to A.E.R., Aug. 13, 1861. Recruits undisciplined: Beatty, *Memoirs*, 17–68. Frontier democracy: Leech, *Reveille*, 75–79. R's discipline: Cox, *Reminiscences*, I, 127. Creighton episode: New York *Times*, May 15, 1898. "Want of officers": R, testimony, *C.C.W.*, Dec. 31, 1861. R instructs: Ross, "Old Memories," 155. R an incessant worker: Reid, I, 315. Votes of thanks: Rosecrans Papers. Lee on weather and rain: Freeman, *Lee's Lieutenants*, I, 555; Lee, *Recollections*, 41. Brigadier's sword and sash: R to A.E.R., Sept. 6, 1861. Mapped Western Virginia: New York *Times*, Sept. 16, 1861. Benham: Reid, I, 318. Lytle's charge: New York *Times*, Sept. 16, 1861. Confusion: R, testimony, *C.C.W.*, Dec. 31, 1861. Gloom in South: Charleston, S.C., *Courier*, Sept. 21, 1861. Captured property: R to A.E.R., Sept. 11, 1861. Exposure produced sickness: Cox, "McClellan," 147 ff. "Wagon-master's work": Cox, *Reminiscences*, I, 123. Cross episode: Cross, "Campaign in West Virginia," 168. Lee's discouragement: Lee, 51. Cox's portrait of R: Cox, *Reminiscences*, I, 111 ff. Reid's portrait: Reid, I, 349. R blames Benham for loss: R to A.E.R., Nov. 19, 1861. Pollard on R's campaign: Pollard, *Southern History*, I, 175. Whooping cough: A.E.R. to R, Nov. 19, 1861. Reports and correspondence: *Official Records*, Series I, Vol. V.

Chapter Four: "That Damned Little Cuss, McClellan"

Adams' comment: Ford, *Letters of Henry Adams*, 35. Wagoning, pack mules: R, testimony, *C.C.W.*, Dec. 31, 1861. Hauling: Freeman, *Lee's*

Lieutenants, I, 574. Offer to resign: Cincinnati *Times,* Oct. 20, 1863. Low spirits, McClellan's troubles: Sandburg, *War Years,* I, 377 ff., 388. "Bottom out of tub": Leech, *Reveille,* 125. R interviews McClellan: R, *Sketch,* 10 ff.; R, testimony, *C.C.W.,* April 22, 1865. R won McClellan's victories: Charleston, S.C., *Courier,* Sept. 21, 1861. McClellan credits Lander: R to A.E.R., April 22, 1862. Radicals; Ben Wade on peace; browbeating; Stanton replaces Cameron; Fremont the martyr; scheme to have McClellan fail: Williams, *Lincoln and the Radicals,* 10, 13, 64, 78 ff., 88–91, 111–113, 117, 120, 123 ff. R to Washington: R, *W.S.R.,* 31. R before Committee: R, testimony, *C.C.W.,* Dec. 31, 1861. Trotter's complaint: West Virginia Writers' Program, *West Virginia,* 507. R invents ambulance: Frost, *Rosecrans,* 5; R, *W.S.R.,* 32. "Plots and counterplots": Williams, 111–113, 117–122, 126. "Some preferred defeat": Burgess, *Civil War,* II, 104 ff. Blenker: Mottelay and Campbell, I, 235; Leech, 114. Stanton's reception of R: R to F.-J. Porter, Sept. 18, 1880, Porter Papers; R to A.E.R., April 22, 1862. "Only live plan": R, *W.S.R.,* 32 ff. "Damned little cuss, McClellan": R, *W.S.R.,* 33. R confers with Banks: R, *W.S.R.,* 33–35. Hartsuff's notes: G. Hartsuff to R, April 15, 1862, Jan. 8, 1863. "Senseless prejudice": R to F.-J. Porter, Sept. 18, 1880, Porter Papers. "Stanton an enemy": R, *W.S.R.,* 35. "Hartsuff will shield me": R to A.E.R., April 22, 1862. "Tide sets strongly": R to A.E.R., April 30, 1862. "Mind your business": Cincinnati *Times,* Oct. 20, 1863. "Actions hostile": R to F.-J. Porter, Sept, 18, 1880, Porter Papers. "Kind with inferiors": Reid, *Ohio,* I, 348 ff. "Temper caused Stanton's hostility": R to F.-J. Porter, Sept. 18, 1880, Porter Papers. Henderson's comment on Jackson: q. in Rhodes, *Civil War,* 131. "Divine interposition": Leech, 173. Reports and correspondence: *Official Records,* Series I, Vol. V; Vol. XII, Part III.

Chapter Five: Under Grant's Command

Five most likely to succeed: Lewis, *Grant,* 425. Grant castigated: Chicago *Tribune,* April 16, 1862. Grant's troubles: Grant, *Memoirs,* I, 316–329; McRaven, *Nashville,* 95; Grant, "Shiloh," 466; Reid, *Ohio,* I, 378; Boyd, *Diary,* 47; Rhodes, *Civil War,* 108. "R bore it handsomely": Reid, I, 321. Western armies: Greene, *Mississippi,* 29 ff. Mumps: Boyd, 51. Battlefield of Shiloh: Boyd, 44, 52. Failure to seize Vicksburg: Greene, 27–34. Dry summer: Boyd, 54 ff.; Best and Hellyer, "Iuka," 176. Wearing "belly band": Adams, *Doctors in Blue,* 200 ff. "Keep body clean": Carrington, *Ohio Militia,* 23, 26. "Sow belly and magets": John Tallman to Jay Tallman, n.d., Tallman Papers. "Men's health improved": R, *W.S.R.,* 37.

Flies thick: Blegen, *Heg*, 103–105. Sherman reassures Grant: Sherman, *Memoirs*, I, 255; Grant, *Memoirs*, I, 377. Hamilton "touchy": Hamilton, *Papers*. Lincoln supports Grant: Sandburg, *War Years*, II, 118 ff. R under Grant: Reid, I, 321; McCalmont, *Reunion*, 541. Chase promises help: S. P. Chase to R, Aug. 12, 1862. Postal service: Blegen, *Heg*, 114; Fitch, *Annals*, 311 ff. Map making: R, *W.S.R.*, 38 ff. Civil administration: R, *W.S.R.*, 37 ff. R and Negroes: R, *Sketch*, 25; Boyd, 63. Grant seldom smoked: Shanks, *Recollections*, 74. Inner defenses for Corinth: R, *Sketch*, 15 ff.; R, "Battle of Corinth," 740 ff. Cool nights: H. Heg to G. Heg, Aug. 16, 1862, Heg Papers. Headquarters: observed by W.M.L., April 1954. Troublous times: R, "Battle of Corinth," 738. Price's multicolored horde: "Member of the G.A.R.," *Picket Line*, 171. Reports and correspondence: *Official Records*, Series I, Vol. X, Parts I and II; Vol. XVII, Parts I and II.

Chapter Six: *Iuka—The Pincers Do Not Close*

Battle and pursuit: Grant, *Memoirs*, 404–413; R, testimony, *C.C.W.*, April 22, 1865. Grant reports Antietam victory: R, *Sketch*, 19. Lagow and Dickey visit R: R, *Sketch*, 20; R, testimony, *C.C.W.*, April 22, 1865. "Corn a'poppin": Interview with Mr. Woodley, Iuka, April 1954. 11th Ohio battery: Beyer and Keydel, *Deeds of Valor*, I, 92 ff. No sleep: R to A.E.R., Sept. 24, 1862. "Why leave me in the lurch?": Fuller, J. W., "Our Kirby Smith," 170. Pursuit: R, testimony, *C.C.W.*, April 22, 1865. "Failure to cooperate lost Price": R to A.E.R., Sept. 24, 1862. Surrender scheme Grant's: A. C. Ducat to R, April 24, 1885. Price holds up answer: Cincinnati *Gazette*, Sept. 29, 1862, reprinted in the Milwaukee *Sentinel*, Oct. 1, 1862. Dubois and McArthur hear R's guns: R, *Sketch*, 22; R, testimony, *C.C.W.*, April 22, 1865. Ducat rides forward with Ord: A. C. Ducat to R, April 24, 1885. "Drunkenness in high places": Cincinnati *Commercial*, Sept. 29, 1862. Sylvester Rosecrans comments: S. H. Rosecrans to A.E.R., Sept. 29, 1862. "Eno's" account of left: Cincinnati *Gazette*, Sept. 29, 1862. R's comment on Grant's reports: R, *Sketch*, 22–24. Hesseltine comments: W. S. Hesseltine to W.M.L., April 27, 1956. Drunkenness on Hamilton's staff: E. Betty to R, Jan. 1, 1863. "Gen'l Intoxication": Boyd, *Diary*, 106. Rosecrans talkative: Reid, *Ohio*, I, 323. "Heavy blow": Maury, *Recollections*, 160. Battlefield: Boyd, 70 ff. Reports and correspondence: *Official Records*, Series I, Vol. XVII, Parts I and II.

Chapter Seven: Corinth

Ducat's transfer: A. C. Ducat to R, April 24, 1885. Weather turned hot: Boyd, *Diary*, 71. Colored engineers' corps: R, "Corinth," 740 ff.; R, *Sketch*, 24. Van Dorn's numbers: "His Comrades," *Soldier's Honor*, 294. "Van Dorn would not send army against fortifications": R, "Corinth," 743. Meeting of R's commanders: Hamilton and Ducat, *Correspondence*, 7. Corinth on the eve of battle: Cincinnati *Commercial*, q. in Milwaukee *Sentinel*, Oct. 16, 1862. R's first positions: R, "Corinth," 744–746. McArthur: Boyd, 85. McArthur's Scotch blood: R, "Corinth," 745 ff. Boyd describes volley: Boyd, 72. Ducat carries dispatch to Hamilton: R, "Corinth," 746 ff.; Gilmore, *Recollections*, 124 ff. Hamilton's slow obedience: R, "Corinth," 746. "Got them where we want them": Cincinnati *Commercial*, q. in Milwaukee *Sentinel*, Oct. 16, 1862. "Ducat was angry": Hamilton and Ducat, 7. R questioned Hamilton savagely: Hamilton and Ducat, 11. Hamilton abused R: E. Betty to R, Jan. 7, 1863. Hamilton and the night attack: Hamilton, "Hamilton's Division," 758. Strengthening Fort Richardson: Cincinnati *Commercial*, q. in Milwaukee *Sentinel*, Oct. 16, 1862. R retired at 4:00 A.M.: R, "Corinth," 748. First shells: McClay, "Defense of Robinette," 168. Van Dorn's second-day attack: Cincinnati *Commercial*, q. in Milwaukee *Sentinel*, Oct. 16, 1862. "Mower is killed": R, "Corinth," 752. Henderson remembered R: Henderson, "Speech at the Dedication of the Chickamauga National Park." Reid's testimony: Reid, *Ohio*, I, 325. Boyd saw Stars and Stripes: Boyd, 73. Battlefield a gambling table: "His Comrades," 23. "No one but Rosecrans": A. C. Ducat to R, April 24, 1885. R feels faint: R, "Corinth," 751 ff. Fuller remembered: J. W. Fuller to R, Dec. 1, 1870. Maury's men in ditch: Boyd, 75 ff. R's message to Maury: Maury, *Recollections*, 171. "Best of ranch": R, "Corinth," 751 ff: Boyd's description of R: Boyd, 76. "McPherson's approach had moral effect": Grant, *Memoirs*, I, 416 ff. "Enemy did not know": A. C. Ducat to R, April 24, 1885. McPherson reaches Corinth: R, "Corinth," 753. "R failed to follow": Grant, I, 417. Forced march exhausts men: Grant, I, 411. Van Dorn and another assault: Maury, 294 ff. Time of battle's end: R, testimony, *C.C.W.*, April 22, 1865. Stanley defends R: Stanley, "Corinth," 278 ff. Reports and correspondence: *Official Records*, Series I, Vol. XVII, Parts I and II.

Chapter Eight: Grant Calls Rosecrans Back

Determined to return: "His Comrades," *Soldier's Honor*, 294 ff. Beginning of the pursuit: Hamilton and Ducat, *Correspondence*; A. C. Ducat to

R, April 24, 1885. Burial party: R, testimony, *C.C.W.*, April 22, 1865. "Few so beset": "His Comrades," 295. Smith feeds R: Smith, "Wisconsin Volunteers," 66 ff. Headlong pursuit: Boyd, *Diary*, 76 ff. R shows order to Ducat: A. C. Ducat to R, April 24, 1885. Importance of battle: Greene, *Mississippi*, 54; Sherman, *Memoirs*, I, 264. Bad feelings: Reid, *Ohio*, I, 327. "Drunkenness": Cincinnati *Commercial*, Sept. 29, 1862. "Grant offended": Sherman, *Memoirs*, I, 261; Reid, I, 326 ff.; Stanley, q. in Mc-Calmont, *Reunion*, 56 ff. Bickham's account: Cincinnati *Commercial*, Oct. 9, 1862. "Victory complete": R to A.E.R., Oct. 15, 1862. Major general: R to A.E.R., Sept. 22, 1862. "Major generals for camp service": R, testimony, *C.C.W.*, April 22, 1865. R's claim just: Williams, K., *Lincoln Finds a General*, III, 447 ff. Flag of truce: R to A.E.R., Oct. 22, 1862. Rumored second attack: Boyd, 81. "Grant's trouble solved," Grant criticizes R: Dodge, "Personal Recollections," 357. Grant writes to Washburne: Grant, *Letters to a Friend*, 22. Pursuit: Eisenschiml and Newman, *American Iliad*, 291; A. C. Ducat to R, April 24, 1885. Reports and correspondence: *Official Records*, Series I, Vol. XVII, Parts I and II; Vol. XLI, Parts I and II.

Chapter Nine: "Fight, I Say!"

Army: Cist, *Army of the Cumberland;* Fitch, *Annals;* Bickham, *Campaign;* Van Horne, *History.* Buell: Hazen, *Narrative,* 167. Elections: Williams, T. H., *Lincoln and the Radicals,* 12 ff., 192 ff., 226. R on replacing Buell: Kniffen, *Rosecrans,* 5 ff. Seniority: Kniffen, 5 ff.; R to A. M. McCook, Nov. 18, 1883; Piatt and Boynton, *Thomas,* 202. R's position: Beatty, *Memoirs,* 185. Weather, personal items, conversations, meetings, etc.: Bickham, 14, 15, 51, 55–57, 62, 121, 132, 136–139, 145, 163. Strategy: R to S. H. Rosecrans, Nov. 1, 1862. Poor conditions: Blegen, *Heg,* 187; F. Knefler to L. Wallace, March 28, 1862, Wallace Papers. R's staff: Fitch, 47, 50–53, 198–200, 271–279. R on "grand divisions": R, *Sketch,* 30. McCook: Shanks, *Recollections,* 249; Reid, *Ohio,* I, 806–809; Fitch, 73–78; Beatty, 235 ff. R's inability to judge commanders: Reid, I, 329, 348; Piatt and Boynton, 196. Martin's estimate of R: *Military History,* 24. Congratulations: R to A.E.R., n.d. Views: S. P. Chase to R, Oct. 25, 1862. Invading East Tennessee: Van Horne, *Army of the Cumberland,* I, 207 ff. R instructs troops: Bennett and Haigh, *36th Illinois,* 306; Rosecrans, Anita, "Mss. Notes." Poor discipline: R, *Sketch.* Army exhausted: N. Y. *Tribune,* Nov. 3, 1862. Tired: Boyd, *Diary,* 81. Desertion: Sandburg, *War Years,* I, 554. Deserters: R, *Sketch,* 33 ff. Medical Corps:

Adams, *Doctors in Blue,* 83. Chaplains: Fitch, 320–326. Catholicity: Bickham, 143. Nashville garrison: R, *Personal Report,* 12. Elections: Sandburg, I, 602, 610 ff. Cunningham mansion: *Art Work of Nashville, Tenn.* Nashville: Bennett and Haigh, 306; Nashville *Dispatch,* Nov. 16, 21, 1862; Tennessee Historical Commission, *Tennessee,* I, 235. Morgan's marriage: Murfreesboro *Rebel Banner,* q. in Nashville *Dispatch,* Nov. 16, 1862. Horses: Fitch, 35; Mrs. J. Polk to R, Nov. 16, 1862. Women: Fitch, 639 ff.; Bickham, 56–63; R to A.E.R., Nov. 22, 1862; Tennessee Historical Commission, 235; Sandburg, II, 74. Cumberland: Nashville *Dispatch,* Nov. 21, 1862. Garesché: Fitch, 49, 246–248; Seitz, *Bragg,* 245. Headquarters routine: Bickham, 140–145; see also Fitch, 257–264. Cumberland: Fitch, 656; Nashville *Dispatch,* Nov. 27, 31, 1862. Johnson and R: Stryker, *Johnson,* 101 ff. Lincoln caricatured in *Punch:* Sandburg, I, 185. Grant and Murphy: E. Betty to R, Jan. 7, 1863; Grant, *Memoirs,* I, 433 ff. Friends: Frances Darr to R, Dec. 6, 1862. "Not ready": R to A.E.R., Nov. 22, 1862. Fires: Nashville *Dispatch,* Nov. 28, Dec. 18, 1862. Heg on army: Blegen, 180 ff. Morgan's raid: Swiggett, *Rebel Raider,* 96. Morgan's wedding: Murfreesboro *Rebel Banner,* Dec. 15, 17, 1862. "Morgan moving": Nashville *Dispatch,* Dec. 18, 1862. "R waiting": Blegen, 156. Christmas: Nashville *Dispatch,* Dec. 20, 24, 27, 1862. "Bragg attacks first": Crittenden, "Union Left," 633. Generals' meeting: Bickham, 136–139. Reports and correspondence: *Official Records,* Series I, Vol. XVI, Parts I and II; Vol. XX, Parts I and II.

Chapter Ten: Descent to Murfreesboro

Weather, army leaving Nashville, R joining troops, headquarters, conversations, sights, smells, sounds, etc.: Bickham, *Campaign,* 147–203. Sheridan on army: Sheridan, *Memoirs,* I, 214, 218. R's intelligence: Cist, *Army of the Cumberland,* 87. Positions: Fitch, *Annals,* 391 ff. Morgan's absence: Swiggett, *Rebel Raider,* 96–99. "No plan": Shanks, *Recollections,* 148 ff.; Reid, *Ohio,* I, 329; Crittenden, "Union Left," 633. Reports and correspondence: *Official Records,* Series I, Vol. XX, Parts I and II; Vol. XXIII, Parts I and II.

Chapter Eleven: Stone River

Weather, vivid details, R's personal conduct of battle, orders: Bickham, *Campaign,* 205–365. Affairs at the Union left: Crittenden, "Union Left,"

632–635. General account of battle: Kniffen, "Stone's River," 613–632 Wood's quip: Kniffen, "Stone's River," 627. Heg sees Bragg's attack mount: Blegen, 184 ff. "Fought according to Bragg's plan": Crittenden, 633. "Defensive plan Rosecrans' ": Polk, *Polk*, II, 173. McCook's rout: F. Knefler to L. Wallace, March 28, 1863. R's horses: Rosecrans, Anita, "Mss. Notes." Yaryan describes R: Yaryan, "Stone River," 169. R as "brave as Caesar": F. Knefler to L. Wallace, March 28, 1863. Reid's tribute to R: Reid, Ohio, I, 334. R meets Sheridan: Gilmore, *Recollections*, 130. R reforms line: F. Knefler to L. Wallace, March 28, 1863. R organizes stand: Blegen, 185 ff. "Artillery saved army": Beatty, *Memoirs*, 154. "We were outflanked": Blegen, 163 ff. Garesché is killed: Gilmore, 130; Fitch, *Annals*, 36. "Confederates fought like devils": Beatty, *Memoirs*, 204. Hazen finds Garesché's body: Hazen, *Narrative*, 83. "Cold night fell": Hosmer, *Appeal to Arms*, 253. "Longest day": Blegen, 166 ff. Brickhouse hospital: Fitch, 676 ff. Headquarters meeting: R, *Sketch*, 36–38; Fitch, 676 ff.; Kniffen, *Army of the Cumberland*, 11. Crittenden on falling back: Crittenden, 653 ff. Piatt on R's condition: Piatt and Boynton, *Thomas*, 211. Mists resemble Confederates: Hazen, 83. "Rosecrans was able": Deaderick, *Strategy*, 72. Discomfort: Blegen, 168. Hood describes R: Hood, *Diary*, Jan. 1, 1863, Hood Papers. Beatty reads Bible: Beatty, *Memoirs*, 156. Orphan Brigade: Buchanan, *Pictorial History*, 168. R orders Carlin's advance: Blegen, 167. McCook's strategem and R's "light division": R, *Sketch*, 39 ff. "Sun came out bright": Blegen, 168. Father Treacy preaches: Fitch, 329 ff. Reports and correspondence: *Official Records*, Series I, Vol. XXIII, Parts I and II.

Chapter Twelve: "Bragg's Nose Between Our Teeth"

R in Murfreesboro: Bickham, *Campaign*, 321 ff., 327, 368 ff. Hospitals: Gilmore, *Recollections*, 119; Fitch, *Annals*, 258 ff. Headquarters: Gilmore, 119; Fitch, 258 ff. Losses: Livermore, *Numbers*, 75, 79, 140. R taught important lesson: Williams, K., *Lincoln Finds a General*, II, 555. R rides crest: Piatt and Boynton, *Thomas*, 214. Bragg compliments R: Fremantle, *Diary*, 121. Stanton relents: G. Hartsuff to R, Jan. 8, 1863. Palmer's compliment: Palmer, *Recollections*, 146 ff. Heg's: Blegen, 185. Gale's: William Gale to Ed Gale, Jan. 5, 1863, Gale Papers. Betty on Grant: E. Betty to R, Jan. 11, 1863. "No victory": Nicolay and Hay, *Lincoln*, X, 281. Army being put in order: Blegen, 172. Railroad smashed: Fiske, *Mississippi*, 254. Feeding of army: Sheridan, *Memoirs*, I, 252 ff. Departmental trains: Fitch, 265–281. Country ruined: Blegen, 172. Army's needs: Sheridan, I, 253. Granger and Army of Kentucky: Van Horne, *History,* I, 288–290. Garfield describes R: Smith, *Garfield,* I, 272 ff., 280. Weather: Beatty, *Memoirs,* 161, 163. R and the Army of the Potomac: Hebert, *Hooker,* 123; New York *Spirit of the Times,* Jan. 31, 1863. Absenteeism: Beatty, 164 ff. Branding: Cleveland *Leader,* n.d., 1862. Stockpiles: Sheridan, I, 259. R popular: R. Yates to R, March 10, 1863. R popular with army, but head marked: Beatty, 172; Stanley, "Corinth," 101, 144. Pup tents: Beatty, 173 ff. "Gift enterprise": Gilmore, 141 ff.; Cist, *Army of the Cumberland,* 150 ff.; McCalmont, *Reunion,* 60, 70. "R's curt dispatches": Smith, I, 237. Operations of Truesdail: Fitch, 346–356. "Complaints from unscrupulous persons": R to A. Johnson, n.d., 1863. Streight: Smith, I, 287. "Vomit treason": R, *Letters to the Voters of Indiana,* 6–8; R, *Letter to the Ohio Legislature,* 1; Cleveland *Leader,* April 10, 1863. "Stanton flew into rage": Cincinnati *Times,* Oct. 21, 1863. Greeley's scheme: Gilmore, 39–62, 92–102, 119, 249. Villard on R: Villard, *Memoirs,* II, 63–66. R at his worst: Beatty, 190–196. Jealousy: Shanks, *Recollections,* 250. Grant's peculiar antipathy for R: Richardson, *Secret Service,* 245. Halstead on Grant: M. Halstead to S. P. Chase, April 1, 1863. "See but two generals": S. P. Chase to R, April 10, 1863. R solicits commanders' opinions and opposes Negro rebellion: Gilmore, "Why Rosecrans Was Removed." R meets Vallandigham: Sandburg, *War Years,* II, 160–164. R declines to become candidate: Gilmore, *Recollections,* 145 ff. Lincoln discusses R: Gilmore, *Recollections,* 145 ff. Lincoln faces his Cabinet: Gilmore, "Why Rosecrans Was Removed." Stanley's opinion: Cox, *Reminiscences,* I, 484; Smith, I, 203. Reports and correspondence: *Official Records,* Series I, Vol. XX, Parts I and II; Vol. XXV, Parts I and II.

Chapter Thirteen: Tullahoma—
"Outstanding Operation of the War"

General account: Kniffen, "Manoeuvering Bragg," 635–637; R, "Campaign for Chattanooga," 130 ff. R pushes wheel: *Western Christian Advocate,* March, 1898. Marching through mud: Stanley, "Tullahoma Campaign," 166–181; Martin, *Military History,* 32 ff. Heg in mud: Martin, 41. Muster roll: Martin, 4. Dialogue between Polk and Bragg: *Official Records,* Series I, Vol. XXIII, Part I, 618–627, q. as direct discourse. McCook's Independence Day celebration: Blegen, 226. Sherman complains: Howe, M.A.D., *Home Letters,* 270 ff. "Should have destroyed his army":

Smith, *Garfield*, I, 305. Comments on campaign: Villard, II, 78, 80; Piatt and Boynton, *Thomas*, 376. Lincoln's comment: Gilmore, "Why Rosecrans Was Removed." Stanley's praise: Stanley, "Tullahoma Campaign," 179. Logistics problem: Seitz, *Bragg*, 310–312. Reports and correspondence: *Official Records*, Series I, Vol. XXIII, Parts I and II; Vol. XXVII, Part II; Vol. XXX, Part I.

Chapter Fourteen: "A Wall Full of Ratholes"

The importance of Chattanooga: Fiske, *Mississippi*, 248; Fish, *American Civil War*, 155. "Strike at its belly": Piatt and Boynton, *Thomas*, 360. R's sevenfold task: R, "Campaign for Chattanooga," 131. Delightful weather: Beatty, *Memoirs*, 235, 295. "Seditious, lying stuff": Democratic State Central Committee of Ohio to R, Aug. 4, 1863; R to same, Aug. 4, 1863. Sanderson and Rousseau visit Washington: R, "Campaign for Chattanooga," 131; R, *Sketch*, 52 ff.; Sanderson, "Letter Diary," Aug. 16, 1863; R, *Personal Report*, 16; J. A. Ripley to L. H. Rousseau, Sept. 9, 1863. Treasury embarrassed: Donald, *Inside Lincoln's Cabinet*, 183. "We were ordered forward": R, "Campaign for Chattanooga," 131. "Rosecrans too able a soldier": Gordon, *Reminiscences*, 194. Hazen's ghost army: Gordon, 195; Hill, D. H., "Chickamauga," 639 ff.; R, "Campaign for Chattanooga," 132. Pickets end truce: Beatty, 321. Heg reaches Tennessee: R, "Campaign for Chattanooga," 132; Blegen, 238. "Mass of centaurs": Gordon, 196. Bragg's lack of information: Hill, 640. "Unsurpassed strategic ability": Gordon, 196. Sand Mountain steep: Bennett and Haigh, *36th Illinois*, 448. "Campfires twinkled": Beatty, 328. "Offer Divine Sacrifice": R to A.E.R., Sept. 6, 1863. Colby applauds: R. Colby to R, Nov. 7, 1863. R's "brilliant and faultless" strategy: Opdycke, "Chickamauga," 669; Rhodes, *History*, 293; Piatt and Boynton, 378. R erred in dispersing: Opdycke, 669; Fiske, 262 ff. Dana meets R: Dana, *Recollections*, 107 ff. "Hey! Sutler": Shanks, *Recollections*, 263. "Wall full of ratholes": Hill, 641. "Battle imminent": Smith, *Garfield*, I, 320. Washington knew Bragg being reinforced: Piatt and Boynton, 386. Lee criticized Southern newspapers: Lee, *Recollections*, 155. Grant wished to take Mobile: Grant, *Memoirs*, II, 20 ff. "Halleck telegraphed too late": R, "Campaign for Chattanooga," 132. "Thick wall of dust": Hill, 167. Line of fires: Piatt and Boynton, 389 ff.; Cincinnati *Commercial*, q. in Milwaukee *Sentinel*, Oct. 3, 1863. Reports and correspondence: *Official Records*, Series I, Vol. XXIII, Parts I and II; Vol. XXX, Parts I–IV.

Chapter Fifteen: Chickamauga—"The Great Battle of the West"

Weather, battle conditions, sounds, condition of men, and other descriptive details: Cincinnati *Commercial*, q. in Milwaukee *Sentinel*, Oct. 3, 1863. Personal details concerning R: Sanderson, "Letter Diary," Aug. 19, 20, 1863. Telegraph: Moore, *Rebellion Record*, VIII, 365. Bierce remembered Chickamauga: Fatout, *Bierce*, 42. Battle accounts: Hill, "Chickamauga," 638–662; R, "Campaign for Chattanooga," 133 ff.; Van Horne, *History;* Cist, *Army of the Cumberland.* "Thousand anvils": Beatty, *Citizen Soldier,* 251. Croxton's jest: Duffield, *Under the Old Flag,* 3. Evening attack: Piatt and Boynton, *Thomas,* 399. Headquarters meeting: McElroy, *Chickamauga,* 2; Dana, *Recollections,* 113. Stanley and McCalmont describe R's exhaustion: McCalmont, *Reunion,* 71, 670. Tired commander: Bennett and Haigh, *36th Illinois,* 465. Polk unready: Hill, 653. R dresses down Wood: Cleaves, *Rock,* 165. Delay proved serious: R, "Campaign for Chattanooga," 133. "Fatal message": R, "Campaign for Chattanooga," 133; Thruston, G. P., "Crisis," 663–665. "Too many orders": Crittenden, "Union Left," 633. "I hold the fatal order": J. W. Burke to R, June 12, 1864. Wood's "dignity": Cist, 223. Stanley's comment on R's order: McCalmont, 20. Break-through: Dana, 115. R's heroism: Thruston, "Crisis," 664; Dodge, "Personal Recollections," 359; Dana, 116. Negley strays from battlefield: Cist, 224; Fitch, M. H., *Chattanooga Campaign,* 670. Garfield and R withdraw: Cist, 225. Garfield's narration to Cox: Cox, *Reminiscences,* II, 10. R helped from horse: Cist, 226. R's Rossville orders: R, "Campaign for Chattanooga," 134; R, testimony, *C.C.W.,* April 22, 1865. "Turning point": Cist, 170. R rode in wrong direction: Swinton, *Twelve Decisive Battles,* 225. Granger, "That's all nonsense": Shanks, *Andrus,* 273. Reports and correspondence: *Official Records,* Series I, Vol. XXX, Parts I–IV.

Chapter Sixteen: The Eyes of the Ferret

"Greatest battle": Fiske, *Mississippi,* 279. Losses: Livermore, *Numbers,* 75, 105, 140 ff. Confederate newspapers assess victory: Richmond *Sentinel,* Sept. 22, 1863; Richmond *Whig,* Sept. 23, 1863. R held prize: Pollard, *Southern History,* III, 128. Chickamauga important: Gracie, *Truth about Chickamauga,* viii. Hill's estimate: Hill, "Chickamauga," 662. Army denounces Stanton: Sanderson, "Letter Diary," Sept. 21, 1863. "Blue with anxiety": F. H. Pierpont to R, Sept. 23, 1863. "Government again incompetent": Ford, *A Cycle,* Vol. II, 89 ff. "Union army a mob": Beatty, *Memoirs,* 254. Forrest recommends an advance: Hill, 662.

Stupendous blunder: Gracie, viii; Hill, 662. Burnside a myth: Beatty, *Memoirs*, 257 ff. "Greeley sneered": Greeley, *American Conflict*, I, 430. "In this war or the next?": Cincinnati *Commercial*, Oct. 20, 1863. Cabinet meeting: Donald, D., *Inside Lincoln's Cabinet*, 199–203. Railroad operation: Weber, *Northern Railroads*, 81; Gorham, *Stanton*, 129; Le Duc, "Little Steamboat," 676. Chattanooga besieged: Fullerton, "Army," 719. R's invention of Pullman car: Adams, *Doctors in Blue*, 83, 108. "Hooker brought a full supply of land transportation": Grant, "Chattanooga," 689. Stanton to Morton at Indianapolis: Indianapolis *Times*, March 13, 1882. Vallandigham's defeat sealed R's fate: Shanks, *Recollections*, 261. Generals bickered: Beatty, *Memoirs*, 257. Dana to Smith: McCartney, *Grant*, 221. Smith to Margadent: U.S. Army, *Report on Smith*, 207. Smith on R: McCartney, 221. Smith on supplying the army: Smith, "Comments," 714–718. McCook and Crittenden: Palmer, *Recollections*, 187. Dana's role: Gracie, 150 ff.; Villard, *Memoirs*, II, 166, 168, 188–200; Cox, *Reminiscences*, II, 7; McCalmont, *Reunion*, 62. Thomas reports Dana's interview: R, ms. in Rosecrans Papers, n.d. Thomas admonishes Garfield: Society of the Army of the Cumberland, *Burial*, 85. Smith's personal letter: U.S. Army, *Report on Smith*, 58. Sanderson on Reynolds and Garfield: Sanderson, Oct. 15, 1863. "Long impassable road": W. F. Smith to Mrs. Smith, Oct. 14, 1863. The *Chattanooga*: Le Duc, 676–678. Rosecrans and Smith visit Brown's Ferry: Smith, "Postscript," 718; Sanderson, Oct. 19, 1863. Rosecrans removed: U.S. Army, *Report on Smith*, 29, 167, 214. Sanderson surprised: Sanderson, Oct. 19, 1863. R confers with Thomas: R, ms. in Rosecrans Papers, n.d.; Howe, *Historical Collections*, 1889, I, 563. "Leave before announcement": R, ms. in Rosecrans Papers, n.d. "Only ignorance or malice": McCartney, *Grant*, 100; R, testimony, *C.C.W.*, April 24, 1865. Final routines: Sanderson, Oct. 19, 1863. Not abandoning Chattanooga: R, testimony, *C.C.W.*, April 24, 1865; U.S. Army, *Report on Smith*, 217. Sheridan's testimony: Sheridan, *Memoirs*, I, 298–302. Villard agrees: Villard, II, 208 ff. "Enemies he made"; Reid, *Ohio*, I, 399. Reports and correspondence: *Official Records*, Series I, Vol. XXX, Parts I–IV.

Chapter Seventeen: "They Slew Him with Poison"

R's leavetaking: Sanderson, "Letter Diary," Oct. 20, 1863; R, testimony, *C.C.W.*, April 24, 1865. Fog: Howe, *Historical Collections*, 1889, I, 562. Party: U.S. Army, *Report on Smith*, 214. R on journey: Paul A. Oliver to J. W. de Peyster, Jr., March 15, 1867. "Sanderson wept": Sanderson,

Oct. 20, 1863. Sheridan's comment: Sheridan, *Memoirs*, I, 299 ff. Grant meets Stanton and relieves R: Grant, *Memoirs*, II, 19–26. Stanton meets Morton in Indianapolis: Indianapolis *Times*, March 13, 1882, reprinted in Washington *National Tribune*, March 20, 1882. R not retreating: Villard, *Memoirs*, II, 212. Grant meets R: Grant, II, 28. Grant meets Thomas: McCartney, *Grant*, 10 ff. Sanderson studies Grant: Sanderson, Oct. 24, 1863. R's "line of retreat": Grant, II, 29. Baldy Smith and Grant: Grant, II, 29–31. Smith's estimate of Grant: McCartney, 222. Brown's Ferry operation: Fullerton, "Army of the Cumberland," 720. Grant claims credit: Grant, II, 44. Court of inquiry into claims: See U.S. Army, *Report on Smith*. Garfield advises R: J. A. Garfield to R, Oct. 23, 1863. Cincinnati reception for R: undated newspaper clipping, Rosecrans Papers. Press reaction: Cincinnati *Times*, Oct. 20, 1863. Palmer's reaction: Palmer, *Recollections*, 190. McCalmont's comment: McCalmont, *Reunion*, 66. Comments and R's letter: New York *Times*, Oct. 21, 22, 1863, Nov. 2, 1863. Shanks's descriptions of generals, including R: Shanks, *Recollections*, 35–97, 258–266. Reid's description of R: Reid, I, 349. Fiske's: Fiske, *Mississippi*, 227. Washington *Post* editor's: undated newspaper clipping, Rosecrans Papers. Richmond *Examiner's* estimate of R: Richmond *Examiner*, Oct. 26, 1863. Henry Adams to Charles Francis Adams: Ford, *Cycle*, 112. Friendly letters: A. Doubleday to R, Oct. 25, 1863; W. R. Truesdail to R, Nov. 1, 1863; J. W. Burke to R, June 12, 1864; A. L. Streight to R, April 11, 1864. R erupts: "O.B.S." to J. A. Garfield, Dec. 7, 1863. "Lies will be propagated": R to R. B. Hayes, Nov. 22, 1863, Hayes Papers. "Lincoln yielded to sinister influence": Howe, *Historical Collections*, 1889, I, 562 ff. Chickamauga produces crisis in Washington: Welles, *Diary*, I, 438–448. Hooker on R: Sandburg, *War Years*, II, 433. Steedman's role: Toledo *Journal*, q. in New York *Times*, March 7, 1879. Sherman's account of Grant's part in R's removal: R, Document designated "B." Lincoln explains to R: J. A. Gilmore to R, May 23, 1864. Lincoln explains to Doolittle: R, Document designated "B." Rawlins explains: J. A. Rawlins to Mary Hurlbut, Nov. 23, 1863. "Chase will lay eggs": Nicolay and Hay, *Lincoln*, VIII, 317. Gilmore's explanation: Gilmore, "Why Rosecrans Was Removed." Garfield's buried letter: New York *Sun*, June 14, 1882. Garfield writes to Chase: J. A. Garfield to S. P. Chase, Feb. 15, April 5, May 5, May 9, June 14, 1863. Garfield's distress: J. A. Garfield to Mrs. Garfield, June 14, 1863. Garfield's "confidential" letter: J. A. Garfield to S. P. Chase, July 27, 1863. "We shall save this army": J. A. Garfield to S. P. Chase, Sept. 23, 1863. Garfield confides in Villard: Villard, II, 185 ff. Stanton questions Garfield: Cox, *Reminiscences*, II, 7 ff. Garfield defends R: Garfield's statement to R, q. in Francis Darr to R, July 16, 1881. Darr quotes Anson

Stager: F. Darr to R, July 16, 1881. Garfield visits Cox: Cox, II, 8–11. "A great mistake": J. A. Garfield to R, Oct. 23, 1863. Blair's account: Montgomery Blair to R, Sept. 21, 1880. Garfield reassures R: J. A. Garfield to R, Dec. 16, 1863. Reports and correspondence: *Official Record,* Series I, Vol. XXX, Parts I–IV.

Chapter Eighteen: Missouri

"Letters of powerful friends": B. F. Wade to R, Dec. 24, 1863. "To Missouri": F. S. Bond to R, Jan. 20, 1864; W. S. Dennison to R, Jan. 2, 1864. Missouri's troubles: Greeley, *American Conflict,* I, 26–32, 35–41, 445–455, 488–492. Lincoln comments: Nicolay and Hay, *Lincoln,* VIII, 473 ff. Dispersal of Missouri forces: R, testimony, *C.C.W.,* April 24, 1865. Resolution congratulating Thomas: Society of the Army of the Cumberland, *Burial,* 20; Smith, *Garfield,* I, 849. Firm friends: J. A. Garfield to R, March 16, 1864. Bond's arrest: F. S. Bond to J. A. Garfield, April 1, 1864, Garfield Papers; J. A. Garfield to R, April 26, May 3, 1864; R to J. A. Garfield, May 8, 1864, Garfield Papers. Order of American Knights: J. A. Gilmore to R, May 10, 1864; Gilmore, *Recollections,* 295; R, testimony, *C.C.W.,* April 24, 1865; Scott, W. F., "Last Fight," 299. Alarm spread: R to S. P. Heintzelman, May, 25, 1864, Heintzelman Papers. "Lincoln afraid of a clash": J. A. Garfield to R, May 30, 1864. "No desire to sustain R": Nicolay and Hay, VIII, 437. Special Order No. 61: St. Louis *Missouri Republican,* April 11, 1864. Lincoln's comment: A. Lincoln to R, April 14, 1864. R and Vice-Presidency: Cleveland *Catholic Telegraph,* May 28, 1928; Mulhane, L. W., "Rosecrans," 255; *Appleton's Cyclopedia of American Biography,* IX, 163. Soldiers' voting: A. Lincoln to R, Sept. 26, 1864. Grant's criticism "harsh": Nicolay and Hay, VIII, 480. Scott's estimate of R's defeat of Price: Scott, W. F., "Last Fight," 292, 325. R's account of Smith episode: R, *Personal Report,* 26. Rawlins' testimony: R, testimony, *C.C.W.,* April 24, 1865. "No reason assigned": R, testimony, *C.C.W.,* April 24, 1865. "Submitted to my wrongs": R, *Personal Report,* 28. Cause of removal: R to W. S. Dennison, Dec. 17, 1864; R to J. A. Garfield, Dec. 30, 1864, Garfield Papers. Reports and correspondence: *Official Records,* Series I, Vol. XXXIV, Parts I–IV; Vol. XLI, Parts I–IV.

Epilogue

R leaves army: U.S. War Dept. to R, Special Order #278, May 28, 1864. R to L. Thomas, Dec. 25, 1866. "Great Decliner": Bancroft, *History,*

VIII, 46; *Biographical Dictionary of the American Congress;* John Wagner to R, Aug. 28, 1876; W. F. Deal and W. F. Stone to R, Aug. 28, 1876. "Frozen out": R to J. Fraser, July 14, 1875. "$500,000 in five years": R to A.E.R., May 23, 1865. 14,000 acres: R to A.E.R., July 14, 1867; Mulhane, "Rosecrans," 254–256; statement, W. S. Rosecrans III to M. M. L., April 1951; Ehrenclou, "The Water Well," 12. "Bring charges": R to A.E.R., Jan. 15, 1866. R's diminished fortunes: N. Y. *Times*, q. in Waukesha, Wis., *Daily Freeman,* June 1, 1957. Southern Pacific: *Amended Complaint,* 1 ff., 22 ff.; statement, W. S. Rosecrans III to M.M.L., April 1951. Minister to Mexico: William S. Rosecrans Diplomatic Paper. "Yankee capitalism": Pletcher, "Rosecrans," 657, 678 ff. Riley and Rosecrans, *Popular Government.* Business ventures: U.S. Patent Office, Letters Patent, Feb. 24, 1880; F. Darr to R, n.d., 1879; statement, W. S. Rosecrans III to M. M. L., April 1951; Safety Powder Company, *Safety Powder Company,* 1–4. Mint: R to J. Fraser, July 14, 1875; R to A.E.R., May 30, 1877; F. Darr to R, July 3, 1877; W. T. Sherman to R, Nov. 21, 1877. Deaths: M. S. O'Connor to R, May 12, 1876; A.E.R. to R, May 12, 1876; S. H. Rosecrans to R; R. P. Gleaner, *Catholic Columbian,* n.d., Rosecrans Papers; *Dictionary of American Biography,* XVI, 162; Parkersburg, W. Va., *Catholic Messenger,* Nov. 1878. Tributes to R and Thomas: Society of the Army of the Cumberland, *Reports,* Vols. I and III; R. W. Johnson, *Memoir,* 255, 263; R, *Proposed Monument.* Relations with Garfield: G. Granger to R, June 6, 1864; Smith, *Garfield,* II, 864; R to J. A. Garfield, Oct. 19, 1877, Dec. 20, 1879, Dec. 13, 23, 1880, Jan. 9, 1881; J. A. Garfield to R, n.d., 1877, Nov. 27, 1877, Jan. 17, 1880, Dec. 28, 1880; T. L. Crittenden to R, July 8, 1880; Cincinnati *Gazette,* June 7, 1880; F.-J. Porter to R, July 19, 1880; F. Darr to R, Aug. 2, 1880; W. S. Hancock to R, July 28, 1880; San Francisco *Alta Californian,* Aug. 18, 1880. Signs of age: undated newspaper clipping, Rosecrans Papers. Dana's complicity: Caldwell, *Garfield,* 232; New York *Sun,* March 8, June 14, 1882; Washington *Tribune,* March 13, 1882; Chicago *Journal,* n.d.; San Francisco *Examiner,* April 2, 1882; Smith, *Garfield,* II, 870. Grant's "back pay" bill: Green, *General Grant's Last Stand,* 268–275; R, *Remarks,* 1–3. R candidate for Presidency: Shakopee, Minn., *Minnesota Courier,* March 16, 1882. Secretary of War: New York *Herald,* Nov. 17, 1884. Grant's *Memoirs:* Green, 154; R, "The Mistakes of Grant." Honors: *Biographical Dictionary of the American Congress;* McElroy, *Chickamauga,* 199; Chickamauga Memorial Association, *Proceedings;* Rev. J. H. Richards, S. J., to R, Jan. 1, 1889. "Money meant little": statement, W. S. Rosecrans III to M. M. L., April 1951. Restoration to rank: Washington *Post,* Feb. 23, 1889; McCalmont, *Reunion,* 65; Mulhane, 262; House of Representatives, Report #3675, *William S. Rosecrans;* F. L. Thomas to

Anita Rosecrans, Feb. 16, 1889; M. Meigs to R, Feb. 23, 1889. Dana "satanic": Chicago *Chronicle,* Sept. 22, 1895. G.A.R. incident: Williams, C.P., *Diary and Letters,* V, 107–109. R ill: Rosecrans, Anita, "Mss. Notes"; Dr. J. J. Huntington to R, April 17, 1898; Mulhane, 254; statement, W. S. Rosecrans III to M. M. L., April 1951. Life at the Rancho: Rosenkrans, Allen, *Rosenkrans Family,* 316 ff.; McCalmont, 65; statement, W. S. Rosecrans III to M. M. L., April 1951; Mulhane, 254. "Dana is dead": M. J. Patton to R, Oct. 19, Dec. 25, 1897. Old age: W. S. Rosecrans III to M. M. L., April 1951. McKinley's tribute: Chattanooga *Daily Times,* Sept. 18, 1895. Laetare Medal: Mulhane, 254. Death and funeral: Rosenkrans, Allen, *Rosenkrans Family,* 218; Rosecrans, Anita, "Mss. Notes"; statement, W. S. Rosecrans III to M. M. L., April 1951; Los Angeles *Times,* March 17, 1898; Columbus, Ohio, *Catholic Columbian,* n.d. Reburial: Society of the Army of the Cumberland, *Burial,* 69. "We will be forgotten": Gordon Granger to R, June 6, 1864.

INDEX